Loring's Division

MAJOR-GENERAL WILLIAM W. LORING, C. S. A.

Ross Massey

Loring's Division
by Ross Massey

Copyright © 2023 Ross Massey
All Rights Reserved

First Printing

The Scuppernong Press
PO Box 1724
Wake Forest, NC 27587

Printed in the United States of America

No part of this book may be reproduced or transmitted in any form or by any means, electronic or mechanical, including photocopying, recording, or by any information and storage and retrieval system, without written permission from the editor and/or publisher.

International Standard Book Number ISBN 978-1-942806-53-0

Library of Congress Control Number: 2023935723

Contents

PART 1: The Narrative

1-Introduction... 1

2-William Wing Loring... 3

3-Mississippi: Birthplace of Loring's Division.. 24
Mississippi Manufacturing at Risk in campaign-Grant launches his final campaign to take Vicksburg-Joseph E. Johnston's Department Command doesn't prevent Grant's crossing-Loring's and Stevenson's offensive plan for Pemberton to take position in Grant's rear-Johnston's Dispatch halts Pemberton resulting in defeat at Champion Hill-Loring covers Pemberton's retreat and Escapes with his Division-Loring unites his division with Johnston's Army of Relief in Jackson-Johnston leaves to command the Army of Tennessee; Loring's Division under Polk

4- Georgia and Loring's Division in the Army of Tennessee.................... 80
Loring's Division to Resaca-South of the Oostanaula River-South of the Etowah River-Lee, Beauregard, Taylor, and Forrest Victorious-Loring's Division commanded by Featherston at Kennesaw Mountain-Johnston outflanked from Kennesaw and retreats across the Chattahoochee River-Hood in command in Georgia-Peach Tree Creek-Atlanta through battle and bombardment-Ezra Church-Cavalry raids, Utoy Creek, and increased shelling of Atlanta-Jonesborough and evacuation of Atlanta-Loring returned to his division-President Davis visits the army at Palmetto-Moving north through Georgia

5-Across Alabama and into Tennessee.. 133
The Searching for a Tennessee River Crossing- Columbia and Spring Hill

6-Franklin.. 143

7-Nashville Bound.. 173
Thursday, 15 December 1864- Friday, 16 December 1864

8-The Retreat 210

9-North Carolina Finale... 221

PART 2: The Soldiers and Units

10-John Adams's Brigade... 232
Adams's units (1864)

11-Winfeild Scott Featherston's Brigade... 242
Featherston's units (1864)

12-Thomas Moore Scott's Brigade.. 249
Scott's Brigade units (1864)

13-Myrick's Battalion of Artillery (1864).. 255

14-Biographical Entries... 265

15-Bibliography.. 341

Index... 346

Part 1: The Narrative

Chapter 1-Introduction

Biographies of generals focus on the general, as they should. They almost never give adequate credit to their men. It behooves us to include the soldiers, and most of them forgotten, who made the general's fame possible. William Wing Loring earned far too little fame for his sacrifices. A biography by James W. Raab did not surface until 1996. The purpose of this book is to remember Loring's Division, as a distinct organization.

James Raab wrote, "'Old Blizzards' Loring was somewhat stout but a vigorous man, about five feet, eleven inches tall. His thinning black hair was beginning to show gray, and he combed it back and allowed it to grow very long for an officer. It hung down around the back of his neck in ringlets and some of his men called him Old Ringlets.'

"His anger could be terrible and his language inconceivable for an officer. In times of danger or excitement, he roared and chafed like a lion. He would roll out big oaths - when he found his artillery or wagons stalled, he cursed them out of the mire – and it almost seemed he could curse cannon up a hill without horses. There was no question that Loring could be a difficult subordinate, yet he was a benevolent superior to his junior officers."

Loring's Division did not have a reputation like Cleburne's Division. It was a latecomer to the Army of Tennessee in 1864. But Loring's didn't lack for aggressive fighting spirit. Loring's Division's breached the enemy's line at Peachtree Creek in the most successful charge in the Atlanta Campaign. Loring's had more buried in the McGavock Cemetery at Franklin than Cleburne's. No division commander was more colourful than was Loring. As a teenager William Wing Loring was fighting Seminoles in his native Florida. He left an arm in Mexico City in the Mexican War, and served in the U.S. Army in the western territories. He ran afoul of Stonewall Jackson in the War for Confederate Independence, but President Jefferson Davis was too wise to waste Loring's abilities, and promoted him.

Davis sent Loring to Mississippi. Loring is remembered for his victory against the U.S. Navy at Fort Pemberton. He is not known for skillfully covering Lt. Gen. John Clifford Pemberton's retreat after Champion Hill. Perhaps more outstanding was his gutsy escape with his division. Spring Hill is known for Schofield's night escape, marching past Hood. Few have heard Loring had pulled off a similar night escape after Champion Hill! Had every division fought as well as Loring's at Peachtree Creek it might have been the great victory which it was intended to be. "Old Blizzards" and his division were great soldiers.

Loring's Division had roots in the Department of Mississippi and East Louisiana. He took command of the 1st Division on 2 January 1863. That division lost some units, so that what became known as Loring's Division was formed by Pemberton on 5 May 1863. He organized it with the brigades known as Tilghman's, Buford's, and Featherston's. Several Mississippi infantry regiments came to Loring in the brigade of Lloyd Tilghman. They would form the nucleus of Adams's Brigade, as it was known in the Army of Tennessee.

Its fame was insured by the dramatic death of John Adams at Franklin. Buford's became Scott's. Thomas Moore Scott led it until wounded at Franklin. Featherston's Brigade changed the least in units, and Winfield Scott Featherston was in all of the division's campaigns. The primary focus of this book is Loring's Division in the Army of Tennessee, where it made deadly charges, proving its valour was equal to any division.

Loring's Division would no doubt be better known had it fought under more successful army commanders, able to win great victories. Two of the three, Pemberton and Hood, had been promoted beyond their abilities. Johnston may have been too, but at least had more of the traits of a great commander. But Johnston failed in Mississippi, and had no offensive victory in Georgia.

A thorough history of Loring's Division could cover hundreds of pages. The battles alone could have been covered in greater detail. The purpose here is to give a good overview of the actions of Loring and his unit commanders, in order to appreciate the entire division. Biographies and battle narratives often only touch on brigade, regimental, and artillery commanders. These leaders deserve biographies of their own, yet they may never be written. A gap is thus left unfilled, but the Biographical Entries section partially fills it. Firsthand accounts left by the soldiers in the ranks are mostly from *Confederate Veteran*. I have incurred several debts of gratitude in the process of writing this book. Loring's Confederate service began in western Virginia. I asked Robert E.L. Krick to glance over the first few chapters. His "largest recommendation" was to improve transitions. He was exactly right. One problem was not knowing what Loring was thinking; a diary might have solved that problem. Likewise, I can't say what his officers thought of him. My solution was to go back and add subheadings. I was gratified Krick thought there is a "steady tendency to be fair." He wrote I am "pro-Loring, but have not carried it so far as to be unreasonable about it." I appreciate all of his comments very much.

Bouanchaud's Battery has devotees. I was having dinner in a New Orleans restaurant in 2001. I was telling my attorney-friend Phil Nugent about their brilliant stand at Nashville. I found it in an obscure source, and was bragging I might be the only person aware of it. A gentleman, Thomas Donnelley, dining a few feet away, corrected me! He knew too! He shared some of his records. Randall Jarreau and I have shared our thoughts on the battery over the years at S.C.V. reunions; he also furnished photos. Jack Rogers is an expert on the battery, sharing his knowledge and passion.

Foremost I would like to thank my wife, Lynda. Her mastery of computers has been an invaluable contribution to this endeavour. She found obscure photos on-line. As far as I have learned, a history of a Confederate division has never been written. There have been a number of regimental histories, and a few brigade histories, but not a division history. I supposed this book might take less than two years; it took more than twice that long. Lynda might have told me she was tired of me talking about Loring's Division, but never did. The Sons of Confederate Veterans held our 125th annual reunion in Saint Augustine in 2020. Lynda and I got to take an SCV tour and see Loring's downtown grave. Leftists screamed profanities at us from an organized parade of a half dozen vehicles. They cannot alter my choice of heroes. I am gratified to have spent time with Loring and his division.

Chapter 2-William Wing Loring

Loring had stormed about on the ramparts of Fort Pemberton screaming "give them blizzards." And henceforth he would be known as Old Blizzards! Loring's command held out and turned back a U.S. army-navy strike for Vicksburg. Unfortunately Loring had limited opportunities to command on his own. With his aggressive personality he seemed to have excelled on his own. We are left to our imagination how well he might have done.

So Loring is part enigma. He frustrated Stonewall Jackson and John Pemberton. They viewed him as uncooperative. Jackson wanted Loring cashiered! But there is room for another opinion. Bishop Charles Quintard, M.D. wrote of Loring in his narrative. He wrote that Loring "was not only a very charming companion but he was altogether a remarkable man. A braver man never lived." And "he was the hero of three wars." Quintard wrote he was the "noblest of men & most gallant of soldiers." We might think Quintard was referring to Robert E. Lee!

Loring's parents wed in Wilmington, North Carolina, where William was born on 4 December 1818. In 1823 Reuben and Hannah Loring moved to the new American territory of Florida. There in America's oldest city, Saint Augustine, young William grew up in the shadows of the former Spanish Fort Castillo de San Marcos. It had been renamed Fort Marion before Reuben Loring bought a house one block south. Another future general for the Confederacy, Edmund Kirby Smith, was born in Saint Augustine, after the Lorings arrived.

Loring's long military career began in Florida when he was only 14 years old. Seminoles were defending their homeland in a guerilla war from 1835 to 1842. Their killings of whites made it appear the two could never assimilate. Loring campaigned with mounted volunteers under future Confederate general Jesse Finley. Loring took part in the battle of the blockhouse at Withlacoochee (Marion Co.). He distinguished himself at the Battle of Wahoo Swamp, Sumter County, and Florida appointed him second lieutenant of his company. Both of these battles were in central Florida, generally near today's Ocala.

The Great Seminole War wound down, and Loring concentrated on his education. He studied at Georgetown for about five months before he returned to Saint Augustine in the spring of 1840. He read law and passed the Florida bar in 1842. He served in the Florida Territorial Legislature. With statehood in 1845 he served in the first House of the State of Florida.

War with Mexico, arising from the border dispute, brought Loring back to the military. President Polk offered Loring a sword with an appointment as the senior captain in Mounted Rifles. Maj. Gen. Winfield Scott advanced from the seaport of Vera Cruz to take Mexico City. The Mexicans had significant fortifications on the two main roads leading into the city from the east and south. Scott sent Capt. Robert E. Lee and Lt. Pierre Gustave Toutant Beauregard to scout a route thru a lava field of black, jagged rocks called the Pedregal. The Mexicans had fortified Padierna, on the far western side of it. Scott's officers thought it was Contreras, a town a little farther south, and thus, the battle has been remembered as Contreras. Maj. Gen. Gideon Pillow commanded the movement, and ordered Loring to take his Mounted Rifles forward and push Mexican skirmishers off a slope east of Padierna. Loring not only pushed them off the slope, but out of Padierna.

Lee had been directing road work that morning and actually went forward with the first two companies of the Rifles. He charted a path for artillery, which included a section under fellow Virginian Lt. Thomas Jackson. Here Loring outranked both of these future Confederate generals, and would fight under them in Virginia. Joseph E. Johnston was another Virginian fighting at Padierna, and Loring would serve under him too.

The Mexicans should have attempted to escape that night, 19 August 1847. Their confidence was their downfall, for as they slept U.S. troops were sneaking to their rear. The morning of the 20th was gray and foggy. The Mexicans had some idea there were U.S. troops behind them, and positioned a detachment to guard it. At 6:00 a.m. U.S. infantry attacked. Loring's Rifles were in a concealed position on the Mexican's flank. They rose to fire, and the Mexicans retreated toward their main line. U.S. troops then attacked from the east and the Mexicans dissolved in a panic. The battle had lasted only seventeen minutes, but the northward pursuit continued all day.

The U.S. Army was outside Mexico City on 12 September, where an attack on the Castle of Chapultepec was made. Mexico City fell two days later. Loring's gallant conduct earned him a brevet to colonel. Unfortunately he was wounded in the right arm, which resulted in amputation. He endured the operation without anesthetic, and even smoked a cigar. Loring claimed the loss of the arm was the proudest moment of his life. There could be no doubt he would be brave enough to lead Confederate soldiers!

Loring's U.S. Army service continued after the Mexican War. James Raab's biography *W.W. Loring: Florida's Forgotten General* has a good chapter on this period. Loring was promoted to full colonel at age 38. This made him the youngest colonel in the army to that time; 22 December 1856. Quintard said, "His frontier services in the U.S. Army were equaled only by that grand soldier, Albert Sidney Johnston."

An impression of Loring at Fort Union, in New Mexico territory, was left by a Yankee cavalry general, William Woods Averill. It is in his memoir *Ten Years in the Saddle*: "The headquarters of the regiment of Mounted Riflemen were at Fort Union. Our arrival at that post Oct. 31, 1857, with several hundred recruits and heavy trains of supplies was an event. Many officers galloped out miles to meet us and the garrison was full of joyous excitement. Those were the most blessed moments of army life-the meetings. For the first time I saw my picturesque Colonel, W.W. Loring, who had left an arm at the Belen Gate, City of Mexico. His erect soldierly figure of medium height, bright black eyes full of expression, straight black hair, mustache, and imperial, easy courtesy and fine conversational ability, altogether made an agreeable and lasting impression upon me. Strange to say, I never saw him again until after a quarter of a century had filled his life with military experiences of the war for the Union and a decade as a Major General in the Egyptian Army."

In 1859 Loring took leave from the U.S. Army to tour Europe, Egypt, and the "Holy Land." Quintard mentions only so much. This was a day when personal travel was mostly for the wealthy. Loring's quest was probably typical. His visit to Egypt would not be his last. He served the Khedive of Egypt after Confederate independence was lost.

When Lincoln ordered an invasion of the Confederacy, Loring must have felt compelled to defend Florida and the splendid new republic. Lincoln had not even been on the ballot in Florida, or nine other Southern states. He offered nothing good for them. Loring traveled for six weeks from New Mexico, to reach Richmond on 20 July. He received an appointment as a brigadier. Robert E. Lee assigned him to command the Northwestern Army; also known as the Army of the Northwest. The Yankees were beat at Manassas the next day, but they were also invading western Virginia from Ohio.

The old western counties of Virginia have been erroneously painted as a pro-U.S. region by many historians. Some areas, such as around Wheeling were, but to paint the area with one brush simplifies the true political feelings. Numerous counties in the southern part of the state were pro-Confederate. Most counties adjoining today's western border of Virginia were. Other counties were divided as in the "border states." Many just wished to be left alone without animosity. Most Virginians hoped disloyalty in the western counties would subside. The region became a complicated theatre of war.

Those counties that bordered modern Virginia are in the Appalachian Ridge and Valley Region. And other counties west of them are too, so that there is a wide strip along the eastern border of today's West Virginia. It was in these mountains and valleys that the Confederacy had to stop the advance of the U.S. Army. Any eastward advance would threaten the operation of the *Virginia and Tennessee Railroad,* which brought troops and supplies to Virginia. This topography hindered Lee and Loring in their strategic options.

The week before Loring arrived in Richmond there had been several defeats of small commands. One defeat resulted in the war's first death of a general, Virginian Robert Selden Garnett. Brig. Gen. Henry Rootes Jackson had temporarily replaced Garnett, but on 20 July Loring was ordered west to take command. U.S. forces had been under George McClellan. His victory in the Rich Mountain Campaign got him promoted to command of the Army of the Potomac in August. He was replaced by William Rosecrans.

Before McClellan left Lee was riding into western counties. He was accompanied by Col. John Washington, a great nephew of George Washington, and Captain Walter Taylor. Lee wrote his wife, "The valleys so beautiful, the scenery so peaceful. What a glorious world Almighty God has given us. How thankless and ungrateful we are, and how we labour to mar his gifts." Then they rode about six miles into today's West Virginia, to arrive at Loring's camp in Huntersville on 3 August. Lee biographer Clifford Dowdy called it a "dirty mountain village." Dowdy also wrote Loring's camp was filthy and disorganized. Dowdy wrote Loring gave Lee a "very cool welcome."

If Loring's camp was filthy he was ultimately to blame, though he had just arrived and had little time to correct housekeeping. Loring had written Richmond on 26 July: One command was "in truth pitiable. Officers and men are absolutely stripped of everything- tents, clothing, cooking utensils, shoes-and I am sorry to believe many may have thrown away their arms." The command was Col. James Newton Ramsey's, who was arrested for granting too many furloughs. He resigned in December and was elected to the Georgia Senate in 1863. Loring was so exasperated he asked, "Is the whole country to be surrendered?" Loring had more pressing problems than camp "filth."

A lack of organization in command structure in the western counties hindered Loring. Douglas Southall Freeman called them quasi-independent columns in his Lee biography. They were under two political generals John Buchanan Floyd was a former Virginia governor and Secretary of War for President Buchanan. President Davis had called on him to raise a brigade of "your mountain rifle-men with their own tried weapons." The other was the last (1860) governor of Virginia, Henry Alexander Wise. Loring wrote Floyd on 31 July, "…I think we can give the enemy a decided blow in the vicinity of Cheat Mountain and also strike the column sent in the direction of Wise. I beg that you will give me the earliest information of the movements of both General Wise and yourself." Neither Floyd nor Wise would join forces with Loring. Both were too involved along the Kanawha.

The next day Loring reconnoitered the enemy position on Cheat Mountain. Lee had instructed Loring to cling to the mountain passes, protect the railroad, and organize a counter offensive as soon as he thought proper. The Virginia Central Railroad ran east to Staunton. Loring reached Monterey, 43 miles west of Staunton. The important Parkersburg-Staunton Turnpike crossed the future state of West Virginia. Parkersburg, on the Ohio River, allowed enemy troops to reach Monterey on the pike. Holding the pike blocked the enemy's advance toward the *Virginia and Tennessee Railroad*. It allowed Tennessee and North Carolina to send troops to defend western Virginia.

Loring had outranked Lee in the Mexican War, but in Confederate service, Lee's rank was full general before Loring arrived. Their assignment to the western counties had great challenges. They were subjected to heavy raids and difficult terrain. All this was exacerbated by the loose command structure that plagued the Confederacy thru much of the war. The "very cool welcome" Clifford Dowdy wrote of was a "distinctly cold reception" according to Freeman. He explained not two weeks had passed since Lee had given Loring "discretionary orders." Freeman well imagined Loring's point of view: "…he had been an Indian fighter while Lee was a headquarters staff lieutenant; and though he was eleven years Lee's junior and was not a West Pointer, he had seen far more field service than his commanding officer, thus suddenly descended on him from the clouds and the mountain top. Had not Loring been brevetted colonel for gallantry in Mexico? When he had been entrusted with command of the Department of Oregon had he not successfully marched a column across the continent?"

Returning to Lee's arrival on 3 August, Freeman's *R.E. Lee* provides insight to the situation around Huntersville. After Garnett's death, Henry R. Jackson ordered a small Virginia brigade, under Col. William Gilham, to advance from Huntersville. Gilham went

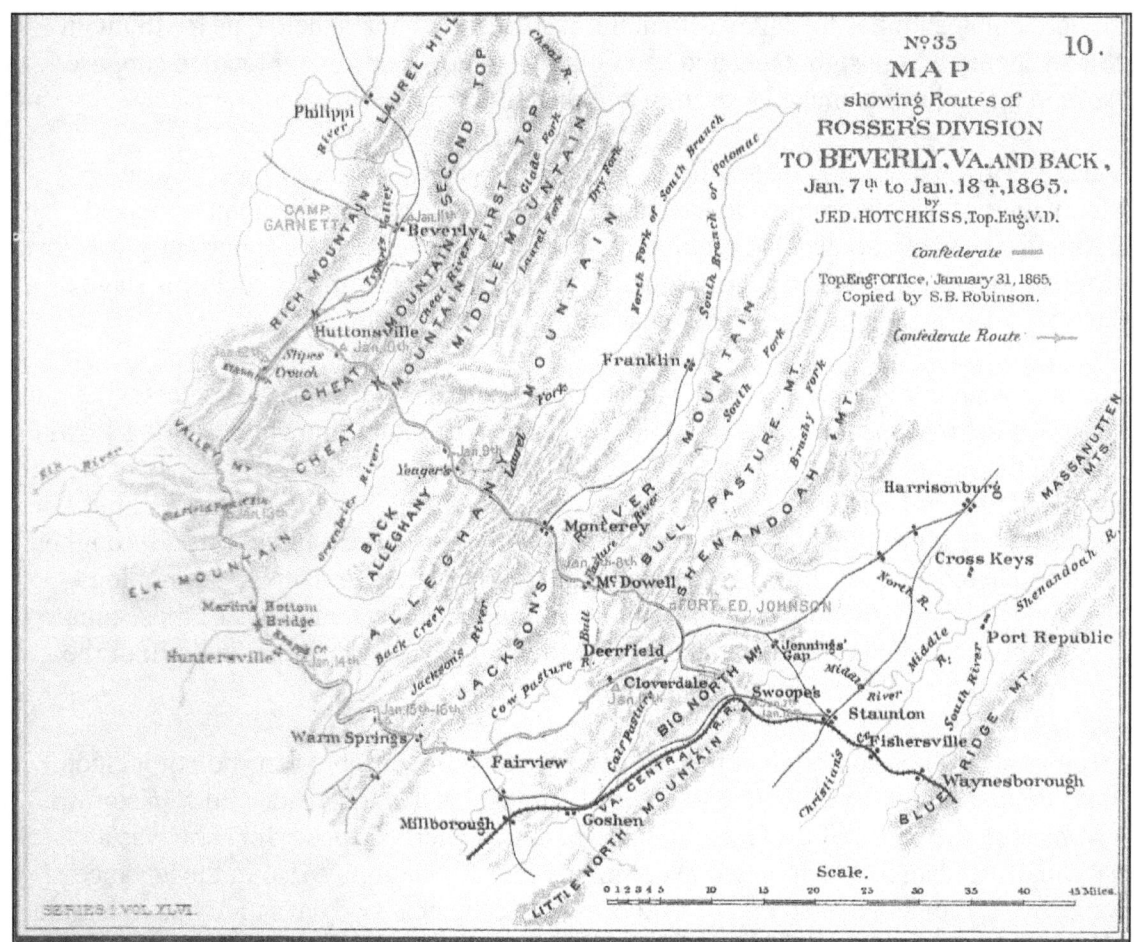

Map above, from the Official Records Atlas, is for one of Brig. Gen. Thomas Rosser's several successful raids into West Virginia. It shows the terrain which Robert E. Lee and William W. Loring campaigned in during 1861. Their efforts were successful enough to protect the *Virginia Central Railroad*, in the Shenandoah Valley, the great connection to Richmond. The *Virginia and Tennessee*, off the map, was a vital connection to supplies and troops coming from the southwest. Millborough was the rail depot to support Loring's advanced base at Huntersville. The U.S. Army held Cheat Mountain, to the north. Lee and Loring occupied Valley Mountain, to the west, in their offensive. Though they were not victorious, neither was the enemy.

Nearly countless battles and raids would take place in this area over the next four years. U.S. troops would campaign to reach and destroy railroads and other points, while Confederate forces would hold them and make counter punches toward the Ohio River. The last great military movement in today's West Virginia was an enemy retreat across the state, after a June 1864 defeat at Lynchburg. Rosser's successful 1865 raid to Beverly is seen above. Troops that campaigned in the area were moving to unite with Lee, when the news from Appomattox reached them. Basil Duke wrote, "That the army of Northern Virginia, with Lee at its head, would ever surrender, had never entered our minds."

forward eighteen miles to Valley Mountain, just west of Yankee held Cheat Mountain. Not an enemy was in sight then, and had Gilham had a larger force, Freeman supposed Jackson might have launched a coordinated attack.

When Loring arrived at Huntersville he was determined to advance toward Cheat Mountain, but was determined to have a well-supplied base first. Freeman criticized Loring for showing no disposition to move fast. He believed a great opportunity was lost "for fear that the soldiers might miss their breakfast!" But Freeman said at this stage of the war Lee was too much of a gentleman to impose his will on Loring.

Freeman went onto point out by 10 August there had been twenty days of successive rain. He called the roads "bottomless in mud." Lee went reconnoitering while "Loring slowly brought the rest of his troops forward." He was moving them from the "newly established advanced base at Huntersville." By 12 August they were all at Valley Mountain, but Lee had not found a line of advance. Walter Taylor went onto serve on Lee's staff throughout the war. He recalled this time, "…but never did I experience the same heart-sinking emotions as when contemplating the wan faces and the emaciated forms of those hungry, sickly, shivering men of the army at Valley Mountain." Ice formed on the night of the 14th, forcing the soldiers to huddle around large fires.

Freeman wrote Lee had brought the rest of his troops forward, but that did not include those to the right under H.R. Jackson. On 12 August his advance under Ed Johnson was advanced to the banks of the Greenbrier River at Traveler's Repose. Johnson was a Virginian, but had been appointed to command the 12th Georgia. Also in the advance were two Virginia units and the 3rd Arkansas. Over the next two days they had to endure plummeting temperatures, frozen roads, and something new to some Georgians, snow.

H.R. Jackson arrived and took command at Traveler's Repose. He named the position Camp Bartow in honour of his Georgian friend Colonel Francis Bartow, who had been killed at Manassas. Johnson had been probing the enemy's Cheat Mountain position across the Greenbrier, and had not found a weak point to strike. But Col. Albert Rust, of the 3rd Arkansas, thought he had found a way to reach the enemy's rear. He had secretly observed their works, with a local guide, and found them vulnerable. If he attacked from the rear, while Jackson attacked in front the enemy would be routed. Jackson approved the strike. Rust's command set out hacking their way through thick rhododendron and mountain laurel. Mysteriously the local guides got lost and after several days Rust's men stumbled back to Camp Bartow.

In early September the poor weather and lack of supplies took their toll on the health of Loring's men. Hospital supplies were short and the mortality rate among the once healthy young men began to climb. Horses and mules suffered as they pulled wagons axle deep in mud. But Lee and Loring kept looking for a way to drive the enemy back.

Off to the east Colonel Rust reported another route of attack. He and a civilian engineer had scouted a way to attack the Yankees on Cheat Mountain. Rust said their left flank was exposed, and that he could launch a surprise attack. That would open the way to a general advance. Rust promised he would not get lost. Lee agreed and on 8 September he issued orders for the attack, in Loring's name. Troops began moving the next day. Lee went forward with two of Loring's brigades, Burke's and Gilham's, on the 11th. Their skirmishing drove back an enemy outpost. This was the first action Lee saw in the war, and presumably for Loring.

At dawn on the 12th, Lee and Loring waited for the sound of Rust's guns. Hours passed and there was no signal of Rust's attack. By noon it was apparent something had gone wrong for Rust. The day passed and still no word from Rust, or H.R. Jackson. The next morning there still was no word. Lee sent his son, Rooney Lee, and Colonel Washington to explore another route of attack. They encountered enemy pickets and Washington fell dead at the first fusillade. Lee was shattered by news of the death of his friend. And that news was more evidence that his first battle was a failure.

So what had happened to Rust? His column safely reached their designated position on the morning of the 12th, unobserved by the enemy. Rust personally captured the first of several pickets. These pickets deceived Rust into believing there were up to 5,000 U.S. troops on Cheat Mountain, and that reinforcements were on the way. There were 3,000 in the vicinity, but only 1,800 on the mountain and around the turnpike. Rust made a reconnaissance and saw the fortified position behind abatis. At that point he felt he could not attack, and withdrew. Rust had been fooled for there were only some 300 enemy troops on the summit, and they had no idea of his presence. His attack would surely have been successful, and Lee's other columns would not have been needed.

Lee wrote Virginia's governor, John Letcher on 17 September. He explained the failure at Cheat Mountain and the difficulties of the campaign. Besides Rust's pullback, the "provisions of the men had been destroyed the previous day by the storm. They had nothing to eat that morning, could not hold out another day…Our greatest loss is the death of my dear friend, Colonel Washington…Our loss is small…Our greatest difficulty is the roads…" Freeman had several criticisms of the campaign. He praised Rust's Arkansas troops, who proved they were superb a year later at Sharpsburg, and he said Rust was no coward. But he had no military experience, and should not have been relied upon to launch the initial attack.

Three days after Lee wrote Governor Letcher he ordered Loring to follow him with most of his force. They were bound for the headwaters of the Kanawha River. The mouth was on the Ohio River. The enemy had advance up the river, leading General Wise to retreat through Charleston on 24 July. The enemy occupied it the next day. Lee was still in Richmond then. General Floyd assumed command of Confederate forces in the Kanawha Valley on 11 August. Rosecrans attacked Floyd at Carnifax Ferry on 10 September, at the time Lee was moving on Cheat Mountain. Though Floyd repulsed the enemy, he realized he was outnumbered and fell back that night. This was the situation as Lee arrived to take department command on 21 September. Floyd and Wise had failed to get along, so that on the 25th Wise was relieved, and sent to a new command in North Carolina. He would later prove himself competent serving under Lee until Appomattox.

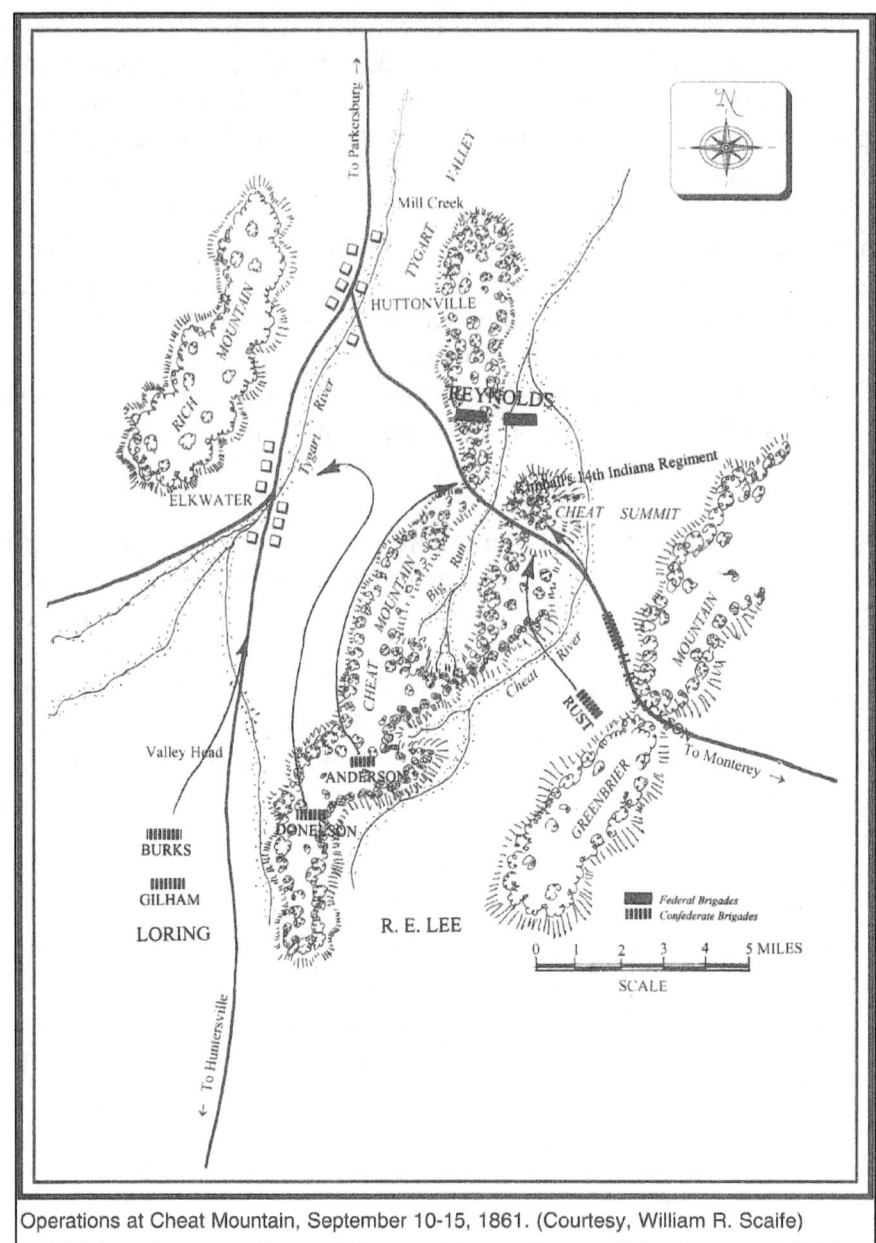

Operations at Cheat Mountain, September 10-15, 1861. (Courtesy, William R. Scaife)

Loring arrived in Monterey on 25 July 1861, on the Parkersburg-Staunton Turnpike, to command the Army of the Northwest. Within a week he rode west toward enemy held Cheat Mountain. He decided a direct assault along the turnpike was impractical, but believed an advance from Huntersville to Valley Mountain pass (Valley Head) would turn the enemy's position. He then began to establish his headquarters and supply base at Huntersville.

Back in Richmond, Robert E. Lee had assigned Loring army command. Lee arrived in Huntersville on 3 August and began his own reconnoitering. There is no evidence Lee usurped power from Loring, though he was ultimately in command. Rust's surprise attack failed to materialize. The operations ended in a stalemate.

But before Wise was sent away, Lee had arrived at his position at Sewell Mountain. Lee agreed it was a good one, and ordered Floyd forward to join Wise. The vanguard of Loring's little army were near. Then on the night of the 5-6 October the pickets thought they heard the Yankees moving up artillery. But when the sun came up it was found that the sound had been wagons withdrawing. Yankee-Rosecrans had decided to shorten his lines of communication and had slipped away.

Newspapers did not see the enemy withdrawal as a success, but as another failure by Lee. He wrote his wife, "I am sorry to say that the movements of our armies cannot keep pace with the expectations of the editors of the papers. I know they can arrange things satisfactorily to themselves on paper. I wish they could do so in the field." Lee had hoped to pursue but the weak horses lacked forage in the mountains. The muddy roads were so bad it took six horses to move a two-horse load. When a wagon stalled it halted the entire train until the stuck wagon could be dragged out of the mud.

Loring had left H.R. Jackson behind holding the line across the turnpike to Staunton. The enemy attacked and had been repulsed, but he was calling on Loring for aid. Lee decided it was not "proper to retain General Loring any longer." On 21 October Lee and Loring departed Sewell Mountain, never to return. Loring returned to his former position while Lee was assigned to the new Department of South Carolina, Georgia, and East Florida. Newspaper editors may have been unhappy, but Lee and Loring had discouraged the enemy from farther advances. That is, they did not advance into today's western Virginia.

Thomas Jonathan Jackson became Stonewall at the great victory at Manassas. Even his Virginia brigade took on the name Stonewall Brigade. The invaders were routed back into Washington City, leaving almost all of northeastern Virginia Yankee-free. But to the northwest they were threatening on two fronts. They were near Winchester, though north of the Potomac in Maryland. They were also in the western counties; counties that would later be essentially confiscated and turned into the illegal state of West Virginia.

Citizens had appealed to the War Department for protection. Secretary of War Judah P. Benjamin wrote to Jackson, who thereby learned on 23 October, that he was to go west and command the Valley District. Jackson and his aides reached Winchester very late on 4 November. He was then in command of 1,700 widely scattered militia. An immediate concern was a reported force of 4,000 Yankees at Romney, 43 miles west of Winchester. On 5 November the War Department ordered the Stonewall Brigade to join Jackson.

Jackson began formulating plans for an offensive against Romney. By 20 November he had a plan and outlined it to Benjamin. He could take the offensive with more troops and wanted Loring and his three brigades. Loring had planned to winter in position to guard the Staunton-Parkersburg Turnpike, but could see Stonewall might have a better chance to attack. By the 14th Loring was headquartered at Staunton, along the way to Winchester. Two of his regiments were there too, but Jackson wanted "all the troops under Loring."

Benjamin sent Loring a copy of Jackson's plan. Benjamin took the middle road and wrote Loring, "if, upon full consideration, you think the proposed movement objectionable and too hazardous, you will decline to make it, and so inform the Department." Loring could have chosen the easier of job of taking defensive positions for the winter, but to his credit he agreed reluctantly to cooperate. He wrote Benjamin, "I consider a winter campaign practicable if the means of transportation sufficient to move this army can be obtained… With warm clothing, good tents, and proper attention by the regimental and company officers there need be no suffering from the climate in the region." It would take weeks.

Loring agreed to begin moving his brigades in stages. He had written Benjamin, "If upon consideration of affairs on this line, you should desire the proposed campaign to be prosecuted, be assured that I shall enter into it with a spirit to succeed." While some writers have portrayed Loring as a self-serving troublemaker, he was cooperating.

Henry R. Jackson had been left in command at Monterey guarding the turnpike approach. But on 25 November he was ordered back to Georgia. Col. Ed Johnson, who had been commanding the 12th Georgia, commanded Loring's troops along the turnpike. Jackson went to command state troops, but would meet Loring again. He would bring a brigade of Georgia troops to the Army of Tennessee while it was defending Atlanta in 1864.

Johnson began to see activity on his front that Stonewall didn't take seriously. During the first week of December Johnson continued to skirmish, indicating the enemy had not abandoned offensive moves along the turnpike. Jackson felt time was being wasted by the slow transfer of Loring's army to Winchester. He wrote Benjamin, "As the Federal forces may move on this place any day, I would respectfully recommend that General Loring be directed not to postpone the marching of his troops." It is interesting to note Jackson did not specify that Federal meant U.S. federal, for the Confederate armies had an even better claim to be a federal army, having the purer federal concept of limiting federal powers!

While Stonewall lobbied Richmond, Ed Johnson, at Camp Allegheny, wrote to Loring, "If it is intended to abandon entirely this position, under the impression that the enemy have left Cheat Mountain, or that if they have not, the roads and climate, & c., will prevent their making incursions into this country, a grave mistake has been committed… If this post is abandoned there will be nothing to prevent their march to Staunton…" Johnson's warning, written on 7 December, was prophetic.

The enemy attacked Ed Johnson's Allegheny Mountain position on 13 December. Johnson believed there were at least 5,000, based on remarks of prisoners, against his "1,200 effective men." He wrote of fighting from 4 a.m. to 2 p.m., where the victory was complete. "The enemy were led into my camp by a Virginia traitor." Loring's withdrawal had been observed and reported as Johnson feared. "I have all along contended that this place would be occupied if we abandoned it." Johnson believed the position could be strengthened, but his force was too small to hold it. Loring received Johnson's report, and advised Richmond later that day (O.R. Ser. 1, Vol. 5, page 459). It was thought good weather led to the attack, and if the weather remained good, they would attack again.

Like Stonewall, Loring had wanted to believe the Yankees around Cheat Mountain would remain inactive for the winter. Loring halted his Winchester bound regiments where they were. He advised Richmond, "…in consequence of the necessity of meeting the enemy at Allegheny, and the uncertainty of their movement, I have determined to keep the command of Colonel Johnson where it is for the present…"

Two days before Christmas, Stonewall again solicited Richmond for "such of Brig. Gen. W.W. Loring's forces as are on and near Allegheny Mountains." Then he speculated, "…that the forces that were recently defeated on the Allegheny will be in Romney before Colonel Johnson leaves his position." Richmond upheld Loring's decision to hold Johnson at Camp Allegheny. Johnson was promoted to brigadier effective 13 December.

Jackson was from northwestern Virginia, and that was a motivator for his offensive ambitions for the area. But as time had passed the reports of the enemy force at Romney grew from 4,000 to 7,000, and then to 11,000. Likewise the enemy overestimated Jackson's force. As Jackson waited Loring had continued to move in stages. Loring said, "I consider a winter campaign practicable if the means of transportation sufficient to move this army can be obtained…With warm clothing, good tents, and proper attention by the regimental and company officers there need be no suffering from the climate in that region." Loring's brigades arrived in Winchester by 27 December. They were about to learn the reality of such shortages.

Loring brought three of the brigades of his Army of the Northwest to Winchester. Virginian William Booth Taliaferro commanded one. He had graduated from William and Mary, and studied law at Harvard. His Mexican War service must have given him some bond to Loring. The 3rd Arkansas was in his brigade and was the only Arkansas unit to serve in Virginia. A second was under Virginia born Samuel Read Anderson. He had settled in the Nashville area and served as a lieutenant colonel of the 1st Tennessee in the Mexican War. His brigade of Tennessee regiments would remain in the Eastern Theatre. Loring's third brigade was under William Gilham. His 21st Virginia was brigaded with two other Virginia regiments. When the Romney Campaign ended, Jackson preferred charges against this fellow V.M.I. colleague for moving too slowly.

One cadet remembered Gilham as an excellent teacher, unlike the unpopular Jackson. The cadet wrote that Gilham "commanded our profound respect, admiration, and love." Gilham paid Jackson a visit, along with the 21st Virginia's Lt. Col. John Mercer Patton. Patton told Jackson, "General, both my regiment and myself are ready to execute your orders, but I feel it my duty to say to you that my men are so foot sore and weary that they could just crawl up barely and if they have any double-quicking to do from the character of your orders, I suppose they will." Jackson told him if that was their condition they would not have to go on the expedition. Patton was a V.M.I. graduate and quickly realized being excluded would not do, and Jackson forgot about it.

One day before 1862 had rung in, Loring signed an autograph book. A lady identified as Elizabeth submitted it to *Confederate Veteran* in 1921 (Volume 29, page 29). She wrote, "Now we turn to a time that left us graves unmarked and memories, the War Between the States, and the year is 1861. This rollicking soldier boy, maybe the type who loves and rides away, signs himself 'Major General Loring,' and his contribution is written in a facetious vein, as follows:

'If I ever forget thee ever,
Then let me prosper never,
But let it cause
My tongue and jaws
To cling and cleave together.'"

Jackson's force set out from Winchester, to drive the enemy from Romney, on 1 January 1862. Romney only had a population of 500, but it was the principal community in the valley of the South Branch of the Potomac River. Controlling Romney probably meant controlling the valley. Jackson had his own Stonewall Brigade, Loring's three brigades, a brigade of militia, and 26 pieces of artillery. This gave Jackson 11,000 men, which is the same as what was believed the enemy had.

The New Year's Day march began with temperatures in the fifties, but the good weather ended in late afternoon. Winds out of the northwest sent the temperature plummeting. Many troops lacked outer clothing. The next morning winds sent blinding snow into the path of the column. Wagons bogged away as the earth turned white, and the roads began to freeze. The column had moved about fifteen miles over two days. Finally that night the wagons came up with food. Loring allowed his brigades to bivouac. Soldiers and teams had suffered in the cold for a day and a half without food, and needed to rejuvenate.

Then Jackson and Loring had their first falling out. Jackson ordered Loring to bring his regiments up, as he wanted to veer north to Bath, and attack an enemy force at sunrise. Loring was furious. He responded, "By God, sir, this is the damnedest outrage ever perpetrated in the annals of history, keeping my men out here in the cold without food!" Loring had been a soldier for thirty years, and followed orders. The men were outraged and called Jackson "Tom Fool Jackson." The Stonewall Brigade was hungry too. It was commanded by Virginian Richard Brooke Garnett, a cousin of Robert Garnett killed at Carrick's Ford. Garnett argued the men had to eat. Jackson could not understand men wanting to eat when they could attack the enemy! He said, "I never found anything impossible with this brigade."

William McComb recalled the Romney Campaign in *Confederate Veteran* in 1914 (Volume 22, page 211). The 14th Tennessee officer recalled Jackson had made "General Loring furiously mad, and he dashed through the camp, ordering everything back in the wagons at once. Part of the bread was half cooked and the rest in dough. Consequently the boys got no supper, and the teams ate very little. But we obeyed orders and prized and shoved wagons from that time until after day the next morning and did not advance three hundred yards. Then, after General Jackson took in the situation the next morning, he ordered us in bivouac and to cook two days' rations. This was our first acquaintance with General Jackson, and unnecessary to say, we were not favorably impressed."

Loring's command was in the lead of Jackson's main column, marching toward Bath, on 3 January. Some 870 militia swung to the west so that Jackson could have a two-pronged attack. They didn't march up to Jackson's expectations, and neither did Loring's lead brigade under Gilham. Jackson was still hoping to overwhelm the 1,400-man garrison at Bath when Gilham encountered enemy skirmishers. Jackson ordered them to sweep them out of the way, but Loring soon countermanded the order and told Gilham to go into bivouac. Jackson lashed out at Loring. During an angry exchange Loring said, "If you should be killed, I would find myself in command of an army of the object of whose movement I know nothing!" Similar complaints would come forth in 1862. Cavalryman Turner Ashby would offer his resignation because "not knowing his movements has made my dutys much more arduous." Richard Ewell would have the same complaint in the Shenandoah Valley.

Jackson finally got his attack on the Bath garrison on 4 January. Three inches of snow overnight had not improved the circumstances. Mountain ranges to the east and west made positioning troops for the attack difficult. Loring's troop positions were not the best, and by mid-afternoon Jackson just rode into Bath, in advance of the skirmishers, and found the enemy escaping and making it across the Potomac River into Maryland.

That night the temperature fell to eight degrees. It was so cold shoe soles froze to the ground. On Sunday 5 January snow fell for most of the day. On Monday there was at least six inches blanketing the ground, and with ice clogging the Potomac, Jackson decided to turn south. The horses suffered too. They did not have winter shoes and on Tuesday Loring's mount slipped, causing the general to be badly bruised. The miserable weather followed Jackson, but some good news materialized. Ashby's cavalry learned the enemy had abandoned Romney! Jackson rode into town on 14 January, and Loring got his three brigades there over the next two days.

Romney turned out to be a poor reward for a miserable campaign. The Yankees had left tents standing and medical supplies. But they also left waste in the muddy streets. It was so deep even the horses struggled. One soldier wrote, "Of all the miserable holes in creation, Romney takes the lead." He called it little more than a hog pen. Charles Todd Quintard would later be a bishop, but was the 1st Tennessee's chaplain here. He wrote, "I cannot begin to tell all that our troops suffered through the stupidity and want of forethought of Major-General Jackson. It is enough to say that we were subjected to the severest trials that human nature could endure. We left Winchester with 2,700 men in General Anderson's Brigade of Tennesseans. That number was reduced to 1,100." He thought "…General Loring ought to demand that he might be allowed to withdraw his forces from the command of Major-General Jackson…"

Jackson aggravated Loring's command further when he and the Stonewall Brigade filed out of Romney, bound for civilized Winchester, on 23 January. Loring and his three demoralized brigades watched the cheering Virginians depart. Some were calling out, "Jackson's lambs," and "There go your F.F.V's [First Families of Virginia]." It did not take long for the anger to manifest itself into Quintard's idea of withdrawing. Jackson was not going to enjoy the "ease and comfort" of Winchester while Loring's froze.

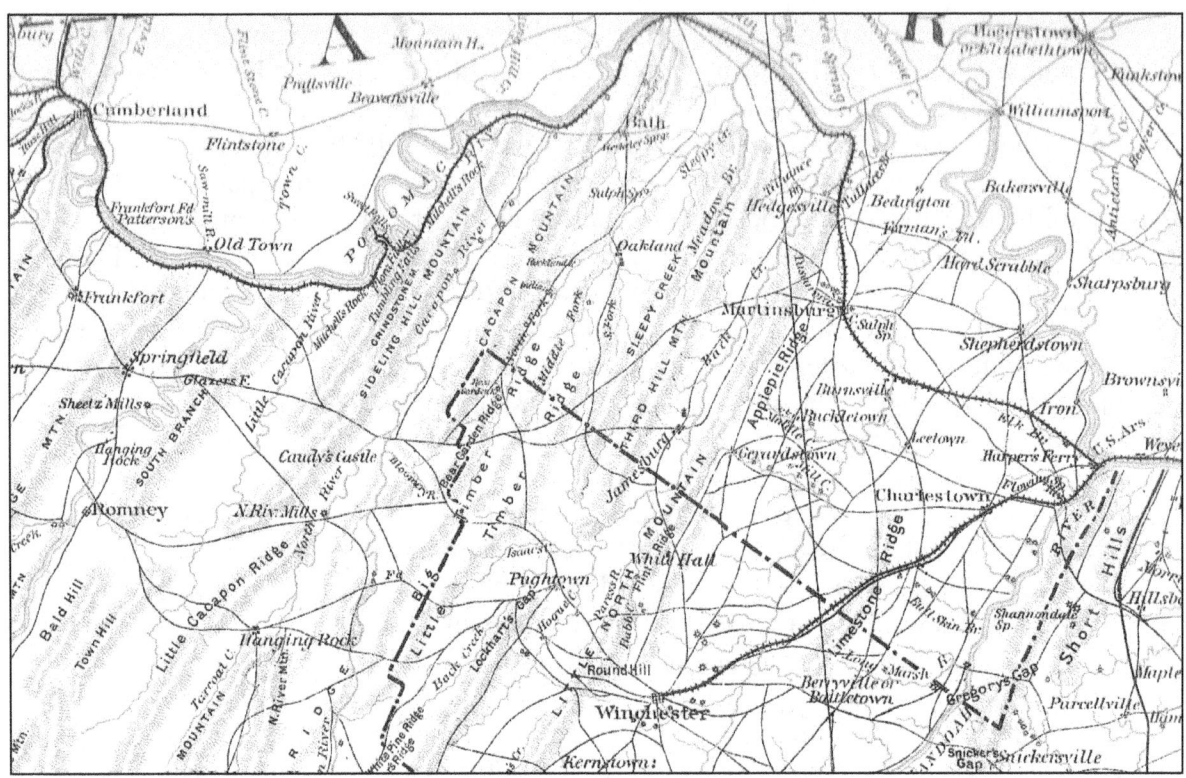

This map shows the area of the Romney Campaign. Stonewall Jackson hailed from the northwestern Virginia area. Naturally he wanted to drive U.S. forces out, but taking and holding the *Baltimore and Ohio Railroad* (running along the Potomac) was the greater strategic goal. It was the U.S. capitol's direct link to Ohio and beyond. Jackson was at Winchester, in November 1861, with three militia brigades and two cavalry companies. Jackson called on Loring's Army of the Northwest to join him. Loring was cooperative and had three of his brigades link with Jackson in December.

Jackson and Loring fought no great battles in the Romney Campaign, for U.S. troops evacuated towns on their approach. In January 1862 they set out for Bath, north of Winchester. The enemy fled from Bath, leaving supplies in their haste for the north bank of the Potomac, into Maryland. Jackson and Loring turned toward Romney, and again the enemy abandoned supplies in another panic. Jackson then returned to Winchester with his choice troops; his old Stonewall Brigade had joined his command. This left Loring and his three brigades in undesirable little Romney. The lack of supplies and freezing conditions led to a petition by 11 of Loring's brigade and regimental officers, seeking an override of Jackson's orders. Loring dispatched the petition to the Secretary of War, thru Jackson.

Some historians have labeled Loring as a troublemaker. But Romney was not even on the railroad. Conditions were such that some regiments had two out of three men unfit for duty. Chaplain Quintard wrote of the stupidity and lack of forethought by Jackson. Clearly there were two sides to the issue of holding Romney. Fortunately President Davis worked out a solution that retained the services of Jackson and Loring.

Raab's biography explains how the fat got in the fire! On 25 January 1862 eleven of Loring's brigade and regimental officers handed him a signed petition condemning the occupation of Romney. Loring dispatched it to Secretary of War Judah Benjamin, and by way of Jackson in Winchester. Jackson submitted his resignation on 31 January, also being upset that he was ordered to bring Loring's army back to Winchester. Joseph E. Johnston appealed to Jackson's patriotism, and Jackson withdrew his resignation. It was good for the Confederacy that he did, for his star was rising higher than Loring's.

Negative implications have been made regarding Loring not getting along with Jackson. But Stonewall would later have trouble with other subordinates. Richard Garnett was in command of the Stonewall Brigade at Kernstown in March. Jackson had come across a larger enemy force than expected. He had left Garnett in the dark as to his intentions, just as he had done to Loring and others. Garnett pulled back at a critical juncture, to save his command. It may have had a part in Jackson's defeat, which was likely anyway. All five of Garnett's regimental commanders in the Stonewall Brigade felt he was justified. But Jackson put him under arrest, many think to shift the blame of his own tactical defeat.

Jackson also had problems with his cavalry chief, Turner Ashby. Much of it was over a lack of discipline in Ashby's handling of his troops. Jackson largely striped Ashby of his command. This led to his resignation, much to Jackson's surprise. This surprised Jackson though he had been on such a course after his conflict with Loring.

Stonewall's cartographer was Jedediah Hotchkiss. He later shared his opinion of Loring, which may have been Stonewall's. General Loring always struck me as lacking in nearly all the qualities necessary for command of an army designed to carry on an offensive campaign in a difficult region. He was always hesitating [in] what to do, was always suggesting difficulties in the way of active operations, and worse than all in my mind, he was always filling himself with brandy and thus incapacitating himself for his duties."

Yet Jackson was not through with Loring. He readied a court-martial charge against Loring, accusing him of neglect of duty and the like. Fortunately President Davis saw the folly of it all, and made sure charges would not be prosecuted. On 19 February 1862 Loring was promoted to major general. Three days later Loring arrived at Norfolk. But he arrived with pneumonia and was confined to a sick bed at the Norfolk Naval Hospital.

Quintard was on hand at Loring's bedside. An enormous historical event was on the horizon in late February. Quintard wrote, "I became interested in the transformation by which the *'Merrimac'* became the *'Virginia'* of the Confederate Navy. One day I slipped off from my patient, General Loring, while he was sleeping, and went to Portsmouth to visit the wonderful craft."

Saturday 8 March 1862 was an unusually clear and bright day. The water was calm with a gentle breeze from the northwest. Captain Franklin Buchanan took the *Virginia* out for her maiden voyage. All aboard and on shore thought it was a trial run. Quintard said he was there to witness what followed; he does not say if Loring did. The *Virginia* kept steaming downriver and into Hampton Roads. The 14-gun *Virginia* took left little time to show her shells could penetrate the fragile hull of the 24-gun U.S.S. Cumberland. One shot wiped out a sixteen-man gun crew. She then rammed the Yankee, and on impact fired a bow gun, killing ten. The Cumberland managed to fire broadsides before she lurched forward, and with a roar, sank bow first. Colours were flying as she went under.

The next morning the *Virginia* steamed back into Hampton Roads and found the enemy's new ironclad, the *U.S.S. Monitor*. The previous day the *U.S.S. Minnesota* had grounded and the *Monitor* was to protect it. For four hours the two ironclads pounded each other. The *Virginia* got aground and the *Monitor* moved closer. But the Virginia fired and wounded their commander. With that the Yankee quit fighting. The *Virginia* was able to get free and falling tide and leaks caused her to return to anchorage. The *Monitor* had saved the *Minnesota* but the *Virginia* had won undisputed control of Hampton Roads.

Quintard said Loring had fully recovered by 11 April. They went down with a party of friends to watch the *Virginia* steam into Hampton Roads. Quintard said the *Monitor* could not be drawn into an engagement. The Peninsula Campaign commenced and Norfolk was evacuated. Loring was in command at nearby Suffolk, and was ordered to evacuate. Thus Loring's time in the Tidewater came to an end.

Loring found a new assignment to the Department of Southwestern Virginia; it was effective 8 May 1862. His headquarters were at Giles Court House. The war in Virginia was in great transition. Stonewall Jackson was about to clear the Yankees out of the Shenandoah, and Lee was about to fight the Seven Days and save Richmond. In August Lee was marching into northern Virginia to defeat the Yankee "miscreant" John Pope. His "Army of Virginia" was outside Washington City, and being reinforced by troops that had fought in the Seven Days under McClellan.

Lee's cavalry was under Maj. Gen. James Ewell Brown Stuart and made a typical dashing Confederate raid, on 22 August, whereby he secured papers related to enemy troop movements. They indicated troops on the Kanawha, facing Loring, were also being sent to Pope. Thus Lee requested that Loring advance. Actually, Loring's cavalry, under Brig. Gen. Albert Gallatin Jenkins had also advanced on 22 August. Jenkins had a cavalry brigade of about 550 men; cavalry brigades were smaller than infantry brigades.

Jenkins was from Cabell County, and his plantation there was on the banks of the Ohio. Like Stonewall, Jenkins had a personal interest in holding the western counties. They defeated the enemy at Buckhannon on 30 August. Vast stores were destroyed, but not before they cast aside their shotguns and armed themselves with new rifles. Jenkins defeated and paroled other enemy forces as he advanced to the banks of the Ohio. On the evening of 4 September his cavalry forded the Ohio River. Jenkins wrote of the exciting crossing and forming the command on an eminence where "the banners of the Southern Confederacy floated over the soil of the invaders. As our flag was unfurled in the splendors of the evening sun, cheers upon cheers arose from the men…"

Jenkins made a considerable march into Ohio. The people feared depredations and even that their homes would be burned. Though many of the men were homeless and their

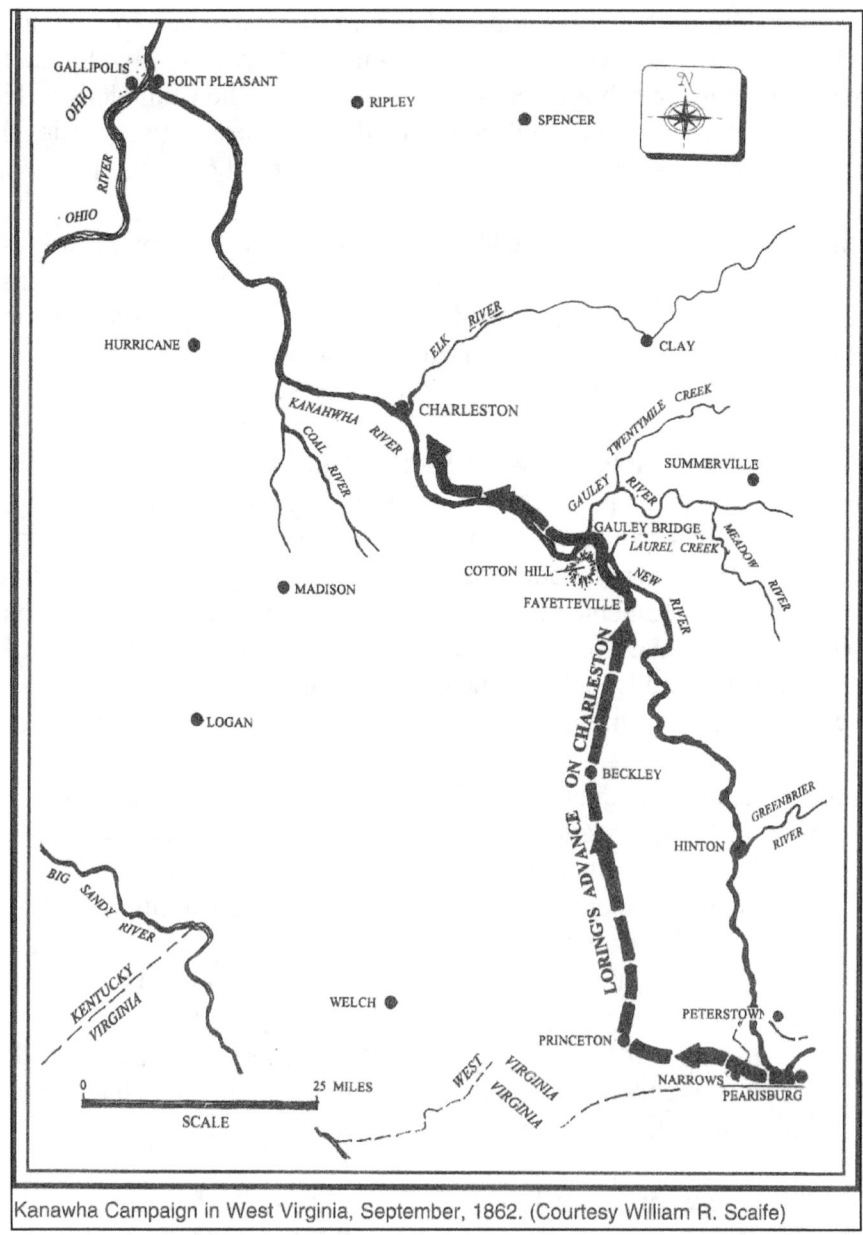
Kanawha Campaign in West Virginia, September, 1862. (Courtesy William R. Scaife)

Loring's victorious Kanawha Campaign was overshadowed by Lee's post Second Manassas advance into Maryland. Lee had hoped Loring would advance with him. Loring first needed to control the Kanawha River Valley. Loring's cavalry, under Jenkins, rode in advance and actually crossed into Ohio. Loring advanced, and the enemy fell back without making a successful stand. They were compelled to abandon immense stores, which Loring estimated at about $1,000,000. He held Charleston, the future capital of West Virginia. Loring won a brilliant campaign. Lee won a tactical victory at Sharpsburg, Maryland, though his campaign failed.

Loring began recruiting, since the U.S. Army had been cleared out. His success led to conflicts with Governor Letcher, and ultimately Loring's request to serve in another department. Loring was sent to Mississippi and there his division was born.

families in exile in Virginia, Jenkins told the Ohioans that his men were not barbarians. They were fighting for their liberties. As they continued they were often by the friendly waving of handkerchiefs and shouts for Jefferson Davis and the Confederacy. Jenkins returned to cross the river at Racine, Ohio. Ironically it was less than ten miles from Buffington Island, where many of John Hunt Morgan's would cross the following July.

While Loring's cavalry had crossed the Ohio River, Lee was advancing toward the Potomac. He had won a splendid victory at Manassas on 30 August. Instructions from Secretary of War George Randolph reached Loring, indicating he was to clear the Kanawha Valley as Lee advanced into Maryland. On 6 September Loring's 5,000 troops advanced. Lee hoped Loring might then join him in the Shenandoah.

Loring drove the enemy from Fayetteville. Their withdrawal became more of a rout. Loring's men were able to supply themselves with new guns, 425 wagons, food, and other equipment. Loring's artillery opened on Charleston, on the Kanawha River, on the morning of the 13th. The enemy made a run toward the Ohio River, leaving stores worth perhaps $1,000,000. By late September Lee had repulsed the enemy at Sharpsburg, but had fallen back into Virginia. Loring was holding Charleston, but Richmond still wanted him to join Lee. Lee praised Loring's campaign, but other trouble was brewing for Loring. He was interfered with by the governor and others in building up his army.

Loring militarily secured the Kanawha Valley for the Confederacy, the only time in the war. He issued a congratulatory address to his troops and a proclamation to the people: "The army of the Confederate States has come among you to expel the enemy, to rescue the people from the despotism of the counterfeit State government imposed on you by Northern bayonets, and to restore the country once more to its natural allegiance to the State. We fight for peace and the possession of our own territory. We do not intend to punish those who remain at home as quite citizens in obedience to the laws of the land, and to all such, clemency and amnesty are declared; but those who persist in adhering to the cause of the public enemy and the pretended State government he has erected at Wheeling, will be dealt with as their obstinate treachery deserves."

Loring's proclamation went onto call on the able-bodied to "defend the sanctities of religion and virtue, home territory, honor and law…" He pointed out oaths to the U.S. government were "…immoral attempts to retrain you from your duty to your State and government." The *Confederate Military History* volume on West Virginia indicated, "Loring had considerable success at first in securing recruits and collecting conscripts, but these accessions were checked by rumours…" of another enemy invasion and complaints to Richmond of Loring's methods. Gov. John Letcher was a problem.

On 22 September Loring wrote Secretary of War George Randolph, "I observe in the late message of the Governor of the State certain wanton and unfounded charges, that, exceeding my authority as a Confederate officer, I had improperly and mischievously interfered with the non-conscripts…" Loring went onto detail his predicament. Instead of support Loring received orders from Richmond, specifically from Gen. Samuel Cooper, to turn over his command to another general and report to Richmond. This seems to have been prompted by an ultimatum Loring had sent regarding Letcher.

Loring was relieved of command at his own request on 27 November 1862. Loring wrote his friend Dr. Charles Quintard, "I had a brilliant campaign in Western Virginia as long as it lasted; we took the Kanawha Valley and waters and levees in the Ohio; I, but for the interference of Randolph with matters of which he was ignorant, and as I am informed, without the knowledge of the President, would have had a campaign which would have been of great service. As it was I saw no prospect in Western Virginia this winter but monotonous inactivity-I applied to be relieved and ordered to an army in the field. It resulted in me coming here [Meridian, Mississippi]."

Of further interest: The Library of Virginia has field maps of the southwestern part of Virginia, found in books that belonged to Loring. They went with reports to the governor.

Loring's staff officers in Virginia per Robert Krick's *Staff Officers in Gray* were:

Barton, Seth M., Lt. Col.: Engineer Officer (EO), 1862
Baskerville, Henry E.C., Capt.: Assistant Commissary of Subsistence (ACS), 1861
Deshler, James, Capt.: Acting Chief Artillery, 1861
Kirker, William H., Maj.: Quartermaster (Q) 1861?-1862
Lee, Hugh H., Lt.: Ordinance Officer (OO), 1861
Long, Armistead L., Maj.: Chief of Artillery, 1861
Mathews, Henry M., Capt.: Engineer Officer (EO), 1861-1862
Porterfield, George A., Col.: Ordinance Officer (EO), 1861
Quintard, Charles T., Lt.: Aide-de-Camp (ADC), 1862
Robinson, Henry, Maj.: Assistant Adjutant General (AAG), 1862
Starke, William E.: Volunteer Aide-de-Camp (VADC), 1861
Stevenson, Carter, L., Lt. Col.: Assistant Adjutant General (AAG), 1861-1862
Whiting, Jasper S.: Lt. Engineer Officer (EO), 1861
Williams, James S., Maj.: Engineer Officer (EO), 1861
Yost, Samuel M., Capt.: Assistant Quartermaster (AQM)

Absent from the list is John Douglas Myrick. Krick lists him in Appendix One as a staff officer of Loring's with no dates of service. Krick indicates Myrick as an Aide-de-Camp (ADC) and Chief of Artillery. Loring's biographer James Raab has Myrick as one of Loring's staff officers in Virginia. In September 1862 Loring sent Myrick to Richmond to request 5,000 more troops. Myrick was likely an ADC at this time, and did not serve as Artillery Chief until Fort Pemberton.

When Loring went to Mississippi it is difficult to tell exactly who went with him, and who did not. Loring wrote Quintard on 28 December 1862, "I have Charlie and Joe Mathews, Hanson Thomas and Henry Robinson with me, the rest of my staff including Fitzhugh who I miss very much, remain in Western Virginia." The Mathews named are not on Krick's list, though Henry Mathews is. Henry Robinson is the only name that Krick lists that Loring mentions making it to Mississippi. Myrick must have come later.

It seems a surprise that five from Loring's staff in Virginia became generals. Carter L. Stevenson rose to major general and commanded Pemberton's largest division at Champion Hill. Fellow Virginian Seth M. Barton commanded a brigade of Georgian's in his division there. James Deshler was killed at Chickamauga, and William Starke was killed at Sharpsburg, leading Stonewall's old division. Armistead Long survived the war and wrote a biography of Robert E. Lee.

Additional staff members for Loring are found in *Confederate Staff Officers 1861-1865*, by Joseph H. Crute, Jr. It lists staffs for Confederate generals, though without all the biographical information Krick includes. He listed about 2,300 staff officers with ties to Virginia service. Those names are not repeated on the following list from Crute; hence, the following should be those that served under Loring in Pemberton's department, or in the Army of Tennessee. I have added pertinent remarks regarding their service.

Armstead, John N., Captain, ordinance officer, March 1863: Krick spells Armistead in an appendix. He lists him as an O.O. to Loring and Pemberton. Loring mentions Armstead at Fort Pemberton.
Banks, Edwin Alexander, Major, CQM, January 1864: Krick includes Banks in an appendix, as a quartermaster to Loring, Lovell, and Pemberton.
Bursley, A. A., Captain, chief of artillery, 16 May, 1863; March 1864: Bursley unknown?
Clarke, John Lytle, Lt. and aide-de-camp, March 20, 1862, major and assistant adjutant general, May 1, 1862: Krick adds born 1833, died 1898.
Cole, Robert G. Major, commissary of subsistence, 6 August, 1861
Ellis, Powhatan, Jr., Captain, assistant adjutant general, January 1864. Raab's biography of Tilghman says the general died in the arms of his adjutant general, Powhatan Ellis. Krick's appendix lists Ellis as AAG to Tilghman, B.R. Johnson, Loring, and S.D. Lee. Then as a major he was AAG to Leo. Polk. He is also shown as being on the staffs of Cleburne, Floyd, John Adams, R. Taylor, F. Gardner, W.T. Martin, and Forrest. Ellis could hardly have served on more staffs. Krick shows him born in 1829; death in 1906.
Farlow, L.G., Major, commissary of subsistence, 20 November, 1864: Krick's appendix lists Farlow for Loring and Buford.
Fitzhugh, Henry H., Major, assistant adjutant general, 26 June, 1862: Crute indicates he was promoted to colonel on 14 September 1862; it may have been to lieutenant colonel.
Harrison, Thomas, Lieutenant, aide-de-camp, 16 May 1863: Krick's appendix shows he was also an aide-de-camp to Baldwin and Hardee.
Hunter, John A., Dr., M.D., 20 September 1862
Jones, J.W., Major, provost marshal, 1864
King, John Floyd, Major, chief of artillery, 20 September 1862; Krick's appendix shows he was ordinance officer for Heth and chief of artillery for Loring. Born 1842, died 1915.
Marshall, Levin K., Captain, assistant adjutant general, 20 August 1863; Krick shows he was assistant adjutant and inspector general, and middle initial of "R."
Marye, Lawrence S., Captain, ordinance officer, 20 September 1862
Mathews, Charles L., Captain, aide-de-camp, 1 May 1862; February 1864
Mathews, H.M., Major, aide-de-camp, 3 March 1862
McCranie, George W., Major, provost marshal, 18 July 1864

McDavitt, James C., Lieutenant, staff duty, per Crute; Krick's appendix shows he was also on the staffs of Leonidas Polk, Maury, and J.E. Johnston.

McFarland, William, rank not shown by Crute, volunteer-aide-de-camp, 16 May 1863

McGuire, Thomas, Major, quartermaster, 15 August 1863; Krick's appendix shows he was also on the staffs of Buford and Featherston.

McKnight, George, Major, assistant adjutant general, March and 2 May 1863; Krick's appendix shows he was born 1833, and died 1869.

Meriwether, Minor, Major, engineer officer, March 1863; Krick's appendix points out he was also an engineer officer for Leonidas Polk, Pemberton, and Price.

Mickle, Belton, Captain, assistant quartermaster, March to 16 May 1863. Loring's report on Fort Pemberton has him as quartermaster. Krick's appendix shows he was also on Villepigue's staff.

Millsaps, Reuben Webster, Major, assistant inspector general, 15 July 1864

Myers, William B., Captain, assistant adjutant general, 15 May and 20 September 1862, and to major on 14 October 1862

Poor, Richard Lowndes, Captain, engineer officer, 20 September 1862

Robinson, John Moncure, Captain, engineer officer, March 1863; Krick's index shows he was also on staffs of Williams, Jones, and Breckinridge. He was born in 1835, died 1893.

Sykes, William, Captain, assistant aide-de-camp, 16 May 1863

Taylor, Henry, Captain, volunteer aide-de-camp, 16 May 1863

Thomas, James D., Lieutenant, aide-de-camp, 1 August 1863

Thorburn, Charles Edmonston, Colonel, assistant inspector general and chief of artillery, 20 September 1862; Krick's appendix shows he was assistant adjutant and inspector general and ordinance officer. *Confederate Colonels* has a biographical entry.

Vernon, S. McD., Lieutenant, engineer officer, February 1864; Krick's appendix shows he was also on Walthall's staff.

Venve (de Veuve?), Henry de, Captain, assistant engineer officer, 16 May 1863: Krick's appendix shows he died in 1898.

Voorhies, A.H., chief surgeon, March 1863, is mentioned in Loring's report on Fort Pemberton. Loring reported he arrived on the 15th.

Watts, W. Ormsby, Major, assistant ordinance officer, January 1864; Krick's appendix shows he was assistant adjutant general to Tilghman, volunteer aide-de-camp to S.D. Lee, ordinance officer for Polk, and acting ordinance officer for Loring.

Whitehead, P.F., surgeon, 1864

Whiting, Joseph ?, (Jasper in Krick's register), Lieutenant, engineer officer, 21 July 1861

Krick explains duties of staff positions. The adjutant general was almost always viewed as the primary staff officer; officially they were assistant adjutant general (AAG). Aide-de-camps (ADC) might perform any chore his general assigned. Engineer officers (EO) were experienced engineers who might scout, eye terrain, improve roads, lay out lines, etc. Inspector generals, or assistant adjutant and inspectors general (AAIGS), had numerous tasks; some were inspection of camps, drills, and equipment. Ordinance officers (OOS) in a volunteer army had no such prewar occupation. Army regulations defined quartermasters as providing quarters (likely tents), transportation, clothing, care of livestock, etc. They were typically majors in divisions (QM) and captains in brigades (AQM). They often dealt with money, as paymasters to troops. Commissary officers dealt with rations; commissary of subsistence (CS), and assistants (ACS).

3-Mississippi: Birthplace of Loring's Division

Ultimately the battle to control the Mississippi River was fought in Mississippi. Loring came to Mississippi as General Ulysses S. Grant was beginning his first campaign to take Vicksburg. Loring fought the invaders over a wide area of the Magnolia State, with much success. The Mississippi River is one of the world's great rivers and taking it was a motivator for the U.S. military. Vicksburg was a sort of Gibraltar of the river, but finding a point to approach it consumed about five months, and almost two more to take it.

A Grant biographer, W.E. Woodward wrote of the Mississippi and the Mississippi Delta, "Perhaps I have not made clear the nature of the country. The river contains the dripping rain of half a continent. One can hardly call it a river; it is one of the wonders of the world; it is to rivers what Pike's Peak is to a pleasant little hill. In that amphibious land one meets creeks and bayous everywhere. Roads end suddenly in a waste of swirling water flowing in the midst of a tangled forest. The river is higher than the land, and levees of earth and stones strive to keep it in its course. But it escapes. Creeks flow from it, running strangely backward and upstream. In these drowned and stricken forests one loses sense of direction. The world becomes a wilderness of yellow water, trees and trailing vines…but not altogether; there stands Vicksburg, on its tall hill, a solid vision in a melting cosmos." Loring might agreeably have reflected with this colorful description.

Before the Confederacy was formed the free and independent states of Louisiana and Mississippi had passed on official word they did not ever intend to close the Mississippi River to trade with the United States. Why would they? And later the Confederate government dittoed their acts. This was not enough for Lincoln and the imperialists. Taking the river was an essential element of Gen. Winfield Scott's "Anaconda Plan." Grant was Lincoln's man to finish the job. After the river was open to U.S. warships Lincoln would later say the river flowed "unvexed to the sea." The imagery has been adored by generations of imperialists, with no thought that Lincoln was doing the vexing!

Before Loring arrived in December 1862, the Confederacy had left native son Earl Van Dorn to guard the approaches into the Magnolia State. He was at some disadvantage as the U.S. Army had enhanced Beauregard's fortifications around Corinth. The town was not only on the *Memphis and Charleston Railroad*, but the *Mobile & Ohio* too. Van Dorn had tried to take it in a two-day battle in October. He failed though many of his units proved themselves, and would soon come to serve under Loring.

Van Dorn's failure at Corinth led to his replacement by John C. Pemberton. In fairness to Van Dorn, it might be considered the fortifications at Corinth were especially significant for 1862. In 1864 there was cumulative evidence of the high failure rate of attacking them for both sides. Van Dorn's attacks at Elkhorn Tavern, or Pea Ridge, had also failed back in March. He may have been too rash to command infantry. Several of his generals were scheming for Van Dorn's removal. He demanded a court of inquiry, which Pemberton granted. It convened on 7 November. One of the officers on it was Lloyd Tilghman, who had surrendered Fort Henry. Allegations were generally disproved, and Pemberton kept Van Dorn to command his cavalry. He went onto prove it was a good decision.

Van Dorn's defeat at Corinth allowed Grant to set up a supply base at Holly Springs. It was begun as his troops entered the beautiful town on 13 November. Grant's advance entered Coffeeville on 5 December. Lloyd Tilghman was there in Lovell's Division. Mansfield Lovell had commanded a division under Van Dorn at Corinth. His days were numbered because he was under scrutiny for losing New Orleans back in April. But here he saw an opportunity to strike the enemy near Coffeeville, and sent Tilghman to take care of them. It was a small affair, but Tilghman's reputation needed help. He remarked "the whole affair was a complete success and taught the enemy a lesson I am sure they will not soon forget."

Capt. J.L. Bond wrote to *Confederate Veteran* (Vol. 5, page, 462) in 1897 on the retreat from Holly Springs, south to Coffeeville. He was in the 12th Louisiana of Villepigue's Brigade. They would later establish a reputation as great fighters for Loring. Bond wrote, "At Coffeeville there was a hot fight and Capt. (Thomas C.) Standifer commanded the skirmish line of our brigade, consisting of about six hundred men. Col. (Thomas Scott) had great confidence in Standifer. Good skirmish-line is the salvation of an army, as it protects the troops from surprise. In the skirmish at Coffeeville Standifer drove back the enemy and demonstrated his high qualities as a commander. He was not only cool and brave, but possessed wonderful magnetism with his men."

Loring arrived in Mississippi in December. President Davis had placed John Pemberton in command of the Department of Mississippi and East Louisiana. Loring would have been a better choice, but at least he got second in command. It didn't take Loring long to have an opinion of Pemberton. In December he wrote Quintard, I "do not think much of the officer in charge." Lt. William Drennan, of Featherston's staff thought that Loring hated Pemberton to such a degree that he would be willing for Pemberton to lose a battle, if it resulted in Pemberton being displaced.

Loring was far from the only one who disliked Pemberton. Drennan also wrote his wife that Loring, Tilghman, and Featherston were "engaged in quite an animated conversation the principal topic being General Pemberton-and the affairs of the Country generally." Drennan was more sympathetic to Pemberton. He continued, "They all said harsh, ill-natured things and made ill-natured jests in regard to General Pemberton."

It is too bad President Davis did not see what Drennan did. Drennan believed: "That there was no harmony-no unity of action, no clear understanding of the aims and designs of our army was apparent and instead of there existing mutual confidence on the part of the Commanding General and his subordinates-there was just the opposite-and it amounted to what in an ordinary matter would have been called distrust."

It has been a mystery to historians why Davis picked Pemberton. Davis scholars seem to agree Pemberton enjoyed an exalted military reputation without having done anything to deserve it. Davis wrote that he was "one of the best Generals in our service," but does not offer insight on his opinion. Three Davis biographers of the late 20th Century have not found an answer. Pemberton, having held Charleston, must have seemed capable.

Maryland-born Brig. Gen. Lloyd Tilghman (left) was living in Paducah, Kentucky when our war for independence commenced. He commanded Fort Henry (map), which was beginning to flood when the U.S. Navy bombarded it. After release from prison Tilghman fought in Mississippi. He blocked an advance by Grant's forces, out of Holly Springs, at Coffeeville. His time under Loring began during the repulse of U.S. forces at Fort Pemberton. When Pemberton created Loring's Division Tilghman had command of one three brigades. He was killed at Champion Hill amidst the guns of Cowan's Battery. Tilghman photo (Southern Historical Collection at the University of North Carolina, Chapel Hill)

Davis had just visited Braxton Bragg and his Army of Tennessee, up at Murfreesborough. Johnston had Bragg send Forrest to tear up the Mobile and Ohio, Grant's primary supply line. Davis felt that the Mississippi River was more important than Tennessee. He told Bragg to fight if he could, or fall back to the Tennessee River. Bragg came close to destroying the enemy's army, before falling back only to the Duck River. Arm chair strategists have never given Bragg the credit he deserves. Had Johnston been in command at Murfreesborough, we might imagine him falling back before the enemy advanced.

Davis made it clear he viewed Pemberton's department as more important than Bragg's. After the enemy got control of the Mississippi River the Confederacy surprisingly went onto function fairly well. But that was not thought possible before. Drennan's thoughts are of interest: "I have always thought Pemberton did well-having as he has had the most important Dept. to defend in the Confederacy-and from the topographical situation of the Country the most difficult one to defend."

Davis traveled onto Mississippi and visited Pemberton's army near Grenada, Christmas Eve. Loring wrote Quintard, "I was in command a few days of this army at which the President and General Joe Johnston were present. The army presented a fine appearance." From Grenada Davis and Johnston went down to Jackson. Portions of the president's magnificent speech follow. Had independence been won it would be a speech read in classrooms across the Confederacy.

"I was among those who, from the beginning, predicted war…not because our right to secede and form a government of our own was not indisputable and clearly defined in the spirit of that declaration which rests the right to govern on the consent of the governed, but because I saw that the wickedness of the North would precipitate a war upon us. Those who supposed that the exercise of this right of separation could not produce war had cause to be convinced that they had credited their recent associations of the North with a moderation of sagacity, a morality they did not possess. You have been involved in a war waged for the gratification of the lust of power and aggrandizement, for your conquest and your subjugation, with a malignant ferocity and with a disregard and a contempt of the usages of civilization entirely unequaled in history. Such, I have ever warned you, were the characteristics of the northern people…After what has happened in the last two years, my only wonder is that we consented to live for so long a time in association with such miscreants and have loved so much a government rotten to the core. Were it ever to be proposed again to enter into a Union with such a people, I could no more consent to do it than to trust myself in a den of thieves…There is indeed a difference between the two peoples. Let no man hug the delusion that there can be renewed association between them. Our enemies are a tradition less and homeless race. From the time of Cromwell to the present moment they have been disturbers of the peace of the world. Gathered together by Cromwell from the bogs and fens of the north of Ireland and England, they commenced by disturbing the peace of their own county; they disturbed Holland, to which they fled; and they disturbed England on their return. They persecuted Catholics in England, and they hung Quakers and witches in America."

Davis went on to say, "They have destroyed the freedom of the press, they have seized upon and imprisoned members of state legislatures and of municipal councils…men have been carried off into captivity in distant states without indictment, without a knowledge of the accusations brought against them, in utter defiance of all rights guaranteed by the institutions under which they live. These people, when separated from the South and left entirely to themselves, have in six months demonstrated their utter incapacity for self-government. And yet these are the people who claim to be your masters." All of this was true. In cities such as Nashville all the newspapers had been taken over, and elected officials removed from office. Tennessee had a military governor. In Maryland the legislators that were to vote the state out of the United States were sent to prison; most or all had been sent to Fort Warren in Boston Harbour.

George Washington had been able to win his ultimate victory at Yorktown with help from the French army and navy. Davis had believed much of what had been done in the first Revolution would come to fruition. France was inclined to help, but would not move unless England did. England never intended to. Davis continued, "In the course of this war our eyes have often been turned abroad. We have expected sometimes recognition, and sometimes intervention, at the hands of foreign nations; and we have had a right to expect it….Put not your trust in princes, and rest not your hopes in foreign nations. This was is ours; we must fight it ourselves. And I feel some pride in knowing that, so far, we have done it without the good will of anybody."

Applause followed the president's speech, and then calls for Johnston. He came forward to redoubled cheers. "Fellow citizens," he said. "My only regret is that I have done so little to merit such a greeting. I promise you, however, that hereafter I shall be watchful, energetic, indefatigable in your defense." A reporter described the outburst of applause as "tremendous, uproarious, and prolonged." Somehow Johnston created believers.

In January 1863 Johnston ordered Van Dorn to Tennessee, creating a serious handicap for Pemberton. He would still be asking for his cavalry back in March. Johnston replied, Van Dorn's cavalry is absolutely necessary to enable General Bragg to hold the past of the country from which he draws supplies." The Nashville Basin counties where Van Dorn operated were important, but Davis was more concerned about Mississippi than the Nashville Basin and Middle Tennessee. The Davis-Johnston conflict of interests would continue. Mississippian Van Dorn would never make it home. He was murdered by a jealous husband on 7 May 1863.

With Loring around Grenada, holding the Yalobusha Line, he was given command of the 1st Division of the Department of Mississippi and East Louisiana. This division was not the same as "Loring's Division," which would be formed in May. This division was composed of two brigades and Thomas N. Waul's Texas Legion. Brig. Gen. Albert Rust commanded one; he had served with Loring in western Virginia. The other was under Lloyd Tilghman, who would be killed at Champion Hill. Several of his Mississippi regiments remained under Loring until the end of the war.

Holly Springs was just south of Tennessee, on the *Mississippi Central*. It was taken to serve as a supply base on 13 November 1862. Earl Van Dorn's ability to command an army after repulses at Pea Ridge and Corinth had been questioned. The Mississippian would not command another army, but would prove competent to command cavalry. He quickly demonstrated that when he destroyed Grant's Holly Springs base in December.

Joseph E. Johnston had reported himself fit for duty on the 12$^{th.}$ He was wounded at the Battle of Seven Pines on 31 May. He had taken a bullet in his right shoulder and within moments a shell struck him in the chest. It knocked him from his horse unconscious, and with that, he lost command of the Virginia army. In conjunction with Van Dorn's raid, he ordered Bragg to dispatch Forrest to raid the railroad behind Grant. These brilliant raids caused Grant to retreat and use the Mississippi River for a supply artery in his subsequent Vicksburg campaigns.

Van Dorn's cavalry raid on Holly Springs on 19 December, along with Forrest's cavalry raid up the Mobile and Ohio Railroad, had dismantled Grant's first drive on Vicksburg. Also, Stephen D. Lee had decisively defeated Sherman's attempt to take Vicksburg, at Chickasaw Bayou. Grant abandoned the idea of a railroad supply line into Mississippi. He shifted to the Mississippi River. This led Pemberton to shift Loring from Grenada to Yazoo City, 45 miles north of Vicksburg.

U.S. Army of the Potomac generals were removed for failed campaigns, and there no doubt this first campaign failed. The editor of Cincinnati's Gazette wrote Salmon Chase, on Lincoln's cabinet. It was from an observer with Grant's army. Included from a lettre: "There never was a more thoroughly disgusted, disheartened, demoralized army than this is under such men as Grant and Sherman…How is it that Grant, who was behind at Fort Henry, drunk at Fort Donelson, surprised and whipped at Shiloh, and driven back from Oxford, Miss., is still in command?" This lettre left out Grant's retreat from Belmont, Missouri. Grant biographer Woodward wrote, "He was not an inspirer of men-and was also a poor battle tactician." But Lincoln saw that Grant was not a quitter.

Leaving the railroad line made sense, especially considering the outstanding Confederate cavalry generals. But water routes had risks too. Confederate torpedoes sank more U.S. warships than did gunboats. The *U.S.S. Cairo* had been sunk 12 miles up the Yazoo River on 12 December. It had struck two mines and sank in eight minutes! The Navy had to go up the Yazoo, past where the *Cairo* had been sunk to prepare a landing place for Sherman to attack southward toward S.D. Lee's position south of Chickasaw Bayou. A U.S. flotilla spent three days clearing torpedoes, or mines, from the Yazoo. Even after Vicksburg was surrendered, the *U.S.S. Baron DeKalb* was sunk by two mines, upriver near Yazoo City.

A joint U.S. Army-Navy force was trying to reach Vicksburg by way of the Tallahatchie River in March. Sherman's Chickasaw Bayou defeat meant a better landing area in the soggy Mississippi Delta was needed. The navy found a way to get inland at a place called Yazoo Pass, five miles down the Mississippi from Helena, Arkansas. They were able to cross Moon Lake and twisted their way to the Tallahatchie with the intention of reaching a landing on the Yazoo River, northeast of Vicksburg. Loring was victorious over them, in what is known as the Yazoo Pass Expedition.

Confederate engineers had been sent to block the move down the Tallahatchie, and were working on a fortification at a ferry site. It was over two miles from Greenwood, and would be named Fort Pemberton. Historians focus on Pemberton's failures; however, the general and his engineers were able to pinpoint enemy avenues toward Vicksburg before they occurred to Grant or his engineers. Loring arrived at Fort Pemberton and approved the site on 23 February. The next day he requested two big guns for the defenses. It was hurriedly built of earth, sandbags, and cotton bales. It was nearly hidden in a narrow bend of the Tallahatchie. It was also in swampy terrain, to prevent infantry from flanking it. Loring had Thomas Waul's Texas Legion to deploy. He also had the 20th Mississippi. His total force was about 2,000 men. Pemberton, headquartered in Jackson, sent Tilghman's Brigade west from Jackson, though his brigade was not at Fort Pemberton.

Loring got the two requested big guns. One was a 32-pounder that had been rifled and banded; it fired 68-pound shells. It could enfilade an 800-yard stretch of the Tallahatchie. The other was actually a large field piece, a 20-pound Parrott that had been captured in the Battle of Corinth. It was positioned to control the sharp bend in front of the fort. Five more guns, one a lowly 6-pounder, were placed between the two large flank guns. They were mounted en barbette, or on wood platforms. They were commanded by Capt. John Douglas Myrick who was Loring's Chief of Artillery, and an aide-de-camp, in Virginia.

The enemy plan was to bring gunboats down the Tallahatchie, followed by transports for infantry. Different sources number the transports at 14, 22, and 27. An engraved stone at the site says 22 transports carried 5,000 troops. The flotilla got into trouble well before it came to the fort. The Confederacy had allies in a very Southern tree, the cypress. The unique trees are usually found in swampy places, where their stalagmite-looking knees reach for the surface. These allies had already ripped blanks out of the bottom of the boats. Of further hindrance were the many trees felled to block their way. Near the upstream side of Fort Pemberton, the *Star of the West* had been sunk to block the channel.

The Star of the West was made famous when she was used to carry 200 artillerymen and marines to Fort Sumter. U.S. President Buchanan's administration had secretly chartered the merchant vessel in December 1860, just after South Carolina seceded. A shore battery sent a shot across her, which turned her back. On 20 April 1861 she was along the Texas coast when she was boarded by Confederates under Earl Van Dorn. They told the Star's officers Confederate troops lay concealed on shore, and were about to blow her out of the water. The bluff worked and the captured ship was taken to New Orleans. She was re-christened *St. Phillip*, though the new name didn't stick to the famous *Star of the West*.

A 1952 piece in The Journal of Mississippi History explains the *Star of the West* avoided capture when New Orleans fell in April 1862 by steaming up the Mississippi to the Yazoo. She was there in 1863 as Loring began planning the defense of Fort Pemberton. He wanted to sink a ship in the Tallahatchie to block enemy gunboats. The Star was the

John Clifford Pemberton
Civilwartalk.com

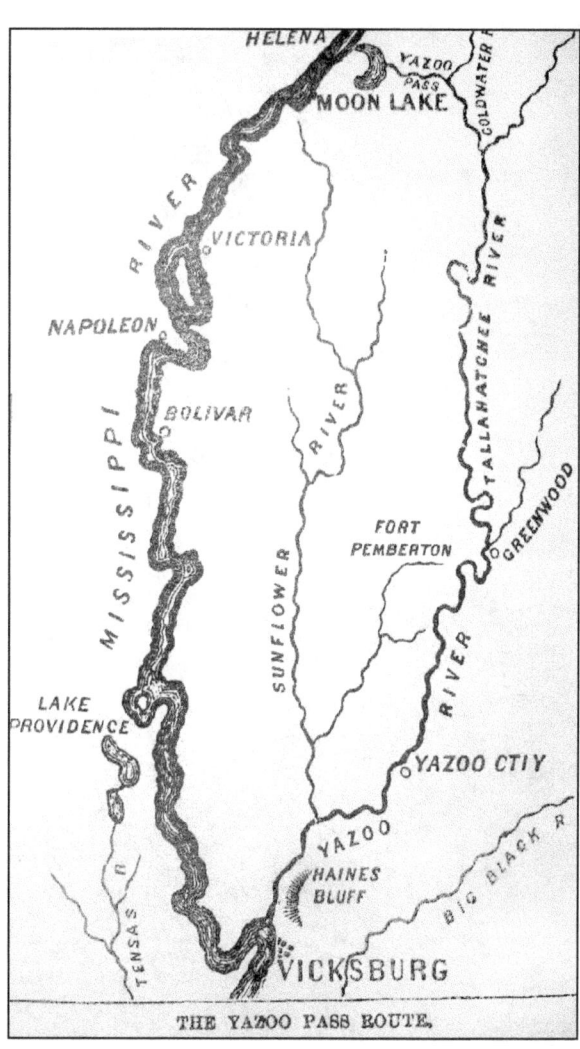

THE YAZOO PASS ROUTE.

The side-wheel steamer *Star of the West* became the Confederate ship *St. Philip* after being captured off Texas in April 1861

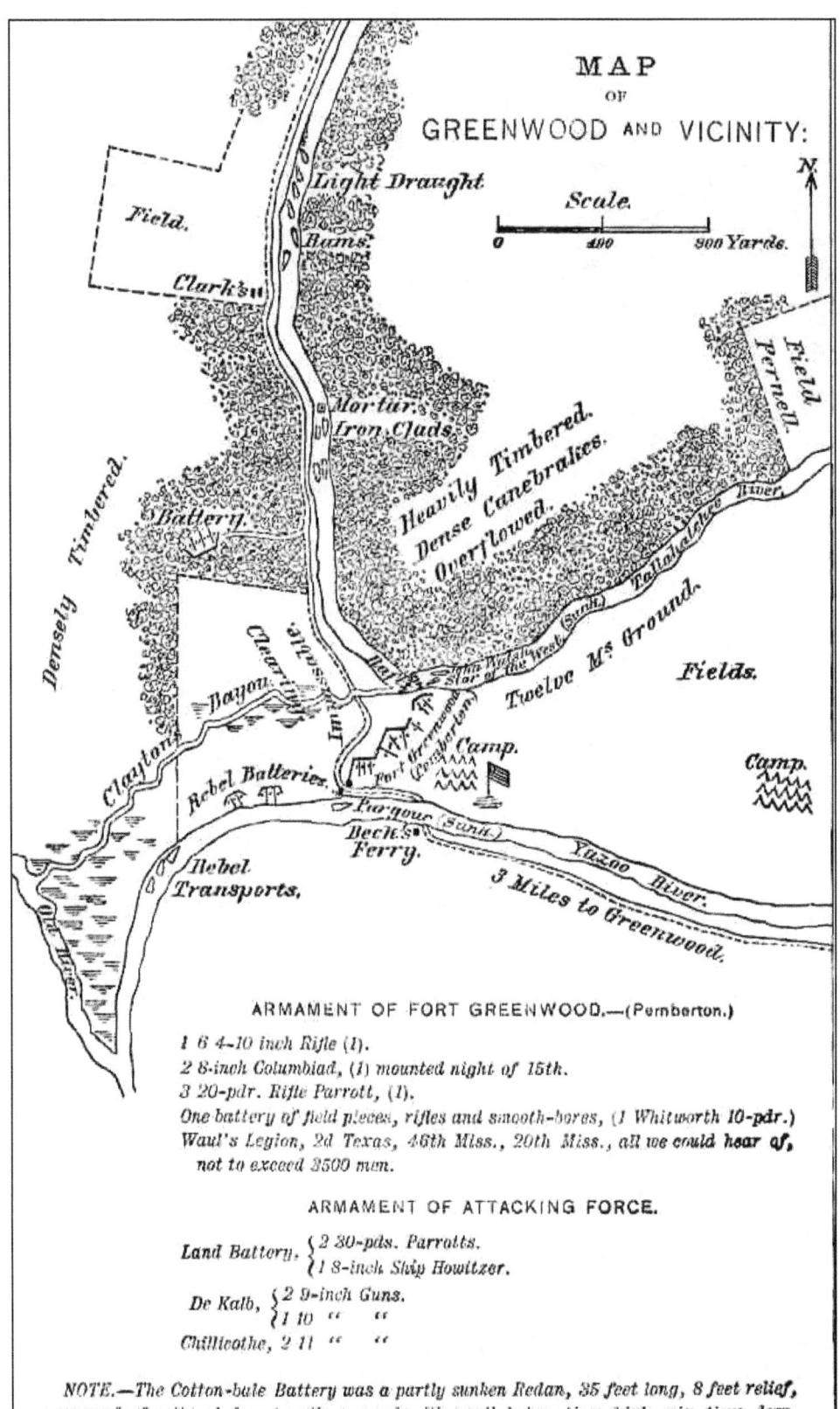

ARMAMENT OF FORT GREENWOOD.—(Pemberton.)

1 6 4-10 inch Rifle (1).
2 8-inch Columbiad, (1) mounted night of 15th.
3 20-pdr. Rifle Parrott, (1).
One battery of field pieces, rifles and smooth-bores, (1 Whitworth 10-pdr.)
Waul's Legion, 2d Texas, 46th Miss., 20th Miss., all we could hear of, not to exceed 3500 men.

ARMAMENT OF ATTACKING FORCE.

Land Battery. { 2 30-pds. Parrotts.
{ 1 8-inch Ship Howitzer.
De Kalb, { 2 9-inch Guns.
{ 1 10 "   "
Chillicothe, 2 11 "   "

NOTE.—The Cotton-bale Battery was a partly sunken Redan, 35 feet long, 8 feet relief, composed of cotton bales, (partly covered with earth,) two tiers high, six tiers deep, embrasures one foot splay, revetted with sheet iron, which blew out soon. Cotton did not burn to any hurtful extent; kept wet by pouring water on. The platforms were 9 by 14, one foot below surface, four inches higher on the rear line.

"Map of Greenwood and Vicinity" from a New York newspaper even calls Fort Pemberton Fort Greenwood. The right side of the map cuts off the mouth of the Yalobusha River as it joins the Tallahatchie to form the Yazoo. Greenwood is just below that point, about three miles away.

FORT PEMBERTON PARK

IN THE 1863 CAMPAIGN AGAINST VICKSBURG GENERAL GRANT TRIED SEVERAL APPROACHES, ONE BEING TO SEND TROOPS ON TRANSPORTS DOWN THE TALLAHATCHIE AND YAZOO RIVERS. HE CUT THE MISSISSIPPI RIVER LEVEE IN FEBRUARY WHICH FLOODED THE SEVERAL BAYOUS BETWEEN THE MISSISSIPPI AND TALLAHATCHIE RIVERS, MAKING A NAVIGABLE CONNECTION. TWENTY-TWO TRANSPORTS (WITH 5000 TROOPS), TWO IRONCLADS, TWO RAMS AND SIX LIGHT DRAFT GUNBOATS MADE UP THE FIRST EXPEDITION, WHICH WAS LATER REINFORCED WITH ANOTHER BRIGADE AND ADDITIONAL VESSELS. IT TOOK SEVERAL WEEKS TO MAKE THE TWO HUNDRED MILE TRIP AS THE BAYOUS WERE NARROW AND TORTUOUS.

APPRISED OF THE FEDERAL PLANS THE CONFEDERATE GENERAL JOHN C. PEMBERTON ORDERED A FORT TO BE CONSTRUCTED TO BLOCK THE ENEMY FORCES. THE ENGINEERS SELECTED A LOCATION WHERE THE TALLAHATCHIE MAKES AN ABRUPT TURN EASTERLY, THE RIVER FLOWING TO THIS POINT IN A STRAIGHT STRETCH, THERE BEING ROOM FOR ONLY TWO GUNBOATS ABREAST. THUS THE CONFEDERATES WOULD BE SHOOTING DOWN A STRAIGHT ALLEY. THE FORT WAS HASTILY BUILT OF COTTON BALES COVERED WITH EARTH, AND NAMED FORT PEMBERTON. IT HAD BUT A FEW LIGHT GUNS, BUT ONE, AN EIGHT INCH RIFLE, WAS VERY ACCURATE. THE FORT WAS MANNED BY 1500 MEN UNDER COMMAND OF BRIG. GEN. W. W. LORING. CUTTING THE LEVEES HAD FLOODED THE AREA AND THE ONLY APPROACH TO THE FORT WAS BY WATER. TO FURTHER IMPEDE THE ENEMY THE STEAMSHIP "STAR OF THE WEST" WAS SUNK IN THE CHANNEL.

THE FEDERAL FLOTILLA ARRIVED AT FORT PEMBERTON ON MARCH 11TH, AND THE TWO IRONCLADS ATTACKED AT 1000 YARDS BUT BOTH WERE DAMAGED. AFTER SEVERAL ATTEMPTS TO REDUCE THE FORT THE FEDERAL FLEET RETIRED TO THE MISSISSIPPI. GRANT HAD FAILED TO REACH VICKSBURG BY THE TALLAHATCHIE-YAZOO ROUTE.

PART OF THE FORT IS INCLUDED IN THIS PARK, AND SOME OF THE ORIGINAL BREASTWORKS MAY BE EASILY RECOGNIZED.

Modern day travelers will find the Fort Pemberton Park easy to access, along U.S. Highway 82, west of Greenwood. Confederate engineers did an outstanding job locating the fort. Its guns could fire at U.S. gunboats descending the Tallahatchie in March 1863. The levees were cut, and along with the bayou and swamp, all of this deterred infantry from landing where the fort could be attacked.

General Loring went atop the fort's earthen wall to shout to his artillerists, "Give them blizzards boys!" He was ever after known as "Old Blizzards." It seems to have been one of the most colourful examples of leadership in the war. Pemberton was no doubt encouraged by the victory and impressed with Loring. He ordered what would be known as Loring's Division in May 1863.

longest around, so she was brought up to be sunk. Two days were spent drilling 250 holes in her hull. On 11 March she made her last run under her own steam, about 100 yards up from the fort. Then she was swung broadside to the current, and the plugs were pulled. After sailing oceans her grave was in the yellow sand of the Tallahatchie. In 1952, during the low water of autumn days, a glimpse of the ship might still be seen.

The Star of the West had been sunk just in time, for the flotilla reached Fort Pemberton on 11 March 1863. They thought their 11-inch Dahlgren was enough to bring them victory. But they had hardly begun their barrage when Loring's one big piece, a 32-pounder rifle, sent a shell into a port. The Dahlgren on the *U.S.S. Chillicothe* was being loaded when the shell exploded. The blood and guts of 13 killed and wounded crew men were splattered through the interior. The *Chillicothe* fired three rounds and withdrew. This first fight lasted about a half hour.

The Chillicothe returned about six hours later, at 4:15 p.m., and opened fire again. Following were the ironclad *DeKalb* and the ram *Lioness*. Loring's gunners returned fire and the 32-pounder ruled again. One fine shot hit a Dahlgren on the muzzle as it was being loaded. Four more sailors were killed and fifteen wounded, and the navy withdrew again. This fight lasted about seven minutes.

Loring reported to Pemberton that evening on the repulse of the gunboats, but he also had an ammunition shortage. He wrote, "Our 32-pounder shot nearly exhausted; they are our main reliance. Received this evening extraordinary dispatch from Major Mayo. For some reason unknown to us, he takes upon himself the responsibility of refusing to send ammunition." There had been eight 32-pounders engaged at Fort Donelson in repulsing the gunboats, so it is bewildering to find Loring short of ammunition for his.

The gunboats had failed twice so that night a cotton bale battery was erected about 700 yards from Fort Pemberton. This work continued on Thursday the 12th. A 30-pound Parrott was moved from the Rattler, followed by another that night. Loring lacked ammunition to interfere with the enemy's threatening position. But Tilghman came from Yazoo City, possibly with the ammunition for he wired Pemberton it was on hand.

On Friday the 13th, the navy reappeared firing their bow guns as the narrow Tallahatchie limited them. They were unable to maneuver and took a beating. Loring had been inspiring his gunners by shouting, "Give them blizzards boys!" He was seen atop Fort Pemberton's earthen wall as George Washington had been seen atop a parapet at Yorktown, as bullets and shrapnel flew about him. Perhaps Washington had been an inspiration to Loring. No doubt Old Blizzards inspired his artillerists.

The flotilla commander was so distressed he called off the day's action. His admiral stated the commander was showing "symptoms of aberrations of mind." Their infantry could never be disembarked due to the muddy terrain. A U.S. Army engineer was disgusted with the navy commander and sarcastically referred to him as "Acting Rear Admiral Commodore Captain Lieutenant Commander Smith!" Loring and his victorious command earned a far better title for their general. He would be known as "Old Blizzards" thereafter!

Lloyd Tilghman seems to have been present. Biographer James Raab has Tilghman coming up to Fort Pemberton from down at Yazoo City. From correspondence in the Official Records it may be seen that Tilghman was in Grenada on 8 March, and also on the 12th. On the 11th Loring wrote to Pemberton that his 32-pounder shot was nearly exhausted, and that it was his main reliance. He complained that a Major Mayo had refused to send it. Tilghman was at the fort on the 13th, at 7:50 p.m., when he confirmed ammunition for the heavy guns had arrived. Tilghman had experience from Fort Henry that must have been helpful to Loring. Fort Henry had a two-mile long field of fire, on the wider Tennessee River. He had also battled a larger flotilla there. Fort Pemberton on the Tallahatchie had an open field of fire of about a half mile. Perhaps Tilghman was more of an adviser. Loring mentions him in his report, dated the 22nd, for rendering aid.

Another attempt to take Fort Pemberton was made on 16 March. The gunboats had failed so the army established a land battery to aide in the landing of troops though the gunboats were still deemed essential in the attack. The commander of the U.S. infantry, Brig. Gen. L.F. Ross, reported, "In view of the shortness of our ammunition, I had arranged for a short and brisk fight at close quarters, and, if successful in silencing their batteries, to make a descent upon the fort with infantry, loaded on the light-draught gunboats, and storm it. The arrangements being all made, and the infantry placed on the boats, we opened the fight. The *Chillicothe* had not been engaged fifteen minutes until she was struck six times, and both of her port-holes closed, by being so battered that the doors to her ports could not be opened. She had to withdraw, and the *DeKalb*, being unwilling to engage alone, also retired." Loring reported the sound repulse to Pemberton at 9:00 p.m.: "We were unable to prevent land batteries from increasing, because we are fearful of not receiving more ammunition in time." He later reported his casualties up to Monday 16th: "1 killed and 4 wounded, and 16 severely burned or injured by the explosion of our magazine. Total of casualties, 21."

General Ross reported on the 17th, "In order to take this fort, we must have ordinance of heavy caliber and plenty of ammunition. Better gunboats must be sent us, if it is expected to accomplish anything with them. I don't believe our two iron-clads can withstand the terrific fire of the guns now on the fort for one hour without total destruction."

Ross reported on the 21st, "We remained in front of the fort until the morning of the 20th, occupying the time by constantly reconnoitering the country thoroughly by strong parties, accompanied by Lieutenant-Colonel Wilson and the officers of my staff, but every attempt to find any feasible point of attack for infantry failed. The rebels' works were so surrounded by swamps, bayous, and overflowed country as to be inaccessible for land forces." As Ross retired up the Tallahatchie on the 21st he encountered Brig. Gen. I. F. Quinby. He had more infantry and ordered Ross back down the river with him.

Also in the next week the Chillicothe apparently came upon a mine. She had fired several rounds when a geyser of water rose up near her bow. The naval commander feared his

The traditional court house monument (above) mentions nearby Fort Pemberton. It guarded the river approach to Greenwood. Pemberton had the fort built to block the enemy from approaching Vicksburg on the Yazoo River. The U.S.S. Chillicothe (below) was built in 1862 to serve on the Mississippi River and its tributaries. It was defeated by Loring's command at Fort Pemberton.

gunboats might be lost to a mine. He must have been apprised of the report of the *Cairo's* sinking. Her skipper reported, "Her whole frame was so completely shattered that I found…that nothing more could be effected than to move the sick and the arms. The *Cairo* sunk…minutes after the explosion, going totally out of sight, except the top of the chimneys." This may have been the best call, for the Confederacy was successful with mines, and as mentioned, the *DeKalb* would be sunk by one in the Yazoo in July.
On 28 March Grant sent Quinby orders to withdraw. Like Ross, he could find no way to take Fort Pemberton. Grant was about to launch his final drive, which would lead the Yankees to cross the Mississippi River south of Vicksburg. Quinby withdrew in April.

Loring of course had no way of knowing Grant's strategy. From his perspective he had simply forced the enemy to retreat. Loring reported his continuing success in the enemy's first and second withdrawals. On 12 April he wrote, "During their short absence we greatly strengthened our lines, and were fully prepared to give them a warm reception. We waited a short time after their arrival, in the hope they would muster courage to attack us, but it seemed that it failed them in the critical moment." Loring was victorious and led Grant to abandon the effort to reach Vicksburg from the north. Loring's report continued, "While our fire was destructive to their crowded camps, our action from right to left alarmed them very much, and on the night of April 4 they commenced embarking, and by daylight they were in rapid retreat up the river."

Loring's reference to his left included Dabney Maury's brigade, temporarily attached, and on the right were Tilghman's. Tilghman had a county map that showed the farm house where Quinby was headquartered. Tilghman had trained guns by a compass and on an appointed signal they opened on Quinby's camp. Regardless of Grant's orders to retire, Quinby may have concluded what Ross had; Fort Pemberton couldn't be passed. Quinby's force had retired to Helena, Arkansas by the night of 10 April, and that was the official end to the Yazoo Pass Expedition for U.S. forces.

Simultaneously with the Yazoo Pass Grant was trying another route to reach the Yazoo. This route was another twisting trek which they called the Steele's Bayou Expedition. This route was not protected by a fort, but it suddenly failed amidst felled trees and Confederate attacks. This expedition concluded on 27 March as the enemy retreated. Loring was not engaged, but a brigade of Mississippians under Brig. Gen. Winfield Scott Featherston was. His brigade was then free to reinforce Loring.

The end of March was a transition for Loring as new units were coming under his command. Featherston's Mississippi brigade began arriving at Fort Pemberton on the 29th. They came as part of a division under Maj. Gen. Dabney H. Maury. He reported that all of Featherston's arrived by 1 April. Loring told Maury his services were no longer needed near the fort on the 8th. Maury returned to Vicksburg without Featherston's. It would become one of three brigades in Loring's Division.

In April Abraham Buford came to Loring. Buford later gained fame commanding one of Forrest's divisions in 1864, but he had infantry bivouacked at Meridian. Several of Buford's units were the nucleus of what would become Scott's Brigade, while others would be dispersed elsewhere. Tilghman's experience with heavy artillery at Fort Henry made him an asset at Fort Pemberton. His brigade, later under John Adams, would remain with Loring. John Myrick commanded the artillery at Fort Pemberton, and he would stay with Loring.

Loring's victory at Fort Pemberton is not only remembered by the monument at the site, but on the courthouse lawn in nearby Greenwood. The county seat of Leflore County began three decades before. *Mississippi* says, "In 1834 John Williams came to the lush swamp as the confluence of the Yazoo and Yalobusha rivers and built a river landing…" Among planters who brought cotton to the landing was the Choctaw chieftain Greenwood Leflore. Ironically the town and county are named after the Choctaw. *Mississippi* goes onto explain the war brought gunboats to the Yazoo, supplanting barges for commerce, and railroads were destroyed. "Even throughout reconstruction much of the rich black Delta lands lay fallow because there were no means of transporting such crops as were grown." Lincoln's imperialism still vexed the Mississippi Valley decades after his death.

The monument by the courthouse was presented in 1913 by the Varina Jefferson Davis Chapter of the U.D.C. *Confederate Veteran*, Volume 21, in 1913, covered the monument dedication. There a many figures of interest. One is a base relief of the pilot wheel of the Star of the West. Another figure is a Confederate officer, with field glasses, watching the battle at Fort Pemberton. The top figure is native son, General Benjamin G. Humphreys. That outstanding officer was not present during the campaign, as he was in Virginia. Also, a model of Fort Pemberton is at the nearby Museum of the Mississippi Delta.

Mississippi Manufacturing at Risk in campaign

Mississippi was not a state generally associated with manufacturing. Its short winters leave most of the year warm to hot. In the days before air conditioning this would have been a difficult climate for factory workers. Yet *Confederate Military History* (Vol. 7, Part 2, page 62) quoted a Jackson newspaper explaining much activity. In March 1863 an editorial in *The Mississippi* claimed: "The subsistence, the clothing and the camp equipage for a tremendous army have been exclusively drawn from the State of Mississippi, and this too, when several of her most populous and productive counties have been under the control of the enemy. Mississippi manufacturers have made nearly all the material used for the army in the whole department."

The Mississippi editorial went onto say that 5,000 garments were made by a Jackson manufacturer weekly. Similar smaller manufacturers were in Bankston, Columbus, Enterprise, Natchez, and Woodville (President Davis's boyhood hometown). Jackson and Columbus had hat factories making 200 a day. "We have a manufactory at Jackson which turns out 50 blankets a day. The Pemberton works at Enterprise, and Dixie works at Canton, make not less than 60 wagons and ambulances a week. A shoe shop was being created and expected to turn out 6,000 pair a month. "The most extensive tannery in the Confederacy is situated at Magnolia, and supplies 600 hides daily. Tents manufactured from Mississippi cloth are the best in the Confederacy, and enough of them are made at Jackson and Columbus to supply the army."

The Daily Southern Crisis was another Jackson newspaper extolling patriotic attributes of the Magnolia State. The 28 March 1863 issue said, "The wheat crop in Mississippi looks very promising-in fact it could not be better. There is a large surface of our soil in wheat, promising flour in abundance after the May harvest. If there are no more frosts this State will furnish wheat enough to supply half the Confederacy in flour for the next year; … but a small crop of cotton planted, which shows the good sense of our people."

Confederate Military History cited another example of Mississippi for the war effort. On 29 April "the corporate authorities of Columbus" wrote to President Davis: "We beg to say that our patriotic planters had, to a large extent, anticipated your recent proclamation, and have planted their broad prairie acres in grain and other articles for the subsistence of the army. In fact, sir, our country is one vast cornfield which is protected from the enemy will, under the smiles of Providence, furnish an amount of provisions that will relieve the western army from all fear of want." Sadly, the enemy was intent on vexing Mississippi.

<u>Grant launches his final campaign to take Vicksburg.</u>
Grant marched south thru Louisiana and find a point to land across the Mississippi. Joe Johnston had said his department with Mississippi and Tennessee was not as practical. Holding the Mississippi River would be more practical if troops in Mississippi were paired with those in Louisiana. Grant was about to prove that correct. Also, Pemberton did not have enough experience to confront a seasoned campaigner like Grant. He was also hampered by the lack of cavalry and an erroneous report from scouts. They discovered the upstream departure of one brigade of about two thousand men. On 13 April Pemberton reported to Davis that "most of Grant's forces are being withdrawn to Memphis." Perhaps Loring's victory at Fort Pemberton contributed to this incorrect conclusion. Pemberton would remain confused until confronted with Grant's seven divisions at Champion Hill.

Pemberton's confusion was an enormous benefit to Grant. He was about to launch a cavalry raid out of southwestern Tennessee, into the heart of Mississippi, and it kept Pemberton confused. Grant's raider, Grierson, made it across the Magnolia state and never had to contend with any serious contention by Confederate cavalry. Loring was at Enterprise on 25 April, southwest of Meridian, where he hoped to ambush them. Grierson came up and demanded surrender.

Loring notified Pemberton, "Enemy appeared here at 1 o'clock and demanded the town. They were represented as 1,500 strong. Colonel [Edward] Goodwin was here with the Thirty-fifth Alabama, who defied them." Loring explained he had hastened with two regiments, and the enemy moved on. Buford also reported to Pemberton. Loring may have been modest of his role, for Buford said Loring's reinforcements led the enemy to fall back. Loring concluded, "I have no hope of catching them on foot."

The reason Loring had no cavalry to pursue was because Johnston had sent Van Dorn up to Tennessee in January. Postwar bickering over this was evident when Johnston wrote, "Mr. Davis represents that General Pemberton's operations were cramped by a want of cavalry, for which I was responsible. He had cavalry enough; but it was used near the extremities of the State against raiding parties…" This rings hollow. At this period another enemy cavalry raid, Streight's, crossed northern Alabama. An awesome pursuit by Forrest's cavalry totally destroyed Streight's command. Had Pemberton had enough cavalry in northern Mississippi, Grierson might have been intercepted and destroyed.

Johnston's authority to transfer Van Dorn reinforces his own belief that Pemberton should have been in a department with Trans-Mississippi troops rather than Bragg. It is interesting for Davis wanted such coordination two years later. On 31 January 1865 he wrote Trans-Mississippi commander Kirby Smith, "I think it advisable that you should be charged with military operations on both banks of the Mississippi…"

Davis had retired to Beauvoir on the Mississippi Gulf of Mexico coast when he wrote *The Rise and Fall of the Confederate Government.* He wrote of Pemberton's inability to discern Grant's intentions as he suddenly conducted the biggest U.S. amphibious landing since the Mexican War. Grant landed at Bruinsburg, south of Grand Gulf. Davis wrote, "At this time the small cavalry force remaining in Pemberton's command compelled him to keep infantry detachments ay many points liable to be attacked by raiding parties of the enemy's mounted troops, a circumstance seriously interfering with the concentration of the forces of his command."

Pemberton was not only lacked the cavalry to pursue Grierson, he had difficulty tracking Grant once he crossed the Mississippi River. Davis quoted Pemberton's report, "With a moderate cavalry force at my disposal, I am firmly convinced that the Federal army under General Grant would have been unable to maintain its communication with the Mississippi River, and that the attempt to reach Jackson and Vicksburg would have been as signally defeated in May, 1863 as a like attempt from another base had, by the employment of cavalry, been defeated in December 1862." But Davis had created the department structure that allowed Van Dorn to be transferred from Mississippi.

Pemberton had a point, but he lacked the leadership qualities to bring victory. He had enough infantry initially. While he was still headquartered at Jackson, Carter Stevenson commanded at Vicksburg. Back in December 1862, President Davis had ordered Carter Stevenson's division away from Bragg's army. Their presence would likely have given Bragg at Murfreesborough a victory more decisive than Chickamauga. But Stevenson and his division had been sent to Vicksburg. Stevenson reacted to Grant's landing to the south by ordering every man to march from Vicksburg to defeat Grant. But Pemberton countermanded the order and only allowed two brigades to go south. Stevenson left on his own might have driven Grant back into the river, and won a magnificent victory.

Pemberton's decisions had not only lost him Loring's respect, but the press's too. On 8 May the editors of the Jackson *Mississippian* sent a disturbing communication to Davis: "The people within this department-soldiers and citizens-do not repose the confidence in the capacity and loyalty of General Pemberton which is so important at this junction. Whether justly or not, we are certain three-fourths of the people in the army and out doubt him." Davis had made one of the worst personnel choices possible. And Davis had already tried to improve the West with a department command organization.

Carter Littlepage Stevenson had been on Loring's staff in Virginia. The Fredericksburg native graduated from West Point in 1838, and was promoted to brigadier general in the winter of 1862. He had a brigade in the Dept. of East Tenn. He commanded a division that took Cumberland Gap without a fight in September, the enemy having retreated to the Ohio River! Stevenson advanced into Kentucky as Bragg and K. Smith were withdrawing. This led to his division joining Bragg's Army of Tennessee in December. But President Davis ordered it to Mississippi. Thus they fought with Loring's Division at Champion Hill in May 1863.

John Stevens Bowen, a Georgia native, was promoted to major general during the Vicksburg Campaign. He demonstrated great ability holding Grand Gulf in the defeat of the U.S. Navy. At Port Gibson he was outnumbered three to one, yet held Grant back for sixteen hours. At Champion Hill his magnificent charge nearly turned the tide of the battle. After Pemberton withdrew into Vicksburg he used Bowen's Division to furnish the troops for a strategic reserve. When U.S. attacks might break thru, the reserve was used. Pemberton's lines were never broken. Bowen played a key role in the 3 July armistice that led to the surrender. He was ill with dysentery and died ten days later in an ambulance, as a paroled prisoner. He is buried in City Cemetery, Vicksburg.

Joseph E. Johnston's Department Command doesn't prevent Grant's Crossing

Johnston felt he had recovered well enough from his Seven Pines wounds to report on 12 November 1862. He would have preferred an army command, but was ordered to assume department command over Bragg and Pemberton. Johnston's headquarters were initially at Chattanooga, but he was in Tullahoma on 1 May when Pemberton wired him that Grant had crossed the Mississippi, landing south of Vicksburg. Johnston wired quickly wired back, "If Grant's army lands on this side of the river, the safety of Mississippi depends on beating it. For that object you should unite your whole force." Uniting the troops scattered across Mississippi and fighting Grant, rather than defending Vicksburg, would continue to be Johnston's goal. Pemberton's would be to hold Vicksburg, which President Davis insisted on.

Davis created the department for he could not manage it from Richmond. But then he destroyed its potential effectiveness by insisting Pemberton communicate directly with him. Johnston as Pemberton's immediate supervisor was thus incapacitated. Davis would do this again in the fall of 1864 when he placed Beauregard in department command over John Bell Hood, and then had direct communications with Hood. Numerous historians have cited the president's inability to keep his hands off military matters, better left to subordinates. If he had better relations with Johnston and Beauregard he might not have interfered. He trusted Robert E. Lee, and generally did not interfere with strategy.

Loring was in Meridian when Grant crossed the Mississippi. The next day Pemberton ordered Loring to take command of troops at Grand Gulf. The once thriving cotton port was on the Mississippi, about 20 miles south of Vicksburg. John Steven Bowen was in command there. The U.S Navy had met a bloody repulse there on 29 April deterring Grant from landing. It was considered the heaviest U.S. naval bombardment to date. Grant pointed out not one gun was silenced at Grand Gulf, in one of the most forgotten Confederate victories of the war, though it is maintained as a Mississippi State Park. Perhaps Grand Gulf is forgotten because the next day Grant found a new landing just downstream. It was just an old plantation landing named Bruinsburg. *Mississippi* described Bruinsburg Landing "affords one of the loveliest views of the Bayou Pierre. Before flowing into the Mississippi the bayou thrusts itself out in two giant arms to embrace cypress woodlands hazy with moss. The landing is a secluded spot today, its few inhabitants living in a primitive logging camp and it shanty boats moored to the shore."

Grant addressed the significance of landing five divisions at Bruinsburg in his memoirs: "When this was effected I felt a degree of relief scarcely ever equaled since. Vicksburg was not yet taken it is true, nor were its defenders demoralized by any of our previous moves. I was now in the enemy's country, with a vast river and the stronghold of Vicksburg between me and my base of supplies. But I was on dry ground on the same side of the river as the enemy. All the campaigns, labors, hardships and exposures from the month of December previous to this time that had been made and endured, were for the accomplishment of this one object."

Grant was then about 12 miles south of Port Gibson. He wanted to reach it before Bowen could destroy bridges over both forks of Bayou Pierre, north of Port Gibson. Also if

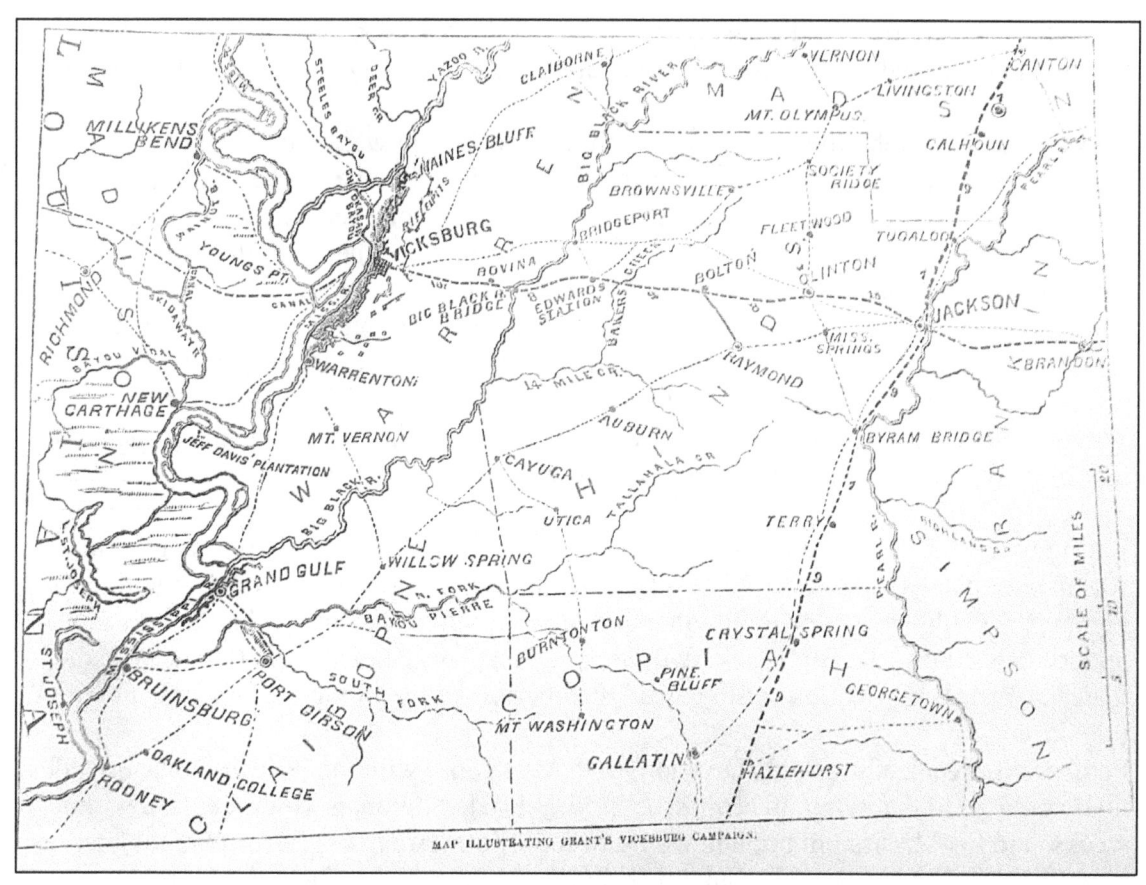

Grant hoped to land troops at Grand Gulf. The U.S. Navy's bombardment on 29 April 1863 failed. It was a grand day for often forgotten C.S. artillerists and engineers.

Grant took Port Gibson and crossed Bayou Pierre, he would be on Grand Gulf's flank. Grant wanted Grand Gulf to use as a base, until one could be created up on the Yazoo.

Bowen warned Pemberton of his risky position, and Loring was dispatched to assist. He thought Loring was coming with two brigades. That would have created a total force of about 7,000, and they might have held Grant south of Bayou Pierre until reinforcements arrived. Instead Loring and Tilghman arrived on the night of the 2nd with only two of Tilghman's regiments. They all agreed they had to move north to avoid being overwhelmed by Grant's army. Bowen ordered the evacuation of Grand Gulf, and Loring took command as they withdrew north toward the Big Black River. It would be the last significant water barrier to Grant's advance on Vicksburg. Loring then counted some 17,000 soldiers, but not enough to hold a Big Black River line. He decided on a shorter line from Warrenton to Big Black Bridge (over the river) through the Lanier plantation.

Loring was far short of the manpower necessary to confront Grant's army. Pemberton was in command and he failed to develop a strategy to push Grant back into the river. Pemberton could have met Grant with equal numbers at this point. He had the divisions under Loring along the Big Black, two more at Vicksburg, and about 6,000 at Jackson. Instead of attacking, as Loring suggested, Pemberton let the initiative remain with Grant.

Pemberton organized Loring's Division, on 5 May 1863, with the three infantry brigades that would go to the Army of Tennessee in May 1864. Tilghman would be dead within weeks, and his Mississippi brigade would become John Adams's. Buford would later be transferred to Forrest's cavalry, and his brigade would become Thomas Moore Scott's. Alabama regiments, along with one from Louisiana would be banded together. Another Mississippi brigade, under Winfield Scott Featherston gave Loring a strong connection to the Magnolia State.

On 6 May Pemberton had about 31,000 men on the Warrenton to Big Black Bridge line. Stevenson's Division was about Warrenton, Loring's about Lanier's, and Bowen's about Big Black Bridge. Pemberton knew Grant was driving toward Vicksburg. He thought the approach would be from one of three directions. It might be toward Edwards, on the *Southern Railroad of Mississippi,* about 20 miles east of Vicksburg. The Big Black Bridge over the Big Black River was just to the west. Or Grant might take what would then have been a more direct route to cross the river, at Hankinson's Ferry, where Loring and Bowen had crossed. The third was toward Loring's position at Lanier's plantation.

Pemberton decided to split Loring's Division to cover the different points. But Loring thought Pemberton had imagined too much. Pemberton wanted the brigades of Buford and Featherston at Big Black Bridge. Loring felt sure Grant would cross the Big Black at Fisher Ferry or Hall's Ferry. He decided to disobey and ordered the two brigades south toward Lanier's. Later that day Pemberton received a direct order from Davis to hold Vicksburg. While they were thinking defensively Loring was thinking offensively.

In *The Personal Memoirs of U.S. Grant,* Grant wrote, "So I finally decided…to cut loose altogether from my base and move my whole force eastward." This has been pointed out

Abraham Buford was born in the Bluegrass Region of Kentucky. Buford raised thoroughbred horses. He graduated from West Point and his gallantry in the Mexican War earned him a brevet to captain. He did not enlist with the Confederates until the Bragg-Smith fall 1862 campaign in the Bluegrass. He established a recruiting camp in Lexington. An infantry brigade was created for Buford in 1863, and became one in Loring's new division. He went onto command cavalry under Forrest, who gave him credit for the great victory at Brice's Crossroads.

Winfield Scott Featherston did not have a military education, but had dropped out of school at 17 to fight the Creeks. He next studied law. Mississippi elected him to Congress. He settled in Holly Springs in 1857 and led the 17th Mississippi to Virginia in 1861. In the victory at Ball's Bluff he encouraged his men: "Mississippians, charge! Drive the damn Yankees into the Potomac or into eternity." He might have said, "…into hell." He transferred west in 1863 to command a Mississippi brigade, which became one of three in Loring's Division. He led them into 'hell' at Peachtree Creek and Franklin. Few generals saw more fighting than Featherston.

as "postwar bombast," for Grant had a 200-wagon train when he moved toward Jackson. Grant wrote, "I, however, had no base, having abandoned it…" Here is another false assertion. Grant had two divisions protecting the wagons and their line back to the Mississippi River. Grant had to have communications stretching back to the river to supply his army with ammunition and other provisions.

Grant's "bombast" was an exaggeration, but it was a bold risk. Winfield Scott had done this on the 260 mile march from Vera Cruz, on the Gulf of Mexico, to Mexico City. Robert E. Lee described it as "like Cortes." Hernando Cortez had founded Vera Cruz in 1510 before his own march on the Aztec capital, later known as Mexico City. Grant wrote in his memoirs that Scott had sent him as quartermaster to procure needed forage. "We procured full loads for our entire train at two plantations, which could easily have furnished as much more." Scott's plan to subsist his army on the country was a sort of blueprint for Grant's march on Vicksburg. Pemberton had met Grant in Scott's advance, so he might have imagined such a move after the naval attack at Grand Gulf.

On 9 May Loring was on the Baldwin's Ferry Road. The ferry crossing was at the Big Black River, southeast of Vicksburg. Loring wrote to Pemberton, "…I believe if a well-concerted plan be adopted, we can drive the enemy into the Mississippi, if it is done in time. They don't expect anything of the kind; they think we are on the defensive." Pemberton was so constricted by his responsibility to hold Vicksburg, he could not move. It wasn't a lack of bravery; he had won two brevets for gallantry in the Mexican War. Loring's proposal was for a force large enough to accomplish the objective. Instead Pemberton ordered one brigade, commanded by Brig. Gen. John Gregg, to march out of Jackson and attack Grant's right as he marched northwest toward the Big Black River railroad bridge.

Gregg marched southwesterly from Jackson on 11 May and reached Raymond that night. Gregg expected Wirt Adams's mounted infantry to take the lead, but that didn't happen. The lack of cavalry was continuing to plague Pemberton's department. Gregg wrote, "Because of this lack of cavalry, I was unable to ascertain anything concerning the strength of the enemy." The U.S. 17th Corps was in his front, but he believed it was a single brigade and set out to capture it! Gregg's aggressive fight so confused the enemy that they lost the initiative, until Gregg skillfully extracted his brigade to withdraw.

Pemberton's department had defeated Grant's previous offenses, but now there were two defeats. Conflicting orders from Davis and Johnston were about to bring far worse ones. Davis wanted him to hold Vicksburg, and it was a logical desire to prevent the enemy from vexing the entire river, and to keep communications with the Trans Mississippi open. Johnston would want Pemberton to join him closer to Jackson and defeat Grant. Had Davis been on the scene rather than struggling with his own poor health, he might have seen the merits of Johnston's proposed strategy. But Davis was under even more pressure because the U.S. Army of the Potomac had been driving toward Richmond. Thought Lee had dealt them an embarrassing defeat at Chancellorsville, Stonewall Jackson had been mortally wounded the night of 2 May.

Jackson lingered, and might have recovered, had it not been for pneumonia setting in. Irreplaceable Stonewall passed away on 10 May. His body lay in state in Richmond. Varina Davis stood with the president beside the casket. She saw a tear escape and fall onto Jackson's face. Someone spoke to him and he ignored them. He later explained, "You must excuse me. I am still staggering from a dreadful blow. I cannot think." Had Davis not been ill during yet another enemy offensive toward Richmond, and then Jackson's death, he might have been on the scene in Mississippi, and not been insistent on Pemberton getting trapped at Vicksburg. One thing is certain and that is he was in no condition to direct the Mississippi campaign from Richmond.

Had Davis been in Mississippi he would have seen the disruption of lives on plantations. The Negroes running off to follow the enemy was a major concern. Sid Champion had a home east of Vicksburg and his land was about to become a battlefield. He was serving in the 28th Mississippi Cavalry, and might have fought on his own land but they were kept in Vicksburg. Champion wrote his wife, "Stevenson and Lee wanting us with them while Gen'l Forney is determined we shall remain in city or at least a portion of us as couriers." John H. Forney commanded one of two divisions Pemberton left in Vicksburg. Stevenson commanded a division with S.D. Lee's brigade, and must have needed cavalry more than Forney. Champion concluded his lettre, four days before the battle, with an appeal: "Tell the negroes it would be better to hang a stone around their necks and plunge into Baker's Creek than to go to them. Starvation, death, with all its horrors will be their portion. I feel for them in that they may be foolish enough to run off. I look upon them like I do my children-to take care of them in sickness and health. May your home be spared is the Eden of all my thoughts. I see you still in my dreams, amid the flowers, may it long be your sweet home." Tragically a Yankee burned their home after the battle.

Joe Johnston went to Mississippi, as other Confederate brigades were moving there. He entered Jackson in the evening of the 13th with part of States Rights Gist's brigade. The South Carolina general had been sent by Beauregard, from Charleston. Johnston realized he had far too few soldiers to hold Jackson, and telegraphed Davis, "I am too late." Johnston had gone to Tullahoma to take temporary, direct command of the Army of Tennessee while Bragg took leave on family matters. Perhaps Johnston could have gone to Mississippi sooner, and left Hardee in command. But Johnston was not physically up to field operations. He may have been fairly well recovered from his Seven Pines wounds but had become ill. He wrote on the Mississippi Campaign in *Battles and Leaders*. When he received the order to go to Mississippi he responded, "I shall go immediately, although unfit for service." He wrote that Davis knew he had been sick for five or six weeks, but does not state what the illness was. He explained, "I arrived in Jackson as nightfall, exhausted by an uninterrupted journey of four days, undertaken from a sick room…" Johnston made this point to deflect unfair criticism from Davis. "…he had no right to expect that I was able to make a night ride of thirty miles, after a journey of four days."

John Adams was at Jackson when Johnston arrived. He could hardly have arrived to worse circumstances. Just to the southwest at Raymond, John Gregg's brigade had just fought the vanguard of Grant's army. As Johnston got to Jackson, Adams wired Pemberton that Gregg was facing 30-40,000 U.S. troops. Obviously Gregg had no choice but to fall back toward Jackson. Adams began wiring other troops to steer clear of Jackson, as Johnston intended to evacuate it. One was fellow West Point Class of 1846 graduate Samuel Bell Maxey, who commanded a brigade on the way up from Port Hudson. Maxey could hardly believe it until Johnston confirmed it.

The morning of the 14th found Johnston retreating north out of Jackson. He knew before he arrived that Grant's army was positioning itself between Jackson and Vicksburg. Communications between Johnston and Pemberton were thus blocked. All the worse, one of Johnston's couriers was a spy, and apprised the enemy of Confederate correspondence. Gregg did an outstanding job of covering the withdrawal from Jackson. About 2 p.m. he received word that the supply wagons were safely out of Mississippi's capital, moving north. Gregg made also made a successful withdrawal. Grant and Sherman entered Jackson behind him, at 4:00 p.m. Jackson was the capitol and railroad junction; hence, it had become a communications and supply centre. The loss of Jackson was a blunder for the Confederacy, for which Johnston and Pemberton were accountable. Pemberton had been headquartered in Jackson until 2 May. When he learned Grant had crossed the Mississippi he had moved to Vicksburg, leaving Jackson vulnerable.

Johnston's goal was to unite his growing force, often called the Army of Relief, with Pemberton's mobile force of 22,971 men. Pemberton had left some troops, including state troops, at Vicksburg, as he moved east toward Edwards Station (about 20 miles west of Jackson). Pemberton had ordered Loring to Edwards Station on the morning of 13 May. He ordered Loring to send out patrols to determine the whereabouts of Grant's divisions. It was nearly midnight when Pemberton learned no enemy division was threatening Edwards Station. Instead, the enemy was marching hard toward Jackson. Early on the 14th Pemberton received an order from Johnston to march farther east, to Clinton. Pemberton responded, "I do not think you fully comprehend the position that Vicksburg will be left in, but I comply at once with your order."

Pemberton had marched east in obedience to Johnston's orders, but began to have second thoughts, for Davis expected him to hold Vicksburg. Pemberton had left enough troops in Vicksburg to hold it while he and Johnston combined their forces, but time was running out. Grant had earlier ignored orders from Halleck, in Washington, to combine his army with the one under Banks downriver, at Port Hudson. Grant did not take counsel of those that would have deterred him. Had he moved toward Port Hudson, it would have given Johnston time to bring reinforcements to Mississippi and combine with Pemberton.

<u>Loring's and Stevenson's offensive plan for Pemberton to take position in Grant's rear</u>
Pemberton had a confusing dilemma with Johnston's order, and was about to be more so. Loring and Stevenson had another idea. They wanted to advance against Grant's supply line. Loring had already tried to get Pemberton to attack Grant before he took Jackson. This time he suggested they march south to the road between Grand Gulf and Jackson. That would put them on Grant's line of communications and supply so that Grant would have to attack them. Loring was backed by Stevenson, who commanded the largest division. Pemberton did not like the plan, but decided to follow it. Loring report claims, "I understood the opinion of the general commanding to be that he did not approve the

move proposed by General Johnston, but coincided with those who were for moving to the enemy's rear." Pemberton was taking risk, for Loring's plan was not what either Davis or Johnston desired. But on 15 May Pemberton's force marched away from the Edward's Station area to an intersection known as Crossroads, south of Champion Hill.

From Edward's Depot (a.k.a. Edward's Station) Loring advised Pemberton: "I purpose marching in the following order, which will enable us to move into line of battle as follows: Tilghman's brigade on the right; Culbertson's battery, two 6-pounders, one 12-pounder howitzer, one 3-inch rifle. Buford's brigade center; Bouanchaud's battery, four 6-pounders, two 12-pounder howitzers, two 3-inch rifles; Cowan's reserve battery, four 6-pounders, two 12-pounder howitzers. Featherston brigade, left; Wofford's battery, two 6-pounders, two 12-pounder howitzers. I expect to keep the reserve battery in rear of General Buford, and to hold Scott's regiment also in reserve." Of the 22 artillery pieces only the three 3-inch rifles were much in favour. The 6-pounders and howitzers would mostly be phased out of Confederate armies by 1864. Napoleons would be desired.

Pemberton's march on the 15th was delayed when it was learned the ford he planned to use to cross Baker's Creek was too swollen to cross. It seems Pemberton's lack of cavalry to scout to the ford led to poor reconnaissance. Perhaps the ford would have been a faster crossing, but a bridge was found upstream and used, though with a delay into afternoon. Pemberton continued south of Crossroads to reach the Raymond Road; this is today's Highway 467. He headquartered in Sarah Ellison's house. Loring reported his division, in the lead, reached there about dark.

Loring wrote that after dark, "Upon this road the enemy was in large force within a few miles of my camp. Being satisfied of this from prisoners taken and from observations of several of my staff sent in advance, very large picket forces were placed in my front, rear, and right flank. Completing my dispositions, I soon after met General Pemberton, to whom information of the near proximity of the enemy in large force was given." Loring went onto say Pemberton knew the enemy was in his "immediate front."

The next morning Loring and others were on hand with Pemberton for a meeting. Between 6:30 and 7:00 they began to hear the first shots of the battle. Enemy cavalry was crossing Turkey Creek, about three miles east, and were exchanging fire with Wirt Adams's mounted infantry. The Mississippians were on the Gillespie plantation. Behind the enemy cavalry were two infantry divisions. A brigade deployed to reinforce the cavalry. Naturally Adams withdrew to the west. In 1.2 miles Adams came to a ridgeline where there was another plantation, that of a Jefferson Davis (not the president). Two of Loring's regiments, the 35th Alabama and the 22nd Mississippi had positioned on the ridge the previous night. They were commanded by Col. Edward Goodwin of the 35th.

J.P. Cannon was in the 27th Alabama, of Buford's Brigade. He wrote, "On May 16, 1863, while we were breakfasting on the remnants of our scanty rations, a sudden volley of artillery in our immediate front announced to us that the Yankees were much nearer to us than we had imagined the night before. It was a genuine surprise to us if not to our commanders and subsequent events tended to confirm our opinion that there was a failure somewhere to realize the situation as it was. Unexpected as it was we had no confusion, but activity was apparent all over the camps in an instant and it required but a few moments to don our accoutrements and be ready for orders."

Johnston's Dispatch halts Pemberton resulting in the defeat at Champion Hill

Pemberton's officers were hearing these first shots of the battle when a dispatch arrived from Johnston. It directed Pemberton to join him on the railroad, at Clinton, about ten miles west of Jackson. That wasn't about to happen. Grant had three of his seven divisions between Pemberton and Clinton. Furthermore, Johnston withdrew northward from Jackson. Pemberton decided to abandon Loring's plan to strike Grant's supply line, and turn the army around to reach the railroad. He could not march into Grant's three divisions to the northeast, but he could attempt to reach the railroad at Edwards Station. This kept him between Vicksburg and Grant, while opening the possibility of a way of uniting with Johnston. Unfortunately for Pemberton, Grant was about to strike.

The Raymond Road led westward to the Lower Crossing of Baker's Creek. During the battle to follow only Loring would block the two U.S. divisions from advancing and cutting that line of retreat. During the battle Pemberton would focus on Stevenson's Division on his left, as that was where virtually all of the fighting took place. It was near the left that the Upper Crossing became cut off by the enemy. Pemberton would order Loring to the left, which might have resulted in the loss of the Lower Crossing too! Historians have generally dismissed Loring as a troublemaker because of his friction with Stonewall, ignoring how many others did as well. Thus they put blame for the loss in this battle with Loring for not complying with Pemberton's orders to leave the Raymond Road and come to Stevenson's aid. Had Loring done so, the two enemy divisions would have been in Pemberton's rear, forcing him to fight on two fronts, with no line of retreat.

Grant was at Clinton, about ten miles west of Jackson on the morning of the 16th Two railroaders had passed thru Edwards Station the previous day and reported Pemberton had passed with a force of about 25,000; he actually had almost 23,000. Grant had 32,000 at hand and they were mostly well rested. Many of Pemberton's had had little sleep, some having been up all night. Grant knew Pemberton was not entrenched and was outnumbered. He decided to attack.

Pemberton was along a road to Raymond on the morning of 16 May when he received an order from Johnston to meet him north of the *Southern Railroad of Mississippi*. This meant Pemberton had to reverse his march to backtrack. To the east, toward Raymond, gunshots could be heard about 6:30 a.m. Grant had two divisions advancing on his left, on the road from Raymond. Loring suggested to Pemberton they better form a line of battle as quickly as possible. Pemberton agreed and soon had Loring's 6,300 men positioned on a ridge overlooking Jackson Creek.

Carter Stevenson had been ordered to headquarters on the Raymond Road at sunrise. He learned they were no longer on the offensive, but complying with Johnston's order to

Pemberton's army had advanced east of Jackson Creek (seen above from 467), hoping to attack Grant as he marched north. Then he crossed back to the west side. Loring's decision to hold the ridge there (below) was and is controversial.

return toward the railroad. Pemberton was hoping to withdraw and not have to fight. This explains his order to Stevenson to move their 400 wagons west of Baker Creek. Once there they were to be "arranged to the right and left of the road in such a manner as would afford an uninterrupted passage to the infantry and artillery." As it turned out the battle was fought and needed ammunition would not be at hand.

Some writers have blamed Stevenson for moving the wagons, including ammunition, west of Baker's Creek. Stevenson's report states, "My division started early on the morning of the battle, under the supposition that the army was about to retrace its steps to join General Johnston, and with that view was weakened by sending one brigade to the rear in charge of the whole baggage train." Pemberton's report clarifies, "Major-General Stevenson was instructed to make the necessary disposition for the protection of the trains then on the Clinton Road (Jackson Road) and crossing Baker's Creek." Pemberton gave the order which resulted in ammunition for Stevenson's and Bowen's Divisions leaving the battlefield. Loring's Division, along the Raymond Road, had its train.

Loring's Division went from the vanguard of Pemberton's advance to the rearguard. Thus Loring was in a position to understand the predicament they were in. He soon advised Pemberton "that the sooner he formed a line of battle the better, as the enemy would very soon be upon us." Pemberton deployed his largest division, Stevenson's with 11,714, on his left. It was on and around Champion Hill, but only about 6,500 were present to fight. His Fourth Brigade, with the 3rd Maryland artillery battery, had been sent west of Baker's Creek to guard the wagon train. Stevenson's three brigades on the field would initially fight five U.S. brigades, numbering about 10,000 troops. Stevenson, like Pemberton, had no battlefield command experience, and not even at the regimental level. He was not an ideal general to command Pemberton's largest division in such a position.

Loring might have resented this; after all Stevenson had been on his staff in Virginia. Also, Tilghman might have resented Bowen, his junior, commanded a division while he only commanded a brigade. Pemberton was apparently upset with Tilghman, and it may have been for something else, for he removed him from command. Robert Lowry was placed in command, but only briefly, for the order not only upset Tilghman, but Loring. Lt. F.W. Merrin, of Culbertson's Mississippi battery, recalled the turmoil, "Here was a pretty kettle of fish. The whole army right close up, face to face, with Grant's army, twice or three times as strong, and our officers are all in a stew! General Loring, who acted as a breakwater between the two on past occasions now again cut the Gordeon knot. The one-armed general rode squarely up to the pompous Pemberton and in language more forcible than elegant, more caustic than clever, informed Pemberton that unless he then and there revoked the order of the day before in reference to Tilghman that he might dispense with his (Loring's) service for the day's battle. Then and there, an order was hastily written by Pemberton on the pummel of his saddle, restoring General Tilghman to command."

Loring had pulled back his blocking forces near Jackson's Creek, and destroyed the bridge. It was a good decision for another ridge to his rear covered the Ratliff Road, which led north to Bowen's and Stevenson's positions. The home of H.B. Coker was on that ridge, where it still remains in the 21st Century. Loring's experience commanding his

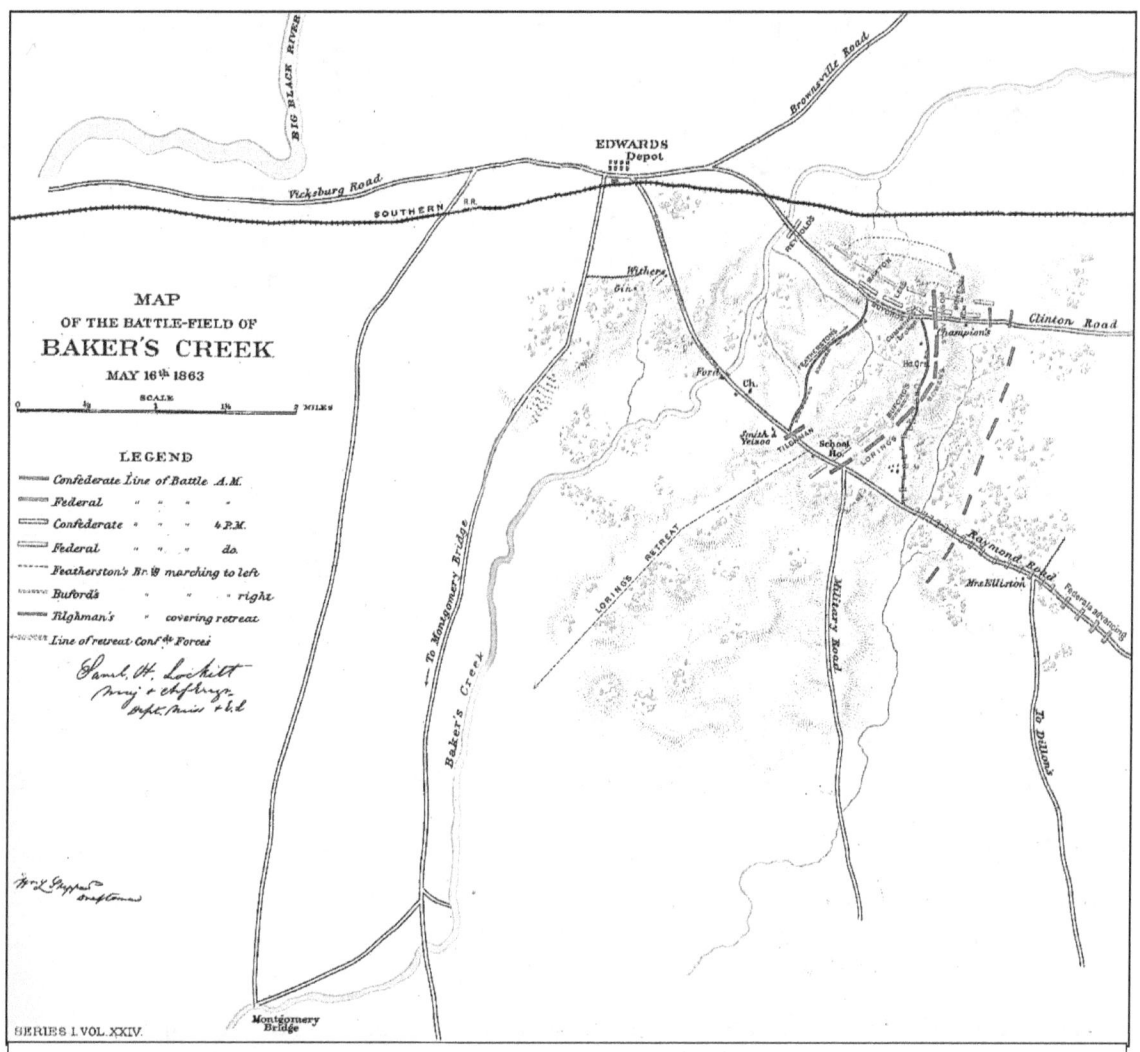

Confederate engineer Samuel Lockett's map (above) refers to the battle usually known as Champion Hill as Baker's Creek. The creek had to be held for Pemberton to retrace his steps to Edwards, in obedience to Johnston's order to move to Clinton; at Edwards, Brownsville Road could be taken to reach Clinton. Grant brought 3 of 7 divisions on the Clinton Road (a.k.a. Jackson Road) and attacked with a numerical advantage. Pemberton and division commander Stevenson lacked battlefield experience.

The first phase of the battle was fought by Stevenson's Division, generally parallel and to the north of the Jackson Road (Clinton Road on map).The unshaded positons of Barton and Lee are correct for the 1st-Phase (10:30-1:30). Loring's position is correct; artillery duel stalled U.S. divisions. The 2nd-Phase (1:30-3:00) saw Bowen reinforce Stevenson and attack and drive U.S. back at Champion Hill. Loring ordered Buford and Featherston north. The 3rd-Phase (3-5:00) saw Bowen run out of ammo and Loring facing north, parallel to Jackson Road. Tilghman and his artillery held 2 U.S. divisions from advancing on Pemberton's rear! The 4th-Phase (5:00 until dark) saw Loring positioned for an attack with Buford and Featherston. Loring reluctantly obeyed Pemberton's order to retreat. Loring covered retreat for Bowen and Stevenson.

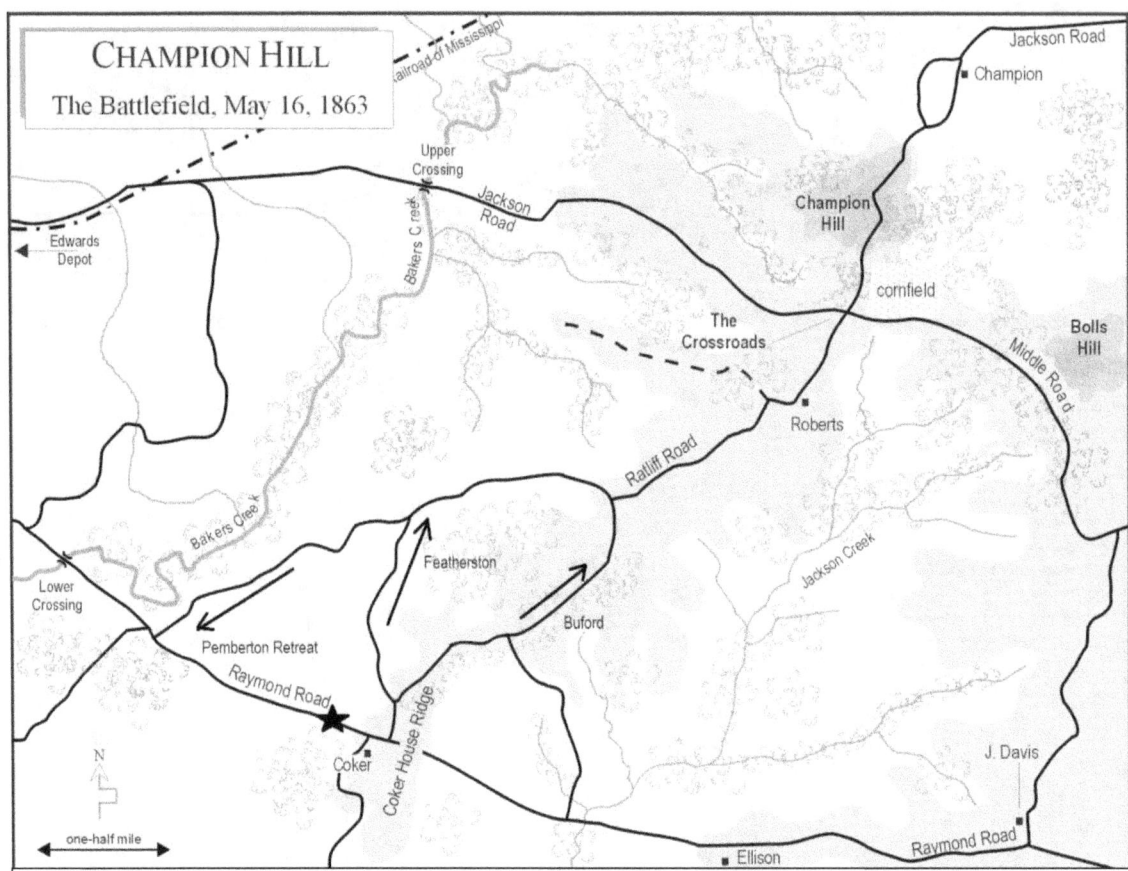

Champion Hill 7 Battlefield Map by Theodore P. Savas from Timothy Smith's, *Champion Hill Decisive Battle for Vicksburg* (2005). Reprinted with permission. Several features added by the author are troops movements and star for Tilghman.

Major Lockett's map had errors, as will be seen when comparing to the map above. Lockett may have never seen the battlefield north of Champion Hill, and that could explain the absence of the Jackson Road running north from the Crossroads. The primary enemy movement came out the Jackson Road to attack Stevenson's Division. Carter Stevenson's brigades were in a generally east-west line as Lockett designates. Lockett indicates Bowen's Division of two brigades, initially faced east, as did Loring. Stevenson's retreat led Pemberton to call on Bowen for assistance.

Bowen's spectacular attack drove the enemy back, but his troops began to run low on ammunition. Pemberton called on Loring to advance. Buford's Brigade was along the Ratliff Road, closest to the Crossroads, and moved first. Two enemy divisions were in position to advance on the Middle Road, toward the Crossroads. Pemberton ordered one of Buford's regiments to protect Bowen's right flank, and then Bowen ordered another one to assist. Not until Buford got into position facing north did he realize the two regiments were gone. Loring moved Featherston's Brigade on a country road, due to a guide's directions, delaying their arrival. Loring united Buford and Featherston and was preparing to attack when Pemberton ordered a retreat to the Lower Crossing. Tilghman's Brigade and artillery (star) held the Raymond Road, insuring the escape.

artillery at Fort Pemberton, and Tilghman's at Fort Henry, must have come into play here, for the artillery fire appeared to hold back the two enemy divisions in their front. But the two enemy divisions were initially under orders not to advance. Loring reported, "…in orders conveyed to me at different times during the day he (Pemberton) instructed me to hold my position, not attacking the enemy unless he attempted to outflank us."

A Confederate Missourian watched as Confederate smoothbores competed against U.S. rifled pieces. He recalled it as "the most splendid artillery duel…that I have ever witnessed in open fields, when both parties were in full view; this lasted for thirty minutes, during which time the guns on both sides were handled in the most skillful and scientific manner." But Loring saw the enemy had the advantage and pulled back to the next ridge, on which the Coker house was located. By 11:00 U.S. troops had repaired the bridge over Jackson Creek and began to line up on Loring's former position.

An Alabama brigade under Stephen D. Lee passed thru the crossroads onto the Jackson Road. Lt. Col. Edmund Winston Pettus rode nearly a half mile north to the bald crest of Champion Hill. Pettus could see a large column of enemy troops approaching from the east on the Jackson Road. Here is another occasion when Pemberton's lack of cavalry was evident. Pettus had to rush back to tell S.D. Lee. Lee explained this to Stevenson, that their marching column was about to be outflanked. Stevenson gave Lee permission to form his brigade on Champion Hill. Stevenson began sending other reinforcements, including artillery, to the hill from which the battle would take its name.

Meanwhile Loring was still on the Coker House Ridge facing the approaching enemy division. The enemy vanguard reached Jackson Creek, east of the ridge, and found the bridge largely destroyed. As their pioneers attempted to rebuild it Loring's artillery opened on them. His smoothbores were no match for the enemy's rifled Parrotts. By 11:00 a.m. the enemy was across the creek. Grant didn't want to bring on a battle until all of his approaching divisions were in place; hence, Loring was not attacked, but he had reason to think he would be. He reported the enemy, "…the enemy throwing forward a heavy line of skirmishers, and showing every indication of an attack in force upon my position, both in front and upon the right flank. General Bowen also informed me that he thought the enemy was moving to the right." Loring might have been flanked. Instead his artillery sporadically exchanged fire with the enemy for several hours.

Grant and corps commander McPherson had been to the north, at the Champion House, positioning divisions as they arrived. Carter Stevenson was watching from atop Champion Hill, and realized the left of Lee's Brigade would be outflanked. He brought up more Seth Barton's Georgia brigade and artillery. They arrived just in time to receive an attack. But on Lee's right, Alfred Cumming's outnumbered Georgia brigade broke. Lee's Alabamians then trailed back too. Barton's Georgians were cut off and retreated west toward Baker's Creek Bridge. Stevenson's retreat ended the first phase of the battle. The second phase of the battle saw Bowen's Division respond to Pemberton's orders to come to Stevenson's relief. Pemberton's line was an upside down "L." Stevenson faced three enemy divisions to the north, while Bowen and Loring faced four to their east. They could see that if they simply pulled out to reinforce Stevenson, four U.S. divisions could march unopposed, behind Pemberton. They might have attacked from the rear and cut off his line of retreat west to Baker's Creek. Yet Bowen's 4,599 troops advanced to the Crossroads, pushed an enemy division north of it, and off Champion Hill. An Arkansan said the enemy line "seemed to fall and tumble headlong to the bottom of the hill."

Bowen's pullout widened the gap between Loring and the main line of battle. Loring wrote that "…General Bowen was summarily ordered in that direction, without warning either to myself or General Buford, commanding a brigade of my division next to him." Writers have criticized Loring for not obeying Pemberton's orders to move north, but the presence of four divisions to the east justified Loring's reluctance. Pemberton sent a staff officer to order Loring to send reinforcements a third time. Loring told Pemberton's officer he had his hands full with the enemy force out the Raymond Road. Pemberton learned of this and sent an aide to Loring to insist reinforcements were needed. Loring then ordered Buford's and Featherston's Brigades toward Champion Hill. This left Loring with Tilghman's Brigade and artillery to face two enemy divisions with artillery.

Pemberton learned Bowen's counterattack failed about 3:00. The battle was about to enter the third phase. Bowen's ferocious Arkansas and Missouri troops had begun running out of ammunition when they ran into 16 U.S. artillery pieces. Bowen's troops felt bayonets would not carry the day, and began stripping cartridges from the dead and wounded. The enemy positioned fresh troops for a counterattack, and Bowen had to fall back. Within the next hour he was pushed back over Champion Hill. Pemberton had just ridden south and found Buford leading his brigade north. The Crossroad was threatened and before Buford could reach it the enemy drove across it. When he left Loring's position down at the Raymond Road he marched north to Crossroads on the Ratliff Road. He reported, "My command double-quicked the distance (about two miles) under a scorching sun, through corn and rye fields, in about half an hour, when I arrived about the rear of the right wing of General Bowen's division, which was falling back in disorder before an overpowering force of the enemy."

J.P Cannon recalled the march from the perspective of one of Buford's men. He wrote, "We double-quicked, it seemed to us, at least three miles under a blistering sun, with not a drop of water in our canteens. When we reached the battle field we were almost exhausted, but dashed into the fray with cheers and yells to encourage our boys who by that time were slowly falling back. Stimulated by our presence some of them rallied and the battle raged furiously again."

Buford approached the Jackson Road at Crossroad, close to 3:30. He wrote, "Across this road our men were hastening in wild disorder and in consternation before a very heavy fire of the enemy." His brigade struggled to move north as troops retreating "continually" broke into his advance. They were "rushing pell-mell from the scene of action and resisting all attempts to rally them." He explained "the enemy held possession of the road, and that I must retake it in order to comply with the command of General Pemberton." Then Buford realized two of his regiments were missing. Pemberton had ordered the 35th Alabama and the 12th Louisiana eastward to confront two U.S. divisions around the Middle Road. Buford wrote, "Two of my strongest regiments were detached from the rear of my brigade…The strength of my brigade at this critical moment was thus unceremoniously and materially reduced, this being done without my knowledge, and without any report being made to me of the fact by the generals who gave the orders."

Pemberton may have felt justified in snatching regiments from Loring, from frustration with Loring's disobedience of orders. The other generals Buford referred to were Cockrell and Green. Fortunately the two regiments allowed Bowen's Division, running out of ammunition, to make a fighting withdrawal. It also gave Loring time to position his division to cover the army's withdrawal.

Brig. Gen. Martin Green's Second Brigade of Bowen's Division was comprised of Arkansans and Missourians. Green saw Col. Edward Goodwin with his 35th Alabama and ordered him eastward to support Wade's abandoned Missouri battery. Goodwin wrote, "The battery men, being reassured by the appearance of the regiment, rushed with enthusiasm to their guns and for an hour worked them with a celerity and daring that I believe never has been surpassed during this war." Luck was with Goodwin, as he said, "The enemy poured volley after volley of shot, shell, grape, and canister upon us, but owing to a fortunate position I only lost one man." Underbrush, including cane, and ravines must have helped shield the Alabamians, for they fought off elements of three enemy brigades. Goodwin finally withdrew as Wade's gunners emptied their caissons, and Green's men retreated across Goodwin's rear. Green solicited Goodwin to pull back and rejoin Buford's Division. They had made a splendid fight and Loring would later confirm they "had distinguished themselves."

Col. Thomas M. Scott's 12th Louisiana was also directed eastward parallel to the Middle Road. Goodwin's Alabamians were south of it as Scott's was moving north. Scott said he arrived as Green's Brigade was retiring southward in great confusion. Though there were two enemy divisions ahead Scott was fired on by two, maybe three. Scott said a heavy fire tore into his ranks, and it was returned with spirit. Rather than stand and take it Scott ordered an advance, which he said was made with "great steadiness and precision." But enemy fire was too heavy; Scott decided on a bayonet charge. He ordered his Louisianans to "make a steady advance in line without yelling, that they might hear my commands; and never was an order more implicitly obeyed." Also, it "caused them to flee in great confusion." But with two divisions to the east, his ability to advance was limited. But he and the 35th Alabama had played crucial roles, covering the retirement of Bowen's men.

Buford was not in position when Pemberton snatched his two regiments away, but was very soon. Before he reached Crossroads he deployed with an open field to his front. The Jackson Road ran across the field running west of Crossroads. The 35th Alabama was to his right, and the 12th Louisianans up northeast of Crossroads. Buford had hoped to attack, but the open field caused him to pause and get aligned.

Buford recalled "I awaited the approach of the enemy, who must advance through an open, clear space. The enemy, however, halted in the road and established a battery. To have charged him from my position, with my brigade reduced in strength and over an open space of several hundred yards, would have cost it half its numbers." He moved his brigade into some timber on the right hoping to find a better route of attack, but found his line was being flanked, on the left and right. He fell back a short distance and found Loring, with Featherston's Brigade, in a "commanding position." The 35th Alabama and 12th Louisiana returned to the brigade at this position.

Pemberton realized Bowen's Division, out of ammunition, could not continue, and that Stevenson's larger division was not able to maintain itself in a cohesive, effective line. Pemberton had a staff officer ride south to look for Loring. Instead of finding him coming toward Crossroads on Ratliff Road, as Buford had taken, somehow Loring, leading Featherston's Brigade, was on a less direct road farther west. Featherston recalled they had gone into "woods and over very rough ground a distance of about two miles." This points out the large area of the battlefield, as large as more prominent fields in the war. Featherston continued, "The march was as rapid as possible under the circumstances; the troops moved at a double-quick most of the way."

Loring had arrived to find fleeing troops from the other two divisions and "there was no one endeavoring to rally or direct them." Buford had just retired as pointed out, and he found Loring positioning Featherston. This was on a ridge about a half mile south of the Jackson Road, and Crossroads. Buford was positioned on Featherston's right, and some of Bowen's (hopefully with some ammunition) to Buford's right. Loring had managed to keep his ordinance train, and it was being positioned for access.

Loring wrote, "Upon the approach of W.S. Featherston's brigade, in rapid march, a considerable force of the retreating army having been rallied behind him, the enemy, who was advancing upon the artillery, fell back in great disorder, Colonel (William) Withers pouring in a most destructive fire upon him. It was here that we witnessed a scene ever to be remembered, when the gallant Withers and his brave men, with their fine park of artillery, stood unflinchingly amid a shower of shot and shell the approach of the enemy in overwhelming force after his supports had been driven back, and trusting that a succoring command would arrive in time to save his batteries, and displaying a degree of courage and determination that calls for the most unqualified admiration." Withers escaped from the field and commanded the artillery at Vicksburg; hence, he and Loring did not serve together again.

Meanwhile, S.D. Lee could not find Stevenson, and rode up to Loring for orders. His brigade and other troops of Stevenson's Division were placed on the far left. Pemberton was in retreat with much of his army. With his direct route of retreat across Baker's Creek to Edward's Station cut, his army was headed for the Lower Bridge. At this time Loring was creating a new line and thinking of launching an attack!

The fourth and final phase of the battle was Pemberton's retreat. Pemberton ordered his army south along the Austin Ridge to reach Baker's Creek at the Lower Bridge. As the battle had raged Maj. Lockett's engineers had rebuilt the bridge! There was also a ford, so that Stevenson and Bowen could retreat west to the Big Black River.

Loring Covers Pemberton's Retreat and Escapes with his Division

Loring was about to order the attack to retake the Crossroads when a courier from Pemberton rode up with orders to retreat. Loring was overcome with aggression and still insisted he would attack. Just then one of Pemberton's staff rode up and insisted Loring must retreat, as the rear guard for Stevenson and Bowen. This may have been for the best because Grant had finally created a solid line with five of his divisions. Loring's role in commanding the final line was critical for he became the rear guard. Featherston was positioned to cover the retreat for most of the army. He gave much of the credit to three pieces of artillery from Bouanchaud's Battery.

Though some units of Stevenson's Division had been forced back in disorder, Loring's brigades were able to cover the retreat and retire in good order. Featherston reported, "My last position on the field was not abandoned until I was ordered by General Loring to do so, and move my command toward the depot as rapidly as practicable." He went onto explain as he retired toward the ford on Baker's Creek he encountered Loring and learned the enemy were in possession of the ford. This was about sunset or later.

Tilghman's Brigade was still alone across the Raymond Road, confronting the two other enemy divisions. He also had artillery to hold off the two lurking enemy divisions. Col. Arthur E. Reynolds of the 26th Mississippi was there and later reported it was to "prevent a flank movement of the enemy down it to on our right." It was far worse, for they could have attacked from behind and taken the line of retreat to the lower crossing on Baker's Creek. Pemberton had snatched two regiments from Buford without telling Loring, and about the time Loring departed Raymond Road with Featherston's Brigade, Pemberton sent orders to Tilghman to move to the far left.

Tilghman had left the Raymond Road, and was moving north, when Pemberton and his escort approached from the opposite direction. Pemberton asked, "General Tilghman, why are you moving your brigade?" Tilghman responded, "I received an order from you to move to the left flank, General Pemberton." But Pemberton, obviously stressed, said, "That order was countermanded almost an hour ago with instructions for you to hold your position! You must move your brigade back to the Raymond Road and prevent the enemy from moving up it and seizing the crossing over Baker's Creek!" The engineer Samuel Lockett had completed the bridge over the creek about 2:00, and rode up. He had been sent with the later order and was just arriving with it due to a broken down horse. Loring's desire to maintain his position on the Raymond Road had finally been fully comprehended by Pemberton.

E.T. Eggleston wrote of Tilghman's last moments for *Confederate Veteran*. He recalled, "General Tilghman came to our position in an open field on foot. He was in particularly good humor and wore a new fatigue uniform. He ordered his son, Lloyd Tilghman, Jr., who was his aide-de-camp, to go with a squad of men and drive some Federal sharpshooters from a gin house on the left of the Raymond Road who were annoying some of Wither's cannoneers." Colonel William Withers was Pemberton's artillery chief, rather than a battery commander.

Eggleston again referred to Tilghman's pleasant manner. It is remarkable in consideration of Tilghman's continuing friction with Pemberton. Tilghman was observing Captain Cowan's battery when he joked with Cowan, "I think you and your Lieutenants had better dismount. They are shooting pretty close to us, and I do not know whether they are shooting at your large gray horse or my new uniform." The officers dismounted and Tilghman shifted his attention to a Napoleon gunner. "I think you are shooting rather too high" and he sighted the gun himself. Then Tilghman returned to a little knoll and lifted his field glasses. As he did an exploding Parrot shell struck him in his stomach.

Loring had seen Tilghman's Brigade was positioned to be his last brigade to withdraw. In the midst of a potential disaster, Tilghman had been killed. Loring raced to the scene. It was recalled in *Confederate Veteran,* Volume 21. The writer had been a teenaged soldier in the 26th Mississippi. He was only 30 feet from Tilghman when a shell fragment passed through the general's body. The boy-soldier had been noting Tilghman's "knightly" presence directing artillery fire. He wrote, "The wildest confusion then prevailed for a short time, and but for the appearance of the daring, one-armed General Loring on his fast-racing, nick tailed roan horse there is no telling what might have happened." He said Loring appealed, "Boys don't let those damn Yankees have that battery!"

Loring was a friend of Tilghman and lamented his death in his report. He wrote of him and his brigade: "The bold stand of this brigade under the lamented hero saved a large portion of this army." Drennan, of Featherston's staff wrote, "…three hours before I had sat and listened to him talking and jesting, full of life and gaiety…and then he was gone to that course from whence no traveler returns." Decades later the *Vicksburg Herald* reported the spot where Tilghman's "noble life ebbed away and the sad earth drank the blood with greedy thirstiness," a unique peach tree took root. Its leaves and fruit were a bright scarlet every year it bore fruit. Tilghman had been killed 10 days before his 20th wedding anniversary.

Loring knew his artillery had given great service in holding onto the Raymond Road, and had to demand more. Private James G. Spencer, of Cowan's Battery, later recalled Loring rode up to Captain Cowan. Loring said, "I intend to save my Division as I have been cut off by the defeat of General Stevenson. I want your Battery to hold this position until sun down, fall back, following my line of retreat."

Loring meant to cross to the west bank of Baker's Creek to reach Pemberton, but as the rear guard he couldn't until Stevenson and Bowen had. One of his staff had gone to get information from Pemberton, who could not be located. Instead he brought Loring word from Bowen: "For God's sake, hold your position until sundown and save the army." Minutes later a message arrived from Bowen. The enemy had gotten across at the upper crossing and outflanked him. The message ended, "Do your best to save your division."

Loring rode to the Lower Crossing near dark and a reconnaissance determined there were no Confederates present. Instead there was enemy infantry and artillery on a ridge on the far side. Buford said, "General Bowen had retired, and when near the ford, it was clearly perceptible that the enemy, with his artillery, was raking the same, and at the same time

The dramatic sculpture of Tilghman at Vicksburg was donated by his two sons in 1926. The stone, located some 17 miles east, marks the point where Tilghman was killed.

advancing his columns in that direction. Finding that it was impossible to cross the creek under the fire of the enemy and the dispositions of his infantry, you ordered me to turn my command to the left, and by going through a plantation, seek a ford lower down."

Loring then had enemy troops in front, to his right, and behind him on the Raymond Road. Loring's biographer explained that General Buford had secured a guide who he thought could lead the division across Baker's Creek, farther down, and onto the Big Black Bridge. The guide had led them to believe it was only three or four miles. Loring was showing evidence of following Pemberton into Vicksburg. But they began to learn it was ten or twelve miles, and that they would not be able to make it. Loring decided he could not make it into Vicksburg. Loring decided to escape the trap, but had to abandon most of his artillery and wagons. One of Buford's Kentuckians recalled "putting fifty rounds of cartridges in our haversacks from an abandoned ordinance train." A story has circulated that Loring was insubordinate in his decision, but it appears he had no choice. Loring reported, "After a full consultation with my brigadiers, all of us were of the opinion that it was impossible to attempt the passage of the Big Black at any point, and in doing so the entire division would certainly be lost. Subsequent events have fully shown that we were right in this determination."

A story in an 1894 issue of *Confederate Veteran* described the night scene. T.A. Manahan wrote, "General Loring came riding down our lines close up to us, and was encouraging the boys and told us that we had been sold, but he would take us out." With over 6,000 troops, or about 27% of the field force, Loring began marching them to the southeast. He had to slip them around the camps of two enemy divisions. In a march similar to the more famous enemy escape at Spring Hill, Tennessee, Loring marched out right under their noses!

T.H. Knight also recalled this march, writing from McGregor, Texas. He saw a rider approach and ask for the general; apparently meaning Loring. The rider and the general spoke, and then the general called, "Attention!" Knight said before the echo of his voice faded every man was on his feet and had his gun. "We then filed to the left and into a dark swamp and struck into an old road, familiar to the man who had come to lead us out. He seemed to be nearly 60 years of age. The word was sent down the line, 'No man must speak above a whisper.' While in the swamp we could hear the Federals not a hundred yards away, who thought they had cut us off, but by marching all night we got away."

J.P. Cannon was in Buford's Brigade and supplied pertinent details of the night march: "Once in the timber we were out of their clutches for the time and welcomed the night soon spreading her mantle around us, effectively concealing us from our bloodthirsty pursuers. We were in an unknown forest without a road or star to guide us, almost surrounded by a foe flushed with victory, wagons and artillery captured and no rations in our haversacks. Staff officers were stationed on the line of march, warning us not to speak above a whisper, as we were passing between two bodies of the enemy. Their camp fires were burning brightly on both sides of the road and we steered as nearly as possible between them and no doubt it was largely due to this that we were enabled to make our escape, for without the lights for a guide we would probably have wandered right into their camps. Slowly and silently as a funeral procession we groped our way through the woods and fields and swamps until midnight when, considering ourselves reasonably safe, the restrictions were removed and we discussed the events of the day, our hazardous retreat and marvelous escape. The opinion was generally expressed that General Pemberton must have handled his troops very badly…No doubt we were largely outnumbered, but it did seem to us that if good generalship had been displayed we should have been able to retreat in order and with much less loss than we sustained."

In an 1896 issue of *Confederate Veteran*, J.V. Greif wrote, "We passed so near the enemy on the night of the 16th that we could hear them talking. As we were approaching a road which crossed the one on which we were marching, General Loring learned that the enemy had a strong picket post at the cross-roads. He dressed a courier in a Yankee uniform and sent him around to come up the road and order the picket withdrawn. They obeyed the order promptly, as we had a clear road." The troops marched all night and into the next day to make their escape!

General Buford's report (O.R. Vol. 24, Part 2, p. 86) succinctly described the escape of Loring's Division: "By neighborhood roads we moved during the night, passing the flank of the enemy, hourly expecting an attack, hearing the enemy conversing as we passed along, and crossing ravines and creeks, which proved the impossibility of moving artillery, and about 3 a.m. Sunday morning reached Dillon's, on the road from Grand Gulf to Raymond, and but a few miles from the battlefield. We then marched to Crystal Springs, on the *Jackson and New Orleans Railroad*, near which we camped Sunday night." Dillon was where Loring had hoped Pemberton could reach Grant's rear.

J.P. Cannon remembered, "At sunrise we stopped long enough to call the roll and ascertained that about one third of the regiment was missing." No doubt many could not keep up on the exhausting march, and some captured. Cannon continued, "After thirty minutes rest we moved on and 'dragged one foot after the other' going into bivouac at sundown, having been on foot thirty-six hours without food and had to go to sleep supperless. Having stacked arms, we threw ourselves on the ground without even a blanket to shield us from the night dew, or a knapsack for a pillow and in a very few minutes the whole division was sleeping so soundly that the explosion of a sixty pound bomb shell would have hardly awakened us."

Maj. J.T. Hogane of the engineer corps thought Loring did well. He wrote for the *Southern Historical Society Papers* (Vol. 11, page 227) in 1883: "There was one man of sense-General Loring. He absolutely refused to go into Vicksburg, and declared to General Pemberton that he would not obey his orders, and he did with about 10,000 men, cut his way out in spite of General Grant's cordon." Loring probably did not tell Pemberton he would not obey his orders, but there was a perception that he had.

Loring unites his division with Johnston's Army of Relief in Jackson
Thus Loring's Division was able to escape Pemberton's surrender at Vicksburg. Loring had marched to Crystal Springs, about 20 miles south of Jackson. He arrived in Jackson

on the morning of 19 May. This brought his division under Johnston's command. Lt. Col. Arthur Fremantle, an English soldier of the Coldstream Guards, happened to be visiting. Fremantle wrote of Loring arriving, "He is a stout man with one arm. His division had arrived at Jackson from Crystal Springs about 6,000 strong." A division field return, found in O.R. Volume 24, Part 3, page 917, lists the three infantry brigades had an aggregate present of 5,778. The artillerymen may have brought the total to 6,000.

Fremantle arrived three days before and wrote that Johnston received him with much kindness. "In appearance General Joseph E. Johnston (commonly called Joe Johnston) is rather below the middle height, spare soldier-like, and well set up; his features are good, and he has lately taken to wear a grayish beard. He is a Virginian by birth, and appears to be about fifty-seven years old. He talks in a calm, deliberate, and confident manner; to me he was extremely affable, but he certainly possesses the power of keeping people at a distance when he chooses, and his officers evidently stand in great awe of him. He lives very plainly, and at present his only cooking-utensils consisted of an old coffee-pot and frying pan-both very inferior articles. There was only one fork (one prong deficient) between himself and Staff, and this was handed to me ceremoniously as the 'guest.'"

Historians have tended to focus on Johnston's retreats. Yet he had strong support through the entire war. Fremantle wrote, "He has undoubtedly acquired the entire confidence of all the officers and soldiers under him. Many of the officers told me they did not consider him inferior to Lee or anyone else." Johnston told Fremantle he was planning to relieve Vicksburg, but with only 11,000 men, he had to be reinforced. Fremantle continued, "General Johnston told me that Grant had displayed more vigour than he had expected, by crossing the river below Vicksburg, seizing Jackson by vastly superior force, and, after cutting off communications, investing the fortress thoroughly, so as to take it if possible before a sufficient force could be got to relieve it." Fremantle said Grant's army was estimated at 75,000, which was about what he ended up with.

Newspaper man Sylvanus Cadwallader wrote *Three Years With Grant*. He summarized the fighting where Loring had the misfortune to be subject to Pemberton's orders. Cadwallader wrote: "With the maneuvers and marches between Jackson and the Big Black, which resulted in separating and keeping apart Gens. Johnston and Pemberton and driving the later behind his intrenchments at Vicksburg, may be said to have ended the tactical features of the campaign. They were splendid beyond description-almost beyond conception-are scarcely equaled in history-and may be profitably studied for all time. They are certain to be handed down to posterity as military classics, for the imitation of future generations."

Cadwallader was essentially correct, but like many writers he failed to note Grant fought Champion Hill with only three of his seven divisions fully engaged. This can be seen in casualties he reported; 410 killed, 1,844 wounded, and 187 missing. This 2,441 total came almost entirely from the three divisions fighting on and around Champion Hill. The two that advanced along the Middle Road, east of Crossroads, had less than one percent. One of the two divisions advancing on the Raymond Road, which Loring faced, had even less. Again, had those two divisions advanced, Pemberton would have been sandwiched in between with nowhere to go. His two escape routes over Baker's Creek would have been cut. It wasn't until after the battle that Grant learned one of his brigades had cut the Upper Crossing. His memoirs fail to mention Bowen's breakthrough or two dozen pieces of artillery positioned to halt him. Much like at Shiloh, Grant's artillery saved him.

Mississippi, the 1938 guide, referred to Champion Hill. It says, "Grant's victory was the decisive stroke of the campaign. It was at least the turning point of the campaign. Pemberton had shown he was too inexperienced on a battlefield to exercise command. Though Grant failed to unite his divisions for what might have been a complete victory, his attacks took the initiative from Pemberton.

Pemberton's staff was not experienced enough to communicate with Loring when orders were issued to his units. Further, Loring's official report pointed out that Bowen had been moved from Loring's left without warning. Loring wrote, "Soon a series of orders came, specifically and with great particularity, for two of my brigades to move to the left, closing the line as often as Bowen moved, and we in this manner followed him."

Loring's report pointed out he had faced what he supposed was a full corps. It was the U.S. 13th Corps (McClernand's). Loring wrote, "During this time I received an order to retire, also one to advance, both of which were countermanded. My whole division, including reserves, was strung out in line of battle, mostly in thick timber. The enemy during these movements remained steadily in front in heavy force, being, apparently, a full corps, occupying a series of ridges, wooded, and commanding each other, forming naturally a very strong if not impregnable position, throwing forward a heavy line of skirmishers, and showing every indication of an attack in force upon my position, both in front and upon the right flank." A brigadier (Burbridge) opposing Loring wrote, "It was my conviction at the time, confirmed by all that I have learned since, that, properly supported by General Blair's division, we could have captured the whole rebel force opposed to us, and reached Edwards Station before sunset." Pemberton was fortunate Loring had the good sense not to obey his orders, and leave the Raymond Road open!

Champion Hill may be considered the turning point in Grant's final approach on Vicksburg. Loring had been correct to convince Pemberton to drive his three mobile divisions behind Grant and his bases on the Mississippi River. Pemberton still had two divisions in the Vicksburg trenches, and Johnston was creating his Army of Relief around Jackson. Pemberton could have chosen his own ground for a battle and Grant's ammunition supply would have been reduced and possibly seriously depleted. Loring was the experienced Confederate officer with a strategy for a decisive victory.

Loring's killed and wounded at Champion Hill had been light. Buford had 11 killed and 49 wounded. Most of those were suffered by Scott's 12th Louisiana in their brilliant fighting on the Middle Road. Featherston had only one killed and one wounded earlier on the Raymond Road. Tilghman's Brigade had 5 killed and 10 wounded. Many of his were by Robert Lowry's 6th Mississippi, which had engaged in heavy skirmishing. Loring's missing was greater, many stragglers not keeping up with the night escape.

The day after Champion Hill Pemberton lost another battle west of Edward's Station. He was trying to hold a crossing at the Big Black River. His objective was to hold a crossing point for Loring's Division. He might have guessed Loring had moved south, rather than north, based on Grant's close pursuit. Pemberton again demonstrated his inexperience in commanding an army in the field. His battle line, composed of just several brigades, was formed west of Edward's Station with the Big Black to their back. They failed to hold and Pemberton's army retreated into Vicksburg.

Grant overestimated the demoralization in Pemberton's army. It existed in Stevenson's Division, but Bowen's knew it had come close to winning Champion Hill. The two divisions that had been left in Vicksburg were ready to fight. They must have served as an inspiration for Stevenson's Division. The fight to save Vicksburg became one of many that brought glory to the fighting men of the Confederacy. Grant soon learned this.

After Grant captured Fort Donelson he thought the Confederacy was about to cave in. Shiloh brought an abrupt transition to his delusion. Likewise, when he launched his first assault on Vicksburg, on 19 May, he found a foe not in the least inclined to retreat. It cost Grant over 1,000 casualties, from Sherman's troops. Pemberton's were slight. Grant made a much larger attempt on 22 May, suffering more than 3,000 dead and wounded. Confederates had even hurled hand grenades in repulsing them. No more costly attacks were made, as he settled on a siege, which ultimately starved Pemberton to surrender.

Grant had to keep Johnston and Pemberton separated. On 25 May he received a report that Johnston had 6,000 or more troops at Mechanicsville. The town lay along a ridge or corridor between the roughly parallel Yazoo and Big Black Rivers. Grant sent some 12,000, but all that force found was John Adams and some mounted infantry. Adams at first shouted orders to attack, but realized he was outnumbered and countermanded the order. The result was he withdrew and so did the intimidated U.S. force. At this point Adams was still an obscure brigadier, but his reputation was improving. In a few weeks he was given command of Tilghman's Brigade.

Johnston was not successful on Mississippi battlefields, but he could inspire soldiers in all ranks. J.P. Cannon wrote, "On May 26th we were inspected by General Joseph E. Johnston, who had taken command of the department a short time previously. He was received with prolonged cheers, his influence renewed confidence in our little command and as reinforcements were coming we felt with him to lead us we might soon attack Grant in the rear, raise the siege and relieve the garrison at Vicksburg."

Johnston received reinforcements in May, but not into June. Grant continued to receive them so that by the middle of June he had about 77,000 soldiers around Vicksburg. It seems Johnston could have attacked Grant from the rear, but Grant had no rear. Grant had an entrenched line of 34,000 facing east toward Johnston.

In the face of Grant's buildup Johnston was ultimately ineffective. J.P. Cannon wrote, "During most of the month of June, the weather was hot and sultry, rendering our marches from one point to another very disagreeable. The dust, shoe mouth deep, stirred by horses, wagons and artillery was so dense we couldn't see ten feet before us. We perspired and wiped our faces with dirty hands, the dust continually accumulating until the skin was covered with a thick coat, so masked our features that we could not recognize our most intimate chum. Our mouths, noses and throats were so stifled with it that we could scarcely breathe. In addition to this, water was scarce and part of the time ponds were the only accessible sources of supply and these were often stirred by hundreds of beef cattle and so hot it almost scalded the throat when swallowed."

Johnston's Army of Relief suffered, but brought no relief to Vicksburg. Cannon wrote, "For five or six weeks we had been wandering around in the territory between Canton and the Big Black, never more than 20 or 30 miles from a central point. In the meantime the thunder of the guns day after day and night after night told us that the heroic little city was still victorious and encouraged us with the hope she would be able to hold out until we could collect a force sufficient to render assistance. We were fully aware of the strength of the enemy and realized that we could accomplish nothing without a desperate struggle, but had all confidence in General Johnston and believed that when the auspicious moment arrived he would lead us to victory."

Johnston's ability to inspire confidence without commensurate results must have had to be experienced first-hand. Cannon continued, "Our idea of generalship was that if our expedition was intended for the relief of Vicksburg, it should be a bold and quick movement. It was irritating to be dallying along at the rate we were going, but we had implicit confidence in General Johnston and hoped all would turn out well." If Johnston had attacked he might have been repulsed. Pemberton later learned the small size of the Army of Relief and said "it would have been folly to attack Grant with double the number." One of his staff said Grant's entrenched force "could have repulsed 100,000."

A new arrival to Johnston in June was Maj. Gen. Samuel Gibbs French. He had been in Virginia where he had been headquartered at Petersburg. Some of the lines that Lee would hold there in 1864 had been laid out by French. On 3 June French left for his adopted home state of Mississippi. French was born in New Jersey, graduated from West Point in 1843, won two brevets in Mexico, and by marriage to a Mississippian came to be a planter. Their home was along Deer Creek in the Delta, north of Vicksburg.

In the 21st Century maps are readily available, but accurate maps in the 19th Century were a rarity. Johnston could not expect to successfully attack Grant without maps or a guide. French wrote of meeting up with Johnston, Loring, and others on 3 July. They were approaching the enemy, and trying to find a route. French wrote, "If there be any one thing in this part of the country more difficult than all others, it is to find a person who knows the roads ten miles from his home. Nine hours were spent in vainly attempting to get accurate information from the citizens respecting the roads and streams. But little could be learned of the country on either side of the Big Black that was satisfactory, because it was so contradictory."

Had Johnston's Army of Relief attacked in June it might have broken Grant's line. As the calendar page turned to July his time ran out. Pemberton received a petition from his

"Federal troops before Jackson, Mississippi" refers to U.S. Army troops, but federal troops might also refer to Confederate troops. Here is the essence of the conflict. The sovereign state of Mississippi seceded from the U.S. federal government and became an independent nation in January 1861. Sovereignty was not surrendered when Mississippi became a state in the new federal government, the C.S.A.

Hylan Benton Lyon came from pro-Confederate western Kentucky. He graduated from West Point in 1856 and saw active service with the U.S. Army before resigning in April 1861. As lieutenant colonel of the 8th Kentucky Infantry he was captured at Fort Donelson. Prisoner exchanges brought him back to the 8th as their colonel. They fought at Coffeeville, winning praise from Tilghman. Vicksburg had fallen when Joe Johnston attempted to hold Jackson. Lyon and the 8th Kentucky again won praise from a fellow Kentuckian, Abraham Buford, as his 8th Kentucky repulsed an enemy advance at Jackson. Buford and Lyon went onto command cavalry under Forrest. Both Kentuckians earned praise from Forrest for their advance at Brice's Crossroads. Lyon was known to exhibit a recklessness akin to desperation.

Hood's 1864 campaign into Tennessee had an offshoot in a cavalry raid by Lyon into Kentucky. Though often ignored in campaign histories, Lyon's raid was similar to John Hunt Morgan's Kentucky raid in December 1862, when Bragg had the Army of Tennessee positioned in Middle Tennessee. He burned courthouses U.S. troops were using as barracks and fortifications. Blockhouses, bridges, freight cars, and depots were destroyed on the *Louisville and Nashville Railroad*. When Lyon learned Hood was defeated he made his way south to Alabama. He wrote that the expedition "was a success beyond my most sanguine expectations. The men were all new recruits, but poorly organized, and armed for the first time…"

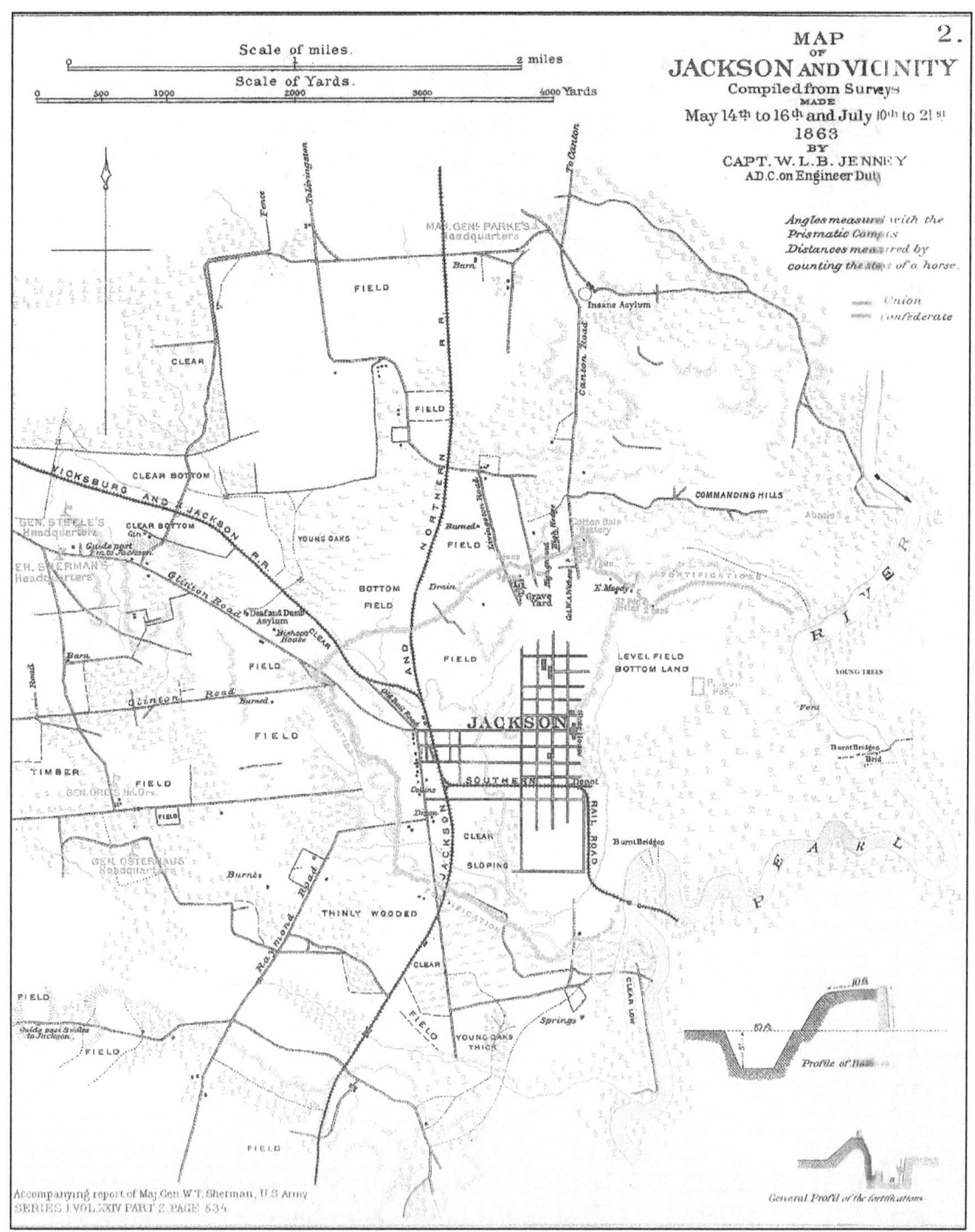

This map was prepared by a U.S. Army engineer, and does not denote positions of Confederate divisions. General French (C.S.) wrote on 11 July 1863, "The order of the divisions that encircle Jackson, from the river above the city to the river below, is as follows, beginning on the right: Loring, Walker, French, and Breckinridge." The positon for Johnston's outnumbered army, with the river at their back, put them into a Vicksburg-like trap. Johnston pulled off a stealthy retreat eastward on the 16th.

starving soldiers. It was titles "Appeal for Help," and signed by "Many Soldiers." It read, "If you cannot feed us, you had better surrender us, horrible as the idea is, than suffer this noble army to disgrace themselves by desertion." Soldiers such as J.P. Cannon recalled waiting for orders to advance, and instead "an ominous silence prevailed in the region around Vicksburg." But there was no explanation, as they waited. "A funeral would not have been more somber."

Johnston learned of the surrender on 6 July and retreated to Jackson. Grant had about 77,000 soldiers so Johnston had little choice. Sherman wrote, "Johnston had received timely notice of Pemberton's surrender and was in full retreat for Jackson. Grant sent Sherman with three infantry corps to pursue. He had close to 50,000 troops.

The word finally came, as Cannon recalled, "At one a.m. on the 6th, we were aroused from our slumbers and officially informed that Vicksburg had surrendered…then with solemn tread and downcast hearts began another retreat toward Jackson. The day was one of the hottest of the summer, the dust stirred by the train of wagons was stifling, no water on the route, many fell by the wayside exhausted. Our canteens were drained before half the morning passed and not another drop of water did we see until 2:00 p.m. We came to a pond in an open field into which 300 thirsty beef cattle had plunged, stirring the slimy mud from the bottom until it was thick as gruel and so hot it almost blistered the throat when swallowed. But we were compelled to drink the filthy stuff and, as bad as it was, it saved the lives of many of the men."

J.V. Greif wrote of the retreat in *Confederate Veteran* in 1904 (Volume 12, page 112). Greif was in the 3rd Kentucky, which was being converted from infantry to cavalry. They had been ready to cross the Big Black River on pontoons when "…we began our retreat to Jackson, with Loring's Division in the rear and Buford's Cavalry covering the retreat. We fought the enemy all the way, and so closely did they press us that they arrived in Jackson almost as soon as our rear guard."

Johnston's army entered Jackson on the 7 July. The next day General French wrote, "I rode around with Gen. Johnston to examine the line. It is miserably located and not half completed." The lines had been laid out by Pemberton's orders earlier in the year. By the 10th French said there was heavy fighting. On the 11th he described the division positions.

Sherman had seen attacks fail at Chickasaw Bayou and at Vicksburg, so he was reluctant to attack Johnston's line. He had about 100 guns and ordered the construction of battery emplacements, outside Jackson, for a siege. He ordered the cannon of four batteries to fire at five minute intervals day and night. J.P. Cannon wrote, "It was a waste of ammunition so far as damage to us was concerned for during the forty-eight hours constant firing we did not have a man hurt by it." Sherman wrote Grant, "I think we are doing well out here, but won't brag till Johnston clears out…If he moves across Pearl River and makes good speed, I will let him go. By a flag of truce today I sent him our newspapers…that, with our cannon tonight will disturb his slumbers."

On the 11th French wrote, "The order of the divisions of the army that surround Jackson from the river above the city to the river below, is as follows, beginning on the right: Loring, Walker, French, and Breckinridge." Johnston's line did not surround Jackson, but had the city to its rear, with his flanks on the west bank of the Pearl River. He continued, "Fighting commenced early this morning, and the firing was rapid all along the line. About 11 A.M. we drove the enemy from their lines…" Sherman wrote, "On the 11th we pressed close in, and shelled the town from every direction." He went onto explain one brigade "got too close, and was very roughly handled and driven back in disorder." That attack was against Breckinridge, and was such a severe repulse that the enemy's brigade commander was relieved of his command.

Buford's Brigade also repulsed an attack. The 12th Louisiana was his right, on the west bank of the Pearl. Buford's line then had breastworks in a straight line, due north and south, on the edge of a cornfield. Across the field, close to the U.S. line, there was a deep gully, running southwest at about a 70-degree angle. Col. Hylan Lyon's 8th Kentucky was positioned in advance on a bare knoll so that they could cover a pass in the gully.

An article, *The Eighth Kentucky at Pearl River* is in *Southern Bivouac*, October 1885. It was written by A.B. This might be Abraham Buford, though he committed suicide in June 1884. A.B. wrote, "On July 11, 1863, heavy columns of the enemy had massed in the woods in front of the pass, and to unfold their position, two companies of the Eighth Kentucky, under command of Lieutenant-Colonel A.R. Shacklett, were deployed as skirmishers five hundred yards in front of the pass. These skirmishers found the enemy lying down in column, with bayonets fixed, and when Colonel Shacklett gave the command, 'Skirmishers in retreat,' the enemy rose, cheering, and charged at double quick. The skirmishers rallied at a run upon the pass and received a volley while executing 'into line, faced to the rear,' and formed in the regiment on the knoll, without cover. The enemy advanced, firing. The Eighth Kentucky held its fire until the enemy neared the pass and was about sixty yards distant, when it delivered a most destructive volley. The enemy recoiled under it, but for a moment only, when they rallied and advanced firing, until within sixty feet, where the opposing lines stood firing face to face and almost hand to hand for ten minutes. The enemy wavered and stubbornly retired into the pass. The Eighth Kentucky was then ordered, 'Backward march, ten paces-lie down-load,' which movement they executed with admirable coolness and steadiness, placing themselves under the cover of the knoll, on which lay the Confederate dead and dying. But soon the enemy showed there was more work to be done, and came rushing forward with loud cheers. Just as their heads began to pop over the Confederate slain, Colonel Lyon commanded, 'Rise up-forward-commence firing,' which order Colonel Shacklett repeated, adding, if the truth must be told, 'Charge them, G—d--- them!' and the regiment did charge into the pass; and the enemy, thus splendidly repulsed, fled to the woods beyond, leaving the Eighth Kentucky in possession of the knoll, and seventy-five of the Second Michigan lying dead upon the field. The conflict was between one hundred fifty men on one side and one thousand on the other."

A.B. concluded, "Immediately after the engagement, Lieutenant-Colonel Shacklett reported to General Loring, who introduced him to General Johnston, who took the gallant colonel's hand in both his own, saying, 'Colonel Shacklett, give me your hand; you have made the most heroic fight of the war.' It was a merited compliment, for the gallant resistance to overwhelming numbers prevented a great disaster, and possibly saved the army of General Johnston."

Johnston learned Port Hudson had fallen and saw no chance of relief. His final hopes were that a cavalry attack on Sherman's artillery-supply line would end the bombardment of his lines and the city. Unfortunately Johnston learned on the afternoon of the 16th that the cavalry failed. He notified Davis, "The enemy being strongly reinforced, and able when he pleases to cut us off, I shall abandon this place, which it is impossible for us to hold. His evacuation seems premature, though Grant could have brought his entire force to bear on Jackson and surrounded it. He had abandoned positions in Virginia and been backed up to Richmond. It is difficult to reconcile his retreats with the overwhelming admiration generated from his armies. To his credit he was able to remove his wounded and artillery before sneaking out the Army of Relief.

Sherman was thus enabled to march into Jackson a second time and supervise destruction in more detail. He referred to it as "one mass of charred ruins." He sent foragers to strip the countryside for about fifteen miles around. He informed Grant, "The inhabitants are subjugated. They cry aloud for mercy." He thought they should have appealed to the "judgment of the learned and pure tribunals our forefathers have provided…" Mississippi women made a particular impression on Sherman thinking "no one who sees them and hears them but must feel the intensity of their hate…begging us with one breathe for the soldiers' rations and in another praying that the Almighty or Joe Johnston will come and kill us, the despoilers of their homes and all that is sacred." But from the Mississippians perspective they must have wondered why their forefathers had ever consented to ratify and common government with the Yankee race.

The war correspondent Cadwallader was in Vicksburg, with similar opinions. He wrote, "General Sherman honestly believes a strong Union sentiment exists. I as honestly disbelieve it. I have conversed with hundreds of families between here and Jackson, and have not found one citizen who could properly be termed a Union man. Many profess a conservatism which in the opinion of the administration in Washington, is treason. Very many more attempt no reserve or concealment, but openly proclaim their attachment to their own government, while drawing rations and supplies from ours…" This was a remarkable complement to the patriotism of those between Vicksburg and Jackson!

Pemberton surrendered his army because they were nearing starvation and the citizens were not much better off. It was the Yankees who were doing the vexing and no doubt citizens had to fake some loyalty to the United States to keep from starving. He wrote, "In one particular the people of Vicksburg and vicinity differ widely from all other communities the fortune of war has thrown among us. While cherishing the utmost bitterness and malignancy towards us, they nevertheless accept our favors and benefactions. They even come as cravens and sycophants to beg favors that were denied when insolently demanded. They lack honesty and sincerity in a markable degree."

A complicated question is who was to blame for the loss of Vicksburg and the army. The finger pointing began before the campaign ended. A somewhat neutral view came from a Confederate engineer, Major Samuel Lockett. He worked closely with Pemberton and saw his difficulty in trying to obey orders from both Davis and Johnston. Lockett wrote, "I saw, or heard read, most of these dispatches. They were very confident in their tenor, and neither those of Mr. Davis nor those of General Johnston exactly comported with General Pemberton's views. He then made the capital mistake of trying to harmonize instructions from the superiors diametrically opposed to each other, and at the same time to bring them into accord with his own judgment, which was adverse to the plans of both. Mr. Davis's idea was to hold Vicksburg at all hazard, and not to endanger it by getting too far from it. Johnston's plan was to cut loose from Vicksburg altogether, maneauver so as to avoid a general engagement with Grant until the Confederate forces could be concentrated, and then beat him. Pemberton wished to take a strong position on the line of the Big Black and wait for an attack, believing that it would be successfully resisted, and then the tables would be turned upon Grant in a very bad position, without any base of supplies, and without a well-protected line of retreat. As I have said, none of these plans was carried out, but a sort of compromise or compound of all these attempts, resulting in the unfortunate battle of Baker's Creek, or Champion Hill, and the disgraceful stampede of Big Black Bridge."

The Texas senator Louis Wigfall wrote Johnston, "Let me warn you against Pemberton. The moment he was whipped at Edward's Station (Champion Hill) he wrote to the President that he has made the fight against his judgment and under positive orders from you. The President will sustain Pemberton at your expense if possible. He must do so to sustain himself in placing an entirely untried man in command of so important an army.."

Beauregard also sympathized with Johnston. He told a South Carolina congressman, "I think gross injustice is done by the administration and its entourage to General Johnston. They have never given him an opportunity to show his true metal; they have tied a leaden weight to his feet, and then told him to see what he could do in a deep, rapid stream!" Beauregard had good reason to sympathize with Johnston, as both had issues with Davis. He also knew Pemberton made himself disliked in Charleston. Beauregard was his replacement there and made critical improvements to the defenses. He won brilliant victories in holding Charleston, and might have held Vicksburg as well.

If we could ask Loring who to blame, his anti-Pemberton bias would push him to blame the Pennsylvania native. Johnston wanted to combine his forces with Pemberton's and fight Grant away from the river city. Pemberton might have found that opportunity had Johnston not sent most of his cavalry, Van Dorn's to Tennessee. The lack of information kept Pemberton and Davis confused by Grant's movements. Davis was in a sickbed thru much of the campaign, and not alert enough to analyze the distant campaign. And Johnston admitted he had not recovered enough to be actively campaigning.

Johnston readily shifted blame. He reported, "…that in his short campaign General Pemberton made not a single move in obedience to my orders and regarded none of my instructions, and, finally, did not embrace the only opportunity to save his army-that given by my order to abandon Vicksburg."

Davis had still more difficulty understanding the campaign once Johnston arrived in Mississippi. When Davis learned Pemberton had surrendered he still defended him. Someone said a lack of provisions led to the surrender. Davis replied, "Yes, from want of provisions inside, and a general outside who wouldn't fight." Though Johnston had failed to relieve Pemberton he was just outside Grant's eastward facing entrenchments when word came of the surrender. Had Pemberton held out just a few days Johnston might have launched an attack which could have allowed Pemberton to escape. Sherman wrote in his memoirs of Johnston in their rear: "Even then the ability of General Johnston was recognized, and General Grant told me that he was about the only general on that side whom he feared."

If any of us had been Jefferson Davis it would have been logical to want to hold Vicksburg. The U.S.-imperialist desire to control the river had motivated many a U.S. soldier to enlist. The symbolism of the river was not lost on Davis. The fact that his home, his brother Joseph's, and friend's as well, were there, was no doubt a personal motivation to hold Vicksburg. Had Davis not been so ill, and preoccupied with the nearby U.S. invasion, culminating at Chancellorsville, he might have seen Vicksburg as a trap.

The similarity of Grant trapping Albert Sidney Johnston's forces at Fort Donelson might have been apparent. Johnston had not given clear instructions to any of the fort's commanders in the days leading up to the surrender. Brig. Gen. John B. Floyd had been up the river at Clarksville. He advised Johnston, "I wish, if possible, you would come down here, if it were only for a single day. I think in that time you might determine the policy and lines of defense." Johnston might have taken a train from his Bowling Green, Kentucky headquarters direct to Clarksville. He might have taken a steamer down to Fort Donelson too, and been back in Bowling Green the same day. He never did.

A.S. Johnston was more concerned with a U.S attack on Bowling Green to direct his generals on the Cumberland River. When Tennessean Gideon Pillow was in command he had wired Tennessee Governor Isham Harris, "Upon one thing you must rest assured, I will never surrender the position…" Kentuckian Simon Bolivar Buckner arrived in Clarksville, and saw Fort Donelson as a trap. Buckner wanted a troop buildup between the fort and Clarksville at Cumberland City. He thought it would be possible to operate against Grant's line of logistics without fear of being cut off by gunboats or Grant's army. He thought the fort was expendable. Floyd outranked Pillow and Buckner, but agreed with the later.

Floyd telegraphed Johnston, "I have thought the best disposition to make of the troops on this line was to concentrate the main force at Cumberland City, leaving at Fort Donelson enough to make all possible resistance to any attack which may be made upon the fort but no more. The character of the country in the rear and to the left of the fort is such as to make it dangerous to concentrate our whole force there; for if the gunboats should pass the fort and command the river, our forces would be in danger of being cut off…"

In Mississippi it was Joe Johnston who saw Vicksburg was a trap. The U.S. Navy had it sealed off and Grant repeated his encirclement as he had at Fort Donelson. Joe Johnston had contributed to Pemberton's lack of intelligence by taking most of his cavalry away, but he was correct about Pemberton consolidating his scattered forces and meeting Johnston to combine their forces for a decisive attack against Grant.

The fall of Vicksburg brought elation to the United States, and particularly to the states of the old Northwest. It has ever since been described as decisive by prominent historians. But we might ask why. The Confederacy fought on for almost two more years, and had adapted to the loss of the Mississippi River by letting the Trans-Mississippi practically fight on with some success. Noteworthy were two failed U.S. campaigns to invade Texas. Two months after Vicksburg surrendered a combined army-navy force was defeated by Dick Dowling and 43 artillerists at Sabine Pass. Another much larger army-navy invasion was defeated the following spring in the Red River Campaign.

War correspondent Cadwallader wrote a letter in Vicksburg on 1 August 1863. He wrote, "Vicksburg is ours, the Mississippi is opened, and people wait anxiously to see the practical results so long predicted. Many have looked forward to this consummation as the ending of the war. Almost all have vaguely hoped and believed that it must, in some way, amount to its virtual ending. To me nothing is plainer than that a majority of the people will be seriously disappointed. The war will still go on. Other armies, and still others, will be raised. Battles as bloody as any that preceded, have yet to be fought. When and how the peace so much desired by all, will be obtained, no man living can tell."

If they could have seen into the future they would have seen Grant was definitely on the road to Appomattox. Braxton Bragg's Army of Tennessee had just hit the U.S. Army of the Cumberland at Chickamauga and delivered a knock out to Rosecrans. Bragg had come so close at Murfreesborough, where Rosecrans barely held the field. Grant was sent to Chattanooga, relieved Rosecrans, and pushed Bragg off of Missionary Ridge.

<u>Johnston leaves to command Army of Tennessee; Loring's Division under Polk</u>
Bragg's defeat at Missionary Ridge in November 1863, and retreat into Georgia, led to his resignation in December. Davis was in a dilemma. He didn't care for Johnston, but he had support within the Army of Tennessee. So on the 16th Johnston was relieved of his duty with the Army of Mississippi, and sent to Georgia to replace Bragg. Leonidas Polk replaced Johnston, and established his headquarters in Meridian. Divisions were commanded by Loring and Samuel French. They were both in the Jackson area.

Loring's Division got a break in November. J.P. Cannon wrote "before November was gone we had substantial log houses covered with boards, cracks chinked and daubed, stick and dirt chimneys and could sit by our own firesides, bidding defiance to the elements-provided the Yankees would be good enough to let us enjoy the fruit of our labor." The paymaster had been more punctual so they "were able to indulge in 'luxuries' such as cabbage, stock peas, and potatoes which we bought from the citizens."

Cannon remembered sober times inspired by their chaplain, and other times. He wrote, "Brother Coffee was a zealous laborer in the Lord's vineyard and certainly had a field where the harvest was ripe for the exercise of his zeal. We made seats of split logs and erected a stand for him in a beautiful grove where he hold services day and night…" Other times, Cannon recalled, "Horse racing also was a frequent amusement. We had a nice level track of 600yards along side our camps which the officers used for exercise of their horses." After the races someone went into town and brought back whiskey." Soon "officers and men were in a glorious state of intoxication, yelling like savages and acting lunatics generally." He also mentioned a splendid drill ground, where "General Buford instituted competitive drills between the different regiments of the brigade, which aroused such a spirit of emulation that we became very proficient in Hardee's tactics."

In January 1864 Loring was at Canton, on the railroad north of Jackson. Though the enemy had destroyed much of Jackson, it was once again serving as a hub for the defense of Mississippi. Loring was busy constructing defenses for the railroads, but Polk found time to review Loring's Division. *Confederate Veteran* (Vol. 11, p.414) ran a piece on the review in 1902 that shows the writer as Col. J. R. Buford; it was likely Lt. Col. James R. Binford; he was in the 15th Mississippi, of Adams's Brigade. The writer said that when the 15th passed the reviewing stand Polk turned to Loring and remarked, "I never saw that drilling equaled at West Point." The result was a competition between the 15th and the 3rd Kentucky of Buford's Brigade. John Adams and Abraham Buford were present, but the judges were the cavalry general, William Hicks Jackson, Col. Thomas M. Scott of the 12th Louisiana, and Col. G.H. Forney of the 1st Confederate Infantry Battalion.

The writer said "that the Third Kentucky had a splendidly drilled regiment, composed of as brave men as ever fought beneath the stars and bars, and we claimed to excel them only in the manual of arms, for as to field movement they in every respect our equals." The prize to the 15th Mississippi was a flag, presented by widow, Mrs. Douglas Latimer.

Henry Ewell Hord was in the drill. He was in the Tennessee Confederate Home when he wrote *Confederate Veteran* in 1904 (Volume 12, page 6): "We of the Third Kentucky always gave the Fifteenth Mississippi credit for being one of the best regiments in the service. The men proved it on many a hard-fought field, but there were others. But don't throw mud on Kentuckians. Of the eight hundred men who participated in the Canton drill, less than one hundred ever saw their 'old Kentucky homes' again. As long as we were in Loring's Division we carried our 'Canton flag,' and it was in all the fights of the division. We were mounted and joined Gen. Forrest in North Mississippi." Hord also wrote, "In every raid that Forrest went on in Kentucky and Middle Tennessee our old Canton flag appeared." J.V. Greif also wrote Confederate Veteran in 1904. He recalled they had a white crescent-blue flag, as Cleburne's Division carried, "…until the ladies of Canton, Miss., presented the regiment with a large silk flag.

Pat Henry wrote to *Confederate Veteran* in 1918 (Volume 26, page 61) of social fun after the drill: "That night in Canton a grand ball was given by the division, and it goes without saying that there were more pretty girls and gallant soldiers participating in that dance than will ever again assemble in that fine little city. The beauty of Madison and Rankin

County was there-girls as fresh and fair as the morning dew, as sweet and pure as the breath of spring stealing o'er a bed of violets. The gallants were typical Southern gentlemen, each honorably vying with the other in courtesies to his 'lady love;' and it was away in the 'wee sma' hours ayant the twae' before General Buford, the master of ceremonies, had the band play 'Home Sweet Home,' when gathering the wraps about their lovely forms, we escorted our partners to their homes, where, promising 'oft to meet again,' we parted to dream of vows plighted, wondering how many would ever be carried into effect.

Though Loring's Division gave the ball, Henry did not mention Loring. He continued, "General Buford was commander in chief at the ball, and a grand commander he was. Six feet tall and weighing about three hundred pounds, his rare and courteous manner won the admiration of the ladies as well as the wonder of the gentlemen. 'Count Fesco' they dubbed him, so royally did he dispense his courtesies."

But Polk had more serious concerns, as Sherman was at Vicksburg with four divisions, or at least 20,000 troops. In November Sherman had been at Chattanooga, where Grant's armies pushed Bragg off Missionary Ridge. Grant had given the key role of taking the north end of the ridge to Sherman. But Cleburne's Division and part of Stevenson's repulsed him. The Army of the Cumberland, under native Virginian George Thomas, broke Bragg's centre. Chattanooga had been saved, yet Sherman was still in command of the Department of Tennessee. It embraced most of the east bank of the Mississippi River. That brought him back to Vicksburg in January 1864.

Sherman wrote, "The rebels still maintained a considerable force of infantry and cavalry in the State of Mississippi, threatening the river, whose navigation had become so delicate and important a matter." Sherman set out to destroy Polk's base at Meridian on 3 February. He hoped to reach the Confederate manufacturing installations at Selma, Alabama. Grant hoped Sherman might also go into Mobile. When Loring detected the movement he began falling back toward Meridian. French pulled out of Jackson, also moving toward Meridian. Polk sent orders for Loring to take command.

Sherman had 7,000 cavalry come down from West Tennessee and expected them to join his four infantry divisions at Meridian. Together they might have advanced to Selma, and as Grant hoped, also down to Mobile. Unfortunately for Sherman, the cavalry ran into a trap set by Bedford Forrest! The Wizard of the Saddle was in the process of building up another command, and only had 2,500 troopers armed. That turned out to be enough when the two forces collided at West Point. Forrest jumped all over the Yankee cavalry, in what he called getting the bulge on them. Once the retreat started it didn't end until they got back into Tennessee. It had taken ten days to get to West Point, but only five to get back. Sherman had no idea what had happened to the cavalry, but after five days waiting for them, he also turned back.

While Polk hoped Forrest might destroy the U.S. cavalry, he felt his infantry was too badly outnumbered to stand and fight Sherman. Loring had maybe 8,000 troops. Polk, in Mobile, advised, "My intention is to fall back on the Tombigbee at Demopolis." It was also on the *Alabama & Mississippi Rivers Railroad* between Meridian and Selma.

General Leonidas Polk, C.S.A.: The Fighting Bishop covers the Meridian Campaign from Polk's perspective. Polk's infantry and trains moved out of Meridian in a well-timed withdrawal. All stores at Meridian and Enterprise were saved, except corn in the shuck. Railroad shops and equipment were saved except for maybe ten cars. The property saved was worth about $12,000,000. Author Shelby Foote wrote that when Sherman got there "he found the warehouses yawning empty and the tracks deserted in all four directions." He also said Sherman was furious about it. Polk and his staff called it "one of the most brilliant efforts of the war."

Polk's positive 'spin' ignores Sherman's destruction of the railroads around Meridian. But Polk had the man to fix the railroads. *Memphis & Charleston Railroad* President Samuel Tate had the *Mobile & Ohio* back in operation, from Mobile to Tupelo, and the *Alabama & Mississippi* from Meridian to the Tombigbee River, in twenty-six days. Bishop Polk may have come up short in stopping Sherman, but Loring was sympathetic. He told Polk, "I see that the papers are finding fault. If necessary I will come out with a statement showing that you did all you could with the force you had."

This was a transition period for Loring's Division from Mississippi to Alabama, as Polk moved from the Meridian area, some 50 miles to Demopolis, Alabama. Once Polk got across the Tombigbee River, on 16 February, it was apparent Sherman was not pursuing. J.P. Cannon wrote, "Once more in camp on the soil of our native state we hoped to remain long enough for our blistered feet to heal and to recover from the arduous campaign of thirteen days and nights' of constant retreating and skirmishing." Cannon had said a serious shortage of shoes and blankets had plagued them.

At Demopolis Loring had a camp set up to receive returning prisoners who had been surrendered at Vicksburg. On 24 February they learned Sherman had returned to Vicksburg and it looked like there would be no active operations for some time. Cannon wrote, "Colonel [James] Jackson of the 27th and Colonel Ives of the 35th Alabama got up a petition asking leave to carry their regiments to North Alabama for the purpose of recruiting. At first General Buford was averse to the proposed expedition but reluctantly yielded and endorsed the application." On 4 March they set out. "A tramp of 200 miles was before us, or those of us who lived north of the Tennessee River, but that was only a trifle when our faces were set homeward. Marching by General Buford's headquarters we gave him three cheers and while the 12th Louisiana band played 'Home Sweet Home' we proudly kept time with the strains."

Cannon said on 18 March all who lived south of the Tennessee were furloughed. Two days later they learned some enemy cavalry was near Moulton, impressing provisions. Colonel Jackson proposed driving them off. Early the next morning they advanced and had several skirmishes. He said the enemy retired "each time when we got near enough for our Enfields to reach them." The British Enfield was a favourite of Confederate infantry. It could use its own .577 calibre slug or a .58 Confederate bullet in its cartridges.

Cannon's home was in Lauderdale County on the north bank of the Tennessee. Instead of a simple homecoming he immediately learned he was in danger of being captured by U.S.

troops or Tories, as at least one of the two passed by daily. Tories were mostly renegade Tennesseans, but some Alabamians. Lauderdale borders Wayne County, Tennessee and the southern part of it had voted against secession. Tories made frequent raids robbing and plundering citizens. They also murdered Confederate soldiers. Cannon wrote, "We put out a sentinel to watch for the Yankees, but the first night passed without an alarm. The next day our faithful old servant, who was on picket, ran in the house and said, 'Hide quick, the Tories are coming.'" Cannon was able to hide but there were so many of these visits he had to hide in the woods during the day.

The Alabamians' furloughs ended on 7 April and Cannon made arrangements to get back to the south bank of the Tennessee. He called it the Confederate side, and felt great relief to be there. Once across they learned there was a company of the 9th Ohio Cavalry near. Colonel Jackson led them back across, they attacked them in their camp, and captured them. On 29 April they got the order to return to Loring's Division, as Polk's Army of Mississippi was moving east to Georgia to join the Army of Tennessee.

Cannon said after seven days of marching they reached Montevallo. It is some 30 miles south of today's Birmingham, and was along Loring's route from Demopolis to Georgia. Cannon wrote, "…our brigade had just left again, so we fell in with Featherston's brigade and a three day march brought us to Rome, Georgia. We then boarded a train and reached Resaca at 2 a.m. on May 12th, where we overtook our command. It seemed almost like home to be with our old brigade once more, but some changes had taken place since we left. The 3rd, 7th, and 8th Kentucky had been mounted and under General Buford were then with Forrest. Colonel Thomas M. Scott of the 12th Louisiana commanded the brigade, Loring the division, and Polk the corps."

President Davis directed Polk, on 4 May, to move at least Loring's Division to Rome. This was the initial step in uniting Polk's Army of Mississippi with Johnston's Army of Tennessee. Loring's move from Montevallo took him 134 miles northeast to Blue Mountain. It was the terminus for the *Alabama and Tennessee River Railroad*. Loring was not to wait to organize his division there but to immediately advance his three brigades to Rome.

May 1864 brought on the U.S. Army offensive known as the Atlanta Campaign. There could be no doubt of it. It was not the first drive toward Atlanta. In September 1863 the U.S. Army of the Cumberland had flanked Bragg out of Chattanooga, and it appeared he might fall back to Atlanta. At least it appeared so to Rosecrans, but he underestimated Bragg. Back at Murfreesborough he had made the same mistake, and nearly got pushed into Stones River. At Chickamauga his army was swept from the field. In no other battle of the war was such a large army routed. Because Rosecrans escaped into Chattanooga historians have tended to downplay the significance of the victory. Had Bragg retreated toward Atlanta, it might have been in jeopardy in September 1863, instead of 1864.

4-Georgia and Loring's Division in the Army of Tennessee

Loring's Division in the Army of Tennessee is the primary focus of this book, and specifically in the 1864 Georgia and Tennessee campaigns. Historians have focused far more on Cleburne's Division and Cheatham's Division. The latter became Brown's in 1864 when Cheatham became a corps commander. Yet the fighting prowess of Loring's was in their league. Loring's broke thru the enemy lines at Peachtree Creek. Brown's and Cleburne's broke thru at Franklin, but they were aided by following on the heels of the enemy retreating from their advance line. Loring's assault ran into the impassible abatis and hedge. They left more dead on the field than any division at Franklin.

Loring's Division had been under Joe Johnston in Mississippi and was in Georgia too. Johnston began the campaign in Georgia with about half the manpower of Sherman's three armies. Grant's 1863 victories at Vicksburg and Chattanooga brought him overall command of U.S. forces for the 1864 campaigns. His memoir states, "The armies were now all ready to move for the accomplishment of a single object." That object was largely destruction of the Army of Northern Virginia and the Army of Tennessee, with both offenses to begin in the first week of May. But Grant wanted to apply pressure across the Confederacy so that no army could expect reinforcements. That success was dampened by repeated defeats. A drive through Louisiana, to invade Texas, had been defeated by Richard Taylor in April. Forces under Kirby Smith drove back a coordinated drive in Arkansas. By the middle of May two more defeats were suffered. Breckinridge won at New Market in the Shenandoah, and Beauregard pushed the Army of the James away from Petersburg into Bermuda Hundred, where he had them "corked up."

The U.S. campaign into north Georgia was to destroy the Army of Tennessee, which happened to be positioned across the *Western & Atlantic*. That railroad running from Atlanta up to Chattanooga was perhaps the most important left to the Confederacy. This line had been an object of two previous enemy efforts. The first was by U.S. raiders who stole the General in April 1862. Their intent had been destruction, enabling their army in north Alabama, to take Chattanooga. It failed largely due to the super human efforts of the train's conductor, William Fuller. He pursued and captured the raiders in one of the great dramas of the war. Another strike, dramatic in its own way, was Forrest's brilliant capture of Streight's mounted infantry at Cedar Bluff, Alabama, a little west of Georgia. In May 1863 Streight was also trying to reach the *Western & Atlantic* when Forrest captured his entire command. The U.S. Army would have to send more than raiders.

By far the greatest effort to strike toward the railroad and take Atlanta had been late in the summer 1863. Rosecrans, commanding the U.S. Army of the Cumberland, began climbing the Cumberland Plateau to reach Chattanooga on 16 August. He telegraphed Washington that it was "a point of secondary importance to the enemy, in reference to his vital one, Atlanta." But Rosecrans was routed by Bragg at Chickamauga in September. It was the largest offensive battlefield victory of the war. Many have said it was a barren victory, but had Bragg retreated down the *Western & Atlantic*, Atlanta might have fallen a year earlier. Though his follow-up siege of Chattanooga failed, much time was won.

Johnston left Mississippi to command the Army of Tennessee in December 1863. Bragg had just lost his Missionary Ridge position overlooking Chattanooga. In a postbellum interview Loring said "not a man in the Confederacy felt that the Union had really accomplished anything until Chattanooga fell." He explained, "As long as we held it, it was the closed doorway to the interior of our country." Bragg knew the magnitude of the loss and resigned from command. Johnston had charisma and won the hearts of the army. Maj. Gen. Benjamin Franklin Cheatham introduced him to his soldiers: "Boys, this is Old Joe." President Davis didn't care for him, but soldiers did.

Johnston inherited the two infantry corps Bragg had organized. Georgia's Lt. Gen. William Joseph Hardee commanded one. Maj. Gen. John Cabell Breckinridge had commanded the other. Bragg's great error at Missionary Ridge had been the useless rifle pits at the bottom of the ridge. Breckinridge didn't see they were a problem and it was his line that broke, while Hardee held his end of the ridge until after the battle ended. Breckinridge and Bragg had a strained relationship going back to Murfreesborough, and Bragg accused him of intoxication on Missionary Ridge.

Breckinridge took a leave of absence to go to Richmond in January. He was honoured by both houses of the Confederate Congress, and met with Kentuckians lobbying for another campaign into the Bluegrass state. He met with fellow Kentuckian John Bell Hood, who was still recovering from his Chickamauga wound. The often quoted diarist Mary Chestnut said, he was the "simplest, most transparent soul I have met…in this great revolution." It turned out Hood was sent to the Army of Tennessee to replace Breckinridge, who was given command of the Department of Southwest Virginia. Johnston would lament his loss, as they had been compatible in Mississippi; however, he expected Hood would live up to his reputation.

The campaign in Georgia has usually been called the Atlanta Campaign. Atlanta was not the capital, nor was it Georgia's largest city. The 1860 U.S. Census tallied Savannah as the largest with 22,292. Savannah was the 6th-largest in the C.S.A., a little behind Memphis. Augusta was next, located at the Fall Line of the Savannah River. It was 12th in the C.S.A. with 12,493, followed by Columbus at 13th with 9,621. Columbus was located at the Fall Line of the Chattahoochee. The river falls 120 feet within three miles of the city, and that had made it one of the first Southern cities to develop industry. Far upriver, beyond navigable water, was railroad-born Atlanta. With 9,554 it was only fourth in Georgia, but 14th in the agrarian Confederacy. Its population would swell during the war with the relocation of industries and the temporary home of refugees.

Sherman did not destroy the Army of Tennessee in Georgia, though he did accept its surrender, as a part of Johnston's command, in April 1865. But Sherman did drive Johnston back to Atlanta and Hood out of the city. Of course it was a prize to Sherman, who had noted "Made in Atlanta" on munitions for some time. Its capture made such as impact on the voters of the United States, that it insured the reelection of Lincoln in November. He received the same number of votes, none, in Georgia as he had in 1860. He had not even been on the ballot in the state, or nine others which formed the C.S.A.

John Bell had received the most votes in Fulton County, of which Atlanta was and is the seat. John Breckinridge came in second, and Stephen Douglas a distant third.

Atlanta was a great hub of railroads that supplied the Army of Tennessee. Railroad facilities in the city were lost. They made rails, and all the repair facilities necessary for locomotives and rolling stock. Atlanta's war related industries were similar to those in Richmond. When Nashville was evacuated the arsenal had been moved. Under the direction of Tennessee's Colonel Moses H. Wright the arsenal became the Atlanta Arsenal. It was a massive operation producing nearly 25 million percussion caps per year, and over 4 million rounds of ammunition. Nashvillian, Major George W. Cunningham moved quartermaster operations from there to create the Quartermaster's Depot. His fine Nashville home was used by several U.S. generals for headquarters. This must have distressed him, but he kept his focus to supervise the Atlanta Depot to produce jackets, pants, shirts, undergarments, hats, and shoes. Cunningham had bragged that he could produce 130,000 jackets and pants per year, and more shirts. This was due to some three thousand outsourced seamstresses, who were often wives of soldiers. The Depot had 40 shoemakers turning out 150 pairs of shoes daily. Hammond Marshall was another Nashvillian who relocated a factory. His sword company became the Atlanta Sabre Manufactory. That so much of this industry had been relocated was much to the credit of Nathan Bedford Forrest's supervision of the February 1862 evacuation of Nashville.

Georgia styled itself the Empire State of the South and the Confederacy spread its operations across the Piedmont Plateau. The Augusta Arsenal produced up to 130 cannon, including Napoleons, from 1862 thru 1864. A number of Army of Tennessee batteries had Augusta pieces. Augusta became better known for the vast gunpowder complex, considered as modern as any in the world. The Columbus Iron Works became the Columbus Arsenal when it received machinery evacuated from the Baton Rogue Arsenal. Columbus cast as many as 70 Napoleons. They had been channeled to the Army of Mississippi and the Army of Tennessee. Columbus also had the Confederate naval yard on the Chattahoochee. Gunboats produced were in a position to steam south thru the Florida panhandle to the Gulf of Mexico. The Findlay Iron Works in Macon were bought and converted to the Macon Arsenal. It produced at least 65 Napoleons, as well as Parrotts. Before Leaving Mississippi, Loring's Division had received 12 of them. Macon also had the Spiller & Burr revolver factory. It had been in Richmond, and then Atlanta until January 1864. It fabricated over 1,500 pieces during the war. Macon is most often remembered for the Confederate Ordinance Labs.

What seems to be forgotten in studies of the Atlanta Campaign is Florida. Georgia's southern neighbor had become a great source of food for Confederate soldiers east of the Mississippi River. Joe Johnston wanted Pemberton to save his army more than hold Vicksburg, and it was the correct strategy. After the Trans-Mississippi was severed, Florida replaced it as a source of food. The only way to get cattle across the Mississippi River was to swim them. It is difficult to believe thousands were swam over in 1864, and reached the Army of Tennessee. Colonel Lucius Bellinger Northrop, the commissary general for the armies, confirmed it in 1865 correspondence.

But in August 1863, the month after Vicksburg fell, large drives of cattle were organized in Florida. Northrop picked a good man, Brevet Major Pleasant W. White, who began the drives. Northrop's bureau called for 3,000 a week from Florida, more than possible. Much of the cattle was hundreds of miles south of Georgia, and no railroad connected the two states. They were often driven to Savannah, if not all the way to Atlanta. By August summer suns had parched much grass for grazing. In December White's men, all across Florida, reported they no longer had herds able to survive the immense length of the drives to Georgia. White estimated 30,000 head had been driven out by his officers from August to December 1863. More had been driven by private parties. New grass was not to be had until spring weather, as early as February in most of Florida.

A Florida newspaper reported their significance on 7 November 1863: "The utmost promptness, energy, and industry are required of every agent and his assistants to secure all the surplus supplies of the country; otherwise the armies in the field cannot be fed. As Florida is now, next to Georgia, the most productive State remaining to the Confederacy, much depends on the Government agents within her bounds."

In December a U.S. general reported, "Two thousand head of cattle are reported to be driven out of Florida every week for the rebel armies." The result was an expedition to cut off the supply of cattle and other food, as well as disrupt railroads. They were badly defeated at Olustee on 20 February 1864. February was significant, for needed grasses. This victory, far to the rear of the Army of Tennessee, insured Florida foodstuffs would reach Lee and Johnston in 1864.

An essential commodity in preserving meats and fish also came from Florida, salt. Before the naval blockade, cheap foreign salt made up most of the South's supply. The great majority of Florida's production was along the Gulf, from around Saint Andrew's Bay and onto Saint Joseph's Bay to Cedar Key. Some Yankees believed the loss of Florida's salt works would be a greater blow to the Confederacy than the loss of Charleston. Much of this production was due to guerilla tactics of Florida cavalry units.

Though Sherman failed to destroy the Army of Tennessee, the capture of Atlanta was a decisive step in the ultimate U.S. victory in 1865. The burning of Atlanta and march across Georgia drove a wedge between surviving industries in Augusta and Macon, and through the capital, Milledgeville. This wedge through the industrial heartland would make another city, second to Richmond. The last significant port for blockade runners had become Wilmington, North Carolina. As 1865 dawned, it would become critical for the survival of the Confederacy. Some would say more important than Richmond itself.

A resolute mindset in Confederate political and military leaders was seen in 1864. President Davis's greeting to the newly elected Second Congress was read by the clerk, in accordance with custom, on 2 May.

"When our independence, by the valour and fortitude of our people, shall have been won against all hostile influences combined against us, and can no longer be ignored by open foes or professed neutrals, this war will have been left with its proud memories a record of many wrongs which it may not misbecome us to forgive, [as well as] some for which we may not properly forbear from demanding redress. In the meantime, it is enough for us to know that every avenue of negotiation is closed against us, that our enemy is making renewed and strenuous efforts for our destruction, and that the sole resource for us, as a people secure in the justice of our cause and holding our liberties to be more precious than all other earthly possessions, is to combine and apply every available element of power for their defense and preservation."

Loring's Division to Resaca

President Davis directed Polk, on 4 May, to move at least Loring's Division to Rome, Georgia. This was an initial step in uniting Polk's Army of Mississippi with Johnston's Army of Tennessee. Loring's move from Montevallo took him 134 miles northeast to Blue Mountain. It was the terminus for the *Alabama and Tennessee Rivers Railroad*. Loring was not to wait to organize his division there but to immediately advance his three brigades onto Rome. Factories there, especially Noble Iron Works, made up an industrial complex of importance in itself.

Sherman held his line north of Dalton with two armies, while the U.S. Army of the Tennessee snuck off the west thru Snake Creek Gap. It was to have easily taken the *Western & Atlantic* at Resaca, placing itself behind Johnston. He had thought it more likely the Yankees would swing farther west thru Rome. Johnston was fortunate that Cantey's Brigade had also arrived from Alabama on the 8th and was at Resaca. It was a brigade against an army, but it was enough to scare McPherson, the enemy commander, into pulling back into the gap.

Sherman had attacked Johnston's line at Dalton on 7 May. That day Loring was advised, "The necessity of your troops reaching Rome, Georgia at once is more pressing every moment." Johnston's staff also sent word for a messenger to meet Loring's brigades and "have them make a forced march from Blue Mountain to Rome, and do not wait for wagons or baggage." Johnston held his Rocky Face line, repulsing attacks, but could not remain with an army in his rear. He could protect his railroad supply line or Rome, but not both. Once at Rome, Loring could move troops by the *Rome Railroad* to reach Resaca on the *Western & Atlantic*.

Johnston then saw Sherman was not moving on Rome, but Resaca; however, a U.S. division would swing over to take Rome on the 18th, when only a handful of Confederates were left to defend it. Loring reported (O.R. 38, Vol.3, p.874) on their arrival at Resaca: "Scott's brigade arrived at Resaca on the 10th of May, followed by Adams' on the 11th, and Featherston's on the 12th. Myself and staff arrived with Adams on the 11th."

Loring's Division was not fully engaged at Resaca. On the morning of 13 May he was ordered to send a brigade forward as the enemy was driving the cavalry in. Loring wrote, "…Scott's brigade was moved forward and took position in line of Bald Knob, about a mile west of town. About 1 p.m. the brigade became warmly engaged, and held the

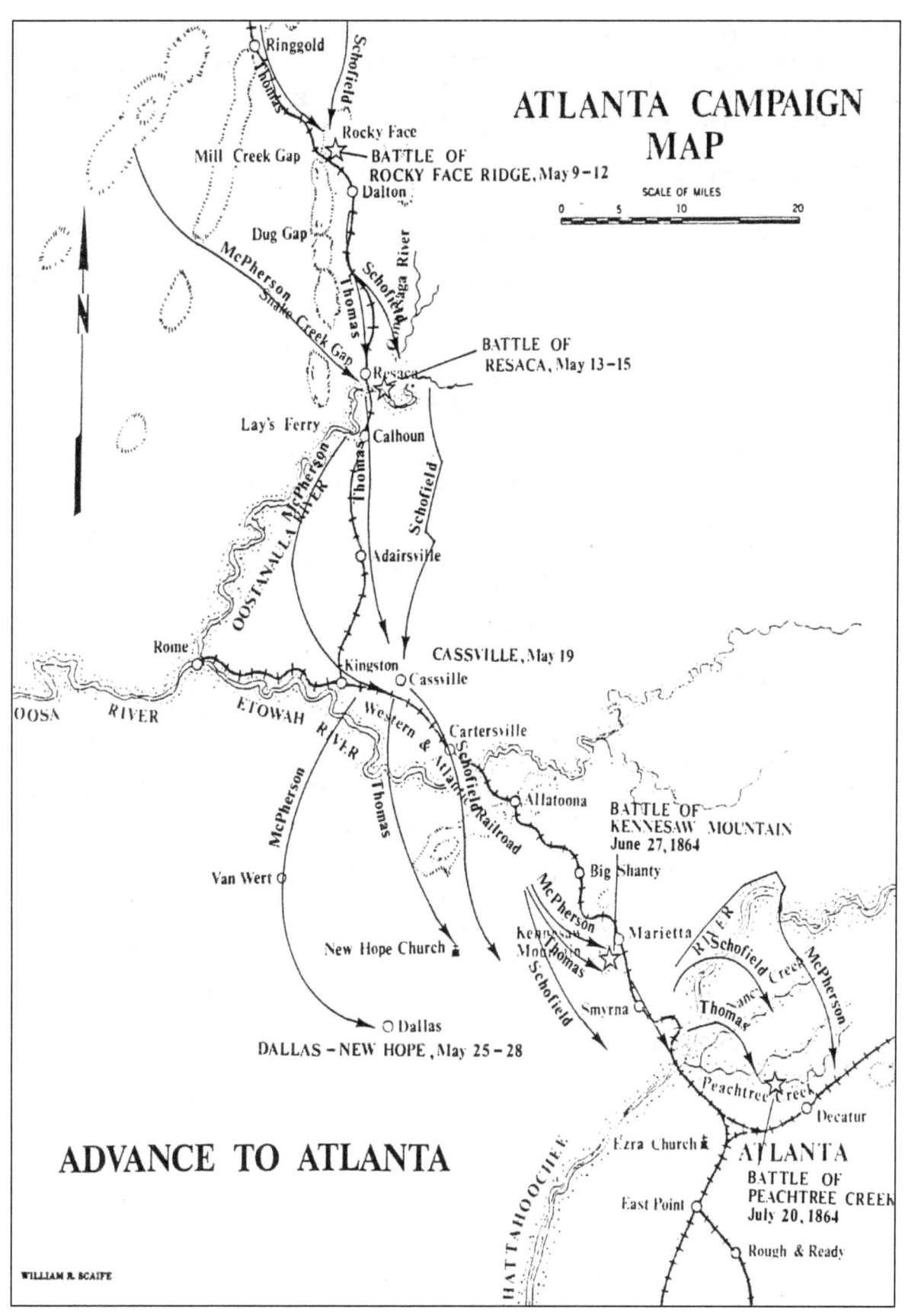

enemy in check three hours, and could have maintained its position longer, but was ordered to retire into our line of intrenchments. It drew off in perfect order and took position on the right of Vaughan's brigade, Cantey's division. Adams' was drawn up on the right of Scott's, with Featherston's in rear as reserve."

The previous chapter concluded with Scott's Brigade moving across Alabama to Resaca. On 13 May J.P. Cannon wrote, "Our forces evacuated Dalton last night and are in retreat. A large force of the enemy reported to be moving on Resaca. At 10 a.m. our brigade was ordered to the front to feel them and watch their movements. We went two miles or more without finding any Yanks, and began to think it was a false alarm, when emerging from the woods into a wheat field, we were suddenly greeted with a shower of bullets from the opposite side of the field." Cannon's entry detailed the fight pretty well as described in Loring's report. He explained the enemy got reinforced, which led Scott's Brigade to "skedaddle." They had a "running fight" back to the main line.

Cannon's entry for Saturday the 14th began, "The night passed quietly. We got a few hours good sleep and felt very refreshed. The troops from Dalton had arrived and all are in good spirits, ready to do their duty when General Johnston, in whom we have the utmost confidence, says the time has come to fight." Johnston's line was four miles long. His left was on the Oostanaula River. Behind him was the Connasauga, which flows south to the Oostanaula. He had confidence in his army to be positioned with rivers to the rear, but he was actually thinking of attacking with his right.

Before Hood launched that attack on the right, Sherman attacked. It was a poorly coordinated effort that was to strike Johnston's line well to the right of Loring's position. Though Johnston had a river to his back Camp Creek was in front of most of his line. It was an impediment to enemy infantry units that became entangled in the attack. One brigade got across and took a quick 200 casualties before Cleburne's rapid-firing troops. One of Schofield's Army of the Ohio divisions never got across Camp Creek, which a soldier remembered was "…hedged on either side by thick bushes and was about waist deep and was very difficult to cross." Another of his division commander's got his division across, but mentioned enfilade fire from salients in Johnston's line. There was also artillery crossfire making 14 May one of the most effective days in the war for the Army of Tennessee's artillery.

Johnston thought he saw an opportunity to push the enemy's left back. A successful attack by Hood's Corps might push their left away from the roads leading back north to Dalton. Johnston knew Hood's reputation for delivering ferocious attacks. One of his divisions under Carter Stevenson, who had taken the blunt of attacks at Champion Hill a year ago, surged forward. With a chilling Rebel Yell they ran over two enemy brigades before being stopped by U.S. artillery. But Hood didn't support Stevenson with Stewart's Division, as he might have, and enemy reinforcements drove Stevenson back.

For Sunday the 15th, J.P. Cannon wrote, "The 'Day of Rest' opened bright and beautiful and we expected a general engagement would take place between the two armies now confronting each other, but we were disappointed. I never saw more enthusiasm among

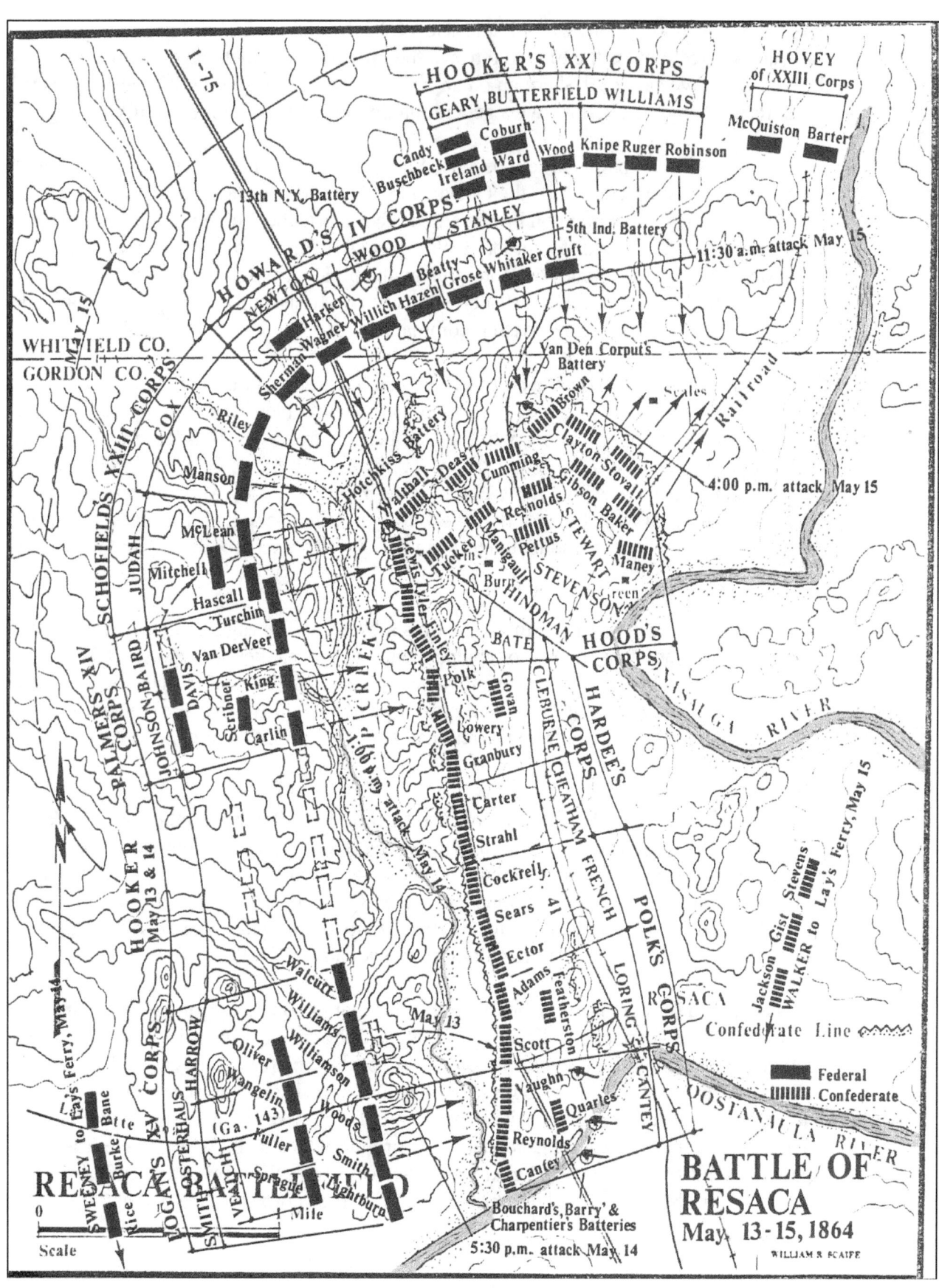

our soldiers or more eagerness for battle. General Johnston has infused new life into the army and we feel now is the time to retrieve the misfortunes which have befallen us in the past and if we can meet Sherman on anything like an equal footing we have no fears of the result. Why we did not have a general battle today I have no means of knowing…"

There was no general battle largely because Sherman didn't initiate one. That morning the Yankees got a brigade across the Oostanaula River, downstream of Johnston's left, at Lay's Ferry. They laid a pontoon bridge and a second brigade crossed to the south bank. Scouts reported it, and Johnston ordered Walker's Division across to drive it away. Johnston had pinned his hopes on Hood to launch another attack which he cancelled, while he waited on William Henry Talbot Walker. In Mississippi, in 1863, Johnston had praised Walker as being a fine division commander.

Sherman's troops on the south bank had a suspicion a large Confederate force was there too, and retreated back across the river. Sherman had not given up on destroying Johnston at Resaca, and decided to use Army of the Cumberland troops to attack Hood's Corps on the right. The troops were 20th Corps troops, commanded by Maj. Gen. Joseph Hooker. He had commanded the Army of the Potomac during the previous May, only to be badly beaten at Chancellorsville by Lee. Bragg's victory at Chickamauga led to the transfer of Hooker, with two corps, consolidated to form the 20th. It was a mix of eastern troops and western troops.

Near noon the three divisions of the 20th Corps advanced. The rugged terrain in front of Hood's Corps enabled his troops to repulse them, but the Yankees may have defeated themselves as much. One of their divisions became so confused its 2nd Brigade fired into the 1st Brigade, and then together they ran through part of the 3rd Brigade. Likewise in another division friendly fire from the rear caused a stampede through the ranks of the 149th New York.

Meanwhile Johnston got Walker's report that he found no Yankees on the south bank. Johnston returned to his plan for Hood to attack. As Hood prepared, Johnston received another report from Walker saying there were Yankees across the Oostanaula, about a half dozen miles to the south. Sherman had ordered them back, driving off pickets who spread the word to Walker. Unfortunately, two of Hood's brigades launched a hopeless attack before word could reach them that the attack had been called off.

Johnston called his corps commanders to his headquarters on the evening of the 15th. Resaca was to be abandoned. Hardee and Polk used the spans of the railroad bridge and another on the turnpike. Hood crossed a pontoon bridge upstream. They were bound for Calhoun, where Walker's Division was waiting. What had Johnston accomplished? Though the battle appears to be a draw the Army of Tennessee held its lines, with the Connasauga at their back, giving Johnston opportunities to attack. Their escape was a strategic defeat for Sherman. His goal was to destroy them. With seventeen infantry divisions in six corps, he could not push Johnston's three corps into the Connasauga.

Loring's Division was not called on to make the aggressive attacks which were made on the right. He reported, "The losses occurring in the division after forming behind the intrenchments resulted from heavy shelling of the enemy and his sharpshooters, there being no heavy engagement on the part of the line it occupied. The entire loss of the division at Resaca up to the time it was evacuated, on the night of the 16th, was 184 killed, wounded, and missing." This was relatively low, though the evacuation began about 10 p.m., and was largely complete at dawn of the 16th.

J.P. Cannon remembered they got a few hours of sleep because, "At 1 o'clock we were roused and formed into line (not line of battle but line of retreat) to our great surprise and regret, for we had hoped to defeat Sherman today and drive him back at least to the Tennessee River." Cannon understood they were badly outnumbered, and emphasized Johnston would "never have an army in better condition or more eager for the fray."

South of the Oostanaula River

The Army of Tennessee was safely across the Oostanaula on the 16th and it seems Johnston might have taken a position to strike Sherman as he crossed. The country was more open and level than in most of northern Georgia. Wasn't there a position not to defend, but to launch an offensive strike? He must have known Lee had success behind the Rappahannock at Fredericksburg, and behind it and the Rapidan at Chancellorsville. It was about 40 miles more to the Etowah River, and the army passed through Calhoun.

Calhoun was six miles down the rails from Resaca, so Johnston was able to reach the town named for the great John Calhoun, on the 16th. Organizing an offensive strike must have been ruled out already, for on arrival he found no defensible terrain. The army was ordered to continue onto Adairsville, another six miles. That night Dr. A.G. Donoho had the longest night of his life. He was at a field hospital with ten seriously wounded men, and no ambulances to evacuate them. Every one that passed was full, and then silence. The cavalry rear guard was departing. Donoho implored them to get him ambulances, and they sent a courier to find one. Loring was almost to Adairsville when he was located, and made arrangements. Donoho wrote, "Just as I could see the gray dawn in the east three ambulances came." One cavalry trooper had remained and "assisted me in getting the men loaded…which occupied some time. Before we got them all in, we could see the enemy advancing, and just as we had the last one, they saw us and opened fire…The last man in, I caught on the hind end of the ambulance, waved my hand to the Yankees, and trotted within our lines."

Cannon's entry for the 17th found Loring's Division near Calhoun. It had gotten a good night's rest after having marched all the previous night in the evacuation of Resaca. He wrote, "Our division being rear-guard, we had our hands full today. Continually pressed by the enemy, we often had to stop and check them, then double-quick to overtake the rest of the command, but our loss has been very light…" Cannon said they formed a line of battle at Adairsville, and Hardee's Corps repulsed an attack. He felt they were "victorious in every battle," though being outflanked and compelled to retreat.

The distance from the Oostanaula to the Etowah is about 40 miles. It is more open and level than most of northern Georgia. At Adairsville Johnston devised his greatest effort to drive Sherman into the Oostanaula, and perhaps onto the Tennessee. From Adairsville the main road and railroad continued south to Kingston. A somewhat parallel, less traveled road, went across the Gravelly Plateau to Cassville, several miles east of Kingston. Johnston correctly guessed Sherman would send his armies on both routes toward the Etowah. Hood's Corps was on the right, as it had been at Resaca. On the 19th Hood was given orders to attack the flank of the advancing Yankee column.

Loring's Division confronted the enemy on the Adairsville-Cassville road. They were to contain their advance until Hood's Corps fell upon their advancing left. Loring's surgeon, Dr. P.F. Whitehead wrote, "Gen. Johnston today…announced that he had arrived to the point which was to be the battle ground. Skirmishing has been going on for several hours and as I write (2 a.m. in the morning) there is not a quarter of a minute that I do not hear a gun. I think the battle will be fought tomorrow notwithstanding we have been retreating for days the troops are in fine spirits and confident we shall whip the enemy."

Johnston's initial position to launch the attack was north of Cassville. It was the county seat of Bartow County, recently named Cass. Georgia renamed it for Col. Francis Bartow who had been killed at First Manassas. A New York soldier recalled it "was a beautiful town." The courthouse was surrounded by stores, four hotels, separate colleges for men and women, and residences. Eight Confederate hospitals treated soldiers from late 1861 until May 1864. Sherman's cavalry burned Cassville in November 1864, and the town was not rebuilt. The *Western & Atlantic* was laid through Cartersville, off to the west and along the Etowah, so it became the seat.

Cassville Monument: Is it death to fall for Freedom's Cause!

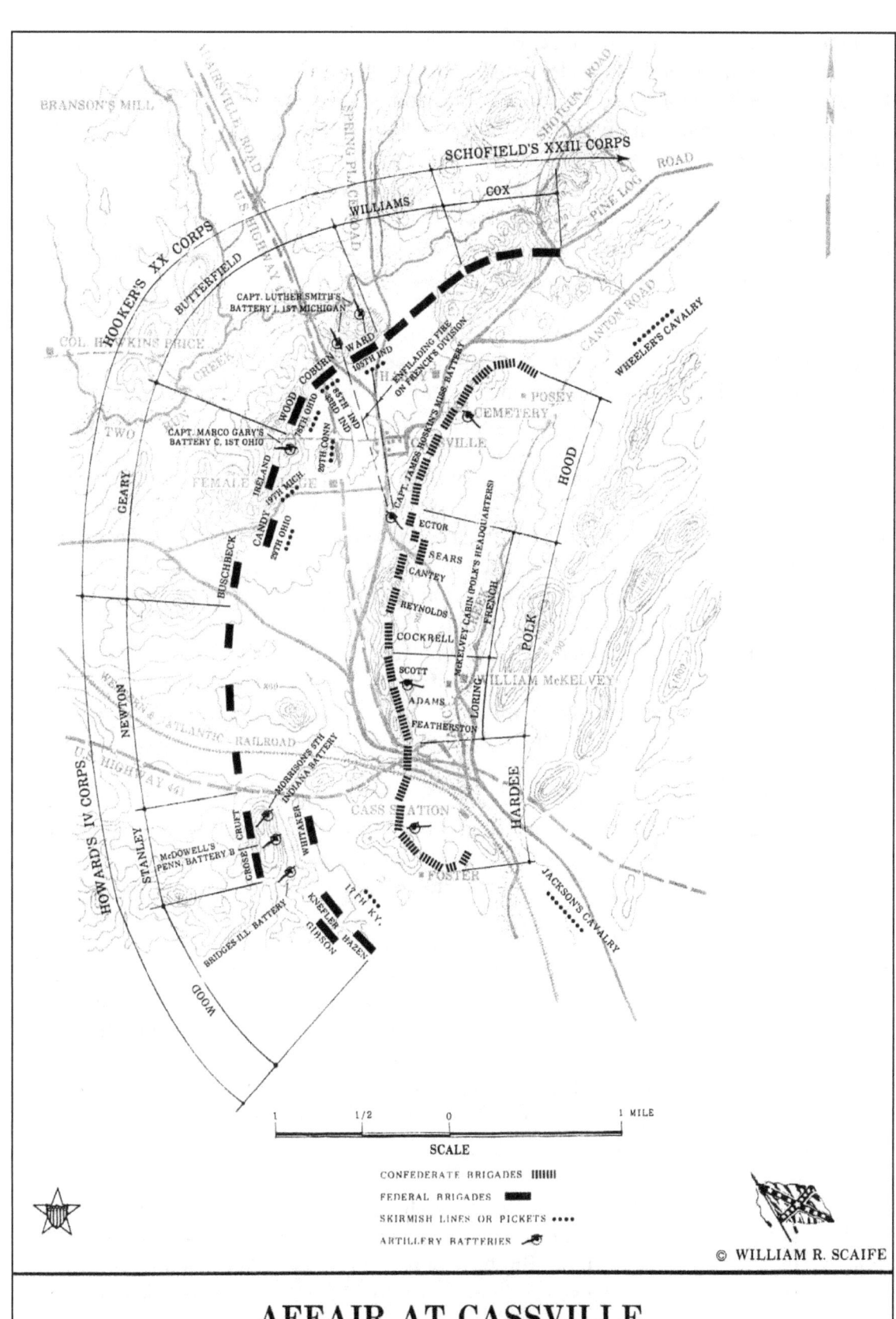

AFFAIR AT CASSVILLE
EVENING OF MAY 19, 1864

As preparations to attack were made, Hood received a report that Yankee cavalry was in his rear. Rather than send a brigade to disperse it, as Bedford Forrest would have done, Hood called off the attack and withdrew. Thus, Johnston lost one his best opportunities to deliver a crushing blow on divided U.S. forces. This was demoralizing to the army which had developed so much respect for Johnston. He had sent around a circular to the army stating, "By your courage and skill you have repulsed every assault of the enemy…You will now turn and march to meet his advancing columns…I lead you in battle!" Perhaps if he had led rather than trusting Hood the army could have dealt a crushing blow. Hood's attacks at Resaca had failed, and it might have led Johnston to stay close to Hood.

The botched attack caused Johnston to retreat through Cassville and position the army on a ridge south of town. Hood's Corps was still on the right, with Polk's Corps the centre. Cockrell's Brigade of French's Division was temporarily attached to Loring's Division. The Missourians had fought well at Champion Hill, and Loring must have welcomed their presence. Johnston had personally laid out this line of about four miles on a ridge. Hardee's Corps had baited Sherman to follow and came up on Polk's left. That night Hood said part of the line could be enfiladed by artillery. French, in *Two Wars*, includes an appendix on Cassville. Though Hood later tried to blame French, and say Polk agreed, French denied it. The appendix includes an 1894 lettre from a member of French's staff. James Shingleur wrote, "There is no doubt upon my mind that Gen. Hood, and he alone, was responsible for our retreat from Cassville." This apparently cleared French, but Hood may not have been entirely to blame either. Johnston was also concerned Sherman was about to cross the Etowah downstream. One of William Hicks Jackson's cavalry brigades, under Brig. Gen. Lawrence Sullivan ("Sul") Ross, had spotted enemy troops across the Etowah, off to the west. It looked like Sherman was to do as he had done on the Oostanaula. Cannon's diary only says, "We had to skedaddle again last night…" But Sergeant Eggleston, of Cowan's Battery, says they had to cross the Etowah because the enemy had crossed it. Though he would regret it, Johnston had ordered another retreat.

South of the Etowah River

High ground on the south bank of the Etowah was known as the Allatoona Mountain Range. Though not actual mountains, Johnston laid out his new line on it. Sherman knew the terrain from his time stationed in Marietta in 1844. He didn't consider attacking it, which would have put the river to his rear. After three weeks of fighting, he let Johnston go, and gave his armies three days of rest along the Etowah. Many of the U.S. troops were from bland landscapes, and were enchanted by the terrain. One Yankee general described "a country picturesque with its natural features, with farms and woodlands as quiet as if there had been no war."

Sherman's new plan was another flanking move to his right, this time about twenty miles southwest of Kingston, toward Dallas. Doing this meant moving away from the railroad, though Kingston would be his base. But he supposed once at Dallas, he could march straight for a Chattahoochee crossing, before Johnston knew he was outflanked, or that Johnston would retreat across the river.

Once again Jackson's outstanding cavalry detected Sherman's move. Again it was Sul Ross, whose Texans provided the intelligence needed. To Johnston's credit he didn't head for the Chattahoochee, but moved southwest to block the advance. His new line ran from Dallas, northeastward for over four miles, to a log meeting house the Methodists called New Hope Church. Stewart's Division of Hood's Corps was positioned along a slight ridge, behind hastily erected log and earth breastworks. Some sheltered themselves behind the grave markers in the church's cemetery. There, on the 25th, they waited.

When the first enemy units ran into Stewart they recoiled. Sherman heard artillery fire and came up. Hooker tried to tell him Johnston was in front, but Sherman scoffed at him. He treated the unfolding battle as a nuisance. It wasn't long before he found out just what a nuisance it was. About 5:00 p.m. bugles sounded amongst some 16,000 U.S. 20th Corps troops. When they approached New Hope Church Stewart's 4,000 plus infantry opened. Hood had seen that they were backed by 16 guns, spewing canister and shrapnel. Hearing the fury, Hood sent a staff officer to see if reinforcements were needed. Stewart calmly replied, "My own troops will hold the position." It was one of Stewart's finest moments. Stewart aide Bromfield Ridley believed his promotion in June was won there. He recalled Johnston exclaimed, "If I can make you a Lieutenant-General for your management you shall have it."

Johnston's left, Hardee's Corps, was south of Dallas, blocking the advance toward the Chattahoochee. Loring's Division was to Hardee's right, as was the rest of Polk's Corps making up the centre. Though not in battle, their lines were under fire. J.P. Cannon wrote on the 26th: "We are getting to be expert with pick and spade and it does not take long to dig a ditch two or three feet deep, and throwing the dirt in front which protects us from the bullets and fragments of shells which are constantly flying around us." He also said the Commissary "sent us two days' rations equal to any four that we have received since the campaign opened." They were mostly getting hard corn dodgers and bacon.

Sherman was confused by the defeat at New Hope Church. His next move was an attempt to swing east of New Hope Church. On 27 May he struck there near Pickett's Mill, from which the battle would be named. Johnston had correctly anticipated the move. Cleburne's Division had been detached from Hardee's Corps and some of Wheeler's cavalry dismounted, to extend the line eastward. About 4:30 p.m. the enemy struck, driving cavalry pickets back. But their fighting withdrawal gave Cleburne time to position his brigade. Cleburne's infantry was trained in rapid reloading so that their three shots a minute destroyed the attack. Cleburne wrote they "slaughtered them with deliberate aim." At 10 p.m. Cleburne gave Granbury's Brigade permission to clear their front. From the enemy perspective the night attackers hit them "like a whirlwind, screaming like demons." Pickett's Mill would not be a battle Sherman would care to remember when he wrote his memoirs.

Enemy losses approached 3,000 at Pickett's Mill. This was in addition to an estimated 1,800 lost at New Hope Church. Johnston's casualties were a fraction, and this helps explain the morale of the army. Cannon's entry for the 27th included: "We have been retreating for three weeks, yet we are cheerful and in high spirits. Usually an army becomes demoralized when it has to fall back continually, but we have enough confidence in our commander to believe that when the opportunity comes he will strike the enemy a blow which will stop his aggressive movements…"

Pickett's Mill was along Little Pumpkinvine Creek. Farther east on the creek, Wheeler's cavalry thought the enemy left was "in the air." This was reported to Hood, who perhaps had thoughts of Chancellorsville. Having won the battle at Pickett's Mill, Hood asked Johnston for permission to withdraw before midnight and strike the enemy on the morning of the 28th. Johnston approved the attack, but by the time Hood marched to make the attack, Wheeler's cavalry advised the enemy left had been withdrawn back across the creek. It was not in the air, but entrenched behind the creek. After the war Johnston used the affair as evidence of another Cassville-like failure on Hood's part. In Hood's 1880 memoir he wrote the cavalry saw the folly of attacking and they "advised me to proceed no further. I reported these facts to General Johnston, and was ordered to return."

Sherman was planning to move back toward the *Western & Atlantic* on the 28th. Johnston anticipated the move, and Wheeler's report of their left having been in the air seemed to have been some evidence. Johnston had won two fights, and had hoped Hood's hoped for attack would make three. Next he hoped Hardee might roll up their line as they began to withdraw. Bate's Division was ordered to test the enemy line in a feeler attack. But first Armstrong's Brigade of Jackson's cavalry was to attack dismounted and fall back if the Yankees were still entrenched. Their attack overran a picket line and three cannon. Bate's artillery was to have fired four shots as a signal to attack. It was obvious the enemy was still in position rather than pulling out, so the signal fire was not made. Sadly Bate's Florida and Kentucky brigades assumed the noise of battle had obscured the signal and launched attacks. They were bloodily repulsed, so that Johnston may have lost 1,000 to 379 stated loss of the enemy. The Floridians and Kentuckians blamed Bate for their losses, and never forgave him. A Kentuckian was quoted in the *Augusta Daily Chronicle* saying the attack "was one of the most wicked and stupid blunders of the war," and that Bate was unfit to command. He was at least responsible for a failure in staff and courier operations. Sadly, low morale in Bate's Division persisted through 1864.

Johnston knew Sherman wanted to move back to the railroad and made it difficult for him to pull out of his entrenchments. He ordered a series of night attacks around Dallas during the last days of May. Cannon's diary entry for the 29th mentions an enemy battery that had annoyed them. He wrote, "General Loring called for volunteers to make an assault on it at midnight. He said it was a hazardous undertaking and he wanted none but brave, determined men to volunteer." But on the 30th he said the attack was not made, and presumed it was decided to the sacrifice would be too great. On the 30th he wrote that the enemy attempted to advance their lines, but "Featherston charged and drove them back."

Dallas was Sherman's only tactical success in the strategic failure of swinging south of Dallas. Rather than move back to the railroad he spent another week on the New Hope to Dallas line. The opposing lines twisted and turned for about ten miles, mostly screened from each other by timber and brush. Sherman's soldiers were hungry, being on three-fourth's rations. Each U.S. regiment had one wagon to supply food from Kingston, about 20 miles away. The roads were poor and travel was slow. Sherman's flanking move had wasted two weeks, and it was time to get the armies back near the *Western & Atlantic*. Their railroad bridge over the Etowah had nearly been rebuilt, and would be on the 11th.

By 4 June Johnston had established a new line called the Lost Mountain line, for the "mountain" on the left, to Brush Mountain on the right. The Dallas to New Hope line had to be stretched out for about ten miles. Jackson's cavalry division had guarded the left and Wheeler's divisions the right. The same was true of the Lost Mountain line. Pine Mountain is east of Lost and stood between two roads leading into Marietta. It is actually a mile-long ridge that is only three hundred feet at its highest point. It was slightly in advance of the main line, and held by Bate's Division, including four artillery batteries.

Sherman dismissed reports that Johnston had these "mountains" heavily fortified. It is reminiscent of his disbelief of the New Hope position being held in force. He made a personal reconnaissance on the morning of 14 June. Hardee had complained about having Bate's Division on Pine, and Johnston accompanied him to take a look that morning. Polk and several other officers were listening to a Florida colonel point out the enemy line. Sherman saw them and said, "How saucy they are!" He ordered artillery to fire on them. A shot shrieked overhead, followed by a second, and then a third. The second shot killed Polk. Johnston and Hardee were overcome with grief. Despite Polk's shortcomings as a general he was beloved by the army. Cannon wrote, "…the Christian soldier, General Polk, was struck in the breast by a cannonball and instantly killed." He said it was a great shock. "We all loved him and had great confidence in him as commander…"

Polk's death led to Loring, the senior major general in the corps, getting command of the corps, still officially called the Army of Mississippi. Loring's first general order included: "In assuming command of this army the major-general commanding cannot refrain from an expression of deep regret at the untimely and unexpected death of its late commander, and shares in common with all officers and men of the command grief at the loss of the patriot general, the memory of whose valor and virtue will long be cherished by his troops." Loring was actually acting commander, as will be seen.

Polk's death made it certain that the advanced position at Pine Mountain was evacuated that night. Lost Mountain was to, on the 18th, but not before a sharp fight took place. Capt. J.L. Bond, of the 12th Louisiana, wrote of the Lost Mountain Line in an 1897 issue of *Confederate Veteran* (Volume 5, page 463). He wrote of the 12th Louisiana, Scott's Brigade, and much of Lt. Col. Thomas C. Standifer. He did not indicate the date, writing: "Col. Standifer was always cool in battle, but very energetic and swift in action; he was self-possessed, but as rapid and terrible as an avalanche. In business he was slow and methodical. At Lost Mountain a Federal brigade charged our regiment and run right through it. I was on the right and Standifer was on the left. The last we saw of the left they were surrounded by the enemy, and we had no doubt but that they were destroyed or captured. We fell back about a mile and a half; were in deplorable confusion and almost panic-stricken, when, to our utter astonishment, we saw the left come marching up with Standifer at the head, and Gen. Scott said: 'I knew he would bring them out.' He had a fine horse killed in doing it. As soon as Standifer rode up his bravery and magnetism calmed the confusion, and perfect order was restored.' In hundreds of episodes the military genius of the man was shown. Scott and Loring both had the greatest confidence in him…Col. Thomas C. Standifer was a grand man, who always helped a soldier in need."

Lost Mountain may seem like an obscure action, but J.P. Cannon also remembered the withdrawal. His 27th Alabama had been on picket duty all night in a drenching rain. Before daylight his picket company got into a "hide and seek" game with the enemy pickets. The firing continued back and forth, but about 2 p.m. a squad of Yankees got possession of a log house between the lines, and Cannon found himself in a crossfire. "It was the worst scrape I ever got into, and I had rather take my chances in a regular battle than another such. They made it so hot that something had to be done and very quickly, or we couldn't stay there; so we sent a courier back and reported the situation to Colonel Jackson, who very promptly brought up a detachment from the regiment, charged the house and drove the Yankees back to their picket-line, much to our relief and great delight…" Jackson had his arm shattered and had to have it amputated. His absence may have been a factor in Cannon's entry for Sunday the 19th: "We were relieved from vidette at 2 a.m. and found that we had been all night without any support, the command having left early in the night. We followed and overtook the division at the foot of Kennesaw…"

Loring biographer James Raab included a story of the difficulty of moving the artillery. It seems to have been in the muddy withdrawal from Lost Mountain. Veteran D.J. Wilson recalled, "On one occasion I was standing on the roadside watching the artillerymen trying to get one of the cannons out of the mud, when I heard someone behind me say, 'Put your shoulder to the wheel.' When I looked around to see who gave the command and saw General Loring. Well, we all got to the wheels and moved it right out."

Lee, Beauregard, Taylor, and Forrest Victorious

The antagonists in Georgia were not unaware of the war elsewhere in the Confederacy. While fighting through northern Georgia U.S. armies were conducting offensives in several states, of interest to Johnston and Sherman. In May Lee won tactical victories in the Virginia "Wilderness." Grant didn't retreat as others before him, and met another defeat at Cold Harbour on 2 June, where he lost about 7,000 troops in under an hour. South of Richmond the U.S. Army of the James were defeated by Beauregard and driven into the Bermuda Hundred defenses.

A joint U.S Army-Navy offensive up the Red River in Louisiana was turned back. Their objective had been an invasion of Texas. Richard Taylor's victory was so impressive he was promoted to lieutenant general, especially impressive as he had no West Point education. Grant and Sherman had preferred an attempt be made to take Mobile instead, making the failed Red River Campaign all the worse. A cooperating column was also defeated and turned back in Arkansas, by troops under General Kirby Smith.

Sherman wrote his wife, "The railroad is taxed to its utmost to supply our daily wants… Thus far we have been well supplied, and I hope it will continue, though I expect to hear every day of Forrest breaking into Tennessee from some quarter. John Morgan is in Kentucky, but I attach little importance to him or his raid. Forrest is a more dangerous man. I am in hopes that an expedition sent out from Memphis or Tupelo about the first of June will give him full employment." The Story of the Confederacy, by Robert S. Henry, points out when Sherman wrote the lettre the enemy was already retreating from Forrest.

Forrest's defense of Mississippi was excellent. Four days before Polk was killed on Pine Mountain, he won one of his most brilliant victories. Sherman wrote that he "sent Sturgis down to take command of that cavalry and whip Forrest." The expedition from Memphis didn't go well. At Brice's Crossroads Forrest hit them on the march and they were badly whipped. Tactics aside Forrest was so busy beating Yankees he didn't have time to raid the railroad behind Sherman. He later wrote that Atlanta would not have been taken without railroads. Johnston was well aware of this and had let Richmond know his desire for Forrest to raid the railroads that led back to the great U.S. supply base at Nashville.

Some of the U.S. troops that had just been defeated up the Red River were the 16th Corps. Grant and Sherman still preferred they take Mobile, but the Brice's Crossroads defeat made defeating Forrest the priority. Maj. Gen. Andrew Jackson Smith and his 16th Corps got the assignment "to make up a force and go out and follow Forrest to the death, if it costs 10,000 lives and breaks the Treasury." Forrest was operating under orders of Lt. Gen. Stephen Dill Lee, commanding the Department of Alabama, Mississippi, and East Louisiana. The Charleston resident had been on the team to negotiate for the surrender of Fort Sumter. Lee had dug in at Chickasaw Bluffs in the last week of 1862 to defeat Sherman's frontal assault at Chickasaw Bluffs. Lee ordered Forrest's badly outnumbered cavalry to make a similar attack against the 16th Corps troops, dug in near Tupelo.

The attacks at Tupelo were bound to fail and they did. That evening Lee called a meeting to discuss the battle. Lee asked, "General Forrest, have you any ideas on the subject?" Forrest replied, "Yes sir, I've always got ideas, and I'll tell you one thing, General Lee. If I knew as much about West Point tactics as you, the Yankees would whip hell out of me every day." He continued, with his voice choking, "I've got five hundred empty saddles and nothing to show for them." The Yankees retreated the next day largely due to a food shortage. Lee's reputation did not suffer so much, for he was called to Georgia before the end of the month. He would command Hood's old corps and launch an unauthorized assault at Ezra Church. Loring was wounded there, back in command of his division.

<u>Loring's Division commanded by Featherston at Kennesaw Mountain</u>

It was not impossible that Sherman would make the mistake of a frontal assault. When Johnston pulled back from the Lost Mountain line on 19 June, Sherman wanted to believe he was retreating to the Chattahoochee. When he found Johnston on the Kennesaw Mountain line, his instinct was to send Schofield's Army of the Ohio, supported by Hooker's 20th Corps, off to slide by Johnston's left. Sherman thought such a large force could reach the Chattahoochee, but Jackson's cavalry slowed them down.

Oakton, Owned By Wilder In 1864 (Now Goodman) Headquarters of Gen. Loring During Battle of Kennesaw Mountain. Marietta, Ga. 1-U-259

On the morning of the 22nd Johnston ordered Hood's Corps from the right to the left in order to confront Schofield. Thus Loring, commanding the Army of Mississippi, became the right, and Hardee's Corps the centre. Rather than just taking a position in front of Schofield, Hood launched an attack without reconnaissance, and it was a costly failure. Brigade commander Brig. Gen. Arthur Manigault wrote it "was a disgrace to the officer who planned it, and showed an amount of ignorance of the enemy's position, and the difficulties to be overcome before he could be reached, for which there could be no excuse. The ground had been ridden over by many officers the day before, at latest, and ought to have been thoroughly understood by General Hood, the greater part of his staff, and particularly his engineers. I formed my estimate of him on this occasion for the first time, and subsequent events only confirmed me in the opinion that he was totally unfit for command of a corps, although he might have deserved the reputation he had acquired as the best division commander in the Army of Northern Virginia."

Hood's attack, known as Kolb's Farm, failed yet Hooker claimed he had "repulsed two heavy attacks." He wanted reinforcements, claiming "three corps are in front of us." Sherman was annoyed with Hooker, for three corps would have been Johnston's army! Sherman wired Halleck the next day "as fast as we gain one position, the enemy has another all ready." Johnston's line was over eight miles long, and Sherman decided it had to be stretched thin. He decided to attack the centre, mostly against Hardee's Corps, but also hitting Loring's left divisions, mostly French's but also part of Walthall's.

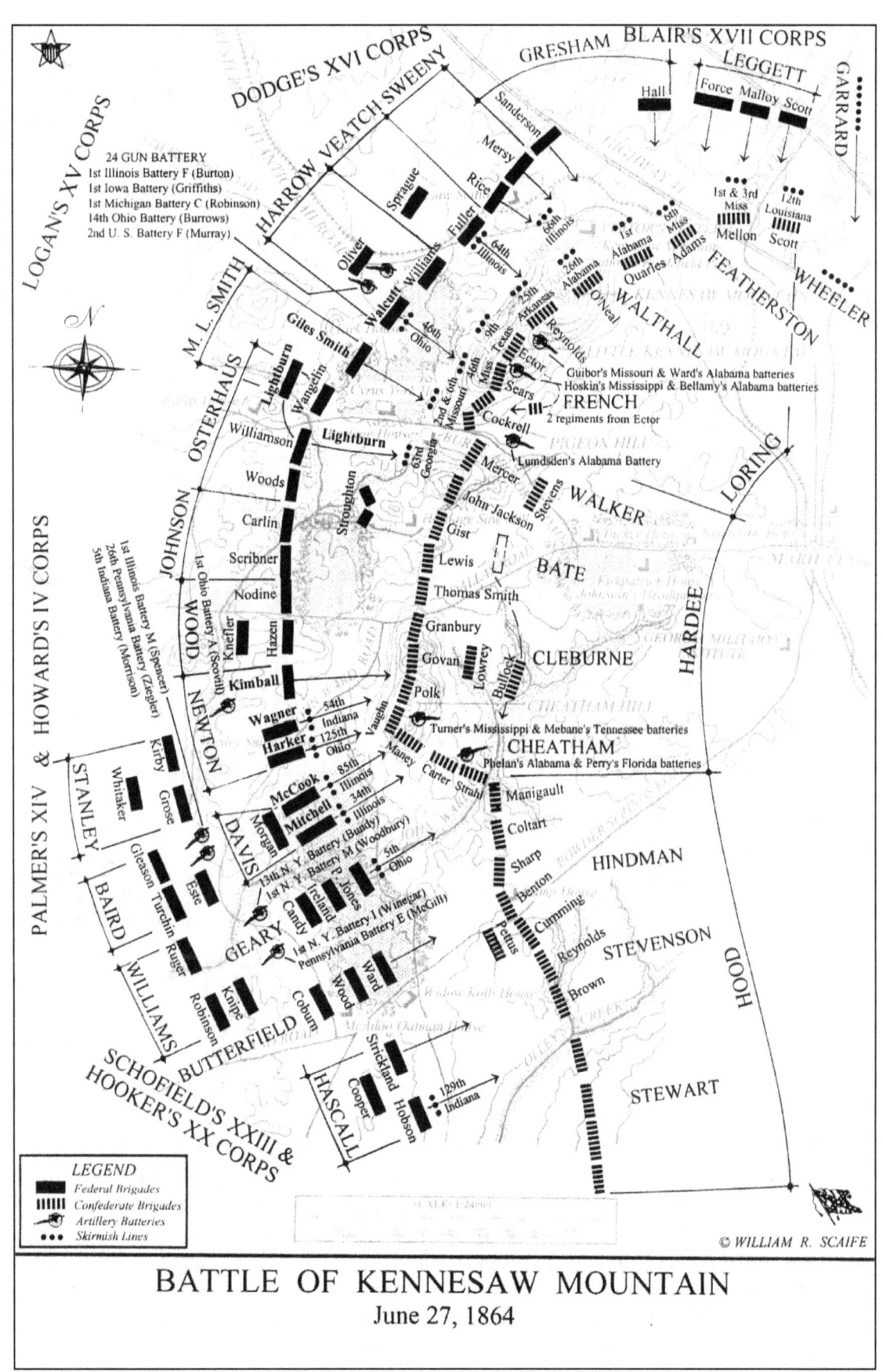

BATTLE OF KENNESAW MOUNTAIN
June 27, 1864

It wasn't long after sunrise on the 27th when some 200 U.S. artillery pieces began shelling Johnston's line. About eight o' clock the shelling faded away and there was a temporary silence. The Yankee infantry stepped forward under a clear sky, as the temperature got hot. Johnston must have been overwhelmed with gratification as he saw their failure. One Yankee saw Hardee's line as "veritable volcanoes…vomiting forth fire and smoke." Johnston's line may have been stretched thin, but there were no flaws in it.

Featherston commanded Loring's, Division at Kennesaw Mountain, and filed the report on 30 June; it may be found in Official Records Volume 38, Part 3, page 878. Featherston explained his position was from the road into Marietta, eastward. Kennesaw Mountain and today's national park are west of the road, which is today's U.S. Highway 41. The position was on the right of the Confederate line, with some cavalry on his right. Though the division did not take the brunt of the U.S. attacks, Featherston's report shows they were fully engaged.

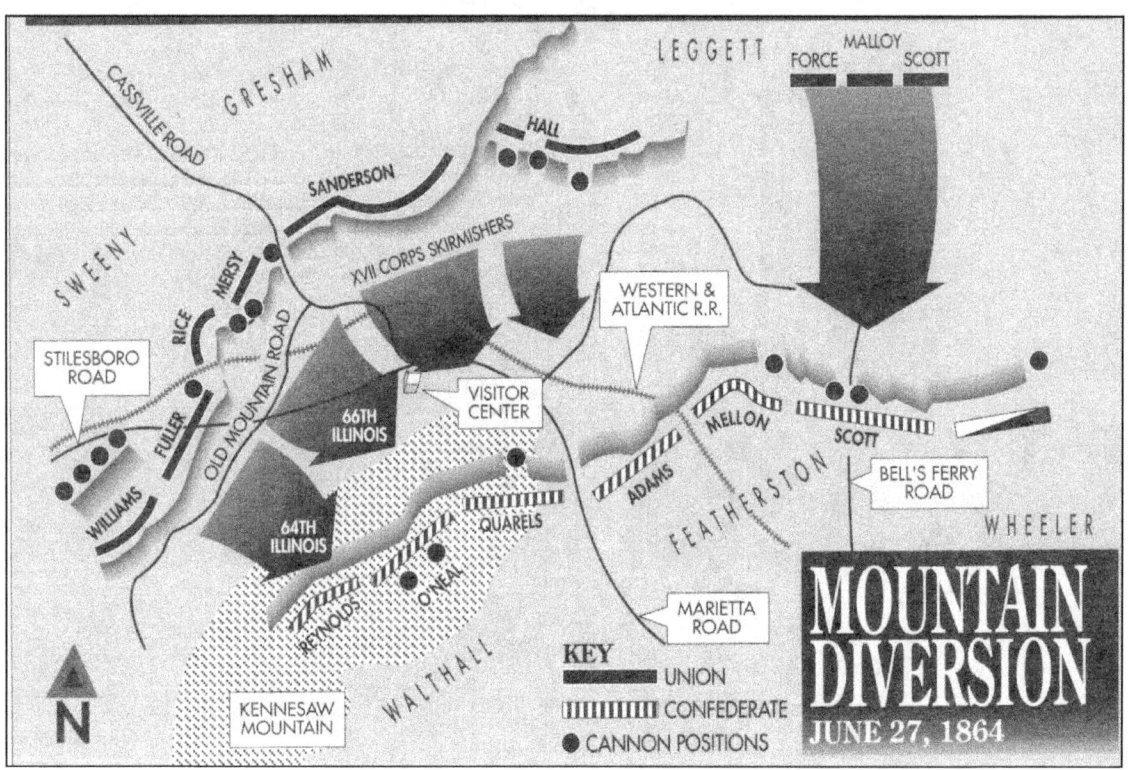

The U.S. division that confronted Loring's Division was commanded by Brig. Gen. Mortimer Leggett. He explained his efforts were largely to create a diversion. He was positioned so that his left was about 100 yards from the Bell's Ferry Road. Garrard's cavalry was refused on his left; this is not indicated on the "Mountain Diversion" map. Leggett complained that his line was "enfiladed by sharpshooters upon hills to my right and also at the left." He extended his front. "At this point we were brought under a cross-fire from three rebels batteries, one on our left, one in front, and one on our right." He claimed he would have needed reinforcements to advance. "The design of my operations being to hold the force in my front….I think we fully accomplished our object…"

Scott's brigade was on the division's right. Featherston write, "About 10 a.m. the enemy advanced in force against the skirmishers of General Scott, on the Bell's Ferry road. They came in one line of skirmishers and three lines of battle. Our whole skirmish line was well intrenched, and General Scott's skirmish regiment (Twelfth Louisiana, under command of Colonel Nelson) held their position against this overwhelming force until the enemy had advanced to within twenty-five or thirty yards of their rifle pits. They poured into the advancing columns repeated volleys of minie-balls, which thinned their ranks and caused them to falter, but did not check them. In this advance the enemy sustained a heavy loss. Colonel Nelson finally withdrew his regiment and fell back to the main line of battle in good order."

Featherston explained the enemy advanced to within about 250 years of the main line when "a concentrated converging fire was directed upon their position by our artillery. Cowan's and Bouanchaud's batteries, of Major Myrick's battalion," and two other batteries "poured into the enemy for the space of one hour a most galling and destructive fire. The artillery was ably and skillfully served, and so terrible was the fire and severe its results that the enemy retired before it…This advance of the enemy in force and in three lines of battle was evidently made with the intent and for the purpose of attacking our forces in the main line of battle." At about 4:00 the 12th Louisiana was able to return to their original position on the skirmish line.

Sergeant Edmund T. Eggleston was in Cowan's and had witnessed the death of Lloyd Tilghman in 1863. In his diary he recorded for Monday the 27th: "Heavy skirmishing this evening in our immediate front. The enemy ran Scott's pickets in this A.M. They afterwards went out and retook their position without firing a gun the enemy having fallen back after driving them in. The 1st Section of our battery shelled the woods for several hours at regular intervals. I went out this evening and examined the ground in front of our battery. We did considerable execution. Killed 25 Yanks and it is thought wounded many more. I saw two of them-a ghastly spectacle."

Featherston's Brigade was commanded by Col. Thomas Mellon of the 3rd Mississippi. The brigade's skirmish line was held by the 1st Mississippi Battalion of Sharpshooters and the 3rd Mississippi. Three enemy regiments appeared to the right, headed toward Scott's line. The battalion of sharpshooters poured "a destructive fire" into them "which caused them to fall back…"

On the division's left, Adams positioned the 6th Mississippi, under Robert Lowry, for his brigade's skirmish line. They had proved themselves at Champion Hill. At about 8 a.m. the left of his line, and the right of Walthall's Division, held by Quarles's Brigade, were charged. The 6th was able to repulse the attack and direct crossfire on those attacking Quarles. When the Yankees retreated they left about 20 entrapped soldiers who had to surrender. At 10 a.m. Lowry's skirmish line witnessed the quick approach of another attack. Lowry shouted encouragements as another attack approached. They fired on the enemy at about 75 yards. Featherston reported "they wavered, broke, and fled in much confusion." Thus, all three of the division brigades easily held their positions.

Loring's Division had easily held their main line at Kennesaw Mountain, thanks to the fine units of the skirmish line and the artillery batteries of Cowan and Bouanchaud. It was one of the finest days for these two batteries, and Featherston noted it in his report. The enemy's artillery had surprisingly little to show for their efforts. Featherston wrote, "A heavy fire from the enemy's artillery in our front was directed at our lines during the evening, but fortunately without effect, the shot and shell passing considerable distance beyond our lines." Featherston stated enemy casualties before him during the battle were in the hundreds, while the division's whole loss was 5 killed and 14 wounded. Leggett claimed to have only 10 killed, and 76 wounded.

Featherston wrote another report from his hometown, Holly Springs, dated 15 November 1867; it may be found in the Supplement to the O.R., Volume 7, page 147. He concluded it, "This brief and imperfect report is made entirely from memory. All of my official reports were lost when General Hood's baggage train was captured at a later period near Jonesborough, Georgia." It is similar to the report above though two artillery batteries were given much credit for the success in holding the right half of the division's line.

Featherston wrote, "Our skirmish line, though very strong, was soon driven in on the right and center, in front of Scott's Brigade and the right of Mellon's. Here the enemy made their heavy advance. Two excellent batteries, [James J.] Cowan's and [Alcide] Bouanchaud's, were placed near the center of Scott's Brigade, and pretty well fortified. These batteries commanded a large public road, running north from Marietta, and running parallel with the base of Kennesaw, and about 1,000 yards east of it…" Featherston said the principal attack on Loring's Division was made at this point, where the two batteries "were directed to give a converging and concentrated fire upon the enemy at this point. The order was obeyed with apparent pleasure, and artillery has been but rarely served so effectively, within my knowledge, during the late war. The firing was rapid, well directed, and very destructive to the compact lines of the advancing foe. As usual, they advanced in three lines of battle."

Kennesaw Mountain was one of the Army of Tennessee's easiest victories. The U.S. casualties were admitted as about 3,000. Confederate estimates were higher. Johnston had about 700. This was the ratio of casualties needed to have a chance of beating them, but it would not happen again. Unfortunately Johnston had little time to enjoy his victory. Sul Ross advised him the Yankee right was closer to the Chattahoochee than Hood's left. It was only a matter of time before the Kennesaw Mountain line would be abandoned.

But while on the Kennesaw line a block of officers, including eight brigadier generals, made it known they wanted Loring to be appointed lieutenant general and permanently assigned to command the Army of Mississippi. The petition was signed on 22 June, but the battle delayed forwarding it to President Davis until the 30th. On the 23rd he issued, "Major-General Stewart has this day been appointed lieutenant-general to command the corps recently commanded by Lieutenant-General Polk." The petition which might have influenced Davis to consider Loring was:

"We, the undersigned officers of the army of Mississippi, feeling a deep interest in the appointment of a successor to the command made vacant by the death of the lamented Lieut. General L. Polk and believing that the Government will lend a listening ear to the earnest wishes of its soldiers when properly expressed and when compatible with the public interest, beg leave to request that Major General W.W. Loring be appointed Lieutenant General and assigned to command of this army." Some of the petitioners had been under Loring for over a year of service going back to at least Champion Hill.

The petition continued, "Many of us have long served under the command of General Loring & all have seen his courage, skill and ability as a commander well tested; and the able and gallant manner in which he has borne himself through all, has inspired us with the most implicit confidence in his leadership & the earnest desire that the request herein made be granted."

Loring or Stewart were worthy of consideration. Each had shined in defensive victories. "Old Blizzards" put himself at risk in an incomparable victory against a joint army-navy attack at Fort Pemberton. Stewart had won notice for the victory at New Hope Church. But Stewart earned his major general's star knocking through the enemy line at Murfreesborough. Another solid offensive role at Chickamauga followed. Davis went to West Point and appreciated an academy graduate with a track record. Perhaps Loring's disagreement with Stonewall was a negative. Loring's miraculous escape from Grant at Champion Hill was too. Davis could have seen Loring making a choice to join up with Johnston's Army of the Relief instead of trying to make his way to Vicksburg as an issue.

Loring returned to his division, which was larger than French's or Cantey's old division. Cantey had too many health related absences. His division became Walthall's. Loring's had 5,175 infantry present for duty at the end of June. This was down 686 from the 10 June return. Kennesaw Mountain only cost the division 22 casualties. Far more casualties seem to have been taken on the Lost Mountain line. No doubt some were on sick roles, and there could have been desertions. The Army of Mississippi officially became Stewart's Corps on 26 July.

Johnston Outflanked from Kennesaw and retreats across the Chattahoochee River

Sherman did what was expected after another battlefield defeat and began flanking Johnston out of his Kennesaw line on 2 July. Of course Johnston was expecting it and had ordered the construction of strong works to the rear. It was the Smyrna Camp line, named for a Methodist campground. It was six miles long, two miles shorter than the Kennesaw line. General Manigault wrote that it was irregular with many salients. It was so tortuous that it confused enemy batteries. He watched as two of them, about 1.5 miles apart, dueled with each other! "It was a ludicrous sight, causing much merriment and shouts of laughter for the space of ten or fifteen minutes, until the two combatants found out their error."

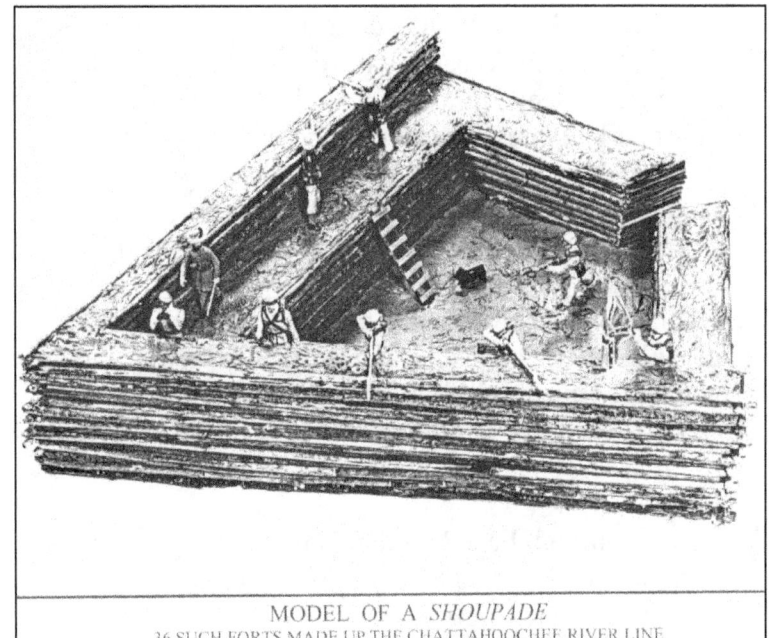

MODEL OF A *SHOUPADE*
36 SUCH FORTS MADE UP THE CHATTAHOOCHEE RIVER LINE

The great Atlanta Campaign historian William Scaife had this model of a shoupade. The vertical exterior walls, 10-12' high, catch the eye first. U.S. artillery shells might have broken the log faces, but the packed dirt, held against the interior logs, may have kept intact. Sherman was very impressed. It seems some artillery shelling might have taken place to determine that question. If Sherman ordered it, the record was not found. The mystery: Why didn't Old Joe try to hold the line?

The Smyrna line was outflanked on 4 July, and Johnston fell back to his final line on the north bank of the Chattahoochee. He positioned the army to protect the railroad bridge over the river, but with the river to his back as he had done at Resaca and Cassville. The line was perhaps the most unique line of fortifications built during the war. Brig. Gen Francis Shoup, Johnston's chief of artillery, knew Johnston would be outflanked again, and had his permission to build a unique line of triangular redoubts. They were built of logs, packed with dirt. Their outer face rose straight up for ten or twelve feet. There was a parapet for infantry to fire from. They were also to be armed with hand grenades. Yankee infantry would not have been able to scale these works, known as Shoupades.

General Shoup oversaw the construction of 36 Shoupades. They were spaced at 240-foot intervals. A conventional entrenched line, backed by artillery, connected them. Shoup believed an 80-man company could hold each one. The entire line could be held by a division. The line protected the railroad, leaving Johnston to swing the rest of his army out to attack Sherman's flank. But nearby river crossings had to be held.

Sherman advanced on the Shoupades, but once he saw them, he was averse to attacking. In his memoir he wrote they "proved one of the strongest pieces of field-fortifications I ever saw." His attacks on fortified lines had failed at Chickasaw Bluffs, Missionary Ridge, Resaca, New Hope Church, and Pickett's Mill, and Kennesaw Mountain. It was almost time for another flanking operation and it, crossing the Chattahoochee, would be the greatest of them all.

Loring's Division learned of his return and Stewart's promotion while on the north bank. Doctor Whitehead wrote, "Lt. Genrl. Stewart will assume command of our Corps this evening. General Loring returning to the Division; the latter is deeply chagrined." That was on 4 July. French wrote on the 7th, "This morning I rode along the lines with Gens. Loring and Shoup. Gen. A.P. Stewart, having been promoted to lieutenant general,

Stewart's bust was placed on the Hamilton County court house lawn in Chattanooga, by the United Daughters of the Confederacy. They recognized his efforts to establish Chickamauga-Chattanooga National Military Park, the nation's oldest and largest.

assumed command of the Army of Mississippi. After the death of Gen. Polk I unhesitatingly said that Gen. Stewart would be promoted. I rode along the whole of his command with him." French did not say why he thought Stewart would get the promotion or if he agreed. French must have known Stewart who graduated from West Point in 1842, a year ahead of himself. No doubt all were impressed with Stewart's victory at New Hope Church. French had been transferred to Mississippi in June 1863, and might not have known Loring before. Loring's lack of a military education, as Stewart was a West Pointer, likely counted against him. Johnston had actually wanted another from Stewart's graduating class, Maj. Gen. Mansfield Lovell.

Loring-Biographer Raab quoted from a 1961 tome, *The Blue and the Gray on the Nile*: "Old Blizzards Loring, a soldier by profession for twenty years, a warrior from the wild west frontier who had a fair claim to having been under fire more times than any other living man was not a man to bear deep resentment and nursed no grudge. But he was sensitive, as a soldier should be, of his honor, his valor, and his judgement, and certainly the leaders of the Confederacy had not accorded him the responsibilities and the opportunities that an officer of his experience and accomplishments could rightly expect after three years, non-stop warfare for 'the cause.'"

Returning to Sherman's greatest flanking operation, in which he bypassed the Shoupades, we find the Army of the Ohio crossed upstream of the railroad bridge. Pontoon boats were loaded on the north bank, out of sight, on Soap Creek. They landed on the south bank, and brushed aside some militia. Johnston absolutely had to control the crossings on the Chattahoochee and failed. These had been surveyed and some defensive earthworks built in 1863. That Johnston had only militia, with one cannon, to contest such a point, shows he didn't share Shoup's confidence in the river line. More Yankees crossed on the 9th, and that night Johnston retreated south of the river, giving up his ninth line.

Johnston had been concerned Sherman might find a crossing, but he thought it would be downstream of the railroad bridge. Enemy troops crossing downstream might break the railroads south of Atlanta. He had sent a staff officer, William Clare, to prepare a detailed description of all potential crossings. Clare sent a report on 4 July, warning of seven such points, and where artillery should be positioned. Unfortunately Johnston's response was lethargic. Johnston failed to place tested troops to guard the Chattahoochee crossings.

On the 11th he shifted some of the blame. He ordered, "Intercourse between the pickets of the enemy and our own is strictly and positively prohibited…Yesterday the enemy had a great interest in finding the fords in the Chattahoochee, and easily attained their object, the pickets by mutual agreement bathing in the river together. The engineers of the enemy most probably mingle with the bathers." All this may have been so, but he clearly failed to utilize the Shoupades and to guard the crossings.

Hood in command in Georgia

President Davis was exasperated with Johnston's failure. He telegraphed Johnston, asking for a specific plan to hold Atlanta. Johnston had been vague about his plans all through the campaign. Once again he stated that he was badly outnumbered, on the defensive, but looking for an opportunity to strike. Efforts at Resaca, Cassville, and Dallas had failed. In a little over two months he had fallen back some 100 miles, and was only six miles from Atlanta. Davis began to fear he would abandon the city without a major battle. It was more than just a military concern. The U.S. presidential election was four months away, and holding Atlanta might insure Lincoln's defeat.

Diarist Mary Boykin Chestnut was the wife of James Chestnut. He had represented South Carolina in the U.S. Senate in antebellum days, was a member of the Provisional Confederate Congress, and in April 1864 was a brigadier general serving on President Davis's staff. Living in Richmond, Mrs. Chestnut had daily contact with such leaders as Lee. She wrote, "Mr. Chestnut told Mr. Davis that every honest man he saw out west thought well of Joe Johnston. The President detests Joe Johnston for all the trouble he has given him, and General Joe returns the compliment with compound interest. His hatred of Jeff Davis amounts to a religion. With him it colors all things. Joe Johnston, whether advancing or retreating, is magnetic; he does draw the good will of those by whom he is surrounded. Being such a good hater, it is a pity he had not elected to hate somebody else than the President of our country. He hates not wisely but too well."

Davis sent Bragg down to Atlanta to see if he could learn more. J.P. Cannon wrote, "General Bragg arrived from Richmond. I guess they are getting uneasy about Atlanta and have sent him to see if something can be done to check Sherman's invasion. It is getting to be a serious matter, but we have the utmost confidence in General Johnston and feel like he will devise some plan to hold the city…" Bragg couldn't get any more out of Johnston, and Davis was so exasperated he ordered command turned over to Hood on the 17th. The news was devastating to the army that adored him.

Hood had been well thought of while serving under Lee. Mary Chestnut wrote about meeting him after he had been promoted to general. "When he came with his sad face-the face of an old crusader who believed in his cause, his cross and his crown-we were not prepared for that type as the beau ideal of wild Texans. He is tall, thin, shy, with blue eyes and light hair, a tawny beard…He wears an appearance of awkward strength." Chestnut went onto quote a Mr. Venable who "had often heard of the light of battle shining in a man's eyes, but he had seen it only once. He carried orders to Hood from General Lee, and found him in the hottest of the fight. The man was transfigured. 'The fierce light of his eyes,' said Mr. Venable, 'I can never forget.'" Davis put a dynamic soldier in place of Johnston. Unfortunately the fierce light would not be seen again.

J.P. Cannon wrote for the 18th, "About 1 p.m. a circular was brought around the lines and read, imparting the sorrowful news that our beloved commander had been removed and General J.B. Hood placed in command. This is a great blow to our cause and had cast a gloom over the whole army. Strong men wept, while others cursed, and not one approved the change." Cannon continued with remarks similar to General Manigault's, that he may have been capable of handling a division, but not an army. Manigault called it our final "calamity." He wrote that it "contributed materially to the downfall of the Confederacy, and possibly caused it." Hood didn't take long to prove them correct. Stewart looked back on it over forty years later. He not only believed it was a "stupendous blunder," but the "coup de grace of the Confederate cause."

Peach Tree Creek

Peach Tree Creek was the significant terrain obstacle to the enemy's advance on Atlanta, south of the Chattahoochee. The creek flowed westward to the Chattahoochee. Its banks were generally steep, often in cane. The terrain may have resembled the Shiloh battlefield as much as any the army had seen. In striking contrast, if they could return today they would find charming suburban neighborhoods on its banks. Today's Peachtree Road follows the period road, though a thoroughly developed cityscape. A small, white marble monument is on Peachtree in front of Piedmont Hospital. It was dedicated on the 80th anniversary of the battle in 1944. The United States was fighting the Second World War and needed Southerners to fight its battles. The area where Featherston's and Scott's men fought may be reached west of Peachtree along Collier Road (more on that follows).

The Atlanta of 1864 was over four miles south of the creek. Captain Lemuel Grant's fortifications had been laid out in an almost-squarish defense perimeter in 1863. It was almost twelve miles. Johnston said he was confident they could be held; however, after the army crossed the Chattahoochee he sent Shoup to inspect them. He was shocked at their weakness, and reported they were "a rather poor line of rifle pits with an occasional earthwork of more pretensions." Much more work would have to be done.

Also, as Johnston was relieved, he and engineer, Lt. Col. Stephen Presstman were laying out an outer line about two miles north of the city, and roughly 5.75 miles of it were parallel to Peachtree Creek. Along the east side of Northside Drive, also U.S. Highway 41, is Loring Heights Subdivision. Georgia's historic marker "Loring's Hill" denotes: "The high hill, within the forks of Tanyard Branch, was occupied by Loring's Division…" The marker explains he advanced astride Tanyard Branch, as it flowed northward to Peachtree Creek. It states Featherston's advanced on the line of the *Seaboard (CSX),* which may have been built over a country road of the period. Using a 21st Century street map, the advance appears close to a mile.

Johnston had planned to strike the enemy in a precarious position, as they crossed the creek. Of course this was to be done to prevent their entrenching. Loring and a number of

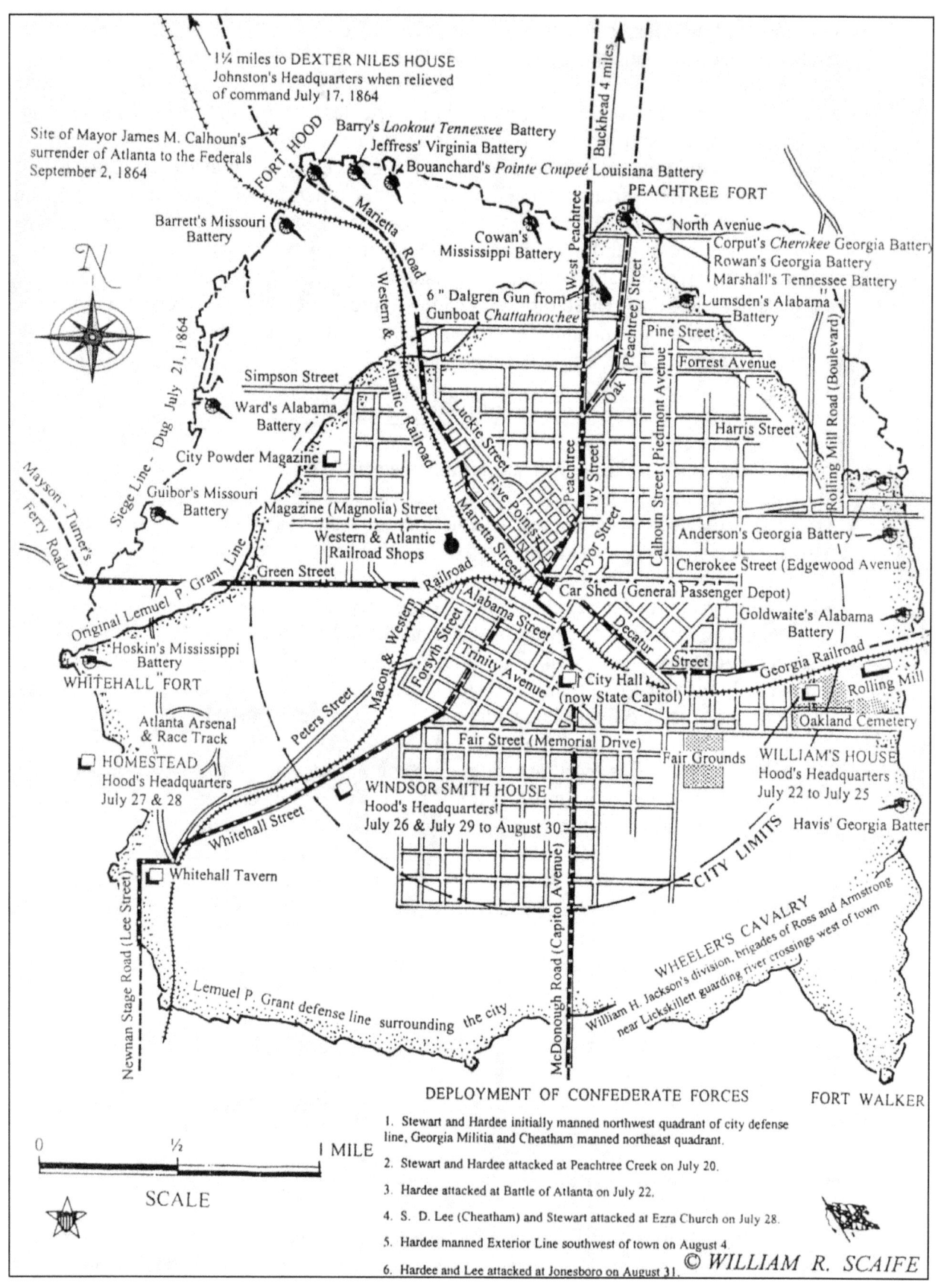

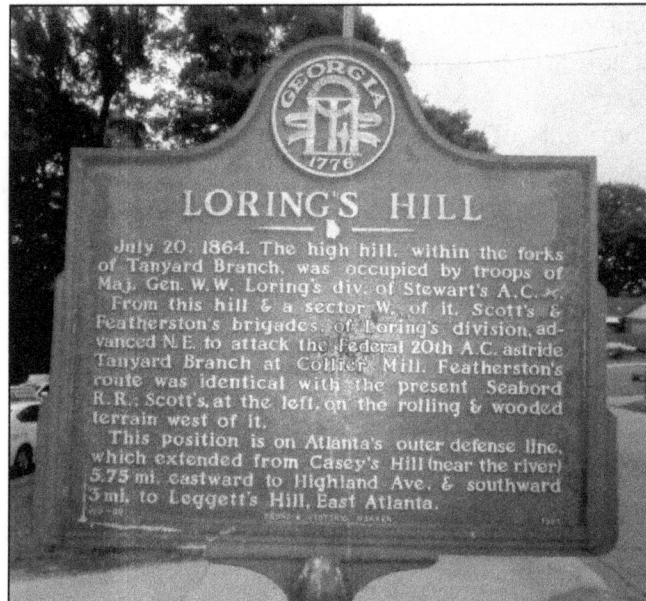

Loring's Hill with Loring Heights are just north of downtown. Interstates 75 and 85 come together in its shadows. Millions of passing vehicles pass unaware of the historic site.

Loring Heights subdivision on Loring Hill off Northside Dr.

his officers were aware of it. Chaplain James McNeilly recalled Loring's bitterness over the failure in a 1918 piece in *Confederate Veteran* (Vol. 26, page 471). Loring had good reason to be bitter as Hardee's brigades, to his right, had failed to advance and support Loring's aggressive advance. Actually Hardee's failure was Hood's as will be seen.

Hood knew of Johnston's plan to strike the enemy with the creek and river to their back. It was to drive the enemy westward toward the angle of the river and the mouth of the creek. Johnston had hoped to attack on 19 July, and so had Hood. His scouts advised him that morning that the Yankees were bridging the creek. But like planning an offensive in a game of chess, your opponent's pieces are not necessarily where you want them when you want them. The three-corps U.S. Army of the Cumberland was not crossing the creek early enough. It was dusk before it had established bridgeheads and the afternoon of the 20th before it was across on the south bank.

It is tempting to assume Johnston would have commanded a better coordinated attack by Hardee's and Stewart's Corps, than did Hood. But he would have also found the enemy's chess pieces out of place. Sherman had sent the Army of the Tennessee to tear up the *Georgia Railroad* by the evening of the 18th. It led east to Augusta and the important powder works, and onto connections for Richmond. That day Hood believed all three of Sherman's armies were between Peach Tree Cree and the Chattahoochee. His flanks were spread out over 18 miles apart. On the 20th they would be 9 miles apart, and Hood would have to shift his old corps, temporarily under Cheatham, to confront the Army of the Tennessee, east of Atlanta. Schofield's Army of the Ohio was way up the north fork of Peach Tree Creek, between the other armies. Sherman was confused with the chessboard too, for he had assumed Hood would move to take out the Army of the Tennessee.

Late in the morning Hood learned of Schofield's position moving up between the other two armies. Hood had planned to attack at 1:00, but now felt he had to delay the attack at Peach Tree Creek. He ordered Hardee to move to the right and connect with Cheatham.

Likewise Stewart had to shift right to keep connected to Hardee. Hood supposed the shift would be far shorter than the mile and a half necessary that consumed about three hours. All of the Army of the Cumberland was across the creek by noon, so any later attack gave them more time to entrench. Hood's opportunity of striking a precariously moving enemy force was over. The wooded terrain made reconnoitering a problem, and he should have decided to call the attack off. This might have been clear to him had he been on the field. At some point, probably after 3:30, Hood did go to Stewart's headquarters. He was still there at 7:15, when he sent a dispatch to Wheeler, advising Cleburne was on his way.

Loring fought the battle without Adams's Brigade, which was on detached duty near the mouth of Peach Tree Creek. Part of Featherston's and Scott's were on detached picket duty, so that he had only about 2,680 infantry for the battle; 1,230 in Featherston's and 1,450 in Scott's. The U.S. 20th Corps was to his front with about 14,600. Confederate brigades to the left and right would also hit the 20th Corps, but all together they still had fewer soldiers. The entrenched positions of the Atlanta Campaign had demonstrated that the defenders might hold their own against double and triple their number. Hood wanted the attack against the entire enemy front, made in echelon. This method failed to bring overwhelming force against any one point, and was almost certain to fail.

Hardee's Corps was the largest of the three corps, at an estimated 18,400 infantry. This was based on an 18 July estimate (O.R. vol. 38, part 5, p.178). They were positioned on Stewart's right, or east flank. Loring was Stewart's left division so Hardee needed to advance for Loring to be successful. Loring reported, "I was informed at an early hour of the intension of fighting a battle on that day, and was requested, in company with my brigadiers, to examine the topography of the country for that purpose. The enemy was reported to be crossing Peach Tree Creek and extending his line on our front. The reconnaissance was thoroughly made, the enemy being about two miles distant."

The morning reconnaissance had been made, but apparently too much time was lost for another. Hardee's right division, Bate's, actually got confused with Clear Creek in their front, mistaking it for Peach Tree Creek, and would take blame for delaying Hardee's attack. The delays gave the enemy time to prepare their line, so Hood seems to have lost the battle before it began. Scouts and couriers must have been busy attempting a reconnaissance. Loring continued, "It was subsequently ascertained that beyond the thick forest in our immediate front several large fields opened out, through which we were compelled to charge, giving my division the most exposed position on the whole line. My orders were as soon as the division on my right had gained the distance of 200 yards mine was to follow in single line of battle without reserve; that we must not stop for any obstacle, and if we came to breastworks to fix bayonets and charge them."

J.P Cannon also commented on the delay of moving Stewart's Corps to link up with Hardee's. "This delayed us till 4 o' clock p.m., when we halted and General Stewart made a little speech in which he informed us that we "were going to assault the enemy in his works, and that we must carry everything, allowing no obstacle to stop us; that the fate of Atlanta probably depended on the result of this battle."

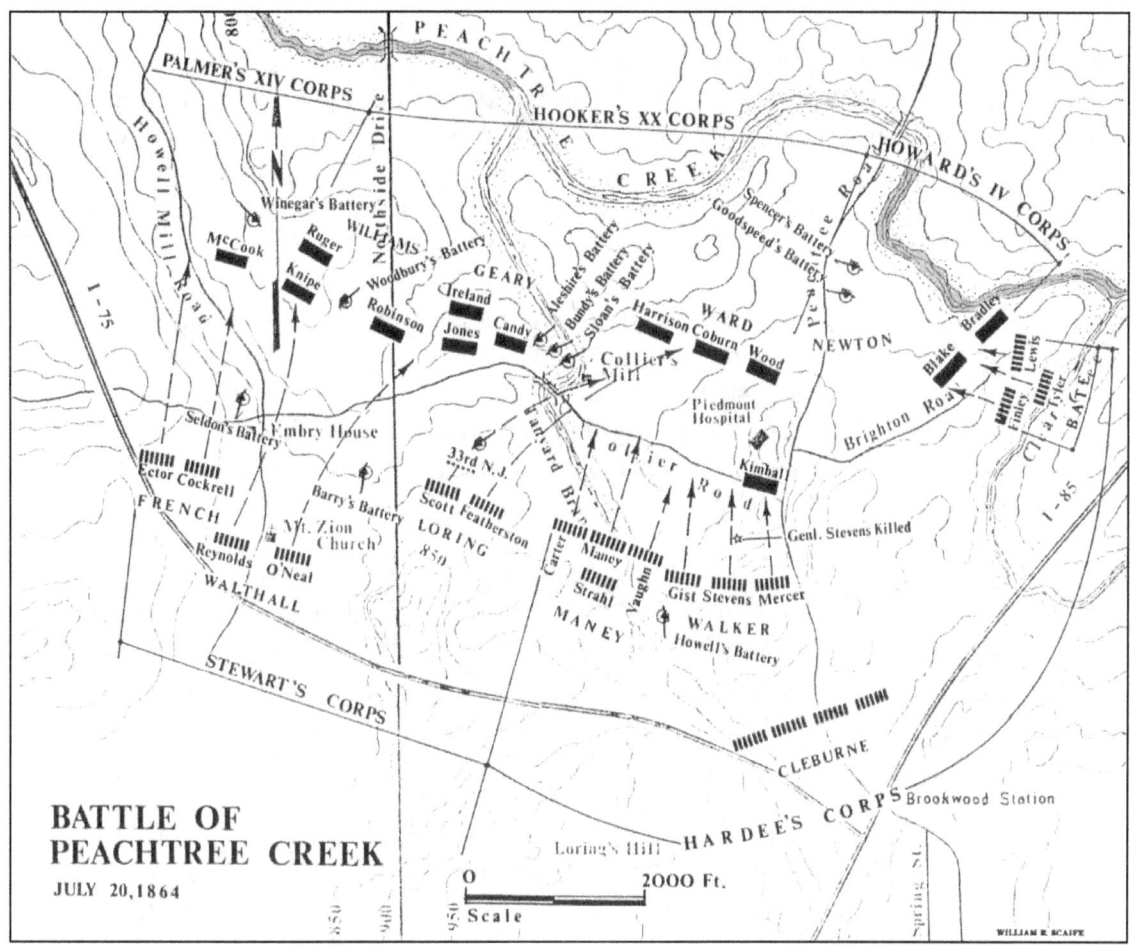

Cannon wrote of the thick forest Loring had mentioned. They had to march through by companies, "for we could never have gone through that tangled mass of timber and brush in line-of-battle. It was a heavy timbered section and the trees had been felled, lapped and crossed until they presented an almost impassable barrier, but we finally made our way through the worst of it and were them halted and wheeled by the left flank into line-of-battle, being then under fire of the pickets."

Loring wrote, "We here merged into the open fields before mentioned. The enemy was in plain view about 700 yards distant on the opposite side of the field, occupying a ridge running east and west, and marked by a line of red earth, which plainly told the work that was before us. The division was halted and the lines rectified." Cannon remembered, "The order to 'fix bayonets, forward, double-quick, march,' was given. We raised the old Rebel yell and rushed on the works, but the yell was soon drowned by the roar of musketry and thunder of cannon..." A Wisconsin colonel remembered Featherston's Brigade coming out of the woods "with a true rebel yell." Loring also recalled the deafening yell, driving the enemy from his position and not stopping until our colours were planted on different points of the breastworks..." It had actually not been made in one charge, but took three efforts to break the enemy's line.

111

An adjutant in the 33rd New Jersey was taking time to read a lettre from his father, until Loring's Division interrupted him. He recalled, "Suddenly and unexpectedly a volley was fired…" The 33rd overlooked an old field near the Tanyard Branch, where the adjutant was sent to check on the sounds of battle. "And there I saw a beautiful sight. Down through the great, open fields they were coming, thousands of them, men in gray, by brigade front, flags flying…I stopped but a few moments to take it all in, and then rode back to report."

Loring's Division had reached their high tide. As they broke through they captured the flag of the 33rd New Jersey. Loring wrote, "This brilliant charge of my gallant division was made so rapidly and with such intrepidity that up to this time we had sustained but comparatively a small loss. As the enemy fled in confusion from his works the steady aim of the Mississippi, Alabama, and Louisiana marksmen of my command produced great slaughter in his ranks. All accounts agree that his loss was very heavy…"

A Pennsylvania general watched as Loring's two brigades came out of the wooded area along Tanyard Branch. He reported, "Pouring out from the woods they advanced in immense brown and gray masses (not lines) with flags and banners, many of them new and beautiful, while their general and staff officers were in plain view, with drawn sabers flashing in the light, galloping here and there as they urged their troops to charge. The battlefield reminded him of Gettysburg. "Not a tree or bush within our range… [escaped] the scars of battle. The appearance of the enemy as they charged upon our front across the cleared field was magnificent." He thought the Confederates "seemed to rush forward with more than customary nerve and heartiness in the attack." The Army of Tennessee's infantry matched courage with Lee's army, regardless of Hood's later implications to the contrary.

From Scott's Brigade, Cannon wrote, "We thought the battle was won and were rejoicing over what we supposed would result in a glorious victory, but Hardee's Corps was repulsed on our right and in a short time the Yankees were pouring a galling fire into us from front and flank, which with an enfilading fire of artillery from our right proved so destructive that we were ordered to retire, leaving our captured guns, but holding onto the New Jersey flag, which we carried out as a trophy." The captured guns were recaptured by Illinois troops armed with Spencer repeater rifles.

Featherston's attack deserves praise, but they were too few to hold on against a U.S. division. He cited a staff officer: "To remain was utter destruction, sheer desperation. Sadly, reluctantly, these gallant men abandoned the point purchased at so priceless a cost, and again shot, and shell, and ball diminished fearfully the ranks already more than decimated by the murderous fire through which they had advanced…Returning from that field of blood crowded with their slain, they met their right making its first advance upon the foe. Falling back beyond a sheltering hill, and forming under the cover of its crest, they maintained their ground till night, in mercy, veiled from view the dark discolored earth where lay so many warriors, brave and true, weltering in their gore."

A.P. Stewart said when his attack stalled, and Walthall's Division had been as well as Loring's, that he had an officer "dispatched to request General Hardee to allow his left division to cooperate with Loring in carrying the line in its front. Before an answer was received a staff officer from the commanding general brought me an order to retire to the intrenched line from which we had advanced, and the conflict terminated." Loring said the fighting continued until dark, and that he withdrew all the dead and wounded possible. His division had 1,062 casualties; the enemy's may have been over double his.

General Scott reported (O.R. vol. 38, Part 3, page 895) that when the attack was thrown back he retreated back to the timber and formed in a ravine. "Here I was soon joined by Major-General Loring, who entirely agreed with me that it was useless to again take the works unless we secured cooperation on our right." All agreed that Cheatham's old division, commanded by Brig. Gen. George Earl Maney, had not advanced far enough. Capt. Augustus L. Milligan commanded the 57th Alabama. He commended Scott, "Our gallant brigadier-general was to be seen in the midst of danger cheering the men with his presence and cool determination." Col. Samuel Ives praised John E. Abernathy, of the 27th Alabama, for capturing the flag of the 33rd New Jersey. Scott's total casualties were 55 killed, 249 wounded, and 86 missing. It seems some of the missing may have been dead and wounded left on the field.

Featherston's report (O.R. vol. 38, Part 3, pages 880-4) offers more details than Scott's. His details agree with those of other officers. But he has the sad decimation of his Mississippi unit commanders. The 1st Mississippi Battalion Sharpshooters advanced in front under Major Stigler. It is ironic he survived in the front line while so many fell. The 33rd under Drake was on the right. Featherston wrote Drake, "a gallant and excellent officer, fell beyond the enemy's first line of works, leading his regiment in the charge and The 3rd under Mellon was left of the 33rd. The 22nd under Oatis was on the left of the 33rd. Featherston wrote they "were both severely wounded after gallantly leading their respective commands to the enemy's first line of works. They will be unfit for duty for some months." The 31st was on the left of the 33rd. Drane "was severely wounded while leading the charge and will be disabled for some time." Featherston mentioned Maj. F.M. Gillespie, of the 31st, also leading their charge and falling near the enemy's works. "In his fall his regiment is deprived of a gallant officer and his country has lost a true patriot." The 40th was on Featherston's far left, and Lt. Col. George Wallace commanded as Colonel Colbert was on sick leave. Wallace was "severely wounded, losing an arm." Major W. Gibbens was also "killed in the full discharge of his duty."

Featherston didn't forget those who bore their regimental colours. Adjutant W.J. Van de Graaf, of the 31st, "a gallant and accomplished officer, a young man of promise and great moral worth, seized the colours of his regiment and bore them to the front after two or three colour bearers had been shot down, and following their example shared their fate. He fell with the colours in his hand." Another adjutant, C.V.H. Davis, of the 22nd, a "gallant and excellent officer, and a young man of ability and promise, seized the colours of his regiment after three colour-bearers had been shot down, advanced with them beyond the enemy's works, and fell dead while calling upon his regiment to dash forward on the enemy's columns." Staff officers were the brunt of many jokes, for being out of the line of fire, and that knowledge may have motivated the two courageous adjutants.

Major Oatis commanded the 22nd Mississippi in Featherston's centre. They and much of the brigade encountered a marsh that disrupted their forward progress. Making it worse, Oatis recalled "we were exposed to a murderous enfilade fire of both musketry and artillery from the left." Hood's hopes for an echelon attack were not practical as the men moved in masses as they tried to pass the marsh. Oatis lamented, "In effecting the passage of this marsh I lost many of my bravest and best officers and men."

Two of Featherston's regimental reports explain the brigade was outflanked on the left and the right. The 40th Mississippi was on the left, with Scott's on their left. Lt. Col. George Wallace was wounded, thus Capt. Charles A. Huddleston wrote the report. He gives a detail lacking in other reports, that they held the enemy's line about 25 minutes before retiring. He wrote "that the regiment moving rapidly, reached the enemy's works about seventy-five yards in advance of the right of brigade on our left, thereby subjecting it (the regiment) to a terrific enfilading fire from the enemy's batteries on the left, which decimated the ranks to a very considerable extent." Once the 40th retired back to woods from which they had advanced, they "kept up a brisk fire with the enemy until the darkness of the evening forbid further activity." Scott's Brigade had broken through the enemy's line, but their advance was not far enough to cover Featherston's left.

The real problem was on Loring's right. The report of the 33rd Mississippi (O.R. 38, Part 3, p. 859) was written by Capt. Moses Jackson, as Colonel Drake was killed. The 33rd was on the far right, which gave Jackson a front line experience to explain how Loring's Division had to fall back. "Not being supported on the right, which rested on the edge of the woods, seeing a heavy column in front of us, and hearing commands given by the enemy to flank us on the right, they advanced their left swinging around us, with a charge and a heavy cross-fire. Seeing our perilous condition, I being on the right at my post, I immediately ordered a retreat. After retreating about a quarter of a mile we saw Wright's brigade in a line of battle in the woods at a halt, which should have engaged the enemy on our right. The failure caused our defeat." From Jackson's point of view the blame rested with the brigades on the right not advancing, but the fault was not theirs.

Hood's report places much blame on Hardee when the blame rests with Hood, who stayed in Atlanta during the battle. Hardee's report (O.R. vol. 38, Part 3, p. 698) explains Hood's order to shift a half a division length could not be followed. For "the fact that Cheatham's corps, with which I was to connect, was nearly two miles to my right instead of a division length. Had Hood been on the field the alternative of delaying the attack or leaving an interval between Cheatham's command and my own could have been submitted to him for decision. He was in Atlanta, and in his absence the hazard of leaving an interval of one mile and a half in a line intended to be continuous, and at a point in front of which the enemy was in force and might at any time attack, seemed to me too great to be assumed." Hardee was correct, and Stewart's Corps should not have attacked. But Hood praised Stewart, who "carried out his instructions to the lettre."

Hood's shift caused Hardee's right division under Bate to be shifted into the confusing tangled valley of Clear Creek. Hood's orders to attack in echelon, beginning with Bate on the far right, were flawed. Hardee reported, "Bate, finding no enemy in his immediate front, was directed to find, and if practicable, to turn their flank, but his advance through an almost impenetrable thicket was necessarily slow. Expecting but not hearing Bate's guns I ordered Maney and Cleburne, whose divisions had been substituted for Walker's beaten troops to attack. At the moment when the troops were advancing to assault I received information from General Hood that the enemy were passing and overlapping the extreme right of the army, accompanied by an imperative order to send him a division at once. In obedience to this order I immediately withdrew and sent him Cleburne's division. The withdrawal of a division at the moment when but two were available compelled me to countermand the assault, and the lateness of the hour, which made it impossible to get Bate in position to attack before dark, left no alternative but to give up the attack altogether."

Though Sherman's crossing of Peachtree Creek had failed to take Atlanta, he had more cards up his sleeve. But neither had Hood won a victory. James McNeilly, the chaplain in Walthall's Division, overheard "half a dozen or more generals and colonels" discussing the removal of Johnston. His recollection is in *Confederate Veteran* (Volume 26, p. 471). He wrote, "…but I listened with eager eyes, for I was devoted to 'Old Joe'…General Loring, who was major general commanding a division, was the chief speaker. He said with great emphasis: 'Gentlemen, I say what I know. In the light of what has happened, I am sure that if General Johnston had been left in command ten days longer he would have destroyed General Sherman's army.'" McNeilly went onto explain that Johnston would have delivered the attack a day earlier, and no doubt, if that had been done, the result could have been a Confederate victory. The remarks at least reveal the lack of respect Hood had at this point of his career.

Hood would have done well to have known what a U.S. surgeon knew. William Grinsted later wrote, "The wounds received in this action were of a severe character, the enemy charging boldly. The rebels received were very severely wounded, many having from three to five wounds, a single wound being the exception. Six died the same night they came in, and some 30 subsequently prior to their transportation."

A staff officer in Featherston's Brigade wrote, "The gallantry, rapidity and coolness, with which these noble men moved through that storm of fire, are above all praise. Heroes, patriots, martyrs, their wounds and death attest their spirit, and set the seal to their devotion. They and theirs deserve well of their country. Privates and officers (line and field and staff) all acted well their parts…Death did his work well that day, unutterable, filled all our hearts and enshrouded our command with gloom. God help the homes and comfort the hearts that dark day made desolate and bereaved."

Featherston and Loring showed emotional devastation. The staff officer continued, "Overwhelmed by a sense of the dread slaughter, Gen. Featherston wept, when reporting the carnage to his Division commander, an undemonstrative man, unaccustomed to emotional display, and inured to war's death dealing work, upon Virginia's blood dyed fields, such destruction overcame even him, a veteran, hardened by many arduous campaigns…" General Stewart addressed the corps after the battle and his concluding remark shows his emotional stress. "Let us leave nothing undone that we can do, and this hated, cowardly enemy, who makes war upon women and children, shall be delivered into our hands, that we may execute upon him the vengeance of Heaven for his crimes."

Featherston's infantry had 616 casualties, more than the 390 Scott reported. This was at least partially due to fighting with exposed flanks. Featherston's 616 casualties were 78 killed, 393 wounded, and 145 wounded. The two brigades numbered 2,700 men. Loring claimed "the enemy's official reports estimating those with my division at 2,500 killed and wounded; again, Loring's infantry lost 1,006. Loring no doubt felt Hood had mismanaged the battle, and was responsible for the needless loss of life. Rev. James McNeilly recalled a bitter conversation between Loring and other officers. They knew Johnston had planned to attack on the 19th, when victory would have been likely. The U.S. Army of the Cumberland had only one division from each of its three corps across Peach Tree Creek. All were across on the 20th; hence, Hood lost any advantage.

Seeing the Peach Tree Creek battlefield is worthwhile, as it is, in disconnected pieces. More than a few historians have pieced together driving tours. Over time landmarks change and historic markers are moved. *All the Fighting They Want: The Atlanta Campaign from Peachtree Creek to the City's Surrender, July 18-September 2, 1864* points this out. Author Stephen Davis notes there is a marker, "*Featherston's Brigade.*" From Peachtree Road, Street as it heads toward downtown, take Collier Road to Ardmore Park. Featherston's "moved down the slope N. toward…" When the marker was placed in the '50's it was along Collier Road near the railroad. People reading the marker led to traffic accidents, which led to their move to Ardmore Park. Tanyard Branch Park is nearby and has a marker for "Scott's Brigade." Besides a colorful newer plaque, there are six "very wordy" tablets. They were set in 1964, and the text must be scrutinized. Davis points out they say 4,796 Confederate casualties. The writer accepted Sherman's false number from a postbellum article. As we have seen, Loring disputed Sherman's numbers.

In concluding Peach Tree Creek, the burial places of Loring's Division should be remembered. Jenkins's *The Battle of Peachtree Creek* illustrates they are to be found in Atlanta and further south. Those killed and left on the field were generally buried by U.S. troops, as they held the field. Later, those found were reentered at Oakland Cemetery in Atlanta. Wounded were transported south to hospitals. Macon had the Ocmulgee Hospital and those who died there may be found in Rose Hill Cemetery. Those who died in Columbus may be found at Linewood Cemetery. Wounded captured by the U.S. Army were often moved by train to hospitals in Chattanooga, and may be buried there. More likely they were taken to the enormous hospital complex at Nashville. Those that died were buried in trenches at City Cemetery, and later reentered at Mount Olivet. Some may have been taken to Louisville and be buried there. Prisoners were taken to several prison camps in the United States including Camp Douglas in Chicago and Camp Chase in Columbus, Ohio. Those who died in Chicago may be buried in City Cemetery, and those at Camp Chase in the Camp Chase Confederate Cemetery.

The monument (left) in Oakland Cemetery honours about 2,500 C.S. soldiers buried there. The cornerstone was laid in 1870, and the completed monument dedicated on 26 April 1874. At 65 feet, it was Atlanta's tallest structure. Skyscrapers were not too far off in the future. It is one of the most interesting sites in the city. Though sacred, it has recently been vandalized by criminals, inspired by several organizations, funded by leftist individuals and hate groups.

Another post card from author's collection is of the arch at Camp Chase's prison cemetery. It was mailed to a Virginia address on 30 April 1915. It was one of several prisons where Loring's soldiers were taken. Perhaps some of their mortally wounded are among the 2,260 claimed on the inscription.

Atlanta through battle and bombardment

Hood had needed Cleburne's Division east of Atlanta, to reinforce Cheatham. The Army of the Tennessee had gotten so close to the city that its shells could fall and kill anyone who happened to be below. The battle along Peach Tree Creek was being fought when the first shell fell. People were walking on Ivy Street when a rattle and a whish were heard overhead. Then there was a deafening explosion, and a cloud of dust. A little girl had been walking with her parents. As the dust settled they saw her lying on her face in a puddle of blood. Her mother and father struggled to their feet, and in a moment they realized she had been killed by an artillery shell. Terror stricken civilians were seen running in every direction, trying to get beyond the incoming shells. The girl was not to be the last citizen killed, not the last child. On 3 August *The Atlanta Register* reported, "About 11 o' clock at night Mr. Nelson Warner, the superintendent of the gas works was sleeping, with his six year old daughter beside him. A round shot fell thru the house landing in bed. The child's body was cut in half. Both of his legs were severed at the thighs. He bled to death over the following two hours."

In 20th Century wars U.S. forces would bomb civilian targets. This heritage had been developed against Confederate cities. Atlanta was not the first. Charleston and Vicksburg endured hell for the cause of U.S. imperialism. Even in a short naval bombardment of Natchez a child was killed.

Correspondence of Sherman makes it clear he didn't value the lives of secessionists. Back in January he had written a staff officer in Huntsville, Alabama: "The war which now prevails in our land is essentially a war of races. The Southern people entered into a clear compact of government, but still maintained a species of separate interests, history, and prejudices." He went onto say, "No man will deny that the United States would be benefited by dispossessing a rich prejudiced, hard-headed, and disloyal planter, and substituting in his place a dozen or more patient, industrious, good families, even if they be of foreign birth."

Southern colonies made a mistake in ratifying the U.S. Constitution, as such Northern attitudes indicate. Sherman went onto say that for "persistent secessionists, why death is mercy, and the quicker he or she is disposed of the better. Satan and the rebellious saints of Heaven were allowed a continuous existence in hell merely to swell their just punishment. To such as would rebel against a Government so mild and just as ours was in peace, a punishment equal would not be unjust." Sherman obviously felt justified in shelling innocent civilians for desiring to have their own country, which was what the founding fathers desired when they signed the Declaration. He cared not for women or children. In June he had written Secretary of War Stanton, "But one thing is certain, there is a class of people, men, women, and children, who must be killed or banished, before you can hope for peace…"

The day after Peach Tree Creek, the 21st, Cleburne found his division in one of the hottest fights of its existence. Hood had to try to stop the Yankee advance and had a bold plan. The enemy's left was in the air. Hood decided to order a vast flanking movement in the style of the immortal Stonewall Jackson. This one would be a little longer at 15 miles. But worse, it had to be made overnight by Hardee's Corps. It included Cleburne's Division, exhausted from their day of hard fighting.

Hood hoped Hardee's attack would fall on the left-rear of McPherson's Army of the Tennessee. But the pieces on the chessboard had been moved before Hardee could make the long exhausting march. His divisions found U.S. brigades entrenched and prepared to repulse his attacks. Cheatham made a frontal assault, and though his troops broke through, they could not resist a counterattack. The resulting stalemate was initially perceived as a victory in Richmond, but as casualties (at least 5,500, if not 8,000) were reported concerns rose over Hood's aggression. Nor could the U.S. be too pleased. Sherman reported 3,722 in repulsing Hood, but one included a favourite general. McPherson had commanded the Army of the Tennessee, and command passed to Howard. He had commanded the 4th Corps in the Army of the Cumberland.

Ezra Church

Sherman's failure to get into Atlanta from the east, by battle and bombardment, led him to send five divisions west of the city to break the *Atlanta and West Point Railroad* north of East Point. Hood quickly discerned the movement. Cheatham had temporarily commanded Hood's old corps, but Lt. Gen. Stephen Dill Lee had just arrived to take command. Lee had not commanded infantry in an offensive action, though he had just been defeated in Mississippi fighting cavalry dismounted in infantry style attacks. Hood's report is clear, that he wanted Lee to hold the Lick Skillet Road. Lee "was to move his forces so as to prevent the enemy from gaining the road. He was ordered to hold the enemy in check on a line nearly parallel with the Lick Skillet road, running through to Ezra Church. General Lee, finding that the enemy had already gained that position, engaged him with the intention to recover that line." Lee's report says he was to "check the enemy." It seems to imply block the enemy's advance; however, it did not prohibit an attack in order to keep them off the road. Lee took two divisions west of Atlanta to block the enemy advance toward the *Macon & Western*.

The ensuing battle on 28 July was known as Ezra Church, for the small Methodist church along the Lick Skillet Road. Lee wasted little time ordering one of his divisions to attack. The Yankees were already dug in and had little trouble repelling the attack. Lee ordered a second division forward, not coordinated with the other. It was repulsed as well. Back in Atlanta Hood realized Lee was doing more than blocking the U.S. advance and sent a dispatch "…not to do more fighting than necessary…" Stewart arrived with Walthall's Division followed by Loring's. Walthall was ordered to attack and failed as had the others. Why did Lee send one division to attack a line of five entrenched divisions?

Loring got orders to deploy and had come to the field on the run. J.P. Cannon thought they "had run about four miles and were quite out of breath…" A soldier in the 3rd Mississippi recalled, "General Lorin' came up in a hurry and ordered us to the left of Lee's Corps and to try and drive the enemy off a hill that they had dug into. The division spread into battle rapidly. The Yankees had us like sittin' ducks in a pond, in the open, and we could only see the smoke from their guns…" A.P. Stewart was wounded, and a few minutes later Loring too. The soldier continued, "As we was movin' into regimental battle lines, General Lorin' wuz shot and toppled from his horse."

An Illinois soldier thought the attackers "fought manfully like Americans." He continued, "Why it was perfect murder. We slaughter them by the thousands but Hood continues to hurl his broken, bleeding, battalions against our immovable lines with all the fury of a maniac. Reason seems dethroned and Despair alone seems to rule the counsels within the walls of Atlanta." All the more peculiar is that Hood and Lee blamed the failure on a "lack of spirit" by their troops. General French was on target writing, "The attack was a failure because it was fought by detailed weak attacks instead of a consolidated force."

Westview Cemetery is on the Ezra Church battlefield, where Confederate units advanced and Darden's Battery was positioned. Westview opened in 1884 and our dead were largely from the Confederate Soldiers' Home in Atlanta. Lt. Edward Clingman was killed in the battle and was reburied in Westview in 1960.

To Hood's defense he had ordered Lee to block the advance. Stewart was acting under Lee's orders when he galloped toward Loring, waving him on. With both generals shot Walthall took command of the corps. Hood had sent Stewart a dispatch, similar to the one to Lee, which Walthall returned with no remarks. Clearly the battle was over before Loring's Division was fully engaged. Walthall didn't think the enemy's line could have been taken with double the force of attackers. Confederate losses were close to 3,000 while the U.S. admitted to 632. Though the U.S. Army had failed to cut the railroad, they had won another defensive victory.

Cavalry raids, Utoy Creek, and increased shelling of Atlanta

As Ezra Church was being fought, Sherman had launched a deep "pincer" movement to the south of Atlanta. The objective was to break both the *Atlanta & West Point Railroad*, coming up from Alabama, and the *Macon & Western Railroad*. Sherman's joint orders to the division under McCook and the two under Stoneman read in part, "…The railroad when reached must be substantially destroyed for a space of 2 to 5 miles, telegraph wires pulled down as far as possible and hid in water or carried away."

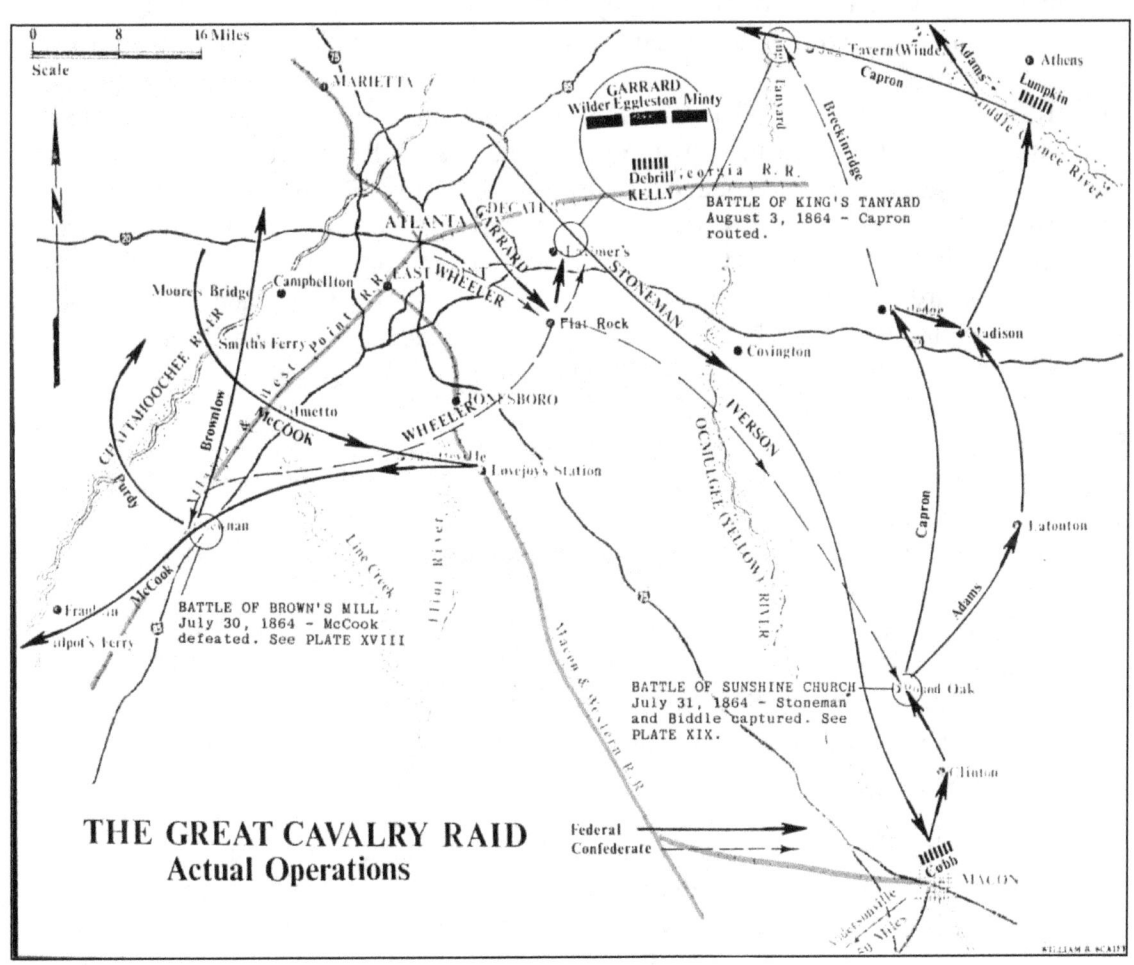

Sherman hoped the pincers would meet at Lovejoy's Station, 26 miles south of Atlanta. From there they might move south toward Macon, tearing up the railroad as they went. General Stoneman had proposed freeing officers in a prison there, and then continuing 50 miles to the southwest to liberate some 30,000 prisoners at Andersonville. If Stoneman broke the railroad, Sherman added, "You may, after having fulfilled my present orders, send General Garrard back to the left flank of the army, and proceed with your command proper to accomplish both or either of the objects named (Macon or Andersonville)…"

Stoneman left Decatur at dawn on the 27th and quickly proved he was no team player. Breaking railroads had less attraction for his ego than liberating prisoners. He rode for Macon with his 2,112 troopers. When confronted near Macon by some 1,500 citizen volunteers and militia, Stoneman lost his nerve. He turned back and found his way blocked at Sunshine Church north of Macon. There were three small Confederate cavalry brigades under Brig. Gen. Alfred Iverson, amounting to only 1,300 men. Iverson, though a Georgian, had commanded a North Carolina infantry brigade in the Army of Northern Virginia. They were shot to pieces on the first day of Gettysburg. Lee felt it was much Iverson's fault and exiled him to Georgia. Iverson did much to restore his reputation at Sunshine Church when he virtually destroyed Stoneman's larger force. His force captured about 500 Yankees, including Stoneman, who found himself in the Macon prison.

Garrard's cavalry division was the largest to make the raid with 3,800 troopers. He told Stoneman he would "try to carry out all order," but was not fully committed to the raid. Garrard never got near the railroad and returned to the army. Sherman wrote, General Garrard…went seven miles; saw some horsemen and came back." He had not even tried to reach the Macon railroad, and that was unforgiveable to Sherman. He wired Thomas, "General Garrard will not attempt anything if there be a show of resistance." Thus ended Garrard's cavalry command, but at Nashville he commanded an infantry division. They would be engaged with Loring's Division on the second day.

The western thrust of the U.S. cavalry pincer movement was McCook's 3,600 man division. They tore up about two miles of the *Atlanta & West Point*. They reached Lovejoy's Station on the *Macon & Western* on 29 July. Stoneman was nowhere to be seen so McCook turned back. Jackson's cavalry division discerned it, and he advised Wheeler, "…I will gain their flank about Newnan. If you can follow and push them in rear, it would be well." The Yankee cavalry was defeated near Newnan at Brown's Mill. Amidst the defeat McCook cried "every man for himself." Remnants drifted back to Sherman. Official returns on 8 August show the division to have 1,139 of the 3,600 who set out to break the railroads. Sherman wired Halleck, "I can hardly believe it, as he had 3,000 picked cavalry."

Sherman was disappointed with the cavalry defeats and attempted to break the railroads, again with infantry. Jackson's cavalry continued their fine scouting and on 5 August let Hood know. A new entrenched line was thrown up to confront the enemy movement. The next day the enemy infantry was thrown back at Utoy Creek. Hood couldn't enjoy the victory though. Sherman reacted to the defeat with orders: "Telegraph to Chattanooga and have two 30 pound Parrotts sent down on cars with 1,000 shells and ammunition. Put them in your best positions and knock down the buildings of the town."

Johnston had begged for Forrest's cavalry to be turned loose on the rails supplying Sherman. Brice's Crossroads in June and Harrisburg-Tupelo in July had preoccupied Forrest. Holding eastern Mississippi and its food supply was obvious, but it was much of the defense for the munitions industry in Alabama. Letting Forrest go was not so simple. Wheeler and Jackson had essentially taken Sherman's cavalry out. Hood decided to turn Wheeler loose on the railroads.

Hood gave Wheeler overly ambitious orders. As he had ordered Hardee on too long of a flank march east of Atlanta, Hood couldn't plan a reasonable campaign objective. Had he just ordered Wheeler to raid up the *Western & Atlantic* and return, reasonable results might have been obtained. But Hood ordered Wheeler to cross the Tennessee River, west of Chattanooga, and raid the two lines coming out of Nashville. Wheeler led some 4,000 cavalrymen north on 10 August. He did little damage and found the Tennessee too high to ford. So he disobeyed orders with a useless raid, northeast into East Tennessee.

Wheeler swung north around Knoxville and finally crossed the Cumberland Plateau for Middle Tennessee. He did minimal damage to the *Nashville & Chattanooga* before swinging over toward the *Nashville & Decatur* (a.k.a. *Alabama & Tennessee*). There were several fights with U.S. forces before he struggled to escape over the Tennessee into Alabama. Wheeler had worn out his command and accomplished little.

On 12 August Hood temporarily attached Scott's Brigade to Cleburne's Division. The victory at Utoy Creek made reinforcing the defenses in that area critical. Cannon wrote, "The enemy is moving large forces to our left, no doubt endeavoring to swing around our rear and cut the railroads on which we depend for supplies. Our brigade was detached and sent to East Point, six miles southwest of the city, and attached to Cleburne's division, making us the extreme left of the army." Shoup directed Scott's Brigade to "occupy the strong work at East Point." Again on the 16th Hood advised A.P. Stewart that Scott's was at East Point. The next day Shoup advised Hardee, "General Hood desires you to notify Scott's brigade to be in readiness to move by rail at dawn, if it should prove necessary." On following days Hood notifies Cleburne several times to have Scott's and Granbury's brigades ready to move. Was Scott's being designated as a brigade Hood relied on?

Stewart had been recovering from his wound in Savannah, as his wife was there. It is possible Loring had gone there too. Stewart's biographer pointed out they barely missed capture when the train bearing them south from Atlanta had to turn back to avoid U.S. cavalry raiders. Stewart returned to resume corps command on 15 August. They were positioned northwest of Atlanta. Early on the 17th he rode to French's headquarters, located behind a redoubt. They rode the line and then returned for breakfast. The redoubt was a favourite target for enemy gunners, causing Stewart to linger rather than be shot.

Stewart no doubt visited Loring's batteries and discussed the enemy's shelling, for Sergeant Eggleston commented on the 18th: "Our artillery opened on the enemy this morning at daylight and attempted to learn the changes that had been made in the positions of his guns if any. They replied to our batty with a few guns doing no damage."

Captain William D. Gale had been assistant adjutant general for Bishop Polk. He was also his son-in-law and had taken leave to escort the body for burial. He wrote his wife on the 19th: "Genl Stewart has returned and assumed command. We all like him very much indeed. He has a son about 18 with him as A.D.C. The Genl is one of the most natural men I ever saw. Perfectly well bred and highly educated, very quiet and sedate, a thorough soldier and in all his actions, precise and military."

The artillery pounding of Atlanta continued, day and night, as Sherman decided to make one more attempt to break the rails with cavalry. Hood believed the victories over the U.S. cavalry had so weakened them, that he dispatched Wheeler to raid northward. But Sherman had another cavalry division, Kilpatrick's. Sherman considered him a damned fool, but the type who might break at least one of the two rail lines to the south. A break of about three miles was made, before Kilpatrick had to retire, having been attacked by Jackson's cavalry. Kilpatrick thought it would take ten days to repair the damage. But in two days, on the 23rd, Sherman wrote, "we saw trains coming into Atlanta from the south, when I became more than ever convinced that cavalry could not, or WOULD NOT, work hard enough to disable a railroad properly…"

On 25 August Sherman's artillery suddenly fell silent. Hood, his army, and Atlanta hoped that it meant Sherman had admitted defeat and was falling back. Sherman, like his friend Grant, wasn't inclined to retreat after defeats. He left one corps to protect the railroad and river crossing points. With his overwhelming force he swung first west and then south to break and hold the railroads. Jackson's cavalry detected the move, and Hood knew what was up. Once again, Hood stayed in Atlanta, sending Hardee to confront the enemy.

Hood seemed to rely on Scott's Brigade to gather intelligence. On the 27th he advised Cleburne, "Generals Lee and Stewart report enemy gone from their fronts. Send some of Scott's men to ascertain facts in your front. Keep your own division well in hand…" As the enemy move toward Jonesborough they were closely observed by Hood's cavalry. Sherman's three armies were headed toward the headwaters of the Flint River on the morning of the 30th. Hood advised Hardee, "When you move let Scott's brigade go to East Point." Cannon's entry for 31 August began: "Just at dusk last night we received orders to go to Jonesboro with all possible haste and had a hard, tiresome march all night, reaching the vicinity of Jonesboro before daylight, when our brigade was immediately ordered back to rejoin our division. We have been attached to Cleburne's division for the past two or three weeks." It isn't clear why Scott's had been selected for the temporary assignment. Perhaps it was to leave Featherston with less responsibility. On the 31st, as Jonesborough was being fought, Hood communicated directly to Scott, advising him, "Be careful not to allow yourself to be cut off. If forced to fall back retire skirmishing. Use sound judgment. Keep us informed." Hood must have had faith in the brigade.

Jonesborough and evacuation of Atlanta

Hardee's offensive was underway against the Army of the Tennessee on 31 August as Sherman's two other armies were breaking the *Macon & Western* at two different points. Hood desired a dawn attack at Jonesborough. But as at Atlanta, another overnight march was destined to fail. Hardee ran into U.S. troops and had to detour. Lee coming up behind Hardee was still waiting for his last three brigades to arrive at 1:30. Another complication was an interval between his corps and Hardee's, under Cleburne. It required a shift of a two-division front. As at Peachtree Creek the delays gave the enemy more time to fortify. The proposed dawn assault had become a 2 p.m. one. Lee was to wait to hear Cleburne's artillery before attacking. Such a signal was confused and failed at Dallas and here again. The attacks were not coordinated, so Lee's attack was bloodily repulsed. Cleburne didn't coordination in the attacks of his divisions in his only time as a corps commander.

Hood mistakenly thought the greatest danger was at Atlanta, and ordered Lee's tired troops to march back after dark. Around 2:00 a.m. Lee was halted at Rough and Ready with orders to position his corps to cover the evacuation of Atlanta. While the Army of the Tennessee had been fighting at Jonesborough, the Army of the Cumberland and Army of the Ohio were marching for a rendezvous. Lee had had to march between them, and it was something of a miracle that he made it. Hardee was left with just his own corps to fight another day. Hardee still faced part of the Army of the Tennessee, but also two fresh corps from the Army of the Cumberland. Hardee's three tired divisions barely held on. That morning, back in Atlanta, Hood began packing up what could be removed by wagons. Many warehouses, especially those with food, were opened so citizens could take what they desired. Train cars of ammunition were blown up.

On 2 September six U.S. infantry corps prepared to finish off Hardee. "Old Reliable, as he was known to some, had vanished in the night. Though his soldiers must have been exhausted, they made the trek six miles south to Lovejoy's Station. A new entrenched line was made, as they wondered what next. About 4:00 the Yankees tested the line, and were quickly repulsed. Sherman took a look at the line and felt it could not have been better constructed had there been a week to build them. There would be no battle.

Up at Atlanta, Mayor James Calhoun and a group of citizens rode out Marietta Street with a white flag. They met a reconnaissance party from the U.S. troops that came down from the Chattahoochee. The mayor made out a note to the nearest U.S. general, "Sir, The fortune of war has placed Atlanta I your hands. As mayor of the city of Atlanta I ask protection for non-combatants and private property." Sherman learned of it on the 3rd, and decided the campaign was over. He had failed to destroy the Army of Tennessee, so taking Atlanta would suffice for the moment.

Loring's Division had the sad experience of seeing the destruction of military property during the evacuation. J.P. Cannon's entry for the 3rd included, "We traveled all night and at daybreak could see the lights from the fires in the city. Daylight brought no rest; on, on, on all day and all night again we dragged our weary limbs and reached Lovejoy Station on September 3rd. We had been two days and nights without sleep or rest, except a few short stops. No doubt Sherman thought he had us 'bagged' this time, but by taking a very circuitous route, passing around the Federal army, which is still at Jonesboro, we reached our destination without any serious mishap." Lee's Corps also arrived on the 3rd. Hood had saved the army and must have felt relief to find Sherman actually disappear from his front, off to occupy Atlanta.

A week after Jonesborough, on 8 September, Sherman resolved to "make Atlanta a pure military garrison or depot, with no civilian population. His orders began: "The city of Atlanta, being exclusively required for war like purposes will at once be vacated by all except the armies of the United States and such civilian employees as may be retained…" Hood wrote to Sherman that the expulsion order "transcends, in studied and ingenious cruelty, all acts ever brought to my attention in the dark history of this war." It made no difference to Sherman. From 12 to 21 September a total of 709 adults (mostly women), 867 children, and 79 servants were taken by train to Rough and Ready, and dumped off.

Confederate citizens and soldiers were disgusted by Sherman's cruelty, but not the voters in the United States. Lincoln's re-election had been in doubt before Atlanta fell. But now most U.S. voters agreed the end was in sight. Had McClellan won, he would not have been inaugurated until March 1865, so the end of the war would have been on the horizon anyway. But for war weary Confederates, whether civilian or military, that was not yet apparent. They did know they could not fight Lincoln as they had for another four years.

<u>Loring returned to his division</u>
With both Stewart and Loring wounded at Ezra Church, Maj. Gen. French was in line to command the corps. He said, "but to my surprise I found that Hood had placed Cheatham in command. I wrote to Hood in regard to the matter. Hood's act was in keeping with the intriguing so ruinous to this army, and I asked to be relieved from serving in it any longer." French's request was turned down.

Loring's wound at Ezra Church led to Featherston with temporary division command again. He had not been severely tested holding the far right at Kennesaw Mountain. J.P. Cannon's entry for 31 July says Cheatham got temporary command of the corps, with no mention of Featherston. Cheatham had just turned over temporary command of Hood's old corps to Stephen D. Lee. Hood wired President Davis, on the 29th, that he wanted John Brown promoted to temporary rank of major-general so that he might command Loring's Division. But Bate was wounded on the Utoy Creek line and Brown took temporary command of Bate's. Bragg learned Maj. Gen. Franklin Gardner, who had done well holding Port Hudson in 1863, had been exchanged. Bragg wanted him to fill in for Stewart or Loring. Gardner went to Richard Taylor, for on 11 August Loring was doing well enough to be expected back. Also, Stewart returned on the 13th.

Featherston might have been promoted and given a division command in July. Fellow Mississippian Edward Walthall was promoted to major general instead and given a division command. Featherston had been a brigadier since March 1862 with the Army of Virginia. Walthall was not a brigadier until December 1862. Walthall proved himself at the division level, and Featherston might have too.

Loring returned to command on 10 September according to a 3rd Mississippi soldier. "We were passed in review yesterday by Uncle Billy Loring. He has just returned to command the division having entirely recovered from his wound of the 28th of July…I would rather be reviewed by General Loring than any other general." Cannon made a similar entry, but for 14 September. "Division review today. General Loring mounted on his old roan, rode down the line, welcomed by cheers from the whole division. He had just returned, having been wounded on July 28th."

President Davis visits the army at Palmetto

Four days after Atlanta fell, on 6 September, Hood wrote Davis: "I am of good heart and feel that we shall yet succeed. The army is in need of a little rest. After removing the prisoners form Andersonville, I think we should, as soon as practicable, place our army upon the communications of the enemy, drawing our supplies from the *West Point and Montgomery Railroad.* Looking to this, I shall at once proceed to strongly fortify Macon. Please do not fail to give me advice at all times. It is my desire to do the best for you and my country." Davis saw it was time to give Hood advice in person, as in the past.

Davis visited the Army of Tennessee in Murfreesborough in December 1862. He might have relieved Bragg of command. Perhaps worse, he sent Stevenson's Division to Mississippi. Bragg might have won the most overwhelming battlefield victory of the war with a reserve division. Davis visited the army after Chickamauga in October 1863. Then Longstreet was allowed to go off on an offensive toward Knoxville. That pretty well insured Bragg didn't have the numbers to fight the U.S. Army outside Chattanooga.

There had been an armistice while the citizens were being evacuated. Before it expired, on the 18th, Hood began moving to Palmetto, on the *West Point and Montgomery*. Davis arrived for his third visit to the Army of Tennessee on 25 September. As in the previous visits he addressed complaints over a commanding general. This time there were too few troops to fear he would take troops from the army. Davis had to listen as Hood asserted he had been placed in command at Atlanta with "an untenable" military position. That doesn't seem to reconcile with his immediate offensive thrust at Peach Tree Creek.

Hood had been put into command mid-campaign and that was a dilemma. But unlike Lee, who took the blame for defeats, Hood didn't. He told Davis that "in the battle of July 20th we failed on account of General Hardee…Our failure on the 31st of August, I am convinced, was greatly owing to him." And he had blamed Hardee for Atlanta on the 22nd. Every time Hood pointed to blame Hardee, three fingers were pointing back at him. Hardee didn't want to serve under Hood either. Davis agreed to relieve Hardee and placed him in command of the Department of South Carolina, Georgia, and Florida. Hardee's Corps became Cheatham's. Davis could move generals around. But Hood blamed the soldiers for "a disgraceful effort." Davis could not solve that opinion.

J.P. Cannon wrote, "President Davis visited us on the 25th, and the next day inspected the army. When riding along the lines many of the men called out loudly, 'Give us Johnston,' or 'Send General Johnston back and we will whip Sherman yet..' and many similar remarks to which the President made no reply."

Of course Davis couldn't imagine putting Johnston back in command, and the idea of putting Beauregard in command was about as disagreeable. He had also relieved him, after Shiloh. Beauregard's stock had shined since then, and Davis knew it. He met with the Creole general at Augusta on 3 October. Beauregard would have liked an active field command. Instead he got the "Military Division of the West" theatre command, over the Army of Tennessee, and Taylor's Department of Alabama, Mississippi, and East Louisiana. Beauregard could command when "present with either army." It turned out he would be too busy for that.

Moving north through Georgia

Hood's abandonment of Atlanta, the supply base and railroad hub, created a logistics dilemma. *Ploughshares into Swords: Josiah Gorgas and Confederate Ordinance* explains: "When one considers the general chaos prevailing throughout the supply organization, the job done in keeping Hood supplied is seen to rank as an accomplishment worthy of Carnot." Georgia's Governor Brown pursued his usual selfish policies of refusing to share. An ordinance offer at West Point, an intermediate supply base, reported he had no ammunition. But Brig. Gen. Robert Charles Tyler was there to oversee an earthwork constructed to guard the West Point Railroad. On 28 September he reported he had found 400,000 percussion caps. Another 2,000,000 were to be dispatched from Virginia, so that Hood had a "comforting number with which to start a campaign.

Loring's Division left Palmetto and moved north, west of Atlanta, to the route of the *Western & Atlantic Railroad.* Featherston reported that his brigade reached Big Shanty (Kennesaw today) on 3 October. He said the enemy held some houses along the railroad, and had converted the depot into a blockhouse. One of Featherston's soldiers recalled, "At Big Shanty, Ga. our brigade was called out front. General Lorin' galloped up to General Featherston, stood up in his stirrups, pointed toward Big Shanty Station, took his hat off and moved about sizin' up the situation, returned a salute to his junior, and trotted back toward the artillery and the first brigade."

Featherston was ordered to attack, which he did with much success. The Yankees had cut loopholes to fire from. Featherston's volleys made it obvious to them they could be overwhelmed, and a white flag was put out. Featherston wrote, "All of the enemy who could not make their escape on the east side of the railroad in the direction of Marietta, were captured-about fifty in number." Featherston reported his own loss as twenty, killed and wounded.

Loring's Division was a little farther north at Acworth on the morning of 4 October. Featherston said the enemy was surrounded by the brigades of Scott and Adams. His brigade was in reserve. "A surrender was demanded and promptly granted, some two hundred of the enemy surrendering." A lettre from Col. James R. Binford, of the 15th Mississippi, was quoted in *Confederate Veteran* in 1902 (Volume 10, page 457). He had written, "We secured 236 prisoners. I remember the number so well because Gen. Adams

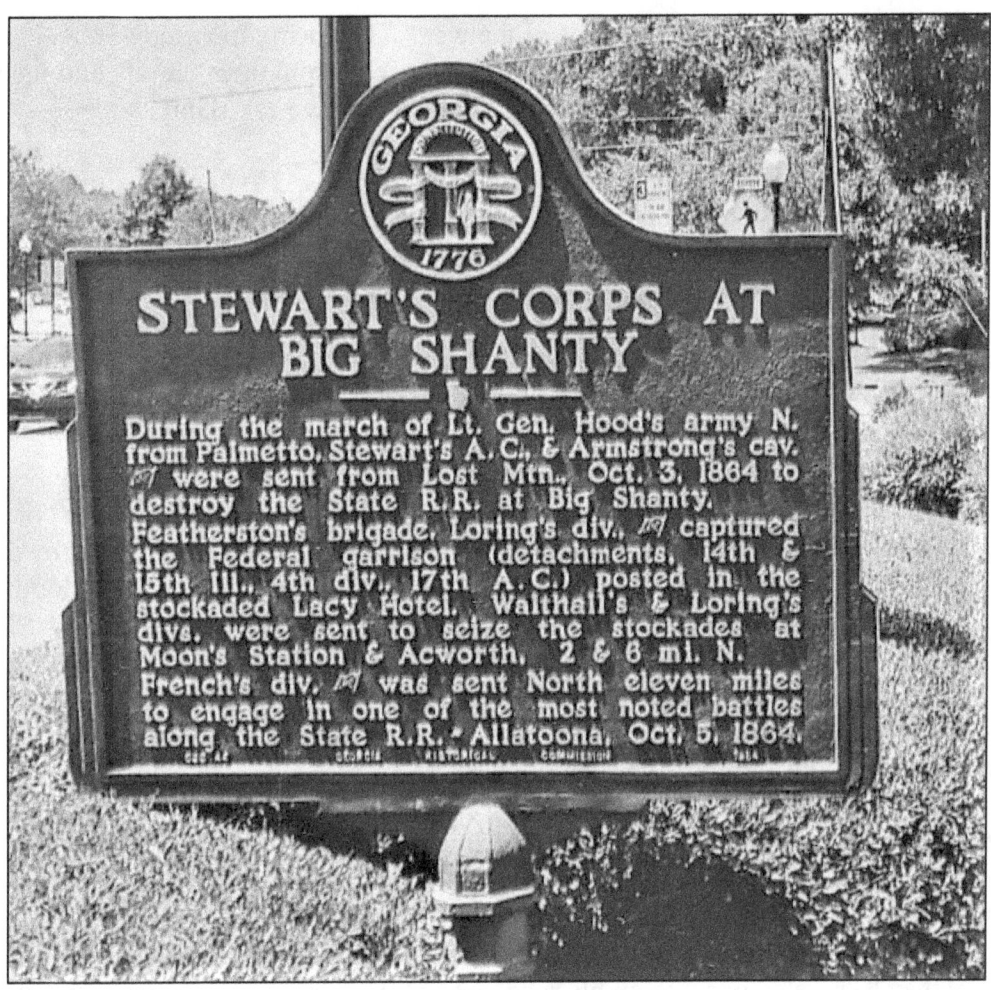

put his brigade in line and then told me to put the Fifteenth Mississippi one hundred paces in front, and said, 'I have sent one of my staff (Maj. Pat Henry, Inspector General) to demand surrender and if they refuse, I want you to charge and take that brick house they occupy.' It was a two-story brick, with an open field in front and a ditch about eight feet wide and six feet deep about thirty feet from the house. I thought (in my wicked heart) it was h---, but told Gen. Adams I would do it. As I reviewed the situation I thought probably I had told him a lie, and almost prayed for the scamps to surrender; and when it was announced that they had done so, I felt relieved and as if my life was saved by their surrender. Gen. Adams then remarked to me that as I was selected to make the charge he thought it right for my regiment to march up and receive the prisoners. We pulled 236 out of that building, and besides captured some horses, stores, and rations. After lying in the rain all the night before, and making this capture without firing a gun, my men felt so good that they concluded to celebrate. We were hungry and wet, and enjoyed the sutler's supplies greatly, which included substantial refreshments."

Featherston wrote, "French's Division left Big Shanty and passed through Acworth to attack a well-fortified enemy garrison at Allatoona. French with about 3,200 soldiers attacked on the 5th. The 1,994 troop garrison repelled French's vicious assaults. Author William Scaife wrote, "Casualties were extremely heavy on both sides in what was one of the most desperately contested battles of the war." The enemy reported 706 and French reported 799. This was about 30% of the troops engaged. From there Hood continued up the railroad tearing up the tracks that supplied Sherman, down at Atlanta.

Wheeler had been sent off on this mission back on 10 August. He finally returned to meet Hood near Cedartown on 8 October. His absence of two months was a failure on the part of both Hood and Wheeler. Had his raiding concentrated on some point in Georgia he might have shut down Sherman's supply line. Furthermore, his service to the Army of Tennessee was near its end. He was about to find most of his cavalry detached to confront the vengeful, hateful invasion of the U.S. Army march for Savannah. Hood would retain Jackson's Division of two brigades, and be joined by Forrest in Alabama.

Beauregard knew Davis had approved Hood's plan to operate on Sherman's supply line. He caught up with Hood at Cave Spring on 9 October. Beauregard agreed to the concept of a raid in force against along the *Western & Atlantic.* Hood had been supplied by the *Atlanta & West Point,* at Palmetto, connecting back to Montgomery. But with Hood moving north the supplies needed a new base, at Jacksonville, Alabama. Beauregard set this up using the *Alabama & Tennessee River (s?) Railroad*. It came out of Selma, which had become a manufacturing centre in the Confederate heartland. The eastern terminus was in the Blue Mountain-Jacksonville area. The later place was his headquarters, where he worked on making it Hood's new supply base.

Sergeant Eggleston explained that on the 9th Cowan's Battery was camped at Cedartown. Loring's Division was on the expedition against the Western & Atlantic with one battery. The balance of the artillery and supply train was left behind. On the 10th Cowan's passed through Cave Springs, and on into Alabama. They traveled fifteen miles that day. The next day they "Traveled over miserable roads in a poor barren piney woods country. Made 16 miles today & camped near the Coosa River."

J.P. Cannon wrote, "On the 10th of October we passed through the battlefield of New Hope Church. This battle was fought on the 25th of May, when the trees were in full leaf, and by getting on this elevated place we could see the line-of-battle stretching out for miles, and trace the exact positions of the two armies by deadened timber from one quarter to half-mile in width." This was a unique experience for an Army of Tennessee soldier to visit one of their battlefields during the war. Eggleston, with Cowan's, had passed it four days before, and "saw acres of timber killed by minnie balls."

Cannon continued, "I had often heard it remarked as being strange that so few men were killed in, considering the number of shots fired, but here was a visible solution of the mystery. The trees between the lines were literally torn to pieces on both sides and, while quite a number of bullets struck as low as a man's head, a large majority of them ranged from 10, 20, and 30 feet from the ground, proving that most of us, under excitement, aimed too high." Many of the bullets had hit soldiers, but no doubt many aimed too high.

Hood's army emerged from the woods of their earlier battles on 12 October. The enemy was protecting the railroad bridge over the Oostanaula with an earthwork fortification.

Hood demanded the surrender of the garrison of some 700 soldiers. The Yankee replied, "If you want it come and take it." Hood decided to go on up the railroad instead. One of Featherston's men wrote, "We reached the R.R. at Resaca...and tore it up as far as Tunnel Hill above Dalton. We stayed all night at Dalton on the night of the 13th. We burnt all the ties and bent iron, and destroyed a great deal of new ties and timber..."

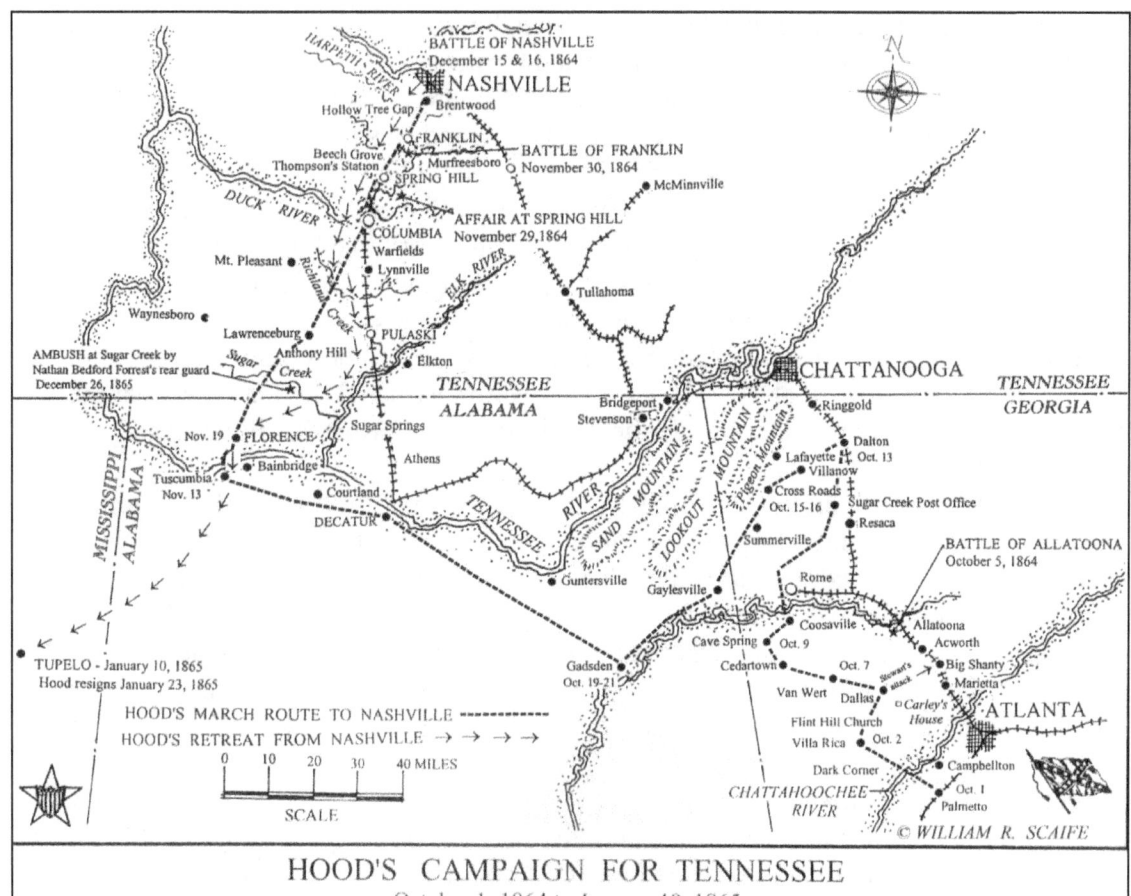

HOOD'S CAMPAIGN FOR TENNESSEE
October 1, 1864 to January 10, 1865

Scaife's map shows the long, difficult trek made by the Army of Tennessee from southwest of Atlanta, then up toward Chattanooga, across Alabama, and then to the outskirts of Nashville. It was all the more difficult in having to cross the Tennessee twice, and then south to Tupelo. As Atlanta was the nucleus of manufacturing in Georgia, and the supply base, it is something that the army didn't starve. Tuscumbia was to be the new base, eventually. Yankee Thomas inherited a well-established base at Nashville. When it was time to fight, he went to the hotel lobby and checked out.

Dalton was a little over twenty miles south of Tennessee and within thirty of enemy held Chattanooga. Hood decided to move west, toward Alabama, and wait for Sherman to attack him. He consulted the higher ranking officers and found they unanimously agreed they were too outnumbered to risk a battle. In 1880 Hood wrote, in *Advance and Retreat*, "In this dilemma, I conceived the plan of marching into Tennessee with a hope to establish our line eventually in Kentucky..." The Kentucky general was not naming

Nashville as an objective, and would not for over a month. But in his 1880 volume, he claimed to be thinking of defeating Thomas and Schofield and capturing their supplies at Nashville before crossing the Cumberland and moving into Kentucky.

Beauregard was still at Jacksonville on 17 October where he officially published his assumption of command of the Military Division of the West. In his typical glorious language he stated the upcoming "efforts to drive the enemy from our soil, and establish the independence of our country." He had made the arrangements for the new base before he left on the 19th to join the army. Hood had moved into Alabama and continued west to Gadsden without notifying Beauregard. Obviously Hood was not inclined to share details so Beauregard began to fear he lacked the responsibility to command the army. Hood said he planned to move north and cross the Tennessee River at Guntersville. Beauregard authorized the move on the evening on the 21st. On the north bank it would be a short march to Stevenson, the junction of the two railroads allowing Sherman's movement of supplies to Chattanooga. The *Memphis & Charleston* had it eastern terminus, as it connected to the *Nashville and Chattanooga*. Hood wanted to be supplied on the former line, with his base along it at Tuscumbia. Beauregard instructed Taylor to see that the lines to Tuscumbia be put in running order. This was a tall order as will be seen.

Hood began the march up to Guntersville without his pontoons. They had been left at the Coosa River and somehow forgotten. Beauregard sent orders to have them brought forward, no doubt incredulous at Hood's lack of planning. He then started north to join the army, but found once again Hood had changed direction. He later wrote that Forrest was still in West-Tennessee and could not join him so far east. Hood told Beauregard the crossing at Guntersville was too heavily guarded. He was then bound for Decatur, which we will see he found the enemy entrenched and not inclined to evacuate.

Sherman had begun pursuit and found Hood's twists and turns hard to follow. He got to Resaca on the 14th, two days late. He hated this type of campaign. Trying to hold Atlanta seemed as hard as taking it. And he had to worry about Tennessee. He had sent Thomas up to Nashville in late September. Forrest had raided out of north Alabama up the *Nashville & Decatur Railroad*. It had also allowed supply trains to keep moving. On the 20th Sherman's columns got to Gaylesville. Hood was about 30 miles southwest at Gadsden. Sherman's pursuit ended. Telegraph connections between Chattanooga and Atlanta were restored the next day. On the 27th trains could run again on the *Western & Atlantic*. Hood's raid had shut it down for over three weeks.

On the 28th Sherman was still at Gaylesville, and learned Hood had left Gadsden for Decatur. Sherman decided to end his pursuit of Hood, and return to Atlanta. Sherman later wrote, "I could not guess his movements as I could those of Johnston, who was a sensible man and only did sensible things…he (Hood) could turn and twist like a fox and wear out my army in pursuit…so divining the object of his movement against our communications, which had thus far been rapid and skillful, I detached all the reinforcements necessary to enable Thomas to defend Tennessee and began my systematic preparations for resuming the offensive against Georgia."

5-Across Alabama and into Tennessee

The Search for a Tennessee River Crossing

Sherman knew north Alabama had suffered at the hands of the U.S. Army, going back to April 1862. He said, "I know that the country about Decatur is bare of provisions, and inferred Hood would have to move westward to draw his food and stores. His men are all grumbling: the first thing prisoners asked for is something to eat." Indeed Hood had to reach Tuscumbia and hope the railroads would be operating.

J.P. Cannon recalled "rations, which had been short ever since we left Lovejoy, had about given out and we were unable to get subsistence from the country. So we turned down the river…" They had last been supplied by a railroad while at Palmetto. Once they reached Tuscumbia they expected to receive supplies on the *Memphis & Charleston*. Though it was not fully repaired, part of it ran east from the *Mobile & Ohio*, at Corinth.

Benjamin LaFayette Smith, a soldier in the 43rd Mississippi of Adams's Brigade, wrote, "Finally Hood started north towards Decatur, Ala., tearing up and burning the cross ties as he marched. When we reached Decatur we had a skirmish with the enemy in which Adjt. Sykes and several more were killed. We remained there all night and the next day started to march west. We soon heard we were going to Tuscumbia…" The railroad they tore up was the part of the *Memphis & Charleston* that led to Chattanooga. While the more direct *Nashville & Chattanooga* was Sherman's primary supply line, trains often returned to Nashville toward Decatur, and then north to Nashville.

Featherston reported they reached Decatur, Alabama on 26 October. Decatur is on the south bank of the Tennessee River, and was the point where the *Memphis & Charleston* crossed the river. There were about 3,000 U.S. troops there in an entrenched line that made a half circle on the south side of Decatur. Each flank rested on the river. There were two fortifications. There were 1,600 yards of rifle pits, with parapets. French wrote, "Loring's Division took position near the defensive works and commenced firing with his batteries on a fort in front."

Hood spent the 27th establishing his line confronting the enemy. On the 28th there was a U.S. sortie. One Yankee recalled, "The affair did not last much more than twenty minutes, and the colored boys had to fall down along the water's edge under the bank of the river, while the enemy ran along above them, and shot down on them." Apparently Featherston's Brigade should get the credit. Also Eggleston, with Cowan's, reported they engaged two gun boats at 4:00 p.m. They fired 32 rounds, striking them several times.

Featherston wrote, "On the 28th, the enemy made an advance upon my front taking shelter and passing up under the river bank until getting within some two hundred yards of the line when they emerged from the cover and marched to the front. The enemy's force could not have been less than one brigade. My skirmish line was driven in but the enemy was easily repulsed by the main line of battle and the skirmish line soon reestablished." Featherston reported his casualties were 27 in killed and wounded."

Hood abandoned his Decatur line on the 29th and marched twenty miles west toward Courtland. The engineers reported it was the closest favourable point to cross the Tennessee. But on arrival the engineers said a crossing could be effected, but not without difficulty. Hood was then some seventy miles west of Guntersville and had burned up five days. He told Beauregard he didn't have the provisions to move into Tennessee, and preferred going to Tuscumbia. It would be the best crossing place and on the railroad.

Crossing the Tennessee at Decatur was probably his last chance to affect the U.S. presidential election. Historians seem to agree the fall of Atlanta brought a war weary U.S. public to see the end in sight. Imagine Hood marching straight to Nashville before Thomas could build up his army. Hood might have made it before the 8 November election, and taken Nashville. This certainly might have taken votes from Lincoln. But the author has seen nothing of Hood considering the politics.

Tuscumbia was to be the base for the campaign into Tennessee. The *Mobile & Ohio* had been put in running order up to Corinth. The headquarters was in Confederate-held Mobile. That no doubt made repairing wartime damage feasible. The *Memphis & Charleston* was essentially formed from a railroad out of Memphis, which had been connected to a northern Alabama road. It seems it had operated with two headquarters. One had been in Memphis and the other in Huntsville, both occupied. From Corinth, it was only repaired eastward to Cherokee, Alabama. The sixteen mile gap to Tuscumbia meant supplies had to be hauled by wagons. The wagon road was in poor condition, further delaying the army's departure.

Beauregard asked Hood for "his plan of future operations…" Hood replied the next day, that "it was not possible for him to furnish any plan of future operations, as so much depended on the movement of the enemy…" Nashville was not yet a stated objective yet. President Davis wired Hood on the 7th and clearly expected too much from Hood and his decimated army. He lectured of the opportunity to take advantage of Sherman's divided forces. "If you keep his communications destroyed, he will most probably seek to concentrate for an attack on you." Davis thought Hood could "beat him in detail" and "advance to the Ohio river." Sherman was a week away from burning Atlanta and taking the war to citizens, without communications. Davis and Hood, Southern gentlemen, had no concept of how hopeless their situation was. Lincoln would be reelected the next day, and that impending disaster wasn't mentioned.

Nashville was not an objective yet and was not when Hood advanced for Tennessee. Beauregard's last day at Tuscumbia was 17 November. He was about to depart to establish his headquarters in Montgomery. In parting he stressed an offensive to strike "the enemy while dispersed. Like Davis, he underestimated Hood's ability to strike without a functioning supply base. The army was too worn out for such objectives.

Beauregard was already in Georgia when he wrote Davis: "On the 16th of November, when about leaving Tuscumbia, Alabama, on a tour of inspection to Corinth, Mississippi, I was informed by General Hood of the report just received by him, that Sherman would probably move from Atlanta into Georgia." Beauregard personally estimated Sherman had 36,000 effectives, instead of 60,000. If correct, Hood might have had confronted another 24,000 troops, meaning those under Schofield would have been close to 50,000. Thus, Hood launched his drive into Tennessee knowing Sherman had marched south. As of then, the cutting loose from a supply line in a war on civilians was not imagined.

J.P. Cannon, of the 27th Alabama, Scott's Brigade, said Forrest's cavalry crossed to the north bank of the Tennessee River on 19 November. Their old brigade commander visited before crossing. "General Buford said he could not pass without seeing his old brigade and it was equally pleasant for us to greet him again. After a general handshaking, he made a little speech in which he said, in part, he 'would like to have us with him if we were mounted, but as that could not be he knew we would do our duty wherever placed, and it was not by the dash of cavalry, but by the heavy blows of the infantry that we might expect to achieve our independence."

A lieutenant in Adams's Brigade wrote his wife on crossing the Tennessee River. William Harvey Berryhill, of the 43rd Mississippi, wrote of crossing it on Saturday the 19th. It was a hard time. "It was raining a very cold rain and we were on the bridge for an hour and a half or more on account of the wagons stalling on the Island ahead." The suffering of the poor horses is horrible. Berryhill's own suffered. He wrote, "I will try to get my horse to you by spring if I do not lose him. I have got him a little crippled. The day that we crossed the river it was raining and the road was full of water and he fell suddenly into a hole up to his shoulders, and in scrambling to get out he cut his left fore leg on the inside of the knee joint and he has been lame since. He is a little stiff, too, but if I had him at home where he could be rested a little I would not take a $1,000 for him."

Berryhill's lettre also mentioned their health problems and no doubt suffered stress to think of them. He also wrote of another stressful issue of money and their future security. "You say that you can get $600 for my Greensboro lot and ask if you must sell it. I am somewhat astonished at you for asking the question for I have told you repeatedly to do with every thing as you thought best, and you know that I wished to sell the place and would have sold it last winter for $500 if you had not been opposed to my selling it, for you said that you wished to reserve a home for you and our children in case I should never get back. If you sell for $600 you get $100 more that I gave for it. And you need the money."

How the army survived the frigid weather of the campaign with shoe and clothing shortages is a testament to their honour and determination. Berryhill's lettre aides us: "About the time I left my regt. On Monday it set into snowing and continued by storms till late in the evening when the sun would show itself occasionally. The wind was high and we had a bitter cold time of it, but I had on 2 prs. drawers and three shirts. One pair of the drawers and one shirt was woolen, but I had lost my gloves and my hands suffered. I had one good sock, too, that I got in the Yankee quarters at Acworth. I put it on one foot over the old ragged one, and the other foot I robed up with a wool rag."

Berryhill continued to write of the day to day marches in southern Tennessee. They had to be alert for bush whackers in Wayne County. It was one of two backward counties in Middle Tennessee that had voted against secession. On the 26th they were in Maury Co.: "Set out at sunrise and got in Murry Co. about 10 o' clock. It is very rich country and beautiful lands and large farms. We passed through Mount Pleasant late in the evening. It is a nice town and is 10 miles south of Columbia. It is as large or larger than Tuscumbia. We camped 8 miles south of Columbia on the farm of Mr. Polk, brother to our late Gen. Polk. There was no end to the riches of the people about here before the war." Artillerist Eggleston also mentioned passing William Polk's, and General Gideon Pillow's. He said, "Came through the finest and most beautiful country I ever beheld…"

Columbia and Spring Hill

On Sunday, 27 November the army moved into position around Columbia. Lee's Corps was on the left, Stewart's in the centre, and Cheatham's on the right. Hood made his headquarters at the Amos Warfield house on Pulaski Pike. The house still stands behind a highway marker titled "Advance and Retreat," as the house has been known. Loring's friend Chaplain Quintard came by to visit Hood. Quintard wrote, "He detailed to me his plan of taking Nashville, calling for volunteers to storm the key of the works about the city and etc. which I do not feel at liberty to write down just now-but 700 men will fill the graves of 700 heroes and receive the laurel crown." This intriguing idea does not seem to reappear again. Perhaps once Hood could spy the U.S. fortified line he dropped the idea. Nashville was finally being named as an objective, though Hood dreamed of Kentucky.

Loring's headquarters may have been nearby. Adams stayed in a log house that belonged to Warfield (see photograph below), and it is also extant. Cleburne stayed there too. Since Adams had parents from Ireland, we might suppose he and Cleburne enjoyed each other's company. Adams was about three years older. It would be the last Sunday of their lives. J.P. Cannon wrote, "When within four miles of Columbia our corps filed to the right. After winding about through fields and woods over small country roads we struck the Pulaski pike. Here our regiment was deployed as skirmishers, and advanced in lie till it encountered the enemy's pickets, when it was halted and ordered to 'rest on arms.'

Schofield at Columbia, facing south, had the Duck River at his back. He crossed to the north bank. J.P Cannon's diary entry for Monday, 28 November, describes Columbia: "We rested very well, sleeping while others watched, till 2 a.m. when we were roused and ordered forward, feeling our way through the darkness, expecting every moment to be fired into, but it wasn't long before the luminous fires and vivid flashes of burning ammunition indicated that the enemy had evacuated. Still we advance slowly and cautiously, entering the town just at daybreak.'

"We were met by citizens of both sexes, who grasped our hands and with tears of joy bid us welcome, so glad to see the Rebels once more. They brought us hot coffee, biscuits, and everything good to eat and how we enjoyed it. Our regiment was made provost-guard and we had a royal time all day. The citizens furnishing us cooked rations of the very best they had, and filling our haversacks to overflowing.'

The enemy, after crossing the river formed line-of-battle on the north bank. When our forces came up a sharp little fight occurred that we witnessed, but took no part in, though stray bullets frequently struck uncomfortably near us, causing us to dodge behind houses for shelter.'

"After the skirmish we began gathering up the commissary stores and other plunder that the Yankees had failed to burn. This kept us busy a good part of the day, but when we were not at work, the younger portion of us were engaged in the more agreeable business of talking to the pretty women."

Hood received a telegram from department commander Beauregard while at Columbia. He let Hood know Sherman was making rapid progress toward the Atlantic. It seemed likely he would turn north and join Grant. He was wearing down Lee in a war of attrition. Beauregard apparently had little idea how many U.S. troops were coming together at Nashville. He wired, "It is essential you should take the offensive and crush the enemy's forces in Middle Tennessee soon as practicable, to relieve Lee." Many books have left this telegram out, but it is essential to understanding Hood's strategy in the campaign. Lee was his hero and he had a direct order to act.

J.P. Cannon wrote of Hood's plan to march around the enemy, and reach their rear at Spring Hill. Cannon said they moved six miles above Columbia to cross the Duck River. Featherston reported they moved by "an unfrequented path in the most direct route for the purpose of reaching Spring Hill before the enemy arrived there. Our artillery and baggage wagons were left behind, being unable to travel the road taken by the troops." This part of the plan was good. Lee's Corps was left around Columbia. Lee was a fine artillery officer, and with almost all of the army's artillery, Hood could be confident of the safety of his rear.

Robert E. Lee has been recognized for his ability in planning timely troop movements. It would have been beneficial for Hood had he acquired that talent. His insufficient planning at Peach Tree Creek, Atlanta, and Jonesborough are evidence of this. Hardee was blamed for movements that could not be made in the expected time frames. Hood failed in his execution at Spring Hill, and had himself to blame. The lack of accurate maps was the essence of the problem. Hood had been led to believe Spring Hill was twelve miles away. As the march progressed it was evident that could not be. Local guides confirmed it would be more like seventeen miles. The partially abandoned Davis Ford route twisted and turned to follow the boundaries of property owners. U.S. troops had the direct macadamized turnpike. What if Hood had crossed Davis Ford and then turned west to strike the enemy position north of Columbia? The attack might have driven the enemy west of the pike. Not only would Hood have controlled the pike the enemy would have had to retreat west. There would have been no direct line of retreat to Franklin. Further, Forrest might have captured their wagons, parked to the north about Rutherford Creek. Instead Hood rode with confidence at the head of the infantry column with the lead brigade, Lowrey's of Cleburne's Division. At least he was at the front.

Writing on Spring Hill has emphasized U.S. troops marching past Hood's encampments on the night of the 29th. It was not both U.S. corps, for a division of the 4th Corps reached Spring Hill about noon, three hours before Hood's infantry began to arrive. The other four divisions arrived well after Cleburne's Division attacked. That is from about 7:00 until after midnight. Bate's Division was positioned near the pike after dark, and U.S. troops crossed his front.

Schofield suspected Hood wouldn't try to cross the Duck and attack with it to his back. As early as the 29th he supposed Hood would cross upriver to the east. Thomas had wired from Nashville that he wanted Hood kept south of the Duck until the 16th Corps troops arrived by transports, just a few days off. Schofield doubted he could stay along the Duck, and moved the immense wagon train north to Rutherford Creek. From his position on the north bank, Hood's pontoons were seen moving east out of Columbia on the 28th. From Schofield's left flank his infantry could tell at least two of Forrest's regiments were riding past. Forrest's cavalry had already crossed and by dark Schofield's cavalry warned him to look out for Spring Hill. Later a captured cavalry man told them the pontoon bridge was being built in the dark, and infantry was poised to cross. A courier was sent to Schofield about 1:00 a.m. Schofield knew Hood was crossing by 7:00. He immediately ordered the 4th Corps to Spring Hill. He ordered one the two 23rd Corps divisions to prepare to leave. That would leave only one division on the north bank of the Duck.

A division of the 4th Corps was arriving at Spring Hill about noon. A message was received warning them a considerable number of Hood's infantry was on the north bank. This gave them time to prepare to defend their claim on the turnpike. Cleburne's Division was over the pontoon about 7:30 a.m. The entire striking column was over two hours later. Almost immediately the column came under fire from enemy infantry. Hood knew by 10:00 his strike column had been seen, and he might have expected U.S. troops to beat him to Spring Hill, but Hood thought Lee's artillery would preoccupy them.

Forrest had driven the U.S. cavalry toward Franklin and turned west to test the enemy line. James Wilson had been sent by Grant to command cavalry for Thomas. Wilson made an erroneous conclusion. He thought Hood was marching on Franklin, and retired his force there, leaving Schofield without cavalry.

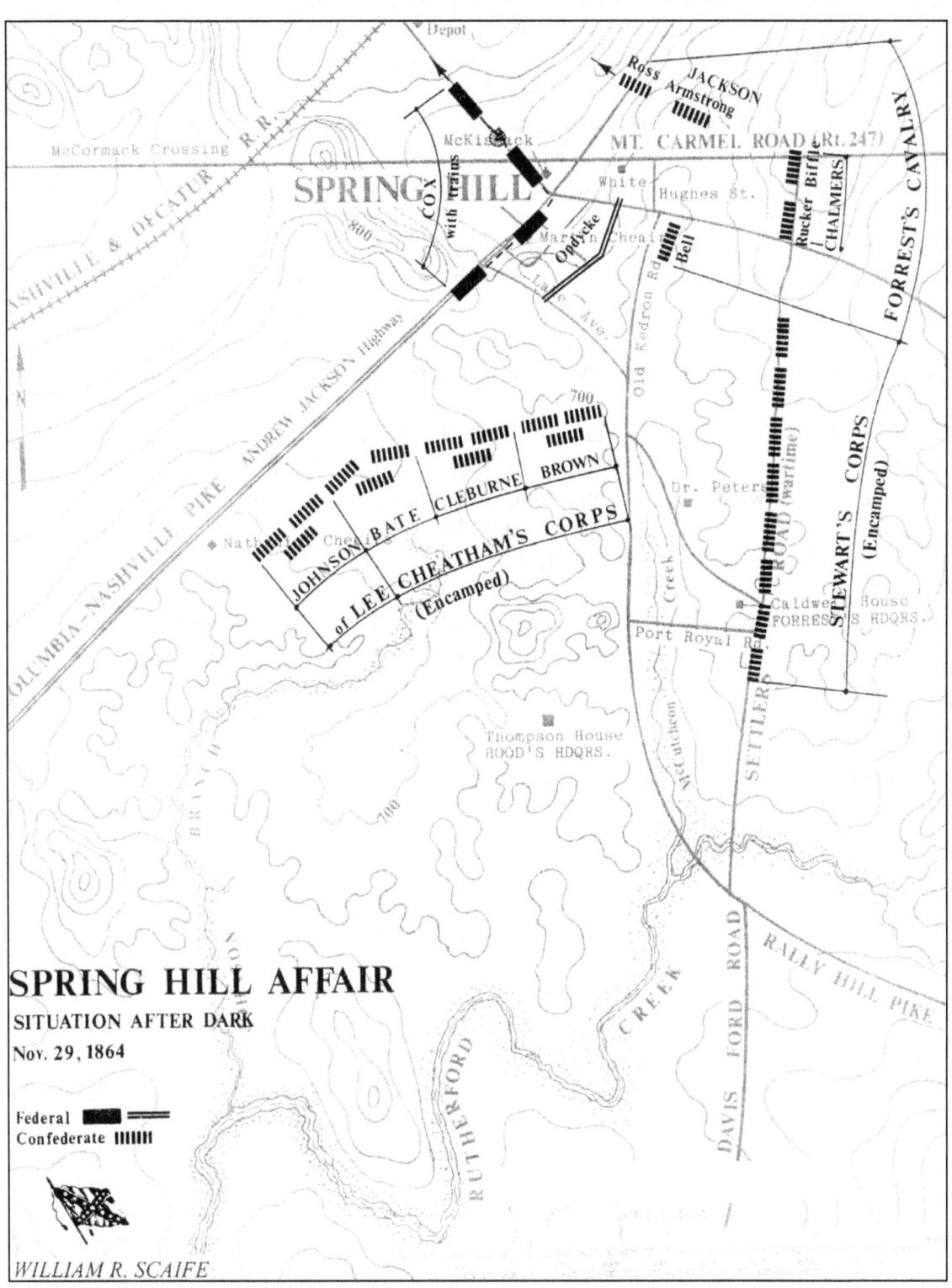

Hood arrived southeast of Spring Hill about 3:00 p.m. at the head of Cheatham's Corps. Forrest had already been on the field about two hours, He had ordered Chalmers to attack and they learned it was not a small force of dismounted cavalry. They were up against artillery backed by infantry. Forrest's troopers had been in the saddle all day, and needed their ammunition wagons to come up. Cheatham recalled, "At this point General Hood gave me verbal orders as follows: That I should get Cleburne across the creek and send him forward toward Spring Hill, with instructions to communicate with Forrest, who was near the village, ascertain from him the position of the enemy, and attack immediately; that I should remain at the creek, assist General Bate in crossing his division, and then go forward and put Bate's command in to support Cleburne; and that he would push Brown forward to join me." Unfortunately Cleburne's direction of attack did not take him across the turnpike. Brown's Division came up on Cleburne's right, and later Bate's Division arrived; however neither became engaged. And virtually all of Cleburne's casualties were in Lowrey's Brigade. Hood did not get near enough to the battle, small as it was, to realize the fighting was not gaining the turnpike. He went to his headquarters at the Absalom Thompson home, Oaklawn, well over a mile south of the closest fighting.

Captain Levi T. Scofield was an engineer with the 23rd Corps. He wrote an account of the campaign in 1909. He recalled that as they approached Spring Hill they were warned not to speak above a whisper. "We could plainly see that the soldiers standing and moving about the flaring lights were Johnnies, and in the quite of the night could hear their voices. An officer was left to repeat the caution to the advancing column."

Loring's Division had no significant role at Spring Hill, as Stewart's Corps acted in a reserve role. Stewart reported to Richmond, when in North Carolina on 3 April 1865. Sir: "In my report of the operations of my corps during my campaign made by General Hood into Tennessee, I omitted the details of what transpired near Spring Hill during the afternoon and night of the 29th of November, 1864. I respectfully submit the following statement and ask that it be filed as part of my report.

"On the morning of November 29 General Hood moved with Cheatham's Corps and mine and Johnson's Division of Lee's Corps (the latter reporting to me), Cheatham's Corps in advance. We made a forced march to get in the rear of the enemy. In the course of the afternoon, about three or four o' clock, I reached Rutherford's Creek, as Cheatham's rear division was crossing. I received orders to halt and form on the south side of the creek, my right to rest on or near the creek, so as to move down the creek if necessary. Subsequently I received an order to send a division across the creek, and finally between sunset and dark an order was received to cross the creek, leaving a division on the south side. Edward Johnson's Division, being in the rear, was designated to remain. Riding in advance of the column about dark, I found General Hood some half a mile from the creek and about as far west of the road on which we were marching..." Stewart went onto explain Hood gave him a "young man of the neighborhood as a guide and told me to move on and place my right across the pike beyond Spring Hill..." It is clear Hood intended for Stewart to block the turnpike to Franklin. Stewart's left was to have been behind Cheatham's Corps. Along the way he came to Forrest's headquarters, which were at Caldwell's house (see map). While talking to Forrest one of Cheatham's staff officers came up. Hood had sent the officer to tell Stewart he wanted his left to on Cheatham's right, which was Brown's Division. When Stewart reached Brown he learned that this alignment wouldn't extend his right across the turnpike. Stewart feared a mistake had been made. It might take all night to accomplish this. He ordered his corps to bivouac while he went to see Hood. It was about 11:00 p.m., so Hood agreed to let his men rest. They had marched all day, having covered close to twenty miles.

J.P Cannon explained the soldiers understood the purpose of the march to Spring Hill: "After a hard day's march we arrived at Spring Hill at dusk, in advance of quite a body of the enemy, and expected to dispute their passage. Instead, we were allowed to bivouac parallel with and only a short distance from the road, where we could hear them passing all night.'

"Having accomplished the very thing which General Hood asked us to, it was provoking to have to lie still and let the golden opportunity slip away from us, without even an attempt to reap the fruit of our forced march, which seemed to be within our grasp. Every private was impressed with the idea that a fearful blinder had been made and many remarks were made uncomplimentary to those in command. Of course, we were not in a position to know who was responsible for the failure."

Featherston did not remark on the fiasco of that night at Spring Hill, and may have had limited knowledge at the time. He said they went into bivouac near 11:00 p.m. He wrote, "At day light the next morning we moved in the direction of Franklin and after entering the turnpike we soon learned that the enemy was not far in advance of us, in retreat. Our march was rapid, Stewart's Corps in front, Loring's Division leading the column." He thought "the enemy hard pressed from the number of wagons abandoned on the wayside…" Loring may have recalled his own similar escape from the Champion Hill battlefield and year and a half ago.

J.P. Cannon said they were more mortified in the morning to learn the game had flown: "We were ordered to fall in promptly and were soon strung out in hot pursuit, pressing them so closely during the day that they were forced to burn about 50 wagons, the smoldering remains of which were scattered along the road for several miles. But no doubt they were rejoicing at their easy escape from a very perilous position. Judging from the way they traveled, they did not intend to allow us to get them into a similar scrape today." The signs of their hurried march must excited many of Hood's soldiers.

Hood and some of his officers had breakfast at the home of a staff officer, Nathaniel Cheairs. The home faced Columbia Pike, just south of Bate's position. The number of officers to blame is a complicated topic. Stewart and Loring were not among them. One officer remembered Hood being wrathy as a rattlesnake, striking at everything. Hood might have noted when he pointed, three fingers pointed back at him. Hood supposed Schofield would retreat all the way to Nashville, and not thinking he would stop at Franklin. Cheatham's Corps had led the advance to Spring Hill, but Stewart's led the way toward Franklin. Brigade for brigade, Stewart's soldiers were as good as Cheatham's.

Hood wrote Stewart before the war ended, on 9 April 1865: "Before leaving for Texas, I desire to say that some of your friends thought that I intended some slight reflection on your conduct at Spring Hill. You did all that I could say or claim that I would have done under similar circumstances myself. The great opportunity passed with daylight. Since I have been informed that your friends felt that my report led to uncertainty as to yourself and troops, I regret that I did not make myself more clear in my report by going into more detail…I only regret, General, that I did not have you with your corps in front on that day. I feel that Tennessee today would have been in our possession."

Lee's Corps played its part well at Columbia. Lee's artillery excellence was showcased. With almost all of Hood's artillery he was able to preoccupy Schofield. Lee also launched a rare amphibious attack. At about the time Hood approached Spring Hill, Lee was launching Edmund Pettus's Alabamians across the Duck River. Two Yankee Kentucky regiments were so distracted by the artillery barrage that they were easily driven back. The Alabamians were eager to pursue but Pettus had to call them back. Their purpose was to create a bridgehead so that a pontoon bridge could be laid. This was done and Lee's force began crossing after dark. They were marching far to the rear as Stewart's Corps was forming southeast of Franklin on the Lewisburg Pike.

Hood (left) didn't function well under Beauregard. Hood seemed self-righteous in the Atlanta Campaign. Davis apparently hoped Beauregard would be able to harness the reckless deficiencies Hood had exhibited. Historians have pointed out promoting Hood higher than division command exceeded his potential. There is no doubt this is correct. The summer of 1863 saw the gallant Hood have an arm mauled at Gettysburg, and then a leg amputated after Chickamauga. No further field duty should have been allowed.

Chapter 6: Franklin

Few towns or cities had such a day as Franklin on the 30th of November. People woke up that Wednesday morning and went about their daily business. They had seen Yankees move through before. Buell and the Army of the Ohio had marched through on their way to Shiloh. The Yankees had begun building Fort Granger in 1863. Cavalry from both armies had come through. This morning the Yankees had to bridge the Harpeth in order to escape. The people knew Hood wasn't far behind.

Frances McEwen recalled, "I was a pupil in the old Franklin Female Institute…The pupils numbered about 175…On…the 30th of November, we assembled at school as usual. Our teachers' faces looked unusually serious that morning. The Federal couriers were dashing hither and thither. The officers were gathering in squads, and the cavalry, with swords and sabres clanking, were driving their spurs into their horses' flanks and galloping out to first one picket post and then another on the roads leading south and southwest of town. The bell called us in the chapel. We were told to take our books and go home, as there was every indication that we would be in the midst of a battle that day." Her home was on Fair Street, a few blocks from the square. At 4:00 she stood in the front door and listened to the sound of the battle near the Carter's, several blocks off. "My father realizing that we were in range of the guns from both armies told us to run down in the cellar." Their house would have been in the line of fire of the artillery at Fort Granger, as it opened toward Cheatham's soldiers near Carter's Creek Pike. Once in the basement "there was a crash! and down came a deluge of dust and gravel. The usually placid face of our old black mammy, now thoroughly frightened, appeared on the scene. She said a cannonball had torn a hole in the side of the meat house and broke her wash kettle to pieces. She left the supper on the stove and fled…into the cellar."

Nearby 19-year-old Fannie Courtney lived a few blocks south of the square. She had watched the Yankees arrive and throw up breastworks. "You would have been astonished to see how quick the work was completed, and with what strength." She asked a passing Yankee if there was to be a battle. He replied, "We will only skirmish with the rebels till we get our wagon trains away…" Soon, Stewart's Corps launched a full scale assault. Miss Courtney was at the dinner table when she heard the roar of artillery. She ran into their yard to listen. "The bullets were falling so thick it was unsafe to remain longer. Men, women, and children were running in every direction, together with unmanageable teams, loose horses and mules…I hastened to the cellar with the rest of my family and neighbors who sought protection with us."

Hood's decision to attack Schofield at Franklin has no known high ranking supporters. Hood's best justification might be his orders from Beauregard to "crush the enemy's forces in Middle Tennessee soon as practicable…" Hood was correct in that he stood a better chance at Franklin than at Nashville. Also, Schofield had to rebuild the bridge on the turnpike to Nashville as the battle was being fought.

Schofield had wired Thomas to send a pontoon bridge so that he could cross the Harpeth. He had left Cox, a division commander in the 23rd Corps, to the home of Fountain Branch

Carter, on the south side of Franklin, on Columbia Pike. Cox wrote Schofield, "spurred forward with his staff to see if it had arrived." Cox and his staff tried to get some sleep, but Schofield "returned, much disturbed at finding no pontoons had arrived." Schofield left Cox to manage the battle, as he and his engineer left "immediately to plan such improvements of the river crossings as should enable him to get the trains and artillery upon the north side of the Harpeth at the earliest possible hour." Cox actually managed the battle. Schofield stayed on the north bank at Fort Granger and at the Trueitt house on the turnpike to Nashville; the house is still a private residence.

Cox continued, "At the river it had been found that by scarping the banks, the ford, though a very bad one, could be used to some extent. Some wooden buildings were dismantled to provide planking for the railway bridge, and a wagon approach to this was made. The lower part of the posts of the country bridge were found to be good, and these were sawn off nearly level with the water, crossbeams and planking were laid upon them, and by noon the army was provided with two passable bridges. The artillery of the Twenty-third Corps passed over first of all at the ford, to gain time, and part of it was placed in the fort on the north bank…" This was Fort Granger, and these guns would blast Loring's Division as it advanced, as will be seen.

Franklin's streets were perhaps grid-locked to use a modern term. Cox wrote, "the town was full of wagons waiting their turn at the bridges, and some of them struggling through the ford." He also claimed that most of the trains were over the river by three o' clock. Hood, operating without an established supply base, could have used the supplies.

His best chance to capture those supplies would have been to take Forrest's suggestion. When Forrest was under Van Dorn they had tested the U.S. defenses. That had been on 10 April 1863. The Yankees had begun construction of Fort Granger and had siege guns there, with infantry and cavalry ready to fight. Van Dorn accompanied William Jackson's division, toward Franklin while Forrest turned east on Henpeck Lane with Armstrong's Brigade. It terminated at Lewisburg Pike, where Forrest began moving toward Franklin. Siege artillery opened on him at the front near John and Carrie McGavock's home, Carnton. U.S. cavalry crossed the Harpeth at Hughes's Ford and struck his flank as he was stretched out over two miles. Obviously Franklin was a tricky place to attack.

Here Forrest was leading Hood's advance in 1864 and he knew the danger of Fort Granger's artillery, and he knew the fords where the Harpeth could be crossed. Forrest met with Hood and others at the Harrison House, extant on Columbia Pike. Forrest said, "If you will give me one strong division of infantry with my cavalry, I will agree to flank the Federals from their works in two hours' time." He might have crossed at Hughes's, or another ford, and struck out for the Nashville Pike. As it passed through Holly Tree Gap, he would have found a defensive position for the infantry, allowing the cavalry the mobility to attack any Yankee wagons trying to escape.

Hood turning down Forrest's suggestion looks all the worse when considering his failure to reconnoiter. Fort Pillow had been one of Forrest's greatest victories, made possible by his reconnoitering prior to the attack. He spent more than five hours, had two horses killed under him and another wounded, injuring him when the horse fell. Forrest valued the lives of soldiers too much for a reckless attack.

Hood didn't have five hours but he had another possibility. He might have concentrated a column, only along Columbia Pike. Longstreet's column breakthrough at Chickamauga was motivated by the failure of Pickett's Charge. Hood led that column and should have been anxious for such a strike. Cleburne spoke of such a column before Franklin, and there is little doubt it could have been successful. Cox explained Columbia Pike, by the Carter House, had been left open so the wagons and artillery could enter Franklin. This is of course where Cleburne's Division punched a hole in the U.S. line, only to be pushed back. Reserves as would have been at hand in a column attack would have given the Army of Tennessee the ability to break the U.S. line and drive it into the Harpeth.

In *Advance and Retreat*, Hood wrote that Cleburne "asked permission to form his Division in two, or, if I remember correctly, three lines for the assault. I at once granted his request…" But Cleburne's column appeared no better than Loring's formation of two brigades in front with one in support. Longstreet's column at Chickamauga was eight brigades in five lines. Stewart's Corps had eight brigades on the field. He attacked the strongest part of the U.S. line considering the obstacles in his path. Had Stewart's Corps been used in a column, following Cleburne, Hood would have broken the U.S. centre.

The setting for the battle was recalled in *Confederate Veteran* (Volume 14, page 261). Featherston's senior surgeon, Dr. G.C. Phillips, of the 22nd Mississippi, watched the battle with Dr. Wall, surgeon of the 33rd. "It seemed as if we were on the rim of a great bowl. Franklin in the bottom, with a low semicircle of breastworks towards us…during this time while the lines were forming it was perfectly still; no sound jarred upon the ear to disturb the beautiful and peaceful scene. I do not like this quietness. It is ominous, and I fear our men are going to be annihilated."

Robert W. Banks, a captain in the 37th Mississippi of Cantey's Brigade, wrote of several unique incidents in his The Battle of Franklin. Stewart's Corps marched from Spring Hill ahead of Cheatham's. They rested on, or near, the DeGraffenried farm. Stewart's map (next page) shows it along Lewisburg Pike, a few miles out. A soldier had made a stop to visit family on the march up, and brought a lot of provisions. Lt. Charles Campbell, of the same company, perceived the abundance and invited others to join them.

Banks wrote it "was a feast deemed fit for the gods. The meal was eaten in haste, each officer with his belt buckled on and side-arms in place, for momentarily they were expecting orders to move upon the enemy in the fortified town. While eating, the impending battle was freely discussed by those eight officers, all of whom were in serious, thoughtful mood. Two only were optimistic. The other six took a gloomy view of the situation. The later frankly expressed the opinion that the approaching battle would end the chapter of their respective lives. They anticipated it would be the finale to their individual endeavors as Confederate soldiers. They had presentiments that when it was over their records for time and eternity would be made up; that for them the curtain would not only be rung down upon the last scene of the last drama of the war, but that with its fall the end to their earthly careers would be at hand. And they substantially so expressed themselves. Sadder prognostications it would be difficult to imagine. Prognostications more swiftly and direfully fulfilled it would be impossible to discover. Before the sun went down six out of the eight received mortal wounds." Two of these were lieutenant colonels mentioned, Farer and Rorer.

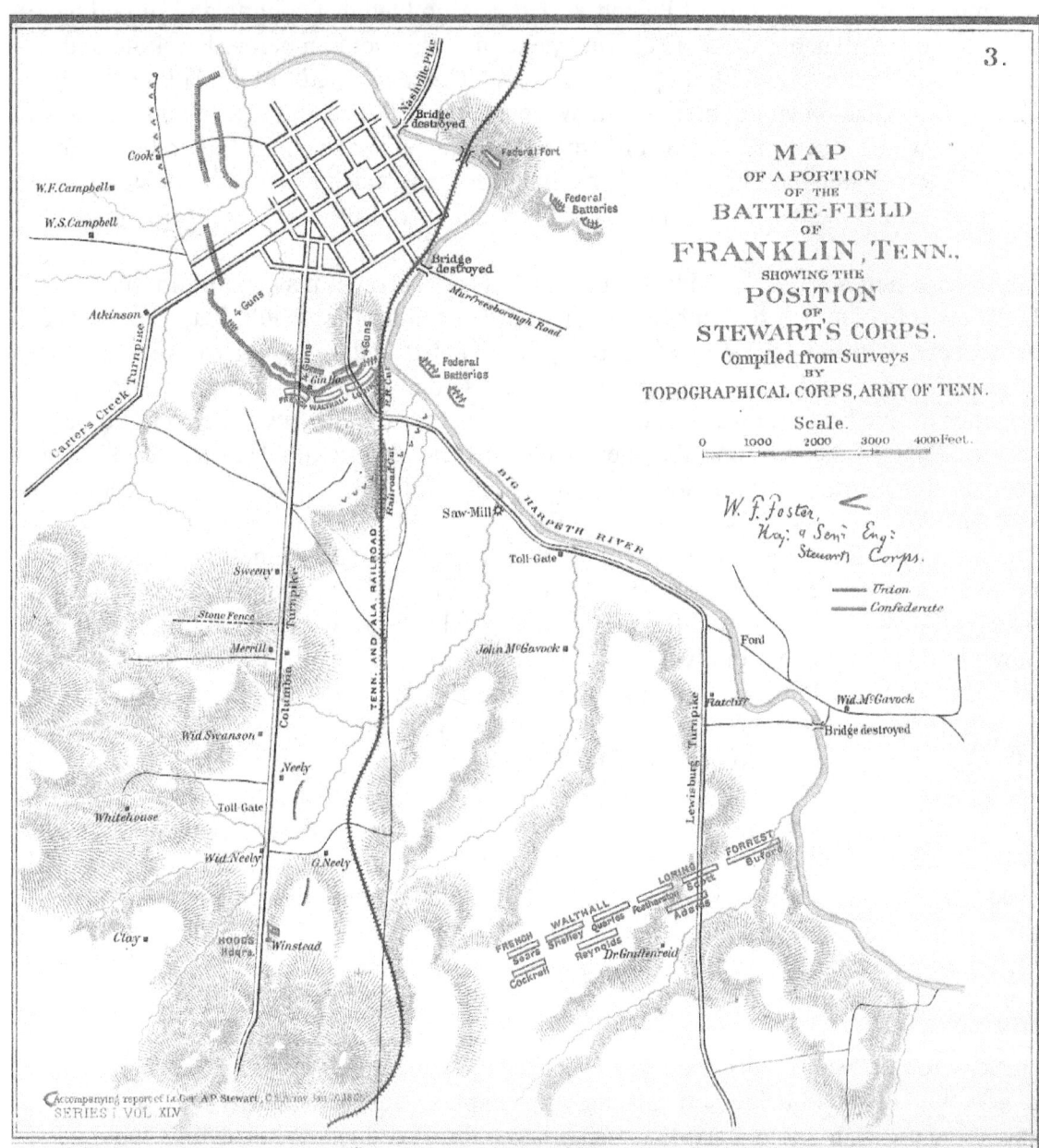

With a battle about to begin, Loring's Division would need a hospital site. Reverend Thomas R. Markham, a chaplain with Featherston's Brigade, rode toward Franklin on the Lewisburg Pike. Markham preached in New Orleans prior to the war, before returning home to Vicksburg. He had known Carrie Winder in Louisiana, and found her home at Carnton, as Mrs. John McGavock. A spring enhanced the site of the magnificent home.

The decision to locate the hospital there brought tragic fame to the site that has endured into the 21st Century.

Hood and his staff rode to the crest of the hill where they were sitting as the troops were getting into position. As our men lined up in three lines of battle, about 300 yards apart, the bands began to play. The doctor heard Dixie, The Bonnie Blue Flag, and The Girl I Left Behind. It was the only time he had ever heard the bands playing at the beginning of the charge. To whose credit it was due, he must be credited for some part in the ferocity of our attacks. The doctor found the "sight was grand and thrilling." They were amazed the U.S. artillery did not open sooner, which only increased the anxiety. "When within 300 yards of their breastworks a cannon boomed from their fort (Granger) across the little river (Harpeth) north of the town. At that point a sheet of flame and smoke burst from the entire crescent of the enemy's breastworks, answered by the Rebel Yell and musketry fire from our own men." After that the smoke of battle obscured their view, but his understanding was that Featherston had led the brigade in three separate charges.

General Loring's fellow division commander, Samuel French wrote in his autobiography, "The sun was sinking in the west, the day was drawing to its close, the tumult and excitement had ceased. The winds were in their caves, the silence that precedes the storm was felt; the calm before the earthquake which by some law of nature forewarns fowls to seek the fields, birds to fly away, and cattle to run to the hills, although withheld from man, seemed to presage an impending calamity, as painful in suspense as the disclosure of any reality. From this feeling of anxiety, sometimes incident to men when held in readiness to engage in a great battle, there came relief by a signal. And what a change! Twenty thousand gallant Confederates at the word of command moved proudly over the open plain to the attack. It was a glorious and imposing sight, and one so seldom witnessed, as all were in full view."

Scott's Brigade came up to a line of hills two miles from Franklin. J.P. Cannon wrote: "Here, while waiting for the rest of the command to come up, we had a good view of the town. The intervening space being almost level, with not a tree to obstruct the view, we could see the enemy' wagons hurrying across the little river and the Yankees themselves in two or three lines throwing up earthworks with the greatest activity.'

"They were evidently preparing to give us a warm reception, which afterwards proved to be about the warmest we had ever met.'

"When the remainder of the army arrived and were taking their places in line, our division (Loring's) was ordered to move by the right flank. We had gone but a short distance when we encountered the enemy's cavalry. Wheeling into line we drove them into the timber above the town. Our cavalry continued skirmishing, but failed to move them any farther. About 3 p.m. our brigade was ordered to the cavalry's assistance and with a yell we charged and then drove them half a mile farther up the river."

Brig. Gen. Thomas M. Scott's last battle was at Franklin. The former commander of the great 12th Louisiana Infantry was the type of courageous officer the Confederate infantryman knew could lead them forward.

Timber above the town does not mean north of Franklin, but upriver, which is east. *Brigadier General Tyree H. Bell, CS.A: Forrest's Fighting Lieutenant* explains Bell's Brigade took position on the far right of the army. They were to attack enemy cavalry on the south bank of the Harpeth. Bell could see the McGavock's home, Carnton, from his position to the southeast near Hughes' Ford. On his immediate left was Scott's Brigade. Their assistance allowed Loring's Division to attack without concern of enemy cavalry. Scott's and Bell's drove the enemy alongside the river and Lewisburg Pike, while Jackson's Division forced their way across at and around Hughes' Ford. An O.R. atlas map (Plate CV-9) for Yankee Wilson's report shows Armstrong's Brigade, of Jackson's Division, across Hughes' Ford. It incorrectly shows Chalmers's, who was on the far left of Cheatham's infantry. It was Jackson's other brigade, Ross's, on the high ground on the north bank. Ross reported that his 3rd and 9th Texas regiments deserved commendation. "By the charge of the Third Texas we gained possession of an eminence overlooking the enemy's position…" This may be seen on the map on previous page.

The area where Scott's and Bell's fought can be found today along Lewisburg Pike. A little south of the entrance to Carnton and the Eastern Flank Park is the parking lot for a Harpeth River Access. Signage indicates this is about the point where Buford's Division fought, and so that includes Bell's Brigade. This is within sight of Carnton, as Bell mentioned. It does not mention Scott's fought alongside them.

The duration of Scott's support of the cavalry is not known. Soon enough they got into position to fight enemy infantry. George Sutton was in the 12th Louisiana and related an incident then, found in a 1920 issue (Volume 28, page 116) of *Confederate Veteran*. Sutton had been severely wounded at Atlanta and was serving with ordinance. He wrote, "Our ordinance train came to a halt some half a mile in the rear of our troops. I saw a regiment form in battle line. As they formed I saw them all kneel down, and some one prayed. I could hear him, but could not understand what he said. I think they were at prayer when the order came to advance, for they arose hurriedly, passed over the hill, and in a few minutes I heard the Rebel yell, and the battle was on." With the enemy cavalry pushed across the Harpeth at Hughes's Ford, Loring's Division passed Carnton, along the Lewisburg Pike. They passed through land preserved as a park.

Eastern Flank Battlefield Park was previously a golf course. The 110 acre city park is located at 1368 Eastern Flank Circle. Signage covers Loring's Division. A concrete walkway traces the route of Scott's Brigade. Signage indicates when Scott's were at about 1,000 yards from the enemy and came under fire from their artillery. The batteries firing toward them had Napoleons and 3-inch Ordinance Rifles. Signage named *Artillery Hellfire* shows the likely coverage area of their fire. *Advancing With Scott's* Brigade signage indicates a point where they were taking casualties from percussion shells and bursting fuse shells. They couldn't respond because they had another ten minutes of marching to get into small arms range. It also points out an exploding shell damaged Scott's spine and internal organs before he reached the enemy's line. He was taken to the field hospital at Carnton. Scott survived but wasn't able to return to command.

Scott's Brigade came up last, having fought with Bell's cavalry. J.P. Cannon continued: "We were entirely detached from our main columns but a left wheel brought us into line facing the upper part of the town, the right of our brigade resting on Harpeth River. General Scott galloped down the line urging us to 'hurry up: that the enemy were retreating and General Hood wanted us to charge and capture them before they could cross the river.' The enemy had several batteries on a range of hills just across the little river which fired over their own lines until the opposing forces got so close together they endangered their own men. Then they concentrated all the guns on us, being on the extreme right and nearest them with nothing but open space between. Our position threw us in direct line with the batteries on the hill which enfilades us every shot, but we pressed forward and when near enough the infantry opened on us with terrible volleys and it seemed as if not one of us could escape the storm of shells, canister, and bullets which were poured into us. Our troops who were massed further to our left had failed to make a breach in the works and before we could reach the works our single line had become so thinned and nearly every officer killed or disabled. With none to command or lead it would have simply resulted in a massacre for us to proceed further. We had reached the railroad cut and took such cover as that afforded and in the abandoned rifle pits of the enemy where we were partially protected and remained until darkness set in." Cannon mentioned the loss of officers; General Scott's wound being the most notable. *Confederate Veteran* (Volume 18, page 138) tells of the 27th, 35th, and 49th Alabama, advancing under Col. Samuel Ives. As they moved forward, roughly parallel to the Lewisburg Pike, shots began coming through the Osage orange hedge. General Forrest was behind the 35th observing, and was nearly hit. The Alabamians advanced through briars and bushes, jumping over logs, trying to reach the hedge.

Joseph Nicholas Thompson, in the 35th Alabama, recalled "their opening on us with grape and canister was too much for us, and we raised a shout and sprinted forward in a run. We were now about 200 yards from them and still they did not shoot except with their artillery, But we could hear them cheering behind their works, but could not see them." Then at about 50 yards "they rose as a blue wave and a wall of fire rose that swept our ranks like hail. Many fell then, but on we went up to them, and when we got to their works we found that we could not get to them on account of a Osage orange hedge in front … so thick that we could not pull it away or cut it. Poor Capt. Stewart, the last I saw of him was trying to cut a path through the hedge with his sword. He fell with four bullets in him. I soon saw that nearly all of our company was killed or wounded…" They began to fall back and a cannon ball took off Thompson's right foot. "Gen. Adams...who had the reserve, rode so close to me that I thought his horse would slip." The old colonel of the 35th, Ives, was struck by 17 bullets, in clothing and in person, yet incredibly lived.

It is easy to conclude no attack should have been made along the Lewisburg Pike. The adjacent Harpeth River protected enemy artillery that enfiladed Loring's Division. The entrenched enemy could not be reached at points until axmen hacked away at the abatis and hedge. Even if Hood could not make close observations, John McGavock or other residents might have given descriptions of the fortified line. Even an advancing skirmish line might have found the abatis and learned it was impassible.

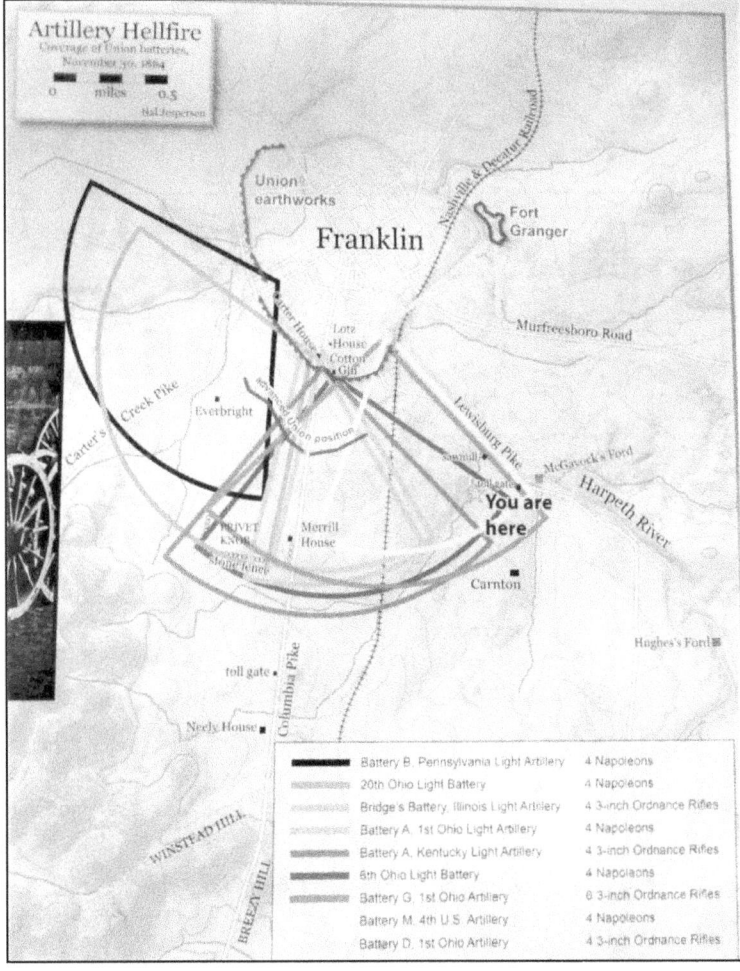

Several Franklin properties allow one to study Loring's advance. The Eastern Flank park is similar to the Pickett and Pettigrew advance at Gettysburg. Both were about a mile long with the Confederates under artillery fire, and unable to respond. Civil War Trails signage points out Loring's soldiers had it worse as just before the enemy breastworks a "tangle of sharpened Osage orange abatis blocked their advance. Unable to break through, some of the surviving officers and men began moving to the left, mixing their units in a confused mass, just as smoke and darkness began to cloak the battlefield." Carnton and the McGavock Cemetery are adjacent.

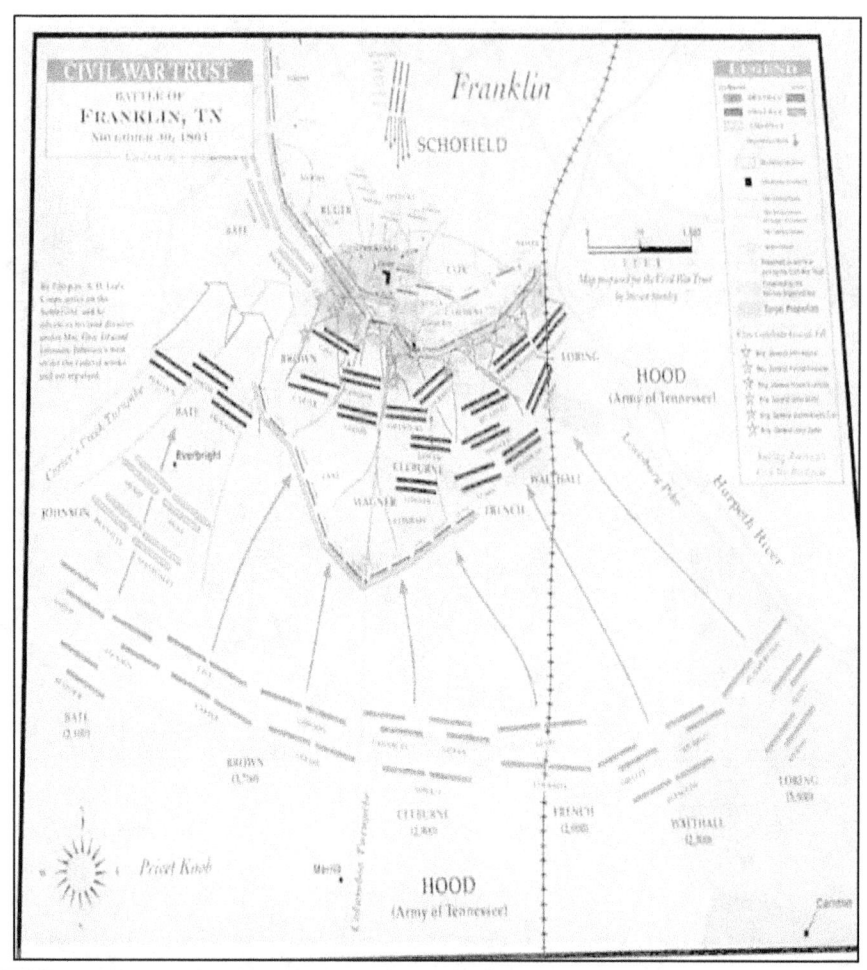

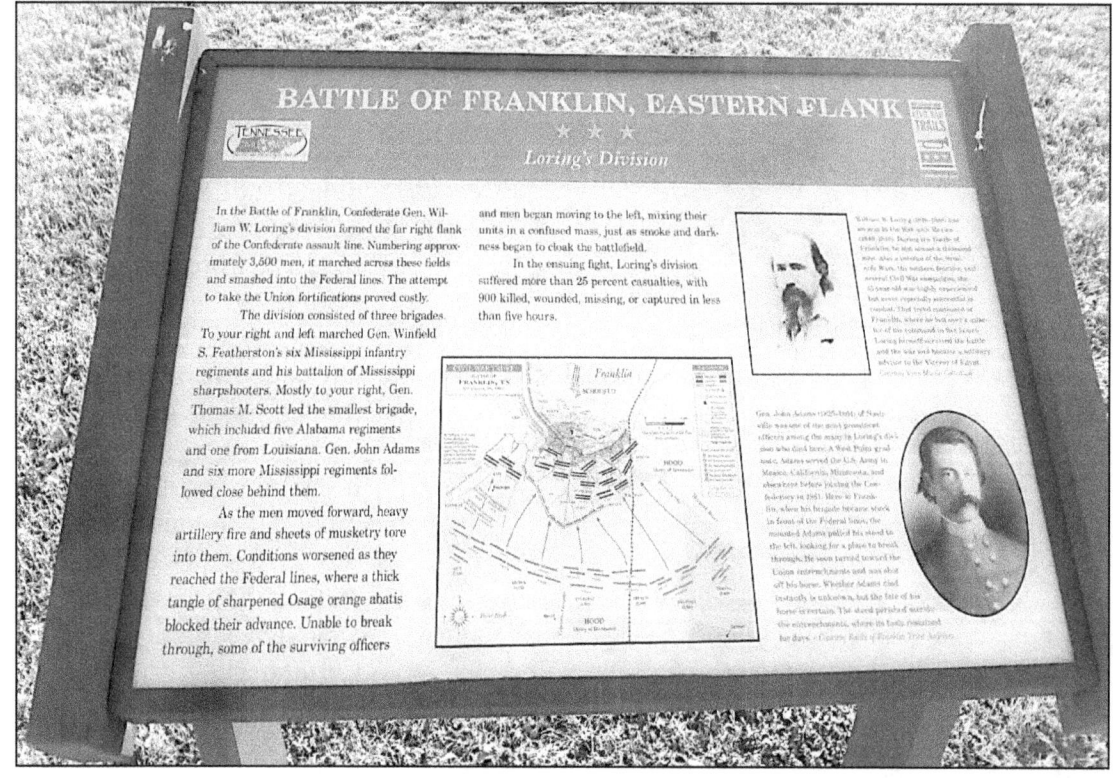

Eastern Flank signage named *Shells from Fort Granger* says it is about one mile north, across the river. It points out 3-inch rifles were in the fort. They were enfilading Loring's Division inflicting heavy casualties as they approached the railroad. It quotes Col. Marcus Stephens of the 31st Mississippi reporting a single shell killed or maimed seven of his men nearby. Heavy artillery may have been in the fort, but is not known to have been engaged. Park Marshall was a Franklin boy at the time of the battle, and later a secretary for General Bate. He wrote in *Confederate Veteran* (Vol. 23, p. 102), "After the battle I saw one of the big eight-inch howitzers that had been in the fort, standing by the railroad embankment, with its wheels cut down as if the retreating army had failed in their attempt to load it on a car. I do not know what large guns were in the fort during the battle…It would be interesting to know of any of the big guns being in action. I have never seen them mentioned in any official way-that is, guns above four-inch field guns. The reports seem to refer to the use in the battle of only three-inch rifles in the fort."

Signage at top and bottom are named *Advancing with Scott's Brigade.* The top indicates: "At this point Scott's brigade entered the range of case-shot shells…the shells acted like large grenades as they burst overhead." They were not alone as Featherston's Brigade advanced on their left. Adams "had a full view of the tremendous losses that Scott's and Featherston's men were suffering and he maneauvered his brigade to your left to find a better path …" Adams was killed in sight of the Carter cotton gin. Signage at the bottom is near the exit from the park onto Lewisburg Pike. It explains: "Within 1,000 yards of the Federal defenses, casualty rates climbed …in range of infantry rifles and canister shot." It explains Scott's crossed the pike (right in photo) and crossed the railroad. Abatis of sharpened Osage blocked their way. As for Scott: "An exploding artillery shell damaged his spine and internal organs. A wagon transported him back to the temporary field hospital at Carnton."

It is possible to follow Loring's advance by leaving Eastern Flank park, and following Lewisburg Pike another half mile. Just before reaching the railroad crossing, turn left into Collin's Farm park; address is 418 Lewisburg Pike. Artillery fire continued to enfilade Loring's line from Fort Granger and then from U.S. artillery firing down the railroad. Of course artillery fire tore into their ranks from straight ahead. The railroad runs alongside Collins Farm. Signals may be seen in the distance, where the pike crosses the tracks.

The Civil Wars Trails sign (left) says Loring's Division "rushed across the ground in front of you…" Earlier in the day U.S. troops "cut down several acres of Osage orange hedges and spread the thorny branches out in front of the works here. Loring's men, trying to hack their way through, faced sheets of musketry and a deafening chorus of artillery fire from your right in the deepening twilight. Men fell in piles, dead or wounded. Some of them crawled on their hands and knees along the tracks, desperately looking for a way around the Union (U.S.) left flank." Artillery behind the breastworks, and up the railroad at McNutt's Hill, prevented Scott's Brigade from making contact with the U.S. line. Featherston's and Adams' fared little better. The sign concludes: "Many of the Mississippi, Alabama, and Louisiana men who died here were buried along the road and tracks, and in front of the breastworks. A year and a half later, they were reburied a mile from here at Carnton in the McGavock Confederate Cemetery. The Williamson County marker, at right, also mentions Adams led his brigade through a ravine (near Meadowlawn?) in an attempt to reach the breastworks farther to the left.

Note: *Embrace an Angry Wind...* has a circa 1884 photo of the repaired Carter cotton gin. In the distance, off to the northeast, may be the site of Fort Granger. As Loring's Division advanced past the McGavock's Carnton toward the entrenched U.S. line, the fort may have been visible, off to their right, during their advance. It was located on a bluff of the Harpeth River known as Figuers Bluff; sometimes as Figuer's Hill. The U.S. Army had nearly been pushed into Stones River during the battle there, outside Murfreesborough. It resulted in the construction there of the enormous Fortress Rosecrans, through which Stones River flowed, and the *Nashville & Chattanooga* passed. Fort Granger overlooked the Harpeth and the bridge for the *Nashville & Decatur*. Another fort, between the two towns, overlooked the road between them, and the turnpike between Nolensville and Triune. Granger is a National Landmark, Rosecrans is part of Stones River National Military Park, and the remains of the Triune fort survive on a knob, privately owned. U.S. line has about 4K gin to RR.

The Carter gin view is remarkable, as no such view has been had of Figuer's Hill, to the north, in anyone's memory. It was the site of Fort Granger. Cleburne's Division attacked toward the gin. Between the gin and Lewisburg Pike saw brigades from all three divisions of A.P. Stewart's Corps become tangled. It was the deadliest single day in the war for the Army of Tennessee. At least 1,756 were killed. The real horror was apparent when the sun rose as most of the dead were in the concentrated area from Columbia Pike to Lewisburg Pike. More had been killed in the two other great Tennessee battles, Shiloh and Murfreesborough. But those battles were two days each, and the dead were spread over some wooded acres. The next morning Rev. Markham, who had selected Carnton as a hospital site, found John Adams's remains. Cleburne's were found nearby, and both taken to Carnton.
Embrace an Angry Wind attributed photo to US Army Military History Institute.

Marshall's account explained where he was standing between the public square and where the road to Murfreesborough came to the Harpeth. The bridge had been destroyed some time before, as had others. Stewart later wrote of artillery fire "from the opposite bank." The map accompanying his report is in the O.R. atlas (Plate LXXIII-3). It shows four enemy batteries across the river. Marshall's map calls that area "Handy's Field. Marshall pointed out "none could have been placed there except by a long detour, as there was no bridge or good ford near the place." He was standing on a street corner when four or five pieces of artillery "reached my corner, turned to the right, went one block to the town end of the Murfreesboro bridge site, and took position…" Foster's map (above) to accompany Stewart's report shows the erroneous position of "Federal Batteries" across the river.

Marshall explained how the fire of these guns "could not only rake the railroad, but, turning a few points to the left, could be made to pass across the river, then across the bend, then across the river a second time, so as to strike Loring's position farther to the south." Marshall perceived that the fire of the guns, to the Confederates, "would well seem to originate on the north side of the river.

A brief description of the U.S. line was made in a lettre Mrs. John Adams received, while living in St. Louis, in 1891. It was from Lt. Col. Baker of the 65th Indiana. He was in command of a skirmish line positioned where Loring's Division was directed. He wrote, "We had during the forenoon thrown up breastworks of earth some ten feet thick and five feet high, behind which our men stood protected; while the enemy came up in an open field and charged upon us. They had no protection, and were mowed down like grass before the scythe. This will explain to you how desperate was the undertaking to dislodge our army from behind this impenetrable breastwork and the sublime heroism of the men who undertook the perilous task and almost succeeded."

The 65th Indiana had at least one company (A) with Henry 16-shot repeater rifles. The firepower of their line near the cotton gin had another enhancement. The ranks were five to six men deep, with those in the rear reloading rifles and passing them to the front. There does not seem to have been a chance for Adams or his brigade to break this line.

Loring Park is in the path of Walthall's right, such as brigades led by Quarles and Shelly. Stewart's left outflanked Wagner, as he almost reached modern Adams Street. French was on the left and Walthall in the centre. His right brigade was Quarles's and they charged forward on Loring's left. A portion of the land has been preserved on Meadowlawn Drive. Featherston's and Adams's both brushed shoulders with Quarles. In 2022 there was no signage but the land can be found between 319 and 321 Meadowlawn.

Save the Franklin Battlefield provides the map below. Sam Huffman shared along with McNutt's Hill visit. "Loring Advance" land appears to be where Adams's Brigade went left, toward the gin, to avoid Osage orange. Signage by the Collins Farm indicates Adams went through a ravine. It seems it is on the far side of the field.

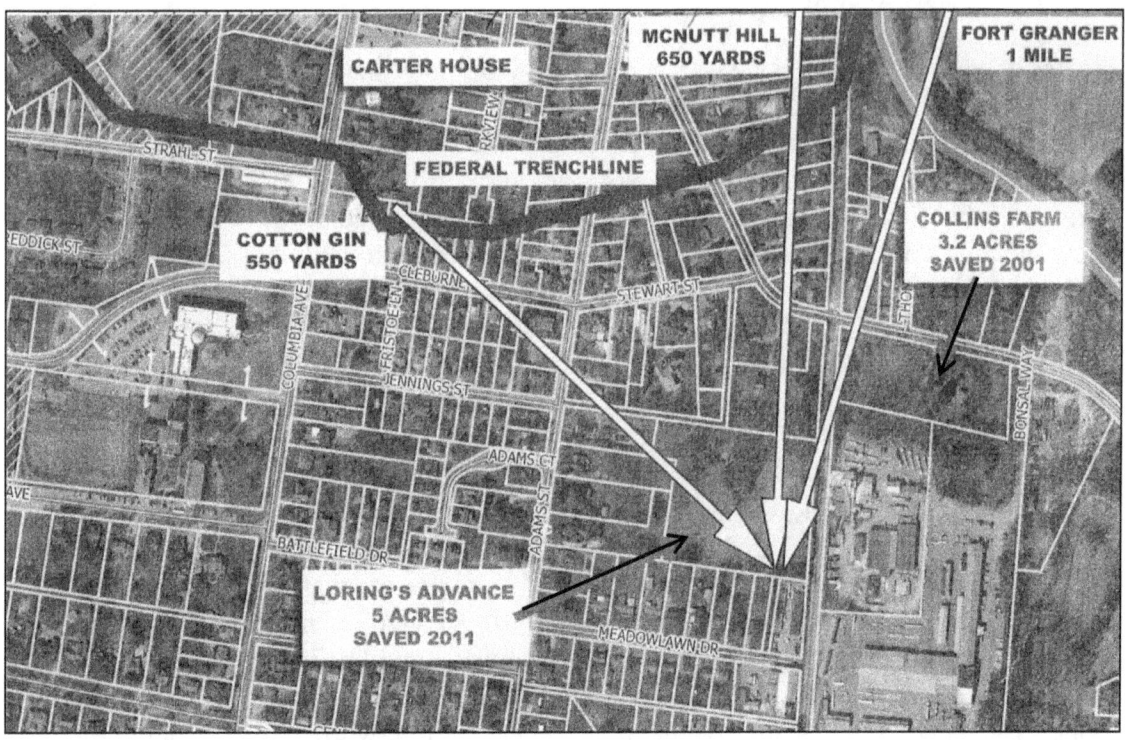

Hood didn't prepare for the wagon wheel departure of the turnpikes out of Franklin. Regiments could get into position a mile or two out, but they might overlap as they advanced. Loring was upset with fellow division commander Edward Walthall before the battle. He rode up to Walthall and heatedly accused him of placing some of his troops so that they overlapped Loring's. James McNeilly was in Quarles's Brigade of Walthall's Division. He recalled, "For a couple of minutes there was a sharp colloquy between the two generals, when General Walthall said, 'General Loring, this is no time for a personal quarrel. When the battle is over, you will know where to find me.'" Hopefully that was the end of their quarrel.

As William Quarles's brigade advanced McNeilly followed them. He had to direct the litter corps. He observed one of Loring's brigades advancing into the area where the enemy cut down an Osage orange hedge to form an impenetrable barrier. McNeilly saw the brigade fall back after suffering terrible casualties. He saw Loring ride among them in an attempt to rally them. He was "commanding, exhorting, entreating, and denouncing," but nothing he said could rally the brigade. Quarles was moving forward on Walthall's right. McNeilly said Quarles's boys tried to help, "but to no purpose." The enemy, firing from their entrenchments, halted Quarles too, "for the bullets were flying thick over and among them." Quarles was wounded and all of his staff on the field were killed.

McNeilly then saw Loring "in full uniform with golden adornments, His sword belt around him and the broad band across his shoulder and breast were gleaming in gold; his spurs were gilt; his sword and scabbard were polished to the utmost brightness; over his hat drooped a great dark plume of ostrich feathers. From spur to plume he seemed a star of chivalry, ready to dash forward…."

McNeilly was spellbound as he watched Loring "for more than a minute [Loring] sat motionless, with his sword in his only hand lifted high above his head and glittering in the light of the sinking sun. As the bullets hissed about him as thick as hail he seemed to court or defy death. With an expression of grief and scorn, Loring looked on the mass of fugitives, and cried out in anguish: 'Great God! Do I command cowards?' General Loring knew there was no coward among them. They had attempted the impossible and failed. Then he galloped after them and, out of range of the enemy, reformed them."

Confederate Veteran (Volume 2, page186) covers Featherston's attack. In the confusion of trying to get around the Osage orange hedge some of Featherston's men got as far west as the cotton gin. In 1894, Don Wilson of the 33rd Mississippi claimed their beloved Captain J.E. Simmons led the men toward the U.S. works. "He went over the main line of works at the gin house and was captured. I was wounded in the hip just at the abatis. The smoke soon settled on us with the darkness, so we could only see by the light of the guns. Our flag bearer was killed on their works." Featherston wrote that their works "were the best I have seen since the beginning of the war." He also wrote "my Brigade made the attack on each side of an old gin-house…" Featherston and Loring said the flag was lost.

Robert Banks wrote, "Brigadier-General W.S. Featherston, who seemed to delight in the shock of battle and, when there was need of personal exposure, courted danger as though it were a mere bauble-a toy to be played with-escaped unscathed. In his brigade the standard bearers of the 3rd and 22nd Mississippi regiments 'planted their colours on the enemy's works, and were wounded and captured with their colours. The colour bearer of the 33rd was killed some fifteen paces from the works, when Lieutenant H.C. Shaw, Company K, carried them forward, and when in the act of planting them on the works, was killed, his body falling in the trenches, the colours falling in the works." Part of his remarks came from Featherston's report on the battle.

Confederate soldiers expected dynamic, courageous leaders. Col. Marcus Stephens gave his 31st Mississippi just that. He wrote, "I…was severely wounded in the right thigh and hip, near the enemy's breastworks, with the flag in my hand, and in an attempt to stick the flag staff in the enemy works. As I fell, Sergt. Hunter rushed up to me. I handed him the flag and as he grasped it in his right hand he was shot in his right arm, and dropped the flag. I told him to change hands and take out the flag, which he did…"

The advances of their colours to the earthworks were acts of dynamic courage. The 22nd had lost at least four colour bearers at Peach Tree Creek. Losing again here, along with their flag, and it appears General Hood's lack of preparations is appalling. These colour bearers and the soldiers they led exhibited heroism beyond what Hood should have expected. Mississippi paid the heaviest price for Hood's poor leadership.

Franklin youth Park Marshall wrote recollections of the battle around the railroad and Lewisburg Pike. He recalled, "…a heavy hedge of Osage orange which ran alongside of the pike and railroad was cut down and placed in front of the works. Fifty yards behind those works and from fifty to 100 yards from the railroad, were two batteries of artillery, one of four guns and one of six, firing over the heads of the men in the works. In the works at the east side of the Lewisburg pike were two guns."

Marshall explained the seriousness of the Osage orange in blocking Stewart's Corps. Possibly his references to Stewart's Corps should have been specifically Loring's Division. Marshall wrote, "Stewart's Corps was split in twain, a part of it under General Featherston turning to the right, passing to the right of the works and along the railroad and riverbank. Some of these Mississippians even crawled on the tracks in an attempt to outflank the U.S. entrenched line. It was to meet this movement that the Federals sent five three-inch rifled guns from their left to the Murfreesboro bridge site and with them raked the railroad as far as the Lewisburg pike, driving Featherston away. The rest of Stewart's corps turned to the left and advanced at an angle, being thus telescoped behind Cleburne." Though Adams's Brigade had been behind Featherston's, Adams's death toward the cotton gin, near where Cleburne was killed, validates Marshall's remark.

Previous photo of signage beside the Collins Farm, on Lewisburg Pike, showed the crossing of the railroad. This view is from that crossing, looking north past the U.S. left. The Harpeth River is at right. Just beyond the curve, on the left, is McNutt's Hill. The U.S. artillery there fired into Loring's right. Some in Stewart's Corps thought there were enemy field pieces across the river. Actually it seems to have been the fire from this position which was not across but downriver. The artillery fire from across the river was from Fort Granger. The fort is up the tracks on the right. Accounts refer to tracks in a cut. Cut may mean a cut on two sides, or only one side as here. Grading may have taken place since 1864 and raised the level of the tracks.

Bishop Quintard explained Adams formed his brigade near Carnton. As the pike approached the U.S. entrenched line the Harpeth River is parallel to the pike here, north of it. They had artillery on that north bank at Fort Granger that enfiladed Loring's line as it advanced. U.S. engineer Levi Scofield recalled "terrific volleys from the batteries on the opposite side of the river." He added their artillery was also in front of Walthall's and Loring's Divisions. It blew gaps in the advancing line. Scofield quoted an artillerist: "At every discharge of my gun there were two distinct sounds –first the explosion, and then the bones." Scofield wrote, "Stewart's living sea, with raging surf, in wave following wave, broke and fell, and plunged onward over the sloping beach in our front."

Quintard wrote, "A more gallant set of officers and men never faced a foe. General Adams was calm, cool, and self-possessed and vigilantly watched and directed the movements of his men and them on for victory or death. He was severely wounded early in the action and was urged to leave the field. A bullet had torn into his right shoulder, and blood was staining his uniform. Adams calmly replied: 'No I will not! I will see my men through.'"

Maj. Patrick Henry, of Adams's staff, wrote *Confederate Veteran* (Volume 21, page 76) in 1913. He said Loring's right flank rested on the Harpeth River as they advanced. Henry wrote, "The brigades of Generals Featherston and Scott were in advance, while Adams's Brigade was in reserve with orders to keep about one hundred yards in the rear of the advancing brigades. The advance of Loring's Division was obstructed by a deep railroad cut, by an abatis, and by a hedge of Osage orange. This abatis was most elaborate, the boughs of the Osage orange hedge being interlocked; while the sharpened planks, sloped so as to strike the breast, were set deep in the ground, nailed to cross pieces. It was almost impossible to get through this hedge, and our heaviest loss was occasioned while our men were trying to pull away the abatis. Let it be remembered that this hedge and abatis were only about thirty feet in front of the enemy's entrenchment, which was protected by head logs."

The bust of Brig. Gen. John Adams is at the Carter House visitor centre, along with other generals killed in the battle. It was sculpted by the late Laura Jane Herndon Baxendale. It was commissioned by the Franklin Memorial Association and unveiled in 1988. It was followed by those of the other four brigadiers: Hiram Bronson Granbury, Otho French Strahl, John Carpenter Carter, and States Rights Gist. All five brigadiers were done by Mrs. Baxendale. A bust of Maj. Gen. Patrick Cleburne was sculpted by Pat Horan and unveiled in November 1982. The late Ronald Clemons was the chairman of the Franklin Memorial Association.

Winstead Hill was Hood's command post. The park there is owned and maintained by the Sam Davis Sons of Confederate Veterans Camp. The memorials to the brigadiers was a special project of a member, the late Milton (Skip) Earle. The Adams memorial has a bonnie blue flag, as he commanded Mississippi troops. When Mississippi seceded on 9 January 1861 a large blue flag with a single white star was raised over the capitol. It was an inspiring spectacle and led the actor Harry McCarthy to write *The Bonnie Blue Flag*. It was second to *Dixie* as a patriotic Confederate song.

Major Henry continued, "As Adams's Brigade reached the open ground in front of the enemy's works, the shots from the enemy passing through the ranks of Featherston's advanced brigade did considerable damage to the reserves (Adams's Brigade), who seeing the front line roughly handled and staggering under the close fire of the enemy, without orders, raised a yell and charged to the rescue. It seemed that the front line had melted from the earth."

Colonel Stephens had led the 31st Mississippi, Featherston's Brigade, in that front line. He had fallen near the works as Adams's line came up. "The 15th Mississippi regiment, which supported my regiment, rapidly formed by their Col. Farrell, who gave the command to charge, and it seemed to me that the regiment was crushed like a dry leaf, they lay so thick, killed and wounded…What was living and unhurt of them fell back and the battle for the time was over, on our part of the line." Farrell had taken mortal wounds.

Henry explained Adams and his staff tried to stop the impulsive charge. "But their fighting blood was to the fore, and go in they would." Adams sent one staff officer, his cousin, Captain Thomas Gibson to follow the right. Adams gave his last known order, "I can be found in the centre if needed." He ordered Henry to go with the left. Henry wrote, "When the left wing of Adams's Brigade reached the abatis under the most galling fire, literally in their faces (the enemy being armed with repeating rifles), and an enfilade fire from the fort (Granger) beyond the Harpeth River, those devoted men tried in vain to pull up the obstruction or force their way through it. But for this we would have captured the works. As it was, many of our men got through and into the ditch around their works, where they remained until the enemy withdrew about midnight."

Another veteran, J.L. Boswell, had another memory of Adams giving a last order. He wrote to *Confederate Veteran* from Plain View, Texas in 1904 (Volume 12, page 454): "As to the last command issued by Gen. Adams I can only say this, that Maj. Garrett, who was commanding the Twenty-Third Mississippi, also of Gen. Adams's Brigade, had halted his men at a rock fence about two hundred yards from the enemy's works. There were two Osage orange hedges in front of us through which Gen. Adams could not ride, making it necessary for him to ride around the ends. He passed directly in front of us for this purpose, and as he did so called out the order, 'Move forward, Maj. Garrett,' and it was not more than three minutes after this that he was shot."

The last scenes of Adams's life must have been clouded by gunpowder as the sun sank off to his left. He must have looked at the entrenched Yankees, intent on Old Charley jumping over their earthworks. He had led his Mississippians around the Osage orange hedge. It would have been an obstacle in times of peace, but here with abatis it might as well have been a mine field. Adams could be seen riding across his advancing line urging the men forward. Adams might also have seen Cleburne's Division breeching the U.S. line by the gin house. This could certainly have attracted him to lead his brigade that way.

Then charging to the U.S. entrenched line, Adams attempted to leap them on his gray horse "Old Charley." It was a jump suited to a steeplechase course, but "Old Charley" came down dead, with his rider shot off. Perhaps nine bullets hit the general. (Sources are OR 45,708 and *Embrace an Angry Wind*). Adams's cousin Thomas Gibson wrote of Adams's last charge in *Confederate Veteran* (Volume 10, page 458): "Riding in front of his brigade, he turned to face his men and said in a cool, calm, deliberate tone: 'Follow me, my men!' In almost less time than it takes me to write, his horse sank down with his front feet resting on the enemy's breastworks, and he was pierced with seven bullets. I have seen it stated from a Federal (U.S.) officer who was in command on that portion of the line, that they could have captured Gen. Adams, but they had to kill him to check his brigade, or else his men would have captured the works. He said he was the bravest man he ever saw."

In 1891 a U.S. officer who witnessed the scene wrote to Mrs. Adams (*CV* 12,482). She no doubt had some idea of the developments leading to the tragic charge. "By this time they were within a few paces and received a terrific volley from our guns. They fell by thousands, and their decimated ranks fell back only to reform and come back again. I doubt if in the history of the world a single instance of such desperate and undaunted valor can be produced. In one of these charges, more desperate than any that followed, General Adams rode up to our works and, cheering his men, made an attempt to leap his horse over them. The horse fell dead on top of the works, and the general, pierced with bullets, was caught under him. As soon as the charge was repulsed our men sprang upon the works and lifted the horse, while others dragged the General from under him. He was perfectly conscious, and realized his condition and asked for water. As he expired, his final words were, 'It is the fate of a soldier to die for his country.'"

More praise from an enemy was recalled by Tennessee Ex-Governor James D. Porter. An enemy officer was met at a meeting of the Confederate Historical Society in Louisville. Porter could not recall his name, but that he had been a regimental commander at the point assailed by Adams's Brigade. The officer said of Adams: "His conduct at Franklin was the grandest performance of the war. I watched him as he led his brigade against our works. He looked like a soldier inspired with the belief that the fortunes of his cause depended upon his own actions; and when his horse leaped upon our works for one moment there was a cessation of firing, caused no doubt by admiration of his lofty courage. Another moment, as he called to his command to follow, a volley was delivered and rider and horse fell dead inside of our works."

After the attack ceased some of the U.S. troops began looking for souvenirs. The flag of the 15th Mississippi was near Adams. Four colour-bearers were shot down, with the fourth losing them. Everything of value was taken from Adams, and even Old Charley's saddle. Adams had brought Old Charley from California, where he had served in antebellum days. Details are from a 1910 *Confederate Veteran* (Volume 18, page 104).

The *Last Moments of General Adams* was done by David Wright in 1963. In 1909 a *National Tribune* news reporter from Washington City said a small tablet told where Adams died. The "old cotton gin had vanished." The tablet may have been along Columbia Avenue. The author's Sons of Confederate Veterans camp (28) placed cenotaph posts for the five brigadiers along Columbia Avenue in 1999. One for Cleburne was on Cleburne Street. They remained for two decades when the city removed them. Leftists have even attacked the Confederate monument in front of the court house. The cause of such disgraceful activities is often attributed to outsiders who have moved to Franklin, escaping from various states the leftists have ruined. They are intent on such ruin in Franklin. Thanks to David Wright.

In 1891 a U.S. officer heard Mrs. John Adams wanted the saddle returned. He wrote her, "There was not a man in my command that witnessed the gallant ride who did not express his admiration of the rider and wish that he might have lived long enough to wear the honors that he so gallantly won." Another U.S. officer wrote, "I doubt if in any history of the world another single instance of as desperate, dauntless valor can be produced."

Quintard wrote: "As a soldier, General Adams was active, calm and self-possessed, brave without rashness, quick to perceive and ever ready to seize the favourable moment. He enjoyed the confidence of his superiors and the love and respect of his soldiers and officers. In camp and on the march he looked closely to the comfort of his soldiers, and often shared his horse on long marches with the sick and broken down men.'

"He was a member of the Episcopal Church, and a sincere and humble Christian. For a year or more before his death he engaged, morning, noon and night in devotional exercises. He invariably fasted on Friday and other days of abstinence appointed by the Book of Common Prayer. He was guarded in all his actions by a thoughtful and strict regard for truth, right, and duty. In all the relations of life he was upright, just and pure. There is no shadow on his memory and he left to his children the heritage of an unblemished name and to coming generations the sublime heroism of a Southern Soldier." He accompanied Adams's body to Pulaski. First taken to his brother's residence, it was then taken to rest by his parent's graves, where Quintard officiated.

Patrick Henry wrote, "Night closed the battle for those not in the ditch of the enemy's breastworks. Those in the ditch, and there were many from all commands, kept up a steady fire until the enemy withdrew. I have often thought what might have been the effect had artillery with which to have fired that gin house standing on the Federal (U.S.) line of battle." Confederate artillery fire hit the Lotz House, which is beyond the gin site; however, this would have been at night.

W.L. Truman, of Guibor's Missouri battery, wrote *Confederate Veteran* in 1923 (Vol. 31, p. 425). They were "on our extreme right, following General Loring's Division, as it moved forward in the attack…" Truman says they were frustrated to be held back. "If General Hood had opened fire with his artillery before he sent in his infantry, which is generally done, we would have knocked all the head logs off of their breastworks, and so demolished their abatis and other obstructions that our infantry would have succeeded." Truman's reflection is correct, but Hood lacked the daylight for such preparations.

Historians of the Western Theatre have taken umbrage with the enormous assault and loss of life being relatively ignored in broad histories of the war. More followed Hood's orders to attack at Franklin than followed Lee's at Gettysburg, and more died. Ask where Hood was when during before Franklin. When the Pickett-Pettigrew assault failed Lee rode out to meet his troops. The English officer-historian Charles Cornwallis Chesney was so enamoured with Lee's actions, he wrote of it through a London publisher in 1863. Chesney knew Lee rode forward to meet the living, knowing an enemy counterattack might follow. Chesney wrote Lee turned to the returning soldiers "back to their duty all who could bear a weapon, whilst using (as has ever been his wont) rather the tenderness of a parent than the sterness of a general…the wounded stopped to cheer their beloved chief; and the groups of loiterers seeking the rear for some trifling hurt, turned back to seek their forsaken colours, and to stand or die with 'Uncle Robert.'…all who looked on him recognized the calm serenity of a hero equal to the crisis of the hour."

No such scene played out for Cheatham's and Stewart's veterans. Had Hood ridden forward that night, on Columbia Pike, he would have found Cheatham's men mostly pinned down on the outside of the main enemy entrenched line. Many of had broken through all three enemy lines, past the Carter House, and maybe past the Lotz House. The Lotz family had huddled in the Carter's basement. There were twenty-four family members and friends there. They were followed by a number of U.S. troops, hiding out. Tod Carter was a staff officer and believed he was about to make a glorious return home. He was mortally wounded just before reaching home. General Granbury may have gotten the farthest of the generals. A courier went for ammunition when the general had passed three lines. Cleburne had died within sight of the Carter's gin. Otho French Strahl may have too, within sight of the Carter property. States Rights Gist did too. John Carter was coming behind and took his mortal wound.

How had Cheatham's soldiers broken through? They had several advantages compared to Stewart's. They first hit an advance line of two brigades. They quickly overwhelmed them, and followed them on their heels. The enemy entrenchment had not been built over Columbia Pike, as wagons had to have a way to continue into Franklin. The entrenched enemy line had to hold their fire to allow their retreating soldiers to retreat past. Parts of Brown's and Cleburne's Division fought their way through and were only turned back by a counterattack of fresh enemy troops. Had Hood allowed a column attack, as Cleburne suggested, the breakthrough could not have been mended.

But for most of Stewart's Corps it had been too obvious they could not penetrate the obstacles before them. It was probably over by 6:30, if not earlier. But rifle fire continued. Their artillery was still spewing canister in Stewart's direction until about 8:00. The enemy had begun a gradual withdrawal after dark, as the bridges had been put in order. Levi Scofield recalled troops, trains, wounded, and prisoners crossed. "The planks were removed from the bridges, and we again took up our retreat to Nashville."

Scott's wounded and dying lay outside the enemy's works. As the bridges were readied for them to retreat, Schofield received word from Thomas: "Send back your trains to this place [Nashville] at once, and hold your troops in readiness to march to Brentwood, and thence to this place, as soon as your trains are fairly on their way." The enemy brigade to Scott's front was preparing to pull out. A Yankee lieutenant thought they ought to stay and wipe hell out of 'em" The brigade commander replied, "There is no hell left in them. Don't you hear them praying?" For wounded Confederates lying before the enemy's works, the danger was far from over. There are numerous accounts of the wounded crying they surrendered. It only made them targets as the Yankees continued shooting.

Recovery of wounded was very risky. Mississippian John Collins wrote to Capt. Thomas Gibson of Adams's staff. *Confederate Veteran* published his lettre in 1902 (Volume 10, page 458). Collins recalled the two met to recover Adams that night. They met near the railroad cut where Thomas Bradley, of the 15th Mississippi, "had attempted to rescue some friend, but found it so hazardous he concluded not to venture farther, and tried to dissuade us from an attempt fraught with so much danger; but, seeing our determination not to heed his advice, he, like the brave boy he was, said: 'Well, I will go back with you.' Always since I have chided myself for being so persistent in pressing forward. You remember that when we got among the dead and wounded piled upon each other I planned as to how we should proceed separately and cautiously, and whichever one should find the body should give a shrill whistle, and the others would go to the call. A few minutes thereafter I came across a poor wounded fellow, who told me to bend down. He informed me that I was in great danger, that the 'Feds' had just passed over him in force, and I could then hear them, after listening carefully; they could not have been over fifteen steps away. I moped about cautiously for a few minutes, looking over the bodies of this one and that one in the hope of finding the body of Gen. Adams. All at once they fired a continuous volley, and in retiring I came across you, wounded, and Bradley also. You remember when we had gotten across the railroad how lustily he called for Collins. It was then I realized the danger, and felt that I was the cause of his getting wounded. I have felt glad, however, a thousand times that you both recovered from your wounds."

In the cold darkness, Hood thought the enemy would be waiting for him in the morning. Patrick Henry had been the acting assistant inspector general for deceased John Adams. Henry wrote to *Confederate Veteran* in 1918 (Volume 26, page 11). He recalled, "About ten o' clock that night I received orders to report to Maj. R.W. Millsaps, inspector general of Major General Loring' s division. Arriving at General Loring's headquarters, I found the inspectors of other brigades. Major Millsaps informed us that we were to report to General Hood, from whom we would receive orders in person. General Hood received us with great courtesy, remarked on the battle, and announced that the corps of General Stephen D. Lee had come up…bringing the artillery of the army; that he desired each brigade inspector to place his respective brigade as near the position it occupied in the battle as possible under cover of darkness…" Capt. William Gale, of Stewart's staff wrote, "I went with Gen. Stewart to Gen. Hood's headquarters. He had determined to renew the attack in the morning. The plan was that all our artillery-100 pieces-which had been brought up, was to open on them at daylight, and at 9 the whole army was to assault the works…" Hood had learned nothing from his failures and was preparing for another assault without reconnoitering. If Loring had been asked he would have pointed out the obstacles before his advance, not to mention enfilading artillery fire.

John C. McQuaide of Cowan's Battery said they were ordered to move "up to pointblank range of the enemy's works, with instructions to open fire on them at earliest daybreak… A very short time before the firing was to commence, and the cannoneers were at their guns, the order was countermanded…I presumed it indicated that the enemy had evacuated Franklin." McQuaide got permission to mount his horse to learn the situation. He came upon Cleburne's lifeless body "and as I looked into the marble features of our hero, our ideal soldier, my first thought was to have the body taken to a place of safety.." McQuaide then saw a friend, Doctor Markham. He was having John Adams's remains loaded onto an ambulance, and they made room for Cleburne. Markham is apparently the same Rev. Thomas R. Markham who had selected Carnton as a hospital site.

Gale continued, "We rode up to a part of the enemy's line, which we still held, to place Strahl's brigade in position, when I was struck by the stillness in the enemy's works, and asked the officer nearest me if the enemy had not gone. He said that they had, as some of his men had been down and found no one there. Further examination convinced me…, and I rode back to our camp-fire, and just as day was dawning I dismounted, wet, weary, hungry, and disheartened, telling Gen. Stewart that Schofield was gone."

Patrick Henry took a friend and courier with him, toward the battlefield to execute the very trying order. He explained, "Just before reaching the field the firing ceased, and we found little torchlights flitting about in our front. Hailing one of these torchbearers, I asked: 'What do these lights mean?' The reply was, 'The enemy has evacuated the works, and we are looking out for the wounded.' Henry sent the courier back to notify Hood.

When the sun came up after Franklin, the scene was unlike any the Army of Tennessee had seen. At least 1,756 Confederates were dead on the field, and more were mortally wounded. A similar number had been killed on other battlefields, but not in one day. At Shiloh, Murfreesborough, and Chickamauga, they were over two days, and the casualties were spread over thousands of largely wooded acres. At Franklin they were concentrated in the small area south of town. J.P Cannon was apparently restrained in his description: "The next morning a sad scene met our eyes when it was light enough to see. Our dead were literally piled on top of each other at the foot of the embankment that alone separated them from the dead Federals in the ditch on the opposite side. Dead and wounded were scattered for hundreds of yards in front of the works. The percentage of loss was equal to, or perhaps greater than, any battle of the war considering the number engaged and the duration of the battle."

Sam Watkins was in Cheatham's Corps, and had served under Loring back in western Virginia. His memoirs were first published in 1882 from articles that had run in the *Columbia Herald*. Watkins wrote of the death angel gathering its last harvest at Franklin. "Kind reader, right here my pen and courage, and ability fail me. I shrink from the task of that dreadful butchery. Would to God I could tear the page from these memoirs and from my own memory. It was the blackest page in the history of the war of the Lost Cause. It was the bloodiest battle of modern times in any war. It was the finishing stroke to the Southern Confederacy. I was there. I saw it. My flesh trembles, and creeps, and crawls when I think of it today. My heart almost ceases to beat at the horrid recollection. Would to God that I had never witnessed such a scene!"

Lt. William Harvey Berryhill, of the 43rd Mississippi in Adams's Brigade wrote his wife: "Near Franklin, Tenn., Thursday, Dec. 1st, 1864-Oh, My Dear Wife, We have passed through terrible scenes and death struggles since I stopped writing this letter on Monday evening, but that you may understand it all I will give an account of our marches… (November 30) When we got within 800 yards they opened terrifick fire of shot, shell, grape and canister, and when the troops got to within 400 yards the musketry united with the cannon and it appeared to come by the millions. I cannot see how any human being could live two moments in such a place. Our Division got to within a few steps of the works and some went upon them. Others could not get there for a thick hedgerow of thorn bushes and after a little while the troops began to faulter and were finally routed and came off in confusion, every man for himself. That is, those that were not killed or wounded. And here, Mary, I am so heartsick that I must stop writing for a while."

Benjamin Smith, also of the 43rd Mississippi, was wounded and lived to write about it: "Hood's army began to form a line of battle in front of the enemy's breastworks there…began one of the severest and most deadly battles of the war." Apparently he was "…bearing our regimental flag, was shot down about 100 yards from the enemy's breastworks. My thigh was broken…between the knee and hip joint, by a …washer ball, which struck a loose knife blade in my right pocket, breaking the blade into a number of pieces. The largest piece found not larger than the finger nail. This wound bled very little, possibly not more than a teaspoon full. I thought when shot about sunset, I would crawl away as soon as it was dark. I made but one effort for I found I could not move an inch. The ground was damp and cold and I soon began to feel chilly. I had only a thin wool blanket." Much of what follows is illegible, but Smith apparently had quite a struggle getting his blanket over himself.

Smith continued with his almost unbelievable story of survival amidst the raging battle and the cruelty of U.S. soldiers. He wrote, "While lying there in range of a battery, a cannonball ploughed in the ground close enough to throw a half foot of dirt on me. Another time a shell burst close enough time a shell burst close enough to me for the concussion to raise my head up off my arm, upon which it was resting. After the battle was over, and things began to quiet down, I called to the Federals, wanting them to come and get me, but they began shooting at me every time I called." Close to midnight the last U.S. troops pulled out, and so quietly there was a delay in the Confederates knowing it.

Sometime between 3 and 4 a.m. Smith was found and taken away on a litter. He wrote, "They carried me a short distance to an ambulance driven by B… E…, a member of the 13th Mississippi regiment, from Starkville. He carried me to Col. John McGavock's home, where seven Confederate generals lay dead on his front porch. It was now about 4 a.m. I was taken in a room laid on the floor before the fireplace. Mrs. McGavock soon brought me some wine, which was all the attention she had time to pay me until about noon, as her house was full of wounded. I was carried to another room and put on a cot and laid on my back. I soon began to feel somewhat comfortable…I did not dare to try to move, for when I did, it pained me greatly." Smith said a surgeon of a Louisiana regiment attended to the wounded in the room he was in." After the Battle of Nashville many wounded in Franklin were captured by the enemy. Smith was one of them, and later had surgery on his leg. He made one more remark about the wonderful McGavocks. He said, "While at the McGavocks, he and his wife were very kind and attentive to us and fed us a good deal at his own expense."

Smith had been mistaken about seven generals laid out. Five had been killed, and John Carter mortally wounded, but he more likely saw four generals. Adams and Cleburne were both found within sight of the Carter's gin, so they were placed side by side in an ambulance bound for the McGavock's. Thomas Gibson of Adams's staff was wounded yet he came by to take his cousin's remains home in Pulaski. Cleburne, Granbury, and Strahl were taken to Columbia, where they were buried temporarily.

For each general to die at Franklin, nearly 300 other Confederate soldiers died. The wife of one got a lettre from Lt. Col. Charles P. Neilson of the 33rd Mississippi. Neilson wrote, "[We found him] lying on his back, and he appeared to be peacefully sleeping. A smile was on his countenance and everything indicated that he had passed away without a struggle…One ball struck him directly in the front, just below the breast bone, passing through. Another struck him on the right side, passing through. Another in the right cheek, and another in the left hand…I found his testament lying on his breast and thinking of his widow far away I put it in my pocket for you…It would certainly be a consolation to you to have received some last message from your loved one, but the unexpectedness of the battle and the circumstances of his death prevented [it]…Your loss is great…but you 'mourn not as one without hope.'"

Col. Noel Ligon Nelson, leading the 12th Louisiana, did not survive. Both of his legs were crushed by a cannon shot. He died at the field hospital at the McGavock's, and is buried there. *Confederate Colonels* says there is a "heartrending letter" describing his last moments, at the Carter House Museum. Capt. J. L. Bond wrote *Confederate Veteran in 1897* (Volume 5, page X63) i: "…at Franklin, the hardest fight of the war, Nelson was killed. He was a brave officer. I saw him dying at the hospital, where I went to have a bullet taken out of my mouth. Both of his legs and arms were shot off. His only murmur was: 'What will become of my wife and little girls?'" Later that year, on page 600, C.E. Merrill also recalled Nelson at the McGavock's home, "…as he lay dying, torn to pieces by a discharge of grape and canister at close range. 'My poor wife and child! My poor wife and child! O M____! Can you not get the surgeon to administer some drug that will relieve me of this torture?' I did try, though my appeals were in vain. I could imagine what he suffered as the cold perspiration gathered in knots on his brow, and of course, knew that death was inevitable."

Merrill continued with an amazing example of human resilience. A Captain Jones of Grenada, Mississippi was also lying on a floor at the McGavock's. Merrill recalled, "One of his thighs had been shattered by a cannon-ball; the bone of the other had been laid bare by a like discharge. One of his arms was also shattered and, as I recall it, one of his hands had been torn away. He was the worst wounded man I ever saw, except that no vital organs had been lacerated, as in the case of Col. Nelson and others. At Capt. Jones's side knelt Dr. George C. Phillips, of Lexington, Miss., the manly surgeon of the Twenty-Second Mississippi, ministering to his wounds. 'Captain, it would subject you to useless pain to amputate your leg,' said the tender hearted young surgeon. 'The wound is fatal or would be by amputation.'

"You are right, Doctor," replied Capt. Jones; "but I don't intend to have that leg cut off, and I don't intend to die. I want to hold on to what is left of me. Why bless your soul!" he added, holding up his shattered hand, as a smile passed over his face, "there is enough left of me to make a first-class cavalryman."

"This was said in reference to the old joke which infantry soldiers good-naturedly were used to getting off on the brave riders of the Confederacy." Merrill concluded by saying he heard Captain Jones's fractured leg grew together and he was still living recently.

Colonel Stephens had been brought to the McGavock's too, and was in the same room with Jones. He said Doctor Wall, surgeon of the 33rd, was in charge of the room. Wall told him that Doctor Roberts, the regimental surgeon of the 31st was going to take his leg off. Stephens said, "Dr. Wall, as you know, I am a physician, and when the war ends everything I have will be gone, but my wife and two children. I will be a very poor man and dependent on my profession for the support of myself and my family, and if Dr. Roberts takes off my leg,…I can never ride a horse, consequently…I cannot practice… Promise me that you will not let Dr. Roberts take off my leg." Wall told him he also thought the leg should come off. Stephens replied, "I…have made up my mind to go with my leg, and I want you to promise me before God, that you will not let him take off my leg." Stephens recalled he grasped his hand with tears in his eyes. "Will you promise?" Dr. Roberts came in later and Dr. Wall let him know the leg was not to come off. Roberts persisted and ordered chloroform. As he prepared bandages Wall told him "if you stick a knife in it, I'll stick a bullet in your head." Roberts folded up his instruments and said, "Let him die." Ironically, Stephens had been work near Franklin and had an uncle living five miles away. He was taken there to recover, returned home, and lived until 1911.

One of the most remarkable lettres written during the war was from William Gale to his wife. She was the daughter of the deceased General Polk, and lived south of Nashville. "I have now one more scene to paint, one more story to tell you, and I am done. I wish I had a pen to do justice to the subject, for in the annals of the war, filled as it is with noble deeds of great and noble men and women, none exceed and few equal in true merit, the noble sympathy of Mrs. John McGavock (Miss Winder). When day dawned we found ourselves near her house-in her lawn-which was in the rear of our line. The house is one of the large old fashioned country homes of the better class in Tennessee, two stories high, with many rooms and every arrangement for comfort. This was taken as a hospital, and the wounded in hundreds were brought to it during the battle, and all the night after. Every room was filled, every bed had two poor bleeding fellows, every spare space niche and corner under the stairs, in the hall, everywhere-but one room for her own family. And when the noble old house could hold no more, the yard was appropriated until the wounded and dead filled that, and all were not yet provided for. Our doctors were deficient in bandages, and she began giving her sheets and table clothes, then her husband's shirts and her own under-garments. During all this time the surgeons plied their dreadful work amid the sighs and moans and death-rattle. Yet amid all this, this noble woman, the very impersonation of Divine sympathy and tender pity, was active and constantly at work. During the night neither she nor any one of her household slept, but dispensed tea and coffee and such stimulants as she had, and that too, with her own hands. Unaffrighted by the sight of blood, unawed by horrid wounds, unblanched by ghastly death she walked from room to room, from man to man, her very skirts stained in blood, the incarnation of pity and mercy. Is it strange that all who were there praise her and call her blessed? About nine in the morning she sent for us-General and Staff-and gave us a nice, warm breakfast, and a warmer welcome. The brother of one of my clerks (McReady) was very badly wounded, and then in her house. I bespoke her kind attention, which she gave until he died."

The McGavocks were not the only citizens to open their home. Frances McEwen had been sent home from school, found the horrible aftermath of the battle on 1 December. "As we approached Col. Carter's house, we could scarcely walk without stepping on the dead or dying men. We could hear the cries of the wounded, of which Col. Carter's house was full to overflowing. As I entered the front door, I heard a poor fellow giving his…comrades a dying message for his loved ones at home. We went through the hall, and were shown to a little room where a soft light revealed all that was mortal of the gifted young genius, Tod Carter, who under the pseudonym of 'Mint Julep,' wrote such delightful lettres to the *Chattanooga Rebel*. Bending over him, begging for just one word of recognition, was his faithful and heartbroken sister." Captain Carter was serving as a staff officer, among the leaders in a charge toward his home. He had been heard to shout, "I am almost home! Follow me boys!" The Carters found him at daybreak and brought him home. Despite medical aid, he died on the 2nd, at age 24.

Frances McEwen went with others "to give water and wine to the wounded. All of us carried cups from which to refresh the thirsty…The dead and wounded lined the Columbia pike for the distance of a mile. In Mrs. Sykes' yard, Gen. Hood sat talking with some of his staff officers. I didn't look upon him as a hero, because nothing had been accomplished which could benefit us…" Going home didn't end the horrors for her. "Ambulances were being filled with the wounded as fast as possible, and the whole town was turned into a hospital. Instead of saying lessons at school the day after the battle, I watched the wounded men being carried in. Our house was as full as could be."

Milton Ryan was in the 14th Mississippi of Adams's Brigade, and on a burial detail. "In places the dead were piled upon each other three and four deep. Sometimes we would find a poor wounded comrade pinned down by several comrades lying on him… We dug trenches two and one half feet deep and wide enough for two to lay side by side. A piece of oil cloth or blanket was spread over their faces and covered up. Every one that could be identified a small piece of plank was placed on their head with their names on it."

.
.
.
.
.
.
.

Chapter 7: Nashville Bound

Nashville occupied by U.S. forces was not the Confederate jewel that it had been before being surrendered in February 1862. It no longer had a capitol for the elected governor, for Lincoln had made Andrew Johnson, military governor. The firms that manufactured materials of war for the Confederacy had generally been evacuated to Georgia. It had been the second largest medical centre in the states. The white population had been intensely secessionist, and now many had crossed over the river to rest under the shade of the trees. Generals Felix Zollicoffer and James Rains were buried in City Cemetery. The glittering prize for Hood would have been the warehouses full of U.S. military supplies. The accumulation of supplies was possible due to railroads, and the Cumberland River. Hood wouldn't have been inclined to stay, with Kentucky on his mind. But he could have established his own base prior to his northward advance.

Nashvillians would have been in a sort of ecstasy to be liberated, as Hood must have imagined. The occupation had been a trying experience. Teenage diarist Rachel Carter considered Johnson a tyrannical devil. "Old Devil called on Pa for $150 today. I wish somebody would blow his brains out." Her father was put in prison until he took the oath of allegiance to the U.S. She compared "such oppression" to the Spanish Inquisition.

Bragg's Kentucky campaign had found few Kentuckians willing to fight for the C.S.A. His subsequent positions in C.S. friendly middle Tennessee had brought the army close, as he headquartered at Murfreesborough. That had been the most realistic hope for Nashvillians until November 1864. Forrest had bombarded Johnsonville and that brought retreating Yankees into the city. But on 1 December they found Schofield's retreating army taking position outside the city. Forrest was close behind, and Rachel Carter wrote of the "greatest excitement here," and that night "Fort Negley looked like an illuminated city." Hopes must have been tempered as U.S. reinforcements arrived on river transports.

Hood moved on toward Nashville, still attempting to follow Beauregard's order to "crush the enemy's forces in Middle Tennessee." Hood took the most demoralized Confederate army, from the sorrows of Franklin, to lay siege to Nashville. It put them into the most lopsided battle of the war. The number of U.S. troops has never been calculated. This is partially due to no return found for something like 12,000 troops brought in by transports. The naval flotilla with them counts. And then there were an unknown number of convalescents, well enough to man the fortified lines. Hood's attempt at a siege against those lines led to what was probably the largest battlefield of the war. It is easy to see the hopelessness in his plan, but he had orders to drive the enemy out of Middle Tennessee. While he enjoyed to comforts of his headquarters at Travellers' Rest, along Franklin Pike, he apparently saw no better strategy.

In the *Decisive Battle of Nashville* Stanley Horn suggested an alternative offensive. "A more artful strategist might have moved quickly with his whole force to Murfreesboro, overpowered its garrison, entrenched himself there, and restored the status quo of late 1862." It was a forward U.S. supply base, and was extremely well fortified. Though there were some 8,000 Yankees there, Hood would have had more than triple their number. It might have required a siege, and his time would have been limited. He would have been off the planned supply line from the Tuscumbia, and might have found it necessary to retake Chattanooga. But it was a more attainable objective than Nashville.

Instead Hood sent Bate's Division of about 1,600 from Franklin to confront the enemy at Fortress Rosecrans, on the edge of Murfreesborough. It was a complex fortification, and far more than Bate's small force could handle. Hood later sent Forrest with Buford's and Jackson's divisions, more infantry, and artillery; it was still not enough. Forrest would be defeated there, in a sense for the first time, but he at least kept the enemy off Hood's rear.

Hood's only cavalry for operations against Nashville was Chalmers's Division, of two brigades. Biffle's small brigade was sent to cover about three miles from the left of the infantry's main line along Hillsborough Pike, to west of Harding Pike. The next day Rucker's Brigade was sent to cover the gap between Biffle and the Cumberland River. Forrest's old regiment, under Lt. Col. David Campbell Kelley, was detached to blockade the river, initially with two 10-pounders Parrotts from Walton's Mississippi battery. They arrived after a convoy of enemy transports brought in at least 12,000 16th Corps troops. They were accompanied by a gunboat flotilla. Kelley captured several transports loaded with 197 horses and mules, miscellaneous supplies, and 56 prisoners. In contrast to Chalmers's small division Thomas was building the largest cavalry force to battle in the Western Theatre. There would be an effective force of 12,500 out of a total of 13,910. Most would fight Hood's infantry, but Chalmers would more than have his hands full. Besides cavalry, Kelley had several fights with the gunboats before and during the battle.

Loring's Division approached fortified Nashville on the afternoon of 2 December. The only city that the U.S. Army had made a greater effort to fortify was Washington. The inner line had been begun in the late summer of 1862, when Braxton Bragg had shot past Nashville in his Kentucky campaign. That seven-mile line had numerous forts. An outer line was added. The land outside their lines had productive land, and what trees had been there were largely gone after the enemy cut trees for over two years.

Hood had no intention of attacking those fortified lines. In *Advance and Retreat* he wrote of his plan "to take position, entrench around Nashville, and await Thomas's attack which, if handsomely repulsed, might afford us an opportunity to follow up our advantage on the spot, and enter the city on the heels of the enemy." Once the battle commenced Thomas left nearly as many troops holding the fortified lines as Hood had on the entire battlefield. The outer line had field artillery, but the inner fortified line had heavy artillery, such as 30# Parrott rifles. Hood's plan was simply unrealistic.

Loring's Division had 2,524 infantry before Nashville. Divisions in the army were the size of brigades, and brigades were the size of regiments. Col. Robert Lowry, formerly commanding the 6th Mississippi, took command of Adam's Brigade after Franklin. Banks wrote that he was "another hero who went through it all unhurt, and yet so nobly did his part that Adams's mantle fell to his shoulders…" Another source has Lowry wounded.

Lowry (below left) was known to be "intellectually a very superior officer and man." The brigade had 1,047 available before Nashville, which was Stewart's largest brigade. Featherston survived Franklin, but only had 781 left to fight. The artillery shell that exploded by Scott at Franklin ended the war for him. Col. John Snodgrass (below right) commanded Scott's Brigade of only 696 veterans. Snodgrass was from Jackson County, in north Alabama, and had been colonel of the 55th Alabama.

J.P. Cannon, of Scott's Brigade, made a diary entry for Saturday the 3rd: "We remained quietly in line till 2 p.m., when we were ordered forward in line-of-battle, charged the enemy's skirmishers and drove them back, advancing in sight of the enemy's works, and were ordered to lie down. Being in plain view of their line, the artillery opened on us and gave us a severe shelling, during which quite a number were killed and wounded."

Cannon's entry for Sunday the 4th indicates they had worked hard all night fortifying, for they knew "the dogs of war" would be turned loose when the sun came up. A terrific shelling did begin and was kept up all day. "The enemy have a strong position, their artillery being posted on commanding eminences, with nothing but open fields between us, while a line of earthworks for the infantry extends as far as we can see. If we are to storm their works, it seems to me it should be done at once as every hour's delay is adding to their strength and no advantage to us." One "commanding eminence" was Lawrence Hill, on today's Ashwood Avenue, east of Belmont Boulevard.

Loring's and French's Divisions held the most advanced, exposed positions in the line. French wrote, "Hood formed his line close as he could in front of their works. My division was on the left of the Granny White turnpike, and ran north of the dwelling of E. Montgomery, who was a cotton planter and neighbor of mine in Mississippi." French was the left end of the line. Claudius Sears made a diary entry for the 3rd: "Drove in the enemy's skirmishers and at night fortified on extreme left on our lines near the Montgomery House." For the 4th Sears wrote, "Enemy gave us a sharp shelling-extended our Division to left on Hillsboro Pike."

Besides Lawrence Hill, the U.S. line came to within a half mile of French's Montgomery Hill position. This was a salient in Stewart's line; it is at the top of today's Cedar Lane, west of Belmont Boulevard. There are traces of his earthworks in a back yard on the northern slope. And just to their north was the U.S. outer line, over an unnamed hill, on today's Linden Ave. It is surprising that Hood's line was ever so close. An historical marker, on nearby 21st Avenue South, named "*IV Corps Jump-Off Line..*," calls the hill a salient in their line.

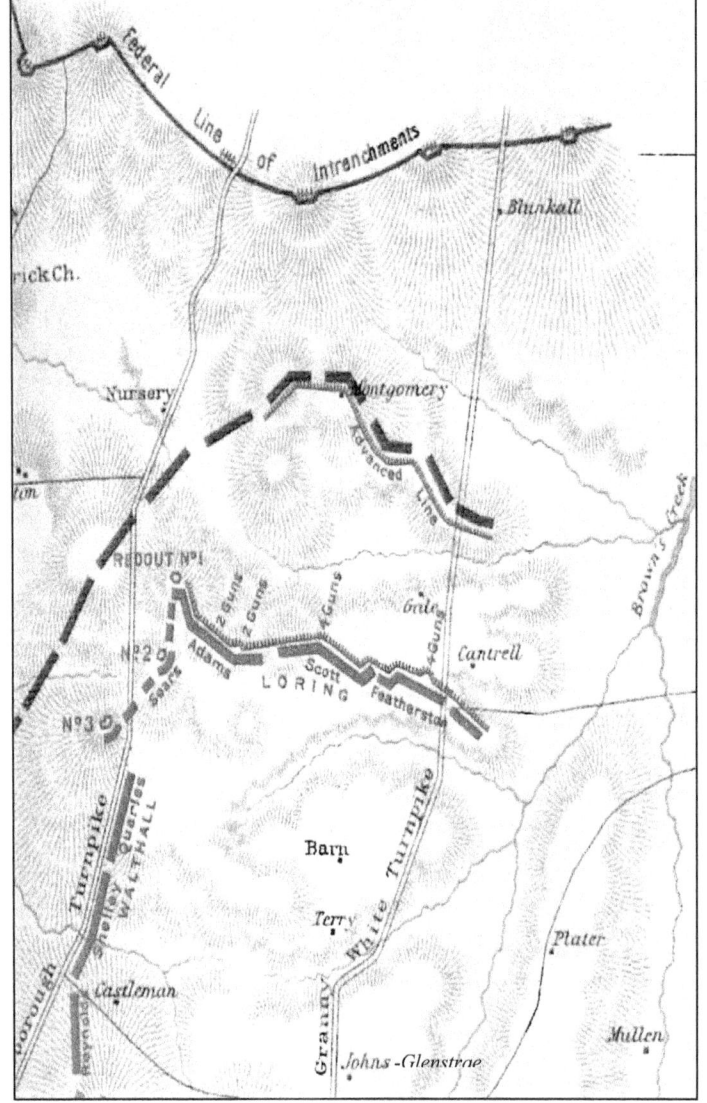

Stewart's Corps map (O.R. plate 73-2) at left shows his initial line. Montgomery house (above) is shown. It had burned in 1862. Hood fell back to a new line on the 11th, leaving the original line as an advance, or picket, line. Hood gave two reasons for the new line; the original line was taking too much artillery fire, and lack of firewood.

When French's line was extended west to Hillsborough Pike, Loring's line must have come close to Montgomery Hill. Walthall's Division was on Loring's right. Neither Walthall nor any other division was so close to the enemy line. Within the week Hood would realize the danger, but first he had to deal with the weather.

The first week of December had been mild in the Nashville area. On the afternoon of the 7th wind and rain came in, followed by a cold, piercing north wind. The next morning the ground was frozen hard. On the night of the 8th a cold rain began to freeze. When the armies awoke on the 9th the ground was covered in ice. Falling rain froze and snow began to coat the ice. This was inconvenient for Thomas as he was under much pressure to attack from Lincoln and Grant. But for Hood's threadbare army it was potentially deadly. Many had no shoes or even a blanket. Few tents had survived and many a Confederate lived by burrowing underground alongside their trenches.

Hood's staff wrote Stewart on the 9th: "General Hood directs that you will push forward, with all possible haste, the work of fortifying the hills in rear of your left upon which you are now working, that you may be in readiness, whenever called upon, to move with two of your divisions and one other division from another corps, with a battery to each of these divisions, to prevent the enemy from re-enforcing Murfreesborough, or to capture the force now at Murfreesborough should it attempt to move off." Hood's creativity in his strategy is impressive. He intended to hold his line south of Nashville while thinking of a way to defeat the force at Murfreesborough, which Forrest was stalemated with. Hood also ordered the extension of Cheatham's right across the *Nashville & Chattanooga* to an earthwork known as Granbury's Lunette. It also overlooked Murfreesborough Pike. He also ordered Biffle's small cavalry brigade to the right, between the lunette and the river. Had Hood sent Stewart before the ice and snow, there was a chance of success.

Hood pulled Stewart's Corps back from the initial entrenched line on the 11th. Hood cited two reasons for pulling back. He said the line was taking too much artillery fire, and he said there were trees for firewood on the new line. Featherston said it was "to protect the men from the enemy's artillery fire." He also reported his brigade was across Granny White Pike. He was the far right of Stewart's Corps. To his right was another Mississippi brigade, Sharp's of Lee's Corps.

Hood may have cited trees for firewood, but J.P. Cannon failed to see them. His entry for Sunday the 11th states: "Last night, under cover of darkness, we moved our line back 400 yards and began fortifying again. We worked hard all night without sleep or rest. This is the coldest day I ever saw. Our position being in the open fields, with no timber for miles to break the force of the wind, which is blowing a perfect gale from the north, no wood to make fires and most of us thinly clad, our suffering is intense. It seems we are bound to freeze unless a change occurs very soon." It was remembered as "Cold Sunday" with lows around ten degrees below zero and a high of twenty degrees. Eggleston's entry was, "A pinching cold day, a sharp cutting wind from the northwest blew all day. We slept on frozen ground last night, but had plenty of blankets and were warm and comfortable." Cowan's must have had large fires to be warm and comfortable!

The weather was hardest on soldiers from the Gulf states, but miserable for all of them. One Tennessean recalled, "Ambition and even life itself, were almost frozen out of us." Sam Watkins wrote, "We bivouac on the cold and hard-frozen ground, and when we walk about, the echo of our footsteps sounds like the echo of a tombstone. The earth is crusted with snow, and the wind from the northwest is piercing our very bones. We see our ragged soldiers, with sunken cheeks and famine-glistening eyes."

While Hood enjoyed the comforts of the Overtons at Travellers' Rest, his army barely survived. Watkins continued, "A few raw-boned horses stood shivering under the ice-covered trees, nibbling the short, scanty grass. Being in range of the Federal guns from Fort Negley, we were not allowed to have fires at night, and our thin ragged blankets were but poor protection against the cold raw blasts of December weather-the coldest ever known. The cold stars seem to twinkle with unusual brilliancy, and the pale moon seems to be but one vast heap of frozen snow, which glimmers in the cold gray sky…"

Scott's Brigade was in Loring's centre, so east of Redoubt One. James Harmon, in the 35th Alabama, wrote, "Hood's army was in a…fix, with provisions short and scanty clothing with cold wintry weather upon us and fuel scarce. We had no shelter of any kind and having to take the weather like a lot of beasts…we poor soldiers were in a pitiful condition…The troops being in this awful condition caused them to weaken very much."

Featherston's 3rd Mississippi had fatigue parties leave their own line to assist in throwing up the redoubts on both sides of Hillsborough Pike. The work continued even though the ground was frozen hard. They said rations were generally an ear of corn a day, but sympathetic area farmers made donations. Cannon's entry for Tuesday the 13th says they were still digging and stretching the lines to a single rank. The snow and ice began to melt by the 14th, and the enemy was about to strike, when Cannon wrote, "The weather has moderated and we enjoy lying around in the sun, but the Yanks won't let us enjoy it for any length of time. When they see a squad of us, they drop over a few shells and we dart into holes like prairie dogs."

French's Division was temporarily broken up before the battle. Cockrell's Missouri brigade had been decimated at Franklin. Cockrell and Loring had battled together since Champion Hill. Cockrell was absent, recovering. The survivors had been sent to the mouth of the Duck River to build a fortified position overlooking the gunboat infested Tennessee River. Kolb's Alabama battery had been sent along with them. Ector's active service ended with the amputation of a leg during the Atlanta Campaign. His brigade's survivors were positioned to cover the Harding Pike. Biffle's small cavalry brigade had been there, but Hood ordered them to cover the area between Granbury's Lunette and the Cumberland River. Ector's line was about three miles long. With 569 effectives, that allowed an average of 190 men per mile, or one man about every 27 feet. French took sick leave due to an eye infection. That left the 210 survivors of Sear's Mississippi brigade in Redoubt Two and Redoubt Three, and maybe in One too, beyond Loring's left.

Amidst the miserable weather Hood had sent a small cavalry raid into Kentucky. Unlike the great cavaliers John Hunt Morgan raided Kentucky with this raid had no impact on

Hood's campaign. Brig. Gen. Hylan Benton Lyon took new recruits, poorly armed, into even colder weather. But Grant was very upset. He wired Thomas, "If you delay attack [ing] longer the mortifying spectacle will be witnessed of a Rebel army moving for the Ohio River, and you will be forced to act, accepting such weather as you find. Let there be no further delay. Hood cannot stand even a drawn battle so far from his supplies or ordinance stores…I am in hopes of receiving a dispatch from you today announcing that you have moved. Delay no longer for weather or reinforcements."

Thomas tried to explain, wiring back later that day, "I will obey the order as promptly as possible, however much I may regret it, as the attack will be made under every disadvantage. The whole country is covered with a perfect sheet of ice and sleet, and it is with difficulty the troops are able to move about on level ground." By the 13th enough melting had occurred that Thomas was preparing to strike on the 15th.

Thursday, 15 December 1864

Somehow Hood knew Thomas was going to attack on the morning of the 15th. The weather may have been a clue. Rain on the 14th led to temperatures near 50 degrees on the 15th. But Hood apparently received some definitive word. James Chalmers had his cavalry division headquarters at Belle Meade, on Harding Pike. He was awakened at 2 a.m. with a warning to expect to be attacked within a few hours.

The most lop-sided major battle of the war was about to commence. Hood's army before Nashville, adjusting for troops off with Forrest, was about 22,000. Thomas probably had over 70,000, and some think he could have had 80,000. It was his supply base, so he had quartermaster troops. It was a hospital base, so he had convalescents. There was also the naval flotilla; it had escorted the transports that brought two 16th Corps divisions from Missouri. Thomas had everything he needed. Hood could not have made it easier for him.

The *Decisive Battle of Nashville* states: "Thomas himself was up early. The gaslights were still glimmering dimly in the city's fog-wrapped streets as the commanding general paid his bill at the Saint Cloud Hotel, checked out with his baggage, and mounted his horse to ride to the front line of the battle." This must be the only battle in history where a general checked out of a hotel and rode a few miles to fight a major battle.

Loring's and Walthall's divisions took the brunt of the U.S. force, swinging out of their entrenchments with a right thrust. Chalmers took some of the hit, but was cut off while holding Charlotte Pike. The eastern end of the entrenched line was Granbury's Lunette. About 8:20a.m. U.S. forces launched a feint which temporarily distracted Hood. It struck the lunette and portions of Brown's and Cleburne's Divisions. It was decisively defeated.

The U.S. plan for the 15th was to attack Stewart's Corps, of no more than 6,136, with three infantry corps, and most of their cavalry. The U.S. Army had over 40,000 available. Lt. Col. James R. Binford commanded the 15th Mississippi of Adams' Brigade. He wrote, "The Brigade (Adams') was on the left of Loring's Division and the 15th Mississippi on the extreme left of the Brigade…" The map by Wilbur Foster shows Loring's line behind or in Redoubt One. Binford would have indicated if the 15th was in a redoubt or fort.

Instead he wrote, "Our position was on the summit of a ridge overlooking a broad valley and where I had a splendid view of the immense number of 'Blue Coats' forming into line." Redoubt One, on today's Benham Avenue, has been preserved by the Battle of Nashville Trust. It seems the position of the 15th was closer to the Unitarian church, southeast of the redoubt.

Stewart's headquarters were at "Glenstrae," the home of Mrs. Johns. It was on the abrupt curve on Granny White Pike (see map above). Loring's line facing north and perpendicular to Hillsborough Pike saw the U.S. 4th Corps. Gale was Stewart's assistant adjutant general. He wrote, "About 9 o' clock it was reported to me that the enemy were advancing in heavy force on the Hillsborough Pike and in front of Gen. Loring. Generals French and Walthall had their troops in bivouac along the east side of the Hillsborough Pike ready to move. I informed Gen. Stewart, who mounted and rode to the point, leaving me to keep my office open and sent dispatches. I had a signal station and sent dispatches to Generals Hood, Lee, and Cheatham, and received others." It seems the fog would have interfered, but Gale makes no mention. Hood had a signal station at Travellers' Rest. Lee may have had one near his headquarters at the Thompson's Glen Levin. It is extant on the east side of Franklin Pike. Thompson Lane led east to Nolensville Pike, where Cheatham had his headquarters at Wesley Greenfield's Flat Rock. He might have had his station at the high point of his line, farther north on Nolensville Pike at Rains' Hill (at I-440 exit).

The first brigade of Stewart's Corps to confront the enemy was Ector's, over on the Harding Pike. They were stretched thin to fill the void between Stewart's main line alongside Hillsborough Pike and Chalmers' cavalry positioned across Charlotte Pike. Ector had been seriously wounded in the Atlanta Campaign, and some 569 survivors were left before Nashville under command of a naval academy student, Col. Daniel Coleman. They witnessed perhaps 18,685 Yankees coming toward them. After firing a few shots they retreated toward Redoubt Four, before 11 a.m. They were asked to stop and make a stand. Their reply was, "It can't be done; there's a whole army in your front."

Lumsden's Battery was in Redoubt Four supported by 100 men from the 29th Alabama. Charles L. Lumsden was a graduate of Virginia Military Institute, where he must have studied artillery under Stonewall Jackson. He was an instructor of Military Tactics at the University of Alabama in 1861, where he recruited his battery. Battery members George Little and James Maxwell wrote *A History of Lumsden's Battery C.S.A.* They wrote of the dense fog in the morning. U.S. infantry and dismounted cavalry were preparing for an assault as their rifled artillery fired on Lumsden's four smoothbore Napoleons. There were probably 24 pieces with their infantry, aligned on a ridge where a portion of today's Estes Road lies. Another two pieces, with the cavalry, were further south and able to enfilade Redoubt Four. This artillery fight consumed over three hours of daylight, from about 11 a.m. to about 2 p.m.

Fog hung around almost all morning. Cannon's entry for the 15th says, "The Yanks took advantage of it in disposing their forces for an attack on our lines." Then enemy artillery drove their pickets in. "Our artillery replied with vigor, and a fearful cannonade was soon in progress all around the line, which continued without intermission for several hours."

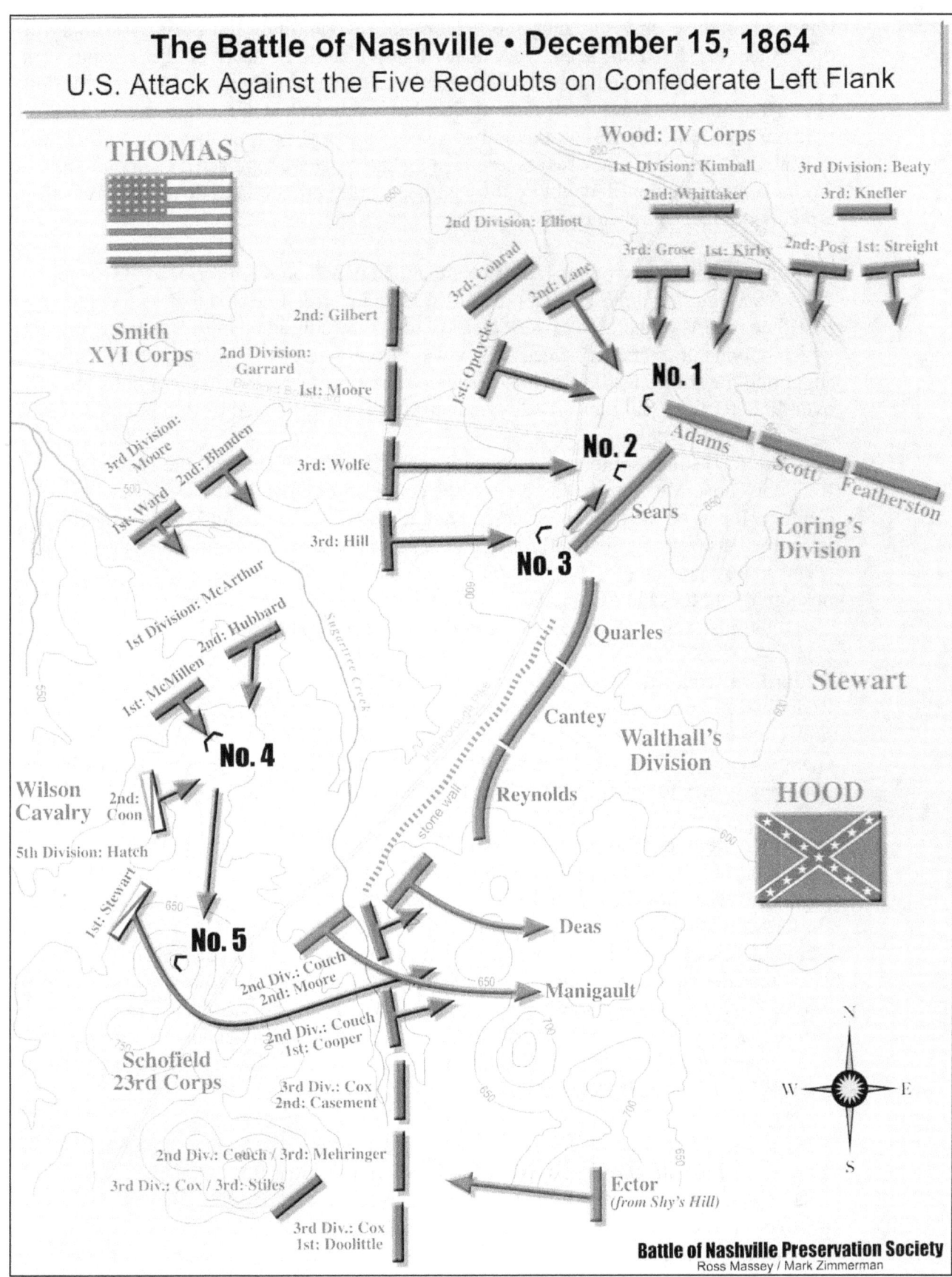

Cannon said the enemy's infantry moved forward several times, but Loring's artillery fire drove them back. "About 2 p.m. very heavy fighting could be heard on the left and, as the sound of the guns receded, it soon became evident they had turned our left wing. We still hoped that our boys would rally and regain what had been lost, believing that we could hold our position. This we subsequently proved, for in a short time they moved forward in heavy columns and made two determined assaults that we repulsed." Cannon's time of 2 p.m. is the assault on Redoubt Four by perhaps 7,000 infantry and dismounted cavalry armed with Spencer repeater rifles.

As Redoubt Four fell two howitzers in Redoubt 5 opened on them. Prior to the author's 2007 *Nashville Battlefield Guide*, previous writers incorrectly stated that #5 had fallen first. The reports of the U.S. cavalry clearly show they continued onto attack the redoubt which only had two artillery pieces. They were from Tarrant's Alabama battery. Infantry supported the attack, leading #5 to surrender. That meant an overwhelming force of well over 40,000 troops had Stewart's line in a vise, having outflanked his left under Walthall.

The U.S. forces took some time between the fall of Redoubt Five and the attack on Redoubt Three. Much of the Redoubt Three could be discerned thru most of the 20th Century. It was on the back of property occupied by Calvary United Methodist Church. From the back right of the building, behind a porte cochere, is a small depression. This seems to be a portion of it, but the view here is of more interest now. Foliage may obscure it, but the land dropping off to the west and south give some idea how Brig. Gen. Claudius Wistar Sears and his men could have seen Redoubt Four fall.

Binford was concerned for his left flank. It seems Redoubt One was to his left-front and Redoubt Two to his left. But his description indicates his idea that his left was not protected. He sent his acting adjutant to Lowry to visit his line. Lowry ordered Binford to change front and charge them. Binford was astonished. He responded that he only had 300 men. Lowry told him he would support him with the brigade.

But Lowry next told Binford to take the 15th and the 14th Mississippi to a fort about a half mile to his left and report to General Sears. This was Redoubt Three. But as he reached it Sears was evacuating it, but ordered Binford to remain and see that the artillery was out. Binford wanted to advance to the redoubt, but said Sears refused. Binford's courage was admirable, but Sears had had a better view of the overwhelming force headed their way. Sears repeated he wanted Binford to see that the artillery was able to be removed. Binford wrote, "I went up to the Fort to hurry them up and to see where the enemy was, but before reaching it, I noticed a terrible going on my left between the enemy and Brantley's and Sharp's Brigades. Our troops were being driven back…" These had been the later arrivals from Johnson's Division of Lee's Corps.

The first two to arrive from Johnson's were Deas's, with 628 effectives, and Manigault's with 838. These brigades had overrun U.S. artillery in battles at Chickamauga and Atlanta, and no doubt many of their bravest had been lost in Georgia. They arrived about the time the redoubts were falling. Stewart wrote they made "feeble resistance, fled, and the enemy crossed the pike, passing Walthall's left. Loring's line not being yet pressed, a battery had been ordered from it, which arriving just at this moment, was placed on a commanding hill, and these same brigades rallied to its support. They again fled, however, on the approach of the enemy, abandoning the battery, which was captured." It was Cowan's that had been sent. Eggleston's entry was more critical than Stewart's report. He wrote, "We went to the left this evening and lost our guns and horses. The infantry ran like cowards and the miserable wretches who were to have supported us refused to fight and ran like a herd of stampeded cattle. I blush for my countrymen and despair of the independence of the Confederacy if her reliance is placed in the army of Tennessee to accomplish it. There are ten men from the battery missing supposed to be killed or captured…All of the Co. papers and records were lost, and all my blankets, and rations. Expect to freeze this winter."

The apparent lack of interest in the battle by the brigades of Deas and Manigault may be understood by reading Manigault's narrative. At Atlanta his brigade had broken through the enemy's position, ordered to retire, and then to re-charge a second time. He wrote his men "did not seem to understand the purpose for which they had been fighting, or the strategy of the generals." Ezra Church and Franklin could not have improved morale.

Binford mentioned seeing Brantley's and Sharp's falling back. They were fellow Mississippians and had fought hard at Ezra Church and in the night attack at Franklin. Lee had praised all of Johnson's Division, never having "seen greater evidence of gallantry…" The carnage of those useless battles had taken too much from them. Stewart wrote they had "come up, but were unable to check the progress of the enemy, who had passed the Hillsborough pike a full half mile, completely turning our flank and gaining the rear of both Walthall and Loring…" The veteran eye of Stewart realized it was time to fall back. He continued, "…orders were dispatched to that effect, when it was found that Walthall had already ordered his line to retire not a moment too soon, and this of itself made it necessary for Loring to withdraw."

Binford saw the two pieces of artillery escape from Redoubt Three. These were from Seldon's Battery, of Alabama. One of his officers "called my attention to the fact that a large force of the enemy was not more than two hundred yards from my left flank, endeavoring to reach my rear. This necessitated an immediate move to the rear with my men…" Amazingly Binford got the 14th and 15th Mississippi into line with the two guns. He thought he was in the rear of Adams' Brigade, and it seems he might have been.

Binford continued, "I was in a quanderry [sic] what to do, for I really did not know where the Brigade was…Just at this moment I was greatly relieved by seeing General Walthall about one hundred yards in my rear, with a flag trying to rally his Division which had been driven back with considerable confusion." Binford then joined Walthall as he could not locate his own brigade.

One of the artillerists in Redoubt Three, from Selden's Battery, wrote a lettre to his father describing the action. Selden's was in Truehart's Battalion, of Walthall's Division. Sears' Brigade of French's Division, was temporarily attached to Walthall's as French had to take leave with an eye infection. French's artillery was in Storrs' Battalion. Sears must have ordered Maj. George S. Storrs to command the section from Selden's as Redoubt Three was in his line.

The artillerist from Selden's wrote of seeing Redoubt Four captured. "The enemy soon began to appear in two lines of battle on our immediate front, and we poured shell and solid shot on them very heavily, causing them to halt. Our ammunition was getting scarce, the major ordered us to reserve our fire. Our infantry support, consisting of about one hundred men of Sayre's [Sears'] brigade (the general himself in our works), continued to fire a few rounds now and then. The Yankees about this time commenced a furious cannonading, and we had to remain idle behind our works."

Above, dramatic sketch shows U.S. brigade commander Col. Sylvester Hill being killed as his troops are about to take Redoubt Three. It shows artillery still in the redoubt. But Sears, his infantry, and the section of Selden's Battery all escaped. Selden's artillerist continued, "We received orders about this time to hitch up and save our guns, as the enemy was not seen coming up the pike, in our rear, and at the same time charging in two or three lines of battle on our front and right flank." The troops in the sketch were apparently some distance from the redoubt when Hill was killed, and found it abandoned before arriving.

Binford stated the two cannon were in his line, and Selden's artillerist wrote of it too, "We got our two pieces about four hundred yards from our works, in a muddy field, where we had to abandon one of them; two of the horses being shot, leaving only four, and they were not able to pull it. Our other gun and our ammunition wagon we brought off. Just as we arrived in this field, the last brigade, either Shelly's (Cantey's old brigade) or Reynolds', being flanked, and the Yankees two hundred yards, in two lines of battle, on their left and rear, broke, General Walthall himself giving the order. From this time it was one perfect stampede for a mile."

While Walthall's Division was in confusion, Binford wrote, "On seeing my men drawn up in perfect order, I was made to feel proud of my brave old Regiment. When he (Walthall) pointing to them said to his men, 'See the old 15th Mississippi, the first regiment I ever commanded, the heroes of Fishing Creek, rally on them. They are always in place and ready.' Then waving his large black plume at the old Regiment he cried out, 'Three cheers for the 15th Mississippi.'"

The location of the rally, 400 yards east of Redoubt Three, may be today's intersection of Graybar Lane and Hopkins Street. Binford described the position of Adams' Brigade as on a ridge, and this intersection in on a southern spur. From they could have seen the other brigades mentioned, being outflanked. The ridgeline must have hidden Loring's main line from view. Once this fall back position was abandoned, the terrain begins a long decent to the east.

Redoubt Three fell before Redoubt Two somewhat behind it on the east side of Hillsborough Pike. The exact times they fell is not known but about 4:00 to 4:15 seems likely. Sears' Brigade provided infantry support to both of them, and possibly in Redoubt One too. This was a salient in Stewart's line. U.S. 16th Corps troops attacked eastward to take #3 and #2. Then U.S. 4th Corps troops attacked southward and eastward to take #1. Since Sears had ordered the evacuation of #3, it seems he would have also ordered the evacuation of #2, and possibly #1. A U.S. colonel had noticed the Confederates at the salient "shifting rapidly to the left (east)" at about 4:00.

185

When the U.S. 4th Corps (13,526 present for duty equipped) began their advance toward Redoubt One and Loring's line (2,524 infantry), Bouanchaud's Napoleon's opened on them with balls and shells. The Yankees sought cover behind a hedge about 75 yards out. Then Bouanchaud's switched to canister. They were positioned in two sections. One was with the 23rd Mississippi of Adams's Brigade, and the other was with Scott's. So both sections were close to the Redoubt One. There is a Metro Historical Commission marker in front of the Unitarian church at 1808 Woodmont Boulevard. It states Loring's Division was there, though incorrectly calling it as the "center of the Confederate main line." A fragment of trench line remains to the left front of the church. Another section is across at 1811 Woodmont in a landscaped area in front of a stone house. Continuing to the right, they are positioned in a southeasterly direction.

The Unitarian church driveway may be on a portion of Adams's (Lowry's) line. A section (circled) runs northwest toward Redoubt One, beyond the houses. The historical marker text: "Trenches about 20 ft. north of this point, held by Loring's Division, were the center of the Confederate main line…" Lee's Corps was the centre, on Loring's right. "…Redoubt No. 1, a key artillery salient 200 yards NW, fired on Federal forces until overrun by General Wood's troops late in the day, when Confederate troops retreated toward Granny White Pike." It is likely that Bouanchaud's initial position was in this view, or within sight of it. The terrain drops off just beyond this scene, making it a logical position for Loring's Corps.

Maj. George Garrett commanding the 23rd Mississippi of Adams's recalled the retreat: "Our army was being withdrawn and then I learned we were to cover the retreat. But a short time and we heard the firing of the pickets, soon they were falling back and took positions in ditch, then we could see the advance line of the enemy. They formed three lines of battle one in the rear of the other and came in order. When the advance line came within reach of my artillery we began to play on them with ball and shell and when they had gotten in close range used grape and canister.'

"I then turned to my men, read them my orders and told them that if we were to be sacrificed for the good of our army and our country that we must submit like men and officers. I wanted them to remember Franklin and if possible revenge our fellow comrades, that they must hold their fire until the enemy came close enough to receive the discharge.'

"They did their duty and did it well as the long line of the enemies dead and wounded in our front bore a solemn testimony. One line after the other would charge with desperate determination. We played upon them with our long range guns and cannons until they came to a hedge I took to be Bodoc, some seventy-five yards in our front, our battery then used grape and canister. The Regiment was commanded to load and fire at will, and the galling fire from both cannon and musketry would cause the enemy to falter and lie down at this hedge to receive one volley after another until it seemed no human could survive. Occasionally we could hear a voice cry out above the din of battle Remember Franklin.'

"On came the second and third lines only to meet similar results. They would rush to this point like demons, did not lack for courage until they reached this point where they were blinded by a terrific fire that belched forth from our line like that of a burning volcano. While they seemed courageous they did sorry shooting, wild and inaccurate which did but small damage."

Major Garrett said that on his right were stationed North Carolina troops. They must have been their two regiments detached from Ector's Brigade, loaned to Loring. Garrett wrote: "After the last line had gotten to the hedge I looked to my right and saw that the NC troops had abandoned the ditches and enemy were coming in south of a rock fence. Then I thought, 'Is it possible that we have been forgotten by our officers thereby dooming us to death or a northern dungeon.' At this time I walked up to the brow of the ridge in my rear hoping to see the officer on his way to relieve us. He was not to be seen but in his stead I saw about three regiments of the enemy who had passed around my left into my rear and were marching toward us. At this time their commanding officer seeing me, rode up to speaking distance and told me to surrender. I told him I thought it was about time as I was completely surrounded. Ordered to raise my flag I told him we had no flag of that kind.'

"He then said, 'Go order your men to cease firing or I will have every d___ one of them shot.' I presume he thought my men were firing on them but it was the overshooting of their own men who were in my front. But I went back to my men who were still holding their portion of the ditches with bulldog tenacity. I gave orders to cease firing and lay down arms." The 23rd Mississippi was likely within sight of today's Unitarian church on the north side of Woodmont Boulevard. The enemy had come past Redoubt Two and was on the south side of today's thoroughfare. Garrett's entry tells how his horse got home.

R.B. Meadows of the 35th Alabama recalled Bouanchaud's "four cannons stationed in our regiment." Perhaps he meant along the line of Scott's Brigade. The withdrawal of Walthall's Division required Loring to abandon his line. Meadows recalled the Louisiana artillerists, "Those noble men turned those four guns with canister shot, held their fire until the Yankees were within about fifteen or twenty feet of their guns, then turned the four guns loose. This gave us a little show to get away."

Louisiana has a biographical sketch of Bouanchaud. "At this critical stage Bouanchaud had the presence of mind to order up his horses from the rear, and that too under a most terrific fire. By this time our infantry was flying in all directions, and the Federals were throwing themselves against Bouanchaud and Darden in overwhelming force. They had already come over our works to the left of these two batteries, and now swept down upon the batteries, capturing Darden's guns, but Bouanchaud, lion-hearted and undismayed, had limbered up and was retiring despite them."

Vicksburg's Captain James J. Cowan (left) had commanded his battery in the overwhelming onslaught at Champion Hill to cover the retreat. Pointe Coupee Parish's Captain Alcide Bouanchaud (right) and his Louisiana battery covered the retreat at Nashville on the 15 December.

An account of Bouanchaud's Battery on the 15th was left by an artillery battalion adjutant, Lieutenant John McQuaide. He recalled: "Bouanchaud and his battery did the grandest piece of fighting on the first day at Nashville done during the whole war; had it not been for him and his battery, General Hood would have been no doubt been completely routed on the first day, because everything on our left gave way before General Thomas expect Bouanchaud's Battery." McQuaide was almost correct, as the battery covered the retreat of almost all of Loring's Division.

Renee Amedee DeRussy was a driver in Bouanchaud's. Some years after the war his comrades asked him to speak to a local camp of the United Confederate Veterans in Louisiana. The *New Orleans Times-Democrat* reported on a paper he read. He seems to describe their withdrawal from the line alongside today's Woodmont Boulevard to a final line along Granny White Pike. DeRussy read his paper, "…our only route led us through a gauntlet and through this we ran to the Granny White Pike. A moment's hesitation meant the loss of a division. Racing wildly past the positions captured by the enemy, we still felt their fire from the guns they had taken and which they turned upon Myrick's Battery (meaning Bouanchaud's), but at last we got thorough. Edward Vignes was lead driver on piece No. 1 and I was lead driver of the caisson of piece No. 2 and it was here that Vignes and myself won the soubriquets from our comrades of 'Little Captains.'"

Bouanchaud's exact position isn't known though in sight of today's Lipscomb University along Granny White Pike. DeRussy continued, "In a moment Vignes stopped and I followed his example and repeated his orders and in an instant our guns were working their utmost, pouring their charges into the enemy. Lieutenant Legendre and Captain Alcide Bouanchaud encouraged us both by voice and example regardless of the shower of shells which rained upon us. So here we stood and fought-the Pointe Coupee Battery fighting unsupported on the open Granny White pike with the heavy blue column crowding in upon it. Bouanchaud worked our four guns to the utmost in the unequal combat, until the gray column, realizing our extremity, rushed to our support." This was the 22nd Mississippi, which DeRussy will get to; first, McQuaide's account mentions.

McQuaide continued: "Under this most terrific and probably hottest fire that any command ever came under, he retired to what is known by field artillerists as sections or half battery, fighting most desperately and hurling death and destruction into the advancing columns of the Federals and thus unaided and unsupported, Bouanchaud and his battery, singlehanded and alone on an open field without protection or shelter, checked and held back the whole of Thomas' right." Again McQuaide exaggerated, though as far as some could see it so appeared. Ector's Brigade ended the day checking much of the 23rd Corps, and U.S. cavalry was checked by Rucker's Brigade.

As Bouanchaud's began to withdraw by sections no infantry was assisting them. McQuaide said, "…there was not a single company going to Bouanchaud's assistance. Generals, colonels, and captains were cursing and pleading-even crying, in vain-to our flying infantry to halt, form, and rally to that battery. An officer cried out, 'Shame, shame! Look at those brave artillerymen; see how calmly the drivers sit their horses under that awful fire! For God's sake rally to their support, or they will be lost.' The great General Loring is one of the generals who was heard to utter such words, and it was one of his regiments, the gallant little 22nd Mississippi (of Featherston's Brigade), that went to Bouanchaud's assistance. This timely aide enabled him to get his battery under cover behind a stone wall." Featherston's right was just east of Granny White Pike. It seems certain their assistance came east of the pike as Stewart's line made a final stand there. McQuaide said they got behind a stone wall. These stone fences may have been on both sides of the pike, and a portion is extant south of Woodmont Boulevard.

DeRussy was aware, "…The Jefferson Artillery (Darden's) was forced to give way, and Captain Bouanchaud's Battery alone defied the Federals. At last a panic appeared to develop and old and tired men were driven from their positions by the storm of fire, but Bouanchaud's remained firm, with his four guns alone replying to twenty. It was a moment of fearful suspense for the Federals were forming for a charge and we knew that if they once got at us they would overwhelm us with numbers and seize our guns, and with the fall of our artillery would come the capture of the entire left flank. Help came, however, and just as Bouanchaud's ammunition was exhausted the Twenty-second Mississippi swept around the foot of the hill and sustained us. Then came the Twelfth Louisiana of Scott's Brigade, and Loring and his 'Whirlwind Division' were irresistible. With his hat tucked under the stump of his left arm, which he had left on the field in the Mexican War, General Loring rode up to Captain Bouanchaud and said: 'Captain, your battery has saved the day.' The blue line came forward, but paused and was lost. For, instead of falling upon us and crushing us by the weight of numbers, it halted and in less than an hour had fallen back again in alignment upon their main line. Then came the orders to move with our division further to the left (south), to take up a new line to the renewal of the battle on the morrow. And a great day in the history of the Pointe Coupee Battery was closed."

Darden's Battery was captured behind Featherston's entrenched line. Stewart mentions a battery that was captured on Loring's line because the horses had been killed or wounded so to the guns could not be removed. This was the sad end to the Mississippi battery, which had a history of glorious service on such fields as Shiloh, Perryville, and Murfreesborough. The U.S. 4th Corps claimed "four brass twelve-pounder field pieces" had been abandoned, enabling them to be captured. But they may have only captured two at this point, for a new position was taken to the southeast along Granny White Pike, near Mrs. Johns. McQuaide said he saw Bouanchaud directing six cannon.

James A. Turpin, of Darden's, later wrote that they were "stationed in an apple orchard just back of the Bradford House." They may have been there after they lost their guns near the main line. Then he seems to confuse where his brother was wounded on Overton Hill, near a peach orchard, on the 16th. He said they were supported by a brigade of Clayton's Division. "Thus, Darden's Battery was also provided new guns from a lesser experienced battery and participated in the fight of the 16th on the far right." Apparently they fought in Stanford's Battery.

Featherston described the aftermath of the fall of the redoubts from his position. He wrote that "the troops on my left had given way, and were falling back through a large open field. Soon after I discovered this General Loring rode up to see about the centre of my line, and ordered me to withdraw my brigade from the trenches and fall back to a line … about a half mile in the rear. This was done in good order but under a very heavy artillery fire." He went onto say his brigade was formed near the Plater house. This is where Brig. Gen. Claudius Sears was taken, about this time, as his leg was hit by an artillery round.

Scott's Brigade was left of Featherston's, where Cannon described a similar scene: "During a lull in the battle, to our dismay, we found that everything to the left of our division had given way and the Federals had swung around and were sweeping down our line not more than two hundred yards distant.'

"Those in front, encouraged by the success of their right wing, made another furious onslaught, and the flanking column bearing down upon us at the same time. Our weak line of one rank could not stand the pressure and it was only a question of retreat or surrender and quite a number of our regiment surrendered on the spot.'

"The remainder of us struck out diagonally toward the rear in order to avoid both lines as much as possible. We fell back in considerable disorder for something near a half a mile. We rallied and opened on them with the effect of checking their advance." This must have been east of Granny White Pike, and possibly in line with Featherston's. His brigade was near the Plater House. It was located east of today's Outer Drive, and north of Greerland Drive. It later became the site of Buford College, for women.

Gale stayed at the Johns's until the Yankees came near Granny White Pike. "I remained in my office until the Yankees advanced to within three hundred yards. I then mounted and made my escape through the back yard with my clerks and joined Gen. Stewart in front of Mr. Platter's." About this time Mrs. Johns was seen by J.A. Turpin, of Darden's Battery, waving to the soldiers to rally them.

Across Granny White Pike from the Johns home site is a Tennessee Historic Commission marker (N 1 14) on the Confederate defenses. It states: "After being outflanked by the advance of the Federal XVI Corps (Smith), Loring and Walthall put their divisions in a defense line west of this road, facing westward. Here, their determined defense brought Federal advances against the Confederate left to a close for the day." Stewart reported Loring was ordered to form along Granny White Pike. He wrote, "This was gallantly and successfully done by this fine division, the corps retiring to a position between the Granny White and Franklin pikes, when night put an end to the conflict."

Nashville Battlefield Guide points out the marker gave to much credit to the XVI Corps. Almost a mile west of the location is where Cowan's Battery was overrun. The XXIII Corps claimed the capture of three of the guns, with assistance from a few hundred dismounted cavalry. It seems more likely that troops from these later bodies fought near the Johns house. A little farther south on Granny White, Brig. Gen. Zachariah C. Deas was attempting to rally his troops. Beautiful 28-year-old Mary Bradford observed this from her home, Zenaida. Hood wrote, "When our troops were in the greatest confusion a young lady of Tennessee, Miss Mary Bradford, rushed in their midst regardless of the storm of bullets and, in the name of God and of our country, implored them to reform and face the enemy. Her name deserves to be enrolled among the heroes of the war, and it is with pride that I bear testimony to her bravery and patriotism."

During the war there were numerous incidents of home loving, patriotic Confederate women rallying the troops when they needed it. Perhaps Nashville was the only battle where at least three women did. While Mary Bradford ran outside, Selene Harding did so four miles west at Belle Meade on Harding Pike. Most of the pikes were named for the

Captain Israel Putnam Darden's Mississippi battery likely lost their Napoleons along the main line; however, J.A. Turpin said they were in an orchard farther south at the Bradford home. One thing is certain, Mary Bradford (right) was one of three women on the battlefield attempting to rally Confederates at dusk.

towns they led to, but it and Granny White were exceptions. Selene was the 18-year-old daughter of William G. and Elizabeth McGavock Harding.

Chalmers was headquartered at Belle Meade, but had left early as a U.S. cavalry division had advanced toward Rucker's Brigade on Charlotte Pike. The naval flotilla engaged Forrest's old regiment and artillery under Kelley too. Rucker fell back from his initial position to one nearly adjacent to Kelley. Kelley and the navy fought to a stalemate, but Rucker's Brigade held on and counterattacked to hold his position across the pike. Ector's Brigade had been on their flank in the morning, but as Rucker fell back the connection was lost. Chalmers wondered if his wagons were still at the Harding's race track along Harding, and near dusk he sent his escort to secure them. But with Ector's gone, U.S. cavalry had surged out Harding and burned the wagons. When the escort realized this they decided to attack that cavalry at Belle Meade.

Selene heard the commotion and ran out the front door. James Dinkins of the escort had admired her while at Belle Meade. He wrote, "Miss Selene was difficult to describe, as she appeared to all of us, "As beautiful as the morning sun, as radiant as the spring, and as sweet as the summer." At first the escort drove the enemy cavalry back, but then ran into "infantry," or perhaps dismounted cavalry. "Bullets were striking the house and trees as we galloped through the yard. I saw Miss Selene standing on the steps, waiving a hand-kerchief, bullets whizzing about her. I called to her, as I passed and grabbed her handkerchief, to go into the house, but she stood like a goddess. She was the bravest person in the crowd." The scars from the Yankee bullets may still be seen on the limestone columns.

Chalmers managed to hang onto Charlotte Pike until after dark. Then he successfully withdrew Rucker and Kelley, with all the artillery. He left the 7th Alabama Cavalry as a rear guard, so that the Yankees didn't know he was gone until the next morning. At the far left, Cheatham held his entire line. The Yankees Cheatham had defeated wouldn't know he was gone until after sunrise. Lee's Corps in the centre had not been attacked and also withdrew without notice from the enemy.

Featherston wrote that his brigade had stayed near the Plater house until about 3 o'clock in the morning of the 16th when they were moved back. They must have been exhausted from a lack of sleep, and poor diet, for the second day. They were "placed in position behind a rock fence, forming the right of Stewart's Corps. Loring's brigades were again placed with Adams's on the left, Scott's in the centre, and Featherston's on the right. Sharp's Brigade of fellow Mississippians, the left of Lee's Corps, was to their right.

Hood had been on Shy's Hill the evening of the 15th and was in position to make observations of the fall of the redoubts along the Hillsborough Pike flank. By chance Ector's Brigade arrived. They had essentially been operating independently since being ordered to hold a skirmish line that crossed Harding Pike, several days before the battle. The morning of the 15th Ector's pickets had witnessed the enormous turning movement roll across their front toward the redoubts. They had fallen back past Redoubt Four, and near dusk found themselves at Shy's Hill.

Much of Hood's success in the Army of Northern Virginia was due to the fighting prowess of Texas infantry. Ector's had two North Carolina regiments which may have been detached and left in the main line. Thus, Texas units were those arriving before Hood. He said, Texans, I want you to hold this hill regardless of what transpires around you." Their spontaneous answer was, "We will do it, General." One of the Texans wrote that they had to fight to keep their hold on the hill. Either before or after Hood ordered the stand, he decided to remain and fight on the 16th.

Hood's main line on the 15th was stretched thin over five miles. There were about 20,000 men behind it, infantry and artillery. Cavalry and at least Ector's Texans were beyond the main line; hence, the main line had about 4,000 men per mile. Hood lacked firepower with his line stretched so thin. His arm was shattered at Gettysburg, where the U.S. Army had four times as many men in three miles, for about 27,000 men per mile. On the busy night of the 15th Hood decided to make a stand on a three mile long line.

Hood's losses on the 15th must have been low. Cheatham's Corps was victorious, and two of S.D. Lee's divisions were not engaged. Stewart's Corps probably lost more captured than killed or wounded. It is possible Hood's total casualties were about equal (500?) to Ector's Texans. Biffle's Brigade of cavalry, which had been beyond the right flank, was also in the main line on the right flank. Hood's main line could have increased to 21,000. Over three miles he seems to have had far too few troops at 7,000 men per mile.

Friday, 16 December 1864

Featherston said he was still near the Plater's until about 3:00 a.m., so Loring may have left at that time. The location of headquarters for Stewart or Loring on the 16th is not clear. Gale wrote, "Our Hdqts. during the night of the 15th were at Mrs. Mullins, tho' I was up until four A.M. re-forming the line with Col. Sevier and others." O.R. atlas plate 73-2 (above) shows a Mullen house almost a mile east of the Johns's. A map for Thomas is the O.R. atlas plate 72, and shows the "Rebel advanced position" for the evening of the 15th and morning of the 16th was situated so that these homes could have still served as headquarters. Also a local history states Stewart "with several of his staff, narrowly escaped capture in the house by a squadron of Federal cavalry…effecting their escape only by leaving untouched a fine breakfast prepared by Mrs. Johns."

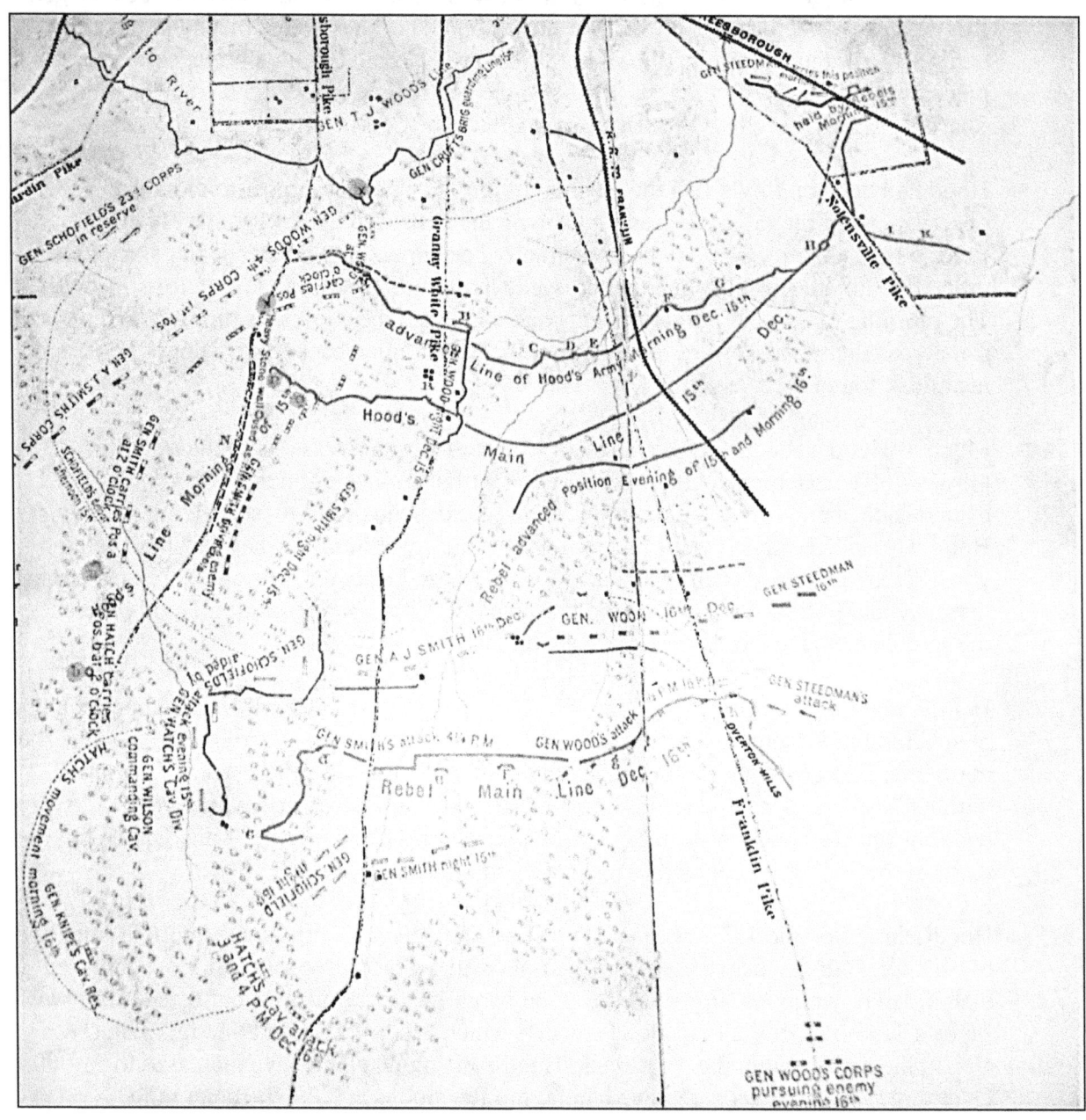

South of the Johns's at Zenaida, the Bradfords found their home in the small gap between the new lines of the two armies. Zenaida had already been turned into a Confederate hospital. Mary had held the arm of a Lieutenant Fitzpatrick during its amputation. They rode out Granny White Pike on a nine mile trek to reach the McCrory place. When they returned they would find the Yankees set up. A 1913 *Confederate Veteran* article stated, "Within the home not a vestige of furniture remained save the piano alone, the top of which had been used for an operating table. Walls and floors were blood stained, and outside the dining room were piles of legs and arms." All of their rugs had been taken up and cut into large pieces to be used for wagon covers. All their clothing and provisions were gone. Fortunately their money hidden under the smokehouse floor remained intact.

Hood had moved his headquarters to Lealand, the Overton Lea house. Perhaps it was headquarters for Stewart and Loring too. It was about 1,000 feet south of Featherston's position, Loring's right. The division right on the 15th was about Granny White Pike. They fell back after dark so that on the 16th their left was on that pike. Shy's Hill was just west of the pike and in sight of much of Loring's line. The division occupied a ready-made line of defense behind a stone fence. The brigades were in line as they had been on the 15th, so that Adams's was the left, Scott's the centre, and Featherston's the right.

Perhaps the most famous stone fence position in the war was at Fredericksburg. Part of Longstreet's Corps held it in the face of repeated attacks. Lee became concerned as the attacks had continued. He told Longstreet he was concerned the line might break. Longstreet replied, "…if you put every man now on the other side of the Potomac in that field to approach me over the same line, and give me plenty of ammunition, I will kill them all before they reach me line." The key words are "over the same line," for his line behind the fence was not outflanked; Loring's Division was.

A Metro Nashville marker located behind the stone fence may be found on Leland Lane, a block south of Battery Lane (named for artillery batteries). Its text explains Loring's Division fought behind the fence. "All Federal (U.S.) attacks were beaten back until the Confederate line was broken a mile to the west (Shy's Hill). The division retreated south through the hills toward Brentwood." See penultimate page of this chapter for view.

Stewart's report includes an explanation of the events of the 16th: "At an early hour in the morning the enemy approached, placing artillery in position and opening a heavy fire, which continued almost incessantly through the day. They confronted us everywhere with a force double or treble our own. Occasional attacks were made on various parts of our line and repulsed, though their chief efforts seemed to be directed against our flanks for the purpose of gaining the roads in our rear. Every attack made on the lines occupied by this corps to the last was repulsed with severe loss to the enemy."

Lee's Corps had been moved from the centre to the right. His line was across Franklin Pike, and then bent south to utilize the high ground of Peach Orchard Hill. Some U.S. reports referred to it as Overton Hill, for the owner John Overton. Lee's soldiers endured heavy artillery fire, and defeated strong feint attacks in the afternoon. They were all rather easily repulsed, in part due to the panic of the United States Colored Troops. Cowan's Battery gunners would have helped repulse them as gunners with Stanford's. Before the day was over every one of Hood's men would have to reach Franklin Pike to escape. All the other pikes had been cut off. Lee's victorious corps made a rear guard stand that allowed time for Cheatham's and Stewart's survivors to reach the pike.

The enemy awoke on the 16th and knew of the major turnpikes, Hood only held Franklin Pike. The previous night a telegram had been sent to Washington: "…From our new line General Thomas expects to be able to drive the enemy at daylight east of the road to Franklin, and so open communication with our forces at Murfreesborough…" But the movement of their forces was so slow that their primary thrust didn't take place until the last hour of daylight. If their operations had begun at daylight Hood might have been pushed east of Franklin Pike, and not escaped into the early darkness. The telegram also kept Grant from coming west himself. Lincoln and his command were that scared.

The weather must have been the primary hindrance to the U.S. offensive. Just as the heavy fog delayed their advance the day before, mist and fog hung over the area. The sun burned off most of the fog by 8:30, and temperatures began to rise toward 65 degrees. But the mist remained and about noon rain was falling. The shallow soil was already saturated from the melted ice and snow. Harder rain fell in the afternoon and colder air moved in. The muddy delays would also hinder Hood's retreat at dusk.

Captain Theodore Carter was in the 7th Minnesota. They had attacked Redoubts Three and then Redoubt Two on the 15th. He wrote to *Confederate Veteran* in 1904 (Vol. 12, page 585). Picking up his story that night: "Although tired out with the day's experiences, the night was so cold that I could get no continuous sleep. We were aroused long before daylight of the 16th and made a long and weary march, halting at some newly constructed works, probably the abandoned Confederate line of the day before." Actually Cheatham had initially been instructed to run his line northeast toward the Bradford House, and then ordered to run his line southeast so as to connect to the stone fence, behind which Loring was positioned. He wrote as they continued "…we came to a road [Granny White Pike?], crossing which we went into a field and into a ravine [Brown's Creek West Fork?] which led up to the rear of the 'Bradford House.' In this ravine we stopped to catch our breath,

and found it a good place to be in, as a brisk cannonading was being carried on over our heads, one of my men being wounded from a piece of shell while resting there."

Carter described the ravine as so narrow that his company was strung out in single file. But then "the regiment coming out of the ravine on to the grounds around the 'Bradford House,' a shell from the Pointe Coupee Battery (Louisiana Troops) burst and killed the rear man of the company in front of mine and the first man of my company." Pieces of the Pointe Coupee were ahead just up Brown's Creek West Fork.

Carter's brigade commander explained the Confederate line was "across the Granny White pike, at the foot of the Overton (or Brentwood) Hills. My right rested on the pike... We pushed forward under a severe fire of the enemy's artillery and musketry, until partly covered by a fence and stone wall running from the Bradford mansion to the pike. Here we halted until the grand charge in the afternoon. Captain Julian's battery was posted about 400 yards in rear of the infantry, and opened and kept up a heavy fire on the enemy's works. In our immediate front was a four-gun battery."

Returning to Cannon's fine diary we find his entry for the 16th. He correctly has Hood's strength as less than 20,000; however, he far underestimates enemy strength as double. It was more than triple. Cannon's entry:

"At daylight the booming of cannon all along the line awakened those of us who were inclined to slumber and foretokened the dreadful ordeal through which we were to pass today. It is seldom the case that an army is in worse condition for meeting its enemy in 'battle's dread array' than ours is at this time. Having suffered numerous defeats in the past six months by an overwhelming force, only yesterday driven from our works, thousands killed and captured, we are now reduced to less than 20,000 effectives.'

"Realizing all these disadvantages, we could but feel dispirited. With a determination to do our whole duty, we nerved ourselves up to the point of making one more heroic effort to stay the tide of the disaster that has befallen us. We awaited the attack with the deepest solicitude.'

"As soon as the sun had dispelled the morning mists we could see two lines of blue drawn up before us, while the artillery from its commanding position was dealing death and destruction in our thinned ranks.'

"The cannonading was terrific and continued almost without intermission during the day. Shells and solid shot passed through the stone fence behind which we were sheltered, scattering stones in every direction and mangling men in a shocking manner.'

"To lie still under such a destructive artillery fire produces a feeling of dread that cannot be described. This is more demoralizing than to be actively engaged in battle; but we had to endure it for six long hours without even a skirmish to divert our attention.'

"Our artillery replied only occasionally, husbanding their ammunition, which was scarce, for the final contest they all knew must come before long. About 4 o'clock p.m. the enemy made an attack on our left, gradually driving our boys back until the fighting seemed to be almost in our rear. The 'hurrah, hurrah, hurrah 'was heard in our front and we knew the 'tug of war' was coming.'

"All dread vanished and excitement took its place. On they came, two lines of blue, through the open field, in a double quick. Our old reliable Pointe Coupee (our brigade battery) opened at once, first with shell and, as they approached nearer, with grape canister. Then a storm of minie-balls was let loose from behind the stone fence, and the yells of Confederates and 'hurrah' of Yankees were drowned under the roar of musketry and artillery. Men were falling on both sides and it seemed for a time that the bayonet would be the means of ending the contest. A few more rounds made it so hot that the enemy began retiring, though only for a short distance. Rallying, they moved forward again, and the battle raged fiercer than before.'

"Still confident that we could hold our position, we defiantly called to them to come on, but they seemed unwilling to come to close quarters, yet determined not to retreat." This is how Hood wanted the situation remembered. In Advance and Retreat he wrote, "I did not, I might say, anticipate a break at this time, as our forces up to that moment had repulsed the Federals at every point…crying out to the enemy, 'Come on, come on.'"

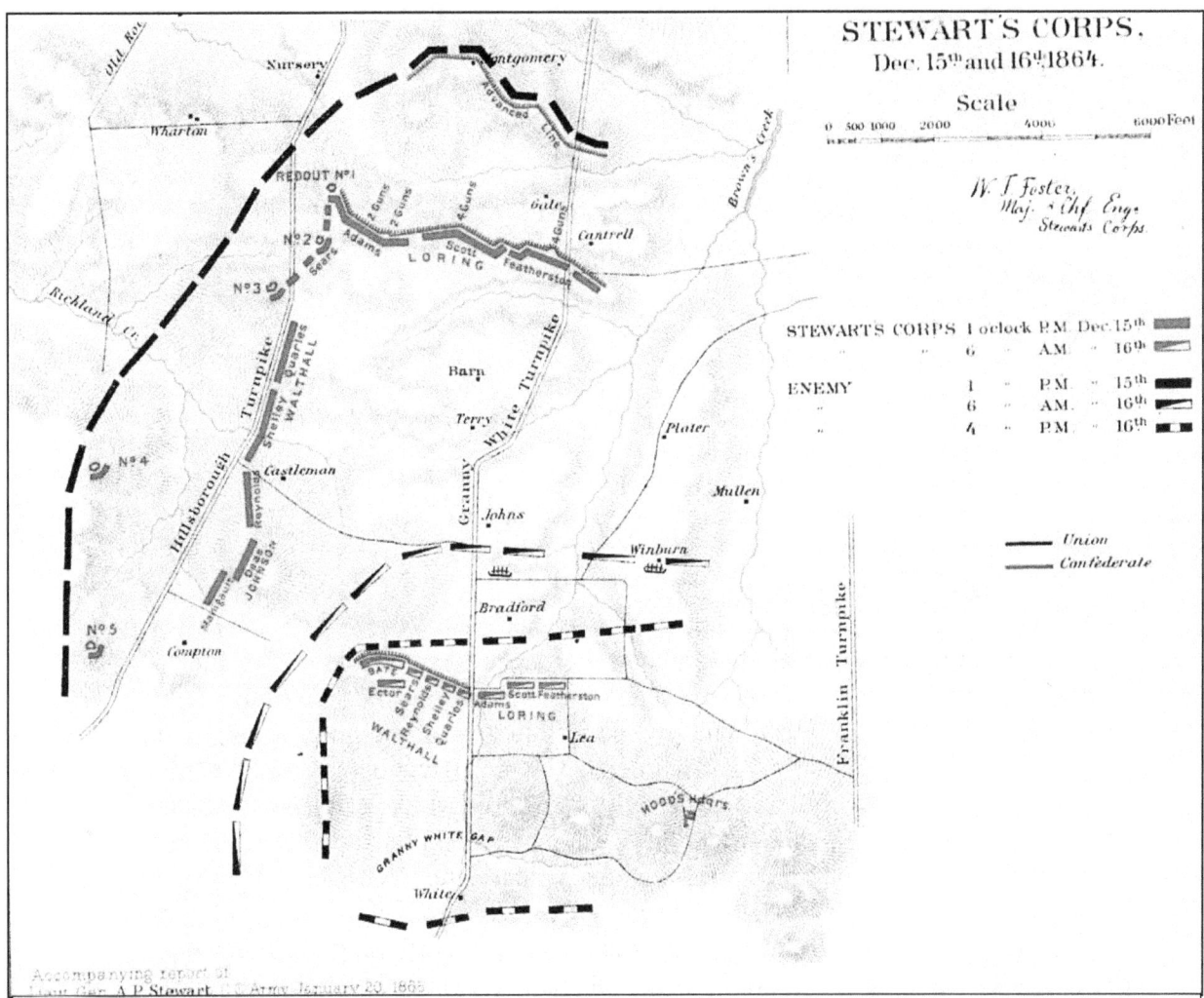

Stewart's map, by Wilbur Foster, shows his line on the 15th and the 16th. Lee's Corps was on Loring's right on both days (not shown). Walthall's Division was on Loring's left both days. Bate's Division was to Walthall's left on the 16th. Bate's turned south (not shown). The other two divisions (Brown's and Cleburne's) of Cheatham's Corps continued south of Bate in a sort of fishhook (not shown) confronting the U.S. line.

Adams' position is behind stone fence, part of which remains on south side of today's Sewanee Road, on east side of Granny White Pike. The original fence makes a turn, on Scott's left, which may still be found. The fence continues in front of Featherston's, and eastward beyond today's Lealand Lane (photos of Metro marker for Stewart's Line, above and below). The road parallel to the fence is found on modern maps as Kirkman Lane. It is abandoned and now private property. Ector's and Reynolds' were pulled out of positions indicated above and sent south on Granny White to confront dismounted enemy cavalry. The cavalry was facing north, as shown This U.S. line probably didn't go as far east as shown. The road parallel to their line appears to be today's Overton Lea Road. Today's Lakeview Drive begins there and leads thru the gap used by Cheatham's, and some of Stewart's, retreating troops. Reynolds' covered the retreat. The middle road seems to be today's Gateway Lane, which led to the Lea House, shown on the map. Hood stayed there on the night of the 15th, and had his headquarters on the lawn on the lawn on the 16th. He had been at Travellers' Rest, extant and open for tours, for two weeks before, east of Franklin Pike.

199

The marker in the photo is at the southeast corner of Granny White Pike and Sewanee Drive (above). Adams's Brigade was on the opposite side of this fence, looking north. Shy's Hill would have been visible west of the pike, across muddy corn fields. The marker says, "…Chalmers's Cavalry Division covered the left flank." That is misleading, for U.S. cavalry was across the pike to the south, and Chalmers was beyond them. A portion of the fence along Sewanee Drive is gone, but continuing east, you may come to a ninety-degree turn. The fence then runs north to another turn (photo below). Scott's Brigade was behind here, and at least a section of the Pointe Coupee was behind the corner, enfilading the attackers. The old Kirkman Lane right-of-way is visible along the north side of the fence.

Loring's Division probably had no idea of the overwhelming force that nearly surrounded Cheatham's Corps on their left. Cannon continued, "During this time we could not what was taking place on other parts of the line. We were feeling rather exultant when, on looking to the left, we saw thousands of blue coats pouring over the hill not 200 yards away. They were sweeping back our lines like chaff before the wind." The hill was the salient point in Cheatham's line, then known as Compton's Hill; today's Shy's Hill. It was renamed to honour Lt. Col. William Shy, who was killed defending it.

General Featherston continued to say that while behind the fence they were "under very heavy artillery fire during the whole day." It was "one of the heaviest I have ever witnessed. There was considerable skirmishing in front, during the day until about 4 o'clock…" Cannon's entry said there was none, so Featherston's Brigade must have.

Loring's left most regiment was the 15th Mississippi under Lt. Col. James Binford of Adams's Brigade. He wrote of their line on the 16th: "On this new line our Brigade was on the left of Loring's Division and the 15th was on the extreme left of the Brigade, the left resting on Granny White Pike." This point has a Tennessee Historical Commission marker titled "Confederate Position…" It is on the east side of the pike at the corner of Sewanee Road. The text on it is misleading. It claims Stewart's Corps was badly mauled on the first day. Actually it made a miraculous escape from three enemy cavalry corps, and several brigades of cavalry. The marker is correct that Cheatham's Corps "extended the line westward, and following the hills curved south. Chalmers Cavalry Division covered the left flank." Cheatham's Corps was not only on Shy's Hill, but extended south over several hills. Chalmers was not on the immediate left, but several miles away.

From Binford's view most of Cheatham's line was "in the rear of Walthall's, and also in the rear of the 15th Mississippi." Hood would have known Cheatham was facing most of the force that confronted Stewart on the 15th. Stewart may have been alarmed to receive an 8 a.m. correspondence from Hood's staff. It began: "Should any disaster happen to us today, General Hood directs that you will retire by the Franklin pike, and Lee is directed to hold it in front of the large ridge, that you may pass to his rear." This is essentially what took place later, as daylight faded away. It also explains, "Cheatham would move by the Granny White pike." Unfortunately U.S cavalry would be across the pike behind Cheatham by afternoon. Their escape would be by other routes.

Stewart shared Hood's concern when he sent Walthall an order at 2 p.m. It read, "Should Bate fall back, keep your left connected with him, falling back from your left toward right and forming a new flank line extending to the hills in the rear." Stewart seems to have been confident Loring's Division could hold behind the fence. As may be seen today, stone fences ran alongside Granny White Pike. Stewart may have imagined Walthall swinging his line behind them, to become perpendicular to Loring's line. At some point Walthall received another order from Stewart's staff instructing him to have "everything in readiness to retire tonight, in accordance of the circular order of today."

But when Cheatham's Corps collapsed, near dusk, Stewart's orders could not be carried out. Binford explained that at that point Cheatham's Corps and Walthall's Division "retiring let the enemy in our rear." He wrote the 15th Mississippi's position "was behind a rock fence, and in front we had an open view of several hundred yards." They were about to be attacked on their front in the midst of a route.

Binford described the perilous position of his 15th Mississippi as Hood's left dissolved: "Walthall's Division retreating and passing to the right within seventy-five yards of my rear, somewhat excited my men and several of the officers called my attention to our retreating columns and the enemy in our rear. About this time our Brigade was ordered to fall back, but the Courier that brought the order failed to give it to me, so the 15th was left in very perilous position of having the enemy both on our left flank and rear, and no support on my right down to Featherston's Brigade, a distance of about two hundred yards." When most regiments would have had all the evidence they needed to retreat, the 15th was about to repulse an attack on their front! Binford continued, "From the first volley the enemy began to fall like leaves before the autumn wind, but…on they came, yet falling at every step. It seemed they would in spite of us reach our line and give us a hand fight across the rock fence. After some minutes I could see no enemy and supposing they had reached the rock fence and were lying down on the opposite side, I gave the command to cease firing intending to call them over as prisoners." But when the smoke lifted he found the ground across the fence strewn with dead and wounded. The rest were in "full retreat." But their overtime stand could not save Hood.

Scott's Brigade was also behind the stone fence, to the right of Adams's. Today a bend in the fence may still be found on Robin Springs Road, north of Sewanee Road. At least a section of Bouanchaud's Louisiana battery was in the fence corner. Their fire was known to inflict high casualties on Minnesota troops attacking parallel to Granny White Pike. James W. Harmon was in the 35th Alabama, of Scott's Brigade. He recalled the enemy "had massed a number of batteries and these began to play on our line with all the vengeance possible. Our regiment being to the left and near the Louisiana battery which we were supporting, had to endure the havoc and crash of these numerous missiles of death in the same manner as the battery at which their firing was concentrated, and which no doubt they were trying to destroy." Thus they lay waiting for the enemy infantry.

Harmon looked north toward today's Battery Lane. He recalled, "There was an open field in front of perhaps about three hundred yards or more in width, back of this field was a skirt of woods, and in these woods the enemy's forces were massed, in several lines of battle, for the purpose of advancing in our front." The enemy troops were from the two divisions brought to Nashville by steamboat as Hood marched up from Franklin. They were also those that attacked Walthall's Division and Bate's on and around Shy's Hill.

Harmon described the attack: "All at once they emerged from the woods in three lines of battle, and were marching straight for our lines when they had gotten fairly into the open field our troops opened fire on them and poured man deadly missiles into their ranks in such an effective manner that they were driven back into the woods with quite a number of their men lying dead and wounded on the field." The enemy's officers described the terrain as Harmon did. But they mention charging as if only one grand and successful charge was made, and in conjunction with the breaking of the line on and near Shy's Hill.

Yet Harmon distinctly described another unsuccessful charge: "They soon rallied and came forward again. The ground was held as before, and at the same time our battery was giving them all the shots possible, and with such deadly effect that they were driven back into the woods the second time with heavy loss."

Loring's line was holding when outflanked. Harmon wrote, "They soon were flanking and closing in around us as fast as they could, having gotten in the rear before our men were aware of it, and while we were holding our ground…a strong force of Federals made their appearance over the brow of a hill, then began to rush down our line, and in this condition many of our men had to surrender…" Harmon was among them.

Continuing with Yankee Theodore Carter's account his regiment had advanced south of the Bradford house. To his right he had seen the Confederate line on the slope of Shy's Hill attacked and taken. It was his regiment's turn to attack and "they advanced on the run until we reached the Confederate rifle pits, made of rails, where we halted for breath. The field was a hard one to travel over, the mud being ankle deep." All accounts agree muddy corn fields were around the hill. "My company was directly in front of the Point Coupee Battery, which had poured grape, canister, and shrapnel into us from the moment we had started, and the supporting line [Scott's Brigade] had also done their share with their rifles. The works, a stone wall built up very high, with rails laid a part of the way from the top and sloping to the ground toward us, had no opening in our front, except a slight notch at the top, just to the left of the battery." The stone wall [actually a fence] still appears high up from the north side because a worn down lane was alongside it.

While Carter's regiment advanced U.S. troops to their right were flanking Loring's line. "We reached the wall just as the 'break' came, and the notch in the wall was so high, and I was so badly used up with the stitch in my side, that the boys had to boost me up to the notch, through which I climbed and dropped to the ground just as my colonel came along inside the line on the gallop, calling out: 'Lay down your arms and surrender.' There were but four or five men in the battery, one the commander, Capt. Alcide Bouanchaud, and they had ceased resisting." The *Louisiana* account says, "Bouanchaud had exhausted all of his ammunition and there remained nothing more for him to do other than attempt saving the few remaining members of his command. He said, 'Men, we can do no more; there is no use remaining here to be shot down or captured!' They went out of that hell, as it were, leaving the plain in front of where their guns had stood that day black with the dark blue uniform of the masses of the dead and dying enemy." Caesar Landry recalled they had "poured double-loaded canister into the advancing column." Their infantry support had been wavering when the fourth gun fell into enemy hands. Landry recalled they were "rather angered by the growing confusion, not to add the intrusive flag" the enemy had planted their flag, so the "cannoneers of the third piece turned their gun directly on the fourth and fire their last round of ammunition at the colours. After this act of justice, the gunners fled to avoid capture."

Atlanta has *Loring Heights* and Nashville has *Loring Court*. This entrance is seen off Battery Lane. The stone fence is in the distance. Loring's position was to right-rear.

Nearby Confederate batteries, such as the Third Maryland, had moved their horses twice to protect them from U.S. artillery fire. Perhaps Bouanchaud was waiting for their horses to be brought up from some distant point. Regardless the sudden, overwhelming enemy flanking movement made saving them impossible. Even the Yankee brigade commander reported their capture as the "splendid Pointe Coupee Battery of four Napoleons…"

Hood had placed Ector's Brigade, under Coleman, on top of Shy's Hill on the 15th. That brigade was in French's Division, who was absent, but his staff apparently remained. His assistant adjutant general was Maj. Daniel Ward Sanders. He wrote in *Southern Bivouac* (August 1885) and explained enemy cavalry had appeared on the high range of hills to the rear, alongside Granny White Pike. Bate's Division was placed on Shy's Hill because "about 11:30 A.M. Coleman was withdrawn from Cheatham's line and moved in rear of the army and drove the dismounted cavalry south over the hills." Cheatham and Stewart were to only have temporary relief from this threat. "At 3:15 P.M. Reynolds' brigade was withdrawn from Walthall's line, sent to the rear to cooperate with Coleman in checking Wilson's cavalrymen, who had gained possession of the hills in the rear of the army and east from the Granny White pike…and the pass through which the pike runs. The line of retreat in the event of disaster to Hood was closed on that pike."

The line on top of Shy's Hill had been laid out in the dark. James L. Cooper was an aide-de-camp for Brig. Gen. Thomas Benton Smith. He wrote, "We had very poor works… Worst of all, we found that the line had been located by the command who occupied the position before us so far back from the crest of the hill that at several points a six-foot man could not see twenty yards in front, thus rendering it possible to mass an attacking party within a few yards of the position and be perfectly sheltered from our fire… This of course was not discovered till after daylight and the enemy gave us no chance to remedy them." As an infantry corps was to their front, another to their left, and cavalry to their rear, artillery shells came from multiple directions, not to mention sniper fire.

Featherston could see the enemy advance on Shy's Hill, after 4:00. "From my position I could see very distinctly the movements of the enemy and our troops. Our troops posted on the hill were driven back by the enemy and gave way. The troops on the right of the hill next gave way and it was not long until the entire line was a moving mass. My Brigade held their position until all the troops on my left had given way and the enemy had crossed the ranks and were moving up on the south side when it was ordered to retire. There were no troops in the line on my right, when my Brigade fell back. Holding about the centre of the line, I saw the necessity of holding my position as long as possible to prevent the enemy from cutting off and capturing our troops on my left."

Featherston's report may imply Scott's Brigade were the troops on his left, or he may have meant troops in general. But J.P. Cannon made it clear they kept fighting to the last: "It is said that our officers now, seeing the day was lost, ordered a retreat. If so, we did not get the order, and continued to maintain the unequal contest, under a galling fire from both front and flank, until the two lines had almost enveloped us. Colonel Weeden, of our regiment, ordered all who could to save themselves.'

"The enemy were closing upon us from front and flank and so near as to order us to surrender. A portion of the regiment stacked arms, but what proportion I am unable, after so long a time, to say. Some of us, however, determined to escape, if possible. A race of half a mile for life and liberty through open, level fields to a range of hills covered with timber was our only hope. We ran in an oblique direction to avoid both lines. Some were killed immediately after leaving the stone fence and many others struck down within the first hundred yards. After that I have no recollection of seeing another member of the regiment. The ground had been frozen, but recently thawed which rendered it very laborious running and many were so exhausted they had to surrender. I passed a ditch of gully where a hundred or more Confederates had taken refuge and, at my suggestion that they better be 'making tracks' replied that they could not run a step further and were compelled to give it up.'

By the time we reached the hills, our squad was reduced to about half a dozen, the remainder who were not disabled or captured having taken some other route. Here the writer had a close call but no damage was done except to disfigure my new uniform which I had worn just one month.'

"We climbed about halfway up the hill, which was very high and steep, to some large trees where we took cover long enough to recover breath and view the scene below. The Federals had broken into a disorganized mob and the fields were dotted with blue coats as far back as we could see. Having left the stone fence with empty guns, we loaded while resting and fired on the enemy, some of whom had reached the foot of the hill. We then retreated further up, loaded, and fired again which had a tendency to check their advance, repeating the same tactics until we were enabled to gain the top.'

"Seeing they had abandoned their pursuit, so far as we were concerned, we sat down on a log for a good long rest. From our elevated position we had a good view of all that was going on below. Lee's corps, which had been our right, making a gallant retreat against tremendous odds, firing volleys, falling back and firing again. It was a grand spectacle, but distressing to us, as we sat there and thought of the dead and dying comrades in the valley below. We thought, too, of the crushing defeat we had suffered, and the train of consequences which must inevitably follow." The hill Cannon refers to must have been what is today known as Laurel Ridge.

R.B, Meadows was in the 35th Alabama, also of Scott's Brigade. He had injured a leg on the 15th and was getting treatment when Shy's Hill fell. "It looked like there was an army corps camped around the ambulance train, soldiers who had gotten away from their comrades in the stampede…after our line was broken. I went to the sergeant in charge of the train, showed him my knee, I could walk with one knee stiff. I asked him what we were going to do and told him that if we were going to fight I could shoot as good as I ever could, but if we were going to run, I would go up the spout. He said we were going to fight it out right there. I said I wanted to go back to my comrades. He said he wanted to send some men back with me, and a note to Colonel Snodgrass, commanding my brigade, to send a guard out there to clean up his camp of the stragglers. I started out with twelve or fifteen men with me." His description indicates Stewart's Corps made some attempt to hold their line. "…got within about a half mile of our line of battle when…(artillery) opened fire on our line. My men commenced falling out of line. Of course, I had no power to stop them. I got to Colonel Snodgrass with one man, gave him the note and went to my command." When Meadows referred to the stampede he may have meant the beginning of the attack. "I looked upon the hill, and to our horror, I saw our line was broken and the enemy was sweeping down on us…(Lt.) Colonel Ashford…was standing just in our rear. He was commanding the regiment of Colonel Ives, who was wounded at Franklin. I stepped back to Colonel Ashford and said to him, 'Colonel Ashford, Look at those men!' That was the enemy coming down on us in plain view with no one opposing them. I said to him, 'Why don't they send somebody to protect our flank?' He would look at me and then at the Yankees when I would ask him to, but he never opened his mouth. He well knew there was no help or relief for us. He knew our fate was sealed. Oh, my God, how I felt! I went back to my place in line."

Meadows may have known Ashford, who was from Courtland, Lawrence County. But he was in the 16th Alabama, Lowrey's Brigade, of Cleburne's Division. And it is peculiar he mentions him as he was killed at Franklin. Lt. Col. Weeden was in command of the consolidated 27th-35th-49th at Nashville. Did Meadows think Weeden was Ashford? Weeden was wounded and captured, while Meadows somehow escaped on his bad leg.

The exhaustion of Loring's troops from lack of sleep, poor diet, and stress was all the worse because of a lack of tents. Many in Adams's Brigade were too weak and exhausted to sleep. In the 6th Mississippi about 50 were capture at the stone fence. Exhaustion and ankle deep mud in adjacent corn fields made running impossible for some.

T.H. Knight of McGregor, Texas, formerly of the 55th Alabama, wrote of Loring's great escape from the Champion Hill battlefield. His reminiscences recalled the retreat from the stone fence. The collapse of the left around Shy's Hill allowed U.S. troops to fire into their rear, while they still confronted three lines of battle. He also had a rare recollection of Loring trying to rally his division on Franklin Pike. Knight wrote:

"We were watching both in front and rear, and decided that we had better retreat, and started in rather bad order in double quick time. Soon we saw that our pursuers were beating a 'double quick' trying to cut us off. It became necessary to actually outrun them, and every man did his best to get away.'

"Our men were being taken prisoners, so I ran across a deep ravine and went up the next hill, where I saw our wagon train getting away. We had from four to six mules to each wagon, and each mule had a driver, and each driver a cudgel in the shape of his hat.'

"It was on a pike road and the noise could have been heard fifteen miles. When I got to the pike I found Major Gen. Loring, who called out, 'All who belong to Loring's Division fall into line.' I suppose he had ninety men." He also recalled rain, sleet, and snow starting as it got dark. He saw barefoot soldiers marching in it, until almost 2 a.m. Lt. Col. Binford also recalled the retreat, in rain and sleet, on the Franklin Pike. He wrote, "My heart almost bled as I saw traces of blood in the icy slush that came from the bare feet of our brave soldiers."

R.B. Meadows referred to the retreat as a "stampede" and so did Maj. Wilbur Foster in a *Confederate Veteran* article in 1904 (Volume 12, page 274). Foster was A.P. Stewart's engineer officer. Foster emphasized, "There is one expression sometimes used to which I wish to enter protest. It has been frequently said that when the line gave way at Shy's Hill a 'panic' ensued and the entire army fled in disorderly route, etc. There was no panic."

Foster recalled that late in the afternoon the high ridge, he called the Brentwood Hills, to the south of Cheatham and Stewart was occupied "by the enemy in strong force. Nobody knew better than the Confederate soldiers in the rifle pits that their line could no longer be maintained, and that only one outlet was open by which to escape inevitable capture. At that moment the line gave way at Shy's Hill, and served as a signal for a stampede to the Franklin Turnpike. This was done, of course, in great disorder; but if 'panic' was there, I failed to see it. This write was in the rush along the foot of the Brentwood hills, and well remembers certain jibes and sarcastic remarks of the men, but no cries of terror. The men simply knew , without being told, that there was but one thing to do, and that was to get to the Franklin Pike; and they did it not because they were panic-stricken, but because it was the proper thing to do." Lee's Corps held the pike allowing their escape.

Lee's Corps was the last to leave the field, and generally in good order, Lee took charge of the rear guard. A member of his staff wrote, "Gen. Lee says his troops were soon

Marker above for Stewart's line (Loring's) was shown above, along stone fence. It is beside Lealand Lane, here looking south toward the high ridge Foster called the Brentwood Hills. Loring's Division had infantry to the north, their front To their rear was "the enemy in strong force." It was dismounted cavalry. They were certainly on the ridge farther west (right in this view). They might not have been "in strong force" directly behind Loring here. Just to the right of this view was a gap through which most of Cheatham's and some of Stewart's retreated. This was made possible by Reynolds's Brigade holding it until they passed on. Today's Lakeview Drive passes through it, and beyond it is Radnor Lake. The man-made lake wasn't there at the time. The road of the period allowed passage onto Franklin Pike.

rallied. Yes, indeed, they were. But who rallied them? On this point Gen. Lee is silent with his accustomed modesty. He caused them to present a good front to the enemy. Let justice be done…There is not a living man who can deny that Gen. S.D. Lee rallied these troops, and to him belongs the credit of saving Hood's army." Lee's men had of course decisively repulsed enemy attacks on and near Franklin Pike. Lee said it "a fortunate circumstance that the enemy was too much crippled to pursue us on Franklin Pike." In a pathetic print, Yankee artists depicted their troops taking Lee's line.

Featherston explained his brigade reformed in Brentwood on the night of the 16th, about four miles south of his position at the stone fence. They had been awake much of the previous night, but from Brentwood they marched onto Franklin, another nine miles.

Scott's Brigade did too. J.P. Cannon said they came into Franklin Pike at Thompson Station; he must have meant Brentwood Station. He concluded his Nashville section:

"When Lee's corps had been driven out of our right, around the base of the hill, it was becoming dark and began to rain. We struck out through the woods but, owing to the intense darkness, could only guess the direction to take and felt like we were about as liable to run into the enemy as our own men. After wandering over hills and hollows, woods and fields till 10 o' clock, we came into the Franklin pike at Thompson Station. The road was full of struggling soldiers like ourselves, all bent on making the distance between them and Nashville as long as possible by daylight. With no officers to command, we continued the retreat all night-every fellow for himself. We arrived at Franklin in the morning where the commissaries were issuing rations lavishly, having no wagons to haul it away, but warned us to be frugal as we might never have a chance at a Confederate commissary. A portion of the consolidated regiment got together here, officers took command, and the continuing retreat was more orderly."

Lee's rear guard stand on Franklin Pike, close to Travellers' Rest, had been critical. But two other rear guard actions took place. Reynolds's and Ector's were still in position on hills east of the pike, facing south. Sanders described Reynolds "with his heroic brigade, intact in its organization, compact and soldierly on its last line, with Wilson's dismounted cavalrymen on the spur of hills west of south of them. As they looked down upon their routed comrades, with many of whom they had fought side by side in the great battles of the Army of Tennessee from Shiloh to this fatal field, the spectacle was of a nature to have appalled even the more heroic hearts…Reynolds comprehending the magnitude of the disaster…promptly moved his brigade from the gap in the north face of the hills to their relief…" Sanders explained the nearby position of Coleman, with Ector's, and how they followed Cheatham's retreating troops as their rearguard, fighting of pursuers.

The third and perhaps the most critical rear guard action was by Chalmers, with Rucker's Brigade. Some histories mistakenly claim Chalmers was on the left of Cheatham. After brilliant fighting on the 15th he pulled out of position and reached Hillsborough Pike. The enemy cavalry he had fought took some time to catch up on the 16th. About 3:15 p.m. Chalmers left Rucker with part of his brigade to contain them, while. He took his escort and Kelley's command to Granny White Pike. Thus while enemy cavalry was behind Hood's infantry, Chalmers was behind the Yankees. After Hood's infantry was routed Wilson mounted a division and thundered out Granny White. The pike ended on Franklin Pike so that without Chalmers blocking his way he could have cut off Hood's retreat. The fighting went on into pitch black darkness, giving Hood's infantry time to escape.

Thomas had fought according to his plan at Nashville, but he made two large mistakes. His cavalry chief had argued the terrain around Shy's Hill was too steep for cavalry. If he had been allowed to take half his force, some 6,000-plus troops, to pass around Hood's right he could have cut off the Franklin Pike escape route. The second mistake was he mistakenly ordered the pontoon train out Murfreesborough Pike. Without the resulting delay Hood might never have made it to Alabama.

Chapter 8: The Retreat

The people of Franklin awoke on the 17th to the depressing site of the army retreating. For wounded Confederates still being cared for it was a greater concern. The possibility of being sent to a U.S. prison confronted them. George E. Estes of the 14th Mississippi, of Featherston's Brigade, was one. He wrote *Confederate Veteran* in 1918 (Vol. 26, p. 442): "I was being cared for, as were many others, by Mrs. James McGavock, just across the Harpeth River from the battle field…" Blessed be her name! She was an angelic mother to us, and her dear daughters and sons, as well as the old-time servants, were so good to us that I always feel indebted to them for my life and comforts that were mine during the stay with them. But, O me! Those pesky Yankees! I wished they had stayed at home and let me get rest until daylight that memorable morning in 1864. But I had to get up…"

This is not Canton, but Mrs. McGavock's home, Riverside (below). It is shown on A.P. Stewart's map (O.R. plate 73-3) above, as the Widow McGavock's. Her husband, James Randal McGavock, passed away in 1862, but the family survived to witness the battle from their home. The house survives under private ownership.

Ross's Texas cavalry brigade, of Jackson's Division, had fought on the north bank, and Estes left with three of them. "One of them had been shot through and through, but seemed less demoralized than any of us. We soon reached the Harpeth River, which looked to me at that time as large as the Mississippi. I saw that the only way to get across that stream was to fly over, wade through, of walk on the waters, as our Saviour did…" Estes and the Texans waded. "Oh how cheerless and chilly was that stream! We soon got across, as wet as the proverbial rat and as cold as a plate of ice cream, but we shook off some of the coldest of water and struck out for Dixie. We soon came to the Lewisburg Pike, which was full of cavalry moving south, all asleep…" This must have been some of Chalmers's Division, providing flank protection as the army marched out Columbia Pike.

Estes continued, "Looking across to the west, we could see troops on the Columbia Pike, but we could not decide whether they were friends or foes. We plodded along as best we could, endeavoring to ascertain the identity of the travelers on the pike. After awhile I saw a possum tied on a fellow's gun, which indicated to me that he was a Rebel."

Featherston said the march was resumed from Franklin on the morning of the 17th. But Lee had to hold the pursuing enemy off on the north bank of the Harpeth River while a pontoon bridge was laid. At 1:00 Lee was wounded by a shell fragment. But he remained on the field until the last of Hood's wagons were across. Then his own corps crossed, and began their withdrawal.

They reached the vicinity of Spring Hill about dark. Lee officially turned over his corps to his senior subordinate, Maj. Gen. Carter Littlepage Stevenson. He had relieved Clayton's Division with Stevenson's already. Still one mile north of the West Harpeth River, Stevenson fought off U.S. cavalry. He had to fight every step of the way to get to the south bank of the small river.

Estes had made his way with a head start on rear guard. "…but I had had no breakfast, and there were no signs of any in the near future. I continued to 'pull mu old freight' for the old friendly Tennessee River with a degree of energy unknown to the common people of America. I passed on with nothing to eat until I crossed the river at Columbia, where I lady to whom I appealed gave me a piece of bread and a drink of cold coffee."

Forrest had been near Murfreesborough when he got word of the battle on the 16th. He began the westward trek to join the army at Columbia. On the night of the 19th Forrest consulted with Hood. Hood had hoped to hold the line of the Duck River, as Bragg had done two years before. Forrest convinced Hood of the deplorable condition of the army, and lack of supplies, made it impractical. He told him, "Give me Walthall with the men he can muster, and I will undertake to hold the enemy until the army as crossed the Tennessee River with all the artillery and all the wagons" The next morning Hood summoned Walthall.

Walthall was staying at Nimrod Porter's home. Porter wrote, "The very heavens are shedding tears for the sufferers in this deadly strife." Walthall left Porter's to meet Hood. Maj. David Ward Sanders of Yazoo City had been on French's staff. That left Sanders free to serve as a volunteer aide-de-camp for Walthall. He wrote of the campaign for *Southern Historical Society Papers* in 1881. It was also be found in *Confederate Veteran* in 1907 (Vol. 15, p. 401). He recorded his recollection as they rode to meet Hood and found him on his horse. Walthall was concerned that as the youngest major general in the army, some might resent his appointment. Hood insisted he was wanted. He replied, "General, I have never asked for a hard place for glory nor a soft place for comfort, but take my chances as they come…I will do my best." Forrest arrived and before him Hood said, "Forrest wants you and I want you."

Post card was mailed from Memphis 1n 1910. Forrest and wife were originally buried in Elmwood Cemetery, but moved to this city park early in the 20th Century. Post cards from mid-century indicate he was the hero of the Battle of Memphis; more of a raid, in AUG 1864. Leftists later seemed to think the statue had been placed to honour his retail slave business. Leftist politicians had the Forrest grave statue forcefully removed in the night, damaging it. The bodies were exhumed and moved to the grounds of the headquarters of the Sons of Confederate Veterans in Columbia. New caskets were made for the Forrests and they were reburied in September 2021. Rain began toward the end of the ceremony and the caskets were moved back into the house. The official pall bearers had left during the rain. The author spent time with the caskets and once the rain ended, was asked to take the general to his final resting place. The statue is being repaired for the site.

Why did Forrest want Walthall rather than Loring? Old Blizzards might seem to have had a better record at higher levels of command. Forrest and Walthall had been on the north end of the field at Chickamauga. Longstreet had been there and called a Walthall attack "masterly." Then cavalry General Joe Wheeler mentioned Walthall as one who could be a

cavalry brigadier, because he "will obey orders." Perhaps the battlefield disagreement between Loring and Walthall at Franklin illustrates Walthall was someone who would cooperate with Forrest's orders.

Eight infantry brigades were selected to form Walthall's infantry rear guard. From his own division, Daniel H. Reynolds commanded his own brigade, paired with Ector's. Featherston commanded his own brigade and Quarles's, from Walthall's Division. Brig. Gen. Joseph Palmer commanded his own brigade, with James A. Smith's attached. Col. Hume Feild commanded Maney's, and Strahl's. After eliminating about 400 soldiers without shoes, the effective total was only about 1,600.

Featherston was remembered by cavalry division commander James Chalmers in 1879. He wrote in the *Southern Historical Society Papers* (#7), "…General Forrest was by unanimous consent selected to cover the retreat from Columbia, and to assist his cavalry, now reduced to three thousand, he was assigned a division of selected infantry, numbering only fifteen hundred, but composed of as brave men and gallant officers as ever lived-not the least of whom was that gallant Mississippian, General Featherstone [sic] whose subsequent conduct at Sugar creek [sic] deserves to be long remembered." Walthall had selected Featherston to command his own brigade and Quarles'.

Scott's Brigade was not part of the rear guard. J.P. Cannon described the retreat from Columbia south. They were blessed that the enemy's pontoon train had wasted days on the wrong roads. This explains Cannon's remark on not being pressed. He continued:

"The enemy did not press us as much as might have been expected, but we had a dreary march through mud and slush for the next day or two. The weather changed from rain to sleet and our clothes froze on us, with many of the boys being bare-footed or nearly so and in this condition we footed it to Pulaski where we arrived on December 21st. Stragglers continued to come in during the night and by the next morning all who were fortunate enough to make their escape from Nashville had assembled. Roll call developed the fact that the 27th Alabama was almost completely wiped out. Of the one thousand who had left home just three years before, only seventeen were present including the line officers. I counted them and entered the number in my diary, so feel sure it is correct…" Sergeant Eggleston's blankets had been lost when they were captured at Nashville. He wrote of the 21st: "Slept on the frozen ground last night with two thin blankets to cover me. Snowed on us through the night. Our poor troops are suffering terribly."

Estes did better south of Pulaski. "…I came to a two-story house that seemed to beckon me under its hospitable roof. I entered it very reluctantly, but with unbounded faith. A lady met me, and I asked her if she would give me shelter just for one night from the wintry blast that was bellowing down through the Tennessee about this time. She replied, 'You can come in out of the weather, but I cannot provide anything but shelter and fire.' I thanked her and entered the room to find twenty or more such Rebels as I trying to get warm and dry." Estes felt he had "drawn the capital prize" when he heard a "thumping upstairs that sounded as if the people were preparing to move, but such was not the case. The lady had taken up the carpet and brought it down for us poor things to cover with, as we were trying to sleep on the benevolent floor. Such acts of kindness to this day I have rarely seen." The next morning Estes "…struck the mud again, accompanied by a large delegation of Hood's army, all in rags and tags, stomachs empty, feet sore, depressed in spirits…by this time I had gotten be a blanket-I won't tell how, but I got one, and its nobody's business where or how I got it."

While most of Hood's army was at Pulaski, or beyond, the enemy's pontoons were still trying to catch up. Thomas had mistakenly ordered them toward Murfreesborough. They got the word and tried to take a muddy country road toward Franklin. They choked in the mud, turned around and headed back to Nashville. There they preceded on the macadamized, though badly rutted, Franklin Pike. They finally made it past Spring Hill. They attempted to bridge Rutherford Creek on the 21st, but a heavy rain storm prevented completing it. It was hours past dark on the 22nd when they finally were across the creek and the Duck at Columbia. Parting shots from Forrest's cavalry and 15-degree weather slowed the enemy's progress. On the 24th the enemy cavalry began trotting through Columbia. The six lost days allowed Hood's escape south of Columbia.

Hood's pontoon train had passed through Pulaski that day and was on the road toward Alabama. Stewart's staff officer Gale recalled "every mind was haunted by the apprehension that we did not have boats enough, or barely enough to make [the] bridge." As the army had moved into and out of Tennessee, anytime a wagon carrying a pontoon had broken down it was usually pushed off the road. After Hood had abandoned efforts to take Decatur and cross the river, the enemy had abandoned it. Roddey's cavalry moved in and found abandoned pontoons. Miraculously there were enough to save the army, and the Alabama cavalrymen moved to begin construction on the river's south bank.

Forrest and Walthall spent Christmas Eve in Pulaski. They stayed busy destroying munitions and other army property abandoned due to weak horses and mules. At daylight on Christmas morning, as the pontoons were being laid on the Tennessee, Forrest moved out of Pulaski. The enemy cavalry was not far behind. Sanders wrote, "it was determined to turn on him. An advantageous position was selected for a line on Anthony's Hill., four miles from Pulaski. Featherston and Palmer, with a brigade of cavalry on each flank, …were put in ambush to await the enemy's approach. "When the attacking force reached the troops lying in wait for them, the latter delivered a destructive fire, and a section of Morton's artillery, masked nearby, opened fire with considerable effect. The enemy retreated in considerable disorder, and Featherston and Palmer promptly pursued and captured a number of prisoners, horses, and one piece of artillery"

Anthony's Hill may be reached on Highway 11, southwest of Pulaski. A highway marker attempts to cover Forrest's rear guard stand on 25 (marker has 26th) December. Featherston was on the northwest side of Highway 11 with Armstrong's cavalry on his flank. Palmer's was on the southeast side, with Ross's on his flank. Chestnut Grove Cemetery has our victorious dead. It may be reached by turning right on Fall River Road. At the top of the hill bear right. Just before the cemetery you might see the period road bed. Several of Featherston's dead are here, including men from the 3rd and 22nd Mississippi regiments.

Forrest and Walthall had retreated south another 14 miles Christmas night to reach Sugar Creek. There was still a large part of the ordinance train there. It had moved in advance of the army, but mules had to be borrowed to hurry the pontoon train to the river. Another rear guard stand was made, and the enemy's cavalry checked. They were still sixteen miles to the river. Sanders wrote, "On the morning of the 27th the march was continued, and the rear guard crossed Shoal Creek about two o' clock in the afternoon." Once again the infantry was drawn up behind the creek, and allowed the cavalry to pass on to the Tennessee. "Walthall with his incomparable infantry, together with the magnificent cavalry and artillery under Forrest, saved Hood's army from annihilation and enabled him to escape south of the Tennessee River." Now contrast Sanders version to Estes's.

Estes found three other soldiers from the 14th Mississippi for companions. "We met no obstacles until we came to Shoal Creek, where we were halted and ordered into line of battle to hold the Yankees in check till out army could get across the creek on an improvised bridge made of fence rails. A rail pen was built in the middle of the stream by placing rail upon rail and rail upon rail till the pen was above the water, and then a man would get each corner and hold down the pen till stringers could be placed from the bank reaching into and upon the rails. After this they would cover the stringers crosswise till a thing somewhat resembling a bridge had been constructed. General Featherston was in command, and he was as busy as a cranberry merchant trying to get the men in some sort of order to resist the Yankee cavalry that was pressing so hard on our disordered ranks. He was flying around here and there and everywhere he could see a man with a gun. He would catch a squad of stragglers and put them in line, then run off for another bunch. When he returned, the first bunch would have run off; so he gave up the effort to make a formidable resistance. But good luck came our way-the Yankees did not make any attack on us, and Hood's army passed on over the creek dry and hungry."

Featherston's Brigade was not the only unit from Loring's Division to allow the army to cross the Tennessee. It had been supposed the U.S. Navy would steam upriver and shell the bridge. Four or five gunboats made it to Florence by Christmas. It was learned the pontoon bridge was being assembled at the foot of Muscle Shoals, about six miles up. Two of the lighter draft gunboats got about two miles, at daylight on the 26th, when they came under fire. The guns were two Napoleons of Cowan's and the one remaining Parrott of Hoskins's. This part of the rear guard was organized by A.P. Stewart. Lt. George H. Tompkins was in command, as he was over Cowan's and the Parrott from Hoskins's.

T.G. Dabney had been with Hoskins's Parrott. He wrote *Confederate Veteran*, from New Orleans, in 1922 (Vol. 30, p. 409). "…We reached Florence (upstream) about dark, and reported to a colonel of Roddy's Cavalry. We were ordered to place our guns in a small lunette work but a little above the water surface. Having had experience in gunboat fighting, I knew that the lunette was a death trap, so I suggested to the colonel that, having a rifle gun, I could use it more effectively on a more elevated position. He then ordered me to place my gun on the spur of a ridge a little farther down the river, and several hundred yards from the river bank, which order I was not slow to obey. About daylight the next morning I was awakened by the sentinel, who reported that the gunboat was coming up the river. There were also two wooden boats, one on each side of the double-turreted monitor that was turning the bend below, The engagement began at once from our side, and the wooden boats dropped back down the river. The gunboat steamed slowly up and came directly across to our side of the river, stopping exactly opposite to my gun, and not over two hundred yards from Tompkins' guns, which were about on level with the gunboats."

The experience of Hoskins's Parrott-gun crew fighting gunboats proved their worth. Dabney wrote, "Tomkins gallantry pitted his twelve-pounders against the 11 or 12-inch Columbiads of the monitor. My gun was too much elevated for the Columbiads to be brought to bear upon it, and she did not fire a shot at me. But poor Tomkins' guns were smashed, and fifteen of his men killed or wounded, Lieutenant Tomkins being among the badly wounded."

By 2:00 p.m. the gunboats had retreated downstream. Dabney's account agreed. He said, "About the middle of the afternoon, when the fifty rounds of ammunition of the Parrott gun had been fired at the gunboat, probably without doing her any material damage, the gun was withdrawn and taken back upriver to the pontoon bridge, where it was crossed over the river about midnight, along with the remnants of Forrest's Cavalry." As the artillery had been firing the engineers assembling the pontoons had listened with anxious ears. They finished as the artillery fire commenced. General Cheatham supervised the crossing of the first wagons, and all safely crossed thanks to Cowan's Battery, the Parrott, and of course the rearguard stands.

Rejoining Estes, after the stand at Shoal Creek: "We passed on through the mud and slush until we finally came in sight of the Tennessee River, with its wide expanse of murky waters bearing down the stream drifts of logs, trees, brush, and everything imaginable. We could see, too, a rickety pontoon bridge hastily and insecurely built. It was serpentine in shape, about twelve feet wide and half a mile long, covered from end to end with all kinds of beasts,, wagons, and, in fact, you could see everything in the shape of humanity except women and dogs. Besides this, there was a Yankee gunboat half a mile or more down the river throwing bombshells, trying to break the bridge; but the shoals prevented it from getting near enough to do any damage." Estes feared the cable holding the pontoon would break as he crossed, but he made it across safely and found his regiment.

On the morning of the 28th Walthall brought the rearguard up to cross. All the wagons, artillery, cavalry, and infantry had safely crossed. The last unit across was the 39th North Carolina (Palmers' ?). The next day Thomas learned Hood had escaped across the river. He ordered "that the pursuit cease." Thomas telegraphed Washington, and the reaction was shock. The former Virginian had been the only one to rout a major Confederate army

yet he hadn't delivered the knockout blow. Grant believed Thomas was too "ponderous" to pursue. The army he had assembled was essentially disassembled, and generally sent to fight elsewhere. As for Thomas, he received the thanks of the U.S. Congress, but didn't have another field command.

J.P. Cannon summarized what we may suppose many of Loring's soldiers thought, "Three years before we had enlisted as twelve-month volunteers, little thinking then that we were entering on such a long and bloody struggle. We had endured hardships and dangers which often times seemed more than we could bear, but there was a function in the life of a soldier which compensates in large measure for the suffering and inconveniences to which we were subjected. Although deprived of comfortable clothing, often destitute of sufficient food, unsheltered from winter winds and snows, we were usually cheered and buoyed up by the hope of accomplishing the object for which we were battling. The memories of past misfortunes and the desperate condition of affairs at that time seemed to concentrate themselves in an overwhelming weight of woe. The future seemed almost hopeless. Our armies were constantly retreating before innumerable, fresh and fully equipped troops. Worn out with hardship and fatigue, hunger and cold, we were in poor condition to bear the vicissitudes of the winter, which was upon us. With no material from which to recruit and little provision for those who had survived, the outlook was gloomy indeed.'

"If the roll of one thousand had been called and answers could have been heard, many would have come from Northern soil, of those who had succumbed to disease contracted in Northern prisons; many more from fields flush with victory; from scenes dark with dire defeat; whose bodies were moldering upon the battlefields of Mississippi, Georgia, and Tennessee. Still others would have answered from widely scattered graves in our own Southland, where the gray moss waved in sympathy and the soft winds whispered a ceaseless requiem through the moaning pines. Now, of those who had survived the hundred days battles and skirmishes of the Georgia campaign and the Slaughter of

Franklin, all, except a mere handful had yielded to overwhelming numbers and were again on their way to Northern prisons."

James Harmon of the 35th Alabama was captured at Nashville on the 16th. He shared the misery and mistreatment typical of Confederates captured at Nashville. Harmon wrote, "When taken prisoners my command was several miles from Nashville, a cold drizzly rain had set in when the tramp began for the city. After a wearisome walk the place was reached where we were packed in an open muddy place under a strong guard all around... All were thoroughly wet, without any shelter whatever,...also without anything to eat and not even a place where one could sit down, for it was nothing but mud under foot...in the place we were crowded to spend that awful night..."

Another day passed for the cold, wet, hungry prisoners. Harmon continued, "We were then removed out of that...place and huddled where there seemed to have been a rock quarry; that certainly was an improvement...yet it was a cold dreary one. The snow was falling thick and fast while we poor mortals were standing there like a lot of sheep in a pen, shivering and nearly frozen to death. They were kind enough to have a few loads of wood hauled, yet as far as I was concerned I never got near a fire...The strongest and most able, crowded around a few smoldering fires, while the great bulk of the men had no chance whatever to ever get near a fire. With many of us, our only chance to keep from freezing was to take all the exercise possible, by moving our hands and feet, and by running around in a ring one after the other." This came after the suffering during the ice and snow before the battle. Even a Yankee agent with the Christian Commission said, "Hood's army has endured fatigues and privations almost beyond belief."

It is difficult to imagine some better arrangements could not be made by the U.S. Army. But the wounded of both armies had to be housed first. Large churches had been used by the U.S. Army after Murfreesborough, and thereafter the city was a hospital centre for sick and wounded. Catholic churches had escaped such use in the past, but no longer. Nashville newspapers reported for the first time the army had taken all the churched "without one exception." The enemy reported their wounded at 2,562 and that may be a low figure. Hundreds of captured Confederates were wounded. After Hood retreated south wounded that were at Franklin were moved to Nashville. On 28 December there were 7,818 sick and wounded in Nashville. Considering 6,421 prisoners were registered between before Franklin to 20 December, the humane thing to have done would have been to parole them, especially since Confederate armies were all but totally defeated.

Instead of paroles it appears the U.S. Army was willing to see prisoners die. Harman said, "After...several days arrangements were made to place us in the Penitentiary. This was surely a grand improvement over previous locations. Yes it was certainly a luxury to be placed under shelter, protected from the cold northern winds, and to have a dry place where on all could spread out blankets, and lie down to rest in sleep." As the days went by the prisoners were shipped north in cold box cars. The first train had left with 311 officers. Most if not all were sent to Johnson's Island on Lake Erie, where more died. Harmon said, "Our destination...was to be Camp Chase Ohio. On this trip men were badly crowded in the box cars. Many were sick and quite a number dies with pneumonia.

One poor fellow that was lying close to me died on the way to Louisville. The exposure had been so great, that it caused a good many to have pneumonia and one by one they passed away."

Major Garrett was captured on the 15th; his wife wrote, "After the battle the Federals placed Major Garrett and other officers in dirty horse cars in which horses had been shipped and which had not been cleaned out and there was no place to sit down or lie except in the filth. The officers were there for several days and then taken to Sandusky, Ohio and forced to walk across the frozen lake covered with deep snow three miles to Johnson's Island, where they were stopped outside and searched and their money and other things taken from them while they shivered in the cold wind and snow. Major Garrett had left his overcoat and the wind blew his hat and they would not let him pick it up. That was December 22, 1864."

The intentional cruelty to Confederates by the U.S. Army surpassed that inflicted on U.S. troops in World War Two. Elizabeth Garrett continued, "In prison they were given about enough fuel to make one good fire and that had to last twenty four hours and a small piece of bread and a piece of salty beef to each officer per day. They slept on bunks. Many stout healthy men starved to death on that allowance, others were wantonly shot down by the guards. Major Garrett was young and well and weighed 165 pounds when he entered the prison and when released he weighed little more than 90 pounds and was not sick a day. The suffering from hunger was intense. They weighed each crumb of bread and divided it and they boiled the beef and drank the saltwater to make them thirsty then filled up on water to try to satisfy their craving for food. They hunted for rats and ate them. Why did Major Garrett live and endure this suffering for months? In answer to prayer." Elizabeth Bouton went on to tell of their marriage; see Garrett's entry.

Sergeant Eggleston's final entry was on 31 December, as they were in Mississippi: "Camped a 8 P.M. a mile from Iuka. A very cold evening. The last of the eventful and disastrous year of 1864! May a merciful Father vouchsafe that the coming year may be more propitious to our cause and may he grant us peace, and independence…We have met many reverses and have lost many brave and gallant souls, but our cause is not hopeless. We can yet achieve our nationality with the aid of the All powerful God of battles-We must bear our reverses with the fortitude of heroes, buckle on the armor and calling on the God of Truth to be our ally resolve to success or perish." ..

Beauregard had left Hood in Alabama before his campaign into Tennessee. He was in Augusta on 6 December, as Sherman's march was essentially enlarging Beauregard's department to include all of Georgia. Augusta is upstream of Savannah, on the Savannah River, which is the border with South Carolina. He found it too being included in his territory, bringing an area far too large to manage. He had about 30,000 troops to hold the 100-plus mile long line from Augusta to Charleston. Beauregard spent time in both places as well as in Savannah, desperate to find a solution to the U.S. war on civilians.

Once across the Tennessee the threadbare Army of Tennessee marched to Corinth. They hoped to find clothing, but didn't. Forrest wrote Lt. Gen. Richard Taylor, "The Army of

Tennessee was badly defeated and is greatly demoralized, and to save it during the retreat from Nashville I was compelled almost to sacrifice my command." Taylor came to visit the army which had moved south to Tupelo. Taylor was the man who had decisively defeated the enemy in the Red River Campaign, and hadn't been acclimated to defeat. He reached Tupelo the first week of January. He wired Davis his view of the army, that "if moved in its present condition it will prove utterly worthless; this applies to both infantry and cavalry." Hood actually wired Secretary of War Seddon, "I respectfully request to be relieved from the command of this army." Beauregard visited the army in Tupelo in mid-January. It was determined to send most of the army to reinforce Hardee in South Carolina, and the rest to Mobile. Beauregard arrived in Mobile on the 21st in order to inspect and assess the fortifications. After four days he was back in Augusta.

Before Hood resigned, he furloughed entire Mississippi regiments. Neither Mississippi brigade commander, Featherston or Lowry, would be present for the last big battle. Snodgrass wasn't either, and perhaps he was allowed a visit home (see his biographical entry). Stevenson still commanded Lee's Corps as it moved to North Carolina. He wrote, "The failure to extend to the troops of Georgia, Alabama, and South Carolina, when passing their homes, the same indulgences as had been granted to those of Mississippi, gave much dissatisfaction and caused large numbers to leave the ranks en route."

In turning over the army to Taylor, Hood expressed hope they would support Taylor and avenge their comrades "whose bones lay bleaching upon the fields of Middle Tennessee." He also said he hoped they would be supplied with more bayonets because "it was the bayonet which gave the soldier confidence in himself, and enabled him to strike terror to the enemy." Hood had learned nothing from Franklin. His total failure in reconnaissance had led to the slaughter of Loring's Division as it tried to hack its way through hedge and abatis. Hood had proved an utter failure at planning from Peach Tree Creek to Nashville.

Sherman presented Savannah as a Christmas present to Lincoln on 22 December, just after Hardee had skillfully evacuated his command into South Carolina. That day U.S. forces had finally crossed their Duck River bridge in pursuit of the Army of Tennessee. Confederates officers were being marched across frozen Lake Erie to prison. At that point Grant desired Sherman to move his command of some 60,000 by sea, to join him in Virginia. But Sherman wanted to march north. He assured Grant that, "I can break up the whole railroad system of South Carolina and North Carolina, and be …either at Raleigh or Weldon, by the time spring fairly opens." Grant had come to realize Hood's demoralized army was no longer a major threat; hence, Grant approved Sherman's plan.

Chapter 8: North Carolina finale: 1865

Sherman spent January refitting his command, and by the time he reached North Carolina he would be reinforced. Fort Fisher fell to a joint army-navy attack on the 15th. The fort protected Wilmington, the last major port open to blockade runners. It was vital to supply Lee's army, as imported items could be brought up the *Wilmington & Weldon Railroad* toward Virginia. Since the fort had fallen, U.S. troops under Maj. Gen. Alfred Terry could advance along the railroad to Goldsboro. Grant had also ordered Schofield to bring his command from Tennessee. They traveled north from Nashville by rail to Maryland, where they boarded transports for New Bern, on the North Carolina coast. Schofield could also follow a railroad, the *Atlantic & North Carolina,* to Goldsboro. Sherman planned to march for the Goldsboro rail junction to unite with Schofield and Terry.

Sherman had more troops than any Confederate general could successfully confront. There was still denial that Sherman, once again advancing in two divergent columns, could continue. His left seemed pointed at Augusta and his right at Charleston. But then he pulled them together and headed for Columbia. The stress was no doubt a factor in the increasingly poor health of Beauregard and Hardee. Age 50 was considered an old man then, and both were approaching it. Loring was too for that matter, and all were being severely tested in 1865. Hardee was trying to hold Charleston, which Beauregard had so brilliantly defended against U.S. attacks in 1863. Yet he had to order Hardee to evacuate it and move toward North Carolina. Beauregard reached Columbia on 10 February. South Carolina's Wade Hampton had come from Virginia, and was to command cavalry and even Lee's Corps, coming from Mississippi. He was promoted to lieutenant general effective on the 14th, so Wheeler came under his command. As Forrest was also, on the 28th, we see the two highest ranking cavalry generals were not West Pointers.

Hampton found Columbia unfortified and with no natural defenses. Hampton's home and family were there yet his small force could offer no resistance for Sherman's converging wings. Beauregard approved Wade Hampton's evacuating it, as Sherman approached it on the 17th. The beautiful city of gardens burned that night, including Hampton's home. U.S. troops took a special delight in burning the property of helpless South Carolinians blaming them, rather than Lincoln, for starting the war.

Beauregard's department had been large before it was expanded into the Carolinas. His health, often poor, was a concern. Lee had become general-in-chief on 6 February, and had doubts he could hold up. He referred to Beauregard's health as "indifferent," which apparently meant mediocre. There had been a continuous call to restore Johnston to command over the Army of Tennessee. Lee agreed saying, "General Johnston is the only officer whom I know who has the confidence of the army and people…" Lee wanted him restored and word reached Johnston on the 23rd. He was to command the army and all the troops in the Department of South Carolina, Georgia, and Florida. Johnston traveled to Charlotte to meet Beauregard, and see if a subordinate role was acceptable. The Creole general, who had more prominent victories than Johnston in 1863 and 1864, admitted his concern over his health. He would not take the field, but forward troops to Johnston.

Hampton, Forrest, and Richard Taylor were the only civilians without military training to attain the rank of lieutenant general. Accolades for Hampton were similar to those for Forrest; "few equals and perhaps no superiors." Another was "a veritable god of war." After the death of J.E.B. Stuart, Lee might have named his nephew Fitz Lee as Stuart's successor. Instead he named Hampton. The significance may also be appreciated in that he was not a West Pointer, or a Virginian. Sherman's invasion of South Carolina led to his transfer and promotion there. Postbellum was a governor and U.S. senator. He lived to 1902. Post card was mailed from Columbia; appears to be 1907. It was placed on the capitol grounds in Columbia to honour his role as a general and as a statesman. Some have been crying of his slave ownership.

Thomas Connelly wrote, in *Autumn of Glory*: "The delay in appointing Johnston proved disastrous…Johnston was no genius at strategy. But if he had been appointed earlier, he might have wrought some order, and concentration might have been effected. Instead, from almost two critical months in 1865, the Confederacy confronted Sherman in the Carolinas with nothing but chaos." Connelly tended toward negative assessments, yet this is a fair point. A Confederate concentration was the sort of thing Beauregard, so worn out, preached. What if Sherman had been defeated in the Carolinas, and his retreat to Charleston or Savannah been blocked by Hampton or Wheeler? Grant had Lee contained at Petersburg. Could Johnston have attacked Grant from the rear? What if Grant had also been defeated? Would worn out Confederates have attacked fortified Washington City?

Joseph E. Johnston knew he was too late. He had known it when sent to Mississippi, and certainly Lincoln reelected and no hope for a negotiated independence. What would he command? Some Army of Tennessee units were sent to the Mobile Bay area, though most were ordered to North Carolina. A.P. Stewart was in command of what was left of the three corps. They made it to the village of Bentonville late on 18 March, and marched one mile beyond at dusk. No fires were allowed and soldiers knew "to make no noise in camp-the enemy are near."

About 4,500 of the Army of Tennessee seem to have made it in time for Bentonville. Perhaps 900 from Cheatham's were on hand; Cheatham didn't make it, so Bate commanded the corps. About 2,700 of Lee's Corps made it. Lee was still absent due to his wound. Stevenson went back to his division when the corps was turned over to North Carolinian Lt. Gen. Daniel Harvey Hill. Stewart's Corps was commanded by Loring, and he was so down with an unidentified illness, he could barely stay in the saddle. About 800 to 900 from five brigades of Stewart's Corps made it to Bentonville; only 459 armed. Joining Johnston's command were Hardee's troops coming up from Savannah, and Department of North Carolina troops temporarily under Bragg. He had served as an advisor to Davis, but returned to his native North Carolina in 1865. He was temporary superseded fellow Tar Heel Maj. Gen. Robert Hoke, to command his Army of Northern Virginia division, comprised mostly of North Carolinians.

Loring's Division was commanded by Col. James Jackson (27th Alabama). After John Adams was killed at Franklin his brigade was commanded by Robert Lowry. He was promoted to brigadier in February 1865. *Bentonville..,* by N.C. Hughes, has the organization with Lt. Col. Robert Josiah Lawrence (14th Mississippi) in command after Lowry. There is no explanation for Lowry's absence; however *Confederate Military History* indicates he was temporarily commanding a cavalry brigade, Gholson's, in Mississippi. Command may have passed to Col. Richard Harrison (43rd Mississippi). The same footnote has Featherston remaining behind in Tupelo to collect men on furlough. He rejoined the army in April, so that Maj. Martin A. Oatis was in command at Bentonville. Scott's Brigade was under Snodgrass at Nashville. Hughes shows the brigade under Capt. John A. Dixon here.

For Johnston to take such an array of forces and form a new army was just the sort of generalship he excelled at. Taking the offensive with it was more amazing. Lee had seen Johnston's cautiousness in previous campaigns. As Sherman's army was entering Fayetteville, to destroy the arsenal, Lee reminded Johnston that a "bold and unexpected attack might relieve us." Several days later Lee stressed, "If you are forced back…and we be deprived of supplies from East North Carolina, I do not know how [my] army can be supported…" Johnston's options were complicated, but his decision was sound. Rather than defend Fayetteville, with its arsenal, or Raleigh, he decided to attack Sherman as he advanced toward Goldsboro. Sherman's left wing was to be ambushed as it marched.

Johnston was at Smithfield, southeast of Raleigh on the North Carolina Railroad, when he asked Hampton if he could strike before Sherman's columns reached Goldsboro. Hampton replied that Cole's Plantation, near the village of Bentonville, would be ideal. At dusk, on 18 March, Sherman's army was 25 miles from Goldsboro, and he was confident the only Confederate force to his front was cavalry. His left wing was on the Old Goldsboro Road, also confident nothing but cavalry was ahead.

Sunday morning the 19th was warm and cloudless in the village of Bentonville. The people may have heard gunfire soon after 8:00 when Yankee foragers encountered Confederate skirmishers. The noise got closer as the Yankees organized to advance. By 11:00 there was fighting at Cole's Plantation. If people arrived at Mill Creek Church expecting a sermon, there may have been little more than a prayer before they hurried off.

Johnston's tactics required something like numerical parity to destroy the U.S. Left Wing and his plan came close to execution. Like other battlefield commanders, on both sides, he found knockout blows hard to deliver. He needed strength in his right and centre. Bad maps played a factor in delaying Hardee's arrival at the centre. But that morning the U.S. 14th Corps ran into Hoke's Division, entrenched across the road, and attacked. Bragg was there, with his seniority, and called on Johnston for reinforcements. As it turned out they were not needed, as Hoke's fine command repulsed the attackers. Johnston recalled this in his postbellum narrative: "…General Hardee, the head of whose column was then near, was directed most injudiciously to send his leading division, McLaws's, to the assistance of the troops assailed." Thus they were not available to launch Johnston's planned attack.

The tiny remains of Stewart's Corps were the centre, along with Lee's Corps to their right, and then Cheatham's to their right. Stewart reported to Johnston that "the enemy attacked the right and centre of our line at 12:45 and were easily repulsed." Thus Loring was not seriously engaged in the repulse, and possibly just as well, as he was ill. The nature of his illness is a mystery. Even his biographer, Raab, doesn't specify it. However "Old Blizzards" had one last attack to make in his Confederate career. He advanced Stewart's Corps in the following counterattack. Besides his own division, Walthall's was also present. French's Division had gone to Mobile. Their advance brought praise from Joe Johnston, who rode up to congratulate Loring and Walthall. Bentonville showed Loring's old troops still had courage left, but the war was long past being won by courage. Hughes wrote they had successfully ambushed one wing of the enemy's forces, before their inevitable defeat. That wing had two corps, the 14th and the 20th.

The different U.S. corps used symbolic badges so that they might be recognized. The 14th Corps used the acorn. Most of the initial fighting was done by the 1st Division of the 14th. Their attack failed and all three Army of Tennessee corps counterattacked along with Taliaferro's Division. The U.S. 20th Corps were entrenching when they heard the 14th routed. One recalled, "Just as we had got a few rails piled up, the whole 14th corps broke pannick stricken, throwing away guns, knapsacks & everything and all running like a flock of sheeps." Another saw what looked like a "stampede." Another said the panic "brought back vividly to our minds a similar scene at the Battle of Chancellorsville." One Yankee general viewed the counterattack "advancing as steadily and calmly as if regiments on review." Nathaniel Cheairs Hughes's volume on Bentonville covers this in a chapter *The Battle of Acorn Run*, as 20th Corps troops called it.

For those familiar with Shiloh and Murfreesborough the outcome might be anticipated. After the driving most of the 14th Corps back for nearly a mile, they confronted artillery, well positioned on high ground. Eight U.S. batteries were positioned to blast the counterattack, tearing gaping holes in the Confederate formations. Loring's Division,

After Bentonville some wounded left the battlefield with Johnston's army, while others were taken to the home of Mr. and Mrs. John Harper. With no surgeon they cared for 54 C.S. wounded, for three months; 31 recovered and went home. Of the 23 that died, 20 are buried here.

Circa 1960s post card shows the Harper House. It has been preserved, and is located next to the visitor centre for the Bentonville Battleground State Historic Site.

under Jackson, was out of ammunition and had to retire. Loring was so ill he turned Stewart's Corps over to Walthall, probably the next morning.

Sherman was marching with the right wing. During the 19th they could hear the left wing fighting the battle. Sherman told Kilpatrick, his cavalry commander that Slocum, the left wing commander, thinks Johnston's whole army is in his front. Sherman refused to think Johnston would bring on a battle. Johnston had abandoned Jackson in 1863, and fallen back to defensive positions in the Atlanta Campaign. Sherman seemed to think Johnston wouldn't consider it in 1865. But this was the last chance for Confederate independence.

Sherman had to adapt to the surprising threat to his Left Wing On the 20th he was coming to the battle with the Right Wing. Wade Hampton recalled, "Early on the morning of the 20th, Brigadier-General Law, whom I had placed temporarily in command of Butler's division…reported that the right wing (U.S.)…had struck the road on which we were on moving down on moving down on our rear and left flank. Hoke then held our left, and General Johnston directed him to refuse his left flank so that he could meet the attack of the approaching force. I prolonged the rear line taken by Hoke by placing Butler's and Wheeler's commands on his left, and while doing this we met and checked a sharp attack. Sherman thus had his whole army united in front of us about 12 o'clock on the 20th, and he made repeated attacks during the day, mainly on Hoke's division. In all of them he was repulsed, and many of his wounded left in front of our lines were carried to our hospitals. Our line was a very weak one and our position was extremely perilous, for our force was confronted, almost surrounded, by one nearly five times as large. Our flanks rested on no natural defenses, and behind us was a deep and rapid stream [Mill Creek] over which there was but one bridge, which gave the only means of withdrawal."

Johnston was fighting with about 16,000 infantry, and 4,000 cavalrymen. He had hoped to destroy Sherman's left wing of 30,000, and with another 30,000 approaching, his opportunity to destroy the left was gone. Johnston thought Sherman only had 44,000, and supposed he could win one of his Georgia campaign style defensive victories. After having the audacity to attack, he must have hated to abandon another battlefield. A great motivation in remaining on the field was the slow process of evacuating his wounded. He had done a magnificent job of saving his wounded in the Atlanta Campaign. There the *Western & Atlantic* was always nearby. But at Bentonville he had to get the wounded to the railroad at Smithfield.

One of Bragg's strong points was attention to the wounded. Even as Murfreesborough was being fought trains had arrived which carried sick and wounded to Chattanooga. With Lee as general-in-chief Bragg had been dispatched to North Carolina. Still there after Fort Fisher and Wilmington fell, he saw he would take a subordinate role to Johnston. He had asked Davis to "relieve me from the embarrassing position." Johnston found a solution as he needed to evacuate his Bentonville wounded. Bragg was sent to Smithfield, on the *North Carolina Railroad*, where he could move wounded by rail.

Tuesday the 21st dawned and Johnston's line was no longer positioned to attack, but to defend the solitary bridge crossing over Mill Creek. Sherman thought Johnston would withdraw on the 20th, but there he was holding his ground. That afternoon, in the midst of a soaking downpour, one of his divisions began a reconnaissance toward Johnston's weak left. Cavalry was on the far left and just beyond it was the bridge. The Yankee's advance caused Johnston and his staff to abandon headquarters. Fortunately Hampton found two mounted regiments and Cumming's old Georgia brigade, from Stevenson's Division. Hardee came up and led a charge and the Yankees were driven back. Too bad for Hardee, for his teenage son was rode with the 8th Texas Cavalry and was mortally wounded.

Hampton's recollections are of much interest, especially since infantry and cavalry of the Army of Tennessee, in their last battle, were successful. "The attack was so sudden and so impetuous that it carried everything before it, and the enemy retreated hastily…other portions of my command struck his flank as he was retiring, and contributed largely to our success." General Johnston tipped his hat to the Georgia infantry. Stevenson wrote of his brigade, "No encomium that I can pass…will be so expressive a recognition of its gallant behavior as the simple statement that it received upon the field the thanks and compliments of General Johnston." Sherman's memoirs are loaded with conceit, such as here, where he stated he ordered his infantry back. With humour Hampton added, "…but if this statement is true, the order was obeyed with wonderful promptness and alacrity."

Though Johnston could take some pride in Bentonville, there was no reason to stay with some 60,000 Yankees holding him against Mill Creek. Late winter rains came down in torrents and continued into the night. A private reflected on the bridge everyone had to cross that night. It "spans a deep creek which runs close to the town of Bentonville, and owing to the recent rains is very much swollen, and not fordable any where; therefore it is very important for us to hold the bridge." The torrents of rain benefitted the process of disengaging, as noise was muffled, keeping enemy curiosity down.

Of 23 Confederates that died in the Harper House, 20 are buried in a mass grave adjacent to this monument. Their burial was unmarked before the militia company Goldsboro Rifles raised money in 1894. The monument was dedicated on 20 March 1895. Wade Hampton delivered the keynote address.

Confederate dead from the battle were buried at various places on the battlefield. Some 360 were moved to a site on Harper House Road. It has roadside marker, "Confederate Cemetery."

General William Hardee's 16-year-old son, Willie, is perhaps the most famous casualty. He was mortally wounded while fighting with the Texas Rangers. He was transported to Hillsborough, where he died three days later. He is buried at St. Mathews Episcopal Church.

Wednesday morning, the 22nd, Yankees began probing forward and found the bridge over Mill Creek in flames. Hampton said some of Wheeler's cavalry had a skirmish as the enemy attempted a crossing. They were repulsed and with that, Bentonville was over. Could Johnston count it as a victory? He had finally abandoned the field, losing 240 killed, about 2,400 wounded, and about 1,500 were captured or deserted. Sherman's total loss was just over 1,500. As in Georgia, Sherman couldn't budge Johnston without flanking him. Here, he had no intention of pursuing Johnston. He had a rendezvous in Goldsboro with the 10th Corps and the 23rd. He would rest and refit, as he had done at Atlanta, before advancing again. Whether or not Johnston could call Bentonville a victory or not, he could take satisfaction in having made one last offensive. Once across Mill Creek he had only fallen back a short march to Smithfield.

Interesting occurrences during this period come from the journal of Bromfield Ridley, a young man on Stewart's staff. On 28 March he went into Raleigh for an overcoat and was turned down because he wasn't a North Carolinian. Governor Vance intervened on his behalf and he left with the "smuggled goods." On the 30th he learned that the wagons that had been left in Tupelo were to arrive in the first week of April. They were left as much of the infantry traveled by trains to Augusta. On the 31st he reported S.D. Lee had arrived with some of troops. Thousands more from Stewart's and Cheatham's corps were near.

Ridley wrote of 4 April: "I witnessed today the saddest spectacle of my life, the review of the skeleton Army of Tennessee, but one year ago was replete with men, and now filed by with the tattered garments, worn out shoes, bare-footed and ranks so depleted that each colour was supported by only thirty or forty men. Desertion, sickness, deaths, hardships, perils, and vicissitudes demonstrated themselves too plainly upon that old army not to recur to its history. Oh, what a contrast between the Dalton review and this one! The march of the remnant was so slow-colours tattered and torn with bullets-that it looked like a funeral procession. The countenance of every spectator who saw both reviews was depressed and dejected, and the solemn, stern look of the soldiery was so impressive-Oh! it is beginning to look dark in the east, gloomy in the west, and like almost a lost hope when we reflect upon the review of today." His entry for the 5th began: "The shades of sorrow are gathering upon us…" They heard of the fall of Richmond and the death of Lt. Gen. A.P. Hill. "Heavens the gloom and how terrible our feelings!" Ridley wrote on the 6th: "It never rains but it pours, and still the bad news comes…" They had learned of the fall of Selma. General Stewart learned of the death of his four-year-old son at Auburn, Alabama. "Notwithstanding his stern military character he is a tender hearted man." On the 8th he wrote that their wagons were now within ten miles.

Johnston was still at Smithfield on 9 April when he reorganized the assorted commands into the Army of Tennessee. Stewart got his corps back with 'new' divisions under Walthall and Patton Anderson. Loring's was the only Army of Tennessee division to survive intact from the 1864 organization. James Jackson had led Loring's Division at Bentonville, and with Loring back it is not clear where the one-armed colonel was. Adams's was now Lowry's Brigade and included the 12th Louisiana, formerly in Scott's. Featherston's Brigade was reinforced by Arkansas regiments from Reynolds's Brigade, Reynolds having lost a leg at Bentonville. The five old Alabama regiments of Scott's Brigade were consolidated into one regiment. Col. Edward Asbury McAlexander, of the 27th Alabama, took command. He had been in command of the post of Cherokee, Alabama during Hood's Tennessee campaign. They were placed in a brigade with five other Alabama regiments, commanded by Brig. Gen. Charles M. Shelley. He had commanded Cantey's Brigade, who had taken so many medical leaves that apparently it was now known as Shelley's. Snodgrass does not seem to have returned, possibly on recruiting duties, and Scott couldn't due to his Franklin wound. Cantey's had been in Walthall's Division.

Johnston marched the reorganized army through Raleigh on the 11th. Ridley wrote, "As we passed the female seminary in Raleigh the beautiful school girls greeted us warmly. Each one had a pitcher of water and a goblet. We drank, took their addresses, and had a big time." On the 12th they "landed" one mile east of Durham Depot. "General Johnston left Raleigh on the cars to meet President Davis at Greensboro…Rumors of Lee's capture in Virginia are rife, but not believed."

Sherman had advanced from Goldsboro toward Smithfield on the 10th. He arrived the next day and found Johnston had gone onto Raleigh. They marched for Raleigh on the 12th, and got word of Lincoln's assassination. Johnston wasn't at Raleigh either, so they passed on through on the 13th. Knowing Johnston could no longer hope to consolidate with Lee, he supposed he would move toward Charlotte. Before he moved he received word from Johnston, requesting a cessation of hostilities with a view of surrendering.

The two commanders met at noon on the 17th, at a point near Durham halfway between the picket lines of the two armies. They rode along looking for a place to meet when they came upon the home of James and Nancy Bennett. They had lost three sons in the war, and found their home assuming historic status. Once inside and out of sight of the others Sherman handed Johnston a telegram from Stanton telling of Lincoln's assassination. He had concealed it from his own army, as their reaction might be beyond his control. The larger issue is the U.S. government was not as willing to agree to Sherman's relatively generous terms. Johnston needed to get word to Davis, so Sherman returned to Raleigh, the two agreeing to meet again at the Bennett's the next day. They met again and sent copies of their agreement to the heads of their governments. There was still a truce but no formal surrender.

Sherman's initial terms, made at the Bennet house were too lenient for the radicals in Washington City. Sherman and Grant met in Raleigh to discuss what terms could be offered. Later that day, 25 April 1865, Grant write his wife, Julia, that the "people who talked of further retaliation and punishment, except of the political leaders, either do not conceive of the suffering endured already or they are heartless and unfeeling." During the so called Reconstruction it was typically the hatred and vengeance of such radicals, and not veterans, whose evil domination of the South inured ill will would exist at least until the 21st Century.

This card was mailed to Mr. H.W. Edwards in Salem, Massachusetts in July 1921. Somehow the card made it to Crossville, Tennessee, where the author bought in 2008. The Bennett Place State Historic Site is at 4409 Bennett Memorial Road, Durham. It is usually open Tuesday thru Saturday from 9:00 a.m. to 5:00 p.m.

Now that the Army of Tennessee knew Lee had surrendered and they were to be as well, desertions multiplied. Stewart and Loring spoke to a large assemblage of soldiers on the 20th. Ridley recalled they "explained the substance of the negotiation and the cause of the armistice…If the terms are agreed upon for peace, we will soon be headed for our dear old homes, even if they are not what they were four years ago."

The news traveled fast. One of the most significant civilian diaries came from a young lady, *Eliza Frances Andrews: The War-Time Journal of a Georgia Girl*. Her home was in Washington, Georgia, which became an artery for Confederates going home, or in the case of President Davis, trying to make it to the Trans-Mississippi. It was also the home of Robert Toombs, who might have been president. He arrived on 21 April. Andrews wrote, "He brought confirmation of Lee's surrender, and of the armistice between Johnston and Sherman. Alas, we all know only too well what that armistice means! It is all over now, and there is nothing to do but bow our heads I the dust and let the hateful conquerors trample us under their feet. There is complete revulsion in public feeling. No more talking about fighting to the last ditch; the last ditch has already been reached; no more talk about help from France and England, but all about the emigration to Mexico and Brazil. We are irretrievably ruined, past the power of France and England to save us now. Europe has quietly folded her hands and beheld a noble nation perish. God grant she may yet have cause to repent her cowardice and folly in suffering this monstrous power that has crushed us to roll on unchecked. We fought nobly and fell bravely, overwhelmed by numbers and resources, with never a hand held out to save us. I hate all the world when I think of it. I am crushed and bowed down in sorrow, but not in shame."

Grant came down to meet Sherman in Raleigh on the 25th. Sherman understood what terms he was authorized to formalize, and met Johnston at the Bennett's for a third time, on the 26th. The terms led to the largest troop surrender of the war for it not only included Johnston's army but also the Department of the Carolinas, Georgia, and Florida. Unlike Lee's surrender, there were no U.S. troops to oversee the surrender. They self-policed their stacking of arms, parking of artillery, and returned captured U.S. flags.

The Army of Tennessee began its final march on 3 May. Johnston was reluctant to part with them and traveled with them from Greensboro, west to Salisbury. There they separated into three columns, traveling in different directions. Ridley's journal gave a rare daily account of the journey. On the 14th he said General Loring's wagon train had stopped one mile south of Abbeville, South Carolina. They were on the route Davis and his entourage had taken out of Abbeville almost two week earlier, headed to Washington, Georgia. He was captured down near Irwinville on the 10th, and for practical reasons, he had recognized his cabinet's dissolution. However, there was never a formal surrender of the Confederate government. Loring's train paused to let traffic ease. What had been Loring's Division was about to disappear. Exactly where Loring went next is unknown.

What can be said of Loring's Division may be said of others. They were fighting to create an independent nation, with a legitimate claim to govern itself. Their sacrifices never paid off. Arthur Fremantle came across Loring's Division in Jackson, after their miraculous escape from Grant's seven divisions. He must have been impressed with their prowess. He began his Confederate journey in Texas, and as he traveled saw odd customs. He opened *Three Months in the Southern States* with a laudatory preface. "Many people will doubtless highly disapprove of some of their customs and habits in the wilder portion of the country; but I think no generous man, whatever may be his political opinions, can do otherwise than admire the courage, energy, and patriotism of the whole population, and the skill of its leaders, in this struggle against great odds. And I am also of the opinion that many will agree with me in thinking that a people in which all ranks and both sexes display a unanimity and a heroism which can never have been surpassed in the history of the world, is destined, sooner or later, to become a great and independent nation." Sadly, Fremantle's prediction didn't come true.

The Confederacy might have become a great isolationist nation, similar to Switzerland. Washington was on the Confederate seal. His 1796 Farewell Address had warned to stay out of foreign affairs. Likewise, Jefferson had advised a course of isolationism. Instead, the states of the C.S.A. became permanently dominated and drawn into U.S. imperialism. As Loring's Division fought their last battle for independence in North Carolina, it is insightful to quote Zebulon Vance as he spoke when inaugurated as governor in 1877. "North Carolina was placed in the hands of [the] designing and ignorant of our people, organized and led by unscrupulous and disreputable adventurers from the slums of Northern politics; as a base…tribe of reptiles which seem to spring like fungi from the rottenness and corruption of revolutionary times." The North would draw the South into the Spanish American War. Instead of Spain, the South would have to survive alongside a communist Cuba in the 20th Century. A political assassination in Europe somehow drew the South into World War One. These were not wars for the South.
Bromfield Ridley's 21 May 1865 journal entry: "The echo of the surrender is still preying upon me, and when I think of the future of the Southland, I am filled with dark forebodings. Had we succeeded, we had been patriots; as we did not, we are called rebels. No monument of marble, nor brass, now to commemorate the sacred principles for which we fought, no shaft to be erected by a nation in our honour, but in our hearts will live the memories and convictions that only force has smothered."

PART 2: The Soldiers and Units

Chapter 10-John Adams's Brigade

Adams's Brigade was named for John Adams. Three of the regiments had been in a brigade commanded by Lloyd Tilghman, who was killed at Champion Hill. Adams had been serving at several posts in Mississippi. Pat Henry recalled in *Confederate Veteran* (Volume 21, page 77), "When General Adams was assigned to the command of this brigade (composed entirely of Mississippi troops) it was resented by officers and men. We thought that we should have a Mississippi brigadier, but this feeling soon passed away, it being recognized that he was a fine soldier, a knightly commander, and a Christian gentleman. We soon learned and appreciated his work, and his untimely death, while it reflected glory on his brigade, brought genuine sorrow and sadness to every officer and soldier of his command. Knowing him as I did, having served so long as inspector of his brigade, I want to say that he was not only one of the bravest but one of the most conscientious and truly religious men I ever knew. He was as modest as a woman, rather retiring in his disposition, of the strictest integrity. He scorned that which was not honorable, and lived in daily communion with his God. I rarely ever knew him to lie down at night that he did not read from his rubric and say his prayers. This was often beset with difficulties on forced marches, but Billie, his faithful servant, generally had a piece of candle stuck in a bayonet or a torch close t the General's pallet or blanket. There was nothing of the fanatic about him, nor did he make parade of his religion; he simply worshipped his God. Even now (1913) the old men of his brigade speak his name in reverence and affection, and as a token of my veneration for him I write these memories."

Where No Sorrows Come: The Life and death of Confederate Brig. General John Adams (2014) by Bryan Lane is the only biography. Adams's West Point roommate was George Pickett. Lane has pointed out Pickett gained fame for a charge he did not lead. Adams led a similar charge to his death, and his name is rarely recalled. Much of this had to do with Richmond newspapers operating through the war and promoting Virginia heroes. Adams was from Nashville where the U.S. government had forced the papers to print their own propaganda. This disregarded the 1st Amendment of their U.S. Constitution.

Adams' biography raises issues of bad habits. They followed him into the C.S. Army. At West Point Adams got a high level of demerits. In 1843 he got 124, in 1844 he got 191, in 1845 he got 132, and in 1846 he got 151. Leonidas Polk tried to get Adams out of Memphis in November 1861. He feared Adams had bad habits. Adams was at Columbus, Mississippi when correspondence revealed objections to his promotion to brigadier. A J.D. Blair wrote, "There is not a civilian, or military man here that believes he was capable of commanding this post." Adams was "a devout worshiper of King Alcohol.", "Col. Adams cannot keep sober if he can get anything to make him otherwise."

President Davis ordered an investigation of Adams. Countering charges of excessive drinking are quotes quite to the opposite of those above. Maj. W.J. Anderson stayed with Adams in Columbus. He said, "I not only never saw him drunk, but do not remember a single occasion when I ever suspected him of being under the influence of liquor. With the regard to the charge of incompetency…there are but few officers more thoroughly acquainted with the duties of Post Commander, and none who could have discharged them with more promptitude and fidelity than Col. Adams." Several others are quoted making remarks supportive of Adams. General Johnston seems to have had an impact, for he wrote of Adams, "He is very valuable." That may as well settle the issue, for Adams went onto serve under Joe Johnston, and next to die under his successor, Hood.

But in January 1863 Adams was in Pemberton's Department of Mississippi and Eastern Louisiana. There were four military districts and Adams commanded the Fourth, out of Jackson. It was by far the smallest with only .5% of the men in the department. His 388 troops were a state unit, 1st Mississippi Battalion, and Bolen's Kentucky cavalry company. He had to deal with housing prisoners for the department. Other units were added, so that by the end of April Adams had 2,403 troops.

Confederate Military History (Vol. 7, Part 2, p. 130) details the 4th District in April 1863:
1st Choctaw Battalion under Maj. J.W. Pierce
1st Mississippi Battalion under Maj. W.B. Harper
14th Mississippi under Col. George William Abert
Company C of the 15th Mississippi under Capt. P.H. Norton
Bolen's and Terry's Kentucky cavalry companies
Third Mississippi Brigade, State Troops under Brig. Gen. J.Z. George

Confederate Military History details the infantry units of Tilghman's Brigade in April with several Mississippi infantry regiments that Adams later inherited. Tilghman's had: 54th Alabama Infantry; this unit was transferred to Buford's Brigade soon after. The 8th Kentucky Infantry was also transferred to Buford's and later became a cavalry regiment. The Mississippi units that remained in Tilghman's and went onto serve in Adams's were:
6th Mississippi Infantry Regiment under Col. Robert Lowry
20th Mississippi Infantry Regiment under Col. D.R. Russell (Daniel Renner Russell)
23rd Mississippi Infantry Regiment under Col. J.M. Wells (Joseph Morehead Wells)
26th Mississippi Infantry Regiment under Col. Arthur Exum Reynolds, Maj. T.F. Parker

Tilghman's death led Arthur Exum Reynolds, of the 26th Mississippi, to take temporary command of the brigade. In August was assigned to the Conscription Bureau, ending his time with Loring's Division. On or about 8 June 1863 John Adams was ordered to Benton, east of Yazoo City, to take command of Tilghman's old brigade. It was also known as the Second Brigade, though that name faded out once in the Army of Tennessee, where it was known as Adams's. It had 3,638 men in the following units:
1st Confederate Battalion under Lt. Col. G. H. Forney.
6th Mississippi Infantry Regiment under the command of Col. Robert Lowry.
14th Mississippi Infantry Regiment: under Lt. Col. Washington Lafayette Doss
15th Mississippi Infantry Regiment: under Col. Michael Farrell.
20th Mississippi Infantry Regiment: under Lt. Col. William N. Brown.
23rd Mississippi Infantry Regiment: under Maj. George Washington B. Garrett.
26th Mississippi Infantry Regiment: under of Lt. Col. Francis Marion Boone.
Lookout (Tennessee) Artillery was under Capt. Robert L. Barry.

Tilghman's death led to Col. Arthur E. Reynolds taking temporary command of his brigade. Thus his raised relief may be seen at Vicksburg National Military Park. Adams arrived to take command before Pemberton surrendered. Though they were not at Vicksburg, they were in the campaign, and recognized here. Another Adams bust at the Carter House in Franklin respects his sacrifice. Pickett is better known, yet not the subject of such sculptures.

Brigade structures were more fluid in the first two years of the war. Going back to December 1862, *Confederate Military History* (Vol. 7, Part 2, page 98) indicates Tilghman's units were just the 14th, 23rd, and 26th. Doss commanded the 14th but the 23rd was under Lt. Col. Moses McCarley, and the 26th was under Maj. T.F. Parker. They had won a victory under Tilghman at Coffeeville, in Pemberton's force. As shown above, additional units came to the brigade in 1863. It continued to evolve into what became Adam's Brigade, while still in Mississippi. One unusual deletion was the 26th. So many Mississippians were lost at Gettysburg they were transferred to Virginia in early 1864.

Adams's Brigade came to the Army of Tennessee in May 1864, in Loring's Division. His brigade of six Mississippi regiments arrived at Resaca on 11 May, with Polk's Army of Mississippi. The regiments were the 6th, 14th, 15th, 20th, 23rd, and 43rd. This organization remains the same thru the campaign in Georgia and into Tennessee.

At Kennesaw Mountain Col. Robert Lowry's 6th Mississippi manned the skirmish line. This may have been a somewhat designated role for them. At Champion Hill half of the 6th had formed a heavy skirmish line to shield Loring's move to reinforce Pemberton's centre. The skirmishers accounted for over half of Tilghman's 57 casualties there.

Loring's Division fought at Peach Tree Creek, without Adams's. They were on picket duty on the Chattahoochee River, and generally not engaged in the Atlanta Campaign, once Hood took command. After the supply base in Atlanta was lost, new uniforms and shoes were generally not available. Adams's Brigade was seen wrapping hay-stuffed rags around their feet. Items of U.S. Army blue could be seen mixed in with anything else that might fit. Blankets were also in short supply. A lack of tools meant trenches might be dug with tin plates. This was the situation as Hood led them into Tennessee. Ice and snow was ahead there. It began melting by 14 December, bringing on the battle outside Nashville.

Adams's soldiers could hear the sound of glazed ice crunching in the puddles of their trenches as they waited. Once thawed the U.S. Army attacked, and their line was so thin there could be several yards between men.

The Army of Tennessee had just gotten their feet on the Tennessee's south bank as U.S. cavalry worked to break the *Mobile & Ohio*. On 28 December they struck south of Okolona, at Egypt Station. Brig. Samuel Gholson's cavalry battled them, but Gholson was severely wounded. Lowry was given temporary command of the brigade. Its units were soon dispersed among other cavalry units, and Lowry is thought to have traveled to North Carolina. Adams's Brigade was named Lowry's by Bentonville; however, Lt. Col. Robert Lawrence of the 14th Mississippi commanded. Lawrence was captured, and in April Col. Richard Harrison commanded the brigade.

Where No Sorrows Come: The Life and Death of Confederate Brigadier John Adams has an image of this flag. It says it was donated by Thomas Gibson to the Tennessee Historical Society in 1907. As with many such donations, the flag became a Tennessee State Museum possession. Gibson was a Nashville cousin of John Adams, and served on his staff.

The Adams biography says a newspaper article, written at the time Gibson presented it says it was "made and presented to Gen. Adams' brigade by a lady of Mississippi in 1863." Author Bryan Lane supposes this is the flag Michael Farrell received from Mrs. Lattimer, of Canton, after this regiment won the drill contest.

This Adams flag has a red Maltese cross on a blue field. Featherston's Brigade also had a Maltese cross flag (see chapter on Featherston's); black cross on a tan field.

6th Mississippi Infantry Regiment, Adams's Brigade

The Military History of Mississippi says the 6th was organized at Grenada, August 1861. It says by the fall they were in Cleburne's Brigade, at Bowling Green, Kentucky. Most of the regiment suffered from typhoid fever and measles. Some died at Nashville hospitals, before Fort Donelson fell. The 6th was at Shiloh, where Patrick Cleburne said it would be "useless to enlarge on the courage and devotion of the 6th Mississippi." *Portraits of Conflict* (Mississippi volume) says they suffered 330 killed and wounded, of 425, at Shiloh. It says no Mississippi regiment ever suffered a higher rate, and that only three other Confederate regiments did. They were nicknamed the bloody sixth. Col. John Jones Thornton was wounded while carrying their flag and couldn't return. Robert Lowry, also wounded, was elected colonel.

The 6th was with Breckinridge in his attempt to liberate Baton Rouge in August. They returned to Mississippi and fought at Corinth in October. The 6th and the 15th Mississippi were in a brigade under Georgian John Bowen. In 1863 they were in a brigade under Lloyd Tilghman, which would later be Adams's. Bowen had moved to Missouri and commanded a Missouri brigade during Grant's final campaign to take Vicksburg.

The 6th began service with the Army of Tennessee when they reached Resaca on 11 May 1864. They were engaged in Johnston's great victory at Kennesaw Mountain. Lowry was in command of the 6th, which was the skirmish line for Adams's Brigade. They repulsed attacks at 8 and 10 a.m. Featherston, in temporary command of Loring's Division, said the enemy never got closer than 70 yards in front of Lowry's 6th. He observed the enemy waivered, broke, and fled, in much confusion. Lowry was shown in command on 10 July. When Loring was wounded at Ezra Church, Featherston again led the division. Lowry temporarily led Featherston's Brigade. The 31 July return does not show a commander.

Loring had returned to division command by the 31 August return, and Lowry was back with the regiment. The 20 September 1864 organization shows Lowry in command. Adams was killed at Franklin and Lowry, though wounded at Franklin, got command of the brigade. The 10 December 1864 organization shows Lt. Col. Thomas J. Borden in command. At Nashville a cold rain began to fall on the 16th. The regiment used captured U.S. rubber ponchos to keep their powder dry. They had been awake late, if not all night. When the retreat began at least 50 were too exhausted to run, and were captured.

Of further interest: *Going to meet the Yankees: A History of the "Bloody Sixth" Mississippi, C.S.A.*, by Grady H. Howell, Jr. Jackson, MS: Chickasaw Bayou Press, 1981

14th Mississippi Infantry Regiment, Adams's Brigade

The Military History of Mississippi says the 14th was organized at Corinth in May 1861. Another source has them organized at Jackson in October. It says the men were from the following counties: Clarke, Lauderdale, Lowndes, Monroe, Oktibbeha, Tishomingo (raised the Tishomingo Rangers), and Winston (raised the Beauregard Rifles).

William Baldwin was the first commander of the 14th, and later rose to brigadier general. *They Sleep Beneath the Mockingbird: Mississippi Burial Sites and Biographies of*

Confederate Generals says he moved with his family from South Carolina to Columbus as a child. As a teenager he joined Captain Abert's "Columbus Rifles" in 1845. In 1861 he was elected their captain, and they became a company in the 14th. Baldwin had risen to colonel of the 14th and prior to Fort Donelson he was placed in command of a brigade of two regiments, the 26th Mississippi and the 26th Tennessee. The 14th Mississippi was under Maj. Washington Lafayette Doss, in a different brigade. They were surrendered at Fort Donelson, and exchanged in October 1862. This brought the 14th to Van Dorn's Army of West Tennessee. George William Abert was promoted to colonel on 18 October 1862. Major Doss was promoted to lieutenant colonel; date not confirmed. Abert's ability to command was limited by "phythesis" (tuberculosis), and it led him to resign on 29 March 1863. He went onto serve as post commander in Meridian.

On to Vicksburg! The Mississippi Central Railroad Campaign has an interesting account of the 14th Mississippi. Grant's first campaign for Vicksburg failed at several points. Among them was Lovell's and Tilghman's victory at Coffeeville. Tilghman reported, "The Fourteenth Mississippi, Major Doss commanding, toward the close became too far separated from the main command, but was abundantly able to take care of itself, and drove back the enemy in their front, killing and wounding a number, including Lieutenant Colonel McCullough, who was shot dead…"

Tilghman was commanding the brigade at Champion Hill, and the 14th does not appear to have been present. Part of the regiment was mounted and with John Adams. Tilghman's death led to Adams taking command about 8 June, and the 14th appears to be present in July. The mounting of the part of the regiment was not unique in Pemberton's department as Johnston had previously ordered Van Dorn to Tennessee. The 3rd Kentucky, from Buford's Brigade, was also partially mounted during this period; however, it went onto be fully mounted and served in Buford's cavalry brigade under Forrest.

The 10 July, and 31 July, returns show Lt. Col. Doss in command. Perhaps he was, but *Confederate Colonels* says he was arrested on 25 June. The 31 August return shows Major Robert J. Lawrence in command of the regiment. The 20 September organization shows Doss in command. But *Confederate Colonels* shows Doss had been promoted to colonel on 16 March 1864. It says Doss, an Oktibbeha farmer, had been a private back in May 1861. He had risen to major by the time they were captured at Fort Donelson. While a prisoner at Fort Warren, in Boston Harbor, Doss was called a "pleasant, clever gentleman."

Reminiscences of the Boys in Gray, 1861-1865 has a response from W.R. Bell of the 14th. He wrote from Houston, Texas. Bell enlisted at the Choctaw Agency in May 1861. Bell recalled Franklin: "Gen. Adams' horse fell on a dead man and as the charge was being made a man fell on the horse. There is no language that could picture that battle, and there is little use for me to try." Bell also recalled, "I helped to bury the dead at Franklin, and I think I could have walked all over the battlefield on dead men." The 10 December 1864 organization still shows Col. Doss in command. Another source says when they were surrendered in North Carolina there were only 40 men, and none were officers.

Of further interest: The Archives in Jackson have lettres of William R. Barry. They are from 24 JUL to 8 DRC 1864. Refer to 2331f. at the Archives. Their first flag is there.

15th Mississippi Infantry Regiment, Adams's Brigade

The Military History of Mississippi says the 15th was organized in Corinth in May 1861. Col. Walter Scott Statham, a Grenada lawyer (possibly attended Dartmouth), led them. He was wounded in the shoulder by an accidental gunshot in September. Command passed to Lt. Col. Edward Cary Walthall.

The 15th was briefly in West Tennessee before being sent to East Tennessee. Their first action was north of Cumberland Gap, at Camp Wildcat. Their first battle was at Mill Springs (a.k.a. Fishing Creek), Kentucky, on 19 January 1862. Zollicoffer made a mistake in advancing his forces to the north back of the Cumberland River. This was upstream of Nashville, and enabled our forces to supply by steamboats. The 15th guarded the landing, where our troops had retreated, and burned the steamer when all had crossed. Maj. Gen. George B. Crittenden wrote, " For an hour…the Fifteenth Mississippi, under Lieutenant-Colonel Walthall and the Twentieth Tennessee…of my centre and right, had been struggling with the superior forces of the enemy…I cannot omit to mention the heroic valour of these two regiments, officers and men." Crittenden's defeat meant the collapse of A.S Johnston's right. The centre was lost when Forts Henry and Donelson fell in February. As Johnston organized his forces at Corinth, Crittenden commanded his reserves. He was relieved of command and replaced by John Breckinridge. Colonel Statham had returned and commanded Zollicoffer's old brigade. Thus the 15th participated in the capture of the Hornet's Nest. Breckinridge attempted to liberate Baton Rouge in August, and the 15th fought there.

The 15th returned to Mississippi to fight at Corinth in October. They were in a brigade under John Bowen. The 6th Mississippi was too, and it would find its way to Tilghman and Adams. Bowen was a Georgian who settled in Missouri and would command a brigade of Missourians during Grant's final campaign to take Vicksburg.

The 15th went with Adams's to Georgia. *Confederate Military History* says, "On June 19, at Moore's mill, Colonel Farrell, with the Fifteenth Mississippi and two companies of the Sixth, captured a number of men from an Ohio regiment, whose attack they had repulsed. This was likely on 19 July when the brigade was near Moore's Mill on Peachtree Creek. Col. Michael Farrell is shown in command on returns for 10 July, 31 July, and 31 August. The 20 September 1864 organization shows Lt. Col. James R. Binford. But Col. Mike Farrell was in command at Franklin, and mortally wounded. The 10 December 1864 organization shows Binford in command.

Of further interest: *A Hard Trip: A History of the 15th Mississippi Infantry, C.S.A.,* by Ben Wynne, Macon, Georgia: Mercer University Press, 2003; and *Portraits of Conflict* (Mississippi volume) has a photo (p. 132) of brothers; one killed at Mill Springs and one wounded at Franklin. There is another photo (p. 177) of a soldier from French Camp.

20th Mississippi Infantry Regiment, Adams's Brigade

The Military History of Mississippi says the 20th was organized in Iuka in July 1861. They were ordered to Virginia in August. They had the distinction of being the first Mississippi troops to serve under Robert E. Lee. By winter they had been ordered to Fort Donelson, where they arrived on 13 February 1862. That night they were put in trenches that they had to clear of snow and water. Floyd and Pillow surrendered the fort and the decided to evade their duty by escaping on a steamboat. The 20th was arrayed in a semi-circle around the landing until the boat made its get away.

They were exchanged and returned to Mississippi in the winter 1863. This brought them to Loring, and the brilliant victory at Fort Pemberton in March. We have seen that Joe Johnston had transferred Van Dorn's cavalry into Tennessee, thereby depriving John Pemberton. This was a crisis and led to the 20th Mississippi serving as cavalry for a short time. A Vicksburg N.M.P. website gives the dates as 15 April to 8 May. They were stationed in Jackson and attached to Tilghman's Brigade. This site says they served under Col. Daniel Renner Russell. But another site says they were under Russell until January 1863, and then Lt. Col. William N. Brown. There is a mention of three companies serving under Lt. Col. Horace Miller. He was promoted to colonel in August, and in command of the new 9th Mississippi Cavalry. But the rest of the 20th Mississippi seems to have been infantry again after Champion Hill. Needless to say they are difficult to untangle.

They arrived at Resaca on 11 May 1864. Brown is shown in command on all organization lists from 10 June to 20 September. Loring's Division saw the most action during the campaign at Peach Tree Creek. Adams's missed it as downstream at Moore's Mill. They were not spared the from Hood's fiasco at Franklin. Brown was wounded twice, which disabled him from field duty for the rest of the war. Lt. Col. W.A. Rorer was mortally wounded. The 10 December organization shows Maj. Thomas B. Graham in command.

Of further interest: *Portraits of Conflict* (Mississippi volume) has pictures of brothers who enlisted at Carrollton, and were captured at Fort Donelson; pages 106-7. It also has a photo of a member from Harrison County; page 307. Also learned, one of the flags of the 20th was a blue field four-foot square with a circle in the centre; lettering was: "Twentieth Mississippi." And, the Mississippi Archives has papers (reference 2334f) of Marion Frances Baxter, and lettres (reference 1262f) of W.A. Rorer, from 1859 to 8 June 1864.

23rd Mississippi Infantry Regiment, Adams's Brigade

The Military History of Mississippi says the 23rd was organized at Iuka in August 1861. It lists some colourful company names. From Tippah County there were the Falkner Guards, Tippah Tigers, Thompson Invincibles, Tippah Rifle Company, and the Molino Rifles. Tishomingo County had the Kossuth Volunteers and the Blackland Gideonites. It says they were known as the 3rd Mississippi at Fort Donelson. Col. Thomas Jefferson Davidson had been given command of a brigade with the 23rd and three other regiments. The 23rd was commanded by Lt. Col. Joseph M. Wells. They were in the attack that drove the enemy back one mile. Of 561 that were at the surrender, a shocking 93 of them died in U.S. prisons. They were exchanged in the fall. Davidson died at Fort Warren Prison in Boston Harbour, and was buried at Hollywood Cemetery in Richmond, Virginia. Wells commanded the 23rd until September 1864, when he resigned due to age and illness. The 20 September 1864 organization shows Maj. George W. B. Garrett in command. He was also at Franklin. The 10 December organization still shows Garrett in command.

Of further interest: *Portraits of Conflict* (Mississippi volume) has a photo (page 8) of a soldier in the 23rd.

Though Davidson died 29 April 1862, over a year before Loring's Division was created. He deserved a better fate than being captured at Fort Donelson. A marker mentions him, commanding a brigade, at a point on the Old Forge Road where a section of his artillery was engaged. Most of the captured officers were sent to Fort Warren in Boston Harbour. Davidson became ill there and died.

The author found Davidson's grave by chance, on a June 2002 visit to Hollywood Cemetery, Richmond, Virginia.

Confederate Colonels says Davidson was born in Tennessee. He fought in one of the Seminole Wars. He married Mary Harbin. He was a merchant and contractor in Ripley, Tippah County, Mississippi. He was known to be "honest, capable, and faithful."

43rd Mississippi Infantry Regiment, Adams's Brigade

Confederate Veteran September/October 2017 has a book review of a new history: *The Camel Regiment: A History of the Bloody 43rd Mississippi Volunteer Infantry 1862-5* by Pelican Publishing. It says the 43rd was organized in northeast Mississippi, in spring 1862. It was well known for their camel mascot, named Old Douglas.

Old Douglas was donated to the 43rd by their colonel, William Hudson Moore. One source says Lt. William Hargrove gave it to him. Hargrove brought the camel in Mobile, apparently after seeing an advertisement in the Mobile Daily Register on 23 March 1860. Hargrove was in Mobile, from his Trinity, Mississippi farm. Other sources incorrectly say it had been part of the U.S. Camel Corps, an experiment initiated by then U.S. Secretary of War Jefferson Davis. The 43rd used Old Douglas to transport the baggage of the officers' mess. He grazed within sight and usually got along with the horses, but not always. At Iuka he had spooked a horse into stampeding through a camp, creating such a ruckus some soldiers climbed trees to avoid the path of destruction. While at Vicksburg, Yankee sharpshooters killed Old Douglas.

The text on the post card reads: "Jefferson Davis, Head of the Confederacy, brought over 25 Mohammedan camel drivers with the idea of using camels for transportation in the desert wastes of the Southwest. The idea ended in failure." That was when he was U.S. Secretary of War. The camels proved their worth, but the experiment was abandoned. The plaque of the monument names Syrian Hi Jolly (Hadji Ali). He was the lead camel driver. The monument is at his grave site at Quartzsite Cemetery in Quartzsite, Arizona. It has been written that Old Douglas was one of those camels, or descended from them. He was imported into Alabama later, proving the camels had some transportation-work value. The Yankee who shot him must have been pleased with his little self.

The Military History of Mississippi mentions several actions of the 43rd in defending Mississippi. They were at Corinth in October; they had 13 killed, 56 wounded, and 156 missing. Colonel Moore was mortally wounded there. At Vicksburg the enemy tunneled under their position, and exploded a mine; six were killed. *Portraits of Conflict* (Mississippi volume, p. 35) has a photo of Lt. Robert E. Barker. There is a story regarding the tunnel, and photo of a corporal in the 43rd, on page 266.

The 43rd went to Georgia in May 1864 with Adams's. The organizations from 10 June to 20 September show Col. Richard Harrison in command. He survived Franklin, and the 10 December organization still shows Harrison in command.

Of further interest: The Mississippi Archives has the handwritten autobiography of Benjamin LaFayette Smith of the 43rd; reference 21577f. *Confederate Veteran*, Volume 17, page 159 has a piece on Nashville, written by J.W. Cook. It is difficult to tell which day he writes on.

11-Winfield Scott Featherston's Brigade

Featherston had his Mississippi brigade in Loring's Division in the Vicksburg Campaign. U.S. forces were trying to reach a position north of Vicksburg, where an infantry assault could be launched. During March 1863 Loring turned the enemy back at Fort Pemberton. Featherston's Brigade was in what U.S. forces called "The Steele's Bayou Expedition." That campaign involved such a twisted network of waterways that it will not be explained in detail here. Featherston's came to serve under Loring in the Fort Pemberton area from 29 March to 1 April. Featherston brought the units found in the 1864 Army of Tennessee campaigns. This made it the oldest, most cohesive of Loring's three brigades.

Champion Hill: Decisive Battle for Vicksburg has references to Featherston. It has quotes from one of his staff, Lt. William Drennan. He thought that "…the greater portion of Loring's Division was in as good fighting trim as could be wished for." It also points out Featherston "saw about as much combat at the head of a brigade (and occasionally in divisional command) as most generals would" during the war.

Featherston's Brigade in campaign for Vicksburg is reason bust placed at Vicksburg National Military Park. Citizens of Mississippi complained to President Davis that too many Northern generals had commands in Mississippi. Pemberton was their primary target. Actually the better reason to have complained about him was his lack of battlefield experience. Another Northerner was Samuel Gibbs French, even though he became a Mississippi planter! French had spent much time in laying out fieldworks in Virginia. Featherston, though born around Murfreesborough, Tennessee, had become a Mississippi attorney at age 19. Thus he had spent most of his life in the Magnolia State. Of more importance was his extensive active battlefield experience. From the victory at Ball's Bluff to Lee's great victory at 2nd Manassas, Featherston had tasted Confederate success. His concerns over the invasion of his home state led him to request a transfer. Featherston's Brigade was formed in the first months of 1863.

Featherston's Brigade arrived in Resaca about 12 May 1864. Featherston commanded Loring's division twice. The first was after Polk was killed. Loring had temporary command of Polk's Corps. Featherston commanded the division for about 15 days. This included Kennesaw Mountain, where the division was lightly engaged, and commanded by Colonel Mellon of the 3rd Mississippi. Featherston was back commanding the brigade before Peachtree Creek, as Stewart replaced Loring as corps commander. Peach Tree Creek was Featherston's most significant action of the campaign. Featherston's lost several flags at Peachtree Creek. The 31st Mississippi lost a 12-star battle flag, of the design issued from Mobile. That flag is in Jackson, Mississippi today. The 33rd lost their Second-National pattern flag, also issued out of Mobile. Loring was wounded at Ezra Church bringing Featherston to command the division the second time. Col. Mellon was wounded at Peach Tree Creek, and had to leave the army. Every unit commander in the brigade was killed or wounded. Col. Robert Lowry came from Adams's Brigade to take temporary command. Peach Tree Creek seems to have been a prequel to Franklin.

At some point when Featherston commanded the division there must have existed some optimism the arrangement would last, for a Featherston's Division headquarters flag was sewn; it was a Maltese cross. There was a debate over if it was captured at Franklin. A Yankee wrote *Confederate Veteran* in 1905 (Vol. 13, page 563) claiming Featherston's colour bearer, carrying his headquarters flag, was shot on the works, that he took the flag, and still had it. He is shown in a photo holding a flag with the cross.

Dr. G.C. Phillips, on Featherston's staff as senior surgeon, wrote to refute the claim in 1906 (Volume 14, page 262). He said the Yankee had been labouring under a delusion. The headquarters flag was not captured and the bearer was not killed. In fact he was still alive. Dr. Phillips did not deny the Yankee had captured a flag from Featherston's Brigade, but it was not the headquarters flag. Featherston and Loring did not mention a brigade flag being lost, but the Yankee certainly appears to have a flag with a cross.

This flag was connected to Featherston's Brigade. It has a black Maltese cross design on a tan field. It is similar to the Adams's blue flag (above) with red-cross. *Echoes of Glory: Arms and Equipment of the Conf.*, by Time-Life has image of French's Division headquarters flag. It's similar to Featherston's, but has a tan or white cross on a black field. It also has similar personal guidon of Maj. Gen. Bradley Johnson.

A field return of Featherston's Brigade at Columbia, on 21 December 1864 is found in the O.R. (Volume 45, Part 1, page 729). It is submitted by Forrest's Assistant Adjutant General, John P. Strange. It was to tally the infantry which Walthall would command during the retreat to the Tennessee River. It shows Featherston had an aggregate of 571, including the general and his staff. It also indicates eight servants. Once they reached safety in Mississippi, Featherston remained to collect troops on furlough and forward them to North Carolina. Col. Wallace Colbert commanded the brigade at Bentonville, and was killed. Featherston didn't arrive in North Carolina until April. Because Brig. Gen. Daniel Harris Reynolds lost a leg at Bentonville, his Arkansas regiments were added to Featherston's. This was done on the 9th; they never took the field again.

1st Mississippi Battalion Sharpshooters, Featherston's Brigade

The Military History of Mississippi says this battalion was formed from (Captain C.K.) Caruthers's Sharpshooters, and three companies of the 25th Mississippi. They were in John Bowen's brigade of Mississippi and Missouri infantry units at Corinth. Cozzens's volume on Corinth quotes Lt. William C. Holmes: "The battalion had assumed a new role in the great science of warfare. We had been drilled in the 'skirmish drill' almost exclusively, and our place in the army was in the front, leading the entire division (Lovell's) in the advance, but always in the rear in the retreat. Individually, to a man, we were anxious to show our hand in the line of warfare set apart to us, for our small size made us the jest of other regiments." They were ordered in front of the 22nd Mississippi, which would also go to Featherston's new brigade, to attack artillery. They drove in Yankee skirmishers and pursued into a railroad cut where Holmes recalled the cannon "belching forth fiery destruction, simply grand in its sublimity." The attack drove the Yankees away and Holmes found himself caring for enemy wounded.

The Sharpshooters were distinguished for daring on the skirmish line at New Hope Church. Maj. James M. Stigler was in command at Peach Tree Creek, where he was wounded. Jenkins has about 110 present, with 5 killed, 20 wounded, and 7 missing. He lists all 32 by name. The 20 September 1864 organization shows Stigler in command. The 10 December 1864 organization shows Stigler still in command. They were in Forrest's rearguard to the Tennessee River. *North Carolina Confederate Military History* has him commanding the 3rd, 31st, and 40th, with no mention of the sharpshooters.

1st Mississippi Infantry Regiment, Featherston's Brigade

The victory at Manassas was news when the 1st was organized at Iuka in August 1861. This is unusual in that the 2nd and 11th were at Manassas. *The Military History of Mississippi* says their companies were from northern counties, from Desoto in the northwest corner to Tishomingo in the northeast. The 1st lost 43 men to measles in the fall of '61, at Bowling Green. They had 331 men at Fort Donelson and they charged against McClernand's Division. The 1st took a hill (with reinforcements?) and captured Schwartz's battery. Before the surrender the 1st had 16 killed and 61 wounded.

After being exchanged the 1st was in Beall's brigade at Port Hudson. They participated in repelling enemy attacks. They were throwing hand grenades, some of which exploded over the parapets prematurely on 3 July. Two soldiers were thus mortally wounded.

When Port Hudson was surrendered the 1st was more fortunate than at Donelson, for our force was largely paroled. Enlisted men, those hospitalized, civilians, and perhaps some officers, brought the number paroled to 5,935. The officers sent to prison camps came to 405. U.S. battle casualties were close to 5,200. Another 4,000 were hospitalized with illnesses and sunstrokes.

The 1st was exchanged and that brought them into the Army of Mississippi, commanded by the former bishop, Polk. This is probably when they went into Featherston's Brigade. The 20 September 1864 organization shows Maj. Milton S. Alcorn in command. The 10 December 1864 organization lists Capt. Owen D. Hughes in command. On 21DEC there were only 67 present, yet they were in Forrest's brilliant rearguard to the Tennessee River. They went onto North Carolina.

3rd Mississippi Infantry Regiment, Featherston's Brigade

The Military History of Mississippi says the 3rd was organized at Shieldsboro in September 1861. They were largely of men from Gulf Coast counties. Company names reflected their Mississippi origins. The Live Oak Rifles mustered in at Ocean Springs. The Sunflower Dispersers were from Sunflower County. The Biloxi Rifles mustered in at Biloxi. The Dahlgren Guards mustered in at Pass Christian, apparently named for Charles Gustavus Ulric Dahlgren. He commanded a brigade of the 3rd and 7th Mississippi.

The regiment had been "raised mainly for the defense of the intricate coast of Mississippi Sound." Governor Pettus wanted the 3rd to protect a point of construction of gunboats. The legislature had made a $250,000 appropriation for the gunboats. Dahlgren was the brother of U.S. Navy Admiral John Dahlgren. The Mississippi Dahlgren was born in Philadelphia, Pennsylvania, and had served in the navy. Apparently he had ideas for the anticipated gunboat construction.

The 3rd went to Georgia and on the 10 June organization they were under Col. Thomas Armour Mellon. He had been in a captain in August 1861, and promoted three times, becoming colonel in April 1862. The 3rd's attack at Peach Tree Creek is illustrated in a colourful Rick Reeves painting, *Attack by Stewart's Corps at Peach Tree Creek*. They suffered 93 casualties (5 killed, 73 wounded, and 5 missing); Jenkins lists them by name. Mellon was in command and wounded in the head by a shell fragment as he was waving his sword. He was taken from the field under a hail of bullets. This ended his service with the regiment, though he recovered well enough back in Mississippi to command state troops. The 31 July, 31 August, and 20 September returns show Lt. Col. Samuel M. Dyer in command. He was wounded at Franklin. The 10 December 1864 organization shows Captain O.H. Johnston in command. The 3rd was in Forrest's brilliant rearguard to the Tennessee River. They were in North Carolina in 1865.

Of further interest: *To Live and Die in Dixie: A History of the Third Mississippi Infantry, C.S.A.,* by H. Grady Howell, Jr., Jackson, Mississippi: Chickasaw Bayou Press, 1991

22nd Mississippi Infantry Regiment, Featherston's Brigade

The Military History of Mississippi indicates the 22nd was organized at Iuka, Tishomingo County, in the summer 1861. They were sent to Columbus, Kentucky, but saw no action there. Their first battle was Shiloh, fighting in the Reserve Corps under Breckinridge. They shared the glories of capturing the Hornet's Nest. They were with Breckinridge in his attempt to liberate Baton Rouge in August. From there they began work on fortifications at Port Hudson. They returned to Mississippi to fight at Corinth in October. They were also in the early phases of the Vicksburg Campaign.

Maj. Martin A. Oatis was in command at Peach Tree Creek. Jenkins book shows 190 present with 97 casualties (26 killed, 66 wounded, and 5 missing) by name. Capt. John T. Farmby took command until Oatis recovered. The 20 September 1864 organization shows Oatis in command. The 10 December 1864 organization shows Oatis still in command. The 22nd was in Forrest's rearguard to the Tennessee River. The army first came to rest at Tupelo. When they moved on for North Carolina Featherston stayed behind to collect the men on furlough. He didn't make it to North Carolina until April. The few effectives of the brigade at Bentonville were commanded by Oatis.

Of further interest: Col. Franz Emile Schaller was assigned to the 22nd on 24 December 1861. He was born in Saxony (now Germany) and had served in the French army. He was wounded at Shiloh, and could only serve intermittently thereafter. His correspondence is available; *Soldiering for Glory: The Civil War Letters of Colonel Frank Schaller*. Also, *Portraits of Conflict* (Mississippi Volume) says the 22nd had at least four colour bearers shot at Peachtree Creek. There is a photo of the fourth. He was in the Swamp Rangers, Company I, from Washington County. Jenkins has seven killed and wounded.

31st Mississippi Infantry Regiment, Featherston's Brigade

The Military History of Mississippi has the 31st being organized at Corinth in April 1862. Their first colonel was Jehu Amaziah Orr. He graduated from Princeton, and went onto become a lawyer in Princeton before the war. Orr was a member of the Mississippi secession convention. He became colonel of the 31st on 9 April 1862.

The 31st was not at Shiloh, but appears to have had their first action in the subsequent enemy advance into Mississippi. The 31st was at Baton Rouge in August 1862. Then they were in the early phases of the campaigning to hold Vicksburg. Featherston was promoted to brigadier in March 1863, and assigned to his new brigade in the Vicksburg area. They became part of Loring's Division, and were so until the end in North Carolina.

Colonel Orr resigned due to poor health on 11 March 1864. He was replaced that day by Col. Marquis De Lafayette Stephens, a former captain of Company D. Stephens was a Williamson County, Tennessee born medical doctor. He studied at the Louisville Medical College, before establishing himself in northern Mississippi's Calhoun County. Like Orr before him, he was a member of Mississippi's secession convention. His military service began in Featherston's 17th Mississippi. Stephens led Featherston's Brigade at several times in 1864.

Featherston's Brigade arrived at Resaca as the battle was beginning. Several men were wounded by artillery fire as the got off the train. *The Military History of Mississippi* details their casualties at Peachtree Creek. Jenkins does as well, listing 181. He explains Stephens was absent sick, and Lt. Col. James W. Drane commanded. He has Drane leading 215 up the Collier Ridge and only 34 returning from the attack unhurt. Their colours were dropped and captured there. Jenkins wrote their flag was returned in 1905, and is in the Mississippi Department of Archives and History. Drane was severely wounded so Captain R. Collins is shown commanding on 31 July and 31 August.

Jenkins continued, "Some sixty-seven souls were sacrificed for their country. Many were buried in unmarked graves on the bloody ridge overlooking Peach Tree Creek. Still more who were mortally wounded were buried in remote cemeteries such as in Macon, Chattanooga, Nashville, Louisville, and Camp Chase, Ohio, and Camp Douglas, Illinois." He has 84.18 percent made their "roll call of sorrow among the highest, if not the highest" in the war. "Moreover, the number of fatal casualties sustained by the 'Bloody Magnolias' number among the highest by any Confederate unit during the war, as well."

The 20 September 1864 organization shows Stephens in command. Stephens may have had a personal interest at Franklin, as he had been born in the county back in November 1829. The 31st had 250 present at Franklin, or 230 per Jenkins. This is higher than the 215 shown for Peach Tree Creek. Confederate army doctors had a higher recovery rate so some slightly wounded must have returned. They lost 45 killed and about 100 wounded. After crossing the railroad and abatis they charged with fixed bayonets. When their eleventh colour-bearer went down Stephens took the flag. As he was about to plant them on the enemy's works a rifle ball shattered his thigh bone. Stephens fell into the ditch and the colours were taken by yet another soldier. He too was shot, but managed to obey an order to carry the colours to the rear. Col. Stephens was carried into enemy lines by a soldier from Nebraska, who thought Stephens would have frozen to death. Stephens was invalided out of the army. Jenkins included a photo of their square battle flag, from the Mississippi Department of Archives and History.

The 10 December 1864 organization shows Capt. Robert A. Collins in command. They were in Forrest's rear guard to the Tennessee River, and onto North Carolina in 1865.

33rd Mississippi Infantry Regiment, Featherston's Brigade

The Military History of Mississippi says the 33rd was organized in Grenada in April 1862. Colonel David Wiley Hurst had been a lawyer in Amite and a delegate to the Mississippi Secession Convention. He voted against, but like others against secession, he became a dedicated soldier. The 33rd did well in Van Dorn's attempt to retake Corinth in October. They were brigaded under Brig. Gen. John Villepigue, with the 39th Mississippi. Colonel Hurst was severely wounded and could not return and accepted civilian judicial duties. Lt. Col. William B. Johnson may have commanded next. Jabez Leftwich Drake was lieutenant colonel on 16 July 1863, and promoted to colonel on 5 January 1864.

Their service in the Army of Tennessee began when they arrived at Resaca, Georgia in May 1864. Drake led the 33rd at Peach Tree Creek. They were on the extreme right of

Featherston's. There was no support on that flank because Wright's Brigade, of Hardee's Corps, didn't go forward. Colonel Drake was killed leading the 33rd, while waving his sword and cheering his men on. His body was found beyond the enemy's advanced line. A Colonel Wood, of the U.S. Army buried Drake on the field. *Confederate Colonels* says Drake was later moved to Oakland Cemetery in Atlanta. Featherston eulogized Drake as "a gallant and excellent officer." Jenkins has some 300 in the 33rd, with 168 falling before dark. The *Military History of Mississippi* says the 33rd lost their flag in this battle. It is now in possession of the Mississippi Department of Archives and History. Jenkins has a photo which shows it as a Second National flag, rather than a battle flag.

Capt. Moses Jackson is shown in command on 31 July and 31 August 1864. But the 20 September organization shows Maj. Robert J. Hall in command. He had been wounded at New Hope Church, and he may not have gone into Tennessee. A lettre from Lt. Col. Charles P. Neilson seems to indicate he was. At Franklin the 33rd lost at least two colour bearers. One was killed at 15 paces in front of the enemy works. A Lieutenant Shaw then carried the flag forward and was killed as he planted them on the works. His body and the flag fell into the enemy's entrenchment. To think of losing two flags in this short period is terrible. Hood commanded both of these offensive battles, and he complained the Army of Tennessee had lost their will to attack.

The 10 December 1864 organization shows the 33rd commanded by Capt. Thomas L. Cooper. Perhaps Neilson was wounded at Franklin. The 33rd was at Nashville, Forrest's rearguard to the Tennessee River, and onto North Carolina in 1865.

40th Mississippi Infantry Regiment, Featherston's Brigade

The Military History of Mississippi has the 40th organized in Meridian on 14 May 1862. Mississippi contained two transportation arteries the U.S. imperialists were intent on vexing. First was the Mississippi River, and the other was the *Memphis & Charleston Railroad*. Thus, the 40th found itself fighting to protect their great state. In the summer they were in Maj. Gen. Sterling Price's Army of the West.

The enemy Army of the Mississippi had a supply base at Iuka. It was nationally known for its abundant mineral springs. The *Memphis & Charleston* laid track through Iuka in 1857 and that brought more tourists and merchants. Price may have had no interest in the springs, but wanted the supply base. He took it on 14 September. Then Ulysses S. Grant brought two converging columns to trap Price on the 19th. Instead Price drove one enemy division back onto another, capturing nine cannon. The 40th assisted in the capture of an Ohio artillery battery at Iuka. That night Price realized how lucky his victory had been, and escaped with his loot, rather than remain to fight four enemy divisions.

Col. Wallace Bruce Colbert commanded the 40th at Iuka, in a brigade under. Brig Gen. Louis Hébert. Division commander Brig. Gen. Henry Little was killed at Iuka. This led Hébert to division command, and Colbert to command his brigade. Price united with Van Dorn's Army of West Tennessee for the attack on the fortified U.S. positions around Corinth. It had the crossing of the Memphis and Charleston, with the Mobile and Ohio. The 40th had their flag captured.

The 40th was placed in another brigade, under Brig. Gen. John C. Moore, during the 1863 Vicksburg Campaign. This brigade was temporarily under Loring, before his division was formed in May. They were in the Siege of Vicksburg. There is a raised relief there of their own Major Robert Campbell. The 40th was exchanged on 11 September 1863. This brought them to Featherston's Brigade. Their service in the Army of Tennessee began at Resaca on 12 May 1864. They had high casualties in the Atlanta Campaign. Lt. Col. George P. Wallace commanded at Peach Tree Creek. The 40th was on the far left of Featherston's. Jenkins has 245 present and casualties of 107 (12 killed, 58 wounded, and 37 missing). The wounded included Wallace who lost an arm.

Capt. W. Bassett is shown in command on 31 July and 31 August 1864. The 20 September organization lists Capt. Charles A. Huddleston in command. Col. Wallace Bruce Colbert had returned before Franklin, for he was wounded there. The 10 December organization lists Colbert in command. On the 21st they had an aggregate present of only 67. They were in Forrest's rearguard. Sadly, Colbert never got home to Mississippi. He was killed at Bentonville in March 1865, and is buried in Raleigh.

Chapter 12-Thomas Moore Scott's Brigade

Scott's Brigade was named for Thomas Moore Scott. He had been colonel of the 12th Louisiana. The 12th had been brigaded under Abraham Buford in Loring's Division, during the Vicksburg Campaign. Buford was reassigned to Forrest's cavalry in March 1864. Scott was promoted to brigadier in May, and part of the brigade that had been Buford's were organized into Scott's.

Some units came to Buford's Brigade, from Rust's, in April 1863. Brig. Gen. Albert Rust had commanded a brigade in Earl Van Dorn's Army of West Tennessee. When Braxton Bragg moved into Kentucky in late summer 1862 he hoped to reach the Ohio River, and wished Van Dorn would reach the Ohio, to his west. Van Dorn wanted to retake Corinth as continued operations to the north could be supplied by the *Mobile & Ohio Railroad,* running thru Corinth. Van Dorn attacked the well-fortified enemy position in October. Beauregard had laid out the defenses after Shiloh and the Yankees had strengthened them to suit their purposes. Rust had advised against the attack saying it would be "impossible to succeed in the attack." An Illinoisan recalled fighting Rust's Brigade: "Reforming, they come again with that cold-blooded yell which has to be heard to be appreciated." Ultimately the attacks were turned back, proving Rust correct. But they might have driven the Yankees from Corinth had not their division commander, Mansfield Lovell, halted the attacks. Rust wrote, "We had come much nearer achieving success than I had hoped for. I believed at the end of the first day's fight the place was nearly taken." Rust was soon transferred to the Trans-Mississippi, and most of his units were assigned to a brigade for Abraham Buford.

Buford is not closely associated with Port Hudson, as his brigade was transferred before the siege began in late May 1863. By then his brigade was attached to Loring's Division. The 10th Arkansas and 49th Alabama remained at Port Hudson; the 49th returned to Scott's after exchange. The Alabama battalions were consolidated into the 55th Alabama.

Confederate Military History (vol. 7, part 2, page 131) details Buford's in April 1863:
4th Alabama Infantry Battalion: 4th was consolidated into 55th Regiment; see below.
6th Alabama Infantry Battalion: 4th and 6th Battalions consolidated into 55th Regiment.
27th Alabama Infantry Regiment: The 27th would be with the brigade into 1865.
49th Alabama Infantry Regiment: The 49th would be with the brigade into 1865.
10th Arkansas Infantry Regiment: The 10th was reassigned to Maxey's Brigade.
3rd Kentucky Infantry Regiment: The 3rd would be detached with Buford and mounted.
7th Kentucky Infantry Regiment: The 7th would be detached with Buford and mounted.

Buford had the following units in May 1863 and at Champion Hill:
27th Alabama Infantry under Col. James Jackson
35th Alabama Infantry under Col. Edward Goodwin; from Rust's Brigade (APR 63)
54th Alabama Infantry under Col. Alpheus Baker
55th Alabama Infantry under Col. John Snodgrass
9th Arkansas Infantry under Col. Isaac Leroy Dunlop; from Rust's Brigade (APR 63)
3rd Kentucky Infantry (4 companies) under Maj. J.H. Bowman; from Rust's Brigade
7th Kentucky Infantry under Col. Edward Crossland
12th Louisiana Infantry under Col. Thomas Moore Scott; from Rust's Brigade (APR 63)
Pointe Coupee Artillery, Companies A & C under Capt. Alcide Bouanchaud attached.
Note: Buford reported the 8th Kentucky Infantry had been in his brigade until two days before Champion Hill. It was mounted and detached.

Companies of the 3rd Kentucky had been mounted and were part of Pemberton's small force of cavalry that dealt with Grierson's Raid. J.V. Greif wrote *Confederate Veteran* in 1904 (Volume 12, page 112) on fighting with Greg's Brigade at Raymond. Greif wrote, "I was a member of Company D, Third Kentucky Regiment, Buford's Brigade, Loring's Division. Six companies of our regiment had been mounted only a short time previous at Meridian, Miss., and under the command of Col. R. P. Thompson, ordered to report to General Gregg, and were with him in this fight and covered his retreat to Jackson." Greif said they were at Champion Hill. They are found with Johnston in the defense of Jackson. The entire regiment would be mounted and go onto serve in Forrest's cavalry in 1864-5.

Henry Ewell Hord wrote on the 3rd Kentucky's transformation to cavalry in a 1915 issue of *Confederate Veteran* (Volume 23, page 473). Hord said Grierson's Raid led to orders that sent them to Enterprise; where Loring fended them off. Hord said, "We reached Enterprise just as they were coming into town, fired one round at them, and they skedaddled." He explained, "That raid convinced the authorities at Richmond that they needed more cavalry in that department; so orders were issued to mount us, the 3rd, 7th, and 8th Kentucky, all old soldiers. General Forrest had us sent to his command. General Buford gave up a fine brigade to come with us." Thus, Scott's Brigade came to be.

Scott commanded in the Atlanta Campaign and Tennessee in 1864. Scott's Brigade was the most vulnerable to enfilade artillery fire at Franklin. Scott barely survived his wound. It incapacitated him to further service. Colonel John Snodgrass commanded at Nashville. He was then on detached duty in the Scottsboro area. Capt. John A. Dixon commanded at Bentonville. J.P. Cannon seems to indicate Scott's Brigade and Cantey's old brigade, under Brig. Gen. Charles Shelley were consolidated on 9 April 1865. Cannon wrote that Shelley had a brigade in Loring's Division.

27th Alabama Infantry Regiment, Scott's Brigade

The men in the 27th were from the following counties: Franklin, Lauderdale, Lawrence, Madison, Mobile, and Morgan. The threat to a U.S. invasion of Alabama by way of the Tennessee River became a concern. Companies were sent to Fort Heiman, Kentucky, and the 27th was organized there in December 1861. The fort was on the Tennessee River. The mouth was on the Ohio River and traveling upstream (south) the most significant town was Florence, Alabama. Tennessee had done a poor job locating Fort Henry, and construction on Fort Heiman had been delayed due to Kentucky's former neutrality. Heiman was just upriver (south) of Fort Henry, Tennessee. The Kentucky-Tennessee border has an angle at the Tennessee River, so a bit of Kentucky is south of Tennessee. Fort Heiman never received its heavy artillery, and had to be evacuated due to the approach of enemy gunboats to take Fort Henry. They escaped east to Fort Donelson.

Col. Adolphus Alexander Hughes was in command of the 27th. He was captured at Fort Donelson, as was Lt. Col. James Jackson. Jackson had been wounded at First Manassas, in the 4th Alabama. He was discharged and that brought him back to Alabama, to serve in the 27th. Hughes died on 2 November 1862, and Jackson was promoted to colonel. The 27th was exchanged in September. *Confederate Military History* says they were at Port Hudson in the winter, and until 31 March 1863. Then they were in Buford's Brigade which was ordered to Pemberton's command in Mississippi. Buford's went to Loring's Division when it was created in May. They were at Champion Hill on the 16th.

The 27th went to Georgia in May 1864. Col. James K. Jackson lost an arm on the Lost Mountain Line, on 18 June. Lt. Col. Edward McAlexander is shown commanding on the 30th. By 10 July the 27th Alabama had been consolidated with the 35th and 49th. General Scott reported on Peach Tree Creek the relatively low casualties of two killed and 31 wounded. Jenkins has them with nine wounded, and lists by names. At Franklin Scott and Ives were wounded. Lt. Col. John Weeden commanded at Nashville, where he was wounded and captured. Though Jackson had lost an arm at Lost Mountain, he returned to lead Loring's Division at Bentonville. He died in 1879 and was buried at his famous home, "The Forks," in Lauderdale County.

Jackson's father built the house in 1822 or thereafter. The card says it had a race track. Visitors were Andrew Jackson, James Madison, and James Coffee. The house was struck by lightning in 1966 and caught fire. The stone columns remain today.

Of further interest: *Tattered Volunteers: The Twenty-Seventh Alabama Regiment, C.S.A.* by Harry V. Bernard, Northport, Alabama: Hermitage Press, 1965
Bloody Banners and Barefoot Boys: A History of the 27th Regiment Alabama Infantry, The Civil War Memoirs and Diary Entries of J.P. Cannon M.D., White Mane Publishing

35th Alabama Infantry Regiment, Scott's Brigade

The 35th was formed at LaGrange College on 12 March 1862. About 750 men came from the northern counties of Franklin, Lauderdale, Lawrence, Limestone, and Madison.***? Colonel Crossland, 7th Kentucky, said the 35th "opened and kept up a hot fire, which broke the enemy line." Samuel Spencer Ives was a captain in the 35th by March 1862. He was wounded at Baton Rouge, and had risen to lieutenant colonel by November. The 35th was in Albert Rust's brigade for Van Dorn's October attack on Corinth. They fought very well overrunning an enemy position and capturing artillery. *Confederate Military History* (vol. 7, part 2, page 131) indicates the 35th was still in Rust's Brigade in April 1863. Rust was ordered to the Trans Mississippi and the 35th was added to Buford's Brigade. Buford was at Meridian on 25 April. Grierson's U.S. cavalry had approached nearby Enterprise. Loring notified John Pemberton that Col. Edward Goodwin and the 35th Alabama defied them. Goodwin was again praised by Loring in his report on Champion Hill, where Goodwin "distinguished himself in the charge…"

Brave Colonel Goodwin died at Columbus, Mississippi on 25 September 1863. Ives was promoted to colonel, probably effective the same day. The 35th went to Georgia in May 1864. The 27th, 35th, and 49th were consolidated. Ives was in command at Peach Tree Creek. Jenkins has casualties there as one killed, nine wounded, and two missing. The 20 September 1864 organization shows Ives commanding the consolidated regiment. He was wounded and disabled at Franklin. The 10 December 1864 return shows Lt. Col. John Weeden over the consolidated regiment. He was wounded and captured at Nashville. Only 55 remained to surrender in North Carolina.

Of further interest: *Regimental History of the 35th Alabama, 1862-1865,* by Leroy F. Banning, Bowie, Maryland: Heritage Books, 1999
Confederate Echoes, A Voice from the South in the Days of Secession *and the Southern Confederacy* by Albert Theodore Goodloe.

49th Alabama Infantry Regiment, Scott's Brigade

The 49th was organized at Nashville, Tennessee in February 1862. The men came from the following counties: Blount, Colbert, DeKalb, Jackson, Lauderdale, Lawrence, Limestone, Madison, Marshall, and Morgan. Shiloh was their first battle. They were in Breckinridge's Reserve. They fought with him at Baton Rouge in August. They were in Van Dorn's army in time to fight at Corinth in October. They suffered heavy losses at both battles, and when Port Hudson surrendered about 500 of the 49th were captured. The 49th had been commanded by Maj. T.A. Street. The 49th was exchanged and reorganized at Cahaba, Alabama. It was assigned to Scott's Brigade. The 49th was so small it was consolidated with the 27th and 35th, on 10 July 1864. Jenkins has their Peach Tree Creek casualties as one killed and fifteen wounded. Col. Samuel Ives was in command. When

Ives was wounded at Franklin command passed to Lt. Col. Weeden. He was wounded and captured at Nashville. In North Carolina Captain W.B. Beason commanded.

55th Alabama Infantry Regiment, Scott's Brigade

The 55th was organized at Port Hudson, Louisiana in February 1863, by consolidating two battalions. One was under John Snodgrass, and was numbered as the 4th or 16th at various times. The other was under John Norwood. The men came from the following northern and northeastern counties: Calhoun, Cherokee, Jackson, Madison, and Marshall. Norwood was captured at Fort Donelson, and late exchanged. Snodgrass was wounded at Shiloh. After the battalions were consolidated the 55th was put in a brigade under Buford, by April 1863. Thus, they were in Loring's Division when it was formed in May. In May 1864 they were with the division as it arrived in Georgia.

Confederate Military History says the 55th was "fearfully mutilated" at Peach Tree Creek. Snodgrass reported, "After the order to charge was given, my regiment moved forward under a terrible enfilading fire of grape, canister and minnie, as well as a galling direct fire, until they passed considerably the first line of the enemy's works. My regiment was considerably scattered, but none left the field." Jenkins has Snodgrass in command of the 55th, on the right centre. He lists 182 casualties by name. Lt. Col. Norwood was so seriously wounded he could not return to duty. The 20 September 1864 organization shows Maj. James B. Dickey over the 55th. He was at Franklin too. The 10 December 1864 organization still has Dickey in command.

Of further interest: *The Forgotten Regiment* by Rex Miller, Patrex Press, Austin, Texas John David Snodgrass, a Huntsville, Alabama attorney, furnished me a copy about 1997.

57th Alabama Infantry Regiment, Scott's Brigade

Confederate Military History says the 57th was organized at Troy in April 1863. Another source says organized in March, and sometimes incorrectly called the 54th. The men came from the following counties: Barbour, Coffee, Dale (?), Henry, and Pike.

They were in the Department of the Gulf in January 1864. Columbus J.L. Cunningham was in command on the returns of 10 June, 30 June, and 10 July. He must have been absent at Peach Tree Creek, as Lt. Col. William Bethune was in command. The 57th was on the extreme right of Scott's Brigade. Jenkins indicates 157 casualties, with 78 named. Bethune was severely wounded, so the report was filed by Capt. Augustus L. Milligan. He wrote, "The long list of casualties in this regiment, will be sufficient evidence of its deep devotion to the cause of Southern liberty and independence."

Cunningham must have still been absent on 31 July, as Milligan commanded. The 31 August return shows Cunningham back, but the 20 September 1864 organization shows Maj. J. Horatio Wiley in command. Cunningham had returned to command at Franklin, and was wounded. The 10 December 1864 return has Wiley back in command.
Of further interest: *The Flags of Civil War Alabama* has a photo a battle flag presented to Company A of the 57th. It is in the Alabama Department of Archives and History, in Montgomery. It was presented in Troy on behalf of Mrs. James Holt Clanton, wife of

General Clanton. It became the regimental colours. It was riddled with minie balls at Peachtree Creek, and survived Franklin, where colour bearer John B. Carter was mortally wounded. Captain J.P. Wood saved the flag when he took it home on furlough in 1865. Wood donated the flag to the Archives in Montgomery on December 10, 1910.

12th Louisiana Infantry Regiment, Scott's Brigade

Guide to Louisiana Confederate Military Units 1861-1865 lists the twelve companies of the regiment and the parishes from which they were recruited. They were organized at Camp Moore. It was one of the largest Confederate training camps, and also has a Confederate cemetery. Today it is Camp Moore State Commemorative Area.

Thomas Moore Scott organized the 12th in August 1861. He seems to have been one of the great fighting generals of the Army of Tennessee. But he was a latecomer. Had his star risen sooner, he might have better etched into our history. They were sent upriver to Columbus, Kentucky in 1861. The Pointe Coupee Battery was too. As the war continued they would be together in Buford's Brigade, which became Scott's.

The men of the 12th spent more than the usual amount of time under naval bombardments in the first half of the war. The fall of Forts Henry and Donelson led to the evacuation of Columbus. They were at Island Number Ten, Tennessee until 17 March 1862. Then they were transferred downriver to Fort Pillow, as was the Pointe Coupee artillery. They were there until it was evacuated on 5 June. Memphis fell due to the defeat of the Confederate naval flotilla the nest day. Thus the 12th and the Pointe Coupee retreated to Mississippi.

Fort Pillow had been under the command of Brig. Gen. John Bordenave Villepigue. He was one of many outstanding Confederate generals. He did well at Corinth with a brigade of two Mississippi regiments. The 12th appears to have been added to his brigade after Corinth, but Villepigue was ordered to Port Hudson on 24 October. He died of a fever there on 9 November. The 12th's part in the 5 December 1862 fight at Coffeeville is mentioned above. A soldier referred to be in Villepigue's Brigade, though he had passed.

The 12th Louisiana found itself transferred about Mississippi and Port Hudson, Louisiana prior to Champion Hill on 16 May 1863. *Champion Hill: Decisive Battle for Vicksburg* has good information on the 12th there. They were in Buford's Brigade, as was the Pointe Coupee. Loring praised Colonel Scott for his fighting, calling him "able and daring." They stayed with Loring and came to the Army of Tennessee for the Atlanta Campaign. At Peach Tree Creek, Jenkins has them taking 66 casualties, and names six of them. The 20 September 1864 organization shows Capt. Evander Graham in command. But Col. Noel Nelson was back in the Tennessee, as he was killed at Franklin. Graham was wounded there. The 10 December 1864 organization has Capt. James T. Davis in command. As the army retreated back into Franklin, Graham rejoined them. Capt. John Dixon may have been in command of Scott's Brigade at Bentonville. The brigade was dissolved on 9 April. A Lt. Joseph Reno may have commanded the 12th on 31 March, but died on 10 April, and Dixon seems to have been in command of the 12th. Graham was promoted to lieutenant colonel on 2 May. Over the course of the war 1,457 men served in the 12th. While 304 died of combat wounds, 302 died of illness.

Chapter 13-Myrick's Battalion of Artillery (1864)

Myrick's Battalion was named for Major John Douglas Myrick. He had been Loring's aide-de-camp in Virginia. Unlike most on Loring's staff in Virginia, Myrick seems to have continued with Loring into 1865. He has been evasive, no photo found.

In Loring's 22 March 1863 report on Fort Pemberton, he wrote, "I cannot speak in too much praise of the courage, coolness, and efficiency of Capt. John D. Myrick, my aide and acting chief of artillery, not only under the fire of the enemy in battle, but at the critical moment of the explosion of our magazine. In the midst of it, when every one was appalled, he stood unfalteringly, and with great heroism rallied his men to his guns." Subsequently Myrick commanded a battalion in Loring's Division before Champion Hill.

Another battery, Charpentier's Alabama, joined Loring's Division in time to fight at Jackson. They were named for Captain Stephen Charpentier when organized at Mobile in October 1861. They served there until June 1863, when they were transferred and attached to Featherston's Brigade. They went to Georgia and were apparently equipped with Napoleons, before being ordered back to Alabama.

Confederate Cannon Foundries states that in January 1863, the Army of Mississippi was stationed at Grenada, with 56 field pieces. Only two were Napoleons. The Macon Arsenal in Georgia began the production of bronze 12-pounder Napoleons. The *Macon Telegraph* reported, in June, "Another beautiful battery of twelve pound bronze Napoleon guns from the Macon Arsenal was on the streets yesterday. Both these batteries will be the pride of our artillerymen. The guns are beautifully shaped, and the carriages and caissons thoroughly made and handsomely painted. We understand the old 6-pounder field pieces have been pretty much abandoned in our service."

Confederate Cannon Foundries states two Georgia arsenals, Columbus and Macon, largely assisted the Army of Mississippi in replacing outdated pieces. It says in the spring of 1864 three batteries in Loring's Division turned in their six 6-pounder guns and six 12-pounder howitzers for twelve Napoleons. It says they went to Barry's, Charpentier's, and Pointe Coupe (Bouanchaud's). Loring's Division arrived in Georgia in May 1864. Macon delivered eight Napoleons in May; four more may have been delivered in June.

During the Atlanta Campaign Bouanchaud's and Cowan's batteries were in the battalion, as was Tennessee's Lookout Battery under Captain Robert L. Barry. They were equipped with Napoleons; this may be seen in the report of the Army of Mississippi's Chief Ordinance Officer Charles F. Vanderford. Charpentier's was only with Loring until Resaca, where a shell killed a few of their horses. The Alabama Archives have a web site that says the battery was sent to Selma to be equipped. This may be an error, as they are said to have received Napoleons from Macon. Also, Selma Naval Gun Foundry seems to have specialized in manufacturing 7-inch Brooke rifles for the navy. Darden's was in Williams' Battalion of the Artillery Reserve. In late September 1864 Barry's was ordered to Macon, Georgia. General Hood ordered them to turn over the battery, horses, and equipment to Captain Darden. Myrick appears to have been present after Nashville. An abstract of an artillery report still lists Myrick commanding the battalion.

Barry's (Tennessee) Battery

This battery was in Loring's Division from 30 May 1863 through the Atlanta Campaign. *Tennesseans in the Civil War* refers to it as Captain Robert L. Barry's Tennessee Light Artillery Company. They were also called Lookout Artillery and Lookout Battery. They were organized in Chattanooga, beneath Lookout Mountain, on 15 May 1862. They were attached to the Post of Chattanooga or at other points in eastern Tennessee until October. Then they were in southern Alabama.

Barry's came to Loring when they were attached to Buford's Brigade, where they were reported on 30 May 1863. Loring's remarkable escape from Champion Hill entailed the abandonment of his artillery, thus he would have been pleased to take in this equipped battery. In July records show Barry's was attached to Adams's Brigade. In November they reported an aggregate of 144 men, armed with two six-pounder smooth bore guns, and two 12-pounder howitzers. By 1863 these were generally inferior pieces. The battery had 41 horses and 23 mules.

In January 1864 Johnston was commanding the Army of Tennessee, as Bragg had resigned. Leonidas Polk commanded the Army of Mississippi, which included Loring's Division. The attachment of batteries to specific brigades was no longer designated. Barry's arrived in May and would be in Myrick's Battalion along with Bouanchaud's and Cowan's. They were upgraded to four Napoleons prior to arrival to service in the Army of Tennessee. General William Pendleton had come from Virginia to inspect artillery in the winter. In March he had said some howitzers should be kept for use in broken and wooded country. This was due to their arching trajectory of fire. But six-pounders were of little use on battlefields dominated by twelve-pounder Napoleons.

Tennesseans in the War indicates that at Peachtree Creek, Barry's was under Lieutenant Richard L. Watkins. It says they went into action on Walthall's line. Walthall's Division was on Loring's left. They silenced an enemy battery and sustained 15 casualties. This may have been their hardest fight of the war. They remained with the army until Hood, who had replaced Johnston, gave them a new assignment on 28 September 1864. Barry's was ordered to turn over the battery, horses, and equipment to Darden's Battery, and report to the Post of Macon, Georgia. Darden's replaced Barry's in Myrick's Battalion. Barry's was around Mobile in the last months of the war. They were surrendered by Richard Taylor on 4 May 1865.

Bouanchaud's (Louisiana) Battery, a.k.a. Pointe Coupee Battery

The battery was originally the Pointe Coupee Battery, when it was organized in August 1861. About a year later it was organized into the Pointe Coupee Battalion, with three companies. Capt. Richard Stewart, a Mexican War veteran, had begun raising the troops in the spring. Recruits came from parishes, including Pointe Coupee, along the Mississippi River. The original battery was sent up the river to Columbus, Kentucky and fired on enemy gunboats during the 7 November battle across the river at Belmont, Missouri. Men from New Orleans came up and formed the nucleus of Company B, so the original battery became Company A.

The fall of Forts Henry and Donelson led to the evacuation of Columbus in February 1862. Company B was at Island Number Ten and A may have been until mid-March. Island Number Ten, Tennessee was located close to the U.S.-Kentucky border, opposite Missouri. Brig. Gen. William Mackall, a native of Cecil County in northeastern Maryland, commanded our forces of about 7,000 men. U.S. forces included a flotilla of gunboats and mortar boats. They shelled the island day and night for 23 days, until it surrendered on 7 April 1862. When it did, Company B was too.

Company A had been sent downriver to Fort Pillow. They served there until it was evacuated on 5 June. The subsequent loss of Memphis led the Pointe Coupee to Grenada, Mississippi. Captain Stewart was trying to create a legion, which were out of favor. He became upset and resigned. This led to Alcide Bouanchaud's promotion from lieutenant and command. Company C was created and joined to create the Pointe Coupee Battalion in August. Company B was paroled in September. Lloyd Tilghman, who surrendered Fort Henry, was paroled and commanded our forces in a victory at Coffeeville, north of Grenada. Sections of the Point Coupee were engaged there.

Battery B came under Loring for his victory at Fort Pemberton. Batteries A and C were attached to Buford's Brigade before Champion Hill. Buford reported they each had four guns, and were commanded by Bouanchaud. They attracted enemy artillery fire and served Loring well all the way to the retreat to Baker's Creek. Most of the battalion fell back into Vicksburg, and were in its garrison for the siege. The surrender effectively ended B and C, though some of the men may have found their way to A. One section of A escaped Champion Hill with Loring's Division. Thereafter the battalion ceased to exist and any parolees from B or C may have joined A. Their history with Loring's above.

French's Division attacked U.S. forts near Allatoona on the *Western & Atlantic*. Myrick's Battalion was also engaged. This monument reads: "Pointe Coupee, Co. A, Louisiana Battery, Allatoona Pass, Oct. 5, 1864."

Louisiana has a quote by General Loring: 'To have served in either of the batteries in my command is glory enough for any one man. In my opinion, however, Capt. Bouanchaud's gallant conduct, and that of his famous battery, in the first day's fight before Nashville, has never in all the history of the war been equaled, and never possibly be surpassed."

Confederates casualties around Nashville are most likely at Mount Olivet Cemetery; however, two from Bouanchaud's may be at the Nashville National Cemetery. The U.S. government cemeteries had a policy against Confederate burials, but misidentifications occurred, and were later discovered. Private Hippolyte Decoux died on 18 December 1864, and may be there. Staff officer John McQuaide remembered Decoux's mortal upper thigh wound on the 15th. Private Edgard Guesnon died on the 23rd. He is listed among the dead in the U.S. cemetery, and also at Mount Olivet. A remnant of the battery fought under Forrest at Selma. Fewer still were at Fort Tyler at West Point, Georgia. It was attacked in one of the war's final battles on 16 April 1865.

Confederate Memorial Hall was established in1891, making it the oldest museum in Louisiana. The excellent collection of artifacts includes many pertaining to soldiers and units from Louisiana. The card (left) was mailed in October 1906 from New Orleans, from a son to father in Cincinnati, Ohio. The author bought card in 2010.

Confederate Memorial Hall's newslettre, of December 2015, has a photo of the restored square battle flag of the Pointe Coupee Artillery. It was displayed on one of the paneled walls (left). Descendants of Capt. Alcide Bouanchaud raised money amongst the family for the restoration. They also loaned a Yankee cavalry sword the captain had picked up on a battlefield. Memorial Hall has Cowan's, Van Dorn's Army of the West pattern.

Cowan's Battery

Cowan's Battery was named for Captain James J. Cowan. It was organized in Vicksburg as Battery G of the 1st Artillery Regiment. Vicksburg had a foundry, A.B. Reading and Brother; they began making cannon in 1861. *Confederate Cannon Foundries* provides a sketch of the firm. By late 1861 they were making cannon. They would turn out both smoothbores and rifled pieces. All of their castings were bronze. Known surviving weapons, as of 1977 copyright, are listed. Readings may have sold pieces to Cowan's.

Vicksburg was home to Cowan's Battery. Newitt Vick, a native Virginian and cotton planter, began marking off lots to sell in 1819. He had died of yellow fever before the town was incorporated in 1825. The city thrived into the 1850s and the 1860 census counted 4,500 residents. That was more than the capital, Jackson. John Bell was the first choice for president, indicating attachment for the union with Northern states. Lincoln's war and relentless shelling by the U.S. changed that. July 4th was not celebrated until the 1940s.

Cowan's Battery was designated as Company G. in the 1st Mississippi Light Artillery Regiment, Company G. Cowan enlisted on 26 April 1862. Perhaps waiting for their guns delayed them. Cowan's had a Van Dorn pattern flag now preserved and displayed at Confederate Memorial Hall in New Orleans. It had minor restoration and remounting in 2014. Funding was from the Society of the Order of the Southern Cross. The connection to Van Dorn was he commanded the department in Mississippi during part of 1862.

Pemberton replaced Van Dorn in October 1862, bringing Cowan's under his command. The entry for Cowan regarding Chickasaw Bayou says, "He successfully performed this duty, repulsing the attack of Sherman's troops, and next took part in the defense of Vicksburg against the Federal (U.S.) fleet. Cowan's Battery, and was attached to Tilghman's Brigade (later Adams's) by 19 March 1863. Tilghman was with Cowan's at Champion Hill when he was killed. Most of Loring's Division escaped but Cowan was cut off "and entered Vicksburg with the scattered remains of General Pemberton's army." Actually Cowan and part of the men did. L.S. Flatau wrote to *Confederate Veteran* in 1910 (Vol. 18, p. 423); his remarks on Tilghman in biographical sketch in appendix. Pemberton's army retreated at Champion Hill, and Cowan's Battery was among the last units to attempt to cross Baker's Creek in the retreat toward Vicksburg. Their guns had to be abandoned near the creek and the men went different directions. "Our battery was divided, part of it following First Lieut. George Tompkins, the other past following Captain Cowan into Vicksburg." Cowan had relatives in the battery, and as they were from Vicksburg, we may suppose they were determined to fight for their home.

Captain Cowan, with his faithful command, occupied an important position in the line of defense during the ever memorable siege of forty-seven days, and surrendered with the besieged army. The history of the privations that came after the place was invested, the nights of sleepless peril, the days of anxious care, in the insufficient, unwholesome food, the life in shelter less trenches, exposed to prolonged cannonading or sudden assault, can never be written." The surrender found Cowan and most of the battery shattered in health. They were declared exchanged on 12 September 1863.

Cowan's went to Georgia with Loring, where they were equipped with four Napoleons. They apparently saw no action before 20 June 1864, as an ordinance report shows the battery expended no ammunition, and had no casualties. Leonidas Polk was killed on the 14th and Loring had temporary corps command. Featherston commanded Loring's Division at Kennesaw Mountain on the 27th. They were on the flank where Cowan's and other division artillery opened a "concentrated converging fire." They continued to pour a "most galling and destructive fire." Even U.S. Army reports gave credit to their firing. Cowan may have taken sick leave as he was not shown in command on the 31 July 1864 army organization. Lt. George H. Tompkins was thereafter in the Georgia and Tennessee campaigns. Louis S. Flatau wrote of Cowan's at Franklin, "My battery was equipped like infantry, and we were ordered to charge with Company E of the Fifteenth Mississippi, so as to turn (enemy's) own guns on them after we had captured them; but what a disappointment…This kind of defense we did not expect." Afterward, "Thousands lay upon that field, dead and dying. You could see squads of these veterans who had fought together, kneeling down around the body of some dying comrade, and their grief was so great they wept like women."

We have seen Cowan's lost their guns on 15 December while attempting to support Ed Johnson's troops who were to extend the left of Walthall's Division, Stewart's Corps. *The Military History of Mississippi* says "they arrived on the gallop, and went into position in time to be run over and lose their guns." The enemy's 5th Division cavalry took them after crossing a hill along today's Castleman Drive, and sweeping over it rapidly, captured them. U.S. division commander Hatch claimed three brass rifled guns. Thus, one of Cowan's pieces escaped.

The Mississippi history incorrectly claimed, "That night the guns of Hoskins' Battery were turned over to Cowan's." But not all four could have been. Their two Parrotts were on detached service with Rucker's Brigade of cavalry. They had been fighting gunboats on the Cumberland, and their night march didn't bring them any closer to Hood's army than Hillsborough Pike. One Parrott didn't make it that far as it was left an axle broken. It is likely the other two guns were Napoleons, and it is likely they were captured at Redoubt One. Regardless, the Mississippi history continued, "thus equipped, they took part in the battle of 16 December." Cowan's may have had the Napoleon they escaped with engaged on the 16th.

T. G. Dabney had been a sergeant with Hoskins's and wrote to *Confederate Veteran* in 1909 (Vol. 17, p. 31). He wrote, "…The writer was brought into personal contact with

General Stewart once during the service. When near the Tennessee River in December 1864, being then sergeant in command of the one remaining gun in Hoskins's Mississippi Battery, he received a personal order from General Stewart to proceed with Lieutenant Tomkins, in command of the two remaining guns of Cowan's Vicksburg Battery, down to Florence, Ala., five miles below, to contest the passage of the Federal gunboat up the Tennessee River to cut the pontoon bridge over which Hood's broken army was retreating from the Nashville campaign. The gunboat was engaged by the three field guns, and the pontoon bridge was not destroyed by her."

The men of Cowan's Battery ended up in the Defenses of Mobile ending their time in Loring's Division. In March they were in Grayson's Artillery Battalion and would remain in it until captured at Fort Blakely, northeast of Mobile.

Darden's Battery

The Military History of Mississippi explains this battery was originally formed as cavalry on 6 May 1861. They were equipped as artillery shortly afterward. They organized at Fayette, between Natchez and Port Gibson, in Jefferson County. Thus they were known as the Jefferson Flying Artillery. They were also known as Harper's, after Captain William L. Harper. They were on their way to Virginia late in 1861 when diverted to Bowling Green, Kentucky. General Albert Sidney Johnston had his Department No. 2 headquarters there, and was badly outnumbered. His force there was the Central Army of Kentucky. Maj. Gen. William J. Hardee commanded the 1st Division, and the Jefferson Flying Artillery was attached.

> Text on this card says the Confederate Memorial in Fayette, Mississippi was erected in 1904 as Jefferson County's tribute to her Confederate soldiers. Perhaps some of Lt. Horace Bullen's (Darden's Battery) family was on hand. He was mortally wounded at Nashville and died there on 7 JAN 65. He was brought home for burial.

Tilghman's surrender of Fort Henry led Johnston to abandon Bowling Green and retreat to Nashville. Johnston hadn't visited the fort, or Fort Donelson, and offered no clear strategy. The surrender of Fort Donelson led him to abandon Nashville. It is interesting that the Jefferson Flying Artillery passed through the city, which they would hope to liberate in December 1862 while at Murfreesborough, and in December 1864.

For the flying artillerists Shiloh was the first attempt to liberate Nashville. Beauregard tended to think more of the Mississippi Valley and an advance toward St. Louis. Thus the newly formed army was named the Army of the Mississippi. But had Johnston lived, figure he would have sought to reclaim what he had lost. Harper's battery was still under Hardee though his division was called the Third Army Corps. There were three brigades and Harper's were attached to Sterling Wood's. His infantry were in the front line of attack on 6 April 1862. They overran the Yankees and charged on through their abandoned camps. The speed of the advance made it difficult for batteries to keep up, and also for fresh infantry ammunition to be moved to correct units. In afternoon Harper's was supporting another brigade. It ran out of ammunition and pulled back, leaving the battery unsupported. A Yankee counterattack nearly engulfed them, resulting in the loss of one gun. *Military History of Mississippi* says on the second day they were down to six men to a gun. In trying to withdraw their horses were shot in their harnesses, forcing them to abandon it. But they found a captured 12-pounder howitzer to replace it. Captain Harper was wounded and Putnam Darden took command.

Beauregard took sick leave after Shiloh and President Davis turned the army over to Braxton Bragg. Bragg had brought the best organized troops to the battle and was promoted to full general. He reorganized the army into two wings, placing the Left under Hardee. Darden's Battery was assigned to Bushrod Johnson's brigade. While the army was in Mississippi "many prominent citizens of Kentucky" visited Bragg and said if the army moved into the Bluegrass state their loyalty to the Confederacy "would be proven." Perhaps so, but another factor is generally ignored. Over a year of dead and maimed soldiers had brought about conscription. The exuberance of 1861 had waned. In the combined Bragg-Kirby Smith drive to liberate Kentucky four tactical victories were won including the last at Perryville. Darden's was successfully engaged with two 6-pounders and two 12-pounders. Bragg won and then realized how badly he was outnumbered. Kentuckians had not enlisted, and there was no reason to remain and risk defeat.

Bragg brought the army south to Tennessee by way of Knoxville. It was Kirby Smith's Department of East Tennessee so Bragg kept moving toward Nashville. The army was now known as the Army of Tennessee. It was positioned over about 60 miles, with the centre at Murfreesborough. Darden's with Bushrod Johnson's brigade was off to the west around Triune. The U.S. Army of the Cumberland began their advance after Christmas. Bragg consolidated his line outside Murfreesborough. Darden's report recalled "the men and horses were very much fatigued by the march and exposure, having slept without tents and exposed to the rain…In this condition we arrived on the battlefield illy prepared to go into the engagement."

Bragg had 37,000 to the enemy's 57,127 yet he launched a devastating morning attack on 31 December. Johnson's Tennessee infantry advanced in Hardee's devastating attack. Johnson called on Darden's to establish counter-battery fire against an enemy battery of Napoleons. Darden's gunners managed to disable one before the Tennesseans charged and captured two more. This was one of three batteries silenced by Darden's. They were so active that they exhausted their ammunition, and even used 100 rounds of captured howitzer shells. When Bragg withdrew several days later Darden's removed seven captured U.S. pieces. Putnam Darden's name was placed on the Confederate Roll of Honour for his service at Murfreesborough.

Bragg scored the greatest offensive field victory of the war at Chickamauga in September 1863. Darden's was no longer attached to Johnson's brigade, but in the Reserve Artillery. They were armed with four Napoleons, perhaps some of the guns they removed from the field at Murfreesborough. Darden's was not engaged on the 19th, but was on the 20th. Johnson's old brigade had been in the lead during Longstreet's brilliant column attack. About 5p.m. Longstreet ordered artillery to support the attacks on the U.S. rear guard at Snodgrass Hill. A Chickamauga National Military Park marker allows the location of Darden's. It is on the east side of LaFayette Road, near the intersection of Poe Road.

The tablet and Napoleon locate Darden's Battery at Chickamauga. The Georgia monument is in the background. The tablet explains the battery under Capt. Putnam Darden crossed the Chickamauga at Alexander's Bridge on the 19th but was not engaged, but under fire.

On the 20th they opened fire about 5:00 p.m. from this point. The enemy was crossing the LaFayette Road near the Kelly house. As Stewart's Division moved forward Darden's advanced. The battle had been won, ending their action.

Darden's escaped Bragg's defeat near Chattanooga at Missionary Ridge. There had been shortages of corn and forage. In October one of Darden's officers warned "for the want of forage my horses are rapidly falling off." The mountainous terrain lacked the pastures needed for grazing. Then they were ordered to join Longstreet, who was moving toward Knoxville. James Turpin wrote *Confederate Veteran*, in 1901, explaining "while waiting for a train at Chickamauga Station the battle of Missionary Ridge commenced, and the order was countermanded" Fortunately that station was behind the ridge allowing their escape into Georgia. Darden's was still in the same battalion, commanded by Lt. Col. Samuel C. Williams. It would go into the Atlanta Campaign in it. It didn't become attached to Loring's Division until after the campaign on 28 September 1864.

Military History of Mississippi explained that in Hood's march to Spring Hill, twenty of Darden's men were along "to take charge of guns expected to be captured." It also states two guns were lost at Nashville, and Lt. Horace W. Bullen; he was mortally wounded and captured. The U.S. Army had a complex group of hospitals established for their own troops as well as prisoners. Bullen lived until 6 January 1865. He probably knew the Confederate dead were being buried in trenches at City Cemetery. They were reburied by Nashvillians later at Mount Olivet Cemetery, in what is known as Confederate Circle.

One of Darden's is still at City Cemetery. James Turpin's piece tells how his brother was killed at Nashville. They had lost guns on the 15th, but were sent to man Napoleons of Stanford's Mississippi battery. They were with Clayton's Division, of Lee's Corps, on the right. They were on Peach Orchard Hill along Franklin Pike. They had dueled with several enemy batteries and disabled two guns. Unfortunately two of their limber chests were exploded. Turpin wrote that White (right) was badly burned by one of the explosions, and "taken to the house of Mrs. John Ewing, seven miles south of Nashville on the Franklin pike, and two weeks later taken to the hospital at Nashville by the Federals for safe keeping. There his wound was not properly treated, and he died on the 17th of January, 1865, and was buried near the center of the old cemetery in Nashville. A monument marks his grave." The marker may still be seen at the corner of Cedar and Poplar. The inscription: "Thou shalt be missed because thy seat will be empty," is from *1st Samuel*.

Note: Different U.S. units at Nashville claimed to have captured a battery when they actually captured a two-gun section or three guns. The 15th Ohio Infantry claimed to have captured Napoleons on the 15th that were likely Darden's. They were in brigade that also claimed brass Napoleons and they were also in a division that claimed four captured. Yet *Military History of Mississippi* states Darden's lost two guns at Nashville.

Turpin's piece said, "Having lost our guns at Nashville, our company was stationed at Selma, Ala., and put in charge of six pieces of artillery there. We were in the battle of Selma, and I and twenty-two of my company were captured one Sunday afternoon about four o'clock, April 2, 1865, by Gen. John T. Wilder's Brigade. We were manning two pieces of artillery on the Plantersville road. We were then marched down the line to be fired on by our own company, and think but for an officer of Wilder's command…who ordered our captors to take us back to the rear, we would have all been killed by our own men. I have always been grateful to that officer…After our capture we were put in a stockade at Selma, and kept there for eight days, then taken out and marched toward Montgomery, Ala., en route to a Northern prison. The second night out I made my escape, and rejoined my command at Meridian, Miss., it having joined Gen. Dick Taylor's forces there after their evacuation of Mobile."

Chapter 14-Biographical Entries

These entries are limited to prominent individuals associated with Loring, his military career, and his division. They do not cover parents, spouses, or children in detail. An essential source is *Generals in Gray*. *The Confederate General* has more detailed entries; it is a six-volume set. Both have photos. Confederate Colonels is also an essential source for colonels; it does not include lieutenant colonels. It has a wealth of information, though in shorter entries. It does not have photographs of all the colonels. Artillery officers are generally more obscure. Most of those in the Army of Tennessee are at least mentioned in *Cannoneers in Gray*. It is a general history of the artillery of the Army of Tennessee, and another essential source.

Adams, John: born 1 July 1825 in Nashville, Tenn., killed 30 November 64 at Franklin

Where No Sorrows Come: The Life and Death of Confederate Brigadier General John Adams, by Bryan Lane, is the biography. It details his family and early life. Here is a summary. His father was Thomas Andersonville, born in Ireland in March 1796, three months before Tennessee became a state. His parents brought him to New York City when he was a teenager. His mother was born in Dumfries, Scotland, and came with her parents to Philadelphia in 1808. Pictures of both parents are in Lane's biography. Both migrated to Nashville, where they met, and were married by a Presbyterian minister in 1819. John was their fourth child, born in Nashville in 1825.They lived on today's 5th Avenue, but soon moved several blocks west to today's 8th Avenue.

John must have had pleasant early memories of Nashville, but in 1837 the family moved south to Pulaski. His father had been in banking and accepted the cashier's job at the Planters Bank. The following year John was enrolled at Pulaski's Wertemberg Academy. His math teacher wrote, "His capacity to learn is very good, and he acquires a knowledge of Mathematics with much more ease than most of the scholars whom I have instructed.." John's French instructor wrote, "He reads, translates and understands readily all that is placed in his hands written in that language." When the time came, John's father called on their U.S. congressman, Aaron Venable Brown of Pulaski, for a recommendation to West Point. Brown wrote the U.S. Secretary of War, "He (Adams) is a young man of good morals and studious habits and I have no doubt, would acquit himself with credit and distinction-It would be a singular favour to him to procure such a situation, as his father has a large family and is in moderate circumstance. He is very desirous of such an advantage, as would be afforded him at West Point." He was accepted and graduated in 1846, in the middle of a class, that included (Stonewall) Jackson and George Pickett.

The major campaigns of the Mexican War had been waged, and won when Adams fought at Santa Cruz de Rosales. Col. Sterling Price, later a Confederate general, launched an invasion from El Paso, Texas in February 1848. Near Chihuahua they were approached by a contingent of mounted Mexican troops under a flag of truce. They informed Price the war was over and a treaty signed. Price had no such word and didn't believe them. He moved to Santa Cruz de Rosales and demanded Mexican General Angel Trias surrender. Trias refused citing the peace armistice. Price allowed five days for a courier to obtain a copy, which hadn't been received five days later. Though Adams was Acting Adjutant with dragoons he volunteered to command a 24-pounder howitzer section. He sent two shells into enemy combatants on a church roof. Another shell struck an ammunition wagon. The Mexican force surrendered that night. Adams received praise for his role in the victory, and was brevetted 1st lieutenant for "gallant and meritorious service."

In the following years Adams saw frontier duty, with skirmishes with different native tribes. In 1852 he was ordered to Fort Snelling, Minnesota. Adams Cousin Thomas Gibson was on his staff. In 1896 Gibson wrote into *Confederate Veteran* (Vol. 5, p.29): "Gen. Adams was married at Fort Snelling, May 3, 1854, to Miss Georgia, daughter of Dr. Charles McDougal, a distinguished surgeon of the U.S. Army. Mrs. Adams, four

sons, and two daughters survive him… Though left a widow with six small children, under the many trying ordeals of the period, Mrs. Adams reared them to be useful men and women." But that was in the future. In 1859 John and Georgia were at Fort Crook, California. Adams was disgusted with citizen soldiers killing natives and destroying their crops. He wrote they may succeed in rendering a harmless tribe "quite formidable." In March 1861 Adams responded to a report, "The white inhabitants of this section are more than anxious to be at war with these Indians. For this reason, the Indians are afraid to go into the valleys for roots and berries, so that I cannot imagine how they live, and must think they merit some consideration for not stealing."

Elsewhere whites in Washington City were anxious to be at war. Abraham Lincoln had called for troops to invade the new Confederate States of America. This drove Tennessee to secede and brought Adams east. He sailed from California to New York City. The U.S. secretary of state wired General Winfield Scott to expect his arrival. Scott planned to act wiring back on 5 August: "I think it desirable that John Adams, a native of Tennessee, who recently resigned a captaincy in the U.S. First Regiment of Dragoons, be arrested and held a political prisoner, as I do not doubt that he designs to take service in the rebel army against us." Fortunately for Adams he had already arrived and was in Nashville on the 7th. Adams was made a captain and sent to command the post of Memphis. His sister and husband lived there, so Adams, Georgia, and children arrived to a family welcome.

Adams Confederate service was not remarkable until his attachment to Loring and his new division in May 1863. That has largely been covered in the chapters above, and the chapter on John Adams's Brigade. Reflections on his death and memory follow.

Bishop Quintard wrote Adams's body was taken to Carnton, the McGavock residence. Quintard said, "Mrs. McGavock rendered every assistance possible and her name deserves to be handed down to future generations as that of a woman of lofty principle, exalted character and untiring devotion." Of course many others worked day and night at the massive hospital, but Carrie McGavock deserves eternal remembrance. Quintard and two of Adams's captains took the body to the residence of the general's brother, Major Nathan Adams, in Pulaski. Quintard officiated at the funeral and the remains were placed beside those of the parents.

Quintard recalled, "As a soldier, General Adams was active, calm and self-possessed, brave without rashness, quick to perceive and ever ready to seize the favourable moment. He enjoyed the confidence of his superiors and the love and respect of his soldiers and officers. In camp and on the march he looked closely to the comfort of his soldiers, and often shared his horse on long marches with his sick and broken-down men."

Of further interest: *Confederate Veteran* (Volume 21, page 336) said Adams's saddle, with a bullet hole through it, is a relic with the Tennessee Historical Society. The saddle is now at the Tennessee State Museum. They also have his uniform frock coat, left by his widow. The U.S. colonel, Casement, who commanded troops at the point where Adams was killed wrote Mrs. Adams in 1891. He explained he saw Adams killed and wrote, "The saddle was taken from the horse and presented to me before the charge was fairly repulsed; that is why I have kept it all these years. It is the only trophy that I have of the great war, and I am only too happy to return it to you. It has never been used since the General used it. It was hung in our attic. The stirrups were of wood, and I fear that my boys in their pony days must have taken them. I am very sorry for it." Casement went onto to say the saddle would be expressed to her, and it is now a relic for posterity.

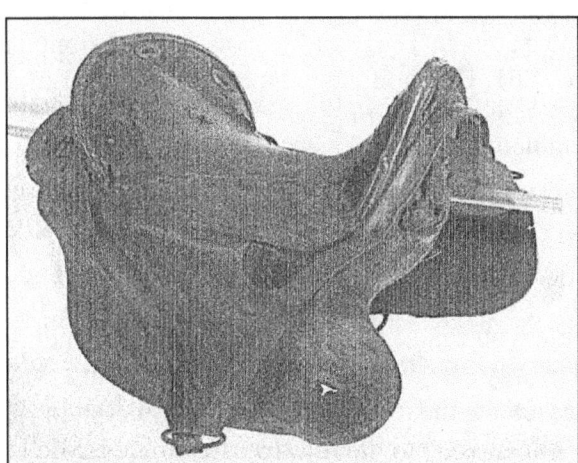

Ronny Mangrum was with the Lotz House when he provided photographs in 1996. The saddle and coat were on loan from the Tennessee State Museum.

Adams is buried in lot with parents in Pulaski's Maplewood Cemetery. Georgianna raised their six children. She was living in St. Louis, Missouri when she passed away in 1905, and buried there.

A tribute to Adams, by Col. James R. Binford, was in a 1902 *Confederate Veteran* (Volume 10, page 457). He wrote, "Gen. John Adams was a knightly man without the royalty usually attached to that class. He was a true type of American, or rather Southern, soldier-ever modest, conservative, brave, and patriotic. He seemed not to know fear. To do his duty at all times and under all circumstances was ever his desire. No truer or braver officer ever gave his life in defense of his beloved Southland." Binford recalled his death, similar to other accounts detailed above. He continued, "History has never done him justice, and I hope Tennesseans will see to it that the page that records his deeds is one of the brightest that adorns Southern history, for she never gave the South a truer, better, or braver officer."

Anderson, Samuel Read: born 17 FEB 1804 in Bedford Co., VA, died 2 JAN 1883

Anderson was one of seven Confederate generals of that name. He immigrated to Kentucky and then to Tennessee. He permanently settled in Nashville. He was second in command of the 1st Tennessee in the Mexican War. Thus Governor Isham Harris made Anderson a major general of Tennessee state troops in 1861, and he was commissioned a brigadier in the Confederate army on 9 July 1861. He commanded a brigade under Loring by September 1861. It was in the Monterey Division of Loring's Army of the Northwest. That division was based out of Monterey, on the Parkersburg-Staunton Turnpike; it was commanded by Brig. Gen. Henry Rootes Jackson. Anderson's brigade fought well at Cheat Mountain. Loring and Stonewall Jackson's separation ended Loring's command over Anderson, who was transferred to Johnston's army in time for the Peninsula Campaign. His Tennessee regiments fought well alongside Hood's at Eltham's Landing on 7 May 1862. His arrival at the critical time won praise from his division commander. But Anderson was 58 and retired from active duty due to ill health, several days after the battle. He worked in conscription for Tennessee for the remained of the war. After independence was lost he returned to Nashville to work in the mercantile business. He died there on 2 January 1883, and was buried in City Cemetery.

Anderson was 57 when his Confederate service began. This was an era when 50 was considered old. His grave in Nashville's City Cemetery has plaque indicating he was a postmaster in the city, 1853-61. His third wife was born Susan Trousdale. After secession she was a member of Ladies Soldiers' Friend Society (L.S.F.S.). The name survives as a civilian reenacting group, from 1984 to the present (2022).

Baldwin, William Edward: born 18 July 1827 in Statesburg, SC, died 19 FEB 64

Baldwin moved at a very early age, with his family, to Columbus, Mississippi. He had an affinity for books and operated a book and stationary store in antebellum days. Once independence was won he hoped to return to the serene enjoyment of his friends and books. He was in the *Columbus Rifles* since 1845. He went off to war with them and was elected colonel of the 14th Mississippi. His gallant leadership of the 14th is detailed above in the chapter on Adams's Brigade. He had no direct connection with Loring's Division.

Baldwin was imprisoned after being captured at Fort Donelson. After exchange he was promoted to brigadier and given command of his own brigade in Mississippi. He was at Vicksburg (bust at left) and the only general opposed to surrendering. He later wrote, "My command marched over to the trenches and stacked arms with the greatest reluctance, conscious of their ability to hold the position assigned them for an indefinite period of time." He died when a stirrup broke and he suffered a fall. He is buried in Friendship Cemetery, Columbus, with several other Confederate generals.

Barry, Robert L.: born MAR 1834, Lumpkin Co., Georgia, died 30 NOV 1918, Decatur

Barry was born and raised in Lumpkin County in the mountainous northern part of Georgia. At a young age he began working at a wholesale dry goods business up in Chattanooga, Tennessee. Barry enlisted on 15 May 1862. The part he played in forming Barry's Lookout Battery or Lookout Battery is not known. The reason they turned over their guns to Darden's Battery isn't known either. H returned to work at the Chattanooga wholesaler postbellum. He was the superintendent of the Confederate Soldiers Home in Atlanta in 1909 and 1910; about age 65. When he retired he lived with a son in Decatur. His obituary called him, "A man of strong and rugged character."

Grave in Decatur Cemetery, Decatur, Georgia

Barton, Seth Maxwell: born 8 SEP 1829 in Fredericksburg, VA, died 11 APR 1900

Barton graduated from West Point in 1849. He spent most of the following decade serving in New Mexico and Texas, where he may have served with Loring. Barton and all three of his brothers served the Confederacy. Loring's concerns about his poor position at Romney, in western Virginia, led Joe Johnston to send Barton there as an engineer. Barton reported, "For a small force this point [Romney] is indefensible." This brought on the irreparable split between Jackson and Loring.

Barton was promoted to brigadier in March 1862. Later in 1862 Barton was assigned to Vicksburg and his brigade was engaged in the victory at Chickasaw Bayou. His Georgia brigade was in Stevenson's Division at Champion Hill. They were captured at Vicksburg and exchanged. Barton got command of Armistead's Brigade, as Lewis Armistead was killed at Gettysburg. Barton's Georgians became Stovall's Brigade in the Army of Tennessee. Barton joined his new brigade in North Carolina. He led them in action at New Berne in early 1864. Ironically, New Berne was the birthplace of Armistead. Barton was captured during Lee's April 1865 retreat toward Appomattox, and spent the rest of the war in prison. Barton died in Washington, D.C. and was buried in Arlington Cemetery. The cemetery was located on the Lee property to penalize them, yet the remains of Confederates rest there.

Baskerville, Henry Embra Coleman: b. 14OCT1817 in Mecklenburg Co., VA, died 1900
Baskerville attended Hampden-Sydney and became a merchant in Petersburg, and then in Richmond. He was Loring's assistant commissary of subsistence beginning in late 1861, but resigned in 1862. He was a wholesale grocer in Richmond, where he died 14 January 1900. He is buried there in Hollywood Cemetery.

Berryhill, William Harvey: born 4 MAY 1828 in Pickens Co., AL, killed 15 DEC 1864

Berryhill's lettres to his wife are more than enough to have this lieutenant in the 43rd Mississippi, Adams's Brigade, added to these entries. He was killed before Nashville. Berryhill and his family moved to Choctaw County, in central Mississippi, in 1834. He married in 1850, and left his wife Mary and seven children when the Yankees killed him. Berryhill wrote his wife the day after Franklin; see Franklin chapter.

Berryhill provides an example of the long lost stories of suffering of the Confederate people. During the 1864 Tennessee campaign Yankees brought hell to Berryhill's family. They burst into his home and destroyed virtually everything the family owned. Dishes were broken. Pillows, mattresses, and linens were slashed with swords. Sacks of flour and meal were ripped open and poured out. Family records were torn out of their Bible.

Their furniture was piled up under the front porch so that a fire could be easily started to burn the house to the ground. As the enemy prepared to leave, they began to set the fires. Mary begged the commanding officer to spare their home, saying that a roof over their heads would be all she would be able to give her children for Christmas. Three-year-old Mattie, who was born with a winning personality and plenty of spunk, interceded also, stepping forward and putting her foot down at burning her house, and charming some of the enemy soldiers. But it was not enough to stop one fire from being set under the porch. Fortunately, as the soldiers left, Mary and the children were able to extinguish it.

Mary Berryhill had saved their home, but on or about Christmas she learned her husband had been killed near Nashville. J.W. Cook, also of the 43rd Mississippi, wrote of it in a 1909 issue of *Confederate Veteran* (Vol. 17, page 159). He mistakenly recalled they were to the left of Franklin Pike. On the 15th they were left of Granny White Pike, which led out to the Franklin Pike. But he says they were first attacked at 10 a.m., which could not have been the main line. It might have been some initial enemy move on the old main line, the skirmish line that crossed Montgomery Hill.

"Late in the afternoon the extreme left of our army gave way when the enemy the enemy began rapidly turning our left flank. To prevent that we were ordered to move by the right flank double-quick. A soldier was shot and fell out of the column. Thinking it was a mess mate, I ran back some one hundred and fifty yards and found it was Lieutenant Berryhill, of the next company, and that he was dead. Retracing my steps as fast as I could, I found that the command was rapidly falling back. Just then Lt. Pat Henry of General Adams's staff, came along and, taking in the situation, stopped about forty of us and commanded us to 'deploy.' In a moment the little skirmish line was formed. He then commanded 'Forward,' and in another minute the line was in the trenches hotly engaging the three long blue lines of enemy, who were trying hard to pass our chevaux-de-frise. We held them long enough to reform our main line of battle, when we were run over and captured." The mention of the chevaux-de-frise seems to confirm this was the 15th, as it would have taken some time to construct; time not available on the 16th.

Brother, S. Newton Berryhill wrote an obituary in the Columbus, Mississippi *Democrat*. It concluded, "In every position he held in the army, Lieut. Berryhill discharged his duties faithfully, won the love and respect of his subordinates, and the confidence and esteem of his superiors. He was a respectful and obedient son, a kind brother, an affectionate husband and father, a good citizen, a faithful soldier, and better than all, an humble follower of his Savior, having lived for years a pious and useful member of the Methodist Protestant Church."

Bethune, William Calvin: born 20 September 1833, died 4 June 1881

Lt. Col. Bethune was in command of the 57th Alabama, Scott's Brigade at Peach Tree Creek. He was severely wounded at Peach Tree Creek. Sgt. Joel D. Murphree wrote his wife afterward. He described the death of his brother-in-law. "…Maj. Arnold was killed in trying to save Lt. Col. Bethune. Col. Bethune was wounded severely and Maj. Arnold went to him, and pulled him into a gully and when he stepped out of the gully was shot dead." Bethune's grave photo may be found on line, and indicates he became a doctor. He is buried in Abbeville, Henry County, Alabama. Another site indicates his house has a Historic Chattahoochee Commission marker. It indicates: "This rare, dual front door, double pen Creole cottage was constructed circa 1840 on the military three-notch road, now Kirkland Street. It is the oldest remaining structure in Abbeville. Earliest known owner was Confederate Colonel Calvin Bethune, M.D. …"

Binford, James R.: born 8 June 1839 at Duck Hill, MS, died 3 October 1918 in Duck Hill
At the beginning of the war he was a student at Kentucky Military Institute. He enlisted in the McClung Rifles which was in the 15th Mississippi, and was appointed adjutant. He quickly proved his bravery at Mill Springs (aka, Fishing Creek) Kentucky where he took the flag forward. Lt. Col. Binford commanded the 15th Mississippi, of Adams's Brigade at Nashville. He was quoted extensively in the chapter on Nashville. He wrote of the death of his wife in *Confederate Veteran* (Vol. 21, page 303) in 1913. He wrote, "On February 28, 1866, I married Frances L. Campbell, a God-given wife (standing behind him in photograph). We shared each other's joys and sorrows…On February 21, 1913, the loving, all-wise Heavenly Father, knowing her patient suffering from disease, said: 'Come up higher.'" The entry for Col. Mike Farrell (below) mentions Binford writing from Duck Hill. He died there and is buried in Duck Hill Cemetery.

Jefferson Davis died at the New Orleans home of Judge Charles Fenner on 6 December 1889, and was interred temporarily in magnificent Metairie Cemetery in New Orleans. Hollywood Cemetery in Richmond had offered Varina a lot and in the fall of 1891 she chose an imposing circular lot. A special train arrived from New Orleans on 30 May 1893. Binford (front far right) was part of the special escort aboard, with 300 family members and guests. His reburial there took place the next day.

Boone, Francis Marion: born 19 JAN 1822 in Lincoln Co., TN, killed 6 MAY 1864

The subject's Boone line emigrated from England to Maryland, then through both Carolinas. Then our subject's father moved to Lincoln County, Tennessee, where he born. South Carolina's great general Francis Marion was the apparent inspiration in his name. The 1830's Chickasaw cession in Mississippi led the family to the newly created Tishomingo County, where they were the first white family to settle. Francis Marion Boone's education there included Rienzi Academy. One of the founders had a daughter named Ursula Patton, and she married Boone on 15 February 1840. Their plantation was near Rienzi, where they raised four children. Boone, his father, and an in-law built twenty miles of Mobile & Ohio roadbed in the area. A new town along the line was Booneville, named for them. These were industrious people that helped create a civilization so it is no surprise to find Boone was elected into the Mississippi legislature.

As Mississippi seceded Boone became involved in recruiting what became the 26th Mississippi Infantry, organized in Iuka, Tishomingo County, on 10 September 1861. Boone was their lieutenant colonel. They fought gallantly at Fort Donelson, only to be surrendered. Boone was in prison at Fort Warren, in Boston Harbour, for about a year. After being exchanged Boone and the 26th were in Tilghman's Brigade. Boone led them at Champion Hill.

It is unusual to find regiments transferred east to the Army of Northern but the 26th was. The Mississippi brigade of Joseph Davis took heavy losses at Gettysburg. Then they learned the U.S. Army was ravaging their homeland. Some desertions resulted, and a new infusion of blood was needed. The 26th arrived on 12 April 1864. Thus they arrived in time to fight in Lee's victory in the Wilderness. Boone was trying to get an unobstructed view of the field when he was shot in the forehead. He was buried in an unmarked grave along the Plank Road. Death left his poor widow with four children.

Borden, Thomas James: born circa 1833 in North Carolina, died 1876 in Mobile, AL

Borden is shown as a lieutenant colonel on the 10 December 1864 organization, as commanding the 6th Mississippi in Adams's. This was due to Colonel Lowry, of the 6th, being in command of Adams's Brigade. Borden enlisted in Brandon in May 1861. When the regiment was consolidated in the spring 1865 he was as supernumerary, thus he was paroled as a private at Citronelle, Alabama on 4 May 1865. He had married Bettie Sarah Byrn (born in Tunica, 1848) in 1860. He is buried at Griffin Cemetery in Moss Point, Mississippi. He and Bettie had five children; she lived until 1925.

Borden is buried in the Borden-Watkins family plot, The urn has his initials on it. It is positioned over grave of his daughter Rinnie's.

Borden enlisted at Brandon, east of Jackson. Moss Point is in the Pascagoula area on the coast. Perhaps his wife was from there.

Bouanchaud, Joseph Alcide: born 16 AUG 1838 in Louisiana, died 7 AUG 1886 at home

Pierre Bouanchaud, born in Nantes, France, was the father of Alcide. He settled in Pointe Coupee Parish and married Charlotte Saizan in 1831. Alcide was born on False River. When he was 14 he was tutored in preparation for a college in Elizabethtown, Kentucky. Upon his return he entered the office of Clerk of Court, Pointe Coupee, as a deputy. In 1860 he married Amelia Herbert, the daughter of a sugar planter. Alcide was a lieutenant in the Pointe Coupee Artillery, which he would later captain as Bouanchaud's. Alcide enlisted on 20 June 1861, apparently in New Orleans. This record was found in a 1920 publication of the Louisiana State Library; *Louisiana Confederate Soldiers and Louisiana Confederate Commands.* A fellow artillery officer, Lt. John McQuaide left quite a tribute regarding Nashville: "I often see that man in my dreams as he was in that hell-hole of fire and bursting shells, just as calm as ever, seizing a sponge staff from a dead cannoneer (H. Decoux was mortally wounded) and using it in his place, again casting his eye along the sights for better range, then speaking cheeringly to the men, never noticing that he was exposed without support." After the war he returned home and became a planter. He later was elected Clerk of Court, and held that position until 1868, when he was elected Parish Judge. His first wife died and he married her sister Eugenia Helene Herbert in 1871. Alcide died nine days prior to his 48th birthday, at home in New Roads. Author Alcee Fortier wrote of Bouanchaud, "…besides being a courageous soldier, a clear headed commander, an impartial and just jurist, and an able advocate also was an upright citizen, always taking an active interest in the public welfare and deporting himself as an accomplished gentleman." The captain was buried at the Saint Mary's Catholic Cemetery; the cemetery is not located at the church.

Bouanchaud is buried in Saint Mary's Catholic Cemetery, New Roads, Louisiana. Randall Jarreau sent the photo to the author in 2008. He pointed out the monument is Woodmen of the World style, and that the cemetery is not located by the church. Alcide's wife, above, was Eugenia Herbert (silent "t" in French pronunciation). The author's wife pointed out she appears to have pierced ears for the ivory earrings

Brown, William N.: born circa 1826 in Tennessee, died 18 JUN 1887 in Gonzales, Texas
Brown was lieutenant colonel of the 20th Mississippi when John Adams took command of Tilghman's old brigade. *Reminiscences of Mississippi in Peace and War* (p. 187) says Brown was from Bolivar County. He was a planter and merchant and served in the Mexican War. That experience led to his becoming captain of the McGehee Rifles, of the 20th Mississippi. *Confederate Colonels* has him captured at Fort Donelson and Vicksburg. He was wounded twice at Franklin, disabling from further field duty. He married Innes Thornton in 1865. They moved to Victoria, Texas by 1880. He was a livestock dealer. He moved to Gonzales, Texas for his health, died there, and is buried there in Masonic Cemetery. A book of Confederate burials in Texas shows a broken grave marker.

Buford, Abraham born 18 JAN 1829 in Woodford County, KY, died 9 JUN 1884
Buford had commanded cavalry in Tennessee, but on 30 January 1863 he received orders transferring him to Pemberton's command in Mississippi. Pemberton did not have a command for him, but Franklin Gardner, commanding at Port Hudson, created a brigade for him. Sterling Price wanted it in the Trans-Mississippi, but it remained in Mississippi.

In early April 1863 Buford's Brigade was at Jackson, Mississippi, where Pemberton was headquartered. In mid-April they were ordered to Bragg's Army of Tennessee. An enemy cavalry raid, under Grierson, was launched into Mississippi on 17 April. The next day Buford was at Montgomery, Alabama when Joe Johnston ordered him to halt. Two of his regiments had already moved east toward Bragg, but the rest were ordered back to Mississippi. By 4 May Pemberton decided Buford was not needed in Jackson. Grant had crossed the Mississippi River and was moving north. Buford was brought to the Big Black River bridge, and the next day was placed in Loring's Division. The brigade was with Loring's for the next ten months, as covered in Mississippi chapter, above. His raised relief below, is at Vicksburg.

Abraham Buford was reassigned to Forrest on 2 March 1864. Buford's Brigade became Scott's. Thomas Moore Scott led it aggressively in the Army of Tennessee. Buford went onto fame with his cavalry division. Forrest gave Buford the credit for the masterpiece victory at Brice's Crossroads. Buford returned to Kentucky after the war, and resumed breeding Thoroughbreds. Financial problems led him to commit suicide. He is buried alongside his wife and son, in Lexington.

Colbert, Wallace Bruce: born 17 NOV 1834 in MS, killed at Bentonville 21 MAR 65
Confederate Colonels says Colbert graduated from the University of Alabama in 1852. He became a planter in Mississippi and served the state in the Secession Convention. Colbert led Hebert's Brigade at Iuka and Corinth. He became a POW at Vicksburg. He led the 40th Mississippi thereafter. Colbert was absent from the 40th at Peach Tree Creek due to illness. He was wounded at Franklin, and killed at Bentonville. He is buried at Oakwood Cemetery in Raleigh. Oakwood is noteworthy as the resting place of six North Carolina governors as well as Colbert's fellow Confederates.

Cowan, James Jones: born 5 AUG 1830 in Warren County, MS, died 1 OCT 1898
Biographical and Historical Memoirs of Mississippi has an entry on Cowan. It says he was one of twelve children. He attended Mississippi College at Clinton, just west of Jackson, and then to Cumberland in Lebanon, Tennessee. He married Miss Maria Louisa Craig in 1850, when he was twenty. He became part owner of a firm, Cowan & Chapin. "Commencing with small capital, he pursued his business so earnestly, so ably and so successfully that upon the outbreak of the war he had accumulated a comfortable fortune. The call for arms met from him a prompt and ready response, and with the enthusiasm, sturdy devotion and disinterested patriotism (U.S.?) that inspired Southern hearts, he left his large business interests and raised and equipped a battery of artillery, well known throughout the bloody conflict which followed as Cowan's battery. Attached at first to Colonel (William) Wither's regiment, the only regiment of artillery ever organized in the Confederate service, he was stationed at Haine's Bluff to defend Yazoo river." See Cowan's Battery, above, for their history.

Cowan's may have fired the last shots in the last significant battle, Fort Blakely. They fought until surrounded. As a prisoner of war Cowan found himself in a sadistic prison. "Enduring all the horrors of prison life on Ship island, a dangerous spell of illness, brought on by anxiety of mind and privations of body, proved nearly fatal, when the end of the conflict secured his release. Broken in health, his fortune swept away, Captain Cowan commenced anew the struggle for a competency, and although he met with varied fortunes and had many ups and downs, he continued to persevere, and is now one of the leading and successful business men of Vicksburg." The entry concluded describing his good health. "He is a fine looking gentleman, his hair and beard quite gray; is five feet ten inches in height, and still, in his upright and dignified carriage, shows evidences of his early military life."

Cowan's business was in cotton, and it probably involved travel. He was visiting Tennessee in 1898 when he was accidentally struck by a train. He died on 1 October and was buried in Cedar Hill Cemetery (a.k.a., The City of Vicksburg Cemetery). Wife Maria is also. His monument is inscribed: "Lord, thou hast been our dwelling place in all generations." They are in good company with some

5,000 Confederate soldiers. Among them are generals, John Bowen, Isham Garrott, and Martin Green. The most unusual burial must be some of the remains of Old Douglas, the camel (see entry for Old Douglas!).

This Vicksburg house was James Cowan's relative. One source has W.T. Cowan, who also served in Cowan's Battery; another has wife of a Cowan. It is more well known as Pemberton's headquarters during the siege. It is a tourist site, where visitors may see the parlour where the decision to surrender was made.

Croom, Cicero Stephens: born 12 DEC 1839 in Quincy, Florida, died 29 JUL 1884 in AL
Croom was well educated, and that was an asset for a staff officer. He was on the staff of Maj. Gen. John Horace Forney. They were captured at Vicksburg, and after exchange Croom served for a time with Loring's Division. He began service at Montevallo, Alabama before the division joined the Army of Tennessee in Georgia. Apparently before the campaign ended he was assigned back to Forney, and they served in the Trans-Mississippi. Croom had moved to Alabama before the war, and returned to marry Mary Marshall on 4 February 1875. He suffered from bronchitis and was hoping to benefit from mountain air around Asheville, North Carolina when he died there on 29 July 1884. Croom papers are at the University of South Alabama in Mobile.

Crossland, Edward, born 30 JUN 1827 in Hickman Co., KY, died 11 SEP 1881 in KY
Crossland had been a lawyer in Clinton, Hickman County, and sheriff. He served as a Kentucky state representative. He was married to Mary Hess. His Confederate service began in April 1861. He was promoted to colonel of the 7th Kentucky on 25 May 1862. They were in Buford's Brigade, thus his brief service in Loring's Division. Postbellum, he was an attorney and judge in Mayfield. He was also elected to the U.S. Congress. He died in Mayfield and is buried there in Maplewood Cemetery.

Cunningham, Columbus J.L.: born 11 AUG 1829 in GA, died 10 NOV 1908 in AL
Confederate Colonels has Cunningham studying law in Tuskegee, Alabama and going on to practice law and edit a newspaper. He had been a second lieutenant in the 1st Alabama, but resigned when his wife, Harriet, became "partially demented." He was a major in the 57th Alabama in April 1863, and colonel, 26 December. During the Atlanta Campaign he is shown as colonel on returns of 10 June, 30 June, and 10 July. The 57th Alabama report for Peachtree Creek was filed by Capt. Augustus L. Milligan, as Lt. Col. Bethune was severely wounded. Milligan still commanded the 57th on the 31 July return. Cunningham returned to command by the 31 August return. The absences may have been leaves to take care of his children, apparently due to Harriet's illness. His service record contains numerous requests for such leaves. He was wounded at Franklin. Postbellum he was a lawyer and judge in Union Springs. He is buried there in Oak Hill.

Daniels, John M.: born 14 FEB 1832 in North Carolina, died 1 APR 1865 in Tennessee
Private Daniels may have never met General Loring, though he served under him in the 15th Mississippi. He lived near Marietta, North Carolina, and married Caroline Grantham in 1858. They lived with his parents for a while but moved to Mississippi and began farming and having children. Daniels enlisted on 1 August 1862. The Army of Tennessee was marching north in Tennessee when one of his daughters died on 17 November 1864, which was Caroline's birthday. Private Daniels was wounded in his left forearm at Franklin. A surgeon operated on him, and he was still recovering when the U.S. Army captured Franklin after Hood's retreat away from Nashville. The enemy captured him and sent him to a hospital in Nashville. He caught small pox and his arm would not heal. He was first buried at City Cemetery, but the Confederates were later moved to Mount Olivet. The Sons of Confederate Veterans Camp 28 organized living history tours at the cemetery for 23 years. Daniels was portrayed in 1995 and 1999.

Darden, Putnam: born 10 MAR 1836 in Jefferson Co., Mississippi, died 17 July 1888
Darden was from Jefferson County, north of Natchez. He graduated from the University of Mississippi at age 20. Biographical and Historical Memoirs of Mississippi state he was "a leader of the people, and was especially warm in his advocacy of the rights of the husbandman, his brilliant mind, his eloquence as a speaker and his sound judgment being all brought to bear in their interests." When The Jefferson Flying Artillery was formed Darden was a lieutenant. Refer to sketch of Darden's Battery above. He returned home after the war and continued farming. He allied himself with the Patrons of Husbandry. He "soon became the most zealous worker in this organization…His fidelity…was rewarded and he was elected master of the Patrons of Husbandry of the United States…" The entry for Darden names his four wives and children borne by them. One of these wives was Mary Love Harper, daughter of his former battery commander, William Harper. They married on 21 January 1868. Putnam died at age 52 and is buried in the Darden Cemetery in Jefferson County (southwest of Fayette).

Deshler, James: born 18FEB1833 in Tuscumbia, AL, killed 20SEP1863 at Chickamauga
Deshler graduated from West Point in 1854. He was in the Utah expedition which may have been his first operation with Loring. If not he served under Loring as acting chief of artillery in western Virginia in 1861. He was shot in a skirmish and on recovery he served as chief of artillery to Maj. Gen. Theophilus H. Holmes. They were in the Seven Days, and Deshler went with Holmes when he was sent to command the Trans-Mississippi. Deshler commanded a brigade at Fort Hindman, where they were surrendered. After being exchanged Deshler's brigade and another Texas brigade were combined and sent to the Army of Tennessee. Deshler was killed by a shell at Chickamauga. He is buried in Oakwood Cemetery in his native Tuscumbia. The brigade became Granbury's in 1864. Brig. Gen. Hiram Granbury and Cleburne were all killed close General John Adams.

Donelson, Daniel Smith: born 23JUN1801 in Sumner County, TN, died 17APR1863
Donelson was a nephew of President Andrew Jackson. The uncle's military talents may have inspired Donelson to attend West Point. He graduated in 1825, but resigned the following year. He returned to Sumner County, north of Nashville, to become a planter. He was active in the militia, and at the time of secession, was the speaker of the Tennessee House of Representatives. As a brigadier general of state troops, he became a brigadier in the Confederate army and was assigned to western Virginia, under Loring, on 9 July 1861. He was in the Cheat Mountain Campaign. By 16 December Donelson and his Tennessee brigade were at Port Royal, South Carolina, thus ending service with Loring. They were sent west in June 1862 to Bragg's army, then at Tupelo. Donelson commanded a brigade in Cheatham's Division, fighting very well at Perryville and Murfreesborough. Active duty must have taken a toll on the 61-year-old. He died at Montvale Springs, Tennessee on 17 April 1863, and is buried at the Presbyterian Church at Hendersonville, Sumner County.

Doss, Washington Lafayette: born 8 JAN 1825 in Pickens Co., AL, died 25 JAN 1900
Doss became a farmer in Oktibbeha County in eastern Mississippi. He was a Mexican War veteran and married Noraline A. Moore. Doss had been a Confederate private in the 14th Mississippi, but was promoted to major 4 June 1861. They were surrendered at Fort Donelson, and imprisoned in Fort Warren. Doss signed the autograph book of Joseph Palmer, a Tennessean who would later command a brigade in the Army of Tennessee. It indicates Doss was from Choctaw Agency, Mississippi. He was exchanged and promoted to colonel of the 14th in October 1862. The 14th was added to Adams's Brigade in July 1863. *Confederate Colonels* points out Doss was arrested on 25 June 1864 on unspecified charges. It also says a fellow prisoner had said he was a "pleasant, clever, gentleman." Doss farmed near West Point, site of one of Forrest's 1864 victories, postbellum. He died at home there, and is buried at Greenwood Cemetery in West Point.

Drake, Jabez Leftwich: born 15 April 1832 in (Huntsville?) Alabama, killed 20 July 1864
Confederate Colonels has Drake as a farmer in Leake County, Mississippi before the war. Leake is just northeast of Jackson. He was married to Samilda Clearman. He had been a lieutenant in the 27th Mississippi in April 1861. By March 1862 he was in the 33rd and promotions followed. He was promoted colonel on 5 January 1864. He was killed at

Peachtree Creek, while waving his sword and cheering his men on. Mathew Andrew Dunn was in the 33rd. He wrote, "We lost our Col. He charged waiving his Sword until he fell." Featherston eulogized Drake as "a gallant and excellent officer. He was buried on the battlefield, but moved to Oakland Cemetery in Atlanta.

Switzerland's *The Lion of Lucerne* inspired this sculpture at Oakland Cemetery. It is for unknown Confederate dead. There is also a Confederate shaft pictured above. Leftists have dumped red paint on it so many times the city may have removed it; site unknown in 2021.

Drane, James W.: born 14 APR 1833 in Columbia County, Georgia, died 8 AUG 1896
Lt. Col. Drane's home is preserved at the French Camp Academy Historic District, on the Natchez Trace Parkway. The James Drane Farmhouse was begun in 1846. His wife was Matilda Shaw. Drane was a politician and housed his family in a log cabin until the house was finished in 1848. It was one of the first frame houses in Choctaw County. It was moved to French Camp in 1981 and restored. Some claim to have seen the image of a man and a woman in the top right-hand window. Might it be the colonel's parents? Or was it the colonel and his second wife, Fannie Hemphill of Rome, Georgia?

Jenkins's Peach Tree Creek volume says, "Born in Georgia, Drane's family had moved to Choctaw County, Mississippi, when he was only three. There, his parents cleared a place in the wilderness in the south part of the county where his father killed 110 deer the first year." The father's father and grandfather were in the Continental Army in the American Revolution. Lt. Col. Drane's company had been The Jackson Rifles. He commanded the 31st Mississippi for the first time at Peach Tree Creek. Jenkins describes him as "naturally energetic" and "always attentive." He wrote Drane was wounded twice as he led the 31st forward up a slope. He had both a head wound and a bullet through his right cheek. He was hit three more times at the crest of the ridge. These last wounds included his left arm shattered by a minnie ball, a shell wound to his side, and a bullet in his right foot. How Drane survived is hard to imagine. Jenkins says he was confined to bed for over twelve months, yet he recovered toward the end of the war.

In 1896 a comrade delivered part of Drane's eulogy: "A braver and truer soldier never entered the Confederate Army. He was always at his post of duty and never flinched in time of danger." Indeed, Drane's five wounds at Peach Tree Creek were some evidence.

Dunlop, Isaac Leroy: born 21 SEP 1835 in York District, SC, died 9 SEP 1864 in GA
Confederate Colonels tells Dunlop was a wealthy planter in antebellum days and worked as a bookkeeper in Warren, Bradley County, Arkansas. He married Elmira C. Franklin. Dunlop was colonel of the 9th Arkansas on 12 January 1862, and led it at Shiloh. General Bowen complimented Dunlop's "cool courage and self-possession." The 9th was in Buford's Brigade by Champion Hill. It would be in Reynolds's Brigade of the Army of Tennessee in 1864. Dunlop died near Lovejoy's Station on 9 September 1864, and is probably buried at the Pat Cleburne Cemetery (below), Jonesborough, Georgia.

Dunn, Mathew Andrew: born 15 DEC 1833 in E. Feliciana Parish, LA, died 30 NOV '64
Lettres of Dunn were published in the *Journal of Mississippi History* in several issues in 1939. Dunn married Virginia Lenore Perkins Hunt of Amite County, Mississippi. Amite and East Feliciana bordered each other; hence, it was natural for them to move there and buy a 320 acre farm in 1859. On 1 March 1863 Dunn enlisted at Liberty, the county seat, in the Amite Defenders, which became Company K in the 33rd Mississippi. It was commanded by Captain Moses Jackson. The colonel of the 33rd was a lawyer in Liberty, David Wiley Hurst. He was severely wounded at Corinth, and could not return to duty.

Dunn wrote his wife, apparently nicknamed 'Stumpy.' In 13 October 1863 he wrote from Meridian. He mentions seeing a scene he hoped "my eyes will never behold again…" of seeing men shot for desertion. In concluding he says to "Tell the Darkies I want to try and come home to See them gather the crop." This was obviously not meant to be offensive. In November they were north of Jackson, at Canton. Dunn wrote that he had tried to get a furlough, but "an order came from Gen Loring today-not to let any off…" On 31 March 1864 he wrote from Demopolis. "I am nearly crazy for a letter to hear how every thing is going on…These beautiful Spring days makes me want to be planting Corn very much, I think if I outlive this war and get back home, I will enjoy farming better than I ever did." On 19 April 1864 he wrote from Montevallo. Many things troubled him. He didn't like hearing of any girls marrying Yankee officers. He heard a woman "had lost pretty well all She had-Supposed to be Stolen by negroes. But she ought not leave her house entirely alone these times." Again his conclusion included, "Tell the Darkeys howdy for me."

Loring's Division was in Georgia in May 1864. On 6 July he wrote from Chattahoochee River, near Atlanta. Dunn is again distressed that he is not receiving lettres from his wife. "I have received nothing from you Since the 20th of May…you can imagine my feelings... I have been looking for a letter from you every day…" He explains Georgia campaign. "We have repulsed the Enemy every time they attacked us. But still they force us to retreat by flank movements-all we ask of them is to meet us Squarely. But they avoid that whenever they can. I don't know how it will terminate. But one thing I feel satisfied about, that is General Johnston will manage the affair as well as any other General-I think he is doing all he can to prevent Sherman from reinforcing Grant in Virginia." Dunn was concerned that Johnston wasn't cutting off Sherman's supplies, but figured he had a reason. He also wrote of Polk being killed. "His death seemed to throw a gloom over the whole army, especially his Corps. I think he was a true Christian as well as a good Commander. He said she can show what he has written to her friends "as I have withheld all Secrets and Soft talk…" As Dunn was a planter he apparently had a servant with him. "Andrew is fatter than you ever saw him. He stays at the Commissary and helps to cook for the Regt. as it Saves a Soldier and he is in a safe place and properly cared for." He tells Andrew takes care of clothes, "And the negroes get more Clothes than they want."

He continued writing the next day, on the same lettre. In his conclusion he says, "Tell Cary to let me know how his puppy is getting on and his name-Tell the Darkies to keep all things Straight. Tell Levi to eat Some catfish for me-Respects to all." He signed off as Mat. He continued on the 8th. "I will remember you all in my petitions to God and I hope he will continue to bless us as he has done."

On 1 August Dunn wrote from Atlanta. He gives details of Peach Tree Creek and of the death of Col. Jabez Drake; entry above. He mentions those they know who were killed or badly wounded. It makes him reflect on his own mortality. "Oh my love if I could only see you and our dear little ones again what a pleasure it would be. But God only knows whether I will have that privilege or not. I want you to try to raise them up right. Train them while they are young-And if I am not spared to see you I hope we will meet in a happier world. I want you to be fully reconciled for it if I am wounded I will be home as soon as I can and if I am killed I hope that I am prepared to go-But my daily prayers are that we may meet on earth again in peace and health…" Dunn mentioned, "Andrew is well-Tell the Darkies they must think of my hardships and try to do the best they can for me at home." After signing he added, "Andrew has just come in with a nice Bucket of rice & squash & a very fancy shirt for me. He keeps me in good clothes…"

Dunn's last lettre in the series is when Hood was marching across northern Alabama, planning to move into Tennessee. It was written from Gadsden on 21 October. Dunn explained they had been operating in Sherman's rear. "I am glad to hear that you are sending me some clothes as I am barefooted & naked. Since we have been on this raid I have worn out every thing I had nearly. It has been an awful time on every thing." He added, "Andrew kept me in such things while I had him…" It appears he started Andrew home to Mississippi. He signs with, "May God bless you; Yours M.A. Dunn."

The lettre from Gadsden may have been Mathew Andrew Dunn's last. He was killed at Franklin. Almost all of the Confederate dead were buried on the field and later moved to the nearby McGavock Cemetery. No state had more killed at Franklin than Mississippi. Their monument claims 424. Many of Featherston's dead are in the Mississippi sections. They include L. Dunn in Section 24. Joseph A. Dunn of the 33rd Mississippi was in Company K and is also in Section 24. They might be relatives.

<u>Dyer, Samuel Morton: born 6 OCT 1829 in Albemarle, VA, died 8 OCT 1892</u>
Dyer enlisted in the 3rd Mississippi in Benton, Mississippi on 25 September 1861. He was a lieutenant colonel when wounded at Franklin. His right leg had to be amputated. Such severely wounded were generally left in Franklin. He was captured there on 17 December as the Army of Tennessee retreated though Franklin. He was sent to Camp Chase, Ohio. He survived the war and married Mary R. Grayson in Yazoo County, on 24 August 1866.

Dyer's father was Francis Bickley Dyer (1798-1838). His mother was Sarah Gassaway White (1801-1883). The 1850 U.S. Census shows Samuel Dyer in Saltville, Virginia. He moved to Mississippi prior to the 1860 Census, which found him in Yazoo County. He was back there per the 1870, as a merchant, and 1880 specifies him as a dry goods merchant. He died in Benton, Yazoo County. His headstone indicates he was a colonel. He is buried in Glenwood Cemetery in Yazoo City.

Elcan, Archibald Liebig: born 20 OCT 1844 in Fayette Co., TN, died FEB 1916 in Calif.
Elcan joined the army before he was 18, in 1862. During most of Loring's service in Mississippi, he was on his staff as an aide-de-camp. In February 1864 he joined the 7th Tennessee Cavalry, which was with Forrest. After the war he read medicine and practiced in Tipton County and in Memphis. He moved to Los Angles, California for his health in about 1906. An obituary is in a 1916 *Confederate Veteran* (Volume 24, page 178).

Farrell, Michael: born circa 1838 in Ireland or New York, died 25 DEC 1864
Let us Die like Brave Men says Colonel Farrell was born in Ireland, and grew up in New York City. Work in brick-laying took him to Grenada, Mississippi. Farrell led the 15th Mississippi at Franklin. *The Battle of Franklin* by Robert A. Banks (Captain Company D, 37th Mississippi) says Farrell, "a young and brilliant officer, was shot through both legs, the left being so badly shattered it had to be amputated. He spent an agonizing night on the field, and the next morning was gentle carried by faithful friends to the nearby home of Honorable John McGavock, where he remained until death relieved him of his sufferings" Death came on Christmas. The *McGavock Confederate Cemetery* indicates he is buried in Section 22.

A tribute to Farrell may be found in *Confederate Veteran* in a 1902 issue Volume 10, page 457). It was submitted by Capt. Thomas Gibson, of Nashville, who was a first cousin of General Adams, and a member of his staff. He quoted from a lettre from Col. James Binford, of the 15th Mississippi. Binford had written to Gibson in 1901: "As to our lamented and brave Mile Farrell, too much cannot be said in his praise. As an officer you know his record, and as a true Southern patriot he fought and died for principle. He did not have a relative in the South, neither did he own one dollar's worth of property. He was a very poor man working at his trade-a brick mason-when the war began, and even the horse he rode and loved so dearly (Old Bullet) was a present to him from his command." Binford also related "a rather strange coincidence in connection" to Farrell's death. The same story is largely told by Capt. Robert Banks, above, before the attacks at Franklin. A number of officers were eating when a captain said he thought he would be killed. This led to discussion and Farrell replied, "O, well, boys, that is a soldier's fate. Let us not complain or shrink from it."

Thomas Gibson donated a unique flag to the Tennessee State Historical Society. An image of it is in Bryan Lane's biography of John Adams. It must have been based on the Polk's Corps flags, yet modified. A newspaper article was written at the time of the presentation and stated, "made and presented to Gen. Adams' brigade by a lady of Mississippi in 1863." Lane indicated this is likely the flag Farrell accepted from Mrs. Lattimer, of Canton, after the 15th Mississippi won the drill contest.

Farrell was remembered again in *Confederate Veteran* in 1906 (Volume 14, page 232). The article has a picture of a Shakespeare volume that belonged to Farrell. It had been given to him by a friend from Mississippi. As Hood's army passed thru Tuscumbia, Alabama it was left for safekeeping. By 1906 it had been sent to Col. James R. Binford of Duck Hill, Mississippi. He was to deposit it in the "Hall of History and Fame of the State of Mississippi at Jackson." Perhaps it is still there.

Featherston, Winfield Scott: born Tennessee, 8 AUG 1820, died 28 May 1891 in MS
Featherston was named for Virginian Winfield Scott of U.S. Army fame, likely for his great service in the War of 1812. Scott was in command of the U.S. Army after Virginia seceded. Featherston's parents may have had second thoughts about their son's name. They had Georgia roots, but he was born near Murfreesborough, Rutherford County, Tennessee. He attended an academy Columbus, Georgia. *Confederate Military History* says while he was in school in Georgia, in 1836, he served as a volunteer against the Creeks. The Creek War had essentially ended with Andrew Jackson's victory at Horseshoe Bend in March 1814, but another conflict arose in 1836. Land speculators in Columbus, Georgia, where Featherston was in school, did much to provoke it. It resulted in various troops, commanded by Winfield Scott, rounding up Creeks and sending them to Indian Territory. Perhaps Winfield Scott Featherston met his namesake. Next he studied law in Memphis. He had a law practice in Houston, Mississippi at age 19. His political interests led him to successful stump speaking and election to the U.S. Congress in 1847, and reelection in 1849. His law practice led to a move to Holly Springs in 1857.

South Carolina boldly led the secession movement as the first state to secede, on 20 December 1860. Yet other Deep South states were also making preparations to secede. Mississippi passed a resolution on the last day of November for a Commissioner to proceed to Kentucky. Featherston was Mississippi's commissioner. Perhaps he had contacts from his days in Congress. Kentucky didn't agree to secede.

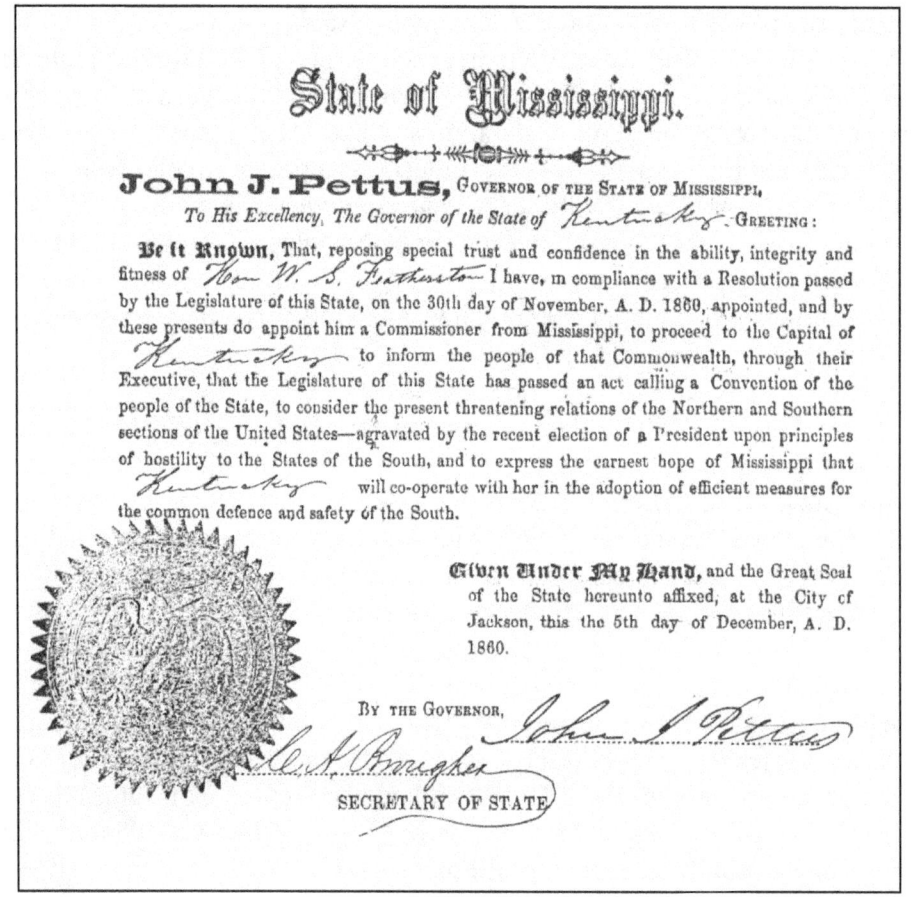

Featherston returned home and recruited an infantry company which became part of the 17th Mississippi. Featherston was elected their colonel. The 17th boarded a train in Corinth on 11 June, and detrained at Manassas Junction six days later. On 16 July 1861 a 35,000 man U.S. Army marched out of Washington City. Beauregard was waiting for them near the railroad junction, Manassas Junction. Featherston's 17th Mississippi was in a brigade commanded by David Rumph Jones. Jones's headquarters were at the Wilbur McLean home. McLean gained notoriety for moving to Appomattox. He was trying to get out the war's way only to find his home where Lee and Grant met. McLean had a ford across Bull Run, and Jones's men were assigned to guard it. It was east of the 21 July battle and Jones was not engaged. *The Confederate General* entry on Jones says he crossed Bull Run late in the afternoon and clashed with the enemy at Little Rocky Run. The U.S. Army had of course been routed and was in full retreat!

Our Virginia army was reorganized on 24 July, and that ended Featherston's time under Jones. His 17th Mississippi was placed in a brigade under Col. Nathan Evans. They won a victory at Ball's Bluff, along the Potomac, on 21 October. Featherston reported on the 17th: "The whole line marched forward in the most admirable order upon a vastly superior force, reserving their fire until within the most effective range; then pouring it in with deadly effect and rushing forward over ground broken in abrupt hills and ravines, and covered with thick woods, without a single halt or waver, until the enemy were literally driven into the river; and this, too, under a heavy fire and after having been under arms almost without intermission for more than thirty-six hours, and while wearied with several long and rapid movements made during the preceding day and night."

Lt. Col. John McGuirk reported, "Colonel Featherston ordered the right and left wings up, thus forming a crescent line, which enabled us with raking fire to cut down the advancing enemy. The men manifested confidence under the coolness of their officers. They seemed fighting a sham battle when above the roar of musketry was heard the command of Colonel Featherston, 'Charge Mississippians, charge! Drive them into the Potomac or into eternity! The sound of his voice seemed to echo from the vales of Maryland. The line arose as one man from a kneeling posture, discharged a deadly volley, advanced the crescent line, and thus encircled the invaders, who in terror called for quarter and surrendered." More than 500 were captured by the Mississippians.

Featherston was promoted to brigadier in March 1862. This drew him away from his Mississippi troops and to command a brigade in a division commanded by Daniel Harvey Hill. The regiments were the 27th Georgia, 28th Georgia, 4th North Carolina, and the 49th Virginia. They were in the retreat up the Peninsula, as U.S. troops under McClellan advanced. Illness prevented Featherston from the battle at Seven Pines. Joseph Johnston was wounded there, which led to Robert E. Lee taking command of the army.

Featherston returned to duty for the Seven Days, but he had a brigade of Mississippi infantry units. D.H. Hill may have had objections to Featherston's sick leave, and didn't want him in his division. Hill has been described as acid-tongued so it may have been as well for Featherston to leave. His new brigade was one of six in Longstreet's Division.

Lee's first great breakthrough was at Gaines' Mill on 27 June 1862. Fruitless attacks on the enemy's high-ground position led Lee to order a massive attack. Lee ordered the largest charge on the entire war. It was a three-mile wide assault made by about 32,100 soldiers of sixteen brigades, including Featherston's. The U.S. line broke on the right, centre, and left, almost simultaneously. Most of the credit went to John Bell Hood's brigade. His remarkable career under Lee later brought him to the Army of Tennessee.

Lee attempted to prevent McClellan from retreating near Glendale, in a battle often called Frayser's Farm. Lee hoped to capture McClellan's huge artillery and supply train, but it had passed. Featherston's and Roger Pryor's brigades recoiled from U.S. artillery fire. They regrouped and charged two more times. One of Pryor's regiments called the battle "The Slaughter House." Featherston was severely wounded in the shoulder. Longstreet commended him for his "gallantry and skill." Lee's army captured about 1,800 Yankees and 18 of their cannon. That night, 30 June, McClellan continued his retreat.

The Seven Days ended at Malvern Hill on 1 July. Over a month late McClellan's massive army was still on the James River downstream of Richmond. There was no reason that Yankee could not commence another drive on the Confederate capital. The enemy was building up another army around Washington City. It was commanded by Pope, and he would have close to 63,000 troops. Lee decided to strike before they overwhelmed him. Lee told Stonewall Jackson he wanted Pope "suppressed." Lee sent Jackson's Corps north to destroy Pope's supply base at Manassas Junction. His foot cavalry marched 62 miles in 48 hours. He first cut the railroad, and then took the depot apart. A lieutenant wrote, "To see a starving man eating lobster salad and drinking Rhine wine, bare-footed and in tatters, was curious." From there Jackson moved to Manassas.

Jackson had carefully chosen his position along an unfinished railroad embankment. It was convenient to Thoroughfare Gap, through which Longstreet's Corp was expected. Jackson launched a surprise attack on a Yankee marching column on the 28th. The actual Second Battle of Manassas opened on the 29th. Pope outnumbered Jackson two to one, but only made a series of uncoordinated assaults. The next morning Pope sent word to Washington that he had won a great victory and was about to pursue. Seldom has a general been more confused. Longstreet's Corps had arrived!

Longstreet had commanded a division but now had a five-division corps. Featherston was in Wilcox's, named for Tennessean Cadmus Marcellus Wilcox. Featherston's report on Second Manassas, for Longstreet, indicated he united "with General Jackson's command on my left at the railroad embankment. General Pryor's brigade was placed on the right of mine…" Cadmus Wilcox was acting as the division commanded, but he was ordered to the right to support Hood. Featherston then had command of his brigade and Pryor's.

Pope resumed his offensive against Jackson, not wanting to believe Longstreet was on the field. Longstreet had an outstanding artillery officer, Stephen Dill Lee. He had eighteen cannon so tightly positioned the cannoneers bumped elbows. When their fire enfiladed the Yankee attackers there could be no doubt, Longstreet was there. One Yankee wrote,

"His batteries followed our every movement in this charge in a way I have never seen equaled before or since."

Return to Bull Run: The Campaign and Battle of Second Manassas has some 600 pages for those interested in both armies in the battle. U.S. troops attacking Jackson's Corps, that were north of the Warrenton Turnpike were impeding Longstreet's advance. Lee wanted Jackson to advance and he would not move forward for more than an hour. This volume points out little is known of Jackson's movements between 4 and 6 p.m. This may apply to Featherston as well, for whatever delayed Jackson may have delayed both.

Featherston's Brigade was Longstreet's far left, on Jackson's right, and it seems he may have waited for Jackson to advance. At 4 p.m., twenty minutes after Jackson repulsed the enemy attack, he had three brigades at the eastern edge of Groveton Woods, ready to move forward. Featherston's and Pryor's were there too. These brigades emerged from the timber, probably just after 6 p.m. One Yankee wrote they were "a perfect phalanx of disciplined veteran troops." When Featherston's Brigade suddenly appeared two New York regiments opened fire. Then confusion took over and they halted their fire. Someone had shouted they were firing on their own men. A Pennsylvania battery kept firing while the infantry broke apart and ran. The artillery tried to escape but before they could the Mississippians were running through the guns. Men and horses were falling as they captured three cannon. Other U.S. batteries were being abandoned, but they had given infantry some time to escape.

Featherston wrote of an attack that followed, "The whole line moved forward in rapid and gallant style. The enemy fled after the first well-directed fire through the woods in the direction of the stone house. All the pieces of their artillery were left upon the field and captured." Longstreet was not pleased with Featherston's report. It seems he had not moved quickly enough. But Stonewall hadn't either. It seems his delay had caused Featherston to wait. Was dissatisfaction with Featherston warranted? It is hard to say.

Lee decided to cross the Potomac to Maryland. The campaign culminated at Sharpsburg, and once again Featherston was absent sick. Col. Carnot Posey's 16th Mississippi had been placed in the brigade prior to 2nd Manassas. Posey commanded the brigade at Sharpsburg. Longstreet was impressed and if Featherston did not return from sick leave Lee would have given Posey the brigade.

Featherston returned to duty prior to Fredericksburg, thus keeping his brigade. They were in rifle pits north of the stone fence, and west of the Orange Plank Road. They came under heavy artillery fire. Confederate *Military History* says, "Featherston's brigade was not actively engaged, but lay in line of battle four of those December days and nights in an open field, without shelter and without fire." This was his last battle in Lee's army.

Featherston's departure from Lee's army was related to the enemy's invasion of Mississippi in December 1862. The first campaign to take Vicksburg failed in December, but it obviously not conclusive. Grant's move down the Mississippi Central Railroad came to an abrupt halt when our cavalry played hell in his rear. Van Dorn destroyed his base at Holly Springs and Forrest raided and disrupted the Mobile & Ohio. Grant quickly moved his supply line to the Mississippi River. Featherston wrote Lee about his concerns over Mississippi. He was interested in having his brigade of Mississippi infantry returned home. Lee would not permit Featherston to leave with his brigade, but did allow him to. The transfer was effective 19 January 1863. Chapter above covers that brigade.

When the Army of Tennessee began leaving Tupelo in the winter 1865, Featherston remained behind to collect men on furlough. Col. Wallace Bruce Colbert, of the 40th Mississippi was in command, and killed at Bentonville. Featherston rejoined the army in early April. He was paroled at Greensboro in May. Perhaps he journeyed directly home to Holly Springs. Few generals saw more combat, and he must have felt lucky to survive.

Featherston resumed his law practice in Holly Springs. He served two terms in the Mississippi House of Representatives, from 1876-78, and 1880-82. In the first term he introduced impeachment legislation to oust the carpetbag governor. After his 1882 term he was a judge (photo at right), and later a member of state constitutional convention of 1890.

Fellow Army of Tennessee brigade commander Alfred Vaughan was a planter near Holly Springs. The devastation Lincoln's war brought to the South was overwhelming. Not only was the money declared worthless, the lack of money led asset values to plunge. The 1860 assessed value of real and personal property in Marshall County was $39,514,886. In 1870 it was $6,609,988. With no money there was no demand.

Old Homes of Mississippi includes Featherston's Holly Springs home, known as the Featherston Place. It indicates the house was built in the 1830's, when Featherston was a child. The lower or basement floor contains the family sitting room, dining room, and kitchen. It is called an English basement style, with the front steps leading upstairs, where the parlor and bedrooms are located.

This post card of the author's collection has 1834 as year of construction. It also credits Featherston, along with Judge J.L. Trotter, with framing the Constitution of Mississippi. While Featherston may be unknown to many students of the war, he is not forgotten in Holly Springs.

A source for Featherston is *They Sleep Beneath the Mockingbird: Mississippi Burial Sites and Biographies of Confederate Generals* by Harold Cross; published in 1994. It says Featherston's "death came quietly at 8:50 p.m. on Thursday, May 28, 1891, in his 72nd year, as his residence in Holly Springs, the result of paralysis caused by a stroke. The funeral was on the following day, a beautiful spring afternoon.

Featherston's monument inscription includes: "Christian Gentleman, Statesman, Soldier & Jurist; he filled the full measure of duty and left to posterity a spotless record and an honored name."

Lizzie M. Featherston passed away on 17 September 1878. Her inscription includes: "On living tablets of the heart, her virtues are engraved; then seek not works of art to record her praise."

Three other generals are here: Samuel Benton, Daniel Chevilette Govan, and Edward Carey Walthall. Featherston's Brigade was under Walthall in the retreat out of Tennessee.

Part of the newspaper coverage of Featherston's funeral at Holly Crest Cemetery read: "The old veterans who had seen him in his might and strength, and had followed him who knew no fear, where death was reaping a rich harvest, followed the helpless clay to its last resting place with tearful eyes and solemn step; the muffled drums and funeral march remind them of the vanity of earthly honors. A sorrowful multitude of all classes and conditions surrounded his grave. They had left their various avocations to do the last honors to a man whose place will be hard to fill in our community. As a man he was brave and generous, as a friend he could hardly be excelled, as a public spirited citizen he was always ready with the powers of his intellect and the force of his mighty will to advocate any cause for the good of is town and country, and by the church of which he was a member and had supported liberally with his counsel and material means his loss will be deeply felt."

French, Samuel Gibbs: born 22 NOV 1818 in Gloucester Co., NJ, died 29 APR 1910
French was a fellow division commander to Loring in the Army of Mississippi and the Army of Tennessee. French graduated from West Point in 1843. He served in Zachary Taylor's army, while Loring was in Scott's, so they probably didn't meet. But French was seriously wounded and formed an acquaintance with the man on the next litter, Jefferson Davis. French bought a Mississippi plantation and their friendship grew.

Davis appointed French a brigadier on 23 October 1861. French was put to work building fortifications. Much of what Lee later defended at Petersburg had been laid out by French in 1862. Davis promoted French to major general on 22 October 1862, even though he lacked the combat experience typical with such promotions. With Grant's invasion into Mississippi ongoing, French was sent to join Joe Johnston's Army of Relief in June 1863. French and Loring may have first met then, as fellow division commanders, and so it would be until the Army of Tennessee laid siege to Nashville.

French had a persistent eye infection in 1864, which at times left him all but blind. After fighting at Franklin, he advanced toward Nashville with the army. But he had to take leave before the battle. During the final months of the war he had a brief assignment at Mobile. After the war he returned to Mississippi for a time. His last years were spent writing his autobiography. He is buried in St. John's Cemetery in Pensacola, Florida.

Gale, William Dudley: born 10 MAY 1819 in Mississippi, died 30 JAN 1888
Gale's parents, Dr. Thomas Gale and Anne M. Green Gale were from Nashville. They had plantations in Jefferson and Yazoo Counties, Mississippi. Gale was born on one known as Holly Bend, on the Yazoo River. In 1858 he married Katherine Polk, daughter of Leonidas Polk. Bishop Polk became a general and Gale became his assistant adjutant general. Loring must have had regular contact with Gale. Their relationship continued after Polk was killed by a shell, and A.P. Stewart replaced him. Correspondence shows Gale as a captain, though he may have been promoted later in the war.

The Gale home was outside of the old Nashville city limits, along today's Gale Lane. It is denoted on most maps of the battle. Katherine likely left it about the time the U.S. Army occupied the city. She was on a Gale plantation in Mississippi, and once again the invaders brought war into her life. She moved with their children and her mother to Asheville, North Carolina. At one point Polk sent Gale there to check on them. Gale would journey to Asheville again when Polk was killed. He escorted them to Augusta, Georgia, where the body lay in state before burial.

Gale not only wrote descriptive articles for *Confederate Veteran,* but Gale's lettres are in the Southern Collection at the University of North Carolina. Staff officers have not gotten the attention they deserve, and Gale certainly seems a subject for a thesis. He wrote of virtually every engagement Polk and Stewart were in. Katherine's recollections and the diaries of other family are in the collection. One noteworthy event was the Gales dining with John Bell Hood in New Orleans in 1874; Hood died there in 1879.

Gale family members are buried in City Cemetery in Nashville. Gale's parents were originally buried there, though later moved to nearby Mount Olivet. Still Gale family members are in city. Most unusual is a badly eroded tombstone that seems to have a raised relief of an angle with its wings embracing a child. But William D. Gale and wife are at Mount Olivet. Katherine's grave shows she was nearly two decades younger, born in 1838; she lived until 1916. Gale descendants remained in Nashville, where a grandson founded an insurance agency that survived into the 21st century. Someone must have a photo of Gale but after searching, the author's wife only found one of Katherine (below). There appear to be other family members beside her, unfortunately cropped out.

Garrett, George Washington Brooks: born 5 MAR 1840, S. Carolina, died 4 MAR 1916
Garrett is subject of a Goodspeed biographical entry. Also a brief biography by his wife is on a Mississippi genealogical site. She said he was born in the Union District, South Carolina. His parents moved to Tippah County, in northeastern Mississippi, in 1851. Garrett joined the Missionary Baptist Church at 16. He was initially a private in the 3rd Mississippi. When they went into camp at Iuka he studied Hardee's manual well enough to train others, and it led to his promotion to second lieutenant.

The 3rd was at Fort Donelson where a bullet cut across the top of Garrett's head and left a scar for life. When the fort was surrendered Garrett was sent to prison. After five months he was exchanged at Vicksburg. So many of the 3rd had died in prison that they were consolidated with the 23rd. Garrett was elected major. The 23rd was in Adams's Brigade, where he suffered more wounds. Elizabeth wrote, "During the Georgia Campaign he was shot through his leg above the knee leaving a scar front and back of his leg, and shot in the foot and ankle. Once he received a partly spent ball in his breast which doubled him forward and the word went the line of soldiers 'Our Major is shot, our Major is shot' and that would have caused a panic, as there was no regimental officer to take his place. As soon as possible he called to them 'No, I'm not killed.' His men were proud of him because he stood for what was right and honourable and they loved him because he led them instead of saying 'Go on boys' and because he protected them and saw to it that they got rations whenever possible." She added, "President Davis appointed and commissioned him Colonel but owing to the fact that there was no mail…he did not receive his commission before he was captured in the battle of Nashville…" and imprisoned until after the war. Thus the major was actually a colonel.

Major Garrett commanded the 23rd Mississippi of Adams's Brigade at Nashville. They were outflanked by the fall of several redoubts (possibly One, Two, and Three). The fall of either Two or Three would have enabled enemy troops to reach his rear. His wife wrote that his division commander, she didn't name Loring, ordered him to hold a certain position. "He and his brave regiment held back the enemy at that point until they were surrounded and when the Federal Officer came up he asked who was the commander and where was the men and when he found so few men he curses and said he thought he was fighting the whole Southern army . When the Confederate general saw from a distance that Major Garrett was captured he wept like a child and said that Major Garrett was one of the finest young officers in the South."

Garrett wrote, "We were then ordered to march to Nashville, placed in the penitentiary. When we started back the officer in charge told us that we could not march over their dead. I told him that we were not disposed to show any disrespect to the dead but we had the consolation in knowing that they were there. I think it would be safe in saying that the number killed outright in our front was greater than that of my command who fought them to say nothing of the wounded. From Nashville we were sent to northern prisons."

We have already read Mrs. Garrett's shocking tale of the U.S. prison on Johnson's Island. The only good news seems to be how his horse was saved as Stewart's line fell. Elizabeth wrote, "Hard Garrett was reared on the plantation of Major Garrett's father and had been Major Garrett's servant in the camps for several years, was with him in the beginning of the battle (Nashville) and asked to stay with him and fight. When Major Garrett was ordered to hold the position he was told to dismount, perhaps to prevent him from being conspicuous, he left his sword, sash, and horse with Hard and told him to go to the rear. After the battle Hard rode the horse home and returned it to Major Garrett's father, for Hard had been emancipated before he ever went with him to the army. After the war Hard became a Baptist minister."

Major Garrett survived prison and made it home. Elizabeth explained his homecoming: "After a few days of rest after his long fast he came to see me and me the pretty ring which he had made for me in prison, It was made out of a button, the gold taken from the gold star in his coat, the silver from a dime, the pearl from Lake Erie, and all the delicate work and carving done with no implements except a pocket knife. I appreciated the gift more because he made it while he was starving.

"His father gave him some land and he went there and under many difficulties rebuilt the dilapidated house, built fences, barns, and stables, garden, etc. and we were married in the winter of 1866. If this were a novel it would close with the marriage. We began a life of hard work and strict economy in a country devastated by fire and sword and pillage, plundered and robbed of everything which the Federals would have, ground down under carpetbag dominion by our enemies. With a brave heart, with cheerfulness, with wonderful perseverance Major Garrett went forward to meet the many trials of life and by the grace of God to endure the losses of three tornadoes, by droughts, by overflows, by Yellow Fever, by five fires, by afflictions and last of all met death, trusting in Jesus Christ and saying in his last hours that God was with him." He is buried in Henry Cemetery, Corinth, Mississippi.

Gibson, James Knox: born 27 July 1845 in Nashville, Tennessee died 1935, Stanton, TN
Gibson was a younger half-brother of Thomas Gibson; his entry follows. James Knox's mother died in 1856. In the spring 1860 his Uncle Nathan Adams persuaded his father to let him live with him and his wife near Stanton, northeast of Memphis. He was able to attend school in LaGrange. He had a German or Prussian military instructor. Thus he had some military education.

Gibson left an account of his time with Adams. James was 18 when he arrived to serve with the brigade before Christmas 1863. Adams's Brigade was at Canton, on the railroad north of Jackson. Much of Jackson had been burned it, but it was again functioning to serve the war effort. When he reported to headquarters Adams saw he "was young and not strong." Gibson said he "had me detailed to serve with Major Thos. P. Adams in the

This is the Gibson Family

Back row left to right- Robert Gibson, Jr., Joseph Gibson, Nathan Gibson, and William Gibson. Front row left to right - Andrew Jackson Gibson, Rosanna Adams Gibson (Mother), James Knox Gibson (as a child, circled), Robert Gibson (Father), Martha Jane Gibson and Thomas Gibson.
James Knox Gibson buried in Stanton Cemetery, Haywood Co., Stanton, Tennessee.

Commissary Dept." Gibson had left home with "a nice heavy overcoat" that Adams liked.
 "He had a new English Gray overcoat and proposed a swap, which we did. I remember once I had gotten away behind our Division and had to work my way on horseback through the Infantry. My new coat had slanting pockets on the sides. I somehow put my left hand in a pocket and one soldier said: 'Look at that boy-has only one arm, make way boys, let him pass.' And I tell you that hand stayed in my pocket…" Gibson wrote from memory, regretting he had not kept a diary. One story must have been in north Georgia.
"I remember going one day up a gulch in the mountains to buy cattle to feed the soldiers, the farmers did not want to sell. I told them they had better sell as we were bound to have the cattle. After awhile I got them to sell and I with several of my drivers started to where I thought the Camp was. We had not gone beyond the range of the cattle before they broke and went up the mountains like deer, so I had to go back and tell the farmer to keep their cattle and to give me the money back, which they did. The cattle was as wild as deer and we could not round them up. I often had to leave our command on business and would have to follow marks left on trees made by the pioneer corps. The mark for Loring's Division was three chops."

Gibson, Thomas: born 20 SEP 1836 near Nashville, Tennessee, died 23 NOV 1917

Gibson was on John Adams's staff. They were from Nashville, where Gibson began working in a large wholesale dry goods house at only 16. Five years later he formed a partnership in a wholesale hat house. Nashvillians were not inclined to favour secession until Lincoln called for troops. Then Gibson enlisted in the Rock City Guards, Nashville being Rock City. While at a training camp he was appointed as a sergeant in the 10th Tennessee. They were captured at Fort Donelson. After exchange his health was impaired and he became an aide-de-camp on the staff of John Adams. He was later Adams's assistant adjutant general. Adams was killed at Franklin and Gibson wounded. He was in the hospital at Macon, Georgia at the close of the war.

Gibson returned to Nashville after the war and successfully reestablished his business. He married Lucy A. McKissack of Spring Hill in 1868. Three years later he engaged in stock raising on her farm. In 1884 he was again engaged in business in Nashville. In 1896 he became librarian for the *Nashville, Chattanooga, & St. Louis Railway*. When he passed away he was survived by his wife and a daughter. He is buried at Rose Hill in Columbia.

Gilham, William: Born 13 JAN 1818 in Vincennes, Indiana, died 16 NOV 1872 in VT

Gilham had been a colleague of Stonewall Jackson at Virginia Military Institute. He wrote a book on drill and tactics used exclusively by the C.S. Army. He married Cordelia Hayden. Gilham led the 21st Virginia before leading a brigade in the Romney Campaign. Jackson preferred charges against him for being too slow; hence, Loring was not the only one to raise Jackson's ire! After the war Gilham taught at V.M.I. and worked as a chemist with a fertilizer company in Richmond. He died at his brother's house in Vermont, and is buried at Stonewall Jackson Cemetery (originally the Oak Grove Cemetery) in Lexington, VA.

Gillespie, Francis Marion: 2 OCT 1828 killed at Peach Tree Creek, 20 July 1864

Major Gillespie of the 31st Mississippi was from Calhoun County in northern Mississippi. His company was *The Dixie Rebels*. He was wounded at Peach Tree Creek. Lt. Col. James Drane was wounded in five places charging the enemy's position on a ridge. Though Gillespie was wounded, he took command and moved the 31st forward! As they went over the ridge they were surrounded on three sides. They met an enemy counterattack with a hand to hand assault. They fought for twenty minutes before the vastly larger enemy force pushed them back. Gillespie's arm wound had a severed artery, and he fell due to loss of blood. Private J.W. Brewer, of the 1st Battalion, spotted the popular officer. Brewer was shot in the neck as he pulled Gillespie to the shade of a tree, where he died. Twenty-four of *The Dixie Rebels* fell that day.

A surgeon (J.H.N.) was quoted on Gillespie in the *Macon Beacon* on 15 August 1864. "Thus fell one of the noblest of men, the purest of patriots and bravest of soldiers. Alas, he is dead, and his hunter's horn shall never again reverberate in the hills of Calhoun, his fond friends will never again be welcomed at his hospitable roof, and the social circle of brave spirits around the camp fire shall never hear that cheerful voice, or welcome that benignant smile, but a kind father, mother, brothers and sisters, shall mourn the loss of the brave soldier, and stout hearts of the brave men have shed many, many tears of affection for him, and methinks when the coming Angel shall distribute chaplets to the noble and brave, none will wear a brighter wreath than the chivalric Gillespie."

Although Mississippi became the 20th state in 1817, counties were formed later. The Chickasaws didn't cede their land until the Treaty of Pontotoc in October 1832. Calhoun County had not been formed, but it appears Gillespie was born within its modern area. Somehow his remains made it back from Georgia for burial at Gunntown Cemetery in Egypt, Chickasaw County. There is a Guntown north of Tupelo; however, Egypt is well to the south; south of Okolona. It was named for a variety of corn grown there, and located along the *Mobile & Ohio*.

<u>Goodwin, Edward: Born 7 SEP 1830, Aberdeen, MS, died 25 SEP 1863, Columbus, MS</u>
Colonel Goodwin graduated from LaGrange College in 1851. The college was one of countless schools destroyed by the enemy during the war, setting education back in the South for posterity. Goodwin became a professor of languages, wrote a novel, and farmed in antebellum days. He married Ann King. He became lieutenant colonel in the 35th Alabama, 12 March 1862, and colonel, 12 November 1862. The 35th was in Buford's Brigade. They put up a great fight at Champion Hill. *Confederate Colonels* mentions his death, but not the cause. He is buried in King Cemetery near LaGrange, Mississippi.

Gen. Richard Harrison, M.D., CSA
(1821-1876)
— Photo courtesy of Mrs. Frank E. Woods

Harrison, Richard: born 3 MAR 1821 in Jefferson Co., Alabama, died 1 November 1876

Harrison's twin brother was Col. Isham Harrison, Jr. He commanded the 6th Mississippi Cavalry, and was killed in action. An older brother was Brig. Gen. James Edward Harrison. A younger brother was Brig. Gen. Thomas Harrison. The parents moved from South Carolina to Alabama, and then to Monroe County, Mississippi. Richard studied at Transylvania and returned to Aberdeen, in Monroe, to become a physician and planter. He was made a first lieutenant after volunteering in the 43rd Mississippi in April 1861. He was promoted to colonel on 10 November 1862. After being captured at Vicksburg he was paroled the 43rd was assigned to Adams's Brigade. He led the brigade during part of 1865. *Confederate Colonels* lists three wives. Like his generals-brothers, Richard moved to the Waco, Texas area. He died at his residence and is buried at First Street Cemetery, as are the Harrison generals.

The First Street Cemetery is also known as Oakwood Cemetery. Another general with a Loring connection buried here is cavalryman Sul Ross. Two other generals are Felix Robertson and his father Jerome Robertson.

Henderson, Derrel Datus: born 10 JAN 1845 in Bankston, MS, died 9 APR 1865 in TN

Private Henderson was in the Choctaw Guards, 15th Mississippi, of Adams's Brigade. The 15th fought in 1862 battles at Mill Springs, Kentucky and then at Shiloh. Henderson was ill during the fighting outside Nashville and had difficulty keeping up once Hood's army retreated. Enemy cavalry put two pistol balls in his left arm, and captured him. While in one of their hospitals at Nashville gangrene set in, and his arm was amputated. City Cemetery was his first place of burial, probably in a trench. The Confederate dead were moved to Confederate Circle in Mount Olivet after it was laid out in 1869. Another brother, William, was also captured in the battle, and died in prison, probably at Camp Chase, Ohio. Another brother had died at Vicksburg, so his widowed father lost three of five sons in the war. Research was done by Tim Burgess, as Henderson was portrayed in the Mount Olivet tours in the 1990s.

Hood, John Bell: 1JUN1831 in Owingsville, KY, died 30 AUG 1879 in New Orleans, LA
Hood has been remembered for his extremes more than most generals. Manigault's remarks got to the point. Perhaps he had been a great division commander. After Cassville and Kolb's Farm, corps command was too much for Hood. Of most interest here is Loring's opinion. James McNeilly heard Loring speak in the aftermath of Hood's poorly planned battle along Peach Tree Creek. Loring spoke with great emphasis when he said, "Gentlemen, I say what I know. In light of what has happened, I am sure that if General Johnston had been left in command ten days longer he would have destroyed General Sherman's army." Instead, over the following week, Hood nearly destroyed his own army at Atlanta and Ezra Church. Hood was responsible for high casualties in both. Franklin was his low point, especially because he apparently didn't reconnoiter. He did a fine job at Gettysburg when he had a division. His corps commander, Longstreet, advised they were to attack the U.S. left on the second day. Hood immediately sent a detail that found Round Top free of enemy troops, but the enemy's supply trains and artillery reserve parked to the rear. It was an invitation to flank and destroy the U.S. left and their line of retreat. It promised a decisive victory like Chancellorsville two months earlier. Longstreet insisted Lee's attack plan had to be followed. Hood implemented Lee's plan and enemy artillery fire quickly took him out, and deprived his division of leadership.

In fairness to West Point-educated Hood, his wartime wounds should have precluded his active field assignments. Just two months after his arm wound at Gettysburg he was critically wounded at Chickamauga. Few survived his type of leg amputation, so close to the hip. He had sacrificed enough on the battlefields for our independence. For him to die from a mosquito bite, with yellow fever, was far from a heroic battlefield death. His wife and a child also died. They are buried in her family vault, at Metairie Cemetery.

Hood was born in Owingsville, Kentucky, in the house at top left. It had a carport added before the 2004 photo. The house above was his childhood home, outside Owingsville. The town is about 40 miles east of Lexington and 90 west of West Virginia. Hood and his wife, Anna Marie Hennen, are buried in her family tomb. It is in Metairie Cemetery in New Orleans; from a 1997 photo; photos by author.

Ives, Samuel Spencer: born 15 AUG 1835 in Masonville, Alabama, died 22 MAR 1917
Colonel Ives had been a Lauderdale County farmer and an overseer in Franklin County in antebellum days. *Confederate Colonels* shows two wives, Amanda Mitchell and Mary Kennedy. It indicates he had been a lieutenant colonel in the 9th Alabama, before serving in the 35th Alabama in 1862. He was a major when they fought at Baton Rouge, but he had achieved his old rank on 12 November 1862. Edward Goodwin was promoted to colonel on the same day. The 35th was in Buford's Brigade. Goodwin's death on 25 September 1863 led to Ives being promoted to colonel. Ives was wounded at Franklin. He returned to Florence, Lauderdale County postbellum, and is buried in Florence Cemetery. Tintype image is courtesy of Alabama Department of Archives and History.

Jackson, Henry Rootes: born 24 JUN 1820 in Athens, GA, died 23 May 1898, Savannah
Jackson served under Loring in Virginia in 1861. He returned to Georgia to command state troops in December. He was later assigned to brigade command in Cheatham's Corps in the Army of Tennessee. In Douglas Southall Freeman's *Lee* he gave glowing praise to Jackson. He wrote, "…Judge Jackson was a Yale graduate, an art lover, a poet, an ex-judge and former United States minister to Austria. Not long before the war, when still under forty, he had declined the chancellorship of the University of Georgia. The people of Savannah had elected him to the Confederate Congress, but as he had served as the youthful colonel of the First Georgia Volunteers during the Mexican War, he had felt that he should enter the army." General Robert Garnett's death in western Virginia led to Jackson briefly commanding the Army of the Northwest before Loring arrived. Freeman pointed out Confederate forces were in chaos and there was the chance for the enemy to make a quick drive on the Virginia Central Railroad. "General Jackson would have been far more at ease if he had been asked to translate an obscure passage in an Horatian ode, or if he had been called on draft a diplomatic note in the most precise Continental style, but in a new capacity and in an unfamiliar country, he had kept his head, had used his strong, native intelligence, and had made in the crises what were, all

things considered, probably the best dispositions possible with the small force at hand." Freeman also commended his modesty in urging Lee to come to western Virginia as he thought a man of greater military experience than himself was needed. Jackson was captured during the retreat at Nashville. Postbellum he returned to his law practice. In 1885 he was appointed U.S. minister to Mexico. He is buried in Bonaventure Cemetery in Savannah. His monument is in lush tropical foliage.

> Henry Rootes Jackson isn't the only brigadier general buried at Bonaventure. Robert Anderson, a Savannah native, has a bust over his grave. Alexander Lawton has an elaborate arch. Claudius Wilson is there. Hugh Mercer may be, if not in Germany.

Jackson's house is at 450 Bull Street. It was erected in 1857 for the British consul. In 1865 the U.S. Army appropriated it, stealing home furnishings. Jackson bought the house in 1885.

Jackson, Col. James: born 21 APR 1822 in Nashville, TN, died 14 AUG 1879, Alabama
Jackson was a planter near Florence. He enlisted in the 4th Alabama and was wounded at Manassas in 1861. He was discharged from the 4th, and recovered at home. Florence, on the Tennessee River, was concerned with the lack of defense at the river forts in Tennessee. Jackson would be lieutenant colonel of the 27th Alabama, and they were sent at Christmas 1861, with 500 slaves, to Fort Heiman. The fort was in Kentucky, roughly across the river from Fort Henry in Tennessee. The slaves provided labour, but no heavy artillery reached the fort, before the gunboats attacked. The 27th escaped to Fort Donelson where it was included in the surrender. Jackson was wounded and lost an arm at Lost Mountain, though some sources incorrectly say at Kennesaw. He missed the rest of the Atlanta Campaign, but returned to lead Loring's Division in North Carolina. Jackson returned to being a planter postbellum. His home, the Forks, is in the entry on the 27th Alabama, above. There is a Region's Bank branch in Florence modeled after the house. He is buried at Cypress Cemetery, Lauderdale County.

Jackson, Moses: born 14 JAN 1822, Amite Co., Mississippi, died 28 NOV 1895 in MS
Jackson came from a line of soldiers. His father was Captain Wiley Jackson, who commanded a company at the Battle of New Orleans. His grandfather was Isaac Jackson, a colonel in the Revolutionary War. Moses Jackson was elected to the Mississippi Senate in 1861. He enlisted in the 33rd Mississippi at Grenada on 10 March 1862. He was in all the battles of the 33rd and took command when Col. Jabez Drake when he was killed at Peachtree Creek on 20 July 1864. At Jonesboro, on 31 August, Jackson received gunshot wounds in both feet and was struck behind an ear with a shell fragment. He could not return to duty until March 1865. He was promoted to lieutenant colonel on 19 April 1865.

Records at the Amite court house written after Jackson passed away read: "As a citizen, he was as loyal and true as he had proved as a soldier. The involvements of office did not allure him to forsake his principles, and even during the darkest days of reconstruction, he did not waiver, but could always be depended on as a bold and aggressive Democrat waging a relentless war upon the rapacious 'carpet baggers.' He was a safe counselor, as no exciting cause could make him lose his equanimity or equanimity. On several occasions he led our citizens, who had been outraged in so many ways by the 'carpetbaggers' and their ignorant and deluded adherents, and he always led them to victory without dishonor. He was repeatedly sent to the Legislative Halls, as Representative and Senator, and gave entire satisfaction to his constituents and to his state. He was a man of strong convictions and had the courage to proclaim them when occasion demanded. He was noted for his prudence and sobriety, and was for many years was a consistent member of the Baptist Church. He lived an exemplary life and died the death of a faithful and unfaltering Christian. Moses passed away Nov. 28, 1895." He is buried in Wiley Jackson Cemetery, Liberty, Amite County, Mississippi.

Dedication at Moses Jackson's Grave
Kneeling L-R-Webb Roberts, Bill Hinson, and Ray Bordon (rip)
Standing L-R- Ed Funchess, Wayne Parker, W.J. Roberts, Jennifer Hughes, Tim Sterling (rip), Virgil Roberts and J.C. Hughes

Jackson, Thomas Jonathan: born 21 JAN 1824 near Clarksburg, VA, died 10 May 1863

General Thomas J. "Stonewall" Jackson Monument, Boulevard and Monument Avenue, Richmond, Va. 21

Jackson and Loring were on the same Mexican War battlefields, though Jackson was fresh out of West Point. Loring was already a veteran, having fought the Seminoles, and outranked Jackson. But when Jackson sought to drive the enemy from western Virginia, Loring did not hesitate to bring three brigades to serve under Jackson. The resulting Romney Campaign showed quirks in Jackson's command style. Fortunately he went onto serve brilliantly until his death at Chancellorsville. His Valley Campaign, Second Manassas, and Sharpsburg were more than enough to justify his promotion to lieutenant general. His remains lay in state in Richmond. President Davis stood by the coffin. Mrs. Varina Davis saw a tear escape and fall to Jackson's face. Congress had just authorized a new national flag; the Second National. It was intended for the roof of the Capitol, but was draped over Jackson's casket. The hull of the packet boat (below) is at Riverside Park, Lynchburg, Virginia.

THE OLD PACKET BOAT (AS IT LOOKS TO-DAY), ON WHICH THE REMAINS OF "STONEWALL" JACKSON WERE CARRIED FROM LYNCHBURG TO LEXINGTON, VA.
PUBLISHED BY G. E. MURRELL, LYNCHBURG, VA.

Jackson, William Hicks: born 1 October 1835 in Paris, TN, died 30 March 1903
Jackson and Loring were together in the Mounted Rifles. From 1857 to 1861 Jackson was a second lieutenant under Loring, who was his senior by about eighteen years. They were both in New Mexico at the time Lincoln called for troops to invade the Confederacy. Jackson tendered his resignation, and traveled with Kentuckian Col. George Crittenden to New Orleans. Loring and Jackson were division commanders in the war, as Jackson was a rising cavalryman. They were in Mississippi in 1863, Georgia and Tennessee in 1864. Jackson was outstanding in Georgia. He and his division kept Johnston informed of Sherman's flanking moves. Jackson developed the plan for the great cavalry victory at Brown's Mill. Jackson gained more fame after the war by marrying Selene Harding. Her family home was Belle Meade, outside Nashville. Jackson's horse sense turned it into one of the greatest thoroughbred farms in the world. The Jacksons are buried at Nashville's Mount Olivet Cemetery. Over 1,500 Confederates rest there, including six other generals.

Brig. Gen. William Hicks Jackson didn't have the opportunities some did to gain notoriety, yet he was greater than some that did. Postbellum, he married Selene Harding. She attempted to rally Chalmers' Escort, during the Battle of Nashville, from her front porch, Belle Meade. The post card, below, was mailed in 1905. Jackson helped turn it into one of the greatest thoroughbred plantations. Enquirer, one of the most famous, was purchased from his old friend. Abraham Buford.

Johnston, Joseph Eggleston: born 3 FEB 1807 in Farmville, VA, died 21 MAR 1891
Johnston served in the Seminole War and might have met Loring there. Johnston also fought in the Mexican War, and they could have met there. Loring was under Johnston in Virginia in the spring of 1862. Loring would come under his command in Mississippi in May 1863. Johnston's arrival in Jackson, Mississippi, on 13 May 1863 put him in direct command over John Adams. They evacuated Jackson the next day in the face of Grant's advance with overwhelming numbers. Two days later Pemberton was defeated at Champion Hill, and Loring's Division escaped to join Johnston's Army of Relief. It not only failed to relieve Pemberton, but had to abandon Jackson a second time. Johnston was called to replace Bragg over the Army of Tennessee in December 1863. This brought Leonidas Polk to command in Mississippi. Loring's Division came with Polk's army to join Johnston's Army of Tennessee, at Resaca, Georgia, in May 1863. Thus Loring served under him until he was removed at Atlanta, and again in North Carolina in 1865. Johnston and his wife are buried in Green Mount Cemetery, in Baltimore, Maryland.

Johnston statue is at Dalton; from a card mailed in 1941. The stained glass window is in the Rhodes mansion in Atlanta. Brig. Gen. Edward Porter Alexander, of Augusta, said he "was more the soldier in looks, carriage & manner than any of our other generals…" Quite a few agreed with him.

Kirker, William H.: born 5FEB1831 in Ohio, died 5MAY1884 likely Charlottesville, VA
Kirker was a quartermaster for Loring in western Virginia. He did not go to Mississippi with Loring, but remained in Virginia. He served on the staffs of J.E.B. Stuart and Wade Hampton. He became a druggist in Charlottesville and is buried in Maplewood Cemetery.

Lawrence, Robert Josiah: born 1825 in Alabama, died 20 August 1887 in Shubuta, MS
Lawrence grew up in La Grange, Alabama. He fought in the Mexican War. In 1850 he began work as a clerk in Mobile. He moved to Shubuta, Clarke County, Mississippi in the 1850s. He married Mary Ledyard. He was a captain in the 14th Mississippi on 28 March 1861. They were captured at Fort Donelson. He was paroled in September 1862 and promoted to major in October. After Tilghman was killed the 14th went to Adams's Brigade; see sketch of 14th above. Lawrence was lieutenant colonel on 16 March 1864; before they reached Georgia. He was promoted to colonel 9 April 1865. He returned to Clarke County and died in Shubuta. He is buried at Magnolia Cemetery in Mobile.

Lee, Hugh Holmes: born 26AUG18 in Clarksburg, VA, died 12JUL1869 in Salem, VA
Lee attended Virginia Military Institute and the University of Virginia. He was Loring's ordinance officer in the spring 1861. He was Stonewall Jackson's the following spring. He was wounded at McDowell and that ended his active duty. He was later in the Auditor's Office in Richmond. He was a lawyer in Salem postbellum, and a legislator. Lee was buried in East Hill Cemetery in Salem.

Lee, Robert Edward: born: born 19 JAN 1807 at Stratford, died 12 OCT 1870
Lee and Loring were in the Mexican War and western Virginia. In Mexico they were in Maj. Gen. Winfield Scott's drive from Vera Cruz to Mexico City. Both were made names for themselves. Loring was in the Mounted Riflemen in Twiggs's Division and Lee, as an engineer, worked with them in the advance. Cerro Gordo was the first major battle of the campaign. Loring's company of riflemen was called on. Scott cited Loring and others with the "highest praise." Scott said Lee was the finest officer in his command. Lee's brief time with Loring in western Virginia is covered in the chapter on Loring. The post card below, postmarked in 1911, is of the Lee statue in Richmond, Virginia.

Lee, Stephen Dill: born 22SEP1833, Charleston, SC, died 28MAY1908, Columbus, MS

Lee commanded Loring's Division briefly, at Ezra Church. Lee was one of the great artillerists in the war. His expertise contributed to victorious actions at Second Manassas and Sharpsburg. When an artillerist was needed at Vicksburg Robert E. Lee agreed to send S.D. Lee. His actions at Chickasaw Bayou, December 1862, were a key in the decisive repulse of Sherman. Department command was given to Lee in May 1864, when Polk went to the Army of Tennessee. Lee won a strategic victory in repulsing a U.S. invasion of Mississippi, though he suffered a tactical defeat at Harrisburg (a.k.a. Tupelo) in July. Historian John Scales explained Lee had never exercised independent command, and lacked tactical patience. That is a polite and succinct explanation. Loring was wounded at Ezra Church, where Lee commanded, and he might have agreed that Lee lacked tactical patience. Postbellum he was the first president of Mississippi State.
Post card at left postmarked 1911.

Lockett, Samuel Henry: born 7 JUL 1837, Mecklenburg Co., VA, died 12 October 1891
Lockett's family moved to Alabama in 1853. He graduated from West Point in 1859, second in the class. He was an outstanding engineer, and met Lloyd Tilghman, and probably Loring, in Mississippi. Lockett was promoted to colonel in August 1864. He taught after the war in Tennessee, and at Louisiana State. Lockett and Loring were together in Egypt in 1876. Lockett was building Fort Gura. Colonel Lockett worked on designing the base for the Statue of Liberty in 1886. Loring was in New York at the time and probably apprised of the work, though he died that December. Lockett was also a railroad contractor in Chile. He died in Bogota, Columbia. His papers are at U.N.C.

Long, Armistead Lindsay: born 3 SEP 1825 in Campbell Co., VA, died 29 APR 1891
Long was one of Loring's five staff members to rise to general. Four of them, including Long, were Virginians. He graduated from West Point in 1850, and served in the artillery until 1861. His first Confederate service was for Loring as chief of artillery. Long was ordered to serve under Robert E. Lee, then in South Carolina. He wrote a biography of Lee, though he had become blind. He died in Charlottesville, and is buried there.

William Wing Loring: born 4 DEC 1818 in Wilmington, NC, died 30 DEC 1886 in NY
In Raab's biography of Loring we find his parents were married in Wilmington, North Carolina in 1812. William Wing, their second son, was born there in 1818. Florida was still Spanish until a few years later. It had become a U.S. territory before the Lorings moved to Saint Augustine in 1823. It had been established by the Spanish in 1565, and is the oldest city in what is today's United States. The old Spanish stone fort, Castillo de San Marcos, towered over the Loring's home. It must have fascinated the boy. The Loring home on corner of Treasury and Saint George Street has been converted into a retail store.

Another future Confederate general, Kirby Smith, was born in Saint Augustine the year after the Lorings moved there. Their age difference was over five years. Loring was already serving with the Florida militia at only 14, and he fought in the Great Seminole War of 1835-1842. Smith was beginning a West Point education and graduated in 1845. His path and Loring's probably crossed as children, and would again.

After fighting Seminoles, Loring focused on his education. Georgetown was selected, and he took undergraduate classes in the 1839-1840 term. He returned to Saint Augustine and began reading law. He practiced and was elected to the Florida legislature, but the Mexican War revived his military ardour. His name became known to President James Knox Polk who offered him the rank of captain in a new regiment of mounted riflemen. Loring was at the end of his third term in Tallahassee and accepted the appointment. He was actually promoted to major, on 12 February 1847, before the regiment embarked for the siege of Vera Cruz. The photograph below is of Loring in the Mexican War era.

The Mounted Rifles which Loring commanded were in Twiggs's Division. On the advance from Vera Cruz to Mexico City he would have known Robert E. Lee. At Cerro Gordo animals could not haul artillery through ravines and around boulders. Loring heard the cry, "Send up the Rifles!" They worked well past midnight to get the artillery in position. It was the first made battle of the campaign, and a great victory. Scott was elated and specifically mentioned Loring, along with several others, for brilliant service. Scott's advance on Mexico City continued with two more victories, and they led to Loring's promotion to lieutenant colonel on 20 August. In the attack on Mexico City a shot shattered Loring's left arm. The surgeon reported, "Loring laid aside a cigar, sat quietly in a chair without opiates to relieve the pain, and allowed the arm to be cut off without a murmur or a groan. The arm was carried on the heights by his men, with the hand pointing toward the City of Mexico." Loring explained seeing the capture of the Castle of Chapultepec was so exciting it drove away all sense of pain." He was made colonel by brevet on 13 September.

Loring's mother reported he was returning to Saint Augustine in November 1847. In December the Florida House and Senate passed a resolution of appreciation for his military service. Winter would have been a good time for him to rest and recuperate. A peace treaty was made with Mexico in February 1848. President Polk recognized Loring with a promotion to full lieutenant colonel. He was to command the Mounted Riflemen in an upcoming march to the new territory, Oregon. Loring left Saint Augustine by August 1848, and returned to Jefferson Barracks in Saint Louis. His old neighbor, Kirby Smith, was there. Loring's rank got him two suites, and he allowed one for Smith. He wrote his mother, "Colonel Loring is an excellent fellow."

Raab's biography covers the rest of Loring's antebellum career in the U.S. Army. By 1857 a state of war existed between the army and Mormons in Utah. In 1858 Loring was called on. In July he was ordered to Fort Union, east of Santa Fe, New Mexico. He was to lead a detachment to Utah. He took a route that saved 200 Miles and became known as the Loring Trail. In 1859 the War Department sent him to Europe to observe armies and training procedures. It led him to France, Great Britain, Prussia, and a number of German states. He was back in New Mexico when Florida seceded in January 1861. In February he wrote Florida's governor, "I always hold myself ready to serve my State and the South, should the time come when my services will be useful to them." Loring held a conference with some officers based out of various posts around Santa Fe. He told them, "For my part, the South is my home, and I am going to throw up my commission and shall join the Southern Army, and each of you can do as you think best." He resigned on 13 May and made his way to San Antonio, Texas. There, on 1 July, he sent a lettre to C.S. Secretary of War Leroy Walker, stating, "I am now hastening to the scene of war… I again offer my services and shall leave here tomorrow via New Orleans for Richmond." He arrived later in July and on the 20th Robert E. Lee assigned then Brigadier General Loring to command of the Northwestern Army in Virginia. Loring's Confederate time is within the text of the chapters above.

Charles Quintard went to western Virginia as a chaplain for the 1st Tennessee Infantry, and served as an aide-de-camp for Loring; see Quintard entry below. He was with Loring when he was reassigned to Norfolk in the winter 1862. Quintard was a trained physician and stayed with him through a case of pneumonia. Quintard visited his family in Rome, Georgia. Norfolk was evacuated and Loring was reassigned to the new Department of Southwestern Virginia. His headquarters were at New River, at the Narrows.

Quintard went there "for a brief visit to the General to whom I was warmly attached, and to make farewell visits to sundry officers and bid my old military companions a final adieu. For my attention it then was to leave the army." He described Loring as "not only a very charming companion but he was altogether a remarkable man. A braver man never lived." And "he was already the hero of three wars-the Seminole War, the War with Mexico and that in which we were then engaged."

The Confederate General entry for Loring has him spending four years in New York City postbellum. He was a banking consultant on Southern investments. In 1869 he went to Egypt, and accepted a commission as a brigadier general from the Khedive, Ismail Pasha. While in service there he won a promotion to a division, and was decorated with the "Imperial Order of Osmanieh." After ten years he returned to the states. Raab's Loring biography has three chapters on his postbellum life.

Loring spent his final years in Florida and New York. He never married. He published a book: *A Confederate Soldier in Egypt.* He died of pneumonia on 30 December 1886 in New York. He was cremated there and his ashes buried at Grace Episcopal Church. There were those who thought his remains should be moved to Saint Augustine. In March 1887 the general was moved, with much pageantry. His funeral was officiated by his longtime friend, Bishop Quintard. He said it was on the 19th of March. "The commanding General of the Army post at St. Augustine acted as one of the pall-bearers, and at the cemetery the body was borne from the gun-carriage to the grave by three Federal and three ex-Confederate soldiers. A salute was fired by a battery of United States Artillery." As the bishop spoke an officer stepped forward with one of Loring's swords, broke it into, and cast it into his grave. An obelisk-memorial stood there, and a nearby Confederate monument added to the unique history of Saint Augustine. On10 August 1973 the general was honoured when the General William Wing Loring Camp, Sons of Confederate Veterans was chartered. The hate and foolishness of the 21st century was not imaginable.

Circa 1920 there was a Saint Augustine Room at a museum at the University of Florida. A favourite niece, Mrs. Spencer, played a large part in seeing that there was a Loring exhibit! It included one of his uniforms, medals, a favourite sword, and furniture and tapestries he had acquired in Egypt. There was even a wax likeness. Her will left funds for the display and for a Loring scholarship. The funds ran out in 1997. The contents of the exhibit are believed to be at the Museum of Florida History. A web site shows a pine camp chest used to carry Loring's personal camp equipment.

Leftist mischief led to Loring's grave and monument being removed from downtown in August 2020.In a pathetic display of leftist guilt, the nearby Confederate monument was too. The monuments were moved to Trout Creek Fish Camp, a private property. Loring's ashes were moved to Craig Memorial Park, off Old Moultrie Road. Fragments of a sword (or two), mentioned above, were found with the ashes. The S.C.V. and the U.D.C. held a grave dedication in January 2021.

Rita Zimmerle, of the Ancient Cities Chapter of the United Daughters of the Confederacy provided photo of Loring's current resting place, below.

Loring's ashes were in downtown Saint Augustine into 2021. Leftists had them removed. They were moved to Craig Memorial Park; it is private property where we may hope they may remain for eternity. His grave obelisk monument is at Trout Creek Fish Camp. The Confederate monument was also moved there.

Lowry, Robert: born 10 MAR 1830 in South Carolina, died 19 JAN 1910 in Jackson, MS
Lowry came directly under Loring when Lowry came to command of Adams's Brigade. Lowry was born in Chesterfield District, South Carolina in 1829 or 1830; his grave has 1829. His parents were in Tishomingo County, Mississippi in 1840. He married Maria M. Gamage, and they had eleven children. Lowry had worked in a mercantile business with an uncle in Raleigh, the seat of Smith County. The uncle was also a judge, which may have led Lowry to read law in Arkansas. His practice may have been in Brandon, as he enlisted as a private in the Rankin Grays in 1861; Rankin is east of Jackson.

Lowry was elected major in the Rankin Grays, which became a company in the 6th Mississippi. At Shiloh they were sweeping through a vacated row of U.S. officers' tents.

The officers of the 6th had reformed the regiment and were beginning to move up an incline. Suddenly U.S. artillery and infantry opened. Lowry was severely wounded. In the short span of less than a half hour the 6th lost 300 soldiers out of 425. That 70.5% loss was one of the several worst by any Confederate regiment during the war. Lowry was elected colonel 23 May 1862. He had established himself as an officer of merit.

Lowry and the 6th went with Breckinridge in his attempt to take Baton Rouge. They were back in Mississippi to fight at Corinth. During the Vicksburg Campaign they fought at Port Gibson in a brigade under General Martin Green. He wrote that Lowry "deserves the highest commendation for his coolness and promptness in executing every order." Within a few weeks the 6th was in Tilghman's Brigade, in time to fight at Champion Hill. Tilghman was killed there and the brigade became John Adams'. Adams was killed at Franklin, and that brought the brigade to another brave commander, Lowry. Once the army reached Tupelo Lowry had temporary command of a cavalry brigade, Gholson's. In the notes of Hughes's volume on Bentonville, his notes (page 259) indicate command of Adams's Brigade passed to Lt. Col. Robert Josiah Lawrence, who commanded at Bentonville. Then command passed to Col. Richard Harrison. The brigade was renamed Lowry's, but if Lowry made it to North Carolina it may have been in April.

The Confederate General has Lowry returning to Mississippi after independence was lost. He served as a state senator from 1865 to 1866. He helped oust the Carpetbagger government to become governor in 1881. He was reelected in 1885. President Davis died in 1889. One of his kindest biographers, Felicity Allen, pointed out Lowry was a pall bearer. He served as Commander of the Mississippi Division of the United Confederate Veterans from 1903 to 1910. During that time he served on a committee to see that funds were raised for a monument to the women of Mississippi. Lowry did not live to see it dedicated, which was done on 3 June 1912. He died at the home of a daughter in Jackson and was buried in Brandon Cemetery; right.

Lowry bought *Ben Venue*, below, in 1882. It was built in 1834, and was on South College Street in Brandon.

They Sleep Beneath the Mockingbird: Mississippi Burial Sites and Biographies of Confederate Generals has a fuller picture of Lowry's postbellum Mississippi lifetime:

"Although Robert Lowry's last eighteen months on this earth were spent battling the long and painful illness of rheumatism, he always maintained a bright and cheerful spirit. He had been a hale and hearty man, a model for leadership in times of turmoil and a great patriarch of his State's efforts to regain its prominence so painfully stripped by the war."

Governor E. F. Noel commented on Lowry's death. Part of his official notice reads: "The angel of death, last night called from life to eternity, one of Mississippi's noblest and most patriotic citizens, ex-Governor Robert Lowry. A soldier without fear, a statesman without guile, and a gentleman above reproach has answered his last roll call." The legislature adjourned and the funeral was held later in the week. Graveside, some of his old soldiers completed the burial, not allowing anyone to use the shovels, as a final tribute of honour to their gallant commander. More of his postbellum life and a tribute in: *The Story of Jackson: Biographical Sketches of the Builders of the Capital of Mississippi*.

Markham, D. D,, Thomas Railey: born 2DEC1828, Jefferson Co., MS, died 12MAR1893
Markham's father, William, owned a mercantile business in Vicksburg, and his mother, Susan, was a founding member of the Presbyterian Church there. Their son graduated from Oakland College, in Rodney, in 1849. He entered Princeton Theological Seminary the same year. He graduated in 1852, and returned to Vicksburg to preach. He moved to New Orleans in 1857 where he continued preaching and married Mary Searles. He was a chaplain during the war, and served in the trenches at Vicksburg. His home was in the city and his wife was pregnant, and died in August from complications in giving birth to twins. Markham became a widower for life. In January 1864 he was exchanged and

assigned to Featherston's brigade. The Atlanta Campaign followed and a younger brother was mortally wounded outside Atlanta. In Tennessee Markham rode along the Lewisburg Pike to located a site for Loring's Division's hospital. He saw someone he had known in Louisiana, Carrie McGavock, at her home, Carnton. A spring convinced him it was a good site, and thus their home's role has insured their memory into the 21st Century. Postbellum Markham was pastor at the La Fayette Presbyterian Church in New Orleans. He is buried at Metairie Cemetery. Confederate Memorial Hall, a great New Orleans museum, has some possessions.

Mathews, Henry Mason: born 29MAR1834 in Greenbrier Co., VA, died 26APR1884
Mathews attended the University of Virginia. He became a lawyer in Lewisburg and a professor at Allegheny College. He was an engineer officer to Loring in July 1861, and an aide-de-camp in 1862. He held that position with Carter Stevenson in July 1862. He held different positions with Stevenson and Pemberton into 1865. He was attorney general for West Virginia, and governor from 1876-1880. His "cheerful expression" must have been an asset. He died in Lewisburg and is buried there in City Cemetery.

McAlexander, Edward Asbury: born 2 MAR1833 in Alabama, died 13 OCT 1870 in Ala.
McAlexander graduated from LaGrange College, which was destroyed during the war. He became a physician in Lauderdale County. He was a lieutenant in the 27th Alabama by 25 December 1861. He was captured at Fort Donelson. After being exchanged he was promoted to lieutenant colonel. Col. James Jackson was wounded on the Lost Mountain line, and command went to McAlexander. He is shown in command on the organization of 30 June. The 27th was consolidated with the 35th and 49th. Colonel Ives commanded and McAlexander may have been second. *Confederate Colonels* indicates he commanded the post of Cherokee, Alabama during Hood's campaign into Tennessee. As Ives was wounded at Franklin, it seems he rejoined the consolidated regiment to command it. He was promoted to colonel in North Carolina on 9 April 1865. Postbellum he was a state representative form 1865-7. He died in Lauderdale County and is buried there, at Florence Cemetery in Florence.

Mellon, Thomas A.: born 13 NOV 1826 near Bolton, MS, died 15 MAY 1873 in MS
Colonel Mellon, of the 3rd Mississippi, Featherston's Brigade, was wounded in the head at Peach Tree Creek. He resigned afterward, but later served as a general of Mississippi State Troops. He served in the Mexican War and became a wealthy cotton planter. After independence was lost he became a commission merchant at Bolton, west of Jackson. Living on the edge of the Champion Hill battlefield must have led to much reflection on what might have been. Mellon is buried at the Raymond Town Cemetery, below.

A September 1865 newspaper story reported a group of bandits attacked a Colonel Mellon in Vicksburg. As he lived at Bolton in Hinds County, just east of Vicksburg, it is almost certain it must have been Thomas Mellon. He killed three of or four of them and made his escape! It is regrettable that no picture was found of this warrior-colonel.

Meriwether, Minor: 1827 in Christian County, KY, died1910 in Saint Louis, Missouri
Meriwether was an engineer officer for Loring, involving Fort Pemberton in 1863. Elizabeth Avery Meriwether, Minor's wife, wrote the intriguing account her life, *Recollections of 92 Years, 1824-1916*. Garrett Meriwether, Minor's father, has been a slave owner, but decided to free them and send them to Liberia. Their ancestors had been brought from Africa to Massachusetts, and later sold south to Virginia. Garrett told her, "They are attached to our family and we are attached to them; it is my purpose to set them free. I think that is best for them, and I think it is best for my son here that he should

live by his own labor rather than by the labor of slaves." Garrett died soon after, but Minor fulfilled his wishes. He took the slaves to New Orleans, where they were sent to Liberia. Minor married Elizabeth in January 1850 in Memphis, where she lived. He worked as a civil engineer, and was recognized by a Memphis newspaper in 1853 for his work on the great railroad tunnel under the Cumberland Plateau where "the accuracy of his work on this great tunnel is recognized as a triumph in railroad engineering." She tells of Minor off in the army and being at Shiloh. Memphis fell to the enemy two months later. While Grant was in charge at Memphis she was treated as a lady, but once Sherman was he order wives of Confederate officers to abandon their homes. She was pregnant

with a son, Lee, and hoped she would be permitted to stay. Lee writes of his response in 1951: "I am not interested in rebel wives or rebel brats; if you are in Memphis day after tomorrow you will be imprisoned for the duration of the rebellion." So it was she and two sons became refugees in Mississippi and Alabama. They returned to Memphis and he continued working as an engineer. A plaque with an image of him has been in the lobby of the Peabody Hotel, indicating he was in "The Engineers Club of Memphis. He left Memphis during one of the yellow fever epidemics. The Meriwethers were living in Saint Louis when he became terminally ill in 1910. In his dying message he asked the United Confederate Veterans camp to attend his funeral in a body. He was buried in St. Louis at Bellefontaine Cemetery, as are two generals, Sterling Price and A.P. Stewart.

<u>Milligan, Augustus L.: 1829 in North Carolina, died 25 July 1889 in Ozark, Alabama</u>
Milligan commanded the 57th Alabama briefly. His obituary says he was born in North Carolina. As a boy he moved to Pike County, Alabama, where he was educated. Then he went to Elba, Coffee County, where he edited a newspaper, The States' Rights Democrat. He served as a county judge before moving to establish a law practice in Newton, Dale County. "Inspired by those grand and noble principles, which made up his character… he joined the glorious old 15th Alabama Regiment, in which he fought for four long years, being actually engaged in thirty-one battles."

Col. Columbus Cunningham was shown in command of the 57th Alabama on the 10 July return. Lt. Col. William Calvin Bethune commanded at Peach Tree Creek, though he was severely wounded. Milligan is shown as commanding on the 31 July return. Cunningham returned to command in time to be on the 31 August return. Cunningham was wounded at Franklin. Major James Horatio Wiley commanded at Nashville. Milligan was captured and sent to Johnson's Island. If he knew his wife died on 17 September he must have been terribly distraught. They had just gotten married in 1861, and sons had been born in 1861 and 1864. Hopefully they were well provided for, as Milligan wasn't released until 7 June 1865. His first wife was Louisa Victoria McEntyre born 22 March 1838. He apparently married her younger sister, Josephine McEntyre (1843-1918).

After the independence was lost he resumed his law practice at Newton, and then to Ozark when the court house was moved. Milligan became sick and died on 25 July 1889. "The dreadful attack of fever, which finally succeeded in overthrowing the physical man, served to strengthen those traits of character, which he possessed, to such an extent that never during the long hours of eight weeks intense suffering, was he heard to murmur once. Milligan is buried at Union Cemetery in Ozark, Alabama, with his second wife.

Milsaps, Reuben Webster: born 30 May 1833 in Copiah Co., MS, died 28 June 1916
Krick's *Staff Officers…* lists Milsaps as a major and assistant adjutant and inspector general for Loring. Crute's *Confederate Staff Officers…* has Milsaps as assistant adjutant general as of 15 July 1864. Milsaps is best remembered for founding Milsaps College in 1889-90. He donated the land in Jackson, Mississippi. In 2021 it is a private liberal arts college with 910 students. He was well educated, attending what is today's DePauw University in Indiana, and then earned a law degree from Harvard. Major Milsaps and his wife are interred in a tomb near the centre of Milsaps College.

Moore, John Creed: born 28 FEB 1824 in Hawkins Co., TN, died 31 DEC 1910 in Texas
Moore was only temporarily under Loring's command in Mississippi. Before Loring's Division was formed in May 1863 his command underwent numerous unit changes; it was known as the 1st Division. Moore graduated from West Point in 1849. In antebellum days he worked as a civil engineer and with a railroad in his native East-Tennessee. He was teaching at Shelby College in Kentucky when the war began. He received an appointment in the Regular Confederate army and was sent to Galveston, Texas to work on its defenses. This led to Moore becoming colonel of the 2nd Texas Infantry.

The 2nd Texas fought at Shiloh where it earned the praise of General Bragg and others. Moore was promoted to brigadier and commanded a brigade in time for Van Dorn's attack on Corinth. His men captured three enemy camps and a redoubt. Pemberton came to command in Mississippi, bringing Moore's Brigade into his command. On 12 March they were sent to Yazoo City, subject to orders from Loring. Loring was victorious over all attempts to take nearby Fort Pemberton. By the end of March the enemy retreated from the area, and Moore's Brigade was only under Loring until late April. They returned to Vicksburg, and were later exchanged. They were at Lookout Mountain and Missionary Ridge, fighting with great success amidst defeats. It seems unfortunate that the War Department had decided to separate Moore from his brigade, wanting him in Mobile. Moore resigned on 3 February 1864, and returned to Texas. He taught there postbellum. He died on 31 December 1910 in Osage, Texas, and was buried there.

Myrick, John Douglas: 30 April 1835 in Hertford Co., NC, died 30 January 1869

Myrick was Loring's Chief of Artillery and Aide-de-Camp in Virginia. He apparently went to Mississippi with him, as he commanded Loring's artillery at Fort Pemberton. He later commanded an artillery battalion in Loring's Division. Myrick is on the roles of University of North Carolina and received a bachelor's degree in 1850. The census for 1850 shows him in Saint Luke's Parrish, Southampton County, Virginia. The county borders Hertford, and it is likely he had a connection as he is shown as a lawyer. Myrick died in Staunton City, Virginia. He is buried at Elmwood Cemetery in Norfolk, Virginia.

Nelson, Noel Ligon: born 1833 in Walton County, Georgia, died 30 November 1864

Colonel Nelson farmed in Claiborne Parish, Louisiana and married Emma Moragne in antebellum days. *Confederate Colonels* shows him as a lieutenant in the 12th Louisiana on 13 August 1861. He was a major in 1862, a lieutenant colonel in 1863, and colonel on 10 May 1864. The last promotion was the same day Thomas Moore Scott was promoted to brigadier. Both of Nelson's legs were crushed by artillery fire at Franklin, and he died that night at the McGavock home, Carnton. He is buried there.

Neilson, Charles P.: born about 1836 in Amite County, Miss., buried Liberty, Amite Co.
Neilson was lieutenant colonel in the 33rd Mississippi in 1864. His father was Richard Moore Neilson (1809-1881). His mother was Jane Elizabeth Sarah Neilson (1810-1880). Neilson seems to have been born in Amite County, which borders Louisiana, but date of birth not found. Charles married Louisa A. Bates (1840-1872) in 1858.

Author Wiley Sword found a lettre from him to a newly widowed wife of one of his soldiers, in the Carter House Archives at Franklin. It was written as if he was present, although Captain Jackson is shown in command since July 1864. Neilson survived the war and dedicated one of the first Confederate monuments, in Liberty, on 26 April 1871.

Dedication of "Liberty Monument" in Liberty, Mississippi: The monument was received for all Confederate veterans by Lt. Col. Charles P. Neilson in April 1871. It was designed and built by a former Confederate captain, A. J. Lewis of Port Gibson. It was one of the first Confederate monuments erected.

Norwood, John Henry: born 23 NOV 1828 at Bellefonte, Alabama, died 12 NOV 1891

Lt. Col. Norwood was at Irving College in Tennessee, before reading law in Bellefonte. He was admitted to the bar in 1852. He was appointed probate judge in 1855, and held that position until enlisting in March 1861. After capture at Fort Donelson he was sent to prison at Fort Warren, Boston Harbour. Records indicate he was six feet tall, with brown hair. Serious wounds at Peach Tree Creek got him permission to return home to recover. Our war for independence ended before he recuperated. He returned to his law practice in 1865. He was buried at Netherland Cemetery in or near Bellefonte. His wife, Mary A. Netherland (1835-1903) rests beside him.

Oatis, Martin Augustus: born 2 April 1833 in Hancock Co., MS, died 26 JAN 1895 in TX
Confederate Colonels has Oatis born in Hancock County on the Gulf coast, but reared farther inland at Monticello and Brookhaven. He graduated from the University of Mississippi with honours, and then studied law at Cumberland's law school, then in Lebanon, Tennessee. He was practicing law in Brookhaven by 1860. He married Helen Teunisson. Oatis was lieutenant in the 22nd Mississippi by 27 April 1861. He was wounded at Shiloh, Baton Rouge, and Peach Tree Creek. No doubt his courage led to promotions. Colonel Wallace Colbert was in command of Featherston's Brigade at Bentonville and killed. Oatis seems to have taken brigade command next. *Confederate Military History* has him commanding his own 22nd, along with the 1st, 33rd, and 1st

Battalion. Oatis was promoted to colonel on 19 April 1865; Featherston had returned. This was the day of Lincoln's funeral, and a few days after Johnston and Sherman began negotiations. Oatis returned to Brookhaven to practice law. He moved to Cleburne, Texas by 1870, and was a probate judge. He is buried there in the Cleburne Cemetery.

Old Douglas: born ?, killed at Vicksburg in 1863
Old Douglas has long been assumed to be a veteran of the U.S. Camel Corps. It had its origins with Jefferson Davis. He was saddened by the death of horses and mules on the wagon trains to California in the 1850s. As U.S. Secretary of War he persuaded President Franklin Pierce to appropriate $30,000 to buy camels in Egypt and experiment with adaptability. They were landed in Texas and so proved to be difficult to manage. But Egyptian camels had not seen rushing water and were afraid of wading streams. Packs designed for mules slipped off, and horses could not stand their presence.

It turns out camels were also brought into the port of Mobile in antebellum years. A *Confederate Veteran* article (JUL/AUG 2021) sets the story on Old Douglas straight. William H. Hargrove, a Trinity, Mississippi planter, saw an ad in the 23 March 1860 issue of the *Mobile Daily Register*. It offered "30 Superior Young Camels, well broke, suitable for any plantation work." Hargrove bought Old Douglas and shipped him by steamboat to Mississippi. When the 43rd Mississippi was formed, in May 1862, Hargrove presented Old Douglas to Col. William Hudson Moore and the regiment. Moore was mortally wounded at Corinth. Old Douglas was killed by a sharpshooter at Vicksburg.

Pemberton, John Clifford: born 10 August 1814 in Philadelphia, PA, died 13 July 1881
Pemberton was graduated in the West Point class of 1837. He won two brevets for gallantry in the Mexican War. The Pennsylvanians marriage to a Virginian led him to adhere to the Confederacy. One unsolved mystery of the war is why Jefferson Davis placed the inexperienced Pemberton in command in Mississippi, which Davis considered

the second most important area after Richmond. Pemberton's entry in *Generals in Gray* points out there was nothing in his Confederate service to warrant his rapid promotions from brigadier to major general to lieutenant general, on 10 OCT 1862. Unfortunately Loring and Pemberton were not a harmonious team. Even worse, Pemberton could not please both the president and Joe Johnston. The result was the surrender of Vicksburg. His loyalty should not be questioned. He took a reduction in rank, and served as a colonel. Pemberton was buried in Philadelphia at Laurel Hill Cemetery. He shares a monument with his wife, Martha Thompson (1827-1907).

<u>Phillips, Dr. George Crawford: born 3 OCT 1835, died 3 NOV 1927 in Akron, Ohio</u>

Phillips was a surgeon for the 22nd Mississippi of Featherston's Brigade. He was a physician in Tchula, Holmes County before secession. He enlisted in the Black Hawk Rifles, which became Company G of the 22nd, on 12 August 1861. He was appointed assistant surgeon. He wrote to *Confederate Veteran* for a 1906 issue, describing Franklin. Phillips was first married to Annie R. Chew, and second to Lucinda L. Dyer. Phillips was visiting a daughter in Akron, Ohio when he died. He was buried in the Odd Fellows Cemetery in Lexington, Holmes County, Mississippi.

Survivors of the 22nd Mississippi Infantry Regiment were apparently having a reunion. Phillips is circled and Lt. Col. H.J. Reid is next to him.

Polk, Leonidas: born 10 APR 1806 in Raleigh, NC, killed 14 JUN 1864 in Georgia

Polk and Braxton Bragg were incompatible. The instances were many. The last was Polk's failure at Chickamauga, which led Bragg to prefer charges of disobedience and neglect of duty. Davis and Polk met in October in Atlanta and in Montgomery to discuss Polk going to Mississippi. Hardee had been there since July, but would be sent back to Bragg and the Army of Tennessee. Johnston was in command in Mississippi but left to take command of the army due to Bragg's resignation after Missionary Ridge. Thus Polk came to command the divisions of Loring and French, and would until he was killed.

Polk entered West Point in 1823, resigned his commission after graduation and attended a seminary. He was ordained in the Episcopal Church in 1830. He was also on a visit to Raleigh and married Frances Ann Devereux. The Diocese of Louisiana was organized in 1838 and Polk became their first bishop. Unfortunately for the Confederacy, Davis made the bishop a general. A daughter, Katherine, married William Gale, and he was on Polk's staff. Immediately after he was killed, Gale went to bring Mrs. Polk to Georgia. She was a sort of refugee in Asheville, North Carolina, as was Gale's wife and other family. Polk was buried at Saint Paul's church in Augusta. He and Mrs. Polk were reinterred at Christ Church Cathedral in New Orleans in 1945, in a crypt under the church.

The scene below is the top of Pine Mountain. It was the highest point in an advance line held by Bate's Division. Timber had been cleared from the steep slopes for cleared fields of fire. Hardee was concerned about the position and asked Johnston to look at it. Polk came along and this caught Sherman's attention. He said, "How saucy they are," and ordered artillery to fire. The first shot scattered Johnston, Hardee, and Bate. Polk lingered and the second shot hit him in the chest, tearing out his lungs. Bate said his death threw a gloom over his division. His "virtues had endeared him to officers and privates…"

Porterfield, George Alexander: born 24NOV1822 in Berkeley Co., VA, died 27FEB1919

Porterfield graduated from Virginia Military Institute in 1844. He was an officer in the Mexican War, a Jefferson County farmer and married Emily C. Terrill. He became colonel of the 25th Virginia, though most of his recruits were captured or dispersed at Philippi. This led him to be chief of ordinance for Loring beginning 9 AUG 1861 to about APR 1862. He later became a banker in Charlestown. He died in Martinsburg, West Virginia, and is buried there in Greenhill Cemetery.

Quintard, Charles Todd: born 22 DEC 1824 in Stamford, Connecticut, died 15 FEB 1898

Quintard came to Loring in western Virginia as an aide-de-camp, on 10 January 1862. The future bishop left Nashville with the 1st Tennessee and that brought them to Virginia. He had studied medicine and became a doctor in 1847. He was ordained as an Episcopal in 1856. Quintard wrote of serving under Loring: "During the march against Romney, General Loring had me commissioned by the Secretary of War as his aide-de-camp. I was very strongly opposed to holding such a commission, and declined to accept it, but I could not leave General Loring in the troubles and anxieties that distressed him, and so as a member of his staff, I traveled around considerably at that time, going from camp to camp.." Quintard continued, "On the 21st of February (1862) I went with General Loring to Norfolk, to which point he had been ordered, instead, as I had hoped, to Georgia, where I would have been nearer my family. At this time he was promoted to Major-General. We went, of course, by way of Richmond where I called with him on President Jefferson Davis… General Loring had a severe chill followed by congestion of the right lung, which was the precursor of an attack of pneumonia affecting both lungs. I watched by his bedside in Norfolk through all his illness…" Quintard got to visit his family in Rome, Georgia. Norfolk was evacuated so when he returned he found Loring with his new command on the New River. "The General and all his staff gave me a most cordial greeting, but the former told me that I had no business to resign and that he had kept the place open for me. If I would not be his aide he had a place for me as chaplain." But his resignation had been approved. Quintard continued, "In June, I had a petition from my old regiment to rejoin it. I had no difficulty getting a chaplain's commission. General Loring wrote me a strong letter, and that, with the aid of a telegram from General Polk, secured it." Quintard would meet Loring again outside Nashville in December 1864.

Postbellum, Quintard was on the Georgia coast, at Darien, when Loring passed away. He officiated at his funeral at Saint Augustine; refer to Loring's entry. Quintard's war diary is a fine source: *Doctor Quintard, Chaplain C.S.A. and Second Bishop of Tennessee*.

Reid, H. J. Reid: born 25 FEB 1827 near Woodville, Mississippi, died circa 1906
Reid served as a private in the Mexican War. By 1850 he was living near Acona, in Holmes County. In 1861 he raised the Black Hawk Rifles and was elected captain of that 22nd Mississippi Infantry company. They fought in Breckinridge's reserve at Shiloh, around such landmarks as the Sunken Road and he Bloody Pond. Reid was promoted to major afterward. Breckinridge's near successful attempt to retake Baton Rouge led to Reid's promotion to lieutenant colonel. They were in Bowen's Brigade at Corinth. Reid's horse was shot and he charged on foot with the 22nd, and they were one of the units given credit for the capture of a 20-pounder U.S. gun named Lady Richardson. Bowen was killed at Champion Hill and after the retreat from Jackson, Reid was in poor health. He was not able to serve in the field again. A 1906 *Confederate Veteran* (Vol. 14, page 132) memorializes Reid a "devoted husband and father," and has his photo.

Reynolds, Arthur Exum: born 29 NOV 1817 in Alexandria, TN, died 1880, Corinth, MS
Reynolds briefly led Tilghman's Brigade, after his death, at Champion Hill, thus he his image is on a raised relief, below, at Vicksburg. On 8 June John Adams was ordered to command it, ending Reynolds's service in Loring's Division. *More Generals in Gray* has Reynolds having studied law in Alabama before moving to Jacinto, Mississippi. It was in Tishomingo County, which was later split, so that it is in Alcorn County, as is Corinth. Reynolds was one of four Tishomingo delegates sent to the Mississippi Secession Convention. The ordinance passed by a vote of 84 to 15. Reynolds and the three others had all voted against. The Tennessee River was along the eastern side, and like a number of downriver counties in Tennessee voting against secession, it seems the commerce connection

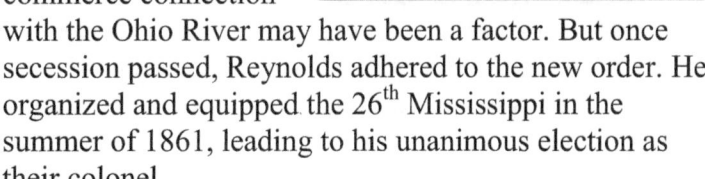

with the Ohio River may have been a factor. But once secession passed, Reynolds adhered to the new order. He organized and equipped the 26th Mississippi in the summer of 1861, leading to his unanimous election as their colonel.

Reynolds and the 26th found themselves in the Army of Northern Virginia in 1864. They fought in the Wilderness where Lt. Col. Francis Marion Boone was killed. Reynolds was wounded at the Weldon Railroad in August, but survived the war. He was elected to Congress but the vengeful Republicans refused to seat him. Reynolds continued his legal career in Corinth. He died in 1880 and is buried in the Jacinto Cemetery.

Robinson, Henry: died by 1894
Robinson reported to Loring to serve as assistant adjutant general on 14 October 1862. When Loring reached Mississippi he wrote Quintard that Henry Robinson was with him. He served as AAG for Adams in 1864. Krick's *Staff Officers...* indicates Robinson became James Longstreet's AAG on 18 March 1865, though he may never have served.

Rorer, Walter A.: born 4 July 1826 in Mississippi killed at Franklin, TN on 30NOV1864

John L. Collins wrote *Confederate Veteran* (Volume 10, page 458) on 20 May 1900. "Colonel [Lt. Col.] Rorer of the Twentieth Mississippi was one of the bravest of the brave on that sad afternoon. A grand and noble character, modest, unassuming, but as brave and determined as a lion. I well remember the esteem and confidence General Adams had in him as an officer and soldier." Collins said in the Atlanta Campaign Rorer lost one or two fingers to a minie ball. He wrapped his hand up as best he could rather than retire from the field. In a *Confederate Veteran* issue from 1902 (Volume 10, p. 457) Col James Binford, of the 15th Mississippi, recalled, "Col. Rorer was lieutenant colonel of the Twentieth Mississippi. He was from the eastern part of Mississippi, and I know but little of his history prior to the war; but he was one of the most daring men I ever knew, and, in fact, he always impressed me as being absolutely destitute of fear. I was told that when we crossed the Tennessee River he remarked that he was going into Tennessee a lieutenant colonel, but coming out a brigadier general or a corpse. Rorer was correct. He was killed at Franklin and is buried there at the McGavock Cemetery.

Russell, Daniel Renner: born Washington, D.C. in 1821, died Carrolton, MS 6 JUN 1870
Russell was a colonel of the 20th Mississippi. He was an officer in the Mexican War, and also was a state auditor for Mississippi, 1851-55. *Confederate Colonels* has two wives, Mary E. Booth, and Julia P. Hall. When Mississippi seceded she sent commissioners to other states. Featherston, for example was sent to Kentucky, and Russell was sent to Missouri. Russell was colonel of the 20th by 27 June 1861. He was not with them when they were captured at Fort Donelson, due to an ankle injury. It appears he commanded them during the spring 1863 when they were mounted, but resigned due to illnesses and general disabilities on 8 August 1863. He had a law practice in Carrolton, about 20 miles south of Grenada, and is buried there in Evergreen Cemetery. Renouard middle name?

Scott, Thomas Moore: born 1829, probably in Athens, Georgia, died 21 April 1876
Though Scott is thought to have been born in Athens, Georgia, he settled in Louisiana in antebellum years. He had been in Claiborne Parish since 1857. His personal papers were destroyed in a fire so limited information survives. He was a mason and was married.

Scott organized the 12th Louisiana in August 1861 and was elected colonel. Once Columbus, Kentucky was occupied the 12th was sent to that Mississippi River position. They later served downriver at Island Number Ten and Fort Pillow in Tennessee, and at Port Hudson, Louisiana. While near Island Number Ten a Yankee spy, Spencer Brown, was captured. He was put in charge of Scott who marched to Tiptonville. In a few days they were on a boat bound for Fort Pillow. Overnight he wasn't given anything to eat. The next morning he asked for Scott to see him. "I asked him if he had orders to starve me, and he, repenting, took me upstairs and gave me a good breakfast." His story gives a glimpse into Scott as a person. As for the spy, he was caught again in 1863 and hung.

The 12th came to Buford's Brigade of Loring's Division before Champion Hill. They made a successful bayonet charge, and won praise from Loring. His Kentucky infantry units desire to be mounted came to fruition. Thus, Buford was assigned to a cavalry command under Forrest in March 1864. Scott was promoted to brigadier on 10 May 1864. He already had command of the Third Brigade, or Buford's, in Loring's Division. As the Army of Mississippi was absorbed into the Army of Tennessee the numerical designation faded away so that it became Scott's Brigade. It really proved its courage at Peach Tree Creek and Franklin. In the later battle Scott was hit by artillery fire and at first reported paralyzed, thus his service was ended.

Lt. Col. Thomas Standifer, of the 12th Louisiana, had been sent back to Louisiana in August 1864. His entry explains he was rounding up absent soldiers and sending them back to the 12th. Scott was to relieve Standifer. Scott's Brigade was dissolved in a 9 April reorganization. Entry for Snodgrass, below, explains.

After independence was lost Scott managed a sugar plantation near the Gulf. Damage to his spine was so severe he probably could do little to relieve his pain. All the worse was U.S. military rule was ongoing. Thomas Jefferson couldn't have imagined this when the Louisiana Purchase was signed. *Generals at Rest* states Scott was found dead in a New Orleans saloon, "apparently of an alcohol overdose." He died on 21 April 1876, and is buried in Greenwood Cemetery in New Orleans. The author made two trips to Greenwood in 1997 trying to confirm his burial place. He is probably buried in the Soldiers Home Tomb though his name is not on any of the vaults. Cemetery records indicate his wife, Mrs. T.M. Scott, bought 44 Pine in 1980. No marker for a Scott was found, but it seems this may be where she is buried.

Snodgrass, John: born 19 MAY 1836 in Jackson County., Alabama, died 19 AUG 1888
The Forgotten Regiment is the history of the 55th Alabama, commanded by Snodgrass. It says his early education was received from a cousin, Alex Snodgrass. That prepared him to continue studies in Huntsville. He was a merchant in Bellefonte, and married Mollie Brown. She filed for an Alabama pension about 1920. Her birthday was 26 August 1842, also in Jackson County, and they married on 13 October 1862.

The Forgotten Regiment says, "John Snodgrass was 6-feet 1-inch tall. He made a striking figure in his gray uniform for he had gray eyes to match. His complexion was fair and his hair was dark. Snodgrass was interested in the militia and the weekly drill sessions that took place in Scottsboro before the war broke out. This appealed to him since he was young, handsome and interested in the ladies. The uniform made a striking figure even more noticeable to the proper ladies of the town." He was also the great-grandson of Revolutionary War Colonel William Snodgrass, who later settled in Tennessee.

Snodgrass was captain of the Jackson County Hornets. They were first sent to Pensacola, and he took leave in October 1861 to marry Mary Jane Brown. While absent the company was assigned to a Mississippi regiment at Fort Pillow. He didn't care for that and this led to the formation of an Alabama battalion he commanded. It was known as the 4th, the 16th, and as Snodgrass's.

The battalion went with Breckinridge in his attempt to liberate Baton Rouge in August 1862. Snodgrass complimented two privates "who boldly moved in advance of the command…They were the first to open fire and the last to quit the field." He praised his battalion for "having advanced and stood under fire, from which older troops and greater numbers had retired." Snodgrass was promoted to colonel on 23 February 1863. His battalion and another joined to create the 55th Alabama at Port Hudson in March. In April the 55th was in Buford's Brigade, which went to Mississippi, where Loring's Division was organized in May. They fought at Champion Hill and escaped with the division. When Buford transferred to the cavalry, the brigade became Scott's. Their history under him is covered above. Most significant episode for Snodgrass was leading the brigade, after Scott was wounded at Franklin. Snodgrass seems to have gone home on leave after Hood's Tennessee Campaign. Perhaps the following story was in the winter 1865.

The Forgotten Regiment includes a family story "that during the war he was at home on leave to see his wife and new baby. The alarm was sounded, 'The Yankees are coming!' Colonel John hastily crawled through a secret door into the attic over the kitchen and a heavy chest of drawers was pulled over the door. The black nurse noticed that one of his army boots had been left in his wife's room; the boot was thrust under the cover of his wife's bed. The house was searched by the Yankees, but the soldiers left without finding either Colonel John or the boot. The piece of furniture that hid the door is treasured today by Colonel John's descendants." The author was able to obtain excerpts of the book from John David Snodgrass, an attorney in Huntsville; he may have become a judge.

Very few Alabama troops of Scott's Brigade made it to North Carolina in 1865. The majority of the brigade consisted of 12th Louisiana soldiers The Mississippi River made furloughs a problem. Scott himself was sent back and never returned to duty. The brigade was under Capt. John H. Dixon, of the 12th Louisiana, at Bentonville. In reorganization on 9 April it was broken up. The Alabama regiments went to Shelley's Brigade. It had been in Walthall's Division. Thus Loring's had Cantey's, Featherston's, and Lowry's.

Postbellum, Snodgrass was engaged in a number of enterprises in Scottsboro. He operated a store, a cotton gin, and was active in Democrat party politics. The *Jackson County Sentinel* published an obituary: "Last Sunday at 11:00 a.m. Colonel John Snodgrass of Scottsboro died at Tullahoma, Tennessee of complications of diseases. Being in bad health he went to the springs at Tullahoma on the 7th inst., for recreation. His condition was, however worse than anticipated, and he gradually grew worse until death resulted. His remains were brought home Sunday night, and after funeral services in the Episcopal Church on Monday morning the remains were laid to rest in the Scottsboro cemetery with Knights of Honor ceremonies. The funeral procession was the largest, perhaps, ever witnessed in Scottsboro."

The Sons of Confederate Veterans (S.C.V.) in Alabama have enhanced the surrender site of Streight's raid. The raid was to destroy industry and railroads in Georgia, but failed to make it across Alabama thanks to Forrest and his cavalry. Today a visit to Cedar Bluff rewards the visitor with interpretative enhancements. One of the pavers memorializes the Colonel Snodgrass S.C.V. camp of Stevenson, Alabama.

Sons of Confederate Veterans camps and their members have set pavers at Cedar Bluff, the site of a Forrest victory. Colonel Pegues was mortally wounded while leading a charge at Gaines's Mill. Camps choose their names and don't limit themselves to generals and colonels. Note pavers for a unit, a sergeant, a lieutenant, and for Admiral Raphael Semmes at top-right.

Standifer, Thomas Cunningham: born 10 NOV 1827, died 10 AUG 1897 in Louisiana

Standifer attained the rank of lieutenant colonel in the 12th Louisiana. He had been a prominent mercantile proprietor in early Rushton, Louisiana. He married Sarah Alabama McLeroy (17 DEC 1837 to 11 MAR 1908). An 1897 *Confederate Veteran* article on Standifer says after the Atlanta Campaign he was detailed to the Trans-Mississippi to gather up men who had joined other commands. It says officers there were disposed to accept men such men and Kirby Smith winked at it. It was a dangerous assignment, but Standifer managed to forward 150 men to the 12th Louisiana. The article concludes he was "a grand man, who always helped a soldier in need." Louisiana History, The Journal of … (Winter 1995) article says he was sent back in August 1864 to collect absentees of the 12th Louisiana. He was there until General Scott, wounded at Franklin, came to relieve him; winter 1865. Standifer is buried in Greenwood Cemetery, Rushton.

Starke, William Edward: born 1814 in Brunswick County, VA, killed 17 SEP 1862

Starke served as a volunteer aide-de-camp to Loring during some part of 1861. He was one of five of Loring's staff to become generals. He had worked as a cotton broker in Mobile, and also in New Orleans, when the war began. He also served as an aide-de-camp to Robert Garnett, who was mortally wounded in western Virginia. Later in 1861 Starke became colonel of the 60th Virginia. He fought well in the Seven Days, and was promoted to brigadier prior to 2nd Manassas. He was with Stonewall Jackson for the capture of Harper's Ferry. Starke was leading Jackson's old division when he was killed at Sharpsburg, Maryland. He is buried in Hollywood Cemetery in Richmond.

Stephens, Marquis De LaFayette: born 9 November 1829 in Tenn., died 15 April 1911

Stephens was born in Williamson County. He studied medicine at the University of Louisville Medical College. He became a physician and teacher in Calhoun County, Mississippi. He married Mary Jane Duff, and was a delegate to the Mississippi Secession Convention. He was a lieutenant in the 17th Mississippi, of which Featherston became colonel. Stephens was granted leave to return home in 1862, and was a captain in the 32nd Mississippi by 7 March 1862. He was promoted to colonel on 11 March 1864, and often led Featherston's Brigade. He was wounded while leading the 31st at Franklin. His thigh was shattered, so that he was invalided. He lived in Water Valley, Mississippi after the war, and is buried there in Oak Hill Cemetery.

Stevenson, Carter Littlepage: b. 21SEP1817 near Fredericksburg, VA, died 15AUG1888

Stevenson was one of five staff members for Loring to rise to general. They would both be major generals commanding divisions in Mississippi under Pemberton, and later with the Army of Tennessee. Stevenson graduated from West Point in 1838, and fought in the Mexican War. After serving on Loring's staff he was colonel of the 53rd Virginia. He was in command at the western tip of Virginia and drove the enemy out of Cumberland Gap. He commanded a division that was taken from Bragg's Army of Tennessee, and sent to Mississippi. He and Loring agreed on strategy prior to Champion Hill. Though captured at Vicksburg (bust at right), Stevenson was exchanged and directed to the Army of Tennessee after Chickamauga. He was with much of his division outside Chattanooga in September 1863. Thus when Loring came to the army in May 1864 Stevenson was again Loring's fellow division commander.

Postbellum he worked at a civil and mining engineer in Caroline County, Virginia. He is buried in Fredericksburg, with his wife. Both markers are nearly illegible. Wife Martha G. appears to have died 24 August 1886. He died two Augusts later. The author arranged for a new grave marker in 2007. It was paid for by the local "Mathew F. Maury S.C.V. Camp," and "General Joseph E. Johnston S.C.V. Camp" in Nashville.

Stewart, Alexander Peter: born 2 OCT 1821 in Rogersville, TN, died 30 AUG 1908

Loring and Stewart did not serve together until Stewart was given permanent command of Polk's Corps. Loring, as the senior major general, had held temporary command. Some would have been happy to see him retain it. As soon as Polk was killed Johnston wired President Davis, "It is essential to have a Lt. Genl immediately to succeed Lt. Gen. Polk. I regard Maj. Genl Stewart as the best qualified of the Maj. Genls of this army. Time is important." Johnston had to have been impressed with Stewart and his division defeating a U.S. corps at New Hope Church. When he sent a courier to inquire whether reinforcements were needed, Stewart replied, "My own troops will hold the position." Davis took Johnston's recommendation to Lee, who didn't know Stewart, yet agreed he might be the best choice. Braxton Bragg was in an advisory role in Richmond; it seems he favoured Stewart. Stewart had been a Bragg supporter in the Army of Tennessee, and had written him in March as a friend. Bragg also carried weight in recommending Hood as Johnston's replacement. Bragg had been appreciative of Stewart breaking through the U.S. lines at Murfreesborough's "Slaughter Pen." That had gained Stewart a promotion to major general. The four West-Pointers may have preferred Stewart as a fellow graduate. Loring wasn't, nor were two other major generals that might have been considered; Cheatham and Cleburne. So Bragg saw Stewart promoted to lieutenant general in June, and Davis ratified it. Hood was new to army command, just as Stewart was to corps command. After Cheatham's Corps failed to block the turnpike at Spring Hill, Hood told

Stewart he should have let his corps lead the advance. It appears Stewart was the best Confederate general on the field; better than Hood or the other corps commanders.

The top house, in Winchester, was one of Stewart's childhood homes. It is in Franklin County, which borders Alabama to the south. Tennessee wasn't seceding fast enough, and they illegally voted to secede from the state, but a county cannot as the states created their counties. The house below was his Lebanon home, where he taught at Cumberland University, before and after the war. The author took photo in 1998, several years before the house burned. Stewart was a University of Mississippi chancellor from 1874 to 1876, and died at Biloxi in 1908. A son settled in Saint Louis in 1869, so when Stewart's wife Harriet died in 1898 she was buried there at Bellefontaine; he and other family are too.

Stigler, James Monroe: born 8 MAR 1835 in Holmes Co. MS, died 26 OCT 1900
Confederate Colonels has Stigler as the Clerk of Court in Holmes County, near the centre of the state, north of Jackson before the war. He was married to Mary E. Wilson. Major Stigler commanded the 1st Mississippi Sharpshooter in Featherston's Brigade. He made it through the retreat, for *Confederate Military History* says in North Carolina he had the 3rd, 31st and 40th. His own sharpshooters may have been with him or consolidated under another unit. He wasn't promoted to colonel until 19 April 1865. This was the day of Lincoln's funeral and several days after Johnston and Sherman began negotiations. Stigler was a farmer in Holmes County after the war. He died in Lexington, Holmes County, and is buried there in the Odd Fellows Cemetery.

Sykes, Columbus: born 23 FEB 1832, killed by tree 7 JAN 1865 at Marietta, Mississippi

Sykes was lieutenant colonel of the 43rd Mississippi, Adams's Brigade, when he was killed by a falling tree. He had been home to bury his brother, W.E. Sykes, the regiment's adjutant, who was killed in skirmishing near Decatur, Alabama in October 1864. Bishop Quintard's memoir says Sykes was buried at his residence. The Kennesaw Mountain N.B. Park has his gloves, sash, uniform frock coat, and civilian linen duster. There is a quote: "Tell my dear wife and children I loved them to the last." He is buried at Odd Fellows Rest Cemetery, Aberdeen, Monroe County, Mississippi.

Taliaferro, William Booth: born 28DEC1822 in Gloucester Co., VA, died 27FEB1898

Taliaferro was graduated from William and Mary in 1841, and then studied law at Harvard. He served as an officer in the Mexican War. After Virginia seceded he was appointed colonel of the 23rd Virginia. Later in 1861 he commanded a brigade in Loring's Army of the Northwest. When Loring was stationed at Romney in January 1863, he was one of several officers who protested to the War Department about Jackson. After Loring was transferred from Jackson's command, he and Taliaferro were separated. His greatest day was likely his command of Battery Wagner, near Charleston, South Carolina. His postbellum career found him in the Virginia Legislature and as a judge in Gloucester Co. He died there at his estate, Dunham Massie," and was buried at Ware Church Cemetery.

Tilghman, Lloyd: born 18JAN1816, Talbot Co., MD, killed Champion Hill, 16MAY1863

Tilghman was born in Talbot County on Maryland's Eastern Shore of Chesapeake Bay. He had attended schools in Baltimore before entering West Point at only 15 years old. He graduated in July 1836, and was assigned to the Dragoons, but resigned his commission in September to work as a civil engineer with the *Baltimore & Susquehanna Railroad*. He married Augusta Murray Boyd in Maine in 1843. The best man was Joseph Hooker, the future Yankee general. Tilghman likely knew Hooker at West Point, as he graduated in 1837. They both served in the Mexican War too.

Tilghman returned to railroad civil engineering after Mexico. The discovery of gold in California in 1849 took American travelers to the Isthmus of Panama, where New York investors were building the Isthmus Railroad. Tilghman worked on it a year, during which time Augusta bore at least one of their eight children. Perhaps concerns over the tropical climate took them back to the states. Tilghman found a new railroad civil engineering opportunity in Paducah, Kentucky in 1852, and it became his home (next page). The General Tilghman Camp, of the SCV, has restored and opened the house.

When Tennessee seceded it was the result of Lincoln's call for troops. This invasion of the Confederacy was unpalatable to many Kentuckians. A recruiting base was just south of the border north of Clarksville. Tilghman arrived with recruits at what became known as Camp Boone. He became colonel of the 3rd Kentucky. It was not long before Tilghman found himself a general and that led him to command Forts Donelson and Henry. The two forts would have 30 guns. Fort Heiman, across the Tennessee from Henry, never received heavy artillery. Too much emphasis was on the Mississippi River, evidenced by Columbus having 140 guns.

Tilghman's surrender of flooded Fort Henry led him to be imprisoned at Fort Warren in Boston Harbor. Officers surrendered at Fort Donelson were there as were political prisoners from Maryland. Most of them were legislators who were going to vote for secession, and the Lincoln administration imprisoned to prevent the vote. No doubt Tilghman renewed some old ties with citizens from the land of his birth. He was invited to join a mess of these Marylanders, and a few days later he was forced to separate. Perhaps Tilghman had some military ideas to bring Maryland into the Confederacy!

Tilghman was exchanged that summer and sent to Virginia. The C.S. War Department sent him to Mississippi, where he was to reorganize exchanged Confederate soldiers. Such a bureaucratic position was at least better than prison, and then another unfortunate duty came his way. He was assigned to a military court to hear charges against Earl Van Dorn for mismanagement of the October 1862 attack of enemy-held Corinth.

December found Tilghman in Lovell's Division in northern Mississippi, facing Grant in his first attempt to reach Vicksburg. Lovell's days were numbered because he was under scrutiny for losing New Orleans back in April. But here he saw an opportunity to strike the enemy near Coffeeville, and sent Tilghman to take care of them. It was a footnote in the combined efforts to take Vicksburg. But Tilghman remarked "the whole affair was a complete success and taught the enemy a lesson I am sure they will not soon forget."

Loring came to Mississippi and in January 1863 Tilghman came under his command. This would be a relationship that seems to have suited Tilghman well enough. And it lasted until his death in the courageous rear guard at Champion Hill. Tilghman must have respected the fellow Mexican War veteran. There was Loring with one arm to show for it. It would have been unusual not to have admired Loring's old red badge of courage.

L.S. Flatan, of St. Louis, wrote *Confederate Veteran* in 1910 (Volume 18, page 423) explaining he was in Cowan's Battery and Tilghman had been speaking him to him. "General Tilghman was a most daring, dashing, splendid officer, and we were fearful that he would be killed...I was the gunner directing and sighting the gun at the time of the advice of General Tilghman, who had a perfect knowledge of the situation of the enemy through his field glasses. His last words to anyone were in the highest compliment to me, praising my excellent marksmanship, except the words he spoke as he fell from his horse after a three-inch rifle shot had cut him nearly in two, and as he careened and fell he said to his son, who caught him, 'Tell your mother; God bless her.'"

Tilghman's reputation was enhanced by death, and a number of laudatory praises may be found. Col. Arthur E. Reynolds took temporary command of the brigade. Reynolds later wrote of Tilghman in *Confederate Veteran*, "As a man, a soldier, and a general, he had few superiors. Always at his post, he devoted himself, day and night, to the interests of his command. Upon the battlefield collected and observant, he commanded the respect and entire confidence of every officer and soldier under him, and the only censure ever cast upon him was that he always exposed himself too recklessly."

Tilghman was one of the great heroes of Champion Hill. Loring reported Tilghman was "carrying on a deadly and most gallant fight. With less than 1,500 effectives he was attacked by from 6,000 to 8,000 of the enemy with a fine park of artillery; but being advantageously posted, he not only held them in check, but repulsed him on several occasions, and thus kept open the only line of retreat left to the army."

Tilghman's wife's father had been first Treasurer of the State of Maine, and she had an uncle who had been a mayor of New York City. Here were some northern connections to New York City that led Tilghman's surviving sons there. In 1902 they went to Vicksburg, where their father had been buried. They had his remains disinterred and reburied at Woodlawn Cemetery in the Bronx.

Photo (above left) is the dedication of the monument on the Champion Hill battle site where Tilghman was killed. Tilghman's sons are kneeling. Several veterans are in the scene. The woman is Mrs. Sid (Matilda) Champion. The card of Tilghman and High School was sent to a woman in Glasgow, Kentucky; postmarked in July 1938. The school merged with another school in recent years.

Vandiver, George: born 1830, Lawrence Co, Alabama, died 9DEC1863 in Nashville, TN
Vandiver's father, also George, died when he was a boy. This left his mother, Pheba, to raise their five boys on their farm. George grew up, married Mary Hall, and they had six children. George enlisted on Christmas 1861, becoming a private in Company C of the 27th Alabama. They found themselves at Fort Heiman, and when it was evacuated they marched to Fort Donelson, where they were surrendered. After being exchanged they came south and served in the fighting to keep the Mississippi River unvexed. He was allowed a visit home in late summer 1863 and was captured. He was sent to Nashville where the enemy used the five-story Maxwell House Hotel as a temporary prison, before shipping our people north. It was nearing completion when Tennessee seceded, and would not be completed until after independence was lost. One late September the prisoners were going down to breakfast when the column was halted on the temporary stairway. It suddenly collapsed with about 200 falling three and four floors. Vandiver's leg was crushed, though 45 others were crushed to death. Vandiver's leg was amputated, yet he did not survive. The sun last came up for him on 9 December 1863. He was buried at City Cemetery, but moved to Mount Olivet after Confederate Circle was established. His marker has his named misspelled as "Wanderer," though a correct marker may have been placed. The local Sons of Confederate Veterans Camp began living history walking tours at the cemetery in 1993; reenactors portrayed Vandiver on several tours.

Wallace, George Phillips: born 22 NOV 1829 in Perry Co., AL, died 30 OCT 1891 in TX
Wallace became a farmer in Attala County, Mississippi. He married Mary Ann Hodge. He was a captain in the 40th Mississippi on 14 May 1862. He was captured at Vicksburg. Lt. Col. Wallace commanded the 40th of Featherston's Brigade at Peach Tree Creek, and a wound led to amputation of left arm. Wallace was in command because Colonel Colbert was absent, sick. Colbert was wounded at Franklin and killed at Bentonville. Wallace was thus promoted to colonel. He became a farmer in Anderson County, Texas after the war, and died there. He was buried in Bethel Cemetery, in Bethel, Tennessee.

Walthall, Edward Cary: born 4APR1831 in Richmond, VA, died 21APR1898 in W.D.C.

Walthall has been described as "the embodiment of the ideal of Mississippi chivalry." Walthall was about 10 years old when his parents moved to Holly Springs, Mississippi. He was a lawyer as a young man. Secession was on the horizon. Walthall was lieutenant colonel of the illustrious 15th Mississippi during the first year of the war. In May 1862 he was elected colonel of the newly organized 29th Mississippi. They were assigned to James Chalmers' Mississippi brigade. That brigade played a key role in spearheading the attacks on the enemy fortifications at Munfordville, Kentucky in September. Two months later he given command of a newly organized brigade; it included the 29th Mississippi. Promotion to brigadier followed in December. In 1863 they fought at Chickamauga and the following battles around Chattanooga. During the 1864 Atlanta Campaign Walthall took command of a division and was promoted to major general. The campaign brought Walthall and Loring together, and they thereafter fought side by side in such significant actions as Peachtree

Creek. Their divisions became enmeshed at Franklin, causing Loring to become upset. Walthall's cool demeanor may have been a reason Forrest wanted him to command the infantry in the withdrawal from Tennessee. He had resumed practicing law postbellum, and served Mississippi as a U.S. senator. He died in Washington, D.C., and was buried in Holly Springs, in the same cemetery as Featherston and other patriots. *They Sleep Beneath the Mockingbird…* has part of the eulogy: "He was almost the last of a long line of Mississippians of historic type and fame…" His entry also has part of a speech at the dedication of a Confederate monument in Jackson: "We did not go to war for slavery…We went to war…to save the constitution as we read it…"

The top house, circa 1848, is known as Walthall's childhood home, though he was a teenager. It is at 290 E. College Street, Holly Springs. Walthall purchased the circa 1856 house below in 1871, and remodeled it to look like his Virginia childhood home. It is at 73 College Boulevard, Grenada. The Walthall Hotel was named for the general! He is buried at Hillcrest Cemetery in Holly Springs. When Walthall was promoted to major general, Samuel Benton was made brigadier and commander of Walthall's Brigade. Brig. Benton is here, as are Brig. Gen. Daniel Govan, and Featherston too.

Waul, Thomas: born 5JAN1813 in Sumter District, SC, died 28JUL1903 Hunt Co., Texas

Waul's Texas Legion was in Pemberton's department in Mississippi, and briefly served in Loring's Division. Legion means a unit with infantry, cavalry, and artillery. Early in the war legions were found impractical, and usually disbanded. Still, Waul's could be found with twelve infantry companies, organized into two battalions, a cavalry battalion, and artillery. In reporting on Fort Pemberton, Loring mentioned Col. T.N. Waul for his "energy, promptness, and good judgment in the discharge of his duty with his Legion in the fortifications during the engagements. I was greatly indebted to him for the assistance he rendered on so many occasions, and which contributed to our frequent successes." Pemberton transferred Waul's Legion out of Loring's Division before retiring into Vicksburg. It was there Waul's made the most brilliant charge of the siege.

Grant ordered a second assault on Vicksburg on 22 May; he would not order another one! There was a brief breach of S.D. Lee's line at the Railroad Redoubt. Lee turned to Waul to counterattack. Waul led a battalion of the Legion forward. Lt. Col. Edmund W. Pettus, of the 20th Alabama, led them. With rifles, and by rolling and pitching cannon balls, they went forward to retake the redoubt. After Vicksburg was surrendered he was paroled and promoted to brigadier in September. He had a brigade in the Red River Campaign, which prevented an enemy invasion of Texas. Then he fought at Jenkins's Ferry, Arkansas, where another enemy thrust toward Texas was driven north. Waul returned to Texas after the war. He practiced law and farmed near Greenville, the seat of Hunt County. He is buried at Oakwood Cemetery in Fort Worth. A raised relief monument to Waul was placed at Vicksburg N.M.P.***

Weeden, John David: born 27 July 1840 in Huntsville, Alabama, died 16 NOV 1908
The author initially confused Lt. Col. John David Weeden with Lt. Col. John Weedon. The later was killed leading the 22nd Alabama at Chickamauga. Another item of confusion was addressed by Weeden in *Confederate Veteran* in 1896 (Vol. 4, page 303). Weeden explained the 49th had been known as the 31st at Shiloh. They were attached to Trabue's "Kentucky Brigade." They were detached to support Hardee, who was fighting Sherman. A biography of A.S. Johnston, by his son, stated, There "they charged at a double quick, routing the enemy and driving them at a run from the field." Weeden wrote the regiment that became known as the 31st was being organized at Talladega in April.

Weeden also wrote the 49th was organized of "brave men of the counties of Madison, Jackson, Marshall, DeKalb, and Cherokee" counties. He was an adjutant at Shiloh. He concluded, "…nothing lacked in soldiership, except good fortune."

Memorial Record of Alabama entry on Weeden was found online at a Lauderdale County site. It has valuable biographical details. It says he was from Huntsville, and that he was graduated from the University of Alabama in 1859. He was practicing law in Huntsville, when he volunteered for the 9th Alabama. In January 1862 he was ordered to Nashville and made adjutant of the 49th. He was promoted to major after Shiloh, and to lieutenant colonel in 1863.

Weeden is on the organization of 10 June as commander, and no other reference is found. Captain Beeson commanded on the 30th. Then the 49th was consolidated with the 27th and 35th. Ives commanded until he was wounded at Franklin. Weeden is shown commanding the consolidated regiment on the 10 December organization. He was wounded and captured at Nashville on 16 December. He was sent to prison on Johnson's Island. Weeden resided and worked in Florence after the war. He was married to Mattie Hayes Patton (1842-1933) in September 1870. They had four children. Weeden was buried at Maple Hill Cemetery in Huntsville (Block 13, Row 17). A website covers burial places of the 49th.

Wells, Joseph Moorehead: born 7 AUG 1811 in Giles Co., TN, died 9 FEB 1896 in MS

Wells was a Methodist minister in Tishomingo County, Mississippi in antebellum days. *Confederate Colonels* lists wives as Sarah L. Burns and Mrs. Mary E. Armour. Wells was a captain in the 23rd Mississippi, and promoted to lieutenant colonel by 5 SEP 1861. They were captured at Fort Donelson, and exchanged in the fall. Well had been in command of the 23rd, but was not promoted to colonel until 24 SEP 1862. He resigned two Septembers later citing age and illness. He was a minister and farmer in Prentiss County after the war. He is buried there in Blackland Cemetery. An obituary called him a "noble old patriot."

Wesson, Laura: born ???   died High Point, April 1865 in High Point, North Carolina
Loring probably never met Laura Wesson, but she deserves to be remembered. *Louisiana History: The Journal of the Louisiana Historical Society* mentions her. It is in an article in the Winter 1995 issue on the 12th Louisiana in North Carolina. It details numerous command changes for the 12th Louisiana, and Scott's Brigade from the end of the Atlanta Campaign to the time the brigade was dissolved on 9 April 1865. Lt. Joseph Reno commanded the 12th briefly, but at least on 31 March. He was sent to a hospital in High Point. Lt. Joseph L. Reno was in command of the regiment on 31 March. He was sent to the hospital. A small pox epidemic and says a "pesthouse" was set up…

Whiting, Jasper Strong: born 13JUL1828 in Lowell, Mass., died 25DEC1862, Richmond
Whiting came to Loring as an engineer officer in July 1861. Perhaps they had met in New Mexico, as Whiting had been an engineer at a mining camp. He was a younger brother of William Henry Chase Whiting, a Confederate general. The older brother was also an engineer. He developed Fort Fisher into the strongest single fortress in the Confederacy. Unfortunately he was mortally wounded there in 1865. Jasper did not survive the war either. He died of scarlet fever in Richmond and is buried there in Hollywood Cemetery.

Wiley, James Horatio: 6FEB1832 in Louisiana, died 13JUN1902 in Flomaton, Alabama
Major Wiley commanded the 57th Alabama after the Atlanta Campaign. Col. Columbus Cunningham was absent on the 10 September return, and Wiley is shown. Cunningham returned for Hood's campaign into Tennessee as he was wounded at Franklin. Wiley is on the 10 December return, when the army was outside Nashville. Tax records indicate he was a retail dealer in Greensboro, Alabama in 1866. The 1870 U.S. Census shows him living in Troy. The 1880 Census has him in Gadsden. The 1900 Census has him back in Greensboro. He is buried at Oakwood Cemetery in Troy; his headstone shows Masonic.

Wiley's father was James McCaleb Wiley (1806-77). His mother was Elizabeth Duckworth Wiley (1806-1842). Horatio married Josephine Antoinette Bayol in Greene County, Alabama. She was born in Alabama in February 1834. She passed away on 9 August 1920 in New Orleans, and is buried there in LaFayette Cemetery #1.

Williams, James Seymour: born JAN1812 in Savannah, GA, died 7SEP1871, New York
Williams was acting adjutant and inspector general for Loring in October and November 1861. He had attended West Point and commanded a company in the Black Hawk war. He worked as an engineer in railroads from 1837 to 1861. Besides Loring's staff he served on two other staffs, Robert Garnett's and Henry R. Jackson's, in 1861. He then served on other staffs, generally in his native Savannah. He again worked in railroads there postbellum. He died in Staten Island, New York.

Withers, William Temple: born 8JAN1825 in Harrison Co., KY, died 16JUN1889 in KY
"Temp" Withers was General Pemberton's chief of field artillery, and fought with Loring during the withdrawal from Champion Hill. He was born in Harrison County north of Lexington, and had a law practice there in Cynthiana. He was an officer in the Mexican War, and badly wounded. He married Martha Sharkey, became a Mississippi planter, and had a law practice in Jackson. In 1861, he was one of three called on to select a recruiting base for Kentucky volunteers. It was just inside Tennessee north of Clarksville, and was known as Camp Boone. The secretary of war asked him to raise an artillery regiment which became the 1st Mississippi Artillery. He was distinguished at Chickasaw Bayou. After Champion Hill he commanded the artillery at Vicksburg. He later served at Mobile. He had to take sick leaves during the war, still suffering from his Mexican War wound, and was retired to the Invalid Corps on 5 March 1865. He returned to his law practice in Jackson after the war. Perhaps oppression from the U.S. forces during the so called Reconstruction led him back to Kentucky in 1871. He bred horses near Lexington, and a house he purchased in 1874, named Fairlawn, is marked with Kentucky Highway Marker 1447 there. He is buried in Lexington Cemetery. An obituary called Withers "a thorough Christian gentleman, a noble and honest man."

Yost, Samuel McPherson: born 13NOV1838 in Union, VA, died in Staunton 21FEB1915
Yost was assistant quartermaster for Loring, Robert Garnett, or both, in 1861. Yost lived in New Mexico before the war, and might have met Loring there. He was later a quartermaster at posts in Winchester and Staunton. He was dismissed by court martial in May 1863. He ran a newspaper in Staunton postbellum; burial there in Thornrose Cemetery.

Bibliography

PUBLISHED SOURCES:
Allardice, Bruce S. *Confederate Colonels: A Biographical Register*. Columbia, Missouri: University of Missouri Press, 2008
Allardice, Bruce S. *More Generals in Gray*. Baton Rouge, Louisiana: Louisiana State University Press, 1995
Allen, Felicity. *Jefferson Davis: Unconquerable Heart*. Columbia, Missouri: University of Missouri Press, 1999
Ballard, Michael B. *Vicksburg: The Campaign That Opened the Mississippi*. Chapel Hill, North Carolina: The University of North Carolina Press, 2004
Banks, Robert W. *The Battle of Franklin: The Bloodiest Engagement of the War* Between *the States.* Souvenir Edition, Franklin Memorial Association, circa 1990
Bearss, Ed. Grant Marches West: The Battles of Champion Hill and Big Black Bridge. *Blue & Gray Magazine*. Volume 18, Issue 5. June 2001
Bergeron, Jr., Arthur W. *Guide to Louisiana Confederate Military Units: 1861-1865.* Baton Rouge, Louisiana: Louisiana State University Press, 1989
Bradley, Michael R. *They Rode with Forrest*. Gretna, Louisiana: Pelican Publishing Company, 2012
Burgess, Timothy L. *Confederate Deaths and Burials in Nashville, Tennessee 1861-65.* Nashville, Tennessee: Author's Corner, 2012
Bush, Bryan S. *Lloyd Tilghman: Confederate General in the Western Theatre*. Morley, Missouri: Acclaim Press, 2006
Carter, Rosalie. *A Visit to the Carter House at Franklin, Tennessee in Photographs, Poems, and Paragraphs.* Nashville, Tennessee: The Blue & Gray Press, 1972
Carter, III, Samuel. The Siege of Atlanta, 1864. New York: Bonanza Books, 1973
Castel, Albert. *Decision in the West: The Atlanta Campaign of 1864*. Lawrence, Kansas: The University Press of Kansas. 1992
Cathey, M. Todd, *Combat Chaplain: The Life and Experiences of Rev. James McNeilly Army of Tennessee.* Macon, Georgia: Mercer University Press, 2017
Chesney, Capt. Charles Cornwallis. *A Military View of Recent Campaigns in Virginia and Maryland*. London, England, 1862
Clemmer, Greg S. *Old Allegheny: The Life and Wars of General Ed Johnson*. Staunton, Virginia: The Hearthside Publishing Company, 2004
Connelly, Thomas Lawrence. *Autumn of Glory: The Army of Tennessee, 1862-1865*, Baton Rouge, Louisiana: Louisiana State University Press, 1971
Cooper, Jr., William J. *Jefferson Davis, American*. New York, New York: Alfred A. Knopf, 2000
Cozzens, Peter. *The Darkest Days of the War: The Battles of Iuka & Corinth*, Chapel Hill, North Carolina and London: The University of North Carolina Press, 1997
Cross, Harold A. *They Sleep Beneath the Mockingbird: Mississippi Burial Sites and Biographies of Confederate Generals.* Murfreesboro, TN: Southern Heritage Press, 1994
Crowson, Noel and Brogden, John V. *Bloody Banners and Barefoot Boys, A History of the 27th Regiment Alabama Infantry CSA: The Civil War Memoirs and Diary Entries of J.P. Cannon M.D.* Shippensburg, Pennsylvania: Burd Street Press, 1997
Crute, Jr., Joseph H. Confederate Staff Officers: 1861-1865. Powhatan, Virginia:

Derwent Books, 1982

Crute, Jr., Joseph H. *Units of the Confederate States Army*. Midlothian, Virginia: Derwent Publishing, 1987

Cunningham, Edward. *The Port Hudson Campaign, 1862-1863*. Baton Rouge, Louisiana: Louisiana Press State University, 1963

Curet, Bernard. *Our Pride: Pointe Coupee*. Baton Rouge, Louisiana, Moran Publishing Company; produced by Bank of New Roads, 1981

Daniel, Larry J. and Gunter, Riley W. *Confederate Cannon Foundries*. Union City, Tennessee: Pioneer Press, 1977

Davis, Burke. *Gray Fox: Robert E. Lee and the Civil War*. New York, New York: Random House Publishing, 1956

Davis, Stephen. *Atlanta Will Fall: Sherman, Joe Johnston, and the Yankee Heavy Battalions*. Wilmington, Delaware: Scholarly Resources, 2001

Davis, William C. *Breckinridge: Statesman, Soldier, Symbol*. Baton Rouge, Louisiana: Louisiana State University Press, 1974

Davis, William C. *Jefferson Davis: The Man and his Hour*. New York, New York. Harper Collins Publishers, 1991

Davis, William C. *The Orphan Brigade: The Kentuckians Who Couldn't Go Home*. Baton Rouge, Louisiana: Louisiana State University Press, 1983

Dowdy, Clifford. *Lee*. Boston, Massachusetts: Little, Brown, and Company, 1965

Drake, Rebecca Blackwell and Bearss, Margie Riddle (editors). *My Dear Wife: Letters to Matilda; The Civil War Letters of Sid and Matilda Champion of Champion Hill*. 2005

Durham, Walter T. *Reluctant Partners: Nashville and the Union* Nashville, Tennessee: Tennessee Historical Society, 1987

Dyer, John P. *From Shiloh to San Juan: The Life of Fightin' Joe Wheeler*. Baton Rouge, Louisiana State University Press, 1961

Elliott, Sam Davis. *Doctor Quintard, Chaplain C.S.A. and Second Bishop of Tennessee: The Memoir and Civil War Diary of Charles Todd Quintard*. Baton Rouge: Louisiana State University Press, 2003

Elliott, Sam Davis. *Soldier of Tennessee: General Alexander P. Stewart and the Civil War in the West*. Baton Rouge, Louisiana: Louisiana State University Press, 1999

Fortier, Alcee. *Louisiana*. Century Historical Association, 1914

Freeman, Douglas Southall. *R.E. Lee*. New York, NY: Charles Scribner's Sons, 1935

French, Samuel Gibbs. *Two Wars: an Autobiography of Gen. Samuel G. French, CSA*. Nashville, Tennessee: Confederate Veteran, 1901

Gillum, James F. *Twenty-Five Hours to Tragedy: The Battle of Spring Hill and Operations on November 29, 1864: Precursor to the Battle of Franklin*: Spring Hill, 2014

Gott, Kendall D. *Where the South Lost the War: An Analysis of the Fort Henry-Fort Donelson Campaign, February 1862*. Mechanicsburg, Penn: Stackpole Books, 2003

Govan, Gilbert and Livingwood, James. *General Joseph E. Johnston: A Different Valor*. Indianapolis, Indiana: Bobbs-Merrill, 1956

Grabau, Warren E. *Ninety-Eight Days: A Geographer's View of the Vicksburg Campaign*. Knoxville, Tennessee, 2000

Grant, Ulysses S. *Personal Memoirs of U.S. Grant*. 2 volumes. New York: Webster 1885

Henry, Robert Selph. *The Story of the Confederacy*. Old Saybrook, Connecticut: Konecky & Konecky, year unknown

Holcomb, Gene (editor) Mississippi: *A Guide to the Magnolia State.* New York, New York: Viking Press, 1938

Hood, John Bell. *Advance and Retreat.* Edison, NJ. The Blue and Grey Press, 1985

Horn, Stanley (Chairman of Civil War Centennial Commission, Tennessee). *Tennesseans in the Civil War.* Civil War Centennial Commission, Nashville, 1964

Hughes, Jr. Nathaniel Cheairs. *Bentonville: The Final Battle of Sherman and Johnston.* Chapel Hill, North Carolina: University of North Carolina Press, 1996

Jenkins, Sr., Robert D. *The Battle of Peachtree Creek: Hood's First Sortie, 20 July 1864.* Macon, Georgia: Mercer University Press, 2013

King, Jr., Spencer Bidwell (editor). *Eliza Francis Andrews: The War-Time Journal of a Georgia Girl, 1864-1865.* Atlanta, Georgia: Cherokee Publishing Company, 1976

Johnson, Timothy D. *A Gallant Little Army: The Mexico City Campaign.* Lawrence, Kansas: University Press of Kansas, 2007

Johnston, Joseph E. *Narrative of Military Operations, Directed During the Late War Between the States.* New York, New York: Appleton and Company, 1874

Kempe, Helen Kerr. *The Pelican Guide to Old Homes of Mississippi (Volume II).* Gretna, Louisiana: Pelican Publishing Company, 1984

Krick, Robert E.L. *Staff Officers in Gray: A Biographical Register of the Staff Officers in the Army of Northern Virginia.* Chapel Hill, NC University of North Carolina Press, 2003

Krumenaker, Lawrence. *Walking the Line: Rediscovering and Touring the Civil War Defenses on Modern Atlanta's Landscape.* Marietta, Georgia: Hermograph Press, 2014

Lane, Bryan. *Where No Sorrows Come: The Life and Death of Confederate Brigadier General John Adams.* Spring Hill, Tennessee: Published by Bryan Lane, 2014

Logsdon, David R. *Eyewitness at the Battle of Franklin.* Nashville, Tennessee: Kettle Mills Press, 2000

Logsdon, David R. *Eyewitness at the Battle of Nashville.* Nashville, Tennessee: Kettle Mills Press 2004

Lokey, Brent. *Riding With the Wizard of the Saddle: A Guided Tour of General Nathan Bedford Forrest's Career.* Nashville, Tennessee: The Dixie Press, 2007

Lytle, Andrew Nelson. *Bedford Forrest and His Critter Company.* Seminole, Florida: The Green Key Press, 1931, 1984

Manigault, Arthur Middleton. *A Carolinian Goes to War: The Civil War Narrative of Arthur Middleton Manigault, Brigadier General, C.S.A.* ed. R. Lockwood Tower. Columbia, South Carolina: University of South Carolina Press, 1983

Massey, Ross. *Nashville Battlefield Guide.* Nashville, Tennessee: Tenth Amendment Publishing, 2007

Mathews, Jr., Byron H. *The McCook-Stoneman Raid.* Georgia: Brannon Publishing, 1976

McAllister, Ruth. *Co. Aytch: Maury Grays, First Tennessee Regiment or a Side Show of the Big Show* by Sam Watkins. Franklin, Tennessee: Providence House Publishers, 2007

McCluney, Jr., Larry A. *On to Vicksburg! The Mississippi Central Railroad Campaign.* Greenwood, Mississippi: Lulu Publishing Services, 2019

McCluney, Jr., Larry A. *The Yazoo Pass Expedition: A Union Thrust in the Delta.* Charleston, South Carolina: The History Press, 2017

McDonough, James Lee and Jones, James Pickett. *War So Terrible: Sherman and Atlanta* New York, New York: W.W. Norton, 1987

McMurray, Richard. *John Bell Hood and the War for Southern Independence.* Lincoln, Nebraska: University of Nebraska Press, 1982

Meriwether, Elizabeth A. *Recollections of 92 Years, 1824-1916.* McLean, Virginia: EPM Publications, 1994

Miles, Jim. *A River Unvexed: A History and Tour Guide of the Campaign for the Mississippi River.* Nashville, Tennessee: Rutledge Hill Press, 1994

Miller, Rex. *The Forgotten Regiment.* Austin, Texas: Patrex Press, 1984

Moore, Jerrold Northrop. *Confederate Commissary General: Lucius Bellinger Northrop and the Subsistence Bureau of the Southern Army.* Shippensburg, Pennsylvania: White Mane Publishing Co., Inc. 1996

Norman, Mathew W. *Colonel Burton's Spiller & Burr Revolver.* Macon, Georgia: Mercer University Press, 1996

Nulty, William H. *Confederate Florida: The Road to Olustee.* Tuscaloosa, Alabama: University of Alabama Press, 1990

O'Brien, Sean Michael. *Mobile, 1865: Last Stand of the Confederacy.* Westport, Connecticut: Praeger Publishers, 2001

Owen, Richard and James. *Generals at Rest: The Grave Sites of the 425 Official Confederate Generals.* Shippensburg, Pennsylvania: White Mane Publishing, 1997

Parks, Joseph H. *General Leonidas Polk, C.S.A.: The Fighting Bishop.* Baton Rouge, Louisiana: Louisiana State University Press, 1962

Parks, Joseph H. *General Edmund Kirby Smith, C.S.A.* Baton Rouge, Louisiana: Louisiana State University Press, 1954

Perry, Milton F. *Infernal Machines: The Story of Confederate Submarine and Mine Warfare.* Baton Rouge, Louisiana: Louisiana State University Press, 1965

Raab, James W. *W.W. Loring: Florida's Forgotten General.* Manhattan, Kansas: Sunflower University Press, 1996

Raab, James W. *Lloyd Tilghman and Francis Asbury Shoup: Two Forgotten Confederate Generals.* Murfreesboro, Tennessee: Southern Heritage Press, 2001

Ridley, Bromfield L. *Battles and Sketches of the Army of Tennessee.* Mexico, Missouri: Missouri Printing and Publishing Company, 1906

Roman, Alfred. *The Military Operations of General Beauregard in the War Between the States: 1861-1865.* New York, New York: Da Capo Press, 1994

Scaife, William R. *The Campaign for Atlanta.* Atlanta, Georgia: self-published, 1985

Scaife, William R. Order of Battle: The Campaign for Atlanta. Atlanta, Georgia, 1992

Scales, John R. *The Battles and Campaigns of General Nathan Bedford Forrest, 1861-65,* El Dorado Hills, California: Savas Beatie, 2017

Scofield, Levi T. *The Retreat from Pulaski to Nashville, Tenn.: The Battle of Franklin, Nov. 30, 1864.* Franklin, Tennessee: Mint Julep Printing, 1996 reprint

Seabrook, Lochlainn. *The McGavocks of Carnton Plantation: A Southern History.* Franklin, Tennessee: Sea Raven Press, 2011

Secrist, Philip. *The Battle of Resaca: Atlanta Campaign 1864.* Macon, Georgia: Mercer University Press, 1998

Shalhope, Robert E. *Sterling Price: Portrait of a Southerner.* Columbia, Missouri: University of Missouri Press, 1971

Sherman, William T. *Memoirs of General William T. Sherman.* New York, New York: Literary Classics of the United States, 1990

Shumate, Joyce Nunn. Old Douglas: The Confederate Camel. self-published, 2019

Silverstone, Paul H. *Warships of the Civil War Navies*. Naval Institute Press, Annapolis, Maryland, 1989

Smith, Hannis S. *The Futile Star of the West*. Jackson, Mississippi: The Journal of Mississippi History, Volume XIV, , January 1952

Smith, Timothy B. *Champion Hill: Decisive Battle for Vicksburg*. New York, New York: Savas Beatie Publishing, 2004

Stern, Phillip Van Doren. Secret Missions of the Civil War. New York, New York: Bonanza Books, 1990

Sword, Wiley. *Embrace an Angry Wind: The Confederacy's Last Hurrah: Spring Hill, Franklin, and Nashville*. New York, New York: Harper Collins Publishers, 1992

Sword, Wiley. *Shiloh: Bloody April*. Dayton, Ohio: Morningside, 2001 revised edition

United Daughters of the Confederacy, Franklin Chapter #14. *McGavock Confederate Cemetery,* Franklin, Tennessee: self-published, 1989

Vandiver, Frank. *Ploughshares into Swords: Josiah Gorgas and Confederate Ordinance*. College Station, Texas: Texas A&M/University of Texas Press, 1952

Venet, Wendy Venet. *A Changing Wind: Commerce and Conflict in Civil War Atlanta*. New Haven, Connecticut: Yale University Press, 2014

Warner, Ezra J. *Generals in Gray: Lives of the Confederate Commanders*. Baton Rouge, Louisiana: Louisiana State University Press, 1959

The War of the Rebellion: A Compilation of the Official Records of the Union and Confederate Armies. 73 volumes, 128 parts, Washington, D.C. 1880-1901

White, Col. Robert. *Confederate Military History: West Virginia*. Atlanta, Georgia, 1899

Williams, T.P. *The Mississippi Brigade of Joseph R. Davis: A Geographical Account of Its Campaigns and a Biographical Account of Its Personalities, 1861-1865.* Dayton, Ohio: Morningside, 1991

Woodward, W.E. *Meet General Grant*. New York, New York: Horace Liveright, 1928

Woodworth, Steven E. *Jefferson Davis and His Generals: The Failure of Confederate Command in the West*. Lawrence, Kansas. University Press of Kansas, 1990

Yeary, Mamie. Reminiscences of the Boys in Gray. Texas, 1912

Yeary, Mamie. *The Gentle Rebel*. Yazoo City, Mississippi: Sassafras Press, 1982

Index

1st Mississippi Battalian Sharpshooters.....101, 113, 244, 332, 346

1st Mississippi Infantry Regiment.......244, 245, 320, 346

3rd Kentucky 70, 76, 79, 237, 250, 334

3rd Maryland Artillery Battery 52, 204

3rd Mississippi Infantry Regiment.......101, 113, 120, 127, 159, 178, 214, 239, 243-245, 284, 294, 316, 332

6th Mississippi..........65, 101, 174, 207, 233, 234, 236, 238, 274, 300, 313, 314

7th Alabama Cavalry 193

7th Kentucky Infantry....250, 252, 278

8th Kentucky Infantry....... 68, 71, 79, 223, 250

12th Louisiana...... 25, 56-58, 65, 71, 76, 78, 79, 95, 101, 148, 149, 170, 228, 249, 250, 254, 319, 327-330, 339

14th Mississippi........172, 182, 183, 210, 215, 223, 233-237, 269, 280, 308

15th Mississippi.........76, 128, 162, 164, 167, 179, 180, 182, 183, 185, 201, 202, 233, 236, 238, 273, 279, 285, 300, 326, 336

20th Mississippi.....30, 233, 239, 276, 326

22nd Mississippi Infantry Regiment........49, 114, 145, 159, 189, 214, 244, 246, 320, 322, 325, 346

26th Mississippi..........59, 60, 233, 234, 237, 274, 325, 346

27th Alabama.......93, 96, 113, 135, 206, 213, 223, 228, 250-252, 303, 316, 336, 339, 341

28th Mississippi Cavalry 47

31st Mississippi Infantry Regiment.....113, 127, 153, 162, 171, 243, 244, 246, 282, 298, 330, 332, 338

33rd Mississippi Infantry Regiment.....114, 158, 170, 247, 283, 284, 304, 319

33rd New Jersey 112, 113

35th Alabama...49, 56-58, 78, 150, 178, 188, 202, 206, 218, 250-252, 299, 302, 316, 339

39th North Carolina (Palmer's) 217

40th Mississippi Infantry..... 113, 114, 244, 248, 249, 277, 290, 332, 336

43rd Mississippi........133, 135, 168, 169, 223, 234, 240, 244, 271, 272, 300, 321, 333

49th Alabama Infantry Regiment..............150, 206, 250-251, 259, 316, 339

55th Alabama Infantry Regiment....175, 207, 249, 250, 253, 328

57th Alabama Infantry Regiment.......113, 253, 272, 279, 317, 340

149th New York 88

Abernathy, John E. 113

Acworth, Georgia ...128. 129, 135

Adairsville, Georgia 89, 90

Adams, John... .....1, 2, 22, 38, 44, 47, 48, 66, 76, 84, 101, 110, 128, 129, 133, 135, 136, 150, 156, 157, 161-170, 172, 174, 179, 183, 185-187, 193, 195, 201, 202, 206, 223, 228, 232-241, 243, 256, 259, 265-269, 271-274, 276, 280, 285, 294-297, 300, 307, 308, 313, 314, 325, 326, 333

Adams, Wirt.................46,49

Allatoona Mountain, Georgia 92, 129, 257

Anderson, Patton 228

Anderson, Samuel Read... 13, 268, 269

Andersonville, Georgia 122, 127

Andrews, Eliza Frances ...230

Ardmore Park, Georgia....116

Army of Relief....... 4, 48, 63, 65, 67, 72, 292, 307

Army of the James.............99

Ashby, Turner..............15, 17

Atlanta and West Point Railroad 119

Atlanta Sabre Manufactory, Georgia 82

Atlanta, Georgia 104-107, 109, 110, 114-128, 130-132, 134, 137, 142, 149, 178, 180, 182, 183, 204, 225-227, 234, 248-250, 254-256, 263, 270, 279, 281, 283, 284, 301, 303, 307, 315, 323, 326, 330, 336, 339, 340

Atlantic & North Carolina 221

Augusta Daily Chronicle ...94

Augusta, Georgia....221, 227, 293, 307, 323, 333

Banks, Robert W. ...145, 158, 174, 285

Bankston, Mississippi.......38, 300

Barry, Robert L........233, 255, 256, 270

Barton, Seth Maxwell .21, 22, 53, 55, 270, 271

Bartow, Francis 8, 90

Bate's Division........110, 115, 126, 138, 140, 141, 153, 174, 199-202, 204, 223, 323

Bath, Virginia 14-16

Bayou Pierre, Mississippi 42, 44

Beauregard, Pierre Gustave Toutant........3, 24, 42, 47, 73, 80, 96, 128, 130, 132, 134, 137, 142, 143, 173,

Beauregard, Pierre Gustave Toutant cont....219, 220-222, 236, 249, 261, 262, 287

Belen Gate, Mexico City 4

Belle Meade Plantation, Tennessee..........179, 191, 192, 306

Benjamin, Judah P. 11, 17

Bentonville, North Carolina 222-226, 228, 235, 244, 246, 249-251, 254, 277, 290, 314, 320, 329, 336

Bermuda Hundred, Virginia 80, 96

Berryhill, William Harvey.. ....135, 136, 168, 271, 272

Bethune, William Calvin 253, 272, 279, 317

Big Black River, Mississippi .44, 46, 58, 62, 64, 66, 67, 70, 73, 276, 341

Big Shanty, Georgia 128-130

Binford, James R. 76, 128, 179, 182- 185, 201, 202, 207, 238, 268, 273, 285, 326

Blue Mountain, Georgia ...79, 84, 130

Bond, J.L.........25, 95, 170

Boone, Francis Marion ...233, 274, 325, 334, 340

Boswell, J.L. 163

Bouanchaud, Joseph Alcide ... 102, 186, 188-190, 202-204, 250, 255- 258, 275

Bouanchaud's Battery (Point Coupee).......2, 49, 59, 188, 190, 203, 257, 347

Bowen, John Stevens ..41, 42, 52-58, 60, 65, 66, 236, 238, 244, 278, 282, 323

Bradford, Mary 191

Bradley, Thomas..............167

Bragg, Braxton......27-29, 40-42, 45, 47, 68, 75, 77, 79-81, 88, 106, 126, 127, 173, 174, 211, 223, 224, 236, 249, 256, 262, 263, 276, 280, 307, 318, 323, 341

Breckinridge, John Cabell 23, 69, 71, 80-82, 236, 238, 246, 252, 314, 325, 328

Brown, William N....233, 239

Bruinsburg Landing, Mississippi 42

Brush Mountain, Georgia...95

Buchanan, Franklin............17

Buckhannon, Virginia.........18

Buckner, Simon Bolivar 74

Buford, Abraham.....1, 2, 22, 23, 37, 39, 44, 45, 49, 53, 54, 56-63, 65, 68, 70, 71, 76-79, 135, 149, 174, 191, 233, 237, 249-254, 256, 257, 276, 278, 282, 299, 302, 306, 327, 328

Cadwallader, Sylvanus ... .64, 72, 75

Calhoun, Georgia.........88, 89

Calhoun, James................125

Camp Chase, Columbus, Ohio ...116, 117. 218, 247, 284, 300

347

Camp Creek, Georgia 86

Camp Douglas, Chicago, Illinois................116, 247

Campbell, Charles 145

Cannon, J.P.....49, 56, 62, 63, 66, 67, 70, 75, 76, 78, 79, 86, 89, 92-96, 106, 107, 110-112, 120, 123-127, 130, 133, 135-137, 141, 148, 150, 168, 175, 177, 178, 180, 182, 190, 197, 201, 205, 206, 209, 213, 217, 250-252

Carnifax Ferry, Virginia 9

Carnton, Tennessee..........144, 146, 149, 151, 153, 155, 161, 168, 267, 315, 319, 344

Carter House, Tennessee 145, 161, 166, 170, 234, 319, 341

Carter, Fountain Branch 143-145, 153, 155, 161, 166, 170, 172, 234, 319

Carter, John B..............254

Carter, John Carpenter....161, 166, 169

Carter, Rachel..................173

Carter, Theodore......196, 197, 203

Carter, Tod...............166, 172

Cassville, Georgia 90, 92, 94, 104, 106, 301

Castle of Chapultepec, Mexico....................4, 311

Cave Spring, Georgia 130

Cedar Bluff, Alabama.......80, 329

Cedar Key, Florida 83

Cedartown, Georgia..........130

Champion Hill, Mississippi.. ...1, 22, 26, 28, 39, 41, 49, 50, 52-56, 64-66, 73, 86, 92, 101, 103, 141, 178, 188, 207, 232, 234, 237, 239, 242, 250-252, 254-257, 259, 271, 274, 282, 299, 307, 314, 316, 325, 327, 328, 331, 333-335, 340

Champion, Sid 47, 335

Chancellorsville, Virginia 46, 74, 88, 89, 94, 224, 301, 305

Charleston, South Carolina... 25, 47, 73, 83, 97, 118, 219, 221, 222, 309, 333

Charleston, Virginia.......9, 19, 20

Chase, Salmon 29

Chattahoochee River, Georgia 81, 82, 92, 93, 97, 102- 107, 109, 125, 234, 272, 282

Chattanooga Rebel, Tennessee....................172

Chattanooga, Tennessee ...42, 75, 77, 79, 80, 81, 105, 116, 122, 123, 127, 131-133, 155, 172, 174, 177, 226, 247, 256, 263, 270, 297, 331, 336

Cheairs, Nathaniel ..141, 224, 343

Cheat Mountain, Virginia ...7, 10, 12, 268, 280

Cheatham, Benjamin Franklin..........80, 81, 109, 113, 114, 118, 119, 126, 127, 136, 140, 141, 143, 145, 149, 166, 168, 177, 180, 193, 196, 199, 201,

Cheatham, Benjamin Franklin cont...204, 207-209, 216, 223, 224, 227, 280, 302, 331

Cherokee, Alabama 134, 228, 316

Chesney, Charles Cornwallis 165, 341

Chestnut, James 106

Chestnut, Mary Boykin.... 81, 106

Chickamauga, Georgia. ... 22, 40, 75, 79- 81, 88, 103, 127, 142, 145, 168, 182, 212, 263, 280, 301, 323, 331, 4336, 338

Chickasaw Bayou, Mississippi 29, 70, 236, 245, 259, 270, 309, 340

City Cemetery, Tennessee 41, 116, 173, 263, 264, 268, 369, 279, 4293, 300, 315, 336

Clare, William 105

Clear Creek, Georgia 110, 115

Clinton, Mississippi...48, 50, 52, 53, 277, 278

Coffeeville, Mississippi ... 25, 26, 68, 234, 237, 254, 257, 334

Coker House Ridge, Mississippi 55

Colbert, Wallace Bruce 113, 244, 3248, 249, 252, 277, 290, 320, 336

Cold Harbour, Virginia.......96

Coleman, Daniel 180, 204, 209, 271

Collins, John 166

Columbia Herald, Tennessee 168

Columbia, South Carolina 221

Columbia, Tennessee 4, 136-138, 141, 142, 144, 145, 166, 168, 170, 172, 210, 211, 213, 214, 221, 244, 297

Columbus Iron Works, Georgia
Columbus Arsenal. 82

Columbus, Georgia 81, 82, 116, 255, 286

Columbus, Kentucky 246, 254, 256, 257, 327, 334

Columbus, Mississippi 38, 39, 232, 237, 252, 269, 270, 272, 299, 309

Columbus, Ohio 116

Confederate Ordinance Labs, Georgia 82

Connasauga, Georgia ... 86, 88

Connelly, Thomas 222

Contreras, Mexico 3, 4

Cooper, James L. 204

Cooper, Samuel 20

Coosa River, Alabama 130, 132

Courtland, Alabama 134, 206

Courtney, Fannie 143

Cowan, James Jones.. .... 60, 102, 133, 177, 183, 188, 215, 256, 258, 260, 277, 278

Cowan's Battery ... 26, 49, 60, 92, 101, 102, 130, 167, 191, 196, 216, 255, 258, 259, 261, 277

Crossland, Edward .. 250, 252, 278

Crute, Joseph H., Jr. 22, 23, 318, 341, 342

Crystal Springs, Mississippi 63, 64

Cumming, Alfred 55, 226

Cunningham, Columbus J.L. 253, 279, 317, 340

Cunningham, George W. 82

Dabney, T.G. ... 215, 216, 260

Dallas, Georgia ... 92-96, 106, 125

Darden, Israel Putnam 188, 192, 255, 262-264, 279

Darden's Battery 120, 190, 191, 255, 256, 261-263, 270

Davis Ford, Tennessee 138

Davis, C.V.H. 113

Davis, Jefferson 1, 6, 16, 17, 20, 25, 27, 28, 38-40, 44, 46-49, 72-75, 79, 21, 83, 84, 102, 103, 106, 107, 126-128, 130, 134, 138, 142, 220, 223, 226, 228, 230, 232, 240-242, 262, 273, 274, 292, 294, 305, 314, 321, 323, 324, 331

Davis, Stephen 116

Davis, Varina 38, 47, 273, 305

Deas, Zachariah C. .. 182, 183, 191

Decatur, Georgia 122, 123, 132-134, 155, 214, 254, 270, 333

Deer Creek, Mississippi 67

Demopolis, Alabama.. 77-79, 283

Department of Southwestern Virginia 18, 311

DeRussy, Renee Amedee 189, 190

Deshler, James 21, 22, 380

Dixon, John A. 223, 250, 254, 329

Donoho, Dr. A.G. 89

Doss, Washington Lafayette 233, 234, 237, 280

Douglas, Old ... 240, 241, 278, 321

Dowdy, Clifford 5, 6

Drake, Jabez Leftwich ... 113, 114, 247, 248, 280, 281, 284, 304

Drane, James W. 113, 247, 281, 282, 298

Drennan, William 25, 27, 60, 242

Duck River, Tennessee 27, 137, 142, 178, 211, 220

Dunlop, Isaac Leroy 250, 282

Dunn, Mathew Andrew 281, 283, 284

East Point, Georgia 119, 123, 124

Edwards Station, Mississippi 48, 50, 65

349

Edwards, Mississippi........53, 229

Eggleston, Edmund T........59, 60, 92, 101, 123, 130, 133, 136, 177, 183, 213, 219

Elkhorn Tavern, Arkansas 24

Enterprise, Mississippi. 38, 39, 78, 250, 252, 329

Estes, George E 210, 213, 215, 217

Etowah River, Georgia ....,89, 92

Ewell, Richard Stoddard....15

Ezra Church, Georgia 97, 119, 120, 121, 126, 183, 236, 243, 301, 309

Farrell, Michael 162, 233, 235, 238, 273, 285

Fayetteville, North Carolina .. 223

Fayetteville, Virginia.........20

Featherston, Winfield Scott. 1, 2, 23, 25, 37, 44, 45, 49, 53, 54, 56, 58-60, 65, 79, 84, 86, 94, 97, 100-102, 107, 110-116, 124, 128, 129, 131, 133, 137, 141, 145-147, 153, 154, 157-162, 175, 177, 178, 189-191, 193-195, 199, 202, 205, 208, 210-215, 220, 223, 228, 235, 236, 242-249, 255, 260, 281, 284, 286-291, 315, 316, 320-322, 326, 329, 330, 332, 336, 337

Figuers Bluff, Tennessee.. 155

Findlay Iron Works, Georgia 82

Finley, Jesse........3

Florida 1, 3- 5, 11, 82, 83, 94, 95, 127, 221, 230,278, 292, 310-312, 343, 344

Florida Territorial Legislature 3

Floyd, John B.....6, 9, 11, 22, 74, 239

Foote, Shelby.......78

Forney, G.H. 76, 233

Forney, John H. 47, 278

Fort Donelson, Tennessee 29, 34, 66, 68, 74,75, 236, 237, 239, 240, 244, 251, 253, 261, 269, 274, 276, 280, 290, 297, 303, 308, 316, 320, 326, 334, 336, 339, 342

Fort Fisher, North Carolina 221, 226, 339

Fort Granger, Tennessee 143, 144, 153-155, 160, 161

Fort Henry, Tennessee......24, 26, 29, 35, 38, 55, 313, 251, 257, 261, 303, 334, 342

Fort Marion, Florida 3

Fort Negley, Tennessee ..173, 178

Fort Pemberton, Mississippi 1, 3, 21-23, 26, 30, 34-39, 55, 103, 239, 242, 255, 257, 316, 319, 330

Fort Union, New Mexico....4, 311

Fortress Rosecrans, Tennessee............155, 174

Foster, Wilbur.156, 179, 199, 207, 208

Franklin Female Institute, Tennessee....................143

Franklin, Tennessee........1, 2, 45, 80, 138-146, 148, 151, 153, 157, 158, 159, 161, 164-168, 170, 171, 173-175, 178, 180, 183, 187, 191, 196, 199, 201, 202, 206-213, 218, 220, 223, 228, 232, 234, 236-241, 243, 245, 247-254, 260, 264, 265, 271, 272, 276, 277, 279, 284, 285, 292, 297, 301, 302, 314, 316, 317, 319, 321, 322, 326-330, 336, 337, 339, 340

Freeman, Douglas Southall 6, 8, 9, 302, 303

French, Samuel Gibbs..... ..67, 69, 70, 75, 77, 92, 98, 103-105, 120, 123, 126, 129, 130, 133, 147, 157, 166, 176-178, 180, 183, 204, 211, 224, 238, 242, 292, 323, 243, 257

Fuller, William....................80

Gadsden, Alabama.........132, 284, 340

Gale, William Dudley.... 124, 167, 168, 171, 180, 191, 194, 214, 292, 293, 323

Gardner, Franklin.....126, 276

Garnett, Richard Brooke ..14, 17

Garrett, Elizabeth.............219

Garrett, George Washington Brooks........163, 187, 188, 219, 233, 240, 293- 295

Gaylesville, Alabama........132

Georgia Railroad..............109

Gibbens, W. 113

Gibson, Thomas 163, 170, 235, 266, 285, 295, 296,

Giles Court House, Virginia 18

Gilham, William ... 6, 8, 9, 13, 15, 298

Gillespie, Francis Marion.. .... 113, 298, 299

Gist, States Rights 47, 161, 166

Goldsboro, North Carolina 221, 223, 227

Goodwin, Edward 39, 49, 57, 250, 252, 299, 302

Grand Gulf, Mississippi ... 40-44, 46, 48, 63

Grant, Lemuel 107

Green, Martin 57, 278, 314

Greenwood, Mississippi ... 30, 33, 36, 38, 280, 327, 330

Gregg, John 46-48, 250

Greif, J.V. 63, 70, 76, 250

Grenada, Mississippi .. 27-29, 35, 170, 236-238, 247, 255, 257, 285, 304, 326

Grinsted, William 115

Guntersville, Alabama 132, 134

Hampton Roads, Virginia.. .... 17, 18

Hampton, Wade 221-223, 225-227, 308

Hardee, William Joseph 22, 47, 76, 81, 188, 89, 92-95, 98, 100, 109, 110, 1312

Hardee, William Joseph cont... 115, 119, 123-125, 127, 137, 220, 221, 223, 224, 226, 248, 261, 262, 293, 3023, 338

Harding, Elizabeth Erwin McGavock 192

Harding, Selene. 191, 192, 306

Harmon, James W ... 178, 202, 203, 218

Harpeth River, Tennessee ... 149, 150, 155, 160, 161, 163, 210, 211

Harrison, Richard ... 223, 235, 241, 300, 314

Helena, Arkansas 29, 37

Henry 16-shot repeater rifles 156

Henry, Patrick 76, 77, 129, 161-163, 165, 167, 168, 232, 272

Hill, Daniel Harvey 223, 287

Hill, Sylvester 184

Hogane, J.T 63

Hoke, Robert 223- 225

Holly Springs, Mississippi.... ... 25, 26, 29, 45, 102, 286, 290, 291, 336, 337

Hood, John Bell. 1, 2, 42, 68, 81, 86, 88, 90, 92-94, 97, 98, 102, 106, 107, 109, 110, 112, 114-116, 118-128, 130-145, 147, 150, 158, 159, 162, 165-169, 172-174, 176-180, 188, 191, 193, 195-199, 201, 202, 204, 208, 209, 211, 213-215, 217-220, 228, 233, 234, 239, 248, 255,

Hood, John Bell cont..256, 260, 261, 263, 268, 279, 284, 285, 288, 293, 300, 301, 316, 328, 331, 332, 340

Hooker, Joseph.. ...88, 93, 97, 98, 333

Hord, Henry Ewell 76, 250

Horn, Stanley 173

Hotchkiss, Jedediah 17

House of the State of Florida 3

Huddleston, Charles A.... 46-48, 114, 249

Hughes, Adolphus Alexander 251

Hughes, Owen D....245

Hughes' Ford, Tennessee.... 144, 149

Iverson, Alfred 122

Ives, Samuel Spencer 78, 113, 1850, 206, 251-253, 302, 316, 339

Jackson and New Orleans Railroad 63

Jackson Creek, Mississippi 50, 51, 55

Jackson, Col. James 78, 79, 96, 223, 225, 228, 250, 251, 316

Jackson, Henry Rootes ... 5, 6, 8, 9, 11, 12, 268, 302, 303, 340

Jackson, Mississippi ... 27, 30, 38, 40, 44, 46-48, 50, 63-65, 68-72, 75-77, 225, 230, 233, 236, 238, 239, 243, 250, 255, 259, 274, 276, 277, 280, 283, 285,

Jackson, Mississippi cont. 295, 307, 313, 314, 316, 318, 325, 332, 333, 337, 340

Jackson, Moses 114, 248, 283, 304

Jackson, Thomas Jonathan 1, 3, 4, 11, 13-18, 22, 46, 47, 50, 103, 119, 180, 265, 268, 270, 288, 289, 298, 305, 308, 330

Jackson, William Hicks 76, 92-95, 97, 122-124, 130, 144, 149, 174, 210, 306

Jacksonville, Alabama 130, 132

Jenkins, Albert Gallatin ... 18-20, 116, 244-249, 251-254, 282

Johns, Mrs. 180, 190, 191, 194

Johnson, Andrew 173

Johnson, Bushrod 262, 263

Johnson, Edward.. ..8, 12, 13, 140, 182, 183, 260

Johnson, William B. 247

Johnston, Albert Sidney....... 4, 238, 261, 262, 338, 331, 332

Johnston, Joseph Eggleston... 2, 4, 17, 23, 27-29, 39, 40, 42, 46-49, 50-53, 63-75, 79-84, 86, 88-90, 92-98, 100, 102-107, 109, 115, 116, 123, 127, 128, 132, 133, 221-230, 233, 236, 239, 250, 256, 268, 270, 276, 283, 287, 292, 301, 306, 307, 32323, 331, 332

Kelley, David Campbell 174, 192, 193, 209

Kennesaw Mountain, Georgia 100, 102-104, 126, 234, 236, 243, 260, 333

Kingston, Georgia.. 90, 92, 95

Knight, T.H................ 62, 207

Landry, Caesar................. 203

Latimer, Mrs. Douglas....... 76

Lawrence Hill, Tennessee 175, 176

Lawrence, Robert Josiah ..2223, 235, 237, 308, 314

Lee, Fitzhugh............. 21, 222

Lee, Hugh................ 21, 308

Lee, Robert Edward..... 3-11, 18-20, 22, 42, 46, 64, 67, 83, 88, 89, 96, 106, 112, 122, 127, 137, 165, 195, 221, 222, 226, 228-230, 239, 242, 271, 274, 287-290, 292, 1301-303 308-311, 331

Lee, Stephen Dill ..22, 23, 29, 47, 53, 55, 58, 97, 119-121, 124-126, 136-138, 140, 142, 167, 177, 180, 182, 183, 186, 193, 196, 199, 201, 206-209, 211, 220, 221, 223, 224, 227, 264, 309, 338

Leggett, Mortimer.... 100, 102

Lincoln, Abraham... 5, 24, 29, 38, 81, 106, 126, 134, 173, 211, 216, 240, 268, 269, 177, 196, 220-222, 228, 229, 259, 266, 290, 297, 306, 321, 332, 334

Linewood Cemetery, Georgia 116

Little Pumpkinvine Creek, Georgia 94

Lockett, Samuel Henry. ... 53, 54

Long, Armistead Lindsay 22, 309

Loring
Egyptian Army............... 4

Loring Heights Subdivision, Atlanta, Georgia......... 107, 109, 352

Loring, Reuben and Hannah. 3

Loring, William Wing.. 1-26, 28-30, 33-39, 41, 42, 44-46, 48-60, 62-67, 69-71, 73, 75-82, 84, 86, 89, 90, 92-100, 102-105, 107-117, 120-123, 125-128, 130, 133, 136, 140, 141, 144-149, 150, 151, 153-158, 160, 161, 165, 167, 168, 174, 176-180, 182, 183, 185-191, 193-196, 199, 201, 203, 204, 206-208, 212, 215, 217, 220, 221, 223-225, 228-231, 233, 234, 236, 239, 240, 242, 243, 246, 249-257, 259-261, 263, 265, 267-271, 276, 278-280, 283, 285, 292, 294, 296, 298, 300-316, 318, 319, 322-331, 333-340

Lost Mountain line, Georgia 95-97, 103, 251, 316

Lotz House, Tennessee .. 165, 166, 267

Lovejoy Station, Georgia.. 125

Lowry, Robert...... 52, 65, 101, 174, 175, 182, 186, 220, 223, 228, 233-236, 243, 274, 313-315, 329

Lumsden, Charles L......... 180

Lyon, Hylan Benton ...68, 71, 179

Macon & Western Railroad 119, 121, 122, 125

Macon, Georgia.. 82, 83, 116, 122, 127, 238, 247, 255, 256, 297, 298

Manahan, T.A. 62

Maney, George Earl........113, 115, 212

Manigault, Arthur.....98, 103, 107, 182, 183, 301, 343

Marietta, Georgia........92, 95, 100, 102, 125, 128, 279, 333

Markham, D.D. Thomas Railey. 146, 155, 167, 168, 315

Marshall, Hammond..........82

Marshall, Park 153, 159

Mathews, Joe 21

Maury, Dabney 37

Maxey, Samuel Bell 48, 250

McAlexander, Edward Asbury 228, 251, 316

McComb, William..............14

McEwen, Frances 143, 172

McGavock, Carrie Winder.. ....144, 146, 267, 315

McGavock, John.....150, 169, 285

McGavock, Mrs. James ...210

McGavock, Mrs. James Randal........................210

McNeilly, James.....109, 115, 116, 158, 301

McQuaide, John C 167, 188, 189, 190, 257, 275

Meadows, R.B. 206, 207

Mellon, Thomas A. 101, 102, 113, 243, 245, 316

Memphis and Charleston Railroad 24, 248

Meridian, Mississippi 21, 37, 39, 42, 75, 77, 78, 237, 248, 250, 252, 264, 283

Merrill, C.E..............170, 171

Merrin, F.W. 52

Mexican War 1, 4, 6, 13, 40, 45, 46, 190, 256, 265, 268, 276, 280, 302, 305, 307, 308, 310, 316, 321, 324-326, 331, 222, 334, 340

Mexico City, Mexico..1, 3, 4, 46, 308, 310, 311, 343

Milledgeville, Georgia.......83

Milligan, Augustus L.......113, 253, 279, 317, 318

Millsaps, R.W. 167, 318

Missionary Ridge, Tennessee 75, 77, 81, 104, 263, 319, 323

Mississippi Central Railroad 29, 237, 389

Mississippi Newspaper 38

Mississippian Newspaper..40

Mobile and Ohio Railroad. 27, 29, 248

Mobile, Alabama 77, 78, 96, 97, 134, 220, 222, 224,

Mobile, Alabama cont...240, 243, 251, 255, 256, 261, 264, 274, 278, 292, 308, 319, 321, 340

Montevallo, Alabama .79, 84, 278, 283

Montgomery Hill, Tennessee 176, 177, 272

Moulton, Alabama 78

Mounted Rifles 3, 4, 306, 310

Murfreesborough, Tennessee 27, 40, 75, 79, 81, 103, 127, 155, 156, 160, 168, 173, 174, 177, 190, 196, 209, 211, 213, 218, 224, 226, 242, 261-263, 280, 286, 331

Muscle Shoals, Alabama... 215

Myrick, John Douglas.... ..21, 30, 38, 101, 189, 255-257, 319

Nashville & Decatur (a.k.a. Alabama & Tennessee) 123, 132, 155

Nashville Battlefield Guide 182, 191

Natchez, Mississippi........ 38, 118, 261, 279, 281

Neilson, Charles P... ...... 170, 248, 319, 320

Nelson, Noel Ligon........ 101, 170, 254, 319

New Bern, North Carolina 221, 271

New Hope Church, Georgia 93, 103-105, 130, 244, 248, 331

353

Noble Iron Works, Georgia. 84

North Carolina Railroad 223, 226

North Carolina troops.....187, 223

Northrop, Lucius Bellinger 82, 83

Oakland Cemetery, Georgia 116, 117, 248, 281

Oaklawn, Tennessee. 140

Ocala, Florida 3

Ocmulgee Hospital, Georgia 116

Old Blizzards
see William Wing Loring ..1, 3, 33- 35, 103, 105, 212, 224

Olustee, Florida 83

Oostanaula River, Georgia 86, 88, 89

Padierna, Mexico..............3, 4

Palmer, Joseph........212, 214, 217, 380

Palmetto, Georgia...127, 128, 130, 133

Patton, John Mercer...........13

Pea Ridge, Arkansas....24, 29

Peach Tree Creek, Georgia.... 107, 109, 110, 116, 118, 127, 137, 159, 220, 234, 239, 243-247, 249, 251-254, 272, 277, 282, 284, 298, 301, 316, 317, 320, 327, 336

Pearl River, Mississippi....70, 71

Pedregal, Mexico.................3

Pemberton, John Clifford 1-3, 21-31,33-42, 44,46-60, 62-67, 70, 72-75, 82, 234, 242, 250-252, 255, 259, 276, 278, 307, 315-319, 321, 322, 331, 338, 340

Perryville, Kentucky.......190, 262, 280

Pettus, Edmund Winston ..55, 142, 245, 338

Phillips, Dr. George Crawford....145, 243, 322, 326

Pillow, Gideon.......4, 74, 136, 239

Pine Mountain, Georgia....95, 197, 323

Plater House, Tennessee 190, 191, 193

Polk, Leonidas. ... 22, 23, 75-79, 84, 88, 92, 93, 97, 102, 103, 105, 124, 136, 171, 232, 234, 243, 245, 256, 260, 283, 285, 292, 293, 307, 309, 323, 324, 331

Polk, President James K. ..310

Polk, William...................136

Pope, John 18, 288

Port Gibson, Mississippi...41, 42, 44, 201, 314, 320

Port Hudson, Louisiana 48, 72, 89, 126, 244-246, 249, 251-254, 276, 327, 328, 342

Porter, James D................164

Porter, Nimrod.................211

Presstman, Stephen..........107

Quinby, I. F..................35, 37

Quintard, Charles Todd .. 3-5, 15-18, 21, 25, 27, 136, 161, 165, 267, 311, 312, 324, 326, 333

Raab, James...1, 4,17, 21, 22, 35, 96, 105, 224, 310-312

Racine, Ohio 20

Rains, James 173, 280

Ramsey, James Newton 6

Randolph, George........20, 21

Raymond, Mississippi 46, 47, 49, 50, 52, 54, 56, 59, 60, 62-65, 250

Rebel Yell........86, 111, 147, 149

Red River, Louisiana ..75, 96, 97, 220, 338

Redoubt One, Tennessee ...178-180, 182, 185, 186, 260

Redoubt Two,Tennesse 178, 182, 185, 188, 196

Redoubt Three, Tennessee 178, 182-185

Redoubt Four, Tennessee 182, 184, 193

Redoubt Five, Tennessee 182

Reynolds, Arthur Exum ... 59, 233, 234, 325, 335

Reynolds, Daniel H.........199, 204, 208, 209, 212, 228, 244, 282

Rich Mountain Campaign... 5

Ridley, Broomfield.. ....93, 227-231

Riverside, Tennessee 210

Robinson, Henry……...21, 23, 326

Rome Railroad, Georgia....84

Rome, Georgia……...979, 84, 281, 311, 324

Romney, Virginia.... ..11, 13-16, 17, 270, 298, 305, 324, 333

Ross, L.F. 35

Rough and Ready, Georgia 125, 126

Rucker's Brigade....174, 189, 192, 193, 209, 260

Russell, Daniel Renner ...233, 239

Rust, Albert. ... 8-10, 28, 249, 250, 252

Rutherford Creek, Tennessee 138, 213

Ryan, Milton....................172

Sabine Pass, Louisiana 75

Saint Andrew's Bay, Florida 83

Saint Augustine, Florida.....2, 3, 310-313, 324

Saint Joseph's Bay, Florida. 83

Sanders, Daniel Ward.....204, 209, 214, 215

Sanders, David Ward.......211

Savannah, Georgia……...222, 223, 302, 303, 340

Scaife, William.......104, 129, 131

Scofield, Levi T......140, 161, 166

Scott, Thomas Moore… 2, 25, 37, 44, 49, 57, 65, 76, 79, 86, 95, 96, 101, 102, 107, 110-114, 116, 123, 124, 128, 135, 148-150, 153, 154, 161, 166, 175, 186, 188, 190, 202, 205, 206, 223, 228, 249-254, 272, 276, 319, 326-330, 339

Scott, Winfield........3, 24, 37, 46, 266, 286, 292, 308, 310

Sears, Claudius Wistar....176, 182-185, 190

Seminoles.. ....1, 3, 305, 310

Seven Pines, Virginia ..….29, 42, 47, 287

Sewell Mountain, Virginia 11

Shacklett, A.R..............71, 72

Shaw, H.C................159, 248

Shelley, Charles M. 228, 251, 329

Shenandoah Valley, Virginia 7, 15, 18, 20, 80

Shoal Creek, Alabama 215, 217

Shoup, Francis 104, 105, 107, 123

Shoupades............... .104-106

Shy, William....................201

Simmons, J.E. 158

Smith, Andrew Jackson....97

Smith, Benjamin LaFayette 133, 169, 241

Smith, Edmund Kirby...3, 40, 41, 45, 80, 96, 262, 310, 311, 330

Smith, James A. 212

Smith, Thomas Benton 204

Smithfield, North Carolina 223, 226-228

Smyrna Camp line, Georgia 103

Snake Creek Gap, Georgia 84

Snodgrass, John 175, 206, 220, 223, 228, 250, 253, 263, 327-329

Soap Creek, Georgia.........105

Southern Railroad of Mississippi 44, 50

Spencer, James G...............60

Spring Hill, Tennessee…....1, 62, 136-138, 140-142, 145, 211, 213, 263, 297, 331

St. Phillip see Star of the West 30

Standifer, Thomas Cunningham….25, 95, 96, 327, 330

Star of the West 30, 34, 38

Starke, William Edward... 21, 22, 330

Stephens, Marcus......153, 159

Stevenson, Carter Littlepage .21, 22, 40, 41, 44, 47, 48, 50, 52-55, 59, 60, 66, 77, 86, 127, 132, 211, 220, 223, 226, 271, 315, 329, 331

Stewart, Alexander Peter... 86, 93, 102-105, 107, 109, 110, 113, 114, 116, 120, 121, 123, 124, 126, 136, 140-143, 145, 150, 155-157, 160, 161, 166-168, 175-177, 179, 180, 182. 183, 185, 189, 191, 193-196, 199, 201, 204, 206-208, 210, 214, 215, 222-225, 227-229, 243, 245, 256, 260, 261, 263, 292, 294, 317, 331, 332

Storrs, George S. 183, 184

Stuart, James Ewell Brown 18, 222, 308

Suffolk, Virginia................18

Sutton, George.................149

Taliaferro, William Booth ....…13

Tallahatchie River, Mississippi ..29, 30, 33-35

Tanyard Branch, Georgia.. ....107, 112, 116

Tate, Samuel......................78

Taylor, Richard....22, 80, 96, 126, 128, 132, 219, 220, 222, 256, 264

Tennessee Confederate Home 76

The Atlanta Register, Georgia 118

The Daily Southern Crisis ....…39

The Great Seminole War 3, 310

Thomas, Hanson................21

Thompson, Absalom........140

Thompson, Joseph Nicholas 150

Tilghman, Lloyd... ..1, 22-26, 30, 34, 35, 37, 38, 44, 49, 52-56, 59, 60, 61, 65, 66, 68, 101, 232-234, 236-239, 257, 259, 261, 274, 276, 308, 308, 314, 325, 333, 335

Tilghman, Lloyd Jr. 59

Tombigbee River, Alabama 77, 78

Toombs, Robert 230

Truman, W.L. 165

Tupelo, Mississippi......78, 97, 123, 131, 220, 223, 227, 3246, 280, 290, 299, 309, 314

Turkey Creek, Mississippi 49

Turpin, James A....... 190-192, 263, 264

Tuscumbia, Alabama.....132-134 136, 280, 285

Tyler, Robert Charles 128

U.S.S. Baron DeKalb.........29

U.S.S. Cairo 29, 37

Utoy Creek, Georgia.. 4, 121-123, 126

Valley Mountain, Virginia..7, 8, 10

Van de Graaf, W.J. 113

Van Dorn, Earl.24, 25, 35,28-30, 39, 40, 73,144, 237, 239, 247-249, 252, 258, 259, 289, 318, 334

Vance, Zebulon................231

Vera Cruz, Mexico.. ......3, 46, 308, 310

Vicksburg Herald Newspaper 60

Vicksburg, Mississippi 3,, 24, 29, 30, 36, 37, 39-42, 44, 46-48, 50, 54, 58, 61-70, 72-75, 77, 78, 80, 82, 83, 103, 118, 146, 188, 234, 236-239, 241, 242, 246, 249, 254, 257-259, 261, 269-271, 276-278, 289, 294, 300, 309, 314-316, 319, 321, 322, 325, 331, 334-336, 338, 340

Weeden, John David...... 205, 206, 251-253, 338, 339

Wesson, Laura 339

West Point and Montgomery Railroad......................127

West Point, Georgia.......6, 41, 48, 67, 68, 76, 77, 96, 97, 103, 105, 128, 221, 222, 232, 258, 265, 270, 280, 292, 301, 305, 309, 310, 318, 321, 323, 331, 333, 340

Western & Atlantic Railroad 80, 84, 90, 94, 95, 123, 128, 130, 132, 226, 257

White, Pleasant W. ...83, 264, 284

Wigfall, Louis 73

Wiley, James Horatio.......340

Wilmington & Weldon Railroad......................221

Wilmington, North Carolina ..3, 83, 221, 226, 310, 342

Wilson, Claudius...........303

Wilson, D.J. 96

Wilson, Don....................158

Wilson, James. 138, 149, 204, 209

Wilson, Mary E. 332

Winchester, Virginia. ..11-17, 332, 340

Wise, Henry Alexander ..6, 9, 11

Withers, William Temple..58, 59, 412340

Withlacoochee, Florida......... 3

Woodville, Mississippi 38, 325

Wright, Moses H. 82, 114, 164, 248

Yalobusha Line, Mississippi 28

Yazoo Pass, Mississippi... 29, 30, 37

Zollicoffer, Felix 173, 238

www.ingramcontent.com/pod-product-compliance
Lightning Source LLC
Chambersburg PA
CBHW080458240426
43673CB00005B/224